Marketing Across Cultures

THIRD EDITION

JEAN-CLAUDE USUNIER

FINANCIAL TIMES
Prentice Hall

An imprint of **Pearson Education**

Harlow, England · London · New York · Reading, Massachusetts · San Francisco
Toronto · Don Mills, Ontario · Sydney · Tokyo · Singapore · Hong Kong · Seoul
Taipei · Cape Town · Madrid · Mexico City · Amsterdam · Munich · Paris · Milan

Pearson Education Limited
Edinburgh Gate
Harlow, Essex CM20 2JE

and Associated Companies around the world

Visit us on the World Wide Web at:
www.pearsoneduc.com

First published 1992
Second edition 1996
Third edition 2000

Library of Congress Cataloging-in-Publication Data

Usunier, Jean-Claude.
Marketing across cultures / Jean-Claude Usunier.-- 3rd ed.
p. cm.
Includes bibliographical references and index.
ISBN 0-13-010668-2 (alk. paper)
1. Export marketing--Social aspects.   2. International business
enterprises--Social aspects.   3. Intercultural communication.
1. Title.
HF1416.U85   1999
658.8'48--dc21   99-25726
                                                                           CIP

British Library Cataloguing-in-Publication Data

A catalogue record for this book is available from
The British Library

ISBN: 0-13-010668-2

Typeset in Stone Serif and Stone Sans
by no. 42

Produced by Pearson Education Asia Pte Ltd
Printed in Singapore (KKP)

10 9   8   7   6   5   4   3   2
04 03 02 01 00

Marketing Across Cultures

We work with leading authors to develop the strongest educational materials in Marketing, bringing cutting-edge thinking and best learning practice to a global market.

Under a range of well-known imprints, including Financial Times Prentice Hall, we craft high quality print and electronic publications which help readers to understand and apply their content, whether studying or at work.

To find out about the complete range of our publishing, please visit us on the World Wide Web at:

www.pearsoneduc.com

Contents

Introduction: Marketing in the global villages   *page* xii

Part 1

The cultural variable in international marketing 1

1 The cultural process 3
 1.1 Culture: definition(s) 4
 1.2 Elements of culture 5
 1.3 Culture and nationality 11
 1.4 Culture and competence 15
 1.5 Culture and social representations 17
 Questions 19
 Appendix 1: Teaching materials 19
 A1.1 Critical incident: An old lady from Malaysia 19
 A1.2 Critical incident: The parable 20
 References 21

2 Cultural dynamics 1: Time and space 23
 2.1 A model of action based on cultural assumptions 24
 2.2 Time: Cross-cultural variability 27
 2.3 Space 33
 2.4 Cultural borrowing and change in societies 41
 2.5 Cultural hostility 45
 Questions 47

Appendix 2: Teaching materials   49
A2.1 Cross-cultural scenario: Inshallah   49
A2.2 Cross-cultural interaction: Engineering a decision   49
A2.3 Cross-cultural interaction: Opening a medical office in Saudi Arabia   50
A2.4 Reading: Language and time patterns: The Bantu case   51
A2.5 Exercise: World picture test   52
References   54

3 Cultural dynamics 2: Interactions, mindsets and behaviours   56
3.1 Concept of the self and others   57
3.2 Interaction models   63
3.3 Culture-based attitudes towards action   72
3.4 How to relate thinking to action   76
3.5 Dealing with desires and feelings   80
3.6 Coping with rules   83
3.7 Cultural assumptions and actual behaviour   86
Questions   89
Appendix 3: Teaching materials   89
A3.1 Critical incident: An American in Vietnam   89
A3.2 Exercise: Seven cultures of the South Seas   90
A3.3 Rationales for section A2.1 (cross-cultural scenario) and sections A2.2
       and A2.3 (cross-cultural interactions)   92
References   95

Part 2

The integration of local consumption in a global marketing
environment   97

4 Cross-cultural consumer behaviour   101
4.1 Culture and consumer behaviour   103
4.2 The influence of culture on selected aspects of consumer behaviour   108
4.3 Investigating the cross-cultural transposability of consumer behaviour
       concepts   113
4.4 Ethnic consumption   118
4.5 Marketing as an exchange of meanings   120
4.6 Conclusion   123
Questions   123
Appendix 4: Teaching materials   123
A4.1 Exercise: 'Dichter's consumption motives'   123
A4.2 Exercise: Investigating the cross-cultural transposability of a consumer
       complaint scale   124
A4.3 Case: Eliot Greeting Card Company (1)   125
References   132

5 Local consumers and the globalization of consumption 136

5.1 Free trade doctrine and the denial of cultural variety in consumers' tastes 137
5.2 The global convergence of consumption patterns 140
5.3 The emergence of a global consumer culture 145
5.4 Local products and consumption experiences 148
5.5 Local consumer cultures and resistance to change 155
5.6 Emergent patterns of a mixed local/global consumer behaviour 160
Questions 163
Appendix 5: Teaching materials 164
A5.1 Case: Disneyland Paris 164
A5.2 Case: IKEA 166
A5.3 Case: Parker Pen 169
References 173

6 The convergence of marketing environments world-wide 178

6.1 Local marketing environments 179
6.2 Marketing: Borrowed concepts and practices 184
6.3 Regional convergence 188
6.4 A diverse marketing environment: The European Union 191
6.5 A changing marketing environment: Eastern Europe and the CIS 197
6.6 A challenging marketing environment: East Asia 200
6.7 Limitations to the world-wide convergence of marketing environments 203
Questions 204
Appendix 6: Teaching materials 204
A6.1 Exercise: Clustering African countries 204
A6.2 Case: Odol 204
References 207

7 Cross-cultural market research 210

7.1 Equivalence in cross-cultural research 211
7.2 Translation equivalence 216
7.3 Measure equivalence 220
7.4 Comparability of samples 223
7.5 Data-collection equivalence 227
7.6 Researching internationally 230
7.7 Conclusion 235
Questions 236
Appendix 7: Teaching materials 236
A7.1 Case: Eliot Greeting Card Company (2) 236
A7.2 Exercise: Hair shampoo questionnaire 237
References 243

Part 3

Marketing decisions for the intercultural environment 247

8 Intercultural marketing strategy 251
8.1 Cost arguments and global strategies 252
8.2 The globalization of competition 260
8.3 International marketing strategies are becoming global 262
8.4 Market segments: Geographic versus demographic 268
8.5 Conclusion 273
Questions 274
Appendix 8: Teaching materials 274
A8.1 Case: Lakewood Forest Products 274
A8.2 Exercise: *Dangerous Enchantment* 277
References 279

9 Product policy 1: Physical, service and symbolic attributes 282
9.1 Adaptation or standardization of product attributes 283
9.2 Physical attributes 284
9.3 Service attributes 290
9.4 Symbolic attributes 297
Questions 302
Appendix 9: Teaching materials 303
A9.1 Case: Lestra Design 303
A9.2 Case: Irish Cream O'Darby 312
References 314

10 Product policy 2: Managing meaning 316
10.1 National images diffused by the product's origin and by its brand name 317
10.2 Consumer product evaluation according to country of origin 319
10.3 National, international and global brands 330
Questions 341
Appendix 10: Teaching materials 342
A10.1 Exercise: Interpreting symbolic attributes 342
A10.2 Case: Soshi Sumsin Ltd 343
A10.3 Case: Derivados de Leche SA 345
References 347

11 The critical role of price in relational exchange 353
11.1 Price as a signal conveying meaning 354
11.2 Bargaining 355
11.3 Price and consumer evaluations 359
11.4 International price tactics 364
11.5 Market situations, competition and price agreements 370
11.6 Managing prices in highly regulated environments 372

Questions 376
Appendix 11: Teaching materials 376
A11.1 Case: Saito Importing Company 376
A11.2 Case: Riva International 377
A11.3 Critical incident: Taman SA 379
References 380

12 International distribution and sales promotion 382
12.1 The cultural dimension of distribution channels: The case of Japanese
    Keiretsus 383
12.2 Criteria for choosing foreign distribution channels 391
12.3 The role of distribution as a 'cultural filter' 393
12.4 Direct marketing world-wide 397
12.5 Sales promotion: Other customs, other manners 400
Questions 405
Appendix 12: Teaching materials 406
A12.1 Case: ComputerLand in Japan 406
A12.2 Case: Aunt Sarah's Fried Chicken 407
References 409

Part 4

Intercultural marketing communications 413

13 Language, culture and communication 415
13.1 Verbal communication: The role of context 416
13.2 Non-verbal communication 422
13.3 Language shaping our world-views 426
13.4 Ethnocentrism, stereotypes and misunderstandings in intercultural
    communication 431
13.5 How to improve communication effectiveness in international business 436
Questions 440
Appendix 13: Teaching materials 441
A13.1 Exercise: Multicultural class 441
A13.2 Exercise: I 'love' cake 441
A13.3 Exercise: Following directions 442
A13.4 Case: Supreme Canning 443
A13.5 Case: Doing business in China: a failure in getting paid 445
A13.6 Critical incident: Scandinavian Tools Company 446
References 450

14 Intercultural marketing communications 1: Advertising 453
14.1 Influence of culture on attitudes towards advertising 455
14.2 Culture and advertising strategy 458
14.3 Culture and advertising execution 462

14.4 Media world-wide: Technological advances and cultural convergence   474
14.5 The globalization of advertising   482
Questions   486
Appendix 14: Teaching materials   487
A14.1 Case: Levi Strauss Company: World-wide advertising strategy or localized
     campaigns?   487
A14.2 Case: Excel and the Italian advertising campaign   490
A14.3 Exercise: Borovets – a Bulgarian ski resort   492
A14.4 Exercise: Slogans and colloquial speech   494
References   494

15 Intercultural marketing communications 2: Personal selling, networking and public relations

15 Intercultural marketing communications 2: Personal selling,
networking and public relations   502
15.1 Intercultural commerce   503
15.2 Networks in business markets   510
15.3 Buyer–seller interactions   511
15.4 Sales force management in a cross-cultural perspective   515
15.5 Public relations across cultures   521
15.6 Bribery: Facts   524
15.7 Bribery: Ethical aspects   526
Questions   532
Appendix 15: Teaching materials   533
A15.1 Case: When international buyers and sellers disagree   533
A15.2 Critical incident: Setco of Spain   534
A15.3 Case: Union Carbide at Bhopal   536
A15.4 Case: Houston Oil Supply   538
A15.5 Critical incident: The *Brenzy nouveau* has arrived!   540
References   543

16 Intercultural marketing negotiations 1: People, trust and tasks

16 Intercultural marketing negotiations 1: People, trust and tasks   546
16.1 The dynamics of trust in relational marketing   547
16.2 The influence of culture on marketing negotiations   552
16.3 Behavioural predispositions of the parties   554
16.4 Underlying concepts of negotiation and negotiation strategies   559
16.5 Time-based misunderstandings in international marketing negotiations   565
16.6 Cultural misunderstandings during the negotiation process   569
16.7 Differences in outcome orientation: Oral versus written agreements as
     a basis for trust between the parties   572
Questions   577
Appendix 16: Teaching materials   577
A16.1 Case: McFarlane Instruments   577
A16.2 Negotiation game: Kumbele Power Plant   579
References   584

17 Intercultural marketing negotiations 2: Some elements of
national styles of business negotiation 588
17.1 Orientals 589
17.2 Western styles 592
17.3 Negotiation styles in other areas of the world 596
17.4 Some basic rules for international marketing negotiations 599
Questions 600
Appendix 17: Teaching materials 600
A17.1 Case: Tremonti SpA 600
References 602

Postscript 605

Author index 609
Subject index 620

Marketing in the global villages

This book is not a classical text of consumer marketing with an emphasis on world markets. Traditional international marketing texts are cross-border extensions of American marketing thought which sometimes blatantly ignore people, languages and cultures and implicitly argue in favour of uniformity. Large multinational companies, such as Mars, Pepsi-Cola, L'Oréal or Nestlé, do not follow traditional textbook recipes: their practice is always much more adaptive to and respectful of local contexts. This text offers a different approach to global marketing, based on the recognition of diversity in world markets and on local consumer knowledge and marketing practices. I invite the reader to undertake an exercise in de-centring. I myself try to break out of my 'Frenchocentric' box, in much the same way as Gorn (1997) invites us to break out of 'North American boxes'. Understanding international diversity[1] in consumer behaviour, advertising, sales, and marketing management becomes the central teaching objective for an international marketing textbook.

This text adopts a cultural approach to international marketing, which has two main dimensions:

1. A cross-cultural approach which proceeds by *comparing* national marketing systems and local commercial customs in various countries. It aims to emphasize what is country specific and what is universal. Such an approach is essential for the preparation and implementation of marketing strategies in different national contexts.

2. An intercultural approach, which is centred on the study of *interaction* between business people, buyers and sellers (and their companies) who have different national/cultural backgrounds. This intercultural view extends further to the interaction between products (and their physical and symbolic attributes) from a definite nation-culture (i.e. a country with a definite and homogeneous national

culture) and the consumers from a different nation-culture, and to the interaction between messages conveyed by marketing communications (brands, packaging and advertising) and consumers from a different culture. To this extent it is inter-action in its broad sense: not only between people, but also between people and messages, and people and products. In this book commerce is emphasized as much as marketing. When the word *commerce* is used in this text, it refers to the complex dimensions of business relationships entwined with interpersonal rela-tions.

The basic assumption behind this book is that culture penetrates our inner being subconsciously and at a deep level. World cultures share many common features. Nevertheless they all display a unique style when such common elements are com-bined: kinship patterns, education systems, valuation of the individual and the group, emphasis on economic activities, friendship patterns, time-related organization pat-terns, the criteria for aesthetic appreciation and so on. The examples that are used in this book are by their very nature eclectic. I have chosen those examples that seem to be both the most striking and pertinent.

I have no wish to describe cultures, either from an insider's point of view, or exhaustively. What I have attempted to provide for the reader is *a method for dealing with intercultural situations in international marketing*. The underlying postulate of this book is that international marketing relationships have to be built on solid founda-tions. Transaction costs in international trade are high: only a stable and firmly estab-lished link between business people can enable them to overcome disagreements and conflicts of interest. In international marketing it is advisable to be very methodical and long term oriented, to select a limited number of partners and opportunities and to develop them to their fullest extent.

Part 1, comprising the first three chapters, is devoted to the cultural variable. These chapters try to define it, to delineate the components of culture and finally to empha-size its dynamic nature. Part 2 deals with the globalization of markets, which is *the* central issue in international marketing; Chapters 4 and 5 examine consumer behav-iour, taking both a local and a global perspective, while Chapter 6 deals with local and regional marketing environments and Chapter 7 with cross-cultural market research. Part 3 presents the general impact of globalization on international marketing strate-gies (Chapter 8), with special emphasis on a key issue for product policy, namely, the dilemma between adaptation and standardization (Chapter 9). Chapter 10 deals with the complex management of meanings related to brand names for international mar-kets and to country of origin images. In Chapters 11 and 12, which concern price poli-cies and the choice of distribution channels, emphasis has also been deliberately placed on the culture-based approaches to such decisions. That is why, for instance, I accentuate bargaining (with its cultural variations) in Chapter 11, and the Japanese *keiretsu* distribution system, in Chapter 12.

Part 4 presents marketing communications in an intercultural environment. It starts with a general overview (Chapter 13) of language, culture and communication issues, which are applied in the next two chapters to advertising issues, personal sell-ing, public relations and to bribery and ethical issues in international marketing. Chapters 16 and 17 are devoted to international marketing negotiations. Table I.1

presents a summary of the basic contents of Chapters 4 to 17, linking culture to marketing issues.

This book is written from both a European and an Asian viewpoint, with many examples relating to these two areas of the world. No international marketing textbook can be considered universal, and this one is no exception. It is written in a slightly less pragmatic and issue-oriented style than most international marketing textbooks. Statements may sometimes be classed as value judgements, since they are not supported by facts and empirical evidence as frequently as is the case in American textbooks. Therefore this book may sometimes seem unusual to native English-speaking readers. I believe they have to regard this appoach as part of the message of the book: it is a more contextual, and therefore less explicit, relationship with the reader.

Each chapter concludes with questions and is followed by an appendix comprising some or all of the following: cases, exercises and critical incidents. An instructor's manual is also available. Since different national versions of this book have been published (Dutch, English, French and German), it may be used in cross-cultural training settings.

TABLE I.1   The impact of cultural differences on selected aspects of marketing

Area of marketing	Cultural differences influence ...	Chapter
Consumer behaviour	Cross-cultural consumer attitudes and decision making	4
	Local consumers and global consumption	5
Local marketing environments	Local infrastructures and marketing knowledge	6
Market research	Equivalence and methods in cross-national market surveys	7
Overall marketing strategy	Global versus locally customized marketing strategies	8
Targeting market segments	Cross-border vs. country clustering	8
Product policy	Adaptation or standardization of product attributes	9
Brand image	Brand and country-of-origin evaluations by consumers	10
Price policy	Bargaining rituals/Price–quality evaluations/Price strategies towards consumers, competitors and suppliers	11
Distribution channels	Channel style and service, producer–distributor relationships	12
Communication	World-views (through language) and communication styles	13
Advertising	Tailoring messages to local audiences' cultural traits	14
Personal selling	Selling styles, sales force management, networking and public relations, bribery and ethical issues in an international context	15
Marketing negotiations	Negotiation strategies, processes and outcomes	16
National style of marketing negotiation	Attitude, organization, scheduling, role of emotions and friendship, communication and interaction style	17

I wish to acknowledge the help of various institutions which during the last ten years have provided me with the opportunity to teach international marketing, and colleagues who have encouraged me to put more and more emphasis on the cultural dimension of international marketing. I thank also Magda Robson and the whole team at Pearson Education who have been instrumental in editing this book. I remain responsible for any errors and shortcomings in the book.

NOTES

1. Diversity is not understood here in its American sense with a strong anti-discrimination stance (reported for instance by Litvin, 1997), but rather in its simplest meaning of 'state or quality of being different or varied', with no value judgement about whether 'diversity' is good or bad. In fact it is neither good nor bad, as shown by Lian and Oneal (1997) through a cross-national study linking cultural diversity to economic development for 98 countries over the period 1960–85.

REFERENCES

Gorn, Gerald J. (1997), 'Breaking out of the North American box', in Merrie Brucks and Debbie McInnis (eds), *Advances in Consumer Research*, vol. 24, Association for Consumer Research: Provo, UT, pp. 6–7.

Lian, Brad and John R. Oneal (1997), 'Cultural diversity and economic development: A cross-national study of 98 countries, 1960–1985', *Economic Development and Cultural Change*, vol. 46, no. 1, pp. 61–77.

Litvin, Deborah R. (1997), 'The discourse of diversity: From biology to management', *Organization*, vol. 4, no. 2, pp. 187–209.

The cultural variable in international marketing

Introduction to Part 1

THE CULTURAL VARIABLE IN INTERNATIONAL MARKETING

In an increasingly interdependent world where barriers to trade and to international exchanges constantly diminish, cultural differences remain the single most enduring feature that has to be taken into account for localizing marketing strategies. Part 1 of this book introduces key concepts in cultural studies that have great influence on the understanding of local markets and the design of international marketing strategies.

Chapter 1 starts by presenting the basic elements of culture and international marketing, providing both general definitions of culture and its main components, such as language and social institutions. For the sake of simplicity, cultural boundaries are often equated with nationality: the limitations of such an assumption are presented. Finally, the chapter reviews how culture affects the development of skills and how certain forms of social representation tend to emerge as a result of meaning being shared in the cultural community. The objective of Chapter 1 is to enable readers to depart from their own cultural conditioning; the end-of-chapter teaching materials are designed for this.

Chapter 2 is an introduction to cultural dynamics, that is, how basic cultural assumptions influence behaviour, and it gives special emphasis to two key dimensions, time and space. These cultural assumptions have an impact on a set of marketing-related issues such as material culture, sense of ownership, preference for durability and so on. The chapter starts by presenting a model of action based on cultural assumptions, which sees final action as a complex outcome of individual decision making framed by deep-seated assumptions about a number of fundamental issues such as how humans relate to nature. It proceeds then to examine cross-cultural variability in the way time is conceived and experienced as well as how people in different cultures manage their relationship to space. Since a great deal of contact and exchange between cultures has taken place over the centuries, the process by which foreign items and customs are borrowed and reinserted in the local scene by various societies is examined. Another important aspect of the inter-cultural encounter is hostility towards unknown people; the last section of this chapter discusses how and why cultural hostility develops in the form of prejudices and negative stereotypes.

Chapter 3 complements the preceding chapter and continues to explain how basic cultural assumptions influence human behaviour and interactions. It examines, first, how people in a particular culture build their concepts of what they are and what others are, which is a basic input in the range of interaction models found in any culture. A number of fundamental issues are then examined, such as: what kind of attitudes towards action are developed? How do people relate thinking to action? How do people deal with desires and feelings? What is the range of cultural variation for coping with rules? This chapter ends with an examination of how cultural assumptions shape actual behaviour. It shows that the influence of culture on behaviour is most often indirect and profound, and moderated by a number of other influences.

1 The cultural process

Not everything is culture based. It would be most dangerous to equate the behaviour of individuals entirely with that of the cultural grouping to which they belong. Furthermore, we often have a rather stereotyped perception of such behaviour, which provides only a shallow, imperfect picture of the operation of a cultural group. Interpretation is often defensive and the analysis neither comprehensive nor fully explicative.

International marketing automatically accords a prominent place to the cultural variable, despite the difficulties of isolating it for direct implementation. One of the principal aims is to identify, categorize, evaluate and finally select market segments. Nation-states are an enduring reality. In many cases, though not all, national territory and the concept of a nation are justified by the existence of groups that are relatively homogeneous on an ethnic, linguistic and religious level. Lack of homogeneity is often at the centre of disputes between different cultural communities. The cultural variable is complex, and the way in which it influences behaviour is difficult to analyze.

The objective of this chapter is to clear the way for the arguments that will be developed later in the book. Initially this involves the definition of culture and its major constituents, and an examination of its relations with nationality (i.e. the concept of national character) and individual psychology (i.e. personality/individual character). Culture is used not only as a guide for communication and interaction, quite subconsciously, with others in one's own community, but also for rather more conscious interaction with people belonging to other cultural communities. I have borrowed from the field of anthropology, particularly cultural anthropology, and also from several other disciplines, sociology, social psychology and cross-cultural psychology.

I strongly urge interested readers to use the notes and bibliographical references at the end of this and the following two chapters, and to refer to the sources mentioned in their original form wherever possible.

1.1   CULTURE: DEFINITION(S)

In French the word *culture* was defined by Emile Littré, in his dictionary which appeared at the end of the nineteenth century, as 'cultivation, farming activity'. The abstract sense probably originated in Germany where the word *Kultur* was used as early as the eighteenth century to refer to civilization. In the Anglo-Saxon world the abstract notion of culture came into widespread use at the beginning of the twentieth century.

Many definitions have been formulated for culture: because it is a vague, abstract notion, there are many candidates for the ultimate definition. Kroeber and Kluckhohn (1952) even devoted an article to a review of the definitions of culture and listed no fewer than 164! This did not prevent them from adding their own. Most of these definitions were the work of anthropologists, generally those who had studied 'primitive' societies (American Indians, Pacific Islanders, African natives and so on). But their definitions also took into account our 'civilized' societies and 'modern' cultures. The use of several definitions, each one adding to the cultural jigsaw puzzle, will help to determine the main aspects of this abstract and elusive concept.

Particular solutions to universal problems

Kluckhohn and Strodtbeck (1961, p. 10) emphasize the following basic points:

1. '. . . there is a limited number of common human problems for which all peoples at all times must find some solution.'

2. 'While there is a variability in solutions of all the problems, it is neither limitless nor random but is definitely variable within a range of possible solutions.'

3. '. . . all alternatives of all solutions are present in all societies at all times, but are differentially preferred. Every society has, in addition to its dominant profile of value orientations, numerous variant or substitute profiles.'

How does culture link the individual to society?

Ralph Linton (1945, p. 21) advanced the following definition: 'A culture is the configuration of learned behaviour and results of behaviour whose component elements are shared and transmitted by the members of a particular society.' At a previous point in his book, Linton clearly indicates the limits of the cultural programming which the society can impose on the individual (1945, pp. 14–15, emphasis added):

No matter how carefully the individual has been trained or how successful his conditioning has been, he remains a distinct organism with his own needs and with capacities for independent thought, feeling and action. Moreover *he retains a considerable degree of individuality*. . . . Actually, the role of the individual with respect to society is a double one. Under ordinary circumstances, the more perfect his conditioning and consequent integration into the social structure, *the more effective his contribution to the smooth functioning of the whole and the surer his rewards*. However societies have to exist and function in an ever-changing world. The unparalleled ability of our species to adjust to changing conditions and to develop ever more effective responses to familiar ones rests upon the residue of individuality which survives in every one of us after society and culture have done their utmost. As a simple unit in the social organism, the individual perpetuates the *status quo*. As an individual he helps to change the *status quo* when the needs arises.

What use is culture to the individual?

According to Goodenough (1971), culture is a set of beliefs or standards, shared by a group of people, which help the individual decide what is, what can be, how to feel, what to do and how to go about doing it. On the basis of this definition there is no reason for culture to be equated with the whole of one particular society. It may be more related to activities that are shared by a particular group of people. Thus individuals may share different cultures with several different groups. When in a particular cultural situation, they will 'switch into' the culture that is operational. The term 'operational' describes a culture that is shared by those among whom there must be co-operation and that is suitable for the task.

Goodenough's concept of 'operational culture' assumes that the individual can choose the culture in which to interact at any given moment or in any given situation. This is of course subject to the overriding condition that the culture has been correctly internalized from past experiences. Although the concept of operational culture is somewhat debatable, it does have the advantage of highlighting the multicultural nature of many individuals in today's societies (bi-nationals, multilingual people, people who have a particular national identity and an international professional culture, employees influenced by corporate culture). It draws our attention to the important issue of the sources of the individual's acculturation.

How to define the 'borders' of a culture

As Child and Kieser emphasize (1977, p. 2):

Cultures may be defined as patterns of thought and manners which are widely shared. The boundaries of the social collectivity within which this sharing takes place are problematic so that it may make as much sense to refer to a class or regional culture as to a national culture.

In colloquial language, when we say 'Texans', or 'Parisians', or 'docs', or 'showbiz' we are referring to cultures as well as to the groups of people who share them. But it is important to consider the following issue: to what extent do the characteristics of these groups relating to certain patterns of thought, belief or behaviour really differentiate them from other cultural groups?

1.2   ELEMENTS OF CULTURE

Culture is much more a process than a distinctive whole, which would be entirely identifiable by the sum of its elements. Its elements are organically interrelated and work as a coherent set. It is not only a 'toolbox' for it also provides people with some 'directions for use' in their daily life in the community. Nevertheless it may be interesting to identify some key elements of culture. Tylor (1913) describes culture as a complex and interrelated set of elements, comprising knowledge, beliefs and values, arts, law, manners and morals and all other kinds of skills and habits acquired by a human being as a member of a particular society.

The biological foundations of culture

The anthropologist Bronislaw Malinowski has evidenced the relationship between the purely biological needs of people and the way in which they are organized and regulated within the framework of the cultural community. For Malinowski (1944, p. 75) there are clearly biological foundations to culture: 'We have to base our theory of culture on the fact that all human beings belong to an animal species. . . . No culture can continue if the group is not replenished continually and normally.' He develops the example of eating habits, which must be regarded as both biological *and* cultural:

Cultural determination is a familiar fact as regards hunger or appetite, in short the readiness to eat. Limitations of what is regarded as palatable, admissible, ethical; the magical religious, hygienic and social taboos on quality, raw materials, and preparation of food; the habitual routine establishing the time and the type of appetite – all these could be exemplified from our civilization, from the rules and principles of Judaism, or Islam, Brahmanism or Shintoism, as well as from every primitive culture.

Malinowski (1944, pp. 86–7) also evokes the cultural relativity of sexual behaviour:

The specific form in which the sexual impulse is allowed to occur is deeply modified by anatomical inroads (circumcision, infibulation, clitoridectomy, breast, foot and face lacerations); the attractiveness of a sex object is affected by economic status and rank; and the integration of the sex impulse involves the personal desirability of a mate as an individual and as a member of the group. It would be equally easy to show that fatigue, somnolence, thirst and restlessness are determined by such cultural factors as a call to duty, the urgency of a task, the established rhythm of activities.

Language

Language has a prominent role as an element of culture. A linguist and anthropologist, Benjamin Lee Whorf (Carroll, 1956, p. 65), a chemical engineer working for a fire insurance company, spent his spare time tracing the origins and grammar of American Indian languages. He is the author of a seminal, and quite controversial, hypothesis, often referred to as the Whorfian hypothesis or Whorf–Sapir hypothesis. Aspects of this theory have been incorporated, either explicitly or implicitly, at many points in this book, particularly those chapters in which language and linguistic issues figure strongly: market research (Chapter 7) – because of questionnaires and interviews, brands (Chapter 10), marketing communications – advertising (Chapters 14 and 15) and negotiation (Chapters 16 and 17). Whorf defines his basic tenet as follows:

The ethnologist engaged in studying a living primitive culture must often have wondered: 'What do these people think? How do they think? Are their intellectual and rational processes akin to ours or radically different?' But thereupon he has probably dismissed the idea as a psychological enigma and has sharply turned his attention back to more readily observable matters. And yet the problem of thought and thinking in the native community is not purely and simply a psychological problem. It is quite largely cultural. It is moreover largely a matter of one especially cohesive aggregate of cultural phenomena that we call a language.

In short, Whorf defends the idea that the language we learn in the community where we are born and raised shapes and structures our world-view and our social behaviour. It influences the way in which we address issues, select those we consider relevant, solve problems and finally act. Although the Whorfian hypothesis has been harshly criticized by many linguists, it remains a *fundamental metaphor*, though not a fully validated scientific theory. We will refer to it as a key issue when describing the pitfalls of intercultural communication (in Chapter 13). Language, especially through tenses and words, shapes time-related behaviour which has an influence on business attitudes (when negotiating or dealing with delivery times or appointments). African Bantu people, for instance, do not have a specific word (as do most western cultures) which clearly differentiates the 'here' and the 'now'. They have a common time–space localizer (see reading A2.4).

Social institutions, material and symbolic productions

Language is an essential part of culture: it is regarded as a reflection of culture. It is the basic input of any culture-based communication process, because everyday life is mostly a matter of interaction through communication in a culturally homogeneous community. But obviously it is not the only element of the culture shared in the community. For instance, the Swiss use different languages but have shared a common culture for several centuries. Accordingly, three other types of element appear to be quite significant:

1. Institutions, broadly defined, because they are the 'spine' of the cultural process, in that they link the individual to the group. This area may include family as well as political institutions, or any kind of social organization within which the individual has to comply fairly obediently with rules in exchange for various rewards (e.g. being fed, loved, paid and so on). These rules are not static and an individual may also sometimes act as a proactive agent of change.

2. Productions (again, broadly defined): not only material productions, but also productions of intellect, artistry and service in so far as they transmit, reproduce, update and continuously attempt to improve the knowledge and skills in the community.[1]

3. Symbolic and sacred elements, because they are the basis for the description (and therefore management) of the relations between the physical and the metaphysical world. Cultures range from those where the existence of any kind of metaphysical world is completely denied to those where symbolic representations of the metaphysical world are present in everyday life. A central preoccupation of cultural communities is to define, through religious and moral beliefs, whether there is life after death and of what kind. The scientific movement, especially at the end of the nineteenth century, has seemed close to eliminating these questions by pushing back the boundaries of the metaphysical world. Nowadays scientists recognize that the metaphysical question will never be resolved fully by scientific knowledge. What is in fact of interest to us is not the answers to these

questions; it is the consequences of moral and religious assumptions, which differ widely across cultures, on individual and collective behaviours.

There is nothing to prevent a particular cultural item from belonging to these four elements of culture simultaneously, which then appear as different layers. For instance, music is at the same time a language, an institution, an artistic production and also a symbolic element.

Productions are diverse: tools, machines, factories, paper, books, instruments and media of communication, food, clothing, ornaments, etc. As a result, we often confuse an influential civilization (which corresponds to the German word *Kultur*) with a cultural community which successfully produces many goods and services. But material consumption or wealth orientation is not definitive proof of cultural sophistication. *There is no hierarchy, apart from the purely subjective, between world cultures.* There are many different cultural attitudes to the material world, its importance and the level of priority in the community's resource allocation given to productions and material achievements.

In *A Scientific Theory of Culture* (1944), Bronislaw Malinowski compiled a list of universal types of institutions across cultures, to which the following refers. The first institution is based on the integrative principle of *reproduction*: it is underpinned by blood relationships and marriage as an established contractual framework. It covers all kinds of kinship patterns – the family as the basic institution formed by the parents and their children. The reproduction principle also incorporates the ways courtship and marriage are legally organized. The extended family must also be considered: clan organization and its nature (matrilineal, patrilineal); the regulation of interclan relationships, etc.

The second type of institution is based on the integrative principle of *territoriality*. Common interests are dictated by neighbourhood and vicinity. Co-operation may be enhanced by the commonly perceived threat of potential foes who are located outside the common territory. This type of institution may range from a horde of nomads to a village, a small town community, a region, a province or, at the largest level, the 'mega-tribe' composed of all the people sharing the same nationality. Initially territoriality is concrete, based on physical space and some kind of fencing or borders. In the modern world, it may be extended to abstract territories (associations, clubs, alumni and so on).

The third integrative principle is a *physiological* one: people in the community are basically characterized by their sex, age, physical traits or defects. This includes institutions such as the sexual division of labour, sex roles, the relationship patterns between age groups and the way minority members of the community are treated (asylums for the mentally ill, or special homes for the disabled).

The fourth principle deals with the *spontaneous tendency to join together*, in order to pursue common goals. This gives raise to various kinds of associations: primitive secret societies, clubs, artistic societies, mutual companies, etc.

The fifth principle is that of *occupational and professional activities*: it deals with the way labour is divided and the kinds of expertise that have been developed. In modern societies, this includes economic organization, the medical system, the legal system and other groups of experts; in fact all those institutions that maintain the fabric of a society: industry organizations, trade-unions, the courts, the police, the army, educational institutions and religious bodies.

The sixth principle relates to the inevitable *hierarchy* within any society: the existence of rank and status positions. This includes the following, *inter alia*: the nobility, the middle class and slaves, or more generally any kind of social class system or caste system. The social hierarchy may follow a variety of criteria: ethnicity, education or the level of riches, etc.

The seventh principle proposed by Malinowski corresponds to the necessity of gathering and co-ordinating these diverse elements into a reasonably coherent whole, that is, *totality*. The political process, whatever it may be (feudal, democratic, theocratic, dictatorial, etc.), expresses the need for totality. It deals with the collective decision process at the highest level. The various strata of totality, such as the individual striving for identity and the community striving for coherence, may compete with each other: that of a minority, that of a state; more generally sub-groups of the mega-tribe of a nation-state. A minority, willing to practise its religion and mores (e.g. polygamy), may be opposed to the state which tries to maintain the global coherence by limiting social customs to the dominant solution (e.g. monogamy). More generally any sub-group of the 'mega-tribe', composed of all the nationals of a particular state, may feel that their particular interests are conflicting with those of the community as a whole. These oppositions will be stronger in 'simple' states (where the nationals are not necessarily homogeneous from a cultural point of view) than in a real 'nation-state' (where the nationals share a common linguistic and cultural background).

Culture as a collective fingerprint: are some cultures superior?

Culture is *the* domain of pure quality. There are no 'good' or 'bad' elements of a particular cultural group. Value judgements should be avoided as much as possible. In this respect culture is entirely qualitative. Culture is identity: a sort of collective fingerprint. Cultural differences exist, but this is no reason for judging a particular culture as *globally* superior or inferior to others. Cultures may be evaluated and indeed ranked, but only on the basis of facts and evidence according to precise criteria and for very specific segments of culture-related activities. Some people may be said to make better warriors, others to hold finer aesthetic judgement, or to be more gifted in the composition of music and so on. But culture is a set of *coherent* elements: straightforward comparison might allow us to indulge in the rather dangerous illusion that it is possible to select the best from each culture and make an 'ideal' combination. However, as we will see later on, it is not quite as easy as that.

A joke about Europeans illustrates this. It goes: 'Heaven is where the cooks are French, the mechanics are German, the policemen are English, the lovers are Italian and it is all organized by the Swiss. Hell is where the policemen are German, the mechanics are French, the cooks are British, the lovers are Swiss and it is all organized by the Italians.' It is easy to see that not only would it be difficult to take the best traits from a culture, while rejecting the worst, but also any attempt to combine the best of several cultures could eventually turn out to be a disaster. This is because *coherence* is needed at the highest level (corresponding to *identity* at the individual level).

The importance of the symbolic dimension

Productions of culture cannot be described only by their physical attributes: they always contain a symbolic or sacred dimension. Mircea Eliade (1956, p. 79) describes how the arts of the blacksmith and the alchemist, the forerunners of modern metallurgy and chemistry, hold a powerful symbolic dimension:

The alchemist, like the smith, and like the potter before him, is a 'master of fire'. It is with fire that he controls the passage of matter from one state to another. The first potter who, with the aid of live embers, was successful in hardening those shapes which he had given to his clay, must have felt the intoxication of the demiurge: he had discovered a transmuting agent. That which natural heat – from the sun or the bowels of the heart – took so long to ripen, was transformed by fire at a speed hitherto undreamed of. This demiurgic enthusiasm springs from that obscure presentiment that the great secret lay in discovering how to 'perform' faster than Nature, in other words (since it is always necessary to talk in terms of the spiritual experience of the primitive man) how, without peril, to interfere in the processes of the cosmic forces. Fire turned out to be the means by which man could 'execute' faster, but it could also do something other than what already existed in Nature. It was therefore the manifestation of a magico-religious power which could modify the world and which, consequently, did not belong to this world. This is why the most primitive cultures look upon the specialist in the sacred – the shaman, the medicine-man, the magician – as a 'master of fire'.

Numerous illustrations of the strength of symbolic dimensions are given throughout the book. In the area of marketing communication, the symbolic dimension is of the utmost importance: products and their advertising communicate through the symbolism of colour, shape, label, brand name and so on. The interpretation of symbols is strongly culture bound.

Traditional societies have always been more consciously involved in symbolic thought and behaviour than modern societies. Since less is *explained*, more must be *related*. For example: Why does the sun shine every day? Should its disappearance be considered ominous? What should be done to satisfy it so that it goes on spreading its generous rays on the fields and rivers? The bloody ritual sacrifices in the pre-Columbian civilizations were heavily charged with symbolic content.[2] Human sacrifices were dedicated to the sun, as were the blood and the living heart which was pulled out of the bodies of living people. The Spanish conquerors were utterly horrified by these sacrifices because they did not understand their meaning. The Spaniards were helped in their conquest by a myth: Mayas and Aztecs were waiting for the return of Quetzalcoatl, a sort of man-god, who had been a benevolent ruler over his people and whose return was to herald a golden age. When the bearded Hernando Cortès landed in Mexico, accompanied by strange creatures (the Indians believed that horses and their riders were a single body), they saw him as Quetzalcoatl.

Of course, symbols are not only related to religious and metaphysical matters; they also extend into everyday life. It is a common mistake to believe that the symbolic dimension has largely disappeared in modern life, forgotten by the modern people who have progressed along the road towards science and knowledge, pushing back the boundaries of the metaphysical world, which will ultimately be eliminated. The illusion of the pre-eminence of science, generated by technological breakthroughs in the nineteenth century, is now largely abandoned by today's top scientists. As Stephen Hawking points out (1988, p. 13):

ever since the dawn of civilization, people have not been content to see events as unconnected and inexplicable. They have craved an understanding of the underlying order in the world. Today we still yearn to know why we are here and where we came from.

1.3   CULTURE AND NATIONALITY

Nationality is one delimitation of individuals belonging to a large group, it is operational and obviously convenient. However, the direction of causality between these concepts of nationality and culture is not self-evident. It is likely that, historically, shared culture has been a fundamental building-block in the progressive construction of modern nation-states. But as soon as these states began to emerge, they struggled against local particularisms, patois and customs, and tried to homogenize institutions. Conflicts in large countries have often had a strong cultural base: the War of Secession in the United States, the rivalry between the English and the Scots in the United Kingdom and the progressive elimination of local powers in the highly centralized French state, all have distinctive cultural elements at stake: language, values, religion, concepts of freedom, etc.

Nevertheless an attempt to equate culture directly with the nation-state, or country, would be misguided, for a number of convergent reasons:

1. A country's culture can only be defined by reference to other countries cultures. India has a country culture in comparison with Italy or Germany, but the Indian subcontinent is made up of highly diversified ethnic and religious groups (Muslims, Hindus, Sikhs, etc.) and languages (there are more than twenty principal languages). India is a deeply multicultural country.

2. Some nation-states are explicitly multicultural – Switzerland, for instance. One of the basic levels of organization is the canton (*Gau* in German), which defends local particularisms. Precise staffing levels have been established in public bodies, companies and banks, which prevent discrimination between linguistic communities whose numbers are unequal: the German-speaking Swiss make up almost three-quarters of the total population, the French-speakers a little more than 20 per cent, Italian-speakers 3–4 per cent and Romansch-speakers about 1 per cent. However, there is a common misconception that Switzerland administers its multiculturalism without encountering any difficulties.[3] The Swiss political system, which was established more than seven centuries ago, enables the people to manage successfully the complex trade-off between an exacerbated compliance with local peculiarities and a common attitude towards anything that is not Swiss.

3. Political decisions, especially during the last century, have imposed the formation of new states, particularly through the processes of colonization and decolonization. The borders of these new states, sometimes straight lines on a map, were often fixed with little respect for cultural realities, and international negotiators obviously had very little in common with the people for whom they were making decisions. Many significant national cultures, such as that of the Kurds (split between the Iraqis, the Syrians, the Turks and the Iranians) have never been accorded the right to a territory or a state. The Eritreans (in Ethiopia) have been given such a possibility after seventy years of civil war.

Sources of culture

The national element is not always the main source of culture when regarded from an 'operational culture' perspective (Goodenough, 1971). Figure 1.1 shows the basic sources of cultural background at the level of the individual. For instance, medical researchers or computer hardware specialists, whatever their nationality, share a common specialized education, common interests and largely the same professional culture. This is developed through common training, working for the same companies, reading the same publications world-wide, and contributing to research where international cross-cultural comparability of purely scientific methods and results is fundamental.

Likewise, the sense of belonging to an important ethnic group may override, and even nullify, the feeling of belonging to a particular nation-state. The Tamil population in Sri Lanka, which makes up about 20 per cent of the total Sri Lankan population and is mostly centred around Jaffna in the north of the island, is strongly linked with the large Tamil community in southern India (numbering 55 million), which supports them in their claim for autonomy. The Tamils are involved in a brutal struggle with the Singhalese community which comprises the largest part of the population. The sense of belonging to a large ethnic group is, in this case, much stronger than the feeling of belonging to a national group.

National/cultural territories with specific, recognized borders are rarely fully homogeneous. The transition from one to another is often facilitated by 'cross-border' cultures. Examples of this are numerous. In the area around the border between France and Spain, for instance, two cultures, which are almost national cultures, exist side by side and offer continuity between the two countries: the Basque country to the west,

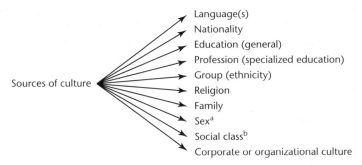

FIGURE 1.1   Sources of culture.

[a]In 1948 the anthropologist Margaret Mead published *Male and Female*, which draws on her in-depth knowledge of several South Pacific and Balinese cultures. It not only depicts their organization of relationships between men and women, the division of labour and roles in the community, but also explains how these patterns may be compared to those of contemporary American society. *Male and Female*, which has continued to be a best-seller, is an excellent and detailed introduction to sex cultures. Although rarely mentioned in this book, which is principally concerned with territory and national culture, the difference between masculine and feminine culture is in fact the most basic cultural distinction.
[b]Social class may be a distinctive source of culture, to a greater or lesser degree, depending on the country. For instance in France and England, where there are traditions of accepted birth inequalities and a strong historical orientation, social class is a very distinctive source of culture; the way one speaks immediately reveals one's social class. However in the United States, Japan or the Scandinavian countries, this is not so marked. But like sex, and unlike most other sources, social class is not a territory-based source of culture.

Catalonia to the east. The painter Salvador Dali, a Catalan born in Figueras (Spain) which is 20 kilometres from the French border, was fascinated by the train station at Perpignan in France – the French part of Catalonia. In reality these two places, on either side of the border, belong to the same Catalan culture, which is sustained by the use of the Catalan language. Other examples show that some people have been able to reach a compromise: the Swedish-speaking minority on the west coast of Finland, for instance, or the Alsatians in France. Alsatians speak a mostly German-based patois, behave in the workplace like Germans and traditionally lean towards a sense of French nationality and the adoption of the French lifestyle outside the workplace. People who belong to these 'cross-border' cultures generally have a privileged position as 'exporters' from one country to another.

Physical and climatic conditions are also a fairly systematic source of differentiation (subtle rather than fundamental). Hence almost every apparently unified country is made up of a 'North' and a 'South'. Even in a country that is homogeneous from a linguistic, ethnic, religious and institutional point of view, such as Sweden, there is a fairly marked difference, at least for the Swedes, between the culture and lifestyle of a southern city and a northern town. This difference may not be so strongly perceived by foreigners, who initially appreciate only their own differences from Swedes and Sweden as a whole.

Cultural homogeneity and relevant segmentation

Most international market segments are based on geographical/geopolitical divisions, which may be also efficient segmentation criteria in cultural terms. However, sociodemographic variables or lifestyles may also be relevant for international segmentation. Should one, for instance, target a transnational ethnic segment, a national segment or a cross-border regional segment? Chapters 6 and 8 examine the issue of regional versus national segmentation, which is particularly important in large countries like the United States and in economic areas such as the European Union (EU).

Homogeneity in certain fields clearly favours the emergence of a coherent culture in a nation-state and hence the possible confusion of culture and country and treatment of the latter as a culturally unified and coherent segment (which could be broken down into sociodemographic microsegments):

1. Linguistic homogeneity.
2. Religious homogeneity.
3. Ethnic homogeneity.
4. Climatic homogeneity.
5. Geographical homogeneity.
6. Institutional and political homogeneity.
7. Social/income homogeneity.

The word 'homogeneity' implies one of the following:

1. The existence, throughout the whole population, of a unique modality (that is, only one religion, or one language) or a reduced standard deviation (in per capita

income, for instance, across all social strata) in comparison with the mean value of the characteristic across the whole population.

2. An accepted diversity, that is, an agreement for maintaining several languages, more or less spoken and/or understood by everybody, or several different religions (as in Germany), but all of them officially recognized and financed by the state.

3. 'Perceived homogeneity', that is, the perception of differences within a country as being acceptable within the national community. For instance, people may observe huge differences in wealth and income but consider it acceptable for various reasons: fatalism, indifference or metaphysical justification.

The concept of national culture

The concept of national culture may seem dangerous in many respects, because it sums up a complex and multiform reality. In short, as a variable it is too artificial to avoid the traps of cliché and stereotype. The following two questions should give a better grasp of the concept:

1. Is this concept coherent and substantial enough to constitute an explanatory variable, not only in the scientific sense, but also from a pragmatic point of view?

2. How does it influence behaviour: can one speak of national character or national culture?

The answer to the first question is clear: the concept of national culture suffers a systematic lack of coherence. It is an 'intersection' of concepts, one being the result of the merging of culture (a mostly anthropology-based concept), and the other, more official, concept being that of the nation-state. As discussed earlier, cultures do not often correspond to nation-states but to linguistic, ethnic, religious or even organizational entities. This is due to the fact that in modern times, the most frequent mode of political organization of individuals within a particular society is that of the nation-state, hence the emergence of this 'intersection' concept of national culture. The vagueness of this concept probably explains why it has been systematically underestimated, especially in international trade theory. Theory-builders, who generally seek to construct formally convincing theoretical explanations, tend to remove such vague variables from their models even if they are explanatory. However, the fact that a construct is not easily measurable is no justification for ignoring it. Despite its limitations, the concept of national culture can still be an interesting Pandora's box.

The second question merits consideration, but the two possible responses as to whether culture directly influences personality cannot be assessed on a scientific basis. Some people favour the idea that the cultural variable directly influences individual psychological characteristics, that is, culture has a distinct imprint on personality. Personality traits exist for which the average individual in one culture scores significantly higher (or lower) than individuals belonging to another culture. This corresponds to the idea of national character or more precisely the concept of modal personality, which has been developed in greater detail by Inkeles and Levinson (1969).[4] This approach largely grew out of enquiries which now seem to have lost some of their relevance: why are certain people more violent, more aggressive, more domineering, collectively more prone to declare war on other nations or to organize and implement genocide? These questions stemmed from the Second World War, especially the Nuremberg trials. Numerous empirical studies have been undertaken, particularly during the 1950s and 1960s, taking as a starting point the formation process of national character (where there could be a divergence between nations): rearing practices, early childhood, education systems, the socialization process of children, etc. Generally the results neither prove nor disprove the existence of national character.

The second approach is that of the anthropologist Ralph Linton in his book, *The Cultural Background of Personality* (1945). According to Linton, individual psychology and therefore personality traits are largely free from the influence of culture (1945, pp. 14–15): 'His [the individual's] integration into society and culture goes no deeper than his learned responses, and although in the adult the greater part of what we call the personality, there is still a good deal of the individual left over.' The question of whether personality is modal (culture-bound) or culture free is not just academic. In Linton's view, individuals may have personalities quite separate from their cultural background. From a 'national character' perspective, one would expect to meet people with an average personality which reflects their culture.

1.4   CULTURE AND COMPETENCE

Some environmental predispositions

Some peoples are considered to be more work oriented and more efficient when it comes to producing material goods. Among the most efficient peoples are those who lost the Second World War: Germany, Japan and Italy. Climate has often been considered an environmental variable which has a strong influence on performance. Box 1.1 contains the beginning of Montesquieu's theory of climates (1748). The physiological explanations are scarcely credible now; it is nevertheless a starting point for the north/south stereotype. The question is: do some countries/climates tend to harden (or soften) people, with the result that they become more (or less) inclined towards activities of war, commerce or industry,[5] and more (or less) efficient in pursuing these activities?

It is a different assumption to say that climate has either a direct influence, that heat physically discourages effort and action, or an indirect influence on skills, through cultural adaptation to climatic conditions. The indirect may be combined with the direct influence because climate may have had a long-term influence on the culture, which would in turn influence skills and behaviour. If the influence is purely direct, air conditioning is obviously a solution for some settings (but for instance, one cannot have an air-conditioned battle). If climate has both a direct and an indirect influence, via progressive genetic adaptation and/or cultural traits acquired through education and socialization, then air conditioning is still necessary but not enough.

National character and educational practices

Research about national character has emphasized the influence of educational practices on the development of adult personalities. Margaret Mead for instance, in her

BOX 1.1

Of the difference of men in different climates

A cold air* constringes the extremities of the external fibres of the body; this increases their elasticity, and favors the return of the blood from the extreme parts to the heart. It contracts⁺ those very fibres; consequently, it increases also their force and elasticity. People are therefore more vigorous in cold climates. Here the action of the heart and the reaction of the extremities of the fibres are better performed, the temperature of the humors is greater, the blood moves freer towards the heart, and reciprocally, the heart has more power. This superiority of strength must produce various effects; for instance, a greater boldness, that is, more courage; a greater sense of superiority, that is, more frankness, less suspicion, policy, and cunning. In short, this must be productive of very different tempers. Put a man into a close warm place, and, for the reasons above given, he will feel a great faintness. If, under this circumstance, you propose a bold enterprize to him, I believe you will find him very little disposed towards it: his present weakness will throw him into a despondency; he will be afraid of every thing, being in a state of total incapacity. The inhabitants of warm countries are, like old men, timorous; the people in cold countries are, like young men, brave. If we reflect on the late** wars, (which are more recent in our memory, and in which we can better distinguish some particular effects, that escape us at a greater distance of time), we shall find that the northern people, transplanted into southern regions⁺⁺, did not perform such exploits as their countrymen who, fighting in their own climate, possessed their full vigor and courage.

*This appears even in the countenance: in cold weather people look thinner.
⁺We know it shortens iron.   **Those for the succession to the Spanish monarchy.
⁺⁺For instance in Spain.

(Source: Montesquieu, 1792, vol. 1, book XIV, ch. 11, pp. 224–5.)

description of American character, notes that adult personality in the United States must be seen as an adolescent peer culture. In this setting, education favours diffuse, depersonalized authority where children face a demand for strong inner moral control. In many European countries, the cheerful, easy-going, informal Americans are often jokingly referred to as being big children.

One of the most efficient ways to study the formation process of national character is to observe education systems and rearing practices; particularly the rearing of small children, up to the age of 5 or 6. Some of the key elements of personality development are here: feeding and nourishing, weaning, personal hygiene and toilet training, the degree and modes of socialization into various parts of the community (with other children, with adults, with the opposite sex), the demands and prohibitions imposed on small children, and finally the reward/sanction systems which help to orientate their behaviour.[6]

Culture and skills

It seems that cultural background has an influence on perceptual and cognitive skills and their orientations and capacities. Segall *et al.* (1990) clearly demonstrate the existence of differences in perception of visual illusions. They base their findings on the following simple theory: if people belonging to various human groups differ in their visual inference systems,[7] this is because the physical environment at which they are used to looking may differ widely from group to group. Some people live in a constructed environment, based on straight lines and sharp angles (especially those of modern buildings and industrial objects), whereas other people live in a more rounded and curvilinear physical setting. The daily environment shapes people's visual inferences: the very same objects are seen differently (where vision is considered as a culturally built interpretation of specific retinal signals).

The variations in levels of competences and skills across cultural groups is another important issue. The first research on the intellectual abilities of non-European people has been undertaken by researchers such as Levy-Bruhl, who classified the thought patterns of primitives as 'pre-logical'. Little by little this somewhat extreme attitude, that 'primitives' could never conceive of anything in the way that we do (we being the modern, westernized people of European culture or origin), has given way to a more reasonable position. Franz Boas became interested in the idea of the psychic unity of mankind: every human group studied presents common traits such as the ability to remember, to generalize, to form concepts and to think and reflect logically on abstract concepts. In fact it seems more likely that differences in ability in specific activities should be attributed to the cultural relativity of skills and competences developed by the individuals in the specific cultural grouping where they have been raised. The scores on intelligence quotient (IQ) tests will always remain relative to the type of questions asked and to the situations evoked in the verbal part of the test (reading, memorization and understanding of texts); even that part of the test which is clearly quantitatively oriented (mathematics, geometry, statistics, logic) requires the handling of abstract and mathematical signs. One cannot claim that it encompasses all the possible facets of human intelligence, or even that it offers total objectivity in the experimental and empirical methods of evidencing them. It is therefore necessary to accept that definitions of intelligence are culturally contingent. This does not mean that all people are equally intelligent, or that IQ tests are of no interest or practical usefulness. It simply means that the results should be interpreted cautiously when tests are administered to people who do not originate from the culture where these tests were conceived and/or are not familiar with this culture.

1.5   CULTURE AND SOCIAL REPRESENTATIONS

The notion of social representation will be used throughout this book, even where there is no explicit reference to it. For instance, the acceptance (or prohibition in some countries) of comparative advertising across countries is related to social representations of the necessity to inform consumers, to allow price competition and even to risk the denigration of one company by another through a comparative advertising campaign (see Chapter 14).

Moscovici (1961) considers social representation (SR) a 'forgotten concept'. He traces it back to Durkheim, for whom it was a class of psychic and social phenomena that relate the individual to the social aspect of collective life. Social representations are miniatures of behaviour, copies of reality and forms of operational knowledge in order to reach and implement everyday decisions. For instance, people may use a combination of social representations in order to make their health-care decisions. Moscovici gives the following example that in the south-west of the United States Hispanic populations concurrently use four bases of knowledge for classifying and interpreting illnesses: the traditional popular medical knowledge, which relates mainly to pains and sufferance; the medical knowledge orally transmitted within Amerindian tribes; the modern (English) popular medical knowledge; and medical scientific knowledge (established and recognized). According to the seriousness of the illness and the availability of money for paying for the cure, Hispanic populations let themselves be guided either by collective representations or by scientific information in order to choose which one of these four sources should be pursued in search of a cure.

Social representations are collective images which are progressively formulated within a particular society. They may be surveyed by public opinion polls. Robert Farr (1988, p. 383) explains that social representations of health and sickness may have a strong influence on consumption patterns. Villagers in many European countries, for instance, tend to moan over the invasion of the countryside by urban development; the entire population compares the constraints of city life to the natural pace of country life. These social representations help to explain the development of natural and organic products, direct from the farm, with no additives or industrial processing, and the diffusion of ecological ideas in modern society.

Jodelet (1988, p. 360) posits social representations at the very intersection of the psychological/individual and social/collective levels. They serve as artificial reference images, as frameworks 'which enable us to interpret what happens to us, possibly even to give sense to the unexpected; categories which serve to classify circumstances, phenomena, individuals with whom we have to deal and theories which enable us to make a decision on these issues'.

The interpretation by people of their daily reality with this sort of preconceived reference framework could be considered pejoratively as reflecting merely their prejudices. However, it would give but a scant idea of the dynamic, collectively verified and validated nature of social representations, which are constantly updated through social situations, individual behaviour and social activities. The media, public opinion polls, news summaries, court decisions and sentences are all sources from which people derive their opinions and stimulate debate and social information processes, which in turn continuously update dynamic social representations.

Social representations do vary across societies. They therefore have a cultural value for the individuals when they have to decide what is, what can be, how to feel, what to do and how to go about doing it (operating culture). Social representations are less profound, as they alter within shorter time spans (ten to twenty years) than basic cultural orientations which change over centuries – the latter are reviewed in the next chapter. But social representations are none the less important – they may oppose basic cultural orientations since their time-scale is short term and they are more suited to the urgent need for collective and individual adaptation to reality.

QUESTIONS

1. In light of the definitions of culture given in this chapter, is it possible for a culture to disappear? Why, or why not? Give an example.

2. A common problem, across cultures, is to attract/be attractive for potential partners. Discuss how, in Kluckhohn and Strodtbeck's terms, there is a range of possible solutions, and how they are differentially preferred across societies. Outline possible consequences for marketing.

3. Discuss the case of multi-language/multi-religion countries (e.g. India, Canada, Switzerland): how can people in these countries share a common culture? On which segments of culture?

4. Discuss the role of education (at home, at school and elsewhere) in the transmission of culture.

5. What is *national character*?

APPENDIX 1: TEACHING MATERIALS

A1.1 CRITICAL INCIDENT: **An old lady from Malaysia**

The frail, old, almost totally blind lady appeared at every clinic session and sat on the dirt floor enjoying the activity. She was dirty and dishevelled, and obviously had very little, even by Malaysian kampong (local village) standards.

One day the visiting nurse happened upon this woman in her kampong. She lived by herself in a rundown shack about 10 by 10 feet [3 × 3 m]. When questioned how she obtained her food, she said she was often hungry, as she only received food when she worked for others – pounding rice, looking after the children, and the like.

The nurse sought to obtain help for the woman. It was finally resolved that she would receive a small pension from the Department of Welfare which would be ample for her needs.

At each weekly clinic, the woman continued to appear. She had become a centre of attention, laughed and joked freely, and obviously enjoyed her increased prestige. No change was noted in her physical status, however. She continued to wear the same dirty black dress and looked no better fed.

The nurse asked one of the rural health nurses to find out if the woman needed help in getting to a shop to buy the goods she seemed so sorely in need of.

In squatting near the woman, the rural health nurse noted a wad of bills in the woman's pocket. 'Wah,' she said, 'It is all here. You have spent nothing. Why is that?'

The woman laughed and then explained: 'I am saving it all for my funeral.'

(Source: Weeks *et al.*, 1987, pp. 24–5. Reproduced with the kind permission of the publisher.)

A1.2   CRITICAL INCIDENT: **The parable**

The leader tells the following parable to the group, illustrating with rough chalkboard drawings if desired:

Rosemary is a girl of about 21 years of age. For several months she has been engaged to a young man named – let's call him Geoffrey. The problem she faces is that between her and her betrothed there lies a river. No ordinary river mind you, but a deep, wide river infested with hungry crocodiles.

Rosemary ponders how she can cross the river. She thinks of a man she knows who has a boat. We'll call him Sinbad. So she approaches Sinbad, asking him to take her across. He replies, 'Yes, I'll take you across if you'll spend the night with me.' Shocked at this offer, she turns to another acquaintance, a certain Frederick, and tells him her story. Frederick responds by saying, 'Yes, Rosemary, I understand your problem – but – it's your problem, not mine.' Rosemary decides to return to Sinbad, spends the night with him, and in the morning he takes her across the river.

Her reunion with Geoffrey is warm. But on the evening before they are to be married, Rosemary feels compelled to tell Geoffrey how she succeeded in getting across the river. Geoffrey responds by saying, 'I wouldn't marry you if you were the last woman on earth.'

Finally, at her wit's end, Rosemary turns to our last character, Dennis. Dennis listens to her story and says, 'Well, Rosemary, I don't love you . . . but I will marry you.' And that's all we know of the story.

(Source: Weeks *et al.*, 1987, pp. 25–6. Reproduced with the kind permission of the publisher.)

Discussion guide

1. Before any discussion takes place, participants should be asked to write down individually on a piece of paper the characters of whose behaviour they most approve, plus a sentence or two explaining their first choice.

2. Participants may be split into small groups of four or five, to share their views and raise relevant issues.

3. The discussion should centre around the cultural relativity of values and their relation to one's own cultural background.

NOTES

1. One may be wary of the ethnocentric (western/modern) bias of the author, in that there is an overemphasis on culture as striving only for the improvement of material productions; in some cultures, the dominant values may be extremely antagonistic towards material preoccupations.

2. The conquest of Mexico by Hernando Cortès is a fascinating example of the almost total destruction of a culture heavily loaded with symbolism (mostly that of the Aztecs and the Mayas) by only a very small group of Spanish invaders. When Cortès's army left the island of Cuba, sailing to Mexico, it numbered only 508 soldiers, 100 sailors and 10 horses. At that time Mexico City had half a million inhabitants.

The Mayas, the Totonacs and the Mexicans were deeply religious people, totally subservient to the will of their gods and the sovereignty of their priest-kings. These people waged a ritualistic war on each other which was based on magic as much as military strategy and in which the desired outcome, decided in advance by the mysterious agreements of celestial powers, was not the conquest of land or the amassing of riches but the triumph of the gods, who received in sacrifice the heart and the blood of the vanquished. Disturbed by the mythical return of the ancestors and of the divine feathered serpent, Quetzalcoatl-Kukulcan, the Indians were blinded, unable to see the actual intentions of those whom they had termed the *Teules*, the Gods. And when the Indians understood that the Spaniards, whom they considered as demi-gods, were involved in a massive slaughter of Mexican Indians, from which none of them would emerge unscathed, it was too late. The Spaniards had taken advantage of their hesitation to penetrate deep into the Mexican empire, to provoke dissension and to conquer lands and take slaves. (Le Clézio, 1988, p. 19).

See also *Historia Verdadera de la conquista de la Nueva Espana*, written by a member of the Cortès troop, Bernal Diaz del Castillo (1968) and *Historia General de las cosas de la Nueva Espana*, written by Bernadino de Sahagun a few years after the conquest (which took place around 1520) and the destruction of the Aztec and Mayan cultures, with the objective of preserving as far as possible the traces of this civilization which had suffered such an abrupt disappearance. For a thorough analysis of culture collisions in colonial history see Urs Bitterli (1989).

3. A famous Swiss novelist, Charles Ferdinand Ramuz, has often set the relations between communities as a background to his novels. *La Séparation des races*, for instance, is the story of the kidnapping of a young girl from Berne by her Valaisan lover and the consequent mobilization of their respective communities.

4 The literature review carried out by Inkeles and Levinson (1969) is certainly the most exhaustive one (100 pages) available. It might appear somewhat dated, but since national character changes over decades and centuries rather than shorter time spans, their review remains largely up to date.

5. War is assimilated here with commerce and industry because, from a historical perspective, war was a *normal* activity. The idea that war produces the vanquished and the victorious, but that they are all losers, is rather a new one. When pursuing colonial wars, commerce and industry were legitimately included in the ultimate goals. The idea of bringing civilization to the barbarians included the extirpation of 'evil' beliefs, magic and sorcery, and their substitution by Christianity.

6. An important figure in these studies of childhood and society is Erik Erikson (1950), who developed a theory of ego development stages (in the Freudian sense) on the basis of field observations of American Indians, Sioux and Yurok, US Americans, Germans and Russians. It is clearly beyond the reach of this book to sum up, even very briefly, the richness of the empirical and theoretical research on national differences which has been published by anthropologists, sociologists and psychologists. The references at the end of this chapter suggest two reviews of such cross-national research: Inkeles and Levinson (1969) and Segall *et al.* (1990).

7. By 'visual inference' is implied the mental system which enables people to transform retinal perceptions into a 'brain image' (Segall *et al.*, 1990, ch. 4).

REFERENCES

Bitterli, Urs (1989), *Cultures in Conflict*, Polity Press: Oxford.

Carroll, John B. (1956), *Language, Thought and Reality: Selected writings of Benjamin Lee Whorf*, MIT: Cambridge, MA.

Child, J. and A. Kieser (1977), 'A contrast in British and West German management practices : Are recipes of success culture bound?', paper presented at the *Conference on Cross-Cultural Studies on Organizational Functioning*, Hawaii.

Diaz del Castillo, Bernal (1968), *Historia Verdadera de la Nueva España*, Espasa-Calpe: Madrid.

Eliade, Mircea (1956), *Forgerons et Alchimistes*, Flammarion: Paris. English translation (1962), *The Forge and the Crucible*, University of Chicago Press: Chicago.

Erikson, Erik (1950), *Childhood and Society*, Norton: New York.

Farr, Robert M. (1988), 'Les Représentations sociales', in Serge Moscovici (ed.), *Psychologie sociale*, PUF Fondamental: Paris.

Goodenough, Ward H. (1971), *Culture, Language and Society*, Modular Publications, 7, Addison-Wesley: Reading, MA.

Hawking, Stephen (1988), *A Brief History of Time*, Guild Publishing: London.

Inkeles, Alex and Daniel J. Levinson (1969), 'National character: The study of modal personality and sociocultural systems', in Gardner Lindzey and Elliot Aronson (eds.), *Handbook of Social Psychology*, vol. IV, Addison-Wesley: Reading, MA, pp. 418-506.

Jodelet, Denise (1988), 'Représentations sociales: phénomènes, concept et théorie', in Serge Moscovici (ed.), *Psychologie sociale*, PUF Fondamental: Paris.

Kluckhohn, Florence R. and Frederick L. Strodtbeck (1961), *Variations in Value Orientations*, Greenwood Press: Westport, CT.

Kroeber, Alfred L. and Clyde Kluckhohn (1952), *Culture: A critical review of concepts and definitions*, Anthropological Papers, no. 4, Peabody Museum.

Le Clézio, J. M. G. (1988), *Le Rêve Mexicain ou la Pensée Interrompue*, Gallimard: Paris.

Linton, Ralph (1945), *The Cultural Background of Personality*, Appleton-Century: New York.

Malinowski, Bronislaw (1944), *A Scientific Theory of Culture and Other Essays*, University of North Carolina Press: Chapel Hill, NC.

Mead, Margaret (1948), *Male and Female*, William Morrow: New York.

Montesquieu, Charles de (1748), *The Spirit of Laws*, translated from the French by Thomas Nugent (1792), 6th edn, McKenzie and Moore: Dublin.

Moscovici, Serge (1961), *La Psychanalyse, son Public et son Image*, Presses Universitaires de France: Paris.

Segall, Marshall H., Pierre R. Dasen, John W. Berry and Ype H. Poortinga (1990), *Human Behavior in Global Perspective*, Pergamon: New York.

Tylor, Edward (1913), *Primitive Culture*, John Murray: London.

Weeks, William H., Paul B. Pedersen and Richard W. Brislin (1987), *A Manual of Structured Experiences for Cross-cultural Learning*, Intercultural Press: Yarmouth, ME.

2 Cultural dynamics 1: Time and space

Culture is sometimes regarded as a somewhat vague concept. The Swedish writer Selma Lagerlöf defines culture as 'what remains when that which has been learned is entirely forgotten'.[1] Depicted thus, culture may appear to be rather a 'rubbish-bin' concept. Its main use would be as a 'synthesis variable': an explanation that serves as a last resort, that is, when all other concepts or more precise theories have been successfully validated. It would also serve as an explanatory variable for residuals, when other more interpretive explanations are unsuccessful.

However, the definition quoted above does have the important merit of identifying two basic elements of cultural dynamics (at the level of the individual):

1. It is learned.
2. It is forgotten in the sense that we cease to be conscious of its existence as learned behaviour.

Yet culture remains present throughout our daily individual and collective activities, and is therefore entirely oriented towards our adaptation to reality (both as a constraint and an opportunity). To this extent it is almost unthinkable that a culture could stand perfectly still, except in the case of those primitive societies that live in quite stable natural and social environments, located in remote places and subject to no exterior interference. At the periphery of a fixed set of basic cultural assumptions, other sources of culture intervene, as a result of which new solutions are used for tackling existing issues or for solving entirely new problems.

This chapter takes as a starting point a model of action based on cultural assumptions (section 2.1). It sets a framework for the explanation of culture-related behaviour which extends throughout this chapter and the next. Basic cultural assumptions that are explained in this chapter relate to time (section 2.2) and to space (section 2.3). Cultures borrow from each other through time and space and section 2.4

is dedicated to this process of borrowing from other cultures and corresponding changes in the importing society. The last section (2.5) is dedicated to cultural hostility: territoriality is the organizing principle of cultures across space and hostility arises from prejudiced views of others and the fear of having space to share with members of alien cultural groups.

2.1   A MODEL OF ACTION BASED ON CULTURAL ASSUMPTIONS

Figure 2.1 presents how basic cultural assumptions in three major areas (time, space and the concept of the self and others) influence interaction models, which, in combination with basic assumptions, shape attitudes towards action. Fundamental assumptions about time, space and the concept of the self and others are explained in greater detail in this chapter and the first section of the next. *Cultural assumptions are statements about the basic nature of reality.* Some of them are based on the 'value orientations' of the anthropologists Florence Kluckhohn and Frederick Strodtbeck (1961) which are often cited – an indication of their analytical power, at least as far as it is perceived by the social scientists. Kluckhohn and Strodtbeck have tested their value orientation theory

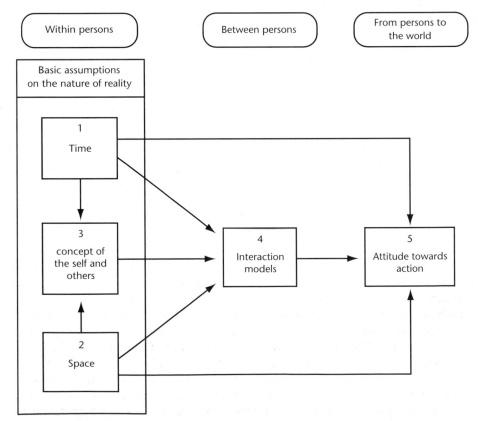

FIGURE 2.1   A model of cultural dynamics.

across five very distinct cultural communities, each one made up of American citizens living in close proximity to each other in the south-western part of the United States, in similar natural environments: 'Two of the populations are American Indian; one an off-reservation settlement of Navaho Indians . . . the other the Pueblo Indian community of Zuni. The third is a Spanish American village which we have named Atrisco. A Mormon village and a recently established farming village of Texan and Oklahoman homesteaders . . . are the two other communities' (1961, p. 49).

Cultural assumptions are basic responses, expressed in a rather dichotomous manner, to fundamental human problems. They provide the members of a particular cultural community with a basic framework for the evaluation of solutions to these problems, combining a cognitive dimension *(people think it works that way)*, an affective dimension *(people like it that way)* and a directive dimension *(people will do it that way)*. Kluckhohn and Strodtbeck (1961, pp. 11, 12) have collected these common human problems under six main categories:

1. What is the character of innate human nature (human-nature orientation): good or evil, neutral, or a mix of good and evil? Is this state of human nature mutable or immutable?

2. What is the relation of humans to nature and supernature (nature orientation): subjugation to nature, harmony with nature or mastery over nature?

3. What is the temporal focus of human life (time orientation): past, present or future?

4. What is the modality of human activity (activity orientation): should people be (being), should people do (doing) or should they do in order to be (being in becoming)?

5. What is the modality of the relationship between humans (relational orientation): linearity, collaterality or pure individuality?

6. What is the conception of space? Is it considered predominantly private, public or a mix of both?

Naturally these modalities are to be found in every society. People *are* and *do*, and there are always children and parents, in the sense that some kind of family nucleus exists everywhere. But different assumptions result in variations as to the kind of response which is dominant in a particular society. We have combined this approach with those adopted by other authors (Hall, 1959, 1966, 1976, 1983, Hofstede, 1980, Triandis, 1983, 1994, Trompenaars, 1993) to depict differences in five tables: basic cultural assumptions in Tables 2.1, 2.2 and 3.1, interaction models in Table 3.2 and attitudes towards action in Table 3.5.

Each of the five tables highlights common problems across cultures, depicts the most important solutions and explains the dominant contrasts. This leads to a detailed inventory of basic differences in cultural assumptions and interaction models, which are mostly the result of learned behaviour. I have tried to give some country illustrations, without too often citing 'typical' cultures, because to do so would be at the risk of stereotyping. Except for Hofstede's four dimensions, which are considered mostly in the realm of 'interaction models', few empirical data are mentioned. For those interested in figures, rankings and scores, I have indicated where they can find such information, to the extent that it is available and significant. My objective is not to classify countries or cultures, but rather to provide readers with an understanding of how cultures differ, and to let them combine this with their own knowledge and experience in order to build their own view of how culture affects our relationships with others and our way of acting.

In doing this, I could not ignore the profound impact of technology on culture. There was the risk that many basic assumptions could be called 'modern' and they would have been naturally compared with what would be classed as 'traditional'. The real world is fortunately more sophisticated: individualism is globally 'modern', but collectivism is not 'traditional' nor even 'conservative'. Many collectivist nations, especially in Asia, have been brilliant achievers in the past twenty years. 'Modern culture' is predominantly based on western values, those held by philosophers, scientists and politicians in the United Kingdom, France and other European countries, during the period when they experienced industrial revolution and colonized other people, and later by the United States, as the dominant political and cultural actor on the twentieth-century world scene. The influence of a cultural assumption being considered as 'modern' is that it is more legitimate, sometimes to the extreme that it is officially considered as the only possible belief. Thus other assumptions tend to be repressed, leading to complex situations where people finally imitate behaviour which does not correspond to the assumptions really prevailing in their culture. Thus, I will try to refer to why and how a certain cultural assumption, interaction model or attitude towards action belongs to 'modern' culture.

At this point in the book, some readers may wonder why I am digging into culture, with apparently little interest in managerial issues, including the focus of the book, that is, international marketing. They will find an initial response in Table 3.5, point (c): I come from an ideology-centred culture where issues are most often addressed first at a very broad level. Later, attempts are made to link culture to action-related issues. My intellectual style is basically French and German: I try to build convincing intellectual frameworks, occasionally at the expense of data. Some readers may consider my statements sometimes to be unsupported by data and evidence. I claim to be culturally relative. The second response is: part of the cross-cultural learning experience resides in being confronted with a different mindset. My belief is that developing cultural awareness is possible just from reading something written with a culturally alien mindset. Cultural assumptions are not completely in the realm of *unbewußtsein* (unconsciousness, deep-seated and inaccessible); in fact, they are rather in the realm of *unterbewußtsein*, that is located at a subconscious level, where interaction and self-questioning can reveal them.

In order to make the link between them, I have tried to refer as often as possible to areas of international marketing on which these cultural differences have an impact. In subsequent chapters in the book they are also used as an explanatory framework for consumer behaviour (Chapter 4), market research (Chapter 7), marketing management (Chapters 8 to 12), advertising communication (Chapter 14), buyer–seller interactions and marketing negotiations (Chapters 15 to 17). The last four chapters build on chapter 13 which is dedicated to language, culture and communication, and explains how language shapes our world-views. Point (e) in Table 3.2 (communication styles) is developed in Chapter 13.

Taking Figure 2.1 as the basis, our exploration starts with the cultural variability in the concept of time.

2.2   TIME: CROSS-CULTURAL VARIABILITY

Most marketing concepts are time based: product life cycle, sales forecasting or the planning of new product launches to name but a few.[2] Normative time in marketing and management seems indisputable, and its very nature is rarely questioned: it is perceived as linear, continuous and economic. However, time, in a cross-cultural perspective, is probably the area where differences are both the largest and the most difficult to pinpoint, because (1) assumptions are very deep seated and (2) formally we adopt a common model of time. People's relationship with time changes with respect to periods of history and the level of human development, according to the technology available for measuring time, to the emphasis given to natural and social rhythms, and to the prevailing metaphysical views. Each vision of time *(Zeitanschauung)* corresponds to a vision of the real world, its origins and destiny *(Weltanschauung)*. Time appears prominently through its social functions in that it allows people to have a common organization of activities and helps to synchronize individual human behaviour. Encyclopaedic approaches to the concept of time (Attali, 1982) show that never has one time pattern eliminated a previous one. Each new time pattern superimposes itself on the one that previously prevailed. As a consequence, individual time perceptions may result from adding or mixing different basic patterns of time. Most of the literature in cultural anthropology considers time perceptions as cultural artefacts. As Gurevitch states (1976, p. 229): 'Time occupies a prominent place in the "model of the world" characterizing a given culture.'

Dimensions of time orientations

Table 2.1 shows time-related cultural assumptions which correspond to four common problems:

1.   To what extent should time be regarded as a tangible commodity (economicity of time)?

2.   How should tasks and time be combined (monochronic versus polychronic use of time)?

3.   Should lifetime(s) be seen as a single continuous line or as combining multiple cyclical episodes (linearity versus cyclicity of time)?

4.   What are the appropriate temporal orientations: towards the past, the present and the future?

As the reader will see, there is some overlap between the prevailing solutions to these four questions. However, I have noted all four basic time assumptions because they need to be considered in order to have a substantive view of what a cultural model of time is. This is exemplified at the end of this section by the Japanese *Makimono* time.

TABLE 2.1   Time-related cultural differences

Basic problem/Cultural orientations	Contrasts across cultures
Is time money? (a) Economicity of time	Time is regarded as a scarce resource or, conversely, as plentiful and indefinitely available.
How to schedule tasks (b) Monochronism versus polychronism	Only one task is undertaken at any (preset) time, following a schedule ('agenda society'), versus dealing simultaneously with different tasks, actions and/or communications (polychronism) for convenience, pleasure and efficiency.
Is time a continuous line? (c) Linearity (L) versus cyclicity (C) of time	Time is seen as linear-separable, cut in slices (L), versus an emphasis on the daily, yearly and seasonal cycles (C).
How should we emphasize past, present and future? (d) Temporal orientations (i) towards the past	People with high past orientation consider that the past is important, that resources must be spent on teaching history and building museums, referring to oral and written traditions and past works. Their basic assumption is that their roots are implanted in the past and no plant can survive without its roots. The converse is true for low past orientation.
(ii) towards the present	People with high present orientation consider that they basically live 'here and now'. Although not always enjoyable, the present must be accepted for what it is: the only *true* reality we live in.
(iii) towards the future	People easily and precisely envisage and plan their future. They are project oriented, prepare for the long term, appreciate the achievements of science, and so on. For them the future is inevitably 'bigger and better'. The converse is true for low future orientation.

Economicity of time

Time may be seen as external to us, and as such to be treated like a tangible commodity. The concept of economic time is based on accurate time reckoning, dependent on precise dating and defined duration. It results in people using their time as 'wisely' as possible, scheduling, establishing timetables and deadlines. Measurement of parking meter time by units of 7.5 minutes or sport performance by the hundredth of a second is typical of economic time as precisely measured and bearing direct and explicit financial consequences. Many European countries as well as the United States are representative of the 'time-is-money' cultures, where time is an economic good. Since time is a scarce resource, or at least is perceived as such, people should try to achieve its optimal allocation between competing ways of using it. Norms tend to be very strict regarding time schedules, appointments and the precise setting of dates and durations in a society where time is strongly felt as economic.

Needless to say, attitudes towards money and the money value of time are inseparable from marketing (Jacoby *et al.* 1976). A strong economic time assumption has wide-reaching influences on consumer behaviour, because products may save time, as household appliances do, or services may be based on time values such as bank loans or life insurance policies. Economicity of time also has an impact on buyer–seller interaction, in the waiting process as well as for dealing together.

Monochronic versus polychronic use of time

Hall (1983) has described two extreme behaviours of task scheduling which he calls monochronism (M time) and polychronism (P time). Individuals working under M time do one thing at a time and tend to adhere to preset schedules. When confronted by a dilemma (e.g. a discussion with someone that lasts longer than planned), M-time people will politely stop the conversation, in order to keep to their schedule. In M-time societies, not only the start of a meeting but also its finish will be planned. P-time, on the other hand, stresses the involvement of people who do several things at the same moment, easily modify preset schedules and seldom experience time as 'wasted'. P-time may seem quite hectic to M-time people: 'There is no recognized order as to who is to be served next, no queue or numbers indicating who has been waiting the longest' (Hall, 1983, p. 47). P-time people are more committed to persons than to schedules. When confronted with a conflict such as the one described above, they prefer to go on talking or working after preset hours and break their schedule, if they have one.

The PERT (programme evaluation and review technique) programming method is an example of a typical 'agenda culture', where M-time is the central assumption. It explicitly aims to reduce a universe of polychronic tasks (they really take place simultaneously, which is part of the problem) to a monochronic solution (the critical path). Management methods, originating in the United States and Europe, favour pure monochronic organization. They clearly push aside polychronic attitudes, which tend to make plans and schedules rather hectic. When it comes to delays and being 'on time', precise monochronic systems give priority to meeting dates and commitments to schedules (Usunier, 1991).

To illustrate sources of tension between people who have internalized different time systems, Hall (1983, pp. 53–4) takes the example of a monochronic woman who has a polychronic hairdresser. The woman, who has a regular appointment at a specific time each week, feels frustrated and angry when she is kept waiting. At the same time, the hairdresser also feels frustrated. He inevitably feels compelled to 'squeeze people in', particularly his friends and acquaintances. The schedule is reserved for impersonal people such as this woman, but since he does not know them personally, keeping to the schedule is not important to him. M or P time is important for business negotiations, buyer–seller interactions in general, or dealing with a foreign distributor (e.g. scheduling a promotional campaign).

Linearity (L) versus cyclicity (C) of time

It is easy to guess that a strongly economic view of time, when it is combined with monochronism, emphasizes the linearity of time. Time is viewed as being a line with a point at the centre, the present. Each portion of the line can be cut into slices, which are supposed to have a certain money value. Basic religious beliefs play a key role in supporting such a linear view of time: Christianity has a one-shot interpretation of worldly life, and people do not live twice (as in the James Bond film title). People wait until the final judgement day to enjoy reincarnation. By contrast, Asian religions, including Hinduism and Buddhism, assume that, on the death of the body, the soul is born again in another body. The belief in regular reincarnation, until a pure soul is allowed to escape the cycle and go to *nirvana*, changes radically the nature of time in a specific life: it is not 'all the time I have got', it is simply one of my 'times' across several lives. For most Asians, cyclicity is central in their pattern of time: *nirvana* is the final release from the cycle of reincarnation attained by extinction of all desires and individual existence, culminating (in Buddhism) in absolute blessedness, or (in Hinduism) in absorption into Brahman. Naturally, patience is on the side of the people believing in cyclical reincarnation of the soul. For Christians, it is more urgent to achieve, because their souls are given only one worldly life. But, as the New Testament puts it clearly, those who do right, even in the very last moment, will be considered favourably.

Another element which favours a cyclical view of time is the degree of emphasis put on the natural rhythms of years and seasons, the sun and the moon. It largely contrasts so-called 'modern' with 'traditional' societies, in as far as 'modern' means technology, mastering nature and, to a certain extent, the loss of nature-related reference points. The Japanese are known for having maintained a strong orientation to nature, even in a highly developed society. Their floral art of *Ikebana* and the emphasis on maintaining a contact with nature, even in highly urban environments, are testimonies to their attachment to the natural rhythms of nature. Even within a country, the relationship to nature influences the model of time adopted by urban as compared with rural people.

Elements of cyclicity are based mostly on metaphysical assumptions or on astronomical observations, but they also include some arbitrary divisions, which are more social than natural. The example of the duration of the week is a good example of the social origins of the reckoning of time cycles. Sorokin and Merton (1937) give the following illustrations of the variability of the week in number of days.

Our system of weekly division into quantitatively equal periods is a perfect type of conventionally determined time-reckoning. The Khasi week almost universally consists of eight days because the markets are usually held every eighth day. A reflection of the fact that the Khasi week had a social, rather than a 'natural', origin is found in the names of the days of the week which are not those of planets (a late and arbitrary development) but of places where the principal markets are held. In a similar fashion the Roman week was marked by *nundinae* which recurred every eighth day and upon which the agriculturists came into the city to sell their produce. The Muysca in Bogota had a three-day week; many East African tribes a four-day week; in Central America, the east Indian Archipelago, old Assyria (and now in Soviet Russia), there is found a five-day week . . . and the Incas had a ten-day week. The constant feature of virtually all these weeks of varying length is that they were always found to have been originally in association with the market.

Elements of cyclicity of time have therefore three main origins: (1) religious assumptions about reincarnation of the soul; (2) natural rhythms of years, seasons and days; and (3) the social division of time periods which is more arbitrary, less natural and 'given', than we assume. Time is naturally both linear and cyclical. I do not argue that one vision of time is 'better' than another. Generally cultures have definite time patterns which combine both views, as is shown later in this section by the example of Japanese *Makimono* time, and by reading A2.4, which presents the Bantu concept of time.

Temporal orientations: past, present and future

The perception of time also tends to be related to temporal orientations *vis-à-vis* the arrow of time. As stated by Kluckhohn and Strodtbeck (1961, pp. 13–15):

The possible cultural interpretations of temporal focus of human life break easily into the three point range of past, present and future . . . Spanish-Americans, who have been described as taking the view that man is a victim of natural forces, are also a people who place the present time alternative in first position . . . Many modern European countries . . . have strong leanings to a past orientation . . . Americans, more strongly than most people of the world, place an emphasis upon the future – a future which is anticipated to be 'bigger and better'.

Being past oriented means that people emphasize the role of the past as explaining where we are now. Europeans are typical of people making this assumption, as are some Asian people. They will tend to restore old buildings, invest in museums, teach history at school, etc. It does not mean that temporal orientation to the past is only based on cultural assumptions. It also depends on individual psychological traits (Usunier and Valette-Florence, 1994). Futhermore, in societies undergoing a rapid process of economic change, past orientation is often provisionally underplayed.

Present orientation is the most logical assumption, in terms of quality of life at least. It means that people favour the 'here and now', believing that the past is over and the future is uncertain, theoretical and difficult to imagine. Religion may play an important role in pushing people towards present orientation, if it emphasizes that only God decides about the future. In terms of temporal orientation the Arabic–Muslim character has been described as fatalistic, rather short term oriented, and not future oriented (Ferraro, 1990). As stated by Harris and Moran (1987, p. 474):

Who controls time? A Western belief is that one controls his own time. Arabs believe that their time is controlled, to a certain extent, by an outside force – namely Allah – therefore the Arabs become very fatalistic in their view of time . . . Most Arabs are not clockwatchers, nor are they planners of time.

Future orientation is naturally related to the view that people can master nature, but also to the view that the future can in some way be predicted or at least significantly influenced. In societies where future orientation is strong, it is backed by the educational system and by an 'imagination of the future' supported by reports on scientific breakthroughs and technological developments.

Combined cultural models of time: The Japanese *Makimono* time

Economic time usually goes with linear time, monochronism and future orientation. It is our 'modern' time, near to R. J. Graham's (1981, p. 335) concept of the 'European-

American (Anglo) perception that allows time to have a past, present and future, and to be sliced into discrete units and then allocated for specific tasks'. This view holds that time can be saved, spent, wasted or even bought, just like money. Even among the cultures that share this pattern of time, there may be significant differences. Lane and Kaufman (1992, p. 15) contrast the prevailing patterns in Northern Europe with those in the United States:

The closed stores on Saturday afternoons and Sundays and short weekday hours are extremely limited by United States standards. Such customs limit the actual clock hours that are available for shopping, reduce weekend employment, etc. The result is a system which encourages recreation and/or social time in the evenings and on weekends, particularly on Sundays. In Europe it is very common to find people taking recreational walks, bike rides, visiting a park or sitting in the cafe. These are not completely foreign to the United States, but seem to exist in Europe on a much grander scale. The use of time in quiet visiting seems to be much greater.

Graham has tried to represent a synthesis of time perception dimensions, not only as a set of different perceptual dimensions, but also as complete temporal systems. He contrasts 'Anglo' time, which he describes as being 'linear-separable', with the 'circular-traditional' time of most Latin-American countries. This perception arises from traditional cultures where action and everyday life were not regulated by the clock, but rather by the natural cycles of the moon, sun and seasons. Graham proposes a third model, 'procedural-traditional', in which the amount of time spent on an activity is irrelevant, since activities are procedure driven rather than time driven. This system is typical of the American Indians, and to a large extent it also typifies Bantu time (reading A2.4). Graham's 'procedural-traditional' time is hardly a 'time' in the western sense.

But it is not as simple as might appear: some people may share different cultures and move from one time model or another, depending on the other people involved and the particular situation, using different types of 'operating cultures' (Goodenough, 1971). As Hall states (1983, p. 58): 'The Japanese are polychronic when looking and working inward, toward themselves. When dealing with the outside world . . . they shift to the monochronic mode . . . The French are monochronic intellectually, but polychronic in behaviour.'

A naive view of Japanese temporal orientations would lead one to assume that the Japanese are simply future oriented. In fact, a very knowledgeable observer of Japanese business, Robert Ballon, argues (in Hayashi, 1988) that the Japanese are neither future nor past oriented. For him the Japanese are present oriented and focused on the here and now. Hayashi explains the difficult attempt at finding cross-culturally equivalent terms by asserting that: 'Many kinds of Japanese behaviour are extratemporaneous' (p. 2), meaning that *they are not time based*. Hayashi explains further what he calls the *Makimono* time. In their model of time, the Japanese tend to posit the future as a natural extension of the present. The Japanese are basically people who work with a cyclical view of time, based on their Buddhist background, and who hold that the souls of dead people transmigrate to newly born human beings, in an eternal cycle. As Hayashi states (1988, p. 10): 'In Japanese cultural time, the past flows continuously toward the present and also the present is firmly linked to the future. In philosophical terms, we might say the past and the future exist simultaneously in the present'.

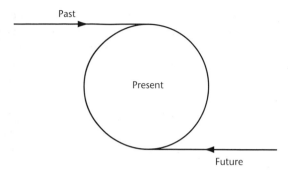

FIGURE 2.2   Japanese *Makimono* time pattern.
(Source: Hayashi, 1988, p. 9.)

Therefore, the linear-separable model of time, found in western cultures, does not predominate in Japan. The notion of continuity is central in Japanese time, just as the notion of discontinuity is central in western models of time. A Japanese definition would say 'the present is a temporal period that links the region of the past with the world of the future' (Hayashi, 1988, p. 18). The notion of continuity as well as the arrow of the future targeted **to** the present are central in the *Makimono* time pattern (Figure 2.2).

2.3   SPACE

The key words for space-related cultural assumptions are 'in' and 'out', member and non-member, belonging or not. Here space is meant in its most general sense: the three-dimensional expanse in which all material objects are located. Let us assume that it is mainly occupied by people; more precisely, groups of people and their properties. Spaces can be physical, such as a town, a county or a country. Space can also be abstract, that is, a grouping of people based on common characteristics such as education, religion or professional associations. Space is the basis for the organizing principle of *territoriality* which we mentioned in the previous chapter. People are by nature territorial: they must define who has ownership and control over certain spaces.

The key problems in space-related cultural assumptions are as follows:

1.   Whether people *are* insiders or outsiders.
2.   What the rights and obligations are for ingroup members.
3.   Whether it is at all possible for outsiders to gain insider status, or a limited part of it.
4.   What the group membership conditions are for those willing to 'enter this space'.

Table 2.2 contrasts space-related differences across cultures.

TABLE 2.2   Space-related cultural differences

Basic problem/Cultural orientations	Contrasts across cultures
Is emphasis put on what people *do* or on what they *are* (based on *belonging* to family, age, sex, religious or social status groups)? (a) Personalization versus depersonalization	Necessity of being personally acquainted with other people if one is to communicate and interact with them efficiently versus ability to communicate easily with unknown persons.
Who is a member of the group and what are the relevant ingroups? (b) Ingroup orientation	Belonging to the ingroup (or reference group: family, tribe, clan, club, professional society, nation, etc.) may be a *necessary condition* for being considered a reliable, *bona fide* partner.
How does one gain membership? (c) Concrete versus abstract territoriality	What are the group membership conditions: for an individual who belongs to the outgroup, what are the prerequisites for assimilation (if any)?
How does one deal with physical space? (d) Group cultures with close physical contact versus individualistic cultures desiring private space	Tendency to live near to one another, and to be undisturbed by such intimacy. Conversely, tendency to feel the need for private space around one's body, and to resent intrusion into this space (Hall, 1966).

People being members of a certain space

Strong *being* emphasis is manifested in what people call themselves and others. In many traditional societies, language designates the people by a term meaning 'human being'. 'Bantu', for instance, means human being. This, more or less, assumes that others are not *real* human beings. Without going so far, the Japanese language gives a good example of a strict division between 'we' and 'they'. Japanese people call themselves *Nihon-jin* and foreigners *Gai-jin* (those from the outside).

In the 'being' orientation emphasis is put on belonging, that is on characteristics shared by a certain set of people:

1. A set of people sharing family ties, a particular social class, a certain ethnic background, a religion or a nationality.

2. Age (youngsters versus older people), sex (male versus female), marriage (married versus unmarried people).

What is specific in a strong being orientation is the underlying assumption that what people *are*, naturally, legitimately and forcefully, influences the roles, power and capacities they have in the society. In the next chapter we will see that there is a strong link between a being orientation and the concept of the self and others, which mediates the being orientation and helps translate it into interaction models. A typical causal chain in the being style is: she is a woman, thus belongs to the group of people in charge of reproduction and nurturing roles, thus cannot work. 'Being' does not necessarily refer to purely individual traits, such as personality.

In contrast, the *doing* orientation assumes that what people are *does not* naturally, nor legitimately, influence the roles, power and capacities individuals have in the society. Thus what is important is what people can achieve, given their talents and abilities. Whereas the being orientation results in 'personalization', the doing orientation results in 'depersonalization'. These words should be taken carefully and interpreted cautiously: they will be discussed in more detail in Chapters 13 to 17, which are dedicated to language and communication, personal selling and international business negotiations. 'Personalization' means that assumptions about what a person can *do* (and what can be done with this person) depend fundamentally on what this person *is*. Therefore it is of prime importance to obtain information on what this person is. Since not all is *prima facie* visible, it means that it will be necessary to spend time exploring who this person is.

In contrast, 'depersonalization' means that it is not important to know who a person is, to decide what this person can do (and what can be done with her). Therefore it is not assumed to be necessary to spend a lot of time discovering who the person is (especially if time is strongly economic). 'Depersonalization' in no way means that there is not interest in what people actually *are*, but that their belonging to certain space characteristics (class, ethnic, age groups, etc.) is considered rather unimportant compared with purely individual, non-space-related characteristics. In the purest version of the doing assumption, character and personality would be considered as unimportant in what individuals can achieve: tasks are viewed as standard and people as interchangeable, deeds are separated from emotions and *doing* belongs to a world of its own, radically separated from the *being*.

Who is a member of the ingroup?

As explained by Triandis (1983, p. 144):

In every culture some people are defined as trustworthy, worthy of cooperation or even self-sacrifice for (ingroup), and other people are seen as 'outsiders' (outgroup). The basis of such distinction varies. In most cultures, tribe and family are crucial; in other cultures, nation, religion, language, or political ideology may be important; in still other cases, occupational group may be all-important. Thus the content of ingroups differs from culture to culture. Also, a person, may belong to one, or to many, ingroups.

There is a natural relationship between the being orientation and the emphasis on group belonging, which has to do with natural law and the right of people to occupy a certain territory. The largest possible ingroups are nations. For many older countries, legitimacy is largely based on one's having ancestors in the place for a long time. In nationality, being legally based on *jus sanguinis* (law of the blood), this may translate, into people being granted a definite nationality only if at least one of their parents is a national. Benefits related to nationality are strongly space related: the right to live, work and enjoy citizenship on a definite territory. On the other hand, certain countries (e.g. the United States and France) base nationality on *jus soli* (law of the soil), that is, being born in the place is enough for a person to obtain citizenship.[3]

This strict opposition delineates two different ways of defining the content of the ingroup (in this case a national group): on the one hand, people emphasize blood and kin; on the other, they do not. But ingroup orientation goes further. It is structured around kin-based loyalties and involves patterns of loyalty and obligation. The family is the basic and smallest ingroup unit, at the other extreme from the nation. Strong ingroup orientation is most often accompanied by a rhetoric based on family relationships, with a dominant father (outside oriented), a protective mother (inside oriented) and sisters and brothers, alternately considered as rivals within the ingroup (because they are competing for parents' love, affection and preference) and allies *vis-à-vis* the outgroup (because they share the same fundamental identity; they *are* of the same kin). The family space is that of the house and the surrounding ground: it is private but not closed to outsiders, who may enter under definite conditions.

Outgroup orientation, in contrast to ingroup orientation, is based on the assumption that there is a fundamental unity of mankind beyond the borders of ingroup spaces, including families, nations and cultures. If the two orientations are roughly opposed, it is not a complete opposition. In certain cultures they coexist, as in the Nordic European cultures which combine a strong sense of national identity (ingroup) with a universal focus manifested in their strong commitment to peace, development of the poorest nations and international organizations (outgroup).

What does membership involve in terms of rights and obligations?

The ingroup bonds involve relationships of loyalty. This loyalty does not extend beyond the borders of the ingroup space. Loyalty is basically about showing allegiance, respecting the values of the ingroup and maintaining a sense of the honour of the group. Loyalty is fundamentally non-reciprocal: people do not expect other ingroup members' loyalty for being loyal themselves. Loyalty is not based on time, except for a sense of eternity: one may wait for fifty years to be rewarded for loyalty or one may never be rewarded; it just does not matter.

Loyalty can be based on kinship or patronage, which is often an extended form of kinship, based on symbolic adoption, that is taking another's child as one's own. The virtue manifested in loyalty is that of maintaining allegiance, even in the face of conflicts with other members of the ingroup or when experiencing unfair treatment from the most powerful members. Strong ingroup orientation increases an insider's loyalty, but simultaneously decreases the feeling of obligation towards outsiders. Morality is space related. It might, for instance, be considered as perfectly virtuous to lie to or steal from people to whom no loyalty is owed. The Mafia is a good illustration of an ingroup-oriented society. Morality is based on a set of values favouring strict loyalty, treason being punished by the death sentence; the godfather who has ordered it goes to the burial ceremony because he still 'loves' the betrayer. Ingroup orientation partly explains behaviourial relativity. Some national groups have a reputation for their compliant behaviour at home (where rules are strictly enforced) and for looser conduct when abroad. When they are away, they not only do not feel the need to observe the rules applying at home, they also consider that, when out of the ingroup space where bonds and loyalty are strong, they do not need to respect others' rules (even those that are similar to those of the ingroup) since outsiders do not deserve loyalty or even interest and respect.

Rights and obligations may be defined according to membership of particular ethnic groups, as in Africa, where only certain ingroups are allowed to be merchants.

Mistrust of and disdain for retail activities explain why merchants are most often foreigners (Lebanese in West Africa, Indians in Zaire), particular local ethnic groups (Dioulas in Ivory Coast) or women (the 'mama Benz' in Benin).

Ingroup or outgroup orientation has a deep influence on the system of ethics and morality in a particular society. Impersonal rules applied by judges to people irrespective of the group to which they belong is typical of low ingroup orientation. A typical case where such orientations are important is when a family member has committed some crime, the family knows about it, but there is no evidence; what does the family do: denounce one of its members or keep silent?

Outgroup orientation values universal rules, applied to everybody: respect for human rights ethics is a typical feature of outgroup orientation. Objectivity and reciprocity are preferred over loyalty; or, to put it another way, loyalty is not to the group, not to people, but to the impersonal rules and values that govern the society as a whole, which is largely why the terms above are 'personalization' (people orientation) versus 'depersonalization' (rule orientation). However, people with outgroup orientation, precisely because they have a more 'depersonalized' approach, are more sensitive to the problems of other human beings, far from their own space. Their tendency to behave in a more universal way in no way means that they are less human.

These differences have a major impact on international business negotiations and personal selling, in particular in relation to how to make contacts. What information should be sought if one is to understand connections between the people one confronts? How are decisions made in a particular ingroup? The differences may also extend in the area of consumer behaviour, especially in the area of decision making where ingroup orientation exerts pressures on consumers' attitudes and buying decisions. Any society combines to varying degrees ingroup and outgroup orientation and organizes them in particular ways. For example, 'affirmative action, equal opportunity' is a strong outgroup motto, typical of the United States. However, the global rule is still that human beings cannot choose their favourite nationality. Yet, were such choice to be available, it would be the purest form of outgroup orientation.

How can membership be gained?

If people are very territorial, it is important to know how to gain access to them, even as an external partner, a business partner in a joint venture for instance, but as a respected partner (bearing in mind that loyalty and morality are mostly values which are applicable to group members only). If we combine the ingroup/outgroup and the being/doing divides, a simple contrast is as follows:

1. When ingroup and being orientation are strong, membership is mostly gained on the basis of *concrete territoriality*.

2. When outgroup and doing orientation are strong, membership is based on *abstract territoriality*.

If membership is based on concrete territoriality, some necessary characteristics are innate or cannot be acquired by adult people, simply because they are related to birth, socialization and education within the ingroup. In cases where it is impossible to gain membership, one must behave as a friendly and realistic outsider, who can target three possible positions in the long run:

1.   A 'tolerated outsider' who is considered as different but useful for practical purposes. This status allows comfortable relationships and, in most cases, is a possible role for developing business. But two aspects have to be kept in mind: (a) such people should not imitate insider status or try to acquire it by too active involvement in the community – 'proactive outsiders' will be reminded, at some stage, of their limited status as a full person; and (b) they should not play insider people off against each other to acquire power and influence: in general, they should not attempt to take advantage of conflict in the ingroup; ingroup conflicts are considered a 'home business', not to be shown overtly, and never to be solved to an outsider's benefit.

2.   A 'recognized outsider': this status is closer to membership, yet is still far from it. Generally a 'recognized outsider' will have been living in the culture for a long period of time, will speak the language fluently and will have established strong relational networks. At a conference some years ago, Robert J. Ballon, a Belgian Jesuit living in Japan for more than thirty years and knowledgeable about Japanese business (mentioned above in relation to Japanese time patterns), explained how he was always considered a pure foreigner, despite his profound knowledge of Japanese society and his very deep involvement with the country. 'Recognized outsiders' often serve the purpose of ambassadors, cultural translators or mediators from the outside world of foreign groups to the ingroup. They are recognized as useful and friendly people by the insiders, yet they would lose their usefulness if they were to become insiders.

3.   'Newly accepted insiders' have taken a further step, crossing the cultural group border. They often can do so because they crossed early enough to be considered as still educable persons, suitable for a profound transformation of their being, as in the case of foreigners who arrived as young adults, completed their education and married locally. Such persons will, however, remain somewhat on the fringes, near to the external borders of the cultural community, often considered as adequate ambassadors or mediators from the ingroup to outgroups.

Membership based on doing and *abstract territoriality* corresponds largely to 'modern culture': outgroup orientation is highly valued and ingroup orientation is often, too quickly, equated with narrow-mindedness, provincialism, hostility towards foreigners and the like. What people have *done* up to now is evidenced by their curriculum vitae (CV). The interview guide for affirmative action compliance programmes considers as discriminatory such enquiries of applicants concerning age, citizenship, marital status, birthplace, education that is not job related, language, etc. – information that, in most countries outside the United States, is considered legitimate for ascertaining who the applicant *is*. In France CVs include this information and are accompanied by a photograph and a hand-written letter, which is sometimes used for assessing the person's character through graphology.

Abstract territoriality is mostly based on professional achievements, evidenced by diplomas, membership of professional bodies, being an alumnus of an ivy league university, and so on. The epitome of abstract territoriality is represented by the *golden boys*. For them *insider* trading is a fraud, showing that the use of their natural ingroup advantages is viewed as evil. The space of 'golden boys' is a mix of top MBA schools, market dealing rooms and a 'club of people constantly connected world-wide'. Just try to imagine how different they are from a Bengali farmer.

Business school graduates (*Grandes écoles* in France), or those holding the title of Doctor in Germany belong to these 'modern groups' that are based on doing and competence rather than being, age, sex and group membership. It is assumed that access to membership is organized on a non-discriminatory and objective basis and that it is in the best interest of society as a whole because the 'best people' are doing the 'appropriate job'. However, even in a doing framework, relational competence never disappears in favour of pure professional competence, simply because managing relationships is a dark side yet an important part of the doing competences. Paradoxically, when abstract territoriality is very strong, it largely re-creates primitive ingroup behaviour, but based on different criteria. The world of academia, for instance, is very 'outgroupist' for sex, nationality, religion or age, but it is very 'ingroupist' when it comes to doctoral degrees and the journals where people publish.

Group membership assumptions are important for marketing negotiations, when facing a national competitive environment as a foreign firm, for making public relations contacts, for the recruitment and promotion of sales people, especially in Africa and the Middle East, and for any situation involving business ethics. The favouring of one party over another, on the ground of personal relationship, in either political or economic affairs, is viewed dimly – indeed it is often called corruption – by outgroup-oriented people, whereas it remains standard practice for ingroup-oriented people.

Pitfalls of excessive ingroup and outgroup orientations

Because extreme positions in space-related assumptions present drawbacks, there is always a combination of both, to varying degrees. Some pitfalls of ingroup orientation are: (1) tribalism – only people of an ingroup based on kin are considered worth interacting with and caring for; (2) localism (we, here) – only people belonging to a small geographical unit are considered interesting people; and (3) provincialism – only values and behaviour that are in use in the community are considered appropriate. On the other hand, the pitfalls of excessive outgroup orientation are: (1) unrealistic universalism – the complete cancelling of borders (the rules of the GATT, the General Agreement on Tariffs and Trade, are partly based on such open-space assumptions) will produce global welfare; if not wrong, this is also far from true; and (2) global village ethnocentrism – if we 'see' what happens everywhere on Earth at any moment a global consciousness will emerge; unfortunately images are global, but their interpretation is not.

Dealing with physical space and other aspects of culture related to space

Territoriality refers also to possessiveness, control and authority over an area of physical space. Individuals need to refer to rules concerning space because they have to defend their space against invasion or misuse by others. The 'language of space' is culturally determined and provides the codes concerning social distance – how far should one stand from other people in order to respect their area of private space? A complete approach to relations with space was proposed by Edward T. Hall (1966) in *The Hidden Dimension*. In this book he developed the concept of 'proxemics' – the term he has coined for the interrelated observations and theories of man's use of space as a specialized elaboration of culture. According to Hall, in western cultures, there are three primary zones of space: the intimate zone (0 to 18 inches; 0–45 cm), the personal zone (18 inches to 3 feet; 0.45–1 m), and the social zone (3 to 6 feet: 1–2 m). Touch can occur for westerners in the intimate and personal zones, but sensory involvement and communication is less intense in the social zone. In fact, what differs across cultures in terms of physical space assumptions is the following:

1.   What are the sizes of the three zones? To what extent do they overlap?

2.   Who is allowed to enter these zones of physical space?

3.   What is considered adequate sensory exchange within definite interpersonal distances?

The last question is important in marketing terms. It relates to the senses, sight, sound, touch and smells in as much as sensory perception is directly related to interpersonal distance. Americans are, for instance, famous for their suppression of personal odours in public spaces, and this has created a mass market for room deodorizers, antiperspirants, mouthwashes and deodorizants. Although smell suppression is globally 'modern' (it has developed strongly outside the United States), it is not clear whether it will remain so in the future, with people striving for a more natural expression of themselves. Chapter 9, which deals with product policy, gives examples of how our sense of physical space mixes with sensory codes in a culturally significant way that enables consumers to attribute meaning to product characteristics.

The list of basic space-related cultural assumptions in Table 2.2 is not exhaustive. Some other aspects need to be mentioned. The availability of inhabitable physical space and the density of population varies greatly across countries, with a profound impact on material culture. The high population density in Japan and in many Asian countries has made it essential to make things 'smaller', so that more can be fitted in. The assumption is that 'smaller is better'. This is a not unimportant reason for the talent of the Japanese for miniaturizing objects. As shown in Chapter 12, Japanese space limitations at least partly explain the distribution system that prevails in that country. Conversely, the availability of space and other resources in North America is a reason for the large size of objects, from cars to servings in restaurants and outdoor advertising posters. The prevalent assumption that 'bigger is better' is probably a significant background explanation for the failure of US car manufacturers to adapt to smaller car sizes after the mid-1970s oil crisis.

Contrasts in physical space should also be considered carefully in physically heterogeneous countries. A good example is Nepal which has both the Himalaya mountains and subtropical plains, in Tharuwan province near India. Cultures are different ways to adapt to an existing reality, and Nepali mountain people exhibit, on average, different values and behaviour from people in the lower areas: interpersonal solidarity and work orientation are stronger, because people would not survive otherwise.

A last area where significant space-related cultural differences are displayed can be found in urban planning, the ways of organizing towns and of relating urban to rural landscape.

2.4   CULTURAL BORROWING AND CHANGE IN SOCIETIES

It would be wrong to give the impression that cultures are truly different and exclusive in their assumptions. Through time and space, cultures intermingle. Negative events such as wars and colonization convey cultural exchange: the Viennese, and through them all the other Europeans, discovered coffee from the Turks when they besieged Vienna during the sixteenth century. It is fascinating to consider the naivety with which, in the process of cultural borrowing, successful cultural artefacts are borrowed from other cultures without the cultural assumptions underlying these artefacts being understood or even imagined. Yan (1991, pp. 51–2) for instance, quotes the reformer Liang Quichao, who wrote in 1897 on the subject of European countries, considered, unlike China, as innovative:

In innovative countries the sovereigns are wise, their mandarins faithful and courageous, their people intelligent and heroic, their politics successful, their business prosperous, their products excellent, etc. Travel in their country brings you such pleasure and joy that you forget to return home. Will you then pose further questions as to the prosperity of these countries?

Isolated cultures, united cultures

Cultures are rarely pure, except in a few areas where people have been almost untouched by foreign influences. An example of such cultural isolation might be Japan which, during the era of the Tokugawa shoguns, withdrew from all contact with outside people and cultures. The Tokugawa period lasted for more than two centuries before the Meiji era, which began in 1868 and initiated a period of increased accessibility of foreign influences to Japan. Reischauer, a specialist in Japanese history, explains in his book *Japan: Past and Present* (1946, 1990) that two centuries of complete peace were enforced with extreme vigour by the Tokugawa regime. The Tokugawa shoguns have left their mark on the behaviour of the Japanese people. In the sixteenth century the Japanese were keen, adventurous and somewhat bellicose. By the nineteenth century they had become docile and humble subjects, awaiting orders from their hierarchical superiors, which they implemented resignedly. Reischauer hypothesizes that collective regimentation under the Tokugawa shoguns led to an inward-looking people who indulged in conformism, which served as consensus. He further notes that, at the beginning of the nineteenth century, antagonism in Japanese society was almost non-existent: the rules of propriety were strictly observed, and violence was extremely rare. Reischauer argues that when the Japanese were confronted with an unknown situation, they displayed very little ability to adapt, much less than other peoples.[4] The Tokugawa period appears good in many ways, especially as regards the general level of education and the development of the arts. However, it largely interrupted the natural evolution of economic and social change. The Tokugawa shoguns preserved an outdated political and social order. Only after the beginning of the Meiji era in 1868 did the Japanese begin to interact with Europeans, who had achieved enormous advances in scientific knowledge during the previous two centuries. The succession of these two periods, one of great isolation and one of openness towards foreign cultures, probably explains the paradoxical relationship of the Japanese with international trade and international marketing. In one sense they are very ethnocentric, but simultaneously they are quite capable of overcoming their ethnocentrism to become, ultimately, highly successful international marketers.

In many other cases, cultures do mix. Contact may inevitably be bellicose, owing to the conflicting interests of countries and their cultures (religion, language, social and political systems) over borders. The perennial conflicts between the region south of the Mediterranean Sea (mostly Arab and Muslim) and the northern region (mostly Christian) are an example of this pattern of conflict/co-operation. Cultural encounters occur even in wartime. When besieged by the Turks in the fifteenth century, the Viennese were introduced by their opponents to a new, tasty and stimulating beverage: coffee. It is through the Viennese as intermediaries that coffee was introduced into the West. Even during the Crusades (tenth to twelfth centuries), warriors on both sides had quiet moments when, for instance, they enjoyed each other's food. In *The Crusades through Arab Eyes* (1985, pp. 128–9), Amine Maalouf describes how the Templars grew accustomed to understanding and accepting the customs and beliefs of the Muslims. In the following extract, Templars, although themselves Christians, side with a Muslim visiting Jerusalem, the Damascene emir Usamah, in defending Islamic religious practices:

When I was visiting Jerusalem, I used to go to Al-Aqsa mosque, where my Templar friends were staying. Along one side of the building was a small oratory in which the *Franj* [an Arab word designating the French, or more generally European, Crusaders] had set up a church. The Templars placed this spot at my disposal so that I might say my prayer. One day I entered, said *Allahu Akbar*, and was about to begin my prayer, when a man, a *Franj*, threw himself upon me, and turned to the east, saying, 'Thus do we pray.' The Templars rushed forward and led him away. I then set myself to prayer once more, but this man, seizing upon a moment of inattention, threw himself upon me yet again, turned my face to the east, and repeated once more, 'Thus do we pray.' Once again the Templars intervened, led him away, and apologized to me, saying, 'He is a foreigner. He has just arrived from the land of the *Franj* and he has never seen anyone pray without turning his face to the east.' I answered that I had prayed enough and left, stunned by the behaviour of this demon who had been so enraged at seeing me pray while facing the direction of Mecca.

Cultural borrowing is general . . . and disguised

Culture is identity, but not pure identity: the basic requirement for the introduction of a new cultural item (a product, a lifestyle, a word, a dance, a song) is that it looks (and in fact is) coherent with the culture that adopts it. That is why cultural borrowing is often disguised, by a change of name or by means of 'reinvention', whereby a local inventor/discoverer is found. It is fascinating to see how many countries seek to claim credit for particular inventions (the Xerox machine, for instance) at the same time.

One may view culture as the accumulation of the best possible solutions to the common problems faced by the members of a particular society. This definition, very

Anglo-Saxon in its problem-solving orientation, does have an advantage: it emphasizes the 'shopping' aspect of cultural dynamics. There have always been different kinds of travellers (explorers, warriors, merchants, colonials, etc.) who have brought back foreign innovations to their native country. Usually by accident or sometimes by an almost systematic process (like the Japanese, because they are overly conscious of their insularity and cultural isolation), societies may find good imported solutions. Jeans, as informal trousers for casual wear, have made their way through all cultures. The fabric originally came from France (*de Nîmes* – denim) and the name from Italy – short for Jean Fustian from Genes (Genoa). Afterwards this 'American' invention made its way back to Italy and most of the countries of the world.

Although cultural opportunism is understandable, it is often hidden by the need to maintain cultural identity. Few societies are prepared to accept that a large part of their culture is really foreign: cultural borrowing is therefore somewhat hypocritical or at least disguised.

Some words and concepts are borrowed easily in their original form when they are obviously related to some well-established stereotype of a particular country: *ersatz* (the high reputation of German chemistry), *leitmotiv* (German music), *showbiz* (US dominance), *élégance* (the French reputation for style), *kamikaze* or *hara-kiri* (the Japanese capacity for self-sacrifice), *mamma* (the Italian sense of the motherly role in the family). Sherry and Camargo (1987) show that that English language has had a profound influence on Japanese marketing: they report a heavy use of English loanwords in Japanese promotional texts and labels. *Mai* (English 'my'), for instance, is used extensively in compounds such as *mai homu* (my home), because the Japanese equivalent would sound too selfish and stress the private over the collective. Beyond the imported word, it is the foreign value, individualism, that is imported.

But, generally speaking, cultural borrowings are disguised and they finally disappear. Numerous words, goods and even lifestyles (the 'weekend', for instance) have been largely borrowed. Such words as 'magazine' and 'assassin' have been directly imported from Arabic. During the Crusades, the Crusaders played endless games of dice, which Arabs call *az-zahar*: a word that the *Franj* adopted to designate not the game itself but *hazard*, the concept of chance (Maalouf, 1985). The example of the Japanese borrowing of Chinese writing more than fifteen centuries ago is a true example of imitation, but also of reinterpretation, which makes this appropriation a genuine element of Japanese culture (see Box 2.1).

The Japanese, when they first read ideograms (which they later called *kanji*) did not immediately recognize them as representing *ideas*, but experienced them more directly as *sounds*. Therefore the *kanji* system works as a pictogram system representing both ideas and sounds. It is further completed by two syllabaries, which represent only sounds: *hiragana* for native words and *katakana* for imported words. The *katakana* syllabary is typical of the Japanese attitude towards cultural imports: they do not object (as the French do, for instance), but at the same time it is a necessity to signal clearly the foreign origin of some words and concepts by writing such words in *katakana*, which represent the same syllables as *hiragana* (an apparent waste of effort).

Other examples of cultural borrowing are numerous: music, clothes, architecture, building techniques, food, recipes, etc. Borrowing sometimes goes as far as pure and

BOX 2.1

The origins of Japanese writing

The Japanese write their language with ideograms they borrowed from China nearly two thousand years ago. Some two thousand years before that, the ancient Chinese had formed these ideograms, or characters, from pictures of things they knew. To them the sun had looked like this ☼, so this became their written word for **sun**. This form was gradually squared off and simplified to make it easier to write, changing its shape to 日. This is still the way the word sun is written in both China and Japan today.

The ancient Chinese first drew a tree like this 朮. This was also gradually simplified and squared, to 木, which became the written word for **tree**. To form the word for **root** or **origin** the Chinese just drew in more roots at the bottom of the tree to emphasize this portion of the picture, 杰, then squared and simplified the character to 本. This became the written word for **root** or **origin**.

When the characters for **sun** 日 and **origin** 本 are put together in a compound they form the written word 日 本 **Japan**, which means literally origin-of-the-sun.

A picture of the sun in the east at sunrise coming up behind a tree 東 forms the written word for **east** 東. A picture of the stone lantern that guarded each ancient Chinese capital 京 squared off and simplified to abstract form 京, forms the written word for **capital**. These two characters put together in a compound form the written word 東 京, Eastern-capital, TÔKYÔ.

The characters may look mysterious and impenetrable at first approach, but as these examples show, they are not difficult at all to understand. The characters are not just random strokes: each one is a picture, and has a meaning based on the content of the picture. The Japanese written language contains a number of these characters, but fortunately not as many as Westerners often assume. To graduate from grammar school a student must know 881 characters. At this point he is considered literate. A high school graduate must know 1,850. To read college textbooks, about three thousand characters are necessary. All these thousands of characters, however, are built up from less than 300 elements, or pictures, many of which are seldom used.

(Source: Len Walsh, 1969)

simple copying, and possibly product counterfeiting. The Japanese have been remarkably skilful at borrowing European music culture, becoming the most important producers of musical instruments world-wide. Even castanets – an ethnically Spanish product – are made in Japan for sale in Spain.

2.5   CULTURAL HOSTILITY

Limits to borrowing clearly appear when it is seen as a threat to cultural coherence. This is especially true of religious practices, social morals and even daily customs. For instance, it is not easy to import polygamy or clitoral excision for babies into cultures where monogamy and child protection are strongly established practices. As previously stated, there must be a minimum level of coherence and homogeneity in cultural assumptions and behaviour in the cultural community if people are to synchronize themselves and live peacefully together.

Racism

Racism is often confused with cultural hostility, whereas in fact it precedes cultural hostility. But cultural hostility does not necessarily imply racism: one may be hostile to people of (some) other cultures, without being a racist. Behind racism there is a theory: that, because of their race (i.e. physiology), some human beings are inferior at various levels (intelligence, creative abilities, moral sense, etc.). The theories of Gobineau and Hitler's *Mein Kampf* are writings which clearly developed and propagated racist views. The following passage on slavery, written by Montesquieu in 1748 (Book XV, Ch. 5, p. 242, my emphasis), exemplifies racism:

Were I to vindicate our right to make slaves of the Negroes, these should be my arguments. The Europeans, having extirpated the Americans, were obliged to make slaves of the Africans, for clearing such vast tracts of land. Sugar would be too dear, if the plants which produce it were cultivated by any other than slaves. These creatures are all over black, and with such a flat nose, that they can scarcely be pitied. *It is hardly to be believed that God who is a wise being, should place a good soul, in such a black ugly body.*

Racist theses and opinions have been progressively abandoned (as scientific theories, at least) over the last two centuries. An issue which is still discussed is that of differing intellectual capacity among people of different races or ethnic groups. It is always measured by IQ tests, which are of western/US origin. Although observed differences across ethnic groups are indisputable, their explanation is debated: some people argue about genetic differences being the explanatory variable, others (Segall *et al.*, 1990) attribute these differences to a series of non-genetic factors. Environmental factors, for instance, such as the absence of a formal education system, on average tend to diminish IQ scores. Such detrimental factors are to be found, significantly, more among groups with low and median IQ scores.

The IQ test itself is biased in as much as it penalizes, by its very construction, those who have been designated from the start as 'culturally inferior'. The IQ test does not take into account many skills and competences, that were unknown to the authors of the test. Moreover, recent studies show that the *inter-individual* variability of genetic characteristics is much larger than the *inter-racial* groups variability (Segall *et al.*, 1990, p. 102). In other words, genetic differences among Europeans, or genetic differences among South African Zulus, are *automatically* significantly higher than the genetic differences between the average European and the average Zulu – a strong anti-racist argument.[5]

Cultural hostility

In contrast to racism, cultural hostility does not imply prior prejudices as to who is inferior or superior according to race or culture. Culture is part of one's own patrimony as a person. There is a strong affective dimension, when one feels that one's proper cultural values are threatened. This feeling may result from either of the following:

1. Simple interactions with people whose cultural values are quite different. One does not feel at ease, communication is experienced as burdensome and there is little empathy. A defensive response may then develop, frequently the case of unconscious (and minor) cultural hostility.

2. Collective reactions. Cases are so numerous world-wide that it would need many pages to quote them exhaustively: Transylvanian Hungarians and Romanians, people in ex-Yugoslavia, Armenians of High Karabakh and Azeris of the Azerbaijan enclave in Soviet Armenia; Walloons and Flemings in Belgium; Protestant and Catholic communities in Ulster; etc. *Identity is a matter of culture rather than race.*

It is not only territorial conflicts but also economic competition that may cause cultural hostility. The Japanese are sometimes considered negatively in the United States, which has a large trade imbalance with Japan. In his controversial best-selling book, *The Japan that Can Say No*, Shintaro Ishihara (1991) argues that anti-Japanese racial prejudice is the main cause of 'Japan-bashing' in the United States. Ishihara, a member of the Japanese diet, quotes what he said to politicians in Washington (p. 27):

I admit that Caucasians created modern civilization, but what bothers me is you seem to think that heritage makes you superior. In the thirteenth century, however, the Mongols under Genghis Khan and his successors overran Russia and Eastern Europe, Caucasians adopted Mongol-style haircuts and shaved eyebrows . . . Just as Orientals of today are crazy about the clothing and hair-style of the Beatles, Michael Jackson and Sting, Occidentals of Genghis Khan times copied Mongolian ways.

Cultural hostility, when directed at successful nations, is often a fairly ambiguous feeling, whereby admiration and envy for the other's achievements go along with contempt for many traits of the envied people and obvious unwillingness to understand the root causes of the other's success. This also results in naive copies of selected cultural artefacts as magical ways of becoming stronger – in *Robinson Crusoe* savages were about to eat Man Friday in order to gain his qualities. In the case of immigrants, Mauviel (1991, p. 73, my translation) comments on the frequent confusion between racism and cultural hostility.[6]

the dominant ideology has been so interiorized that a new, very subtle rhetoric enables us to avoid any direct, frank response to the problems concerning immigrants – the most important issue is not to be accused of 'racism'. And one places under this word the most dissimilar elements, which often have nothing to do with race in its biological acceptance . . . The media especially like the meaningless expression 'everyday racism'. As for the phrase 'ethnic group', which has replaced the word 'race', those who use the expression would have a hard time trying to define it.

There are differences across countries: Mauviel shows that the Italians are not so reluctant to speak openly on cultural hostility problems. The Italian press 'lets reality be

BOX 2 .2

Nigerian women of Chambave

Hundreds, if not thousands, of Nigerian women – graduates in chemistry, law and other subjects, nurses, etc. – came to Italy in search of a better life. Most of them end up walking the streets, or are love traders on the *tangenziali*, the freeways round cities, and even on country roads. The most striking example to me, because of its symbolic meaning, is that of the 'train of sin', from Turin to Aosta, which brings thirty to forty Nigerian women every summer evening on the 9.15 p.m. bus to Chambave, which is located between Aosta and San Vincenzo; they are joining their 'shift' on highway 26. These *pendolari del amore* (commuters) have lost the dream that they previously held, namely that of being salespeople for Italian shoes. One should not be astonished that the mayor [of Chambave], surrounded by the local council and the population of the valley, has organized a silent protest march. However, there is clearly a flourishing market, if one just looks at the evidence of the numerous cars with roaring engines that wait for the women. One may guess what the relations are between this village of nine hundred people and the African women, who are no longer prepared to accept being kept out of sight. In these matters, the most shocking hypocrisy is the rule; only conspicuous incidents that attract people's attention, like those at Chambave, help us to become aware of these new forms of shameful exploitation, a direct consequence of the under-development of the countries of the South.

(Source. Mauviel, 1991, pp. 01–2. Reproduced with permission.)

seen, it does not cover it with an embarrassed veil, it allows the publication of the most diverse opinions'. He describes, for instance, the case of the Nigerian women at Chambave (near Torino) which 'as revealed by the press, demonstrates the irresponsibility of those who vow to have multiracial or multi-ethnic societies' (Box 2.2).

Part 4 further examines the mechanism of cultural hostility, which is sometimes increased by language and communication problems. Intercultural misunderstandings may stem from a lack of competency in the other's language, or from the natural tendency to adopt defensive stereotypes. It often results in a snowballing cultural hostility.

QUESTIONS

1. Discuss cultural variation in solutions which have been found across societies to the four common problems listed below:
    (a) How to secure oneself (to feel secure, subjectively, and to protect oneself, objectively) against unforeseeable negative events (a grave illness, an incident, etc.).

(b)   How to treat the oldest in the community, when they cannot work any more.

(c)   Who should have access to education, on what criteria, and how should its cost be financed, given that the resources available for education, private and public, are not infinite? To what extent should education be given to *all* members of a particular society, irrespective of their age, social class and personal capacities? On which bases should access to education be organized?

(d)   How should couples, the basic unit for the reproduction of the species, be formed? What role should love, common ethnic or social belonging, age or (even) sex play in such a process?

2.   Discuss the marketing implications of differing cultural solutions to points (a) and (b) in question 1, in terms of the existence of certain products or services, provided by the market, the state or mutual bodies, organized within the family group or by a traditional community.

3.   What is the influence of space availability (mostly determined by population density in a definite country or area) on material culture? Give examples.

4.   Indicate how the following products and services are 'loaded' with time, in terms of time used in consumption, time-saving device, durability, waiting time, seasonality, time projections in the past and the future, etc. (As an example, Box 7.1 describes the time load in life insurance policies.)

(a)   a dishwashing machine;

(b)   a haircut;

(c)   obtaining cash from your bank;

(d)   spending two-week vacations at *Club Méditerranée*;

(e)   fresh orange juice versus dried orange juice (i.e. concentrated powder).

5.   How would you expect consumer behaviour to vary across cultures for the five products/services above? (Cite one example per case.)

6.   You try to park your car. A sign indicates that parking in this area is limited to fifteen minutes. Another sign reads: 'Long-term parking, 300 metres'. What do these explicit signs suggest concerning temporal culture in this country?

7.   Define what would be the most important criteria for recruitment in a being-oriented society as compared with a doing-oriented society.

8.   In most countries, police and judiciary positions are subject to a condition of nationality (being a national is a requirement for entering the service) whereas in universities and research centres positions are open to applicants regardless of their nationality. Why?

9.   Find examples of cultural borrowing (in everyday life, in the press, in people's behaviour, in work as well as leisure activities, the arts, etc.).

10.   The scooter was invented just after the Second World War on a Californian airport, by putting a body on a motorcycle; this allowed quick movement on the tarmac. The invention was industrially developed by the Italians in the 1950s and 1960s. In the 1970s, the Japanese began to sell scooters world-wide. What does this suggest in terms of cultural borrowing?

11. Try to elaborate on the following assertion: 'The usual traffic in marketing and business texts is that it generally starts with the American text and this is then translated into other languages or sometimes used in the original version'. What are the problems likely to be encountered by non-US educators and practitioners when using such materials? On the other hand, what are the advantages of using them?

APPENDIX 2: TEACHING MATERIALS

A2.1 Cross-cultural scenario: Inshallah

Stefan Phillips, a manager for a large US airline, was transferred to Dhahran, Saudi Arabia, to set up a new office. Although Stefan had had several other extended overseas assignments in Paris and Brussels, he was not well prepared for working in the Arab world. At the end of his first week Stefan came home in a state of near total frustration. As he sat at the dinner table that night he told his wife how exasperating it had been to work with the local employees, who, he claimed, seemed to take no responsibility for anything. Whenever something went wrong they would simply say *'Inshallah'* ('If God wills it'). Coming from a culture which sees no problem as insoluble, Stefan could not understand how the local employees could be so passive about job-related problems. 'If I hear one more *inshallah*,' he told his wife, 'I'll go crazy.'

QUESTION

What might you tell Stefan to help him better understand the cultural realities of Saudi Arabia?[7]

(Source: Ferraro, 1990, p. 118.)

A2.2 Cross-cultural interaction: Engineering a decision

Mr Legrand is a French engineer who works for a Japanese company in France. One day the general manager, Mr Tanaka, calls him into his office to discuss a new project in the Middle East. He tells Mr Legrand that the company is very pleased with his dedicated work and would like him to act as chief engineer for the project. It would mean two to three years away from home, but his family would be able to accompany him and there would be considerable personal financial benefits to the position – and, of course, he would be performing a valuable service to the company. Mr Legrand thanks Mr Tanaka for the confidence he has in him but says he will have to discuss it with his wife before deciding. Two days later he returns and tells Mr Tanaka that both he and his wife do not like the thought of leaving France and so he does not want to accept the position. Mr Tanaka says nothing but is somewhat dumbfounded by his decision.

QUESTION

Why is Mr Tanaka so bewildered by Mr Legrand's decision?

1. He believes it is foolish for Mr Legrand to refuse all the financial benefits that go with the position.

2. He cannot accept that Mr Legrand should take any notice of his wife's opinion in the matter.

3. He believes Mr Legrand is possibly trying to bluff him into offering greater incentives to accept the offer.

4. He feels it is not appropriate for Mr Legrand to place his personal inclinations above those of his role as an employee of the company.

(Source: Brislin *et al.*, 1986, p. 158. Reprinted by permission of Sage Publications, Inc.)

A2.3 Cross-cultural interaction: Opening a medical office in Saudi Arabia

Dr Tom McDivern, a physician from New York City, was offered a two-year assignment to practice medicine in a growing urban centre in Saudi Arabia. Many of the residents in the area he was assigned to were recent immigrants from the much smaller outlying rural areas.

Because Western medicine was relatively unknown to many of these people, one of Dr McDivern's main responsibilities was to introduce himself and his services to those in the community. A meeting at a local school was organized for that specific purpose. Many people turned out. Tom's presentation went well. Some local residents also presented their experiences with Western medicine so others could hear the value of using his service. Some of Tom's office staff were also present to make appointments for those interested in seeing him when his doors opened one week later. The meeting was an obvious success. His opening day was booked solid.

When that day finally arrived, Tom was anxious to greet his first patients. Thirty minutes had passed, however, and neither of his first two patients had arrived. He was beginning to worry about the future of his practice while wondering where his patients were.

QUESTION

What is the major cause of Tom's worries?

1. Although in Tom's mind and by his standards his presentation was a success, people actually only made appointments so as not to hurt his feelings. They really had no intention of using his services as modern medicine is so foreign to their past experiences.

2. Given the time lag between sign up and the actual day of the appointment, people had time to rethink their decision. They had just changed their minds.

3. Units of time differ between Arabs and Americans. Whereas to Tom his patients were very late, the Arab patient could still arrive and be on time.

4. Tom's patients were seeing their own traditional healers from their own culture; after that, they could go on to see this new doctor, Tom.

(Source: Brislin *et al.*, 1986, pp. 160–1. Reprinted by permission of Sage Publications, Inc.)

A2.4 Reading: Language and time patterns: The Bantu case

Cultural and linguistic unity of the Bantu area

The Bantu area spreads along the southern side of a line which starts from Douala, Cameroon, by the Atlantic Ocean, and finishes at the mouth of the Tana river in the Indian Ocean. It divides northern and southern Africa. The Bantu area covers most of the southern cone of this continent.

These wide territories (several million square kilometres) are occupied by Bantu people, with the limited exception of some other small ethnic groups. The cultural unity of this people has been established on the basis of common linguistic features. As early as the middle of the nineteenth century, W. Bleek (quoted by Kadima and Lumwanu, 1989) had recognized that Bantu languages shared common lexical elements and many grammatical forms. In taking Bleek's work one stage further, anthropologists, historians and linguists have tried to identify the common social and cultural traits which allow a particular area to be classified as Bantu.

Alexis Kagame (1975), for instance, has studied Bantu linguistic systems, especially their underlying structures. He has collated what he terms 'compared Bantu philosophy'. The convergence of authors when describing the conception of time in Bantu cultures is quite marked.

The unification of time and space

At the heart of the Bantu's intuition of time lies the postulate of a very close relation between time and space. Within this postulate none of these basic dimensions of reality exist without the others. Alexis Kagame reveals this conceptual link.

Ontologically, Bantu culture puts into one of four categories whatever may be conceived or said.

1. The being – of intelligence (man).
2. The being – without intelligence (thing).
3. The being – as localizer (be it place or date).
4. The being – modal (incidentality, or modification of the being).

The major assumption made by Kagame is that translation of Bantu words in metaphysical categories is possible. He therefore translates *ha-ntu* by the being-localizer. This common word expresses the unity of space (place) and time (date). In the Bantu language this term means both the 'there' of locus and the 'now' of time. It is an indivisible localizer, both spatial and temporal.

The localizing prefix *ha-*, which forms *ha-ntu*, and its variants *pa-ntu* and *ka-ntu* are found in the eastern zone of the Bantu territory. Its equivalent in the western zone is *va*, whereas it is *go* in the southeastern part of the Bantu area. The idea of unification between space and time in Bantu languages is shared by Emil Pearson, who has lived in the southeast of Angola since the 1920s. He writes in his book *People of the Aurora* (1977, p. 75):

In the Ngangela language there is no word, as far as I know, for 'time' as a continuous, flowing passage of events or the lack of same. Time is experiential or objective, that is, it is that which is meaningful to the person or thing which experiences it. *Time and space are cognate incidents of eternity.* The same word is used for both 'time' and 'space' (the latter in the sense of 'distance').

'Ntunda' can either express meaningful time or meaningful space. For example: 'Ntunda kua i li' – 'There is some distance'; and 'Ntunda i na hiti' – 'Time has passed'. The related verb 'Simbula', means 'delay', the thought being of awaiting 'meaningful time'. To the European the African may seem to be idling away useful time, whereas the latter, according to his philosophy, is awaiting experiential time, the time that is right for accomplishing his objective. 'Time' is locative, something that is virtually concrete, not something abstract. The locatives 'Ha', 'Ku' and 'Mu' are used for expressing 'time' as well as 'place'. Example: 'Ha Katete' – 'In the beginning' (as to either time or place); 'Ku lutue' can mean either 'in front' or 'in the future'. 'Mu nima' can mean 'behind' as to place, or 'after' as to time.

Bantu time experience

Two significant points sharply contrast the way Bantus experience time with the western way of experiencing it within a technological environment. First, Bantus have no theoretical substantive to designate time as an entity *per se*, which can be quantified and measured. Second, for Bantus, the temporal dimension is intrinsic to the event itself. It is not an abstraction as in most Occidental developed cultures. To these cultures it appears as a content which flows regularly from the past to the future, through the present; a flow in which everything moves at the same speed, being 'in time'. For Bantu peoples time has no real value, no meaning, without the occurrence of an event which will serve as a 'marker'. The intuition of time only becomes effective when an action or an event happens: warriors' expedition, arrival of the train, rainfall, starvation on the increase. Time then becomes individualized. It is drawn out of anonymity. It is not anybody's time which would be abstractedly defined. It is concrete time concerning people I know. Instead of considering time as a straight railway track, where events may happen successively, it will only be spoken of as 'the time of this . . .' or 'the time of that . . .', or time which is favourable for this and that. That is why, on many occasions, there is no point in giving dates, that is to refer oneself to ideal time coordinates. History is not a series of dates, but a link between various events. Everything possesses its own internal time. Each event occurs at its own time.

(Source: Usunier and Napoléon-Biguma, 1991, pp. 95–114. Reproduced with the kind permission of the publisher and the co-author.)

A2.5 Exercise: World picture test

Objective

To clarify participants' understanding of countries and cultures of the world through their knowledge of geography.

- *Participants*: Three or more persons. Facilitator.
- *Materials*: Paper and pens.
- *Setting*: No special requirements.
- *Time*: At least thirty minutes to one hour.

Procedure

1. Each participant is given a sheet of paper and a pen and asked to:
   (a) draw a map of the world as best they can within a five minute time period;
   (b) name as many of the countries as they can;
   (c) checkmark any country they have visited for a week or longer;
   (d) exchange papers with other members of the group and discuss what differences are evidenced in what the other person put into their drawing and/or left out of the drawing.

2. Discuss the following points:
   (a) Does a person's awareness of the shape of a country reveal that person's awareness of the shape of the culture?
   (b) When a person leaves out a country, what does this mean?
   (c) When a person leaves out a continent, what does this mean'?
   (d) What country did the person place in the centre of the map and what does that mean?
   (e) When a person draws a country out of place in relation to other countries, what does this mean?
   (f) Were they better acquainted with countries they had visited?
   (g) When the person objects violently to doing the drawing, what does that mean?
   (h) How well did persons draw home countries of other group members?
   (i) What do the persons plan to do as a result of what they learned in this exercise?

   (Source: Weeks *et al.*, 1987, pp. 107–8. Reproduced with the kind permission of the publisher.)

NOTES

1. This aphorism (my translation) is attributed to the Swedish writer Selma Lagerlöf by Karl Petit (1960, p. 100). Selma Lagerlöf is the author of, among other works, *Gösta Berling* (1957), Editions Je sers: Paris, a unique account of the Swedish soul.

2. The concept of time, and therefore of time-related behaviour, has been studied in numerous fields (Jacoby *et al.*, 1976; Feldman and Hornik, 1981). Contributions are to be found in such diverse disciplines as psychology, economics, sociology, theology, linguistics, mathematics, physics, literature and anthropology.

3. In the real world nationality laws are much more complicated and, in many cases, combine the two bases, kin and soil, as relevant criteria for the award of nationality.

4. Reischauer's book is now published under the title *Japan: The story of a nation*. The text has been updated since it was first published as *Japan, Past and present*, and the new version does not contain the ideas about the consequences of the Tokugawa period on Japanese behaviour, perhaps because they were resented by Japanese readers. Even distant historical events and periods may still be controversial today, when different interpretations are at stake.

5. See Ch. 5 of Segall *et al.* (1990, pp. 93–112), which asks 'Are there racial differences in cognition?' and which offers an in-depth review of the empirical studies of the difference in intellectual performance across ethnic groups.

6. Mauviel remarks that numerous studies have been dedicated to immigrant populations as such, but little research is concerned with the relations between the native lower-class population and

the immigrant communities (this is true of France, and probably many other countries). This explains why we know little about cultural hostility, which has been more or less taboo as a research topic, probably because of the fear that unveiling somewhat negative attitudes could encourage their expression. This taboo is especially strong in countries with a significant colonial history (the United Kingdom, France, the Netherlands), which explains a certain feeling of guilt.

7. The rationales behind the alternative explanations for A2.1, A2.2 and A2.3 can be found in section A3.3.

REFERENCES

Attali, Jacques (1982), *Histoires du Temps*, Librairie Arthème Fayard: Paris.

Brislin, Richard W., Kenneth Kushner, Craig Cherrie and Mahealani Yong (1986), *Intercultural Interactions: A Practical Guide*, Sage: Newbury Park, CA.

Feldman, Lawrence P. and Jacob Hornik (1981), 'The use of time: an integrated conceptual model', *Journal of Consumer Research*, vol.7, March, pp. 407–19.

Ferraro, Gary P. (1990), *The Cultural Dimension of International Business*, Prentice Hall: Englewood Cliffs, NJ.

Goodenough, Ward H. (1971), *Culture, Language and Society*, Modular Publications, no. 7, Addison-Wesley, Reading, MA.

Graham, Robert J. (1981), 'The role of perception of time in consumer research', *Journal of Consumer Research*, vol. 7, March, pp. 335–42.

Gurevitch, A. J. (1976), 'Time as a problem of cultural history', in L. Gardner *et al.* (eds.), *Cultures and Time: At the crossroads of cultures*, Unesco Press: Paris.

Hall, Edward T. (1959), *The Silent Language*, Doubleday: New York.

Hall, Edward T. (1966), *The Hidden Dimension*, Doubleday: New York.

Hall, Edward T. (1976), *Beyond Culture*, Anchor Press/Doubleday: Garden City, NY.

Hall, Edward T. (1983), *The Dance of Life*, Anchor Press/Doubleday: New York.

Harris, Philip R. and Robert T. Moran (1987), *Managing Cultural Differences*, 2nd edn, Gulf Publishing Company: Houston, TX.

Hayashi, Shuji (1988), *Culture and Management in Japan*, Tokyo: University of Tokyo Press.

Hofstede, Geert (1980), *Culture's Consequences: International Differences in work-related values*, Sage: Beverley Hills, CA.

Ishihara, Shintaro (1991), *The Japan that Can Say No*, Simon & Schuster: New York.

Jacoby, Jacob, George J. Szybillo and Carol K. Berning (1976), 'Time and consumer behavior: an interdisciplinary overview', *Journal of Consumer Research*, vol. 2, pp. 320–39.

Kadima, K. and F. Lumwanu (1989), 'Aires linguistiques à l'intérieur du monde Bantu: Aspects généraux et innovations, dialectologie et classifications', in Théophile Obenga (ed.), *Les Peuples Bantu, migrations, expansion et identité culturelle*, Editions L'Harmattan: Paris, pp. 63–75.

Kagame, Alexis (1975), 'Aperception empirique du temps et conception de l'histoire dans la pensée Bantu', in *Les cultures et le temps*, Payot/Unesco: Paris, pp. 103–33.

Lane, Paul M. and Carol Felker Kaufman (1992), 'The United States chases time; Europeans pursue life: A cross-cultural comparison of perceived time', *Proceedings of the first Conference on the Cultural Dimension of International Marketing*, Odense, pp. 1–18

Maalouf, Amine (1985), *The Crusades through Arab Eyes*, Schocken Books: New York.

Mauviel, Maurice (1991), 'La Grande Misère de l'antiracisme français', *Intercultures*, no. 12, January, pp. 69–82.

Montesquieu, Charles de (1748), *The Spirit of Laws*, translated from the French by Thomas Nugent (1762), 6th edn, Mckenzie and Moore: Dublin.

Pearson, Emil (1977), *People of the Aurora*, Beta Books: San Diego.

Petit, Karl (1960), *Dictionnaire des Citations*, Marabout: Verviers.

Reischauer, Edwin O. (1946), *Japan: Past and present*, Alfred A. Knopf: New York.

Reischauer, Edwin O. (1990), *Japan: The story of a nation*, 4th edn, McGraw-Hill: New York.

Segall, Marshall H., Pierre R. Dasen, John W. Berry and Ype H. Poortinga (1990), *Human Behaviour in Global Perspective*, Pergamon: New York.

Sherry, John F. Jr and Eduardo G. Camargo (1987), '"May your life be marvellous:" English language labelling and the semiotics of Japanese promotion', *Journal of Consumer Research*, vol. 14 (September), pp. 174–88.

Sorokin, Piritim and Robert Merton (1937) 'Social time: A methodological and functional analysis', *American Journal of Sociology*, vol. 42, pp. 615–29.

Triandis, Harry C. (1983), 'Dimensions of cultural variation as parameters of organizational theories', *International Studies of Management and Organization*, vol. XII, no. 4, pp. 139–69.

Triandis, Harry C. (1994), *Culture and Social Behavior*, McGraw-Hill: New York.

Trompenaars, Fons (1993), *Riding the Waves of Culture*, Nicholas Brealey: London.

Usunier, Jean-Claude (1991), 'Business time perceptions and national cultures: A comparative survey', *Management International Review*, vol. 31, no. 3, pp. 197–217

Usunier, Jean-Claude and Constantin Napoléon-Biguma (1991), 'Gestion culturelle du temps: Le cas Bantou', in Franck Gauthey and Dominique Xardel (eds.), *Management Interculturel: Modes et Modèles*, Economica: Paris, pp. 95–114.

Usunier, Jean-Claude and Pierre Valette-Florence (1994), 'Perceptual time patterns ("Time styles"): A psychometric scale,' *Time and Society*, vol. 3, no. 2, pp. 219–41.

Walsh, Len (1969), *Read Japanese Today*, Charles E. Tuttle: Rutland, VT, and Tokyo.

Weeks, William H., Paul B. Pedersen and Richard W. Brislin (1987), *A Manual of Structured Experiences for Cross-cultural Learning*, Intercultural Press: Yarmouth, ME.

Yan, Chen (1991), 'L'Europe vue par l'empire du milieu', *Intercultures*, no 12, January, pp. 45–56.

3 Cultural dynamics 2: Interactions, mindsets and behaviours

Let us start with this short excerpt from Adam Smith in the *Wealth of Nations*, where he comments about the 'Education of youth' (1776, 1976, p. 286):

If the teacher happens to be a man of sense, it must be an unpleasant thing to him to be conscious, while he is lecturing his students, that he is either speaking or reading nonsense, or what is very little better than nonsense. It must too be unpleasant to him to observe that the greater part of his students desert his lectures; or perhaps attend upon them with plain enough marks of neglect, contempt, and derision. If he is obliged, therefore, to give a certain number of lectures, these motives alone, without any other interest, might dispose him to take some pains to give tolerably good ones.

This text seems to be marked by common sense and its conclusion appears indisputable. However, my objective is that, after reading this chapter, you will be able to give some reasons, based on culture, why such a teacher as the one imagined by Adam Smith may survive perfectly well, although many students have left his class. There are few domains where cultural relativity is as strong as in education and teaching.

This chapter complements the previous one. Figure 2.1 showed that, among the basic cultural assumptions, some were related to cultural models of time, others to space, which in turn influence the dominant profile in terms of concept of the self and others. The first section in this chapter is dedicated to concepts of the self and others. They are central to the explanation of how people interact (section 3.2) and thus, finally, which attitudes people develop towards action (sections 3.3 to 3.6: 3.3 on why and how to act; 3.4 about relating thinking to action; 3.5 on wishes and feelings as they relate to action and 3.6 on coping with rules). This material is all organized around common problems, explained in the three tables (3.1 to 3.3) which relate to Figure 2.1. The last section in the chapter (3.7) discusses how basic cultural assumptions translate into everyday behaviour, especially in the work environment.

3.1   CONCEPT OF THE SELF AND OTHERS

The concept of the self and others does not relate directly to how a society is organized. It deals with how the organization of a society is internalized by people and reflected in the view that they hold of themselves in comparison with others. It is largely about people within a society having responded positively and unconsciously to membership conditions, and thus being largely unaware of those conditions that were necessary for becoming an 'appropriate' member of the society. In fact, men and women, children and older people have basic assumptions about the why and how of their presence in this society, and these assumptions differ across societies.

The concept of the self is a kind of modal view of what people *are* in the society and therefore what they are allowed to *do*. Basic assumptions are related to the main sociodemographic categories (age, sex, social class), but also to idealized conduct in particular roles (the perfect man, businessman, child, etc.). The ideal patterns are shown by books, films, possibly TV series, or any other kind of cultural artefact that conveys subliminal normative messages. If we take only the category of films, we have an abundance of identification possibilities, from Eliott Ness in *The Untouchables*, to Clyde Barrow in *Bonnie and Clyde*, or to the Sioux-white squaw in *Dances with Wolves*, etc. In viewing these, we constantly collect messages on how to behave. We find heroes to be desirable models. Naturally most people have a certain degree of realism and they do know in fact that these characters are not their heroes. The concept of the self has major implications in the area of consumer behaviour (Belk, 1988): our possessions are a major contributor to and reflector of our identities; by ascribing meaning to what we buy and consume, our possessions become the means by which we strive to assert, complete or attain our 'ideal' self (Wong and Ahuvia, 1995).

Table 3.1 presents major categories in the area of concepts of the self and others.

Human nature: good or bad?

A basic assumption about *innate* human nature concerns whether it is good, evil or neutral, that is subject to both good and negative influences. This combines further with the view that this basic nature may or may not be changeable. Indicative of these hidden assumptions (people are largely unaware of them) are attitudes at first contact. A friendly and open-minded attitude towards people whom one does not know is a good indicator of the assumption that innate human nature is good. When visiting the United States, Europeans are often amazed by how well they are received by people with whom they have never been in contact before. Although this cannot be explained solely by assumptions about human nature, it is clear that there is a strong positive belief in the American mentality towards new people: they are viewed as basically good and able to improve themselves by education and commitment (human nature is also seen as changeable). One may interpret this as having a functional side in relatively new countries: generally, films of the 'Western' genre portray 'bad' Indians and 'good' European settlers. The assumptions of this human nature orientation are fairly straightforward: 'civilized' = good; 'uncivilized' (Indians, gamblers, desperados) = bad.

TABLE 3.1   Concepts of the self and others

Basic problem/Cultural orientations	Contrasts across cultures
How should we treat unknown people? (a) Is human nature basically good or bad?	Unknown people are considered favourably and shown confidence or, conversely, they are treated with suspicion when met for the first time.

Appraising others
(b)   When appraising others, emphasis placed on:
   (i)   age
 	
   (ii)   sex
   (iii)   social class
	Who are the persons to be considered trustworthy and reliable, with whom it is possible to do business?
	   (i) older (younger) people are seen more favourably;
	   (ii) trustworthiness is based on (sex or not);
	   (iii) social class plays a significant role (or not) in concepts of the self and others.

Appraising oneself
 	
(c)   Emphasis placed on the self concept perceived as culturally appropriate:
   (i)   self-esteem: low/high
 	
   (ii)   perceived potency: low/high
   (iii)   level of activity: low/high
	To give the correct appearance one should behave:
	
	– Shy and modest versus extrovert or even arrogant behaviour.
	– Power shown or hidden.
	– Busy people or unoccupied/idle people are well regarded.

Relating the individual to the group (d) Individualism versus collectivism	The individual is seen as the basic resource and therefore individual-related values are strongly emphasized (personal freedom, human rights, equality between men and women); versus the group is seen as the basic resource and therefore group values are favoured (loyalty, sense of belonging, sense of personal sacrifice for the community, etc.).

In contrast, the Latin Europeans and South Americans do not start from similar premises, which makes first contact with them more difficult. The novels of the Colombian writer Gabriel Garcia Marques are typical of the view that human nature is basically bad. Novels reflect a view of basic human nature held by a particular people. But complete assumptions about human nature are of a dialectic nature (they include the reverse proposition and present a totality, that is, the apparent contradiction between the two opposing views is resolved at a higher level of thinking); they would read more as:

- Human nature is basically good, but . . .
- Human nature is basically bad, but . . .
- Human nature lies somewhere between good and bad, and . . .

The two sides of each basic assumption coexist in most religions, which strive to improve individuals, especially through the social morals that they develop. We need to have some reference points to evaluate others. They are largely culture based.

The dynamics of friendship are necessarily related to assumptions about human nature. If human nature is assumed to be good, then friendship develops quickly, but it is not necessarily very profound: since many people are supposed to be good, it is not felt to be as necessary to make a selection of 'real' friends. When it is assumed that human nature is generally bad, friendship develops more slowly because there is some initial distrust; this process resembles the behaviour of dogs, which bark at each other before socializing. Friendship will generally be more limited, in terms of numbers, and more profound: a circle of friends may be a protective barrier against a society globally perceived as somewhat unfriendly, if not hostile. Human nature orientation, although a very fundamental concept, is not directly related to action. It is indirectly important in marketing negotiations where people are simultaneously collaborating and competing, adversaries and partners. It may also be reflected in the creation of advertising messages in depicting bad versus good characters as credible support for the message itself.

Appraising others

Appraising others serves a multitude of purposes: making friends, choosing business partners, targeting potential customers, selecting a tenant and so on. Apart from personality traits which we appraise by intuition, there are a number of clues, such as age, sex and behaviour, which we use to appraise with an interpretive grid which is quite largely cultural. Let us illustrate the basic clues and how culture-based interpretations may diverge.

Age may be associated with inexperience, lack of seriousness and character, or, in contrast, with openmindedness, creativity, ability to change things and to undertake new projects. Naturally these contrasted qualities are present in all young people of all cultures. What is more interesting is how a certain culture values older people (Japan, Africa) or younger people (the United States). The probable reason for such differences is that qualities typically found at the more highly valued age are implicitly perceived as more congruent and favourable for the overall development of the society.

Emphasis on age is associated with other cultural orientations such as power distance, which is explained later in this chapter. It is also related to the dominant family models prevailing in a particular society: where the family is nuclear and the family structure fairly weak, the authority image linked to parents' role will also tend to fade away, as will the positive emphasis on older age groups as being in the 'adequate' age bracket. Where, on the contrary, an extended family is dominated by a patriarch, his role will favourably influence the image associated with the corresponding age bracket. On average, 'modern culture' values younger people because changes are extremely rapid (e.g. TV advertising revolves around young blondes, shaggy-haired surfers or yuppie-like professionals), whereas in 'traditional culture' the elders were a source of wisdom and guidance for the community, their age being valued consequently.

Sex is probably the most important cultural difference, because of the definite roles and self concepts imposed on boys and girls by culture. In *Male and Female*, Margaret Mead puts it in the following terms (1948, pp. 7–8):

The differences between the two sexes is one of the important conditions upon which we have built the many varieties of human culture that give human beings dignity and stature. In every known society, mankind has elaborated the biological division of labour into forms often very remotely related to the original biological differences that provided the original clues. Upon the contrast in bodily form, men have built analogies between sun and moon, night and day, goodness and evil, strength and tenderness, steadfastness and fickleness, endurance and vulnerability. Sometimes one quality has been assigned to one sex, sometimes to the other . . . Some people think of women as too weak to work out of doors, others regard women as the appropriate bearers of heavy burdens . . . some religions, including our European traditional religions, have assigned women an inferior rôle in the religious hierarchy, others have built their whole symbolic relationship with the supernatural world upon male imitations of the natural function of women. In some cultures women are regarded as sieves through whom the best guarded secrets will sift; in others it is the men who are the gossips.

The place of women in society has been greatly changing over the last century. Some basic rights have been long denied to women, such as voting, and in many societies the place of women is still very different from that of men. Until a few years ago, the electoral status of women was still not completely equal to that of men even in advanced countries like Switzerland (in very traditional cantons – Appenzell). For a variety of roles and capacities in the society, women are dependent on men, mostly on an economic basis. Not allowed to work outside the home, and often not permitted to buy outside or manage the family budget, as in some traditional Muslim countries, they are kept in the role of pure home-insiders. World-wide differences in the self concept of women and the concept held by men of women are striking.

Gisela Frese-Weghöft, a teacher working for the German development agency in Gadima, North Yemen, explains the case of a young woman, aged 24, that is, too old to be married, who works at home with her sewing machine as a dressmaker. She earns money – which she does not need because she is cared for by the family.

From time to time she asks her brothers to buy some jewellery with the money. Sometimes she gives presents of jewellery to her sisters or gives the money to her brothers when she has too much. It is understood that a woman cannot manage money. The sewing supplies are purchased by the men of the family, since like most women in Gadima, she is strictly forbidden to go to the souk (market-place). Some of the simplest women have invented a trick to bypass this prohibition. They disguise themselves with a dirty black sharshaff and old plastic sandals, and pretend to be one of the country women who sell their vegetables at the souk. In doing this, they should not speak much, so that nobody may recognize their voice or their pronunciation; women recognize each other, even when veiled. During these secret walks to the souk, they procure what their husbands never bring back or have erroneously purchased. (1989, p. 90, my translation.)

Social class and castes. All societies place people in particular strata. In economic-oriented societies they may divide people into the 'haves' and the 'have-nots', but other criteria are feasible based on birth or education, even in the absence of obvious wealth or income criteria. Wong and Ahuvia (1995, p. 82) argue that 'Americans generally see one's social class as primarily reflecting one's personal income level which in turn is believed to reflect (at least in part) one's individual professional merit. But to the interdependent Chinese, class does not belong to oneself, but also to one's group, usually one's family, relatives, and kinship clan.' Like many other elements of the concept of the self and others, social classes are important for consumer behaviour, people expressing their class differences, real or fantasized, by consumption.

Social stratification is based on somewhat different criteria across cultures. Castes are a special kind of social stratification, which, in the case of India consists in four major hereditary classes: the Brahman, Kshatriya, Vaisya and Sudra, into which Hindu society is divided. Social classes, and social stratification in general, exist consistently across cultures, thus probably explaining the success of Marxism for quite a long period of time. But the degree of emphasis on social stratification varies across societies, thus, perhaps, explaining the differential success of Marxist and communist regimes across countries. In countries where the emphasis on social stratification is strong, people in higher classes appraise themselves as *being substantially different* from others, in lower classes. This can extend to speaking the language differently (or even a different language), prohibiting inter-class marriages, distinguishing oneself by specific tastes and lifestyles. Bista (1990, p. 79) describes the Hindu caste system in the following terms:

one has to engage in activities that are appropriate to one's caste. Those whose fate is to be workers continue to work, but this work does not necessarily lead to any form of result or reward. The caste principle admonishes that actions have to be without desire, i.e. without a goal. There is a purpose to action, but it is a purpose known only to a supernatural agency. Individual aspirations are inconsequential and behaviour is submissive to a controlling force that is unknown. Learned Hindus emphasize that the material world is *maya*, an illusion, and claim that this is not worth taking seriously.

Appraising oneself

People hold a certain view of themselves, and prefer spontaneously to choose the one which will be perceived as culturally appropriate by others in the ingroup. Triandis (1983) distinguishes three main areas of cultural contrast. The first is self-esteem, which can be low or high according to whether a person thinks of himself or herself as good or not too good. Low self-esteem results in displaying modest and self-effacing behaviour, whereas higher self-esteem results in demonstrating more assertiveness and self-assurance. Asians, on average, clearly have lower self-esteem than westerners. The reader must be cautious when interpreting these sentences: this is only a standard assumption dictated by culture; it does not mean that Asians deserve less esteem but rather that they assume that they deserve less.

The second contrast in self concept is perceived potency, that is, the extent to which people view themselves as powerful and able to accomplish almost any task or to exercise power. The French proverb *'Impossible n'est pas français'* is a typical high-perceived-potency saying. Where the appropriate level of personal activity is seen as high, people will boast about their being 'workaholics', will work at weekends, and will generally be satisfied with overworking. When, by contrast, the appropriate image of the self is based on a low level of activity, as in the Hindu case quoted above, the standard attributes of a normal self concept will be: few hours spent in the office, low involvement in work-related issues, having time available for pure inactivity.

Individualism and collectivism: A first note

These are mentioned in Table 3.1, in the box 'Concept of the self and others', because my belief is that they are deeply ingrained in our view of the 'borders' of our self. Individualists have a more clear-cut view of where 'oneself' stops ('I, me, mine' as John Lennon's song says) and where 'others' start, whereas collectivist persons have much more fuzzy borders between their self and that of near others. The common problem, across all societies, is how to define the borders between persons and the groups they belong to, in order to ensure the smooth and efficient functioning of society.

The 'rice argument' is frequently advanced for explaining the differences between individualism and collectivism. Rice culture needs the co-ordinated flooding of rice fields which promotes dependence among the group members and requires common action. Conversely, the basic staples in the west are based on 'individualist' cereals (wheat, barley, oats, etc.), where the farmer's achievements depend mostly on his or her own individual efforts.

Individualism is based on the principle of asserting one's independence and individuality. All societies have individuals and groups, but *individualism* stresses the smallest unit as being that where the solution lies. Individualist assumptions are the following:

1. It is at the level of individuals that initiative, effort and achievements can best be developed, because people are separated and *different* (i.e. divisibility).
2. Individual achievements can be added to each other without loss (the sum equals the parts: the additive model).
3. Therefore, society has to maximize individual freedom, emphasize achieving individuals and value persons (the freedom orientation).

These assumptions are not necessarily 'true'. One may subscribe to them because of intellectual conviction, especially assumption 1, or to get personal leeway, as is the consequence of assumption 3. They are 'true' to the extent that they are largely a self-fulfilling prophecy. The obvious problems arise from assumption 2: collective action is, generally, not the direct result of simply adding individual deeds. The process is more complex, and this brings grist to the collectivist mill, which displays the following assumptions:

1. It is at group level, and not at the individual level, that initiative, effort and achievements can best be developed, because people are not really separate from each other; they belong to a *common* reality (the organic view).
2. Collective achievements are fundamentally different in nature from individual achievements, and the combination of parts (if such a computation is even possible) is much greater than the parts themselves (the multiplicative model).
3. Therefore, society has to maximize group coherence and social harmony, even at the expense of individual freedom, and if need be, by downsizing individual achievements (the concord orientation).

Collectivism is associated with 'traditional culture' whereas individualism is a strong component of 'modern culture', especially in the area of consumption, a splendid domain for enjoying individual freedom and expressing difference from others. Belk (1985), for instance, notes that, since the Middle Ages, the awareness of self has become less shared and more individualistic, this being evidenced by the growing popularity of self-oriented objects such as mirrors, self-portraits, chairs (rather than benches), etc.

Modern individualism has its roots in sixteenth- and seventeeth-century England, is based on the ideas of English and Scottish philosophers (More, Bacon, Hume, Locke) and was effected by the Act of Habeas Corpus, the first legal edict forbidding the Sovereign to jail somebody without lawful reason. This was furthered by the French *Déclaration des droits de l'homme et du citoyen*, in 1789. The French were only followers of the British, but they have been good exporters of the concept of human rights, even though neither the British nor the French practised them all the time, especially in their colonies. The United Nations Universal Declaration of Human Rights is in the same vein: it favours an individual-based view of what is a 'good' society. The individualist view of human rights is typical of Amnesty International, which has heated debates with some Asian governments, who maintain, rightly, that they hold a different view of what human rights are.

The individualist/collectivist divide is a strong but not a simple difference. In individualist societies, people still belong to groups, live in communities and conceive of themselves as integrated into a larger whole. In collectivist societies, people still feel a need to express their personal identity, and strive often for individual success and self-actualization. Thus, what differs fundamentally is the initial assumptions.

The 'modern' aspect of individualist assumptions is now heavily challenged by the rise of collectivist nations, in Asia and in South America, and their achievements in international trade and their high rate of economic growth at home. The debate between individualism and collectivism is not yet finished; they are a little bit like water and oil, not really mixable, apparently mixed when shaken vigorously, but separating afterwards.

3.2   INTERACTION MODELS

Individualism and collectivism refer to concepts of the self and others (as assumptions located *within* persons) as well as to a model of interaction *between* people. Table 3.2 lists other aspects of what are considered to be culturally appropriate interaction models in particular societies. Most of these interaction categories are based on Hofstede (1980a, 1980b). Although Hofstede developed these concepts in relation to organizational issues and through collection of data at the corporate level, they are largely transferable to society as a whole. There are many publications devoted to the impact of cultural differences on management and organization (that is, *within* companies). The impact of national cultures on various issues has been assessed, such as structure, hierarchical relationships, management of expatriate personnel and variation in motivation patterns across cultures (see, for instance, Hofstede, 1980b; Laurent, 1983; Adler, 1991). These issues are clearly outside the principal remit of this book, which is to consider the interaction of companies with their environment, that is, markets, customers, distribution channels or various influential groups (consumer movements, regulatory

TABLE 3.2   Interaction models

Cultural orientations	Contrasts across cultures
Equality or inequality in interpersonal interactions (a) Power Distance (PD)	Hierarchy is strong, power is centralized at the top (high PD); power is more equally distributed and superior and subordinates have a sense of equality as human beings (low PD).
Interacting *with* others or *for* others (b) Masculinity versus Femininity	Assertiveness and personal achievement are favoured (masc.) versus caring for others, adopting nurturing roles and emphasizing quality of life (fem.).
Dealing with uncertainty (c) Uncertainty avoidance (UA)	Tendency to avoid risks (high UA), to prefer stable situations, uncertainty-reducing rules and risk-free procedures, which are seen as a necessity for efficiency. Or, conversely, a risk-prone attitude (low UA) where people as individuals are seen as the engine of change, which is perceived as a requirement for efficiency.
Relying on oneself or on others (d) Self-reliance versus dependence	Do people rely on their own forces, find motivation and control within themselves (self-reliance) or do they need to find outside support, motivation and control from their environment (dependence)?
Developing appropriate communication with others (e) Communication styles	See Chapter 13 on Language, culture and communication.

authorities, etc.). Nevertheless a summary of the advances made in cultural differences and organization studies is worthwhile, for two reasons at least. First, Hofstede's four dimensions of national cultures, although they have been measured for management and organization practices, also make sense for marketing and sales. Second, many issues in this book are on the fringes of marketing management and organizational issues: sales force stimulation, business negotiation and global marketing strategies; and consumer behaviour issues, in particular decision making. The stability of these dimensions across replications has been shown (Sondergaard, 1994), and they have been used extensively in cross-cultural studies in international marketing.

National cultures and the relativity of managerial practices

The cover story of an issue of *Fortune* magazine accurately features the difficult question of the transposability of management styles: it shows an American with slanting eyes eating (or, more probably, trying to eat) a hamburger with chopsticks. Geert Hofstede was one of the first researchers to question the adaptability of US management theories and practices to other cultural contexts. Empirical studies for Hofstede's work were undertaken between 1967 and 1973 within a large multinational company, in 66 of its national subsidiaries. The database contains more than 116,000 questionnaires: all categories of personnel were interviewed, from ordinary workers to general managers. Out of 150 questions, 60 deal with the values and beliefs of the respondents on issues related to motivation, hierarchy, leadership, well-being in the organization, etc. The questionnaire was administered in two successive stages (1967–9 and 1971–3) so as to verify validity by replication. Versions of the questionnaire were drafted in twenty different languages. Not all subsidiaries are included in the final analysis; depending on the data under review, 40–55 countries are finally comparable. The results drawn from this data were further validated by a systematic comparison with the results of thirteen other studies (Hofstede, 1980b, 1983).

Interviewees all belonged to the same multinational corporation, IBM, which has a very strong corporate culture shared by its employees. Consequently there was no variance on this dimension across the sample. Each national sample allowed for a similar representation of age groups, sex and categories of personnel, thereby avoiding a potential source of variance across national subsidiaries' results. Finally the only source of variance was the difference in national cultures and mentalities. Hofstede, by means of factor analysis of the respondents' scores, was able to derive four main conceptual dimensions on which national cultures exhibit significant differences. One of these four dimensions is *individualism/collectivism*, which we have already mentioned in the previous section. In collectivist countries there is a close-knit social structure, where people neatly distinguish between members of the ingroup and members of the outgroup. They expect their group to care for them in exchange for unwavering loyalty. In individualistic societies, social fabric is much looser: people are basically supposed to care for themselves and their immediate family. Exchange takes place on the base of reciprocity: if an individual gives something to another, some sort of return is expected within a reasonable timespan. The other three dimensions are explained below. They correspond to the first three cells in Table 3.2.

Power distance

Power distance measures the extent to which a society and its individual members tolerate an unequal distribution of power in organizations and in society as a whole (see Box 3.1). It is shown as much by the behavioural values of superiors who display their power and exercise it, as by the behavioural values of subordinates who wait for their superiors to show their status and power, and are uncomfortable if they do not personally experience it. In low power distance societies, members of the organization tend to feel equal, close to each other in their daily work relationships: when the real hierarchical distance is high, power may be delegated. In high power distance societies, superiors and subordinates feel separated from each other; it is not easy to meet and talk with higher-ranking people, and the real power tends to be very much concentrated at the top. At society level, power distance translates as shown in Box 3.1.

BOX 3.1

More equal than others

In a peaceful revolution – the last revolution in Swedish history – the nobles of Sweden in 1809 deposed King Gustav IV whom they considered incompetent, and surprisingly invited Jean Baptiste Bernadotte, a French general who served under their enemy Napoleon, to become King of Sweden. Bernadotte accepted and he became King Charles XIV; his descendants occupy the Swedish throne to this day. When the new King was installed he addressed the Swedish parliament in their language. His broken Swedish amused the Swedes and they roared with laughter. The Frenchman who had become King was so upset that he never tried to speak Swedish again. In this incident Bernadotte was a victim of culture shock: never in his French upbringing and military career had he experienced subordinates who laughed at the mistakes of their superior. Historians tell us he had more problems adapting to the egalitarian Swedish and Norwegian mentality (he later became King of Norway as well) and to his subordinates' constitutional rights. He was a good learner, however (except for language), and he ruled the country as a highly respected constitutional monarch until 1844.

One of the aspects in which Sweden differs from France is the way its society handles *inequality*. There is inequality in any society. Even in the most simple hunter-gatherer band, some people are bigger, stronger or smarter than others. The next thing is that some people have more power than others: they are more able to determine the behaviour of others than vice-versa. Some people are given more status and respect than others.

(Source: Hofstede, 991. Reproduced with the publisher's permission.)

Masculinity/femininity

Individualism should not be equated with selfishness. When responding to the common problem: 'do we interact *with* others or *for* others?', responses are made on the basis of dominant value systems, which would roughly correspond to male/assertive and the female/nurturing roles. A society is masculine when dominant values favour assertiveness, earning money, showing off possessions and caring little for others. Conversely, feminine societies favour nurturing roles, interdependence between people and caring *for* others (who are seen as worth caring for, because they are temporarily weak). This dimension has been so called because, on average, men tended to score high on one extreme and women on the other, whatever the society.

In typically feminine societies, such as the northern European countries, the welfare system is highly developed, education is largely free and easily accessible, and there is openness to admit that people may have problems: patience and helpfulness are shown to those who are in trouble; both boys and girls learn to be modest and to have sympathy for the underdog. In typically masculine societies, whether individualist like the United States or collectivist like Japan, weaker people find, on average, less support from society at large; people learn to admire the strong, such as Rambo in the United States. The common problem behind the masculinity/femininity divide could perhaps be phrased differently: should we help people (at the risk of their being weakened by a lack of personal effort) or should we not (at the risk, for them, of being even worse)? Obviously, the response is not easy.

Uncertainty avoidance

A common problem faced by people in any society is how to deal with uncertainty. There are basically two ways: the first is based on the assumption that people have to deal with uncertainty, because it is in the very nature of the situations we face. The future is by definition unknown, but risks can be evaluated, and people and institutions can manage them. The other extreme is marked by risk aversion, which results in the assumption that uncertainty is bad and everything in society must be made in such a way as to reduce uncertainty.

The dimension of uncertainty avoidance measures the extent to which people in a society tend to feel threatened by uncertain, ambiguous, risky or undefined situations. Where uncertainty avoidance is high, organizations promote stable careers, produce rules and procedures, etc. 'Nevertheless societies in which uncertainty avoidance is strong are also characterized by a higher level of anxiety and aggressiveness that creates, among other things, a strong inner urge to work hard' (Hofstede, 1980a). Hofstede points out that 'uncertainty avoidance should not be confused with risk avoidance . . . even more than reducing risk, uncertainty avoidance leads to a reduction of *ambiguity*' (1991, p. 116).

The cultural relativity of management theories

Table 3.3 shows the value of the dimensions discussed above for fifty-three countries/regions. Figure 3.1 presents a diagrammatic map of countries when individualism and power distance are combined. Hofstede's main tenet concerns the *cultural relativity of management theories*. These theories are rooted in the cultural context where they were developed, with the result that any simple direct transposition is difficult. As regards motivation, Hofstede shows the linkage that exists between US-based motivation theories and American culture. For instance, Abraham Maslow's 'hierarchy of needs' and McClelland's theory of the achievement motive are directly related to two dimensions of US culture: its strong masculinity and its individualism. People are seen as being motivated in an overtly conscious manner by the expectancy of some kind of results from their acts: they are basically motivated by extrinsic reasons and rewards. In contrast, Freudian theory, which has not been greatly applied by US management theorists, represents the individual as being pushed by internal forces, often unconsciously, the id and the super-ego interacting with the ego. According to Hofstede, Austria, where Freud was born and where he drafted his theories, scores significantly higher than the United States on uncertainty avoidance and lower on individualism. This may explain why motivation is more related to internalized social values. 'Freud's superego acts naturally as an inner uncertainty-absorbing device, an internalized boss' (Hofstede, 1980a).

TABLE 3.3   Values of Hofstede's cultural dimensions for 53 countries or
regions

Country/region	Dimensions			
	Power distance	Uncertainty avoidance	Individualism	Masculinity
Arabic countries[a]	80	68	38	53
Argentina	49	86	46	56
Australia	36	51	90	61
Austria	11	70	55	79
Belgium	65	94	75	54
Brazil	69	76	38	49
Canada	39	48	80	52
Chile	63	86	23	28
Colombia	67	80	13	64
Costa Rica	35	86	15	21
Denmark	18	23	74	16
East African region[b]	64	52	27	41
Ecuador	78	67	8	63
Finland	33	59	63	26
France	68	86	71	43
Great Britain	35	35	89	66
Greece	60	112	35	57
Guatamala	96	101	6	37
Hong Kong	68	29	25	57
India	77	40	48	56
Indonesia	78	48	14	46
Iran	58	59	41	43
Ireland	28	35	70	68
Israel	13	81	54	47
Italy	50	75	76	70
Jamaica	45	13	39	68
Japan	54	92	46	95
Malaysia	104	36	26	50
Mexico	81	82	30	69
Netherlands	38	53	80	14
New Zealand	22	49	79	58
Norway	31	50	69	8
Pakistan	55	70	14	50
Panama	95	86	11	44
Peru	64	87	16	42
Philippines	94	44	32	64
Portugal	63	104	27	31
Salvador	66	94	19	40
Singapore	74	8	20	48
South Africa	49	49	65	63
South Korea	60	85	18	39

TABLE 3.3   *Continued*

| Country/region | Dimensions | | | |
	Power distance	Uncertainty avoidance	Individualism	Masculinity
Spain	57	86	51	42
Sweden	31	29	71	5
Switzerland	34	58	68	70
Taiwan	58	69	17	45
Thailand	64	64	20	34
Turkey	66	85	37	45
United States	40	46	91	62
Uruguay	61	100	36	38
Venezuela	81	76	12	73
West African region[c]	77	54	20	46
West Germany	35	65	67	66
Yugoslavia	76	88	27	21
Overall mean	57	65	43	49
Standard deviation	22	24	25	18

[a]Saudi Arabia, Egypt, United Arab Emirates, Iraq, Kuwait, Lebanon and Libya.
[b]Ethiopia, Kenya, Tanzania and Zambia.
[c]Ghana, Nigeria and Sierra Leone.

Interaction clashes

As shown in Chapter 15, the differences on the dimensions illustrated above have to be taken into account when designing sales force stimulation systems across national subsidiaries which have different cultural contexts. In masculine, individualistic countries, where there is also lower uncertainty avoidance, extrinsic rewards should be preferred (bonuses, gifts, holidays, monetary incentives). In societies which are more feminine, and/or more collectivist, and/or with higher uncertainty avoidance, intrinsic rewards should be chosen because they fit with profound inner values.

Hofstede also examines the direct transposition of the American MBO (Management By Objectives) in France, where it became the DPPO *(Direction Participative Par Objectifs)*. MBO stems from a society where:

1. Subordinates are independent and feel sufficiently at ease with their bosses to negotiate meaningfully with them (low power distance).
2. Subordinates as well as superiors are willing to face ambiguity (low uncertainty avoidance).
3. The outcome is considered important by superiors and subordinates (high level of masculinity).

DPPO enjoyed brief success at the end of the 1960s but had become a flop by the mid-1970s. Indeed in the French cultural context DPPO created anxiety, in a country where hierarchy is traditionally strong (high power distance) and where that structure protects people against uncertainty. MBO assumes a depersonalized authority (role

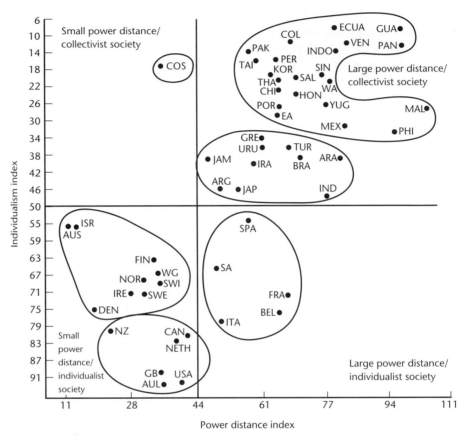

FIGURE 3.1   Map of 53 countries ranked on power distance and individualism indices.

(Source: Hofstede, 1980b.)

authority) whereas, according to Hofstede, from their childhood French people are used to high power distance and strongly personalized authority. Despite efforts to introduce Anglo-Saxon management methods, French bosses do not easily decentralize management and delegate authority.

In a study at Insead, reported by Hofstede, O. J. Stevens asked students of various nationalities to write their own diagnosis of and solution to a small case study about a conflict between the sales department and the product development department. The French saw the problem basically as one that the hierarchy should solve, a solution being sought from the chairperson. The Germans blamed the absence of formal rules and written procedures. The English saw the problem as resulting basically from a lack of interpersonal communication. Stevens concluded that 'the implicit model of the organization for most French was a pyramid (both centralized and formal); for German a well-oiled machine (formalized, but not centralized); and for most British a village market (neither formalized, nor centralized)' (Hofstede, 1980a, p. 60).

Organization types may be more adapted to some cultures than to others. In a matrix organization, for instance, there is a double hierarchical linkage (with a product division at the European level and a subsidiary general manager at the country level): this is not accepted very well by either the French or the Germans. For the French, it violates the principle of unity of command; for the Germans, it thwarts their need for organizational clarity and will not be deemed acceptable unless individual roles inside the organization are unambiguously defined.

Self-reliance versus dependence

Being self-reliant or showing dependence has naturally to do with assumptions about the concept of the self. For example, the valuing of elders in the community will tend to decrease the legitimacy of self-reliance among younger age groups. Similarly for sex: traditional sex roles promote dependence among women. Even social class may have an influence in as much as an implied family model reigns over cross-class relationships, people in higher social classes behaving patronizingly towards those in lower classes. In industrial relations for instance, the 'paternalist' orientation of factory owners towards their workers typifies the role of the boss as a father and the employees as 'children'.

Self-reliant people rely on their own forces and find motivation and control within themselves, whereas dependence implies that they need to find outside support, motivation and control from their environment. As summarized in Table 3.4, low power distance and uncertainty avoidance, combined with high individualism and masculinity, will be related to more self-reliance (the US case; the best examples of extreme contrast are generally the Latin countries like Chile, Portugal or Brazil, see Table 3.3). The typical westerner is on average more self-reliant than the average Easterner. And the typical northern European is more self-reliant than the typical Latin European.

Two assumptions are central in developing either self-reliance or dependence among individuals: (1) the locus of control – whether a person considers that events are contingent upon his or her own behaviour or are under the control of powerful, unpredictable and complex external forces; and (2) the implicit family role that underlies typical interaction patterns.

The first basic issue in relation to self-reliance versus dependence is whether people consider they have an external or an internal locus of control (Rotter, 1966). People with internal locus of control will show more self-reliance, because they believe in their ability to manage their own world and to control it by themselves. The locus-of-control concept was not developed by Rotter in a cross-cultural perspective, but rather at an individual level. However, it applies fairly well as a contrasting dimension across cultures.

The second issue in relation to dependence versus self-reliance is the kind of family role that a particular culture favours: in Latin societies, for instance, the parent/child relationship remains a very strong underlying model for interaction, and even in situations which are normally assumed as being between equals, some people may unconsciously and spontaneously develop parental attitudes. If conflict develops the superior will easily develop the attitude of a 'critical' parent (in the terms of Eric Berne's transactional analysis),[1] leaving little option for their counterparts but to behave as a 'compliant child' ('obeying') or, on the contrary, as a 'rebel child', or finally leaving. Parent/adult roles underlying models of interaction clearly place many relationships in the realm of dependence: functional relationships will be based on

TABLE 3.4

Hofstede's dimension	Influence on self-reliance/dependence
Individualism	Increases self-reliance
Power distance	Promotes dependence
Masculinity	Increases self-reliance
Uncertainty avoidance	Promotes dependence

filial dependence, whereas dysfunctional relationships will be played in the conflict mode. For people who come from societies where self-reliance is standard behaviour, it is often extremely irritating not to be treated as an adult, equal in rights and obligations, but, symbolically, as a child. France is a good case in point: many aspects of the French culture favour dependence, with the major exception of a strong individualist orientation. This results in a pattern of varying dependence, where people constantly play a game of dispute and reconciliation in teamwork, where true self-reliance can only be fostered by creative activity and/or working independently.

3.3   CULTURE-BASED ATTITUDES TOWARDS ACTION

Action is about changing the world, even in a minuscule way. Large categories of actions do not involve any problem: they are repetitive and programmed; they are daily or seasonal routines. Non-routine tasks require a more complex course of action, because they involve problematic features:

1.   They must be based on a clear sense of purpose (why act?).

2.   They involve the future, largely unpredictable, that is risk taking.

3.   They need input from the past (taking lessons from previous experience).

4.   They imply the need to articulate collective and individual interests.

5.   They need to 'relate the hand to the brain, the heart and the mouth'.

Expressed metaphorically, this last feature means that action (hand), in a cross-cultural perspective, can hardly be separated from how people think (brain), how they relate their wishes and desires to actions (located somewhere between brain, heart and mouth), and how they mix feelings with deeds (located clearly in the heart, for most cultures). Table 3.5 details the main contrasts across cultures in terms of attitudes towards action.

Most marketing and managerial action displays the problematic features given above. They are non-routine tasks, especially in an international context. Individuals and organizations have naturally a lot of leeway in making and implementing decisions, but most interpretive clues are given by their cultural background.

Basic cultural assumptions, and combinations of these, have an influence on the way we cognitively evaluate real-world situations and the issues that face us. Some examples will demonstrate that we do know how to construct our reality but only within our native cultural community.

TABLE 3.5   Attitudes towards action

Basic problem/Cultural orientations	Contrasts across cultures
Why act? (a) Degree of fatalism: mastery of nature versus subjugation to nature; existence and degree of legitimacy of a Promethean (proactive) view of human life.	People believe that it is possible to cope with any problem or any situation and that, to mankind, nothing is impossible; evil is when one does nothing ('master of destiny'); the converse is the belief that there are many situations where people cannot do anything; destiny binds us and we should not try to find alternatives (fatalistic orientation); evil is when one does not accept one's own destiny ('subjugation').
What is action? (b) 'Speech' versus 'deed' orientation	Contrast between cultures which value speech as action and those which separate them; contrast between a clear sequencing of action and a fuzzy view of action.
How to relate thinking to action (1) (c) Ideologism versus pragmatism	Ideologism: thinking patterns, communication (style of speech) and actions should always be set within the context of broad ideological principles (religious, political, social, legal, etc.); versus pragmatism: precise issues must be addressed; a practical attitude is favoured: orientation towards problem solving and concrete results.
How to relate thinking to action (2) (d) Intellectual styles	Differences in assigning a dominant role to theory, data, speech, modesty and virtue in assessing truthful propositions that need to be put into action.
How to relate wishes and desires to action (e) 'Wishful thinking' orientation (WT)	WT cultures tend to emphasize enthusiasm, imagination of the future and the capacity of desires to *shape* reality; non-WT cultures emphasize the principle of reality: desires and wishes have to be checked objectively against the constraints of the real world.
How to relate feelings to action (f) Affective (A) versus neutral (N) cultures	People in N cultures separate feelings from actions, do not mix friendship with business; in A cultures, mixing both is seen as inevitable and positive.

TABLE 3.5 *Continued*

Basic problem/Cultural orientations	Contrasts across cultures
How to deal with rules (g) Obeying practical rules versus coping with ideal rules	Rules can be made which are respected, discussed and implemented quite strictly or there may be a discrepancy between ideal rules and what people can actually do, leading them to undertake behaviour that involves exploring and bypassing rules.

Why act?

Not everyone is preoccupied with doing, acting, being efficient and achieving tangible results which can be appraised by others. From an existential point of view this preoccupation with 'doing' is not really justified: in the long term we will all be dead, as Keynes said. Moreover, assuming that we do all care about efficiency, there are many different ways of achieving it. Montesquieu (1748, 1792, pp. 228–9) illustrates the spontaneous irritation of people who are 'doing' oriented towards those who are more 'being' oriented when, in *The Spirit of Laws*, he comments on what he calls *indolent nations*:

The Indians believe that repose and non-existence are the foundations of all things, and the end in which they terminate. Hence they consider entire inaction as the most perfect of all states, and the object of their desires. To the supreme Being they give the title of immoveable. The inhabitants of Siam [Thailand] believe that their utmost happiness consists in not being obliged to animate a machine or to give motion to a body.

Not only are the Indians and Siamese[2] (the Thai people) more 'being' oriented, they also have a quite different view of the relationship with nature from westerners (subjugation to nature rather than mastery over nature). As noted previously, their religions include belief in reincarnation: on the death of the body, the soul transmigrates or is born again in another body, as outlined above. Life therefore is not seen as 'one shot', but more as a cyclical phenomenon. This puts less pressure on people to be 'doing' oriented but also means there is more inducement to *be* blameless and virtuous since that will influence the status of further reincarnations; inaction is one of the surest ways to lead a blameless life.

The idea that we have a soul plays a substantial role in the sense of purpose that feeds our actions. It is only in the recent, 'modern' times that people have envisioned as a quite legitimate world-view that we are only made of material substances, whose molecules are recycled through flame or decay at the end, according to burial custom. As the Swiss psychologist, Carl G. Jung, explains, it is a fairly new idea in world cultures:

Under the influence of scientific materialism became all that was not to be seen with eyes and touched with hands dubious, and even more, questionable, because suspected of metaphysics. Was only considered as 'scientific', and thus as altogether admissible, either what was recognized as material or what was derived from sensory perceptible causes. (1931, 1990, p. 9, author's translation.)

Both ideas (having a soul or not) have their merits and it is obviously difficult to find supportive evidence for either one. Thus, it is more interesting to investigate the consequences for action of the assumption that we have a soul. The idea of a soul generally coexists with that of God. *Metempsychosis* (the migration of the soul from one body to another) is a very strong belief which arises as a response to an important common human problem: what is the relation between the physical world and the metaphysical world? Believers (people raised in the cultures where this belief is prevalent) are more patient, seemingly less 'doing' oriented, simply because achieving position in lives to come is more important than what is achieved in one's present life. Without discussing metempsychosis, let us look at some fundamental monotheist assumptions:

1. God as supernatural force, both protective and threatening.

2. God being almighty and therefore easy to offend.

3. God asking human beings to accept their destiny as it comes to them.

4. God also asking them to do as much as they can to act rightly and justly.

Fatalism is a belief that directly influences action, not necessarily in terms of acting less, but rather in terms of acting *differently*. It clearly posits the locus of control as being outside, in the metaphysical environment. It also provides convenient explanations for unpredictable events, which allow people to resume activity quickly after catastrophes (earthquakes, fires, car accidents). Fatalism makes mourning easier and facilitates the acceptance of strongly negative personal events, a bankruptcy for instance.

Where Christianity fundamentally differs from Islam is on assumption 3. The Christian creed more strictly separates the worldly from the heavenly sphere ('Render unto Caesar the things which are Caesar's; and unto God the things that are God's'). Furthermore, there is a less personal and direct relation to God than in Islam, since, at least in Catholicism, it is largely mediated by the Church. This frees the tendencies towards mastery over nature, since God gives mankind leeway in relation to worldly enterprises. To a large extent, the punishment in the Promethean myth is forgotten. In Christian religions, the way is cleared for proactive attitudes.

What is action?

Another important distinction to be made is whether a culture tends to classify words, speeches and, more generally, acts of communication, in the 'deeds' category. In many cultures there are popular sayings which effectively condemn speech on the basis that it is not real action ('do, not talk'). In the real world, life is more complicated: communications are a category of act, and their potential influence on others is beyond doubt. But whether communication (in what particular form?) is considered as being significantly related to action, differs across cultures.

Let us take the example of poetry, which in Islam is highly esteemed. One can be fascinated by poetry, by the beauty of words and songs (and the fact of being fascinated can lead to the message of the poetry being acted on), as this commentary on the life of the Prophet illustrates:

Thus, Mohammed was sitting in the great courtyard of the Caaba, surrounded by the faithful, foreigners and Qureichits. The melodious music of the verses of the Koran was playing while the Prophet was gazing at the audience; the sparkle in His eyes and the beauty of the songs held the people spellbound. The people kept on repeating: 'If You are a prophet, perform a miracle for us, so that we may believe in You.' And the messenger of God invariably answered: 'O Arab People, is not the miracle powerful enough, that your everyday language has been chosen for the Book, in which a single verse makes us forget about all your poems and all your songs?' It is said that, on hearing this response, non-believers committed themselves to convene all the poets of Arabia, so that they might create at least one verse, a few words, the beauty of which would match that of the Koran. The poets arrived at Caaba and began to perspire under the torrid sun. They toiled, they spared themselves no anguish in seeking to perform what had been requested of them. But as soon as they began to recite their works, even the fiercest opponents to the Prophet themselves were compelled to admit that none of their words could rival the verses of the Koran. Poetic spirit is so greatly esteemed among Arabs that many of those who were in the Caaba at that moment knelt down and were converted to Islam. The unrivalled beauty of the language had convinced them of its heavenly origin. (Mohammed Essad Bey, 1934, pp. 98–9, author's translation.)

The word 'poetry' comes from the Greek word *poio*, a verb meaning to 'make', to 'produce', to 'build'. Such an etymology, which is at first sight surprising, sheds some light on the opposing value judgements of the usefulness of poetry, which are made according to different basic cultural assumptions. On the one hand it may be seen as rather distanced from action in the real world, on the other as a direct source of inspiration for action. Indeed if a 'classical' model of action is assumed, i.e. one that is culturally European/western based, the following sequence occurs:

1. Analysis of the problem and the issues at stake.
2. Gathering of relevant information
3. Listing and evaluating possible solutions.
4. Selecting the 'best' decision.
5. Implementation: that is, mainly articulating individual and collective action since the implementation process is generally scattered among numerous diverse agents, whereas the decision itself tends to be more individualized, or at least taken by a limited number of people.
6. Appraisal of the outcome, control of the difference between target and actual outcomes, and possibly feedback to a previous step in the sequence.

This sequence may be easily criticized for being culturally non-universal: Japanese people have no word for decision making (Lazer *et al.*, 1985), and action/decision/control processes are viewed mainly as implementation issues. This is why they first insist on consulting each one of a large group of people at various levels in the organization, who will comment on how to do something (not necessarily on why). But even if we were to accept that this sequence is true, it would still involve a great deal of cultural relativity.

3.4   HOW TO RELATE THINKING TO ACTION

In relating thinking to action, the categories considered are the following:

1. How should issues be addressed: broadly, with the premise that *the parts always represent the whole*, or narrowly, considering that *focus is the key to relevance* when acting?

2. What are the proofs that a certain course of action, based on previous reflection, is the right one: (a) data; (b) theory; (c) personal conviction; (d) virtue because it is morally correct to think and do so?

Ideologists versus pragmatists

If future partners do not share common 'mental schemes', it could be difficult for them to solve problems together. Buyers and sellers, for instance, should share some joint views of the world, especially on the following questions:

1. What is the relevant information for acting?

2. How should this information be sought, evaluated and fed into the decision-making process?

An important distinction in the field of cross-cultural psychology opposes ideologism to pragmatism (Glenn, 1981; Triandis, 1983). As Triandis (1983, p. 148) expresses it: ideologism versus pragmatism, which corresponds to Glenn's universalism versus particularism, refers to the extent to which the information extracted from the environment is transmitted within a broad framework, such as a religion or a political ideology, or a relatively narrow framework. This dimension refers to a way of thinking.

Ideologists will use a wide body of ideas which provide them with a formal and coherent description of the world: Marxism or liberalism, for instance. Every event is supposed to carry meaning when it is seen through this ideologist framework. On the other hand, the pragmatist attitude first considers the extreme diversity of real world situations, and then derives its principles inductively. Reality will be seen as a series of rather independent and concrete problems to be solved ('issues'). These issues will make complete sense when related to practical, precise and even down-to-earth decisions. Typically, ideologists will *take* decisions *(prendre des décisions)*, that is, pick a solution from a range of possible decisions (which are located outside the person who decides). Conversely, pragmatists will *make* decisions, that is, both decide and implement: decisions will be enacted, not selected.

Triandis hypothesizes that complex traditional societies will tend to be ideologist ones, whereas pluralistic societies or cultures experiencing rapid social change will tend to be pragmatist. This distinction may also be traced back to the difference between the legal systems of *common law* (mainly English and American) and the legal system of *code law* (mainly French and German). Whereas the first type favours legal precedents set by the courts and past rulings (cases) the latter favours laws and general texts which are intended to build an all-inclusive system of written rules of law (a code). Codes aim to formulate general principles so as to embody the entire set of particular cases.

The ideologist orientation, which is to be found mostly in southern and eastern Europe, leads negotiators to try to establish principles before there is any detailed discussion on specific clauses of the contract. Ideologists have a tendency to prefer and promote globalized negotiations in which all the issues are gathered in a 'package deal'. The pragmatist attitude corresponds more to northern Europe and the United

States. It entails defining problems of limited scope, then solving them one after the other. Pragmatists concentrate their thinking on factual aspects (deeds, not words; evidence, not opinions; figures, not value judgements). They are willing to reach real-world decisions, even if they have to be down-to-earth ones.

Communication may be difficult when partners do not share the same mental scheme. The most unlikely situation for success is an ideologist-oriented contractor/supplier who tries to sell to a pragmatist-oriented owner/buyer. The ideologist will see the pragmatist as being too interested in trivial details, too practical, too down-to-earth, and incapable of looking at issues from a higher standpoint. Pragmatists will resent ideologists for being too theoretical, lacking practical sense, concerned with issues that are too broad to lead to implementable decisions.

What information is relevant for action? How should it be used?

The dimensions of ideologism and pragmatism are, to varying degrees, combined. It would be a mistake to consider Americans as pure pragmatists with no leaning towards ideology. In fact they identify problems clearly and precisely as 'issues'. They collect evidence systematically and their attitude is matter of fact. To be 'down to earth' is a positive expression in English, whereas its French equivalent may often be pejorative *(être terre à terre)*.[3]

But it is also true that the free-market/individual-oriented ideology has a strong presence in the United States, and is enshrined in the Constitution, in anti-trust legislation, in corporate law and so on. However, it is rarely present on a daily basis, when information directly relevant to action is gathered or discussed. Ideology is generally accepted unquestioningly. It is therefore somewhat irrelevant to debate practical matters, as an ideologist would.

Conversely, one may well be conscious of pragmatic considerations when ideology and ideas are the object of debate. In international business negotiations there is often discussion of principles, which may seem inconsequential owing to the inevitable generality of such discussion. However, it may lead to a substantive outcome later on. The fundamental skill of diplomats (who are, in many respects, experts in matters of culture) is to obtain the acceptance and underwriting of basic principles by their counterparts, the effectiveness of which is only apparent at a later date.

Actual (empirical) reality versus potential reality: Which should be preferred?

A mistake frequently made is to believe that reality is simple, in the sense that it is directly related to our perceptions and the ways in which we act on it and try to change it. It is what we call 'common sense', that is, shared meaning which makes sense in the cultural community *simply because we share it*, even though it may appear nonsense to people belonging to other cultural communities. The English language is more realistic than the French language here, saying common sense (shared meaning) as opposed to the French *bon sens* ('good sense'), a value judgement which is sometimes wrong. Indeed our relation to the real world is heavily filtered by a series of convergent factors:

1. Our perceptual apparatus is partly culturally formed (see sections 1.4 and 9.4).

2.   We implicitly choose to limit the search to certain categories of facts and represent them in a particular way.

3.   We admit the truthfulness of these facts according to criteria which are determined in part by our cultural background. When and how they are established as true (meaning that there is a consensus about their being a part of the real world) is also culture based.[4]

4.   Even when these facts have been established as true, there still remain different readings and interpretations of them, depending on culture-based values and social representations.[5]

We may favour either *actual/empirical* reality, that is, the ways in which we experience reality here and now (or the way it is revealed by empirical science), or *potential reality*, that is, the reality we imagine and dream about but which also motivates us to achieve. Potential reality is in a sense the *possible* future of actual reality. Our sense of potential reality relies much more on imagination than on actual perceptions. Since it is beyond the reach of our perceptions and we cannot experience it, we have to envisage potential reality. Potential reality is a rich ground for action, because it directly supports our Promethean desires to exert mastery over nature. It helps us to achieve objects and to undertake projects which can make us feel equal to gods ('space conquest' projects, for instance).

Galtung (1981) uses this distinction between actual reality and potential reality in order to contrast what he calls the 'intellectual styles' of four important cultural groups:[6] the 'Gallic' (prototype: the French), the 'Teutonic' (prototype: the Germans), the Saxonic (prototype: the British and the Americans) and the 'Nipponic' intellectual style (prototype: the Japanese). Saxons prefer to look for facts and evidence which result in factual accuracy and abundance. As Galtung states (1981, pp. 827–8) when he describes the intellectual style of Anglo-Americans:

data unite, theories divide. There are clear, relatively explicit canons for establishing what constitutes a valid fact and what does not; the corresponding canons in connection with theories are more vague . . . One might now complete the picture of the Saxonic intellectual style by emphasizing its weak point: not very strong on theory formation, and not on paradigm awareness.

Galtung contrasts the Saxonic style with the Teutonic and Gallic styles, which place theoretical arguments at the centre of their intellectual process. Data and facts are there to illustrate what is said rather than to demonstrate it.

Discrepancy between theory and data would be handled at the expense of data: they may either be seen as atypical or wholly erroneous, or more significantly as not really pertinent to the theory. And here the distinction between empirical and potential reality comes in: to the Teutonic and Gallic intellectual, potential reality may be not so much the reality to be even more avoided or even more pursued than the empirical one but rather a *more real reality*, free from the noise and impurities of empirical reality. (1981, p. 828.)

However, Teutonic and Gallic intellectual styles do differ in the role that is assigned to words and discourse. The Teutonic ideal is that of the ineluctability of true reasoning *(Gedankennotwendigkeit)*,[7] that is, perfection of concepts and the indisputability of their mental articulation. The Gallic style is less preoccupied with deduction and intellectual construction. It is directed more towards the use of the persuasive strength of words and speeches in an aesthetically perfect way *(élégance)*. Words have an inherent power to convince. They may create *potential reality*.

Finally the Nipponic intellectual style, imbued with Hindu, Buddhist and Taoist philosophies, favours a more modest, global and provisional approach. Thinking and knowledge are conceived of as being in a temporary state, open to alteration. The Japanese 'rarely pronounce absolute, categorical statements in daily discourse; they prefer vagueness even about trivial matters . . . because clear statements have a ring of immodesty, of being judgements of reality' (Galtung, 1981, p. 833).

These distinctions are important for any situations where a certain course of action has to be based on favourable arguments, for instance in assessing the quality of a marketing strategy and when doing market research. After the failure of a marketing campaign, people will tend to emphasize different issues: should they, for instance, (1) find supporting evidence of what went wrong, (2) convince sales people to be more enthusiastic about the product, (3) re-think the theory behind the strategy, or (4) improve the quality of the troops in charge of implementation?

3.5   DEALING WITH DESIRES AND FEELINGS

Management is based on the principle of reality, and not on the principle of pleasure (in Freudian terms), and therefore there is little interest in looking at people's desires and feelings, which are considered to be in the realm of the purely subjective, and deserving of being treated as almost non-existent. However, in a cross-cultural perspective, they are important, because people have different ways of relating their actions to their desires and feelings. In this section we are dealing with the two corresponding cells, (e) and (f), in Table 3.5.

How to relate wishes and desires to action

As noted above, words and deeds may either be classified in two separate categories or combined. They may be set opposite each other on the basis that words are empty or hollow, or joined on the basis of the action of words on others: speech implies influencing and often, consequently, causing someone to act. Most acts of authority are only words. To illustrate some culture-based misadventures in the relationship between words and deeds, Box 3.2 presents the example of the role of wishful thinking (WT) in the international negotiation of a delivery date.

Of course, every culture mixes the use of actual/empirical reality and potential reality. But cultures differ in the ranking of these, and in the degree of distrust of potential reality. Obviously potential reality is more dangerous to deal with: it is easier to speak about it than to act on it. Facts are not 'stubborn' if they are remote and vague. An important issue for cultural action styles is the problematical link between what one says and what one does. WT is important in any action that deals with the future and with potential reality: in bidding situations, the management of delivery delays, the announcement of prices, attitudes towards new projects, or in an advertising campaign where arguments unknowingly based on wishful thinking may 'explain why' the audience should be convinced by the message.

BOX 3.2

Wishful thinking

When selling industrial equipment or turnkey projects on world-wide markets, it is always necessary to stipulate one delivery date or more. The effects of such an announcement may be severe: the buyer may cancel the order because the date is too late. However, this date rarely depends exclusively on the person who sets it. One may spontaneously leave some time between the announced date (an actual reality) and the real delivery date (a potential reality), surmised from the previous performance of the seller's organization. Wishful thinking (WT) is a necessary input in this process: it explains why the initially announced delivery date may be very different from the ultimate one. Wishful thinking is a true 'art of communication' which is preferred more in Latin cultures than in Anglo-Saxon cultures. There is no expression in French for *wishful thinking* (except perhaps *des voeux pieux*), so the English expression is used in French. The negative consequences of WT, such as deceitful behaviour, are much less emphasized in Latin than in Anglo-Saxon cultures. The fact that the phrase 'wishful thinking' is rather pejorative, shows that, normatively, in Anglo-Saxon cultures, it should be avoided, whereas in Latin cultures expressing desires appears more natural. Naturally, in addition to the cultural background there are also some personalities and psychological profiles which are more prone to wishful thinking.[8]

WT consists in first thinking, then saying, how one wants things to be, not how they are. Since nobody knows exactly how things will be in the future, a non-WT oriented person will try to say how he or she thinks quite realistically they will be, not as he or she wants them to be. WT deals with the future: when a culture is weakly future oriented, its use is easier. People do not worry about periods which they do not clearly envisage. If a culture clearly divides words from deeds (do what you say, say what you do), the use of WT is inhibited. When, on the other hand, speech is considered as a prominent modality of action, WT may possibly become a necessity (to galvanize people, while at the same time evoking an improbable future). WT is closely related to present orientation: it is a convenient way to escape from the constraints of longer-term realities by focusing on the here and now. It dodges problems to be solved, and hides divergences and possible conflicts. But this is only in the short term.

A seller with a strong WT communication has the tendency to tell a client spontaneously that the delivery date requested is entirely feasible. The seller also manoeuvres verbally around past realities which may not be wholly reassuring: a six-week delay in the last shipment, for instance. The buyer may also have a WT communication framework, and is in fact 'buying' friendly relations rather than hard data, preferring to be 'happy now'. On the other hand, if the buyer is not WT-prone, the seller is judged negatively and the order is not placed, unless there is some compelling rational argument such as a shortage of this type of supply, particularly high quality or exclusive technology.

(Source: Adapted from Usunier, 1989, pp. 89–90.)

Affective versus neutral cultures

The contrast between affective and neutral cultures is closely related to the being/doing divide in basic cultural assumptions and to dependence in the models of interaction. If people are strictly doing oriented they generally tend to disregard what directly expresses the being. Feelings and affectivity are seen as being in the purely personal and private, individual, domain. Anglo-Saxon cultures, for instance, tend to suppress feelings and to view their direct expression as alien and even inappropriate for effective interaction to take place. Trompenaars phrases it as follows (1993, p. 63): 'Members of cultures which are affectively neutral do not telegraph their feelings but keep them carefully controlled and subdued. Neutral cultures are not necessarily cold or unfeeling, nor are they emotionally constipated or repressed.' In response to a question asking if they would express their feelings openly, if they felt upset about something at work, the highest score of neutrality was for the Japanese (83 per cent), followed by (the former West) Germany (75 per cent) and the United Kingdom (71 per cent). The Dutch are in the middle (55 per cent), whereas American people express their emotions more easily than the British, with only 40 per cent in favour of neutrality. Finally Italy and France are clearly more affective cultures, with only 29 per cent and 34 per cent respectively agreeing that they would not express their feelings openly.

In fact the practical problem which all cultures have to face is not an easy one: over-suppression of emotions and feelings may result in flawed interaction, that is, poor results in terms of action. People may discover quite late in a situation that personal antipathy is a major obstacle to further interaction. On the other hand, giving people a free hand to express all that they feel is somewhat dangerous, because feelings may be superficial or short-sighted and may needlessly offend the other party. The feelings/action issue is important for the choice of partners, for improving communication and reducing misunderstandings in marketing negotiations, when managing sales personnel, establishing relationships with foreign distribution channels, or when preparing locally appropriate advertising materials.

Every culture has certain codes and rituals that allow for a compromise between the two extreme positions. What varies is the starting assumption.

1.   Expressing emotions is legitimate and useful for action (affective cultures).
2.   Expressing emotions needs to be separated from action (neutral cultures).

It needs, however, to be refined, by the addition of two further caveats:

1.   As emphasized by Trompenaars, people have no fewer emotions in neutral cultures than in affective cultures; perhaps the contrary is true. Since feelings and emotions are contained, they may pile up and result in hidden negative feelings.
2.   Much is based in personality traits and individual interaction; culture, in this area, should not be overestimated. Much is universal rather than culture-specific in the area of feelings and emotions.

Chapter 13 on language, culture and communication explores the issue of affectivity versus neutrality in more detail.

3.6   COPING WITH RULES

Rules and basic assumptions

A rule is an authoritative regulation or direction concerning method or procedure. Rules are formalized norms which generally comprise a scale of sanctions according to the gravity of the breach. Rules can be made which are respected, discussed and implemented quite explicitly, or there may be a discrepancy between ideal rules and what people can actually do, leading them to behaviour involving the exploring and bypassing of rules. Some typical indicators of rule-related behaviour deal with speed limits, traffic lights, queueing at banks or bus stations, how income statements are filled in, and so on. A naive interpretation of rules would be that they are made to be respected. The real function of rules is more complex. Written rules are fairly standard across cultures. But, the first precaution is to read rules in the light of basic assumptions and interaction models (see Tables 3.6 and 3.7):

1. A positive human nature orientation (HNO) leads to the designing of rules where sanctions are small and often a positive reinforcement, a reward for respecting the rule, will be preferred to a penalty. People are viewed as capable of being trusted to respect the rules and of getting benefit out of them (HNO good), whereas high sanctions and severe enforcement are the case in cultures with an HNO-bad assumption. Table 3.6 presents four ideal types of rule, and behaviour in relation to the rule, based on the type of HNO and the level of power distance. In this table, the HNO assumption must be understood in a somewhat comparative way between the ruler and the ruled: 'good' means that the ruled view themselves as 'better' than or equal to the ruler; 'bad' means that the ruled view themselves as 'as bad' as or 'even worse' than their rulers.

2. The level of power distance in a particular society has an influence on (a) the design of rules; (b) their implementation. Low power distance results in general in people being associated in some way with the design of rules, and in their being applied with a sense of fairness and equity to everybody, included those with larger power in the society (remember, as Hofstede points out, that power is unequally distributed, even in low power distance societies). In contrast, high power distance results in people being subject to rules, in the design of which they were not involved. Furthermore, rules apply more strongly to those with less power, the most powerful being seen as somewhat beyond the reach of rules that apply only to 'ordinary people'.

3. As noted in the discussion in the previous chapter on space-related assumptions, strong ingroup orientation often leads to the syndrome of rules that are 'applicable only here' (that is, in the native community, not outside).

4. The inner drive to respect the rule: guilt (*inner feeling* of responsibility for committing an offence) versus shame (a painful *emotion, directed to the outside*, resulting from an awareness of having done something dishonourable as a group member).

Types of rules and rule-related behaviour

Anglo-rules, including those of northern European countries, are basically 'pragmatic' rules: people generally comply with the rule out of a sense of responsibility built on positive motivation; rules are understood as helping society to work more smoothly and better and everyone is supposed to benefit from their being respected. In this picture, people are universally at ease with their rules, even if they sometimes break them (nobody is perfect in any society).

'Challengeable rules' correspond to those that exist in Italy or France where power distance is fairly high and ordinary people view themselves as having a better human nature than those at the top. It is not seen as wrong to investigate the extent to which rules can be transgressed. Most often rules come directly from the top, without any 'instructions for use'. Rule exploring means looking for the margins of interpretation. The only way to explore a new rule is to breach it discreetly from the start in order to know whether it is intended to be applied seriously or whether it is one more empty text that nobody will respect.

'Mechanical rules' would be found in the German or Swiss case; they are made democratically because power distance is low, but there is distrust of people. Sanctions are explicit and implemented fairly literally: as in the well-oiled machine model of Stevens (the German model of organization as described by Hofstede; see section 3.2), respect for rules has a fairly mechanical and automatic side: they are applied literally.

The last stereotypical case is to be found in many developing and Third World countries with high power distance and negative assumptions as to the nature of human beings, powerful or not. Rules are often very strict, formal and somewhat unrealistic. Chapter 11 develops the example of foreign exchange control systems, which lead to the bypassing of the rule by over- or under-invoicing. Oppressive rules oblige people who have been subject to long-term rule to bypass the law and induce rulers into corrupt behaviour (they can implement unimplementable rules with some leniency in exchange for a bribe). Oppressive rules lead to a strange atmosphere, where there is a high discrepancy between what people say they will do and what they actually do, a sort of systematic social schizophrenia (for instance the policeman will change money in the forbidden parallel exchange market). The idea of possible discrepancies between ideal patterns and actual behaviour was expressed by Linton (1945, pp. 52–4):

TABLE 3.6   Type of rules and behaviour according to HNO and power distance

	Power distance	
HNO	Low	High
Good	**Pragmatic rules** (responsible compliance)	**Challengeable rules** (exploring behaviour)
Bad	**Mechanical rules** (automatic compliance)	**Oppressive rules** (bypassing behaviour)

All cultures include a certain number of what may be called ideal patterns . . . They represent the consensus of opinion on the part of the society's members as to how should people behave in particular situations . . . comparison of narratives usually reveals the presence of a real culture pattern with a recognizable mode of variation . . . it [the ideal pattern] represents a desideratum, a value, which has always been more honoured in the breach than in the observance.

Box 3.3 shows how rules more complex than those officially displayed result partly from opportunistic behaviour, and partly from their being difficult to respect. In any country, an examination of the basic rules relating to the functioning of society (e.g. traffic, queueing, taxation) and how they are actually implemented, quickly provides a fairly good idea of local patterns in dealing with rules.

Universal versus local rules

Table 3.7 contrasts universal rules with local rules: universal rules are assumed to be applicable even beyond the borders of cultures and countries. An example lies in US laws being applicable extraterritorially, such as anti-trust rules or the anti-corruption

---

BOX 3.3

Brazilian traffic lights

When I travel to Brazil, I stay in Rio de Janeiro with friends who work for the Brazilian census bureau (IBGE). There, I have learnt that the rules for traffic lights are not really the same as elsewhere. It is not as simple as 'red = stop', 'green = go'. Sometimes cars just do not stop when it is red for them. There seems to be no rule. Investigating more carefully, I gradually discovered that the rule is largely situation-specific. In the case of heavy traffic, it tends generally to be well respected, which shows a certain common sense on the part of Cariocas. In the case of lighter and smoother traffic, it depends mostly on the relative size of streets (not to mention the driver's personality and propensity to take risks). Those coming from a smaller street must take care before they benefit from their green light: people on the larger street may cross the red lights after slowing down a little bit, but without stopping. Thus, out of rush-hours traffic lights are semi-optional for those driving on major avenues. The last case comes at night: one should never stop at red lights even when lawfully required to do so. One night as we were coming back from an IBGE party at Jacarepagua (a nice suburb of Rio), Roberto explained to me, as he drove across the town to Flamengo without apparently noticing traffic lights, that, a year ago, he had been assaulted by a man who had threatened to shoot him through the side window of his car. Naturally, he had given him all his money and was fortunate enough to get back home unhurt. The rule at night is therefore: never stop at a traffic light, it is better to slow down to catch the green and if necessary cross on the red.

TABLE 3.7   Universal versus local rules

Type of rule	Universal rules	Local rules
Ingroup orientation	Weak	Strong
Inner compliance dynamic	Guilt	Shame

legislation, FCPA, examined in Chapter 15. The legal concept of extraterritoriality is typical of outgroup orientation, and the US legal extraterritoriality is often resented by other sovereign states as as intrusion into their home affairs. On the other hand, strong ingroup orientation, as mentioned above, leads to the feeling that rules are only local, they apply to the people here, on their territory and not outside.

People who favour universal rules are characterized by an inner compliance dynamic based on guilt, that is, self-reproach caused by an inner feeling that one is responsible for a wrong or offence. The moral punishment is to a large extent interiorized within the psyche as in the Freudian concept of *schuld* (in German: debt, fault, culpability). Conversely, the inner compliance dynamic for ingroup-oriented people is based on shame and is more outer directed: it has to do with losing face, having one's honour threatened, that is risking rejection by the other group members. Local rules are territory bound and concern breach of loyalty to the ingroup.

Adopting a more open view of how people attribute meaning to rules makes sense for a large array of international marketing issues. As far as consumer behaviour is concerned, rules on waiting, attitudes towards queuing, theft from stores by consumers, the attention paid by consumers to instructions for use (of pharmaceuticals, food), the attitude towards filling in market research questionnaires, giving truthful information and, more generally, any ethical issue that involves social responsibility of manufacturers, service providers or consumers have to be examined with a view to their cross-cultural relativity.

3.7   CULTURAL ASSUMPTIONS AND ACTUAL BEHAVIOUR

As outlined in Chapter 1, all societies face common problems, and although there is a dominant solution, alternatives are always present, and they combine in a dialectic way. Let us take the example of how individual and collective actions are to be combined. Japanese people are often depicted as collectivist, in contrast to the Americans who are deemed more individualistic. There is undoubtedly an element of truth in this distinction, but it is necessary to outline its limits. For the word 'individual', let us substitute three words which encompass most of its various facets: *human being, person* and *individual*; and for 'collectivity' let us substitute the words *group, community* and *society*. Who is more humane, more personal and more sensitive in interpersonal relations, more attentive and understanding than the average Japanese person? Who cares more about the community than the average American, whose objective is to 'socialize in the community'? In the United States the word 'community' is used extensively. Indeed Americans and Japanese share a common problem (as defined by Kluckhohn and Strodtbeck, 1961): that of combining individual actions and collective undertakings.

This problem may be solved only by a process which is essentially dialectic. In any society there exists a dominant cultural assumption about what the *first* (but not the *sole*) priority should be: either the individual is the most important (as in the United States); or else the group is the basic survival unit to which the individual must be subordinated (as in Japan). Then comes the reverse cultural assumption, which dialectically complements the basic assumption: that the community is where people integrate to build a common society, and their reciprocal links should be strictly and explicitly codified (United States); or (Japan) that the utmost level of sensitivity must be developed in interpersonal relations so that the working of the group is kept as smooth as possible.

The basic cultural assumptions described in the previous sections are in fact deep-rooted beliefs which generate basic values. Indirectly they guide our daily behaviour, but they may also clash with it. By their very nature they are subconscious, as is the process by which they shape our interaction with others and our conduct. There is some leeway for other sources of influence: for instance, we use social representations to make decisions. We are influenced by other values and other standards of demeanour, such as work rules, company codes of conduct, lifestyles or friendship patterns which work closer to the surface than basic cultural assumptions. These standards of demeanour help people to manage adjustments in the short term; they change over much shorter periods of time (ten or twenty years) than basic cultural assumptions (probably formed over centuries). This leads to two questions:

1. To what extent do less profound levels of culture, e.g. corporate culture or educational culture, influence people?

2. To what extent do people, more or less consciously, feel a contradiction between these different sources of prescriptive behaviour?

Taking their views from Schein's (1981) culture model, Derr and Laurent (1989) present what they call the 'levels of culture triangle' (see Figure 3.2). Basic assumptions are at the bottom of the triangle: values and behavioural norms which derive from the society in its present state. At the top of the triangle are behavioural standards, which are prescribed in a much more direct and explicit way, which Derr and Laurent call 'artefacts': for instance, company procedures, business ethics codes and generally all those standards that unashamedly seek to shape employees' behaviour (inside the company). Whereas cultural assumptions are based on national culture, 'artefacts', values and norms are based on organizational culture.

Multinational companies (MNCs) offer their employees the most fruitful opportunities for intercultural exchange. One might believe that, despite differences in national culture, the values shared by executives in MNCs do converge, as they spend years working with different people. In order to grasp differences in cognitive styles, Laurent (1983) asked managers of different nationalities to indicate their agreement or disagreement with the following statement (item 24 of Laurent's questionnaire on management styles): 'It is important for a manager to have at hand precise answers to most of the questions that his subordinates may raise about their work.'

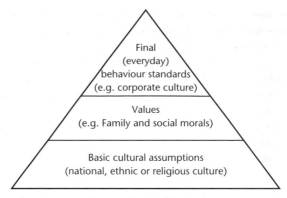

FIGURE 3.2 Basic cultural assumptions and actual behaviour.

(Source: Derr and Laurent, 1989.)

Figure 3.3 reproduces the results (the percentage of respondents replying in the affirmative) for various national groups. Obviously Swedes do not need omniscient managers (10 per cent). Among westerners at the other extreme, the Italians (66 per cent) and the French (53 per cent) believe that managers should have precise answers to most of their subordinates' questions. It seems that most Anglo-Saxon and northern European people tend to see managers as problem solvers, whereas Latin and Asian people see them more as *experts*.

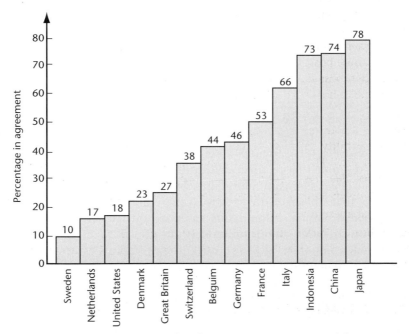

'It is important for a manager to have at hand precise answers to most of the questions that his subordinates may raise about their work.'

FIGURE 3.3 National differences in subordinates' expectations towards their superiors.

(Source: Laurent, 1983 and Adler *et al.*, 1989.)

These differences were observed in people working in their home country. Laurent (1989) asked the same question of executives who had been working for a long time in MNCs where teams had been built up from a large number of different nationalities. One would expect to observe a decrease in the differences between national groups of managers. Surprisingly, the situation is exactly the opposite. Laurent has observed in MNCs an increase of differences across national groups. This suggests that, behind superficial agreements, people's basic cultural assumptions are reinforced. When a corporate culture tries to shape a manager's (or more generally an employee's) daily behaviour, it succeeds from the outside (because people are concerned about their job and career). But it only scratches the surface of people and does not significantly affect the two bottom levels of Figure 3.2. Moreover, since values are forced upon them, not only do they fail to impinge on basic cultural assumptions, but they even reinforce them.

QUESTIONS

1. Are there cultural roots to personal modesty?
2. Which examples would you suggest to exemplify American individualism?
3. In many countries, there is an institution called 'parliamentary democracy'. On which basic cultural values is it based, in your opinion? Is there a relationship between the development of marketing and parliamentary democracy?
4. Given country scores on Hofstede's four dimensions, what do you expect would be the problems encountered by a typical boss from country X in managing a typical employee from country Y (even at the risk of some sterotyping and sweeping generalization)?
   (a) An American boss managing Japanese subordinates.
   (b) A Japanese boss managing French subordinates.
   (c) A French boss managing Swedish subordinates.
   (d) A Swedish boss managing Japanese subordinates.
5. A conversation is in progress between a British manager and a French manager concerning a common (large) project. The project is at a very early stage (examining its feasibility, setting deadlines for construction, planning of steps in building process, etc.). The Frenchman is very enthusiastic and argues: 'Let's go, we can do it; *impossible n'est pas français!* [impossible is not a French word]'. The Englishman feels somewhat uneasy about the turn of the conversation. Why?
6. Are there Japanese individualists? Why?
7. A sign indicates: 'Parking time limited to 10 minutes. Be fair.' Which views of time and rules does this reveal? Try to imagine signs with different information for people who have a different approach to rules.

APPENDIX 3: TEACHING MATERIALS

A3.1 Critical incident: An American in Vietnam

An American in Vietnam recalls an illuminating story told him by a Vietnamese who complained about a lack of understanding between the two allies. They were discussing the fate of a province chief named Vong, once hailed by the Americans as the best province chief in Vietnam. Vong was accused of embezzling some 300,000 American dollars earmarked for an airstrip, and was tried and sentenced to be executed. It seemed a harsh sentence, considering the corruption prevalent at the time, and the American asked the Vietnamese if he agreed.

'No,' the Vietnamese said, 'Vong should be executed because he's a stupid man'.

'Stupid? Because he got caught?' the American asked.

The Vietnamese impatiently shook his head. 'No, no, not because he took the money', he said. 'That is not important. But you know what this stupid man did? He pacified six more hamlets than his quota. This caused the general who gave him the quota to lose face, and that is stupid.'

The perplexed American said, 'In America, he'd get a medal for exceeding his quota.' The Vietnamese shook his head and said, 'You Americans will never understand the Vietnamese.'

QUESTION

What aspects of the incident are significant in describing the difference in opinion between these two persons?

(Source: Weeks *et al.*, 1987, p. 22. Reproduced with the kind permission of the publisher.)

A3.2 Exercise: Seven cultures of the South Seas

You will find below a short excerpt from Margaret Mead's book *Male and Female*. She introduces briefly each of the seven South Seas peoples, who live in fairly diverse natural settings and have different kinds of activities and social organization.

QUESTIONS

For you, this is an exercise in imagination. You are asked to perform the following task, which is both easy and complicated: starting from Margaret Mead's basic cultural descriptions, try to characterize the selling styles of these seven peoples. For instance, consider the following questions for each of these societies:

1. Is selling considered a socially respectable activity?
2. Who is the more powerful: buyer or seller?
3. What is the communication style (hard/soft)?
4. Are people long-term transaction oriented (buyer and seller tending to be loyal to each other in the long run)?
5. What kinds of sales argument (seduction, force, blackmail, etc.) would be used?
6. Does selling exist at all? Is selling meaningful? Why?

The Samoans

The Samoans are a tall, light-brown-skinned Polynesian people living on a small group of islands, part of which belong to the United States. Their way of life is formal and stately. Chiefs and orators, village princes and village princesses, patterned groups of young and old, combined together to plant and reap, fish and build, feast and dance, in a world where no one is hurried, where food is plentiful, nature is generous, and life is harmonious and unintense. They have been Christian for over a hundred years, and have fitted the tenet of Christianity into their own traditions, wearing beautifully starched cottons on Sunday, but still barefoot, and proud of their own way of life.

The Manus of the Admiralty Islands

The Manus people are a small, energetic tribe of fishermen and traders who build their houses on piles in the salt lagoons, near to their fishing-grounds. Tall, brown-skinned, lean and active, with nothing but their wits, their skill, and an ethics which says that the ghost of the dead will penalize the unindustrious, they have built a high standard of living which they maintain by continuous hard work. Puritan to the core, committed to effort and work, disallowing love and the pleasures of the senses, they take quickly to the ways of the Western world, to machinery, to money.

The Mountain Arapesh

The Mountain Arapesh are a mild, undernourished people who live in the steep, unproductive Torricelli Mountains of New Guinea, poor themselves, and always struggling to save enough to buy music and dance-steps and new fashions from the trading peoples of the sea-coast, and to buy off the sorcerers among the fiercer people of the interior plains. Responsive and cooperative, they have developed a society in which, while there is never enough to eat, each man spends most of his time helping his neighbour, and committed to his neighbour's purposes. The greatest interest of both men and women is in growing things – children, pigs, coconut-trees – and their greatest fear is that each generation will reach maturity shorter in stature than their forebears, until finally there will be no people under the palm-trees.

The cannibal Mundugumor of the Yuat River

These robust, restive people live on the banks of a swiftly flowing river, but with no river lore. They trade with and prey upon the miserable, underfed bush-peoples who live on poorer land, devote their time to quarrelling and head-hunting, and have developed a form of social organization in which every man's hand is against every other man. The women are as assertive and vigorous as the men; they detest bearing and rearing children, and provide most of the food, leaving the men free to plot and fight.

The lake-dwelling Tchambuli

The Tchambuli people, who number only six hundred in all, have built their houses along the edge of one of the loveliest of New Guinea lakes, which gleams like polished ebony, with a back-drop of the distant hills behind which the Arapesh live. In the lake are purple lotus and great pink and white water lilies, white osprey and blue heron. Here the Tchambuli women, brisk, unadorned, managing and industrious, fish and go to market; the men, decorative and adorned, carve and paint and practise dance-steps, their head-hunting tradition replaced by the simpler practice of buying victims to validate their manhood.

The Iatmul head-hunters of the Great Sepik River

On the big, slow-moving river into which the Yuat River drains, for which the mountains where the Arapesh live is one watershed, to which the Tchambuli lake is connected by canals, are the swagger villages of the Iatmul people, head-hunters, carvers, orators, tall and fiercely, brittlely masculine, where women serve as spectators to the endless theatricality of the men's behaviour. Rich in sago swamps that provide them with a steady food-supply, well fed on fish that the steady industry of the women provides, they have built magnificent ceremonial houses, and beautifully carved war-canoes, and accumulate in their big villages the art-styles, the dance-steps, the myths, of all the lesser peoples about them, outstanding among their neighbours, and vulnerable in the intensity of their pride.

The Balinese

The Balinese, who can be numbered in hundreds of thousands, not in a few thousands like the Samoans or a few hundreds like the New Guinea peoples, are not a primitive people, but a people whose culture is linked through Asia with our own historical past. Light, graceful, wavy-haired, with bodies every segment of which moves separately in the dance, they have a highly complex and ordered way of life that in its guilds and Hindu rituals, its written records and temple organizations, its markets and its arts, is reminiscent of the Middle Ages in Europe. Crowded on a tiny island with a beautiful, highly diversified, changing landscape, they have turned all life into an art. The air is filled with music day and night, and the people, whose relations to each other are light, without enduring warmth, are tireless in rehearsal for a play where those disallowed feelings will be given graceful stylized expression.

(Source: Mead, 1948, pp. 52–5. Reproduced with permission.)

A3.3   Rationales for section A2.1 (cross-cultural scenario) and sections A2.2 and A2.3 (cross-cultural interactions)

A2.1   Scenario: Inshallah

This scenario can best be understood by first appreciating the very different views in US culture and Saudi culture concerning 'locus of control'. In the United States it is believed that ultimately people are responsible for their own destiny. If something goes wrong, it is believed, it is frequently possible for the individual to *do* something (that is, to change certain behaviour) to bring about the desired outcome. In Saudi Arabia, and indeed throughout the Arab world, people are taught from an early age that all things are subject to the direct will of Allah. All plans for the future (including, of course, business plans) are viewed with a sense of inevitability and will be realized only if God wills it. This is not to say that people in the Arab world would not work hard to help bring about the desired results. Rather, they believe that despite the effort, the desired ends will not happen unless God is willing. Perhaps Stefan would have been less frustrated if he had translated *inshallah* to mean 'if possible' or 'God willing' rather than as a knee-jerk response used to absolve oneself of all responsibility for one's actions.

(Source: Ferraro, 1990, p. 162.)

A2.2   Interaction: Engineering a decision

1. There is little evidence for this in the story. While the financial benefits are relevant, to Mr Tanaka they are probably a minor consideration in the situation. Please choose another response.

2. It is quite probable that, coming from a male-dominant Japanese society, he does think it odd that Mr Legrand should mention his wife's opinion. However, the decision not to go to the Middle East also appears to be Mr Legrand's personal inclination so this does not fully account for Mr Tanaka's bewilderment. There is another explanation. Please choose again.

3. It is unlikely that Mr Tanaka would consider this. There are factors far removed from personal gain dominating his concern. Please choose again.

4. This is the most likely explanation. In Japanese and many other collectivist societies a person is defined much more as a collection of roles (parent, employee, servant, official) than by his or her individual identity. Therefore, fulfilling these roles to the best of one's ability is regarded as more important than one's personal inclinations. Thus Mr Tanaka would see that Mr Legrand's responsibility as a company employee would be to accept the position whether or not he is personally happy about the idea. Mr Legrand's refusal is thus bewildering and makes him think that his belief in Mr Legrand's dedication has been completely misplaced. Mr Legrand, however, comes from a culture where individual freedoms are highly valued and so exercises his right to refuse the offer with little compunction. The cultural conflict thus resides in different strengths of values applied to the roles occupied by a person in the culture.

    (Source: Brislin *et al.*, 1986, pp. 177–8. Reprinted by permission of Sage Publications, Inc.)

A2.3   Interaction: Opening a medical office in Saudi Arabia

1. It is unlikely that people would sign up solely to satisfy a newcomer's feeling. There is a better explanation. Please select again.

2. If there is a considerable time lag between when a person makes a decision and the action upon it, it is possible that they may change their mind. However, there is no indication in the incident to support this. Please select another response.

3. Units of time reference differ markedly between Arab and American cultures. To an American, the major unit of time is five minutes. Fifteen minutes is a significant period of time. To an urban Arab, the unit of time that corresponds to our five-minute block is fifteen. Thus, when the Arab is thirty minutes late (by the clock), he is not even ten minutes late by his standards. This is the best answer. Tom's patients may still arrive.

4. While the patients may be seeing their own traditional healers, they would not necessarily do so in the strict sequence suggested by this alternative. There is a more precise explanation. Please choose again.

    (Source: Brislin *et al.*, 1986, p. 179. Reprinted by permission of Sage Publications, Inc.)

NOTES

1. Berne's theory (Berne, 1961, 1964) is based on a view of the self as composed of three strata: the Parent, the Adult and the Child. Transactions between human beings can take place at the same level or across levels of the self, for instance when a person sends a message based on his Parent to the Child of another person. What I am suggesting here is simply that some cultures may favour Adult–Adult transactions in interpersonal relationships whereas others tend to promote Parent–Child transactions, especially in hierarchical situations.

2. Siam is the name originally given by the French to the present Thailand: Siamese are therefore Thai people.

3. This means implicitly: compared to Latins, such as myself. We are generally much less cautious in taking such steps, if indeed we ever stop to identify them clearly. Even the style of this book reveals that I come from an ideologist-oriented society (French). The expressions 'matter of fact'; and 'down to earth', which are both positive in English, may be translated by *être terre à terre*. The French language also has two expressions, but one is pejorative and the other is positive – *avoir les pieds sur terre* (*Harrap's Concise French–English Dictionary*, 1984, Harrap: London, p. 369).

4. Those who wish to enlarge their world-view by freeing themselves, at least partially, from the mental programmes brought to them by culture, risk being misunderstood. This is in fact a legitimate reaction on the part of other members of the group. By trying to escape a single cultural programming, such people exhibit a definite lack of humility in setting themselves apart from the community. Furthermore, any homogeneous human group feels quite threatened when members of the group overstep the threshold of non-conformity. They may finally be understood (because the message is useful as an instrument of change that is needed in the society), or live alone, or be beheaded (e.g. Sir Thomas More).

5. Clifford Geertz in *Local Knowledge* (1983) quotes a long passage from a Danish traveller and trader, L. V. Helms, who when travelling in India accurately reports the ritual of the cremation of a dead man and his three (living) widows. Helms describes very carefully the background to the incident, which took place around 1850. He is horrified by the ritual, amazed by the absence of reaction of the crowd attending the event and stunned by the lack of fear of the three women who throw themselves alive into the flames. Geertz emphasizes the relationship of culture to moral imagination: what is seen as sheer barbarism by one culture is experienced as wholly normal by another. Another more recent example of cross-cultural differences in the interpretation of facts is given by the totally divergent views during the Gulf War about Saddam Hussein (whose actions are well known): bloodthirsty dictator to some, hero of the Arab world to others. When Saddam Hussein fired Scud missiles at Saudi Arabia and Israel, interpretations of this simple act were also totally divergent. For an interpretation of the Gulf War reportage as representing advertising for weapons, see Ottosen (1992).

6. The article by Johan Galtung which we quote deals with the intellectual style of academics. Since it describes 'intellectual styles' in general (not only the style of the intellectuals), this framework is used as depicting 'ideal types'. Johan Galtung, a Norwegian, is a renowned scholar in the field of peace research. His numerous articles and books are an important source of reflection on national culture and the conflicts between cultural communities.

7. The concept of *Gedankennotwendigkeit* is typical of German thinking patterns, where abstraction is taken to its limits. It is not by chance that German philosophers have a world-wide reach. The German language is probably the richest in the world in terms of abstract words. It favours pure conceptual thinking. The construction of *Gedankennotwendigkeit* is itself proof (sorry: an illustration) of this: *denken* means 'to think', *Gedanken* are 'thoughts'; *Not* means 'necessity', *wenden* is 'to turn', *-keit* is a suffix which abstracts the whole as 'the state of

being . . .'. As a result of this rebus, *Gedankennotwendigkeit* is something like *'the state of being turned into necessary (unavoidable, pure) thoughts'* (*Langenscheidt German–English Dictionary*, 1970, used for the translation of component words, Basic Books: New York).

8. To use a (very elementary) Freudian distinction: the denial of WT employs the anal principle of tightening oneself up and controlling one's behaviour, when strongly integrating reality as a constraint; conversely, the use of WT denotes oral behaviour: favourable words (*paroles*), which describe reality in a much more pleasant way than it actually is, provide wishful thinkers (and above all, wishful *speakers*) with a mouth pleasure. This oral behaviour thwarts the frustrations of reality, like the little child that sucks its thumb when something has made it unhappy.

REFERENCES

Adler, Nancy J. (1991) *International Dimensions of Organizational Behavior*, 2nd edn, PWS-Kent: Belmont, CA.

Adler, Nancy J., Nigel Campbell and André Laurent (1989), 'In search of appropriate methodology: from outside the People's Republic of China looking in', *Journal of International Business Studies*, vol. XX, no. 1, p. 69.

Belk, Russel W. (1985), 'Cultural and historical differences in concepts of self and their effects on attitudes toward having and giving', *Proceedings of the 12th Annual Conference of the Association for Consumer Research*, ACR: Provo, UT, pp. 754–60.

Belk, Russel W. (1988), 'Possessions and the extended self', *Journal of Consumer Research*, vol. 5, pp. 139–68.

Berne, Eric (1961), *Transactional analysis in Psychotherapy*, Grove Press: New York.

Berne, Eric (1964), *Games People Play*, Grove Press: New York.

Bista, Dor Bahadur (1990), *Fatalism and Development*, Orient Longman: Calcutta.

Brislin, Richard W., Kenneth Kushner, Craig Cherrie and Mahealani Yong (1986), *Intercultural Interactions: A Practical Guide*, Sage: Newbury Park, CA.

Derr, C. Brooklyn and André Laurent (1989), 'The internal and external career: A theoretical and cross-cultural perspective', in M. B. Arthur, D. T. Hall and B. S. Lawrence (eds.), *Handbook of Career Theory*, Cambridge University Press: Cambridge.

Essad Bey, Mohammed (1934), *Mahomet*, Payot: Paris.

Ferraro, Gary P. (1990), *The Cultural Dimension of International Business*, Prentice Hall: Englewood Cliffs, NJ.

Frese-Weghöft, Gisela (1989), *Ein Leben in der Unsichbarkeit*, Rowohlt: Hamburg.

Galtung, Johan (1981), 'Structure, culture and intellectual style: An essay comparing Saxonic, Teutonic, Gallic and Nipponic approaches', *Social Science Information*, vol. 20, no. 6, pp. 817–56.

Geertz, Clifford (1983), *Local Knowledge*, Basic Books: New York.

Glenn, E. (1981), *Man and Mankind: Conflict and communication between cultures*, Ablex: Horwood, NJ.

Hofstede, Geert (1980a), *Culture's Consequences: International differences in work-related values*, Sage: Beverly Hills, CA.

Hofstede, Geert (1980b), 'Motivation, leadership and organization: Do American theories apply abroad?', *Organizational Dynamics*, Summer, pp. 42–63.

Hofstede, Geert (1983), 'National cultures in four dimensions: A research-based theory of cultural differences among nations', *International Studies of Management and Organization*, vol. XII, nos. 1-2, pp. 46–74.

Hofstede, Geert (1991), *Cultures and Organizations: Software of the mind*, McGraw-Hill: Maidenhead.

Jung, Carl Gustav (1931), 'Das Grundproblem der gegenwärtigen Psychologie' in *Wirklichkeit der Seele*, DTV: Munich, 1990.

Kluckhohn, Florence R. and Frederick L. Strodtbeck (1961), *Variations in Value Orientations*, Greenwood Press: Westport, CT.

Laurent, André (1983), 'The cultural diversity of Western conceptions of management', *International Studies of Management and Organization*, vol. XII, nos. 1–2, pp. 75–96.

Laurent, André (1989), presentation to the European Foundation for Management Development Seminar 'Cultural shock', EFMD Annual Conference in March, Marseille.

Lazer, William, Shoji Murata and Hiroshi Kosaka (1985), 'Japanese marketing: Towards a better understanding', *Journal of Marketing*, vol. 49 (Spring), pp. 69–81.

Linton, Ralph (1945), *The Cultural Background of Personality*, Appleton-Century: New York.

Mead, Margaret (1948), *Male and Female*, William Morrow: New York.

Montesquieu, Charles de (1748), *The Spirit of Laws*, translated from the French by Thomas Nugent (1792), 6th edn, McKenzie and Moore: Dublin.

Ottosen, Rune (1992), 'The media and the Gulf War reporting: Advertising for the arms industry?', *Bulletin of Peace Proposals*, vol. 23, no. 1, pp. 77-83.

Rotter, J. B. (1966), 'Generalized expectancies for internal versus external control of reinforcement', *Psychological Monographs*, vol. 80, no. 609.

Schein, Edgar H. (1981), 'Does Japanese management style have a message for American managers?', *Sloan Management Review* (Fall).

Smith, Adam (1776), *The Wealth of Nations*, University of Chicago Press edition: Chicago, IL., 1976.

Sondergaard, Michael (1994), 'Hofstede's Consequences: A study of reviews, citations and replications,' *Organization Studies*, vol. 15, no. 3, pp. 447–56.

Triandis, Harry C. (1983), 'Dimensions of cultural variation as parameters of organizational theories', *International Studies of Management and Organization*, vol. XII, no. 4, pp. 139–69.

Trompenaars, Fons (1993), *Riding the Waves of Culture*, Nicholas Brealey: London.

Usunier, Jean-Claude (1989), 'Interculturel: La parole et l'action', *Harvard-L'Expansion*, no. 52 (Spring), pp. 84–92.

Weeks, William H., Paul B. Pedersen and Richard W. Brislin (1987), *A Manual of Structured Experiences for Cross-cultural Learning*, Intercultural Press: Yarmouth, ME.

Wong, Nancy and Aaron Ahuvia (1995), 'From tofu to caviar: Conspicuous consumption, materialism and self-concepts in east-Asian and Western cultures', *Proceedings of the Second Conference on the Cultural Dimension of International Marketing*, Odense, pp. 68–89.

Part

2

The integration of local consumption in a global marketing environment

Introduction to Part 2

THE INTEGRATION OF LOCAL CONSUMPTION IN A GLOBAL
MARKETING ENVIRONMENT

Globalization has taken place at a rapid pace over the last half-century. The continuous expansion of cross-border marketing has been backed by the progressive elimination of barriers to trade, and the emergence of a global consumer culture. Although global convergence seems undeniable, some basic traits of local consumption experience tend to resist to change. The general objective of this part is to show how global and local patterns coexist in both consumer behaviour and marketing environments. The cross-cultural approach to international marketing which is presented in Chapters 4 to 7 should enable future international marketers to understand local consumer behaviour in its full complexity. This approach allows adaptation of the design and implementation of market research across national markets when research instruments and data collection procedures are not similarly understood and do not produce equivalent findings cross-nationally.

Quite often basic concepts have been developed in a specific cultural environment, generally that of the United States, and it is necessary to investigate whether the consumer behaviour concepts and theories used cross the borders of cultures without losing part of their relevance and explanatory power. Consequently, Chapter 4 deals with the cross-cultural dimension of consumer behaviour theories. It starts by assessing how culture affects consumer behaviour and highlights its influence on selected concepts such as loyalty, involvement and dissatisfaction. The chapter also examines the topic of ethnic consumption. The last section in this chapter takes as its premise that marketing is based on exchanges of meanings between marketers and consumers. This perspective makes much sense in international marketing since meaning is directly based on language, and linguistic diversity remains quite high cross-nationally.

The encounters between local consumers and increasingly globalized consumption items are complex, contradictory and sometimes problematic. Chapter 5 first explains how the trend to globalization has been ideologically supported over the last two centuries by the free trade doctrine and how this doctrine tended to view products merely as commodities and to deny cross-national variety in consumers' tastes and consumption habits. Analysis of global trends in consumption patterns shows striking convergence at a broad, quantitative level: the utilitarian needs for reasonably priced, mass-produced products and services are strong drivers behind this fast-paced change. The emergence of a global consumer culture is based on increasing aspirations for a world-standard package of goods and services whose performance is highly predictable. However, the meaning attributed to products and consumption experiences remains to a large extent embedded in local contexts, that of shared habits within the cultural and linguistic groupings. Examples are given of how products whose consumption is becoming global, such as beer, are locally reinterpreted and vested with specific meanings which must be taken into account when designing marketing strategy. In some cases, local consumer cultures can be strong enough as to develop resistance to globalized consumption if it is perceived as detrimental to local cultural and economic interests. In most cases, however, the emergent pattern is that of a mix of local and global consumer behaviour based on kaleidoscopic ways of assembling diverse consumption experiences and making sense of them in everyday life.

Because of increased economic integration world-wide, marketing environments and practices converge at regional and global levels. Chapter 6 first shows how local marketing environments have borrowed and transformed concepts and practices coming mainly from the United States. Regional convergence is also taking place because of free trade areas and customs unions: three sections examine diversity and change in three major regional areas (the European Union, Eastern Europe and the CIS, and East Asia). The chapter concludes with a consideration of the limitations to the world-wide convergence of marketing environments, showing that some key distinguishing features, such as language, will remain deep obstacles to wholly standardized marketing strategies.

When market research takes place across borders, a number of survey instruments, such as questionnaires, scales, sampling techniques, interview techniques, etc., may not fit with the target contexts where data has to be collected. Chapter 7 exposes the technicalities of cross-cultural market research, that is, the problems posed by the possible inequivalence of instruments and methods across research contexts. The chapter reviews equivalence issues, such as conceptual, functional, translation, and measure equivalence which are examined in successive sections and illustrated by real-life examples. The issue of samples and sampling procedures is addressed because of the need of international marketing decision makers for findings which can be consistently compared across cultures and markets. Chapter 7 also examines how local respondents may react to survey instruments and which sort of data biases result from their unfamiliarity with the chosen data collection techniques. As a consequence, international research is often less technical than domestic research in terms of scientific survey instruments and needs more inputs of action research: this is illustrated in the last section with the example of the Japanese style of researching markets.

Chapter

4 Cross-cultural consumer behaviour

'*Sehen Sie Mercedes mit anderen Augen. Die neue E-Klasse ist da*' says a 1995 Daimler-Benz poster for their new E-Class car ('Look at Mercedes with other eyes. The new E-Class arrives'). That is what this chapter is all about: looking with other eyes. It deals basically with the influence of culture on consumer behaviour. Looking with the 'same eyes' means that theories, underlying models, concepts and views of what consumers are, what their motives are, and how they behave are assumed to be universal. One may 'add glasses to the same eyes' so that what was previously invisible comes to light. But what Mercedes asks its potential consumers to do may be necessary: changing the eyes in order to have a different perspective. Table 4.1 sums up four perspectives, starting from the view that both consumers (the object) and underlying consumer behaviour theories (the eyes) can be either universal or specific.

Table 4.1 should not be interpreted with the view that a particular cell corresponds to a better perspective than another. However, they display strong contrasts. The first perspective, in its purest form, is now rarely found except in the text on globalization of markets by Levitt (1983) and more generally when consumers are viewed as truly global. It may make sense for particular classes of consumers, such as business people

TABLE 4.1 Consumer behaviour in a cross-cultural perspective

	Consumer behaviour theories	
Consumers	Universal	Specific
Universal	(1) Global perspective	(3) Ethnic consumption perspective
Specific	(2) 'Imported' perspective	(4) Cultural meaning perspective

travelling world-wide and their families ('the global nomads'). The global perspective has been widely used and in some cases has led to the design of successful marketing strategies. Kotler's *Marketing Management* is now in its eighth edition (1994): it is a world-wide success which started at position 1 and has steadily shifted to position 2. It has been translated into many languages and to various national contexts. For instance, the adaptation of Kotler's book to the French context by Dubois is also in its eighth edition.

Hirschmann (1985) describes the ideological base of American consumer behaviour research as promoting conceptualizations and conjectures in a definite framework, where individuals, who actively seek information, make personal decisions which lead to pragmatic goals. She challenges these assumptions by looking at primitive aspects of consumption in definite US ethnic groups (Black, Italians, WASPS (White Anglo-Saxon Protestant), Jews). The view that underlying theories and concepts have to be challenged is even more clearly relevant when one is looking at international markets. In the 'imported perspective', the examples are tailored to the local markets and marketing environments but the basic theories are not changed. The imported perspective may sometimes enable one to discover significant differences in consumer behaviour (CB) that require adaptation, but it is not always sufficient. As stated by Van Raaij (1978, p. 699), 'We should encourage researchers in other cultures to study their own reality rather than to replicate American studies'.

That is why, in this chapter, I will progressively move towards questioning the cross-cultural transposability of CB theories. My personal view, broadly stated, is not that CB concepts are cross-culturally invalid; that is, a lot is common. This is evidenced by the success in cells 1 and 2. But it is important to assess the cultural relativity of both consumers and the underlying models that are applied if we really want to understand their behaviour. It is even more important to know what one is looking for: similarities or differences. Both exist; it is just a matter of being clear about which models one applies: those that let differences emerge or those that favour the discovery of similarities.

Section 4.1 discusses the influence of major cultural traits on consumer behaviour. It starts with the question of whether the hierarchy of needs applies cross-culturally. Not only whether people locate their needs at different levels in the hierarchy, across cultures, but also, are the major assumptions in this model valid across cultures? The next topic is the influence of individualism and collectivism on consumers' attitudes and buying behaviour. Finally, I examine the influence of institutions, social conventions, habits and customs on consumer behaviour.

Section 4.2 examines the impact of culture on selected aspects of consumer behaviour. Since it is not feasible to deal with all aspects of consumer behaviour, a table (Table 4.2) lists the types of cultural value and behaviour that have an impact on consumer attitudes, decision making and buying behaviour. The table also suggests issues to be addressed in order to reach a better understanding of cultural differences in the area of consumer behaviour. The final part of the section reviews in more detail how consumers' loyalty, involvement, perceived risk, cognitive style, the legal environment and consumerism are affected by cultural variation.

Section 4.3 goes further in explicitly emphasizing the difficulties of directly transferring some consumer behaviour constructs cross-culturally, based on the example of consumer dissatisfaction. We use consumer behaviour concepts with a somewhat – not totally – ethnocentric attitude and we must sometimes re-calibrate our understanding by centring around the common problem (how do cultures solve a *similar* problem *differently*?).

Section 4.4 examines the influences of ethnicity on consumption patterns. As we argued at the end of Chapter 2, cultural borrowing is intense and immigrants bring with them their values and behaviour. Ethnic consumption is a major dimension of cross-cultural consumer behaviour in two respects: (1) ethnic consumption has introduced modifications to the consumption patterns in those countries which were traditionally opened to immigration; and (2) certain ethnic products have reached world-class status by being adopted in most countries of the world, through migration and travels.

Marketing is a process involving communication and exchange: consumers buy meanings as well as objects. Accordingly, section 4.5 focuses on the way in which cultural background influences communication and exchange. Two examples are used to illustrate this: the role of emotions in Japanese marketing and the role of symbolic linkage between objects and persons in the Italian style of marketing.

4.1   CULTURE AND CONSUMER BEHAVIOUR

Although consumer behaviour has strong universal components, its cultural variations cannot be ignored (Dubois, 1987). Without giving an exhaustive list, there are some essential points of cultural influence on consumer behaviour which are worth considering in some detail:

1.   Hierarchy of needs, which shapes demand across product categories.

2.   Culture-based values, especially individualistic or collectivist orientations, which influence purchasing behaviour and buying decisions (individual versus family).

3.   Institutions which influence consumer behaviour, in that most consumption is either rooted in or mixed with social life, a large part of which is institutionalized.

Hierarchy of needs

Culture influences the 'hierarchy of needs' (Maslow, 1954) on at least two levels: first, one of the basic axioms of Maslow's theory is not true in every culture – namely, that needs at a definite level must be satisfied in order for higher-order needs to appear; second, similar kinds of needs may be satisfied by very different products and consumption types. In Maslow's hierarchy of needs, physiological needs are at the bottom because they are the most fundamental; safety needs (being sheltered and protected from dangers in the environment) emerge when physiological needs are satisfied; and then come needs for friendship and love relationships, which Maslow calls social needs. The next level, esteem, is the desire for respect from others, which is strongly supported by status-improving goods. The last and final need, when all other levels have been satisfied, is the need for self-actualization, which encompasses the development of one's own personality.

The level of economic development naturally has some influence: in a less developed economy people usually have more basic survival needs. However, some cultures (for example Hindu) encourage the needs of self-actualization (the highest level), the satisfaction of which does not necessarily imply material consumption. The need for safety (shelter, basic personal protection) is not satisfied according to the same criteria in different cultures. Thus one of the basic axioms of Maslow's theory – that needs must be satisfied at a definite level in order for the needs higher up in the hierarchy to appear – is not true from a cross-cultural point of view. In many Third World countries one may deprive oneself of food in order to be able to buy a refrigerator, thereby replacing the satisfaction of a physical need of safety with the satisfaction of a need of social status and self-esteem (Belk, 1988). The whole area of conspicuous consumption, which is fairly well documented, is in direct contradiction to the hierarchy of needs. As noted by Solomon (1994, p. 426), the term 'conspicuous consumption' was coined by Veblen who was initially inspired by anthropological studies of the Kwakiutl Indians.

These Indians had a ceremony called a *potlach* where the host showed off his wealth and gave extravagant presents to their guests. The more one gave away, the better one looked to the others. Sometimes, the host would use an even more radical strategy to flaunt his wealth. He would publicly destroy some of his property to demonstrate how much he had. This ritual was also used as a social weapon: Since guests were expected to reciprocate, a poorer rival could be humiliated by inviting him to a lavish potlach. The need to give away, even though he could not afford it, would essentially force the hapless guest into bankruptcy.[1]

What this example suggests is that consumer motivations are rooted in the dynamics of social life. Slightly caricatured, Maslow's picture of motivation describes an individual, starting from the belly and extending to the brain: although relevant, it cannot provide a universal view cross-culturally. Mendenhall *et al.* (1995) show that the general findings of studies that have investigated the cross-cultural transposability of Maslow's hierarchy of needs offer mixed support: seven studies support it strongly, three partially and it is refuted by ten research studies. The general message about Maslow's hierarchy is that: (1) the needs themselves are fairly consistent across cultures; (2) their rank ordering varies across cultures; and (3) the degree of emphasis on specific needs and the link between satisfaction at different need levels is also culture bound.[2]

Individualism and collectivism

Most of the available marketing literature depicts individual consumers who make their own decisions. Although industrial marketing literature deals with organizational purchase and buying centres, and the effects of family decisions on consumer behaviour have been meticulously studied, the individualistic conception remains very much at the heart of the mental picture of marketing. The family is seen as an interacting group of individuals, all influencing each other. An *organic* conception of the family as a single decision-making unit is not easily grasped. Moreover research methods themselves are not totally unbiased: are the people questioned representative and can they be considered as reflecting family behaviour? Who should be questioned and in what circumstances?

However, various authors within the field of cross-cultural marketing have pointed out the role of the group as an organic entity, as opposed to a casual collection of individuals who share information and some common interests and constraints, living together within the family cell. This is especially true in Asia.[3] Redding (1982, pp. 104, 112–13), for instance, emphasizes that:

> In most Asian cultures there is a particular grouping to which a person belongs, which involves him in patterns of obligation and behaviour of a special kind . . . It would, for instance, be naive to suppose that the buying power of a teenage market in a Western country would be equivalent to one in, say, Hong Kong or Singapore. The discretion over the use of income is heavily influenced, in the case of the Chinese teenager, by the expected contribution to the family. The tradition of deference to parental wishes also affects buying patterns in clothing, leisure expenditure, etc., especially as it is normal to live at home until marriage.

In addition, a Chinese individual must always take into account all the members of his family when he takes a purchase decision, compared with an interactive decision-making process undertaken by the husband or wife in the West where important household expenditure is concerned. Yau (1988, p. 49) describes the Chinese relational orientation in the following way: 'Chinese have to observe and act according to the norms prescribed for each instance of interpersonal relations. Thus the king must be kingly, the minister ministerly, the husband husbandly, the wife wifely, brothers brotherly, and friends friendly.' In the East the model of the 'extended family' has survived apparently westernized ways of life (Laurent, 1982); it has a powerful influence on many purchase decisions. Even Chinese people, who may sometimes appear quite individualistic oriented when outside their national context, remain strongly bound by their family ties. Yang (1989) describes the influence of what she calls 'familism' on their behaviour as individuals, as family members and as consumers (Box 4.1).

Institutions, social conventions, habits, and customs.

Institutions, such as the state, the Church and trade unions also have an influence on the marketing environment. In distribution, the French Catholic hierarchy has generally been opposed to Sunday trading (Dubois, 1987). In Germany, the trade unions strongly opposed an extension of store opening hours: stores closed at 6:30 p.m. each working day, at 2 p.m. on Saturdays and were closed on Sundays; this was legally compulsory and no store could open outside these authorized times without being heavily fined. The result was that German consumers were obliged to shop on Saturday mornings, and to carry out their purchasing quickly. Mail order was a good substitute for going to shops when stores were open only a few hours a week, given that many consumers were kept at their offices by salaried work. As a result, mail order sales are highly developed in Germany, with giant enterprises having developed in the industry such as Neckermann, Bertelsmann and Quelle.

On the other hand, some products are in a sense institution dependent, whatever their mode of distribution or consumption: examples are marriage-related goods such as a wedding dress or the products featured on wedding lists, or many kinds of traditional gift that are offered for specific occasions.

Of all the cultural conventions that structure daily life in the consumption domain, the most important is probably eating habits. As emphasized by Wilk (1995, p. 372):

BOX 4.1

The role of familism in Chinese consumer behaviour

The single most essential concept to characterize Chinese culture is undoubtedly familism (Ballah, 1970; Yang, 1972). Confucius himself defined five fundamental human relations, three of which relate to family relations: parent and child, husband and wife, and brother and sister. All five of them had roughly equal weight in terms of importance. Later, some of his influential disciples, however, made filial piety the most important among the five (Hsieh, 1967). In any event, a Chinese individual's relationship with family members is a permanent one, which is never grown out of. The Chinese definition of family is often very broad, including various lineages and generations. The single most influential group on an individual's behaviour is his family members, usually extended family members. The influences of family members on an individual's behaviour are extremely extensive; often they extend to areas definitely considered private by Western standards. In contrast to their relationships with their families, Chinese people's relationships with secondary groups beyond the family are usually ill-defined and sometimes non-existent.

The consequences of this emphasis on familism and filial piety are many. First, a Chinese individual's behaviour often cannot be considered as an act reflecting his own preferences or will. It is often the result of a consensus or compromise of himself and his family members, or a take-over by his family's, most often his parents', preferences or wills. Second, social harmony is highly valued in a society whose basic social unit is the extended family (Chien, 1979). To maintain stable and peaceful coexistence is more important than anything else when there are a lot of people who are interdependent and interconnected with each other, constantly involved at any given time and place. Third, an individual's relationships with core family members are not only strong and spontaneous but also collective. The bonds are so natural that they are also very casual. They usually do not need deliberate cultivation by way of saying 'I love you' all the time or showering each other with gifts (Hsu, 1971). Finally an individual's relationship with other non-family members are usually formalized but peripheral. The affections of strangers are not deliberately sought after but can be naturally developed. Strangers are also likely to become a part of the 'extended' family and to be treated accordingly but not until trust has been established between them and a Chinese individual (Fei, 1948). In other words, the Chinese intergroup relationships are often limited to two types; i.e., family (inside) and non-family (outside). Other group memberships are not usually sought and therefore not easily established.

(Source: Yang, 1989. Reproduced with the kind permission of the publisher.)

'Food is both substance and symbol; providing both physical nourishment and a key form of communication that carries many kinds of meanings.' Variations, in addition to the social interpretation of eating habits, exist on the following points:

1. The number of meals consumed each day.

2. The standard duration of a meal, and the position of meals in the daily schedule.

3. The composition of each meal. The portions may differ in size, comprising various kinds of food (local ingredients or cooking style); the nutritional content may be composed so that the eater can cope with long or short time periods without further calorific input during the day.

4. What are the beverages accompanying the meal (water, coffee, tea, wine, beer and so on) and what is their 'status': refresher, energizer, coolant, relaxer, etc.; see Box 4.2)?

5. The social function: either as a communal meal where people entertain themselves by eating and chatting together, or simply as a means of feeding oneself, without any symbolic, personal or collective connotation. A meal may be considered merely as 'fuel' or as a daily 'social event'.

6. Is the food ready-made or is it prepared from basic ingredients? Are there servants to help prepare the meal? What is the cultural meaning of the meal being prepared by the housewife or by her husband, and for particular persons in particular situations?

BOX 4.2

Café au lait *and 'slow food'*

In France, many people start the day with a simple *café au lait*, coffee with milk (a real poison according to doctors); in Germany, the United Kingdom and the United States, people start with a larger breakfast, but eat less than the French at noon. My American students have always been astonished by the two-hour break for lunch: they always tended to consider it as a 'loss of time', without seeing that this was part of the socializing process in and out of the family, depending on whether the meal is at home or outside. The regularity of meal hours is another difference which may have far-reaching consequences. Americans are more ready than other people to eat at 'non-standard' hours. For McDonald's and other fast-food restaurants this is a big opportunity in terms of activity scheduling. People do not rush to eat at very specific hours as they do in some European countries, where it is quite difficult to maintain the 'fast' aspect of service, since staff have to face high peak demand, especially at noon. As a result, the restaurants become 'slow food' restaurants, with customers waiting up to twenty minutes to be served. But European people do not mind that very much: what they want from the McDonald's is not speed; on the contrary, they like to stay longer than the restaurant itself would like them to stay. What they look for is probably cheap and pleasant food, with a modern American image.

The list of cultural variations in eating habits is endless, because nothing is more essential, more universal (food is vital) and at the same time more accurately defined by culture than eating habits. Eating habits should be considered as the whole process of purchasing food and beverages, cooking, tasting and even commenting on it. In many countries, commercials advertising ready-made foods (canned or dried soups, for instance) faced resistance from the traditional role of the housewife, who was supposed to prepare meals from natural ingredients for her family. As a result, advertisers were obliged to include a degree of preparation by the housewife in the advertising copy for such foods.

4.2   THE INFLUENCE OF CULTURE ON SELECTED ASPECTS OF CONSUMER BEHAVIOUR

Table 4.2 presents selected aspects of consumer behaviour which can be influenced by cultural differences. It is not to be considered exhaustive.[4] Some of these issues are developed at greater length later in this and other chapters.

Independent versus interdependent self

Consumers buy objects for the value they provide. In valuing things, consumers may attribute private and/or public meaning (Richins, 1994). Public meanings as defined by Richins are the subjective meaning assigned to an object by outside observers (non-owners) of the object, that is by members of the society at large (p. 505–6). The public meanings emerge through socialization and participation in shared activities and they are reinforced in social interchanges. Private meaning are the sum of the subjective meanings that an object holds for a particular individual. Some of the private meanings may derive from socially shared interpretations, but some of them are unique to the consumer because they are associated with private and even intimate experiences. Both Asians and westerners see the self as divided into an inner private self and an outer public self based on social roles. In looking at the person, the important issue is more how the concept of the self distinguishes westerners and Orientals (and how it is articulated with the concept of others), rather than the mere divide between individualism and collectivism, which can be considered as the other side of this reality, that is, at the social rather than personal level. Markus and Kitayama (1991) have outlined two construals of the self: independent and interdependent.[7] The independent self corresponds to the western conception; it is based on assumption 1 of individualism as cited in Chapter 3: people are seen as inherently separate and distinct. The inner self is the regulator of activity and, in the area of consumption, personal preferences are supposed to reflect a person's tastes, values and convictions; expression of self is encouraged, especially in the area of consumption. The slogan is 'be yourself', that is, act in accordance of your private self (Wong and Ahuvia, 1995).

On the other hand, the 'interdependent self' of most Asians, is based on assumption 1 of collectivism as presented in Chapter 3. People are seen as not fully separable, that is, they are connected to each other by a multitude of overlaps and links: they

TABLE 4.2   The possible impact of cultural differences on selected aspects of consumer behaviour

Aspect of consumer behaviour	Impact of cultural differences: values involved/issues to be addressed
Perception	Perception of shapes, colours and space[5] varies across cultures. See section 9.4.
Motivation	Motivation to own, to buy, to spend, to consume, to show, to share, to give.[6]
Learning and memory	Level of literacy/Memory as it is shaped by the education system (see below, section 4.3)/Familiarity with product classes shaped by education.
Age	Do people know their age?/Respective valuation of younger and older people in the society (section 3.1)/Influence processes across age groups for the buying decisions/How is purchasing power distributed across generations?
Self-concept	See Table 3.1.
Group influence	Individualism/collectivism. To what extent are individuals influenced in their attitudes and buying behaviour by their group? How does consumer behaviour reflect the need to self-actualize individual identity or to manifest group belonging?
Social class	Are social classes locally important? Is social class belonging demonstrated through consumption? What type of products or services do social-status-minded consumers buy? Are there exclusive shops? (See Table 3.1.)
Sex roles	The sexual division of labour; who makes the decisions? Shopping behaviour; who shops: he or she or both of them?
Attitudes change	Resistance in general to change in consumer behaviour (possibly related to high level of uncertainty avoidance, past orientation, fatalism) and resistance to change in particular areas when change could clash with local values and behaviour (e.g. resistance to *fast-food* restaurants in France).
Decision making	Family models (nuclear family versus extended family). The influence of children on decision making. Compulsive buying.
Purchase	Loyalty/Purchasing environment, especially legal marketing environment/Influence of salespersons on clients (see sections 15.1 and 15.3).
Post-purchase	Perceptions of product quality (see Chapters 9 and 10, and section 11.3). Consumer complaining behaviour/Dissatisfaction/Consumerism.

share a common substance. As a result, identity lies in familial and social relationships. People with interdependent selves tend to value the criteria of appropriate social
conduct in their consumption behaviour. In the case of new product adoption, Chiou
(1995) notes that individuals in Asian societies have to consider the wider implications
of their actions and it causes consumers to identify certain role behaviours and to have
less personal freedom in adopting new products. Wong and Ahuvia (1995) cite the case
of a Japanese 'style manual' which provide explicit instructions on what to buy and
how to behave and which explains that 'to be a Japanese is to live always in dread of
what others think of you'. Independent and interdependent selves are reflected in the
concept of belonging to a certain *class*.

Loyalty

Consumers can be loyal, that is, they repeat their purchases on a regular basis, buying
the same brand. Loyal consumers prefer to be sure of what they buy. However,
by doing this they reduce their opportunity to find other, and perhaps better,
choices which would provide them with more value for their money. Other classes of
consumers try new brands, shift from one brand to another when a new one is
promoted, take advantage of temporary price rebates: they are basically disloyal
consumers.

Disloyalty is the natural counterpart of *loyalty* (to a brand, a product, a store, etc.):
what is culturally meaningful is to observe which one of these two opposite attitudes
is considered as the legitimate, fundamental behaviour. In the United States *brand loyalty* is very carefully surveyed and explanatory variables (demographics or lifestyles or
situational variables) are researched. Standard behaviour is implicitly assumed to be
that of disloyalty, although there are large classes of loyal consumers. A consumer
supposedly shifts from one brand to another (brand switching), because it is standard
behaviour to test several competing products successively, thereby fostering price competition, or to respond spontaneously to the stimuli of advertising and sales promotion. Equally, it is assumed that consumers are not especially rewarded by their
practice of buying the same brand and/or shopping in the same store (they can be
'brand loyal' and/or 'store loyal'). The fact that consumers may enjoy the same stable
environment, of which their favourite products would form a basic constituent, is
somewhat underestimated.[8] Stated in a different way, it is assumed that consumers
enjoy change more than stability. Of course, in the United States, there are large
groups of loyal consumers: habits and stability are a reality for many Americans. But
the number of these groups is, in all probability, less than in some other countries
where brand loyalty is normal behaviour.

Loyalty is a key concept in collectivist cultures, which spreads from people to product, in as much as they are extensions of the self. There is an unusual level of single
brand dominance in many Asian markets (Robinson, 1996) with one brand accounting for 40–50 per cent of market share over quite a long period of time. Chiou (1995)
argues that consumers in collectivist (Asian) societies tend to be more loyal on average, because (1) they tend to rely more on information found in their reference group
– often by word-of-mouth communication – rather than on information diffused by
the media; and (2) they tend to follow the group consensus until there is significant

evidence showing that the new product is better. Where consumers are more fundamentally loyal, often less brand-conscious and less used to rational price/quality cross-
brand or cross-product comparisons, it may be assumed that marketing strategies have
to be different from those in countries where consumers frequently shift from one
brand to another. In the former case it may be necessary to build a loyal consumer base
from scratch, whereas in the latter case it may be more effective to persuade disloyal
consumers to switch from other established brands, and then to try to turn the newly
developed consumer base into a loyal one.

Consumer's involvement

The involvement of the consumer in product purchase or consumption varies across
cultures. Yang (1989) depicts the Chinese consumer as being in a low-involvement situation when products are used for private consumption: they are likely to adopt a
rather simple cognitive stance, favouring the physical functions of the product and
being mostly concerned with price and quality. There is a high level of purchasing
involvement when the Chinese consumer buys products for their social symbolic
value. Since people greatly value social harmony and the smoothness of relationships
within the extended family, the social significance of a product is highly important: it
may express status, gratitude, approval or disapproval.

Perceived risk

Perceived risk is an important variable in consumer behaviour, and differs according
to its breakdown into various components: physical risk, financial risk, social risk etc.
(Van Raaij, 1978). Whereas people in certain cultures may be more susceptible to physical risk (because the mortality rate is low, death is feared and avoided), others may be
more sensitive to social risk (because a purchaser may risk the loss of face in other
people's eyes). Let us take an example: when buying a car, in a country where road
safety is not a high priority the perceived physical risk is low; where mileage is non-
relevant, because gas is so cheap, there is a low perceived financial risk; but where an
engine breakdown is a disaster, because of little or no available maintenance, there is
a high perceived reliability risk. The perceived risk is quite different from that experienced by the average purchaser of a car in a western European country. However, when
purchase contexts are highly standardized world-wide, such as in the case of compact
disks, there are only minor differences in risk-reducing behaviour across cultures
(Mitchell et al., 1996).

Consumer cognitive styles

The cognitive style assumed by the classical models of consumer behaviour (Howard
and Sheth, 1969; Engel et al., 1986) is that of an individual reviewing opportunities,
evaluating alternatives, rationally searching for information, relying on opinion
leaders and word-of-mouth communication, who is influenced by the social environment and situational factors. This person is additionally swayed by the stimuli of
marketing strategies (particularly advertising and sales promotion), tries to choose the
best alternative, progressively forms the intention to purchase, and finally (perhaps)
actually buys the product. These models have a rather linear, analytical and abstract
style. Many authors claim that Asian consumers tend to have a quite different

cognitive style: the Chinese as well as the Japanese have a more synthetic, concrete and contextual orientation in their thought patterns (Lazer *et al.*, 1985, Yau, 1988, Yang, 1989). Sections 3.4 and 7.6 show how intellectual approaches vary across cultural groupings to such an extent that the diversity of cognitive styles cannot be ignored.

Legal marketing environment

To a large extent marketing regulations reflect views on whether consumers are predominantly considered as self-reliant (it is assumed that consumers are informed and responsible people) or dependent individuals who find themselves at a disadvantage in relation to the marketer. If assumed to be dependent, they need to be protected against abuses. If considered self-reliant, they still need to be protected if they have not reached the age of self-reliance (children) or against what is considered as harmful to public morality.

1. Many Latin countries consider that private interests cannot exploit the taste of the public for gambling, and, as a result, lotteries are state monopolies; promotional campaigns that take the form of competitions are considered to be immoral, whereas they are permitted by Anglo-Saxon countries. Certain countries forbid promotional gifts or strictly limit their value, whereas other countries authorize them without any restriction. A possible reason for these diverging regulatory attitudes derives from the differences in response to the following question: are people capable of a rational economic evaluation of the value of the gift, capable of relating it to the full price they pay? Finally, are they considered able to come to a sound buying decision, even though they may have been unduly influenced? Section 12.5 examines the cultural relativity of regulatory approaches and consumer responses *vis-à-vis* sales promotion.

2. Moral approbation or the condemnation of certain practices often leads to public debate which in turn influences the regulatory authorities when introducing legislation. For example there are different levels of acceptance of the use of nudity in television or magazine advertising, which lead to moral controversies in the public domain when foreign advertisements, introduced by the means of imported magazines or satellite broadcast, are perceived as shocking by the local audience. Another example is offered by the attitudes of regulators towards advertising targeted to a children's audience. Children are easy to influence, and it is sometimes argued that excessive need creation, which parents cannot always satisfy, may destabilize family relationships. The following topic is also often debated: how should children be hired and compensated for taking part in a television commercial? Some European countries have such stringent regulations that many local commercials, targeting children as consumers, are produced in the United Kingdom, where regulation is more flexible.

3. Agreement with the morality of certain kinds of representation, in advertising in particular: the role of women, representations of 'ideal' people which leads to a desire to identify oneself with those depictions. Chapter 14 presents the cultural relativity of attitudes towards advertising in general, advertising copy and the type of media used.

4.3   INVESTIGATING THE CROSS-CULTURAL TRANSPOSABILITY OF CONSUMER BEHAVIOUR CONCEPTS

Any element of consumer behaviour can be seen (inspected, filtered) through cross-cultural lenses. For example 'word-of-mouth communication' seems a fairly robust concept: in any culture, people discuss informally and exchange information on their consumption experiences. Where little relevant information is available, movie films for instance, or new products, or when consumers have a low level of familiarity with a complex product, people tend to seek information from acquaintances. However, it may be hypothesized that word-of-mouth communication will be stronger in collectivist and ingroup-oriented societies, where outside information provided by an impersonal marketer will be seen as less reliable than opinions from relatives and acquaintances.

The best solution for investigating cross-cultural transposability is always to start from the 'common problem' in Kluckhohn and Strodtbeck's (1961) terms. For instance: why and how can a consumer express dissatisfaction with a product or a service? The basic concept found in the consumer behaviour literature is not based on all solutions to the common problem but on the dominant normative solution in a particular culture, generally western and more specifically, American. Other alternatives must always be looked for, especially the alternative that the problem may be *without* solution.

The example of consumer dissatisfaction

Attitudes towards consumerism vary across national contexts and the importance given to the consumer movement varies according to certain basic premises:

1. Is it legitimate that consumers should make their dissatisfaction known? This is not the case in societies where very long periods favourable to supply (when, for decades, the local supply has been systematically lower than the demand) have implanted the opposite idea. Shopping in eastern Europe illustrates the extent to which a customer complaint can seem an absurd step to take.

2. Is it legitimate for consumerists to force a producer, whose product is of dubious quality, to close down? In other words, may consumers cause job losses and take away the livelihood of workers who are not ultimately responsible for the situation?

I pose these questions not out of a desire to adopt any particular position but merely to demonstrate that it is not inherently obvious that the defence of the consumer has a wholly positive social value. Thus expressing dissatisfaction frankly and openly may be considered to be partially illegitimate.

Constructs such as consumer dissatisfaction have been used for assessing cross-cultural differences in consumer attitudes. Richins and Verhage (1985) have studied differences between US and Dutch consumers relating to their dissatisfaction and complaining behaviour. Their questionnaire was reviewed by a panel of Dutch experts and as a result they made some minor changes to the wording of the questions. They looked for the conceptual equivalence of the dissatisfaction concept: does it have the same meaning, socially and individually, for the US and the Dutch people to be 'dissatisfied with a product or a service'? Richins and Verhage found 29 per cent of the variance to be attributable to national differences, the most salient ones being as follows:

Dutch consumers perceive more inconvenience and unpleasantness in making complaint than do American consumers . . . Dutch consumers were less likely than Americans to feel a social responsibility to make complaints . . . Seemingly contradicting this finding, however, Dutch consumers are more likely than Americans to feel bothered if they don't make a complaint when they believe they should, a sort of guilt. Perhaps this seeming contradiction indicates that Dutch respondents tend to feel a personal rather than social obligation to make complaints. (1985, p. 203.)

The word 'construct' relates to a concept which has several underlying dimensions, and may be measured quantitatively by identifying these various dimensions. The construct 'consumer dissatisfaction and complaint behaviour' (Richins, 1983) identifies five domains of attitude towards complaining:

1. Beliefs about the effect experienced when one complains.

2. Perceptions of the objective cost or trouble involved in making a complaint.

3. Perception of retailer responsiveness to consumer complaints.

4. The extent to which consumer complaints are expected to benefit society at large.

5. The perceived social appropriateness of making consumer complaints.

Investigating cross-cultural transposability may be done by enquiring whether each of these subdimensions makes sense in a particular national/cultural context. Exercise A4.2 proposes to go further in the investigation by using a consumer complaint scale developed by Singh (1988).

Cavusgil and Kaynak (1984) propose an interesting enlargement of the consumer dissatisfaction concept to the case of developing countries. They distinguish between micro-level sources (e.g. excessive prices, misleading advertising, lack of performance) and macro-level sources of consumer dissatisfaction (e.g. low income, inflation), with the possibility of interaction between the two levels. They state: 'In general micro-level sources appear to lead, over time, to a diffuse, latent discontent with the state of the marketplace; that is to a macro-level dissatisfaction. Unsatisfactory experiences with specific products and services seem to be reflected in a disillusionment with all institutions in the society' (1984, p. 118). Moreover, the complaining behaviour does not have the same meaning at all if buyer and seller know each other personally, as either acquaintances or relatives: 'Personal relationships with vendors often prove advantageous. Usually food shoppers get to know how far they can trust a food retailer, and can negotiate prices and other terms' (Cavusgil and Kaynak, 1984, p. 122).[9]

Looking with other eyes: Questioning about consumer behaviour

'Looking with other eyes' implies decentring oneself. To explain this, I will use a personal example of experience as a consumer – see Box 4.3.

BOX 4.3

Differences between Europeans and North Americans in the use of automatic cars

Europeans overwhelmingly have manual gear-boxes. This is in sharp contrast to the USA where the opposite situation prevails. When in the USA, I have enjoyed the smoothness of automatic cars and long drives with less fatigue, because you save hundred of movements. Back in France, I decided to buy a Ford with an automatic gear-box. It is not a standard feature of cars in Europe and I had to pay extra money ($1,500) and wait a little longer to get the automatic car. After two years, I had to sell the car, because I was leaving the place for some time and I could not take it with me. Selling a car with an automatic gear-box in a European country turned out to be a difficult task. I had started with an attractive price, but I found no prospective buyer, although the car had not done many kilometres and was well maintained. Finally, after several weeks of inserting advertisements in local newspapers, I found a bus driver who was sick of changing gears and bought it for a little more than one-third of the price I had paid two years before. Europeans do not 'like' automatic cars.

If we try to apply the perspectives in Table 4.1, the universal approach provides few clues for understanding this case. The 'imported' perspective provides many more insights. The first is that in European countries automatic cars are associated with high social status. Large and expensive cars have automatic drive more often than do medium or small cars. Another argument is the driving licence requirements: people are allowed to learn and pass the licence exam only with a manual gear-box car. In most European countries, there is only one exception: handicapped persons are allowed to use automatic cars to obtain their licence. In the United Kingdom, future drivers can take their test in an automatic without being disabled, but they get a restricted licence that only allows them to drive automatic cars. Learning plays a key role in the resistance to change of Europeans: having been educated on manual cars, they tend to stick to them. Another argument that the imported perspective would probably bring to light is that many Europeans still believe that automatic gear-box cars are reputed to have high petrol consumption (or poor gas mileage in US terms). Nowadays, this is not true since technology has made progress which makes the differences almost nil, and in fact in favour of automatic cars for urban traffic. But the last argument, which appeared to me the strongest when I tried to sell my car was the symbolic argument (*'c'est une voiture d'infirme'*). Most people saw automatic cars, in the middle range of the market, as being only for handicapped persons, that is, *not for them who are not disabled.*

If we sum up on the basis of the perspectives presented in Table 4.1:

- Perspective 1 incurs the risk of transferring too directly because CB in this area is specific.

- Perspective 2 probably allows the discovery of social status and resistance to change arguments.

- Perspective 3 would help the researcher to identify a small 'ethnic' target, that of North American expatriates (although many of them love manual gear-boxes which to them look more sporty).

Only perspective 4 reveals the symbolic argument which is the major obstacle to buying such cars for European people (automatic being associated with handicap), even though they are much more comfortable to drive, as speedy and as fuel efficient as other cars.

Radical questioning

Coming back to the differences in 'motivation' presented in Table 4.2, let us take some examples of radical questioning, that is trying to assess to what extent motivations are radically different. The motivation to own, for instance, is based on the notion of ownership. The English verb 'to own' has no equivalent in Swahili, the dominant language in East Africa. Possession, that is, the rights of individuals over objects, is much more limited in scope. Motivation to spend may also be radically altered by negative views of money. Motivation to save may be altered by a lack of future orientation, and the feeling that one should not bet about one's future (see Box 7.1). Motivation to buy may be low when objects and material culture are discarded, as in Hindu culture, and this is independent of purchasing power. Motivation to consume may be largely hindered by a strong ecological stance, as in Denmark or Germany where sensitivity to environmental problems has practically eliminated plastic bottling in favour of reusable glass. Motivation to show is naturally related to the self concept, which varies across cultures. Motivation to share is altered by the prevailing pattern of property and the individualist/collectivist divide.

Motivation to give also varies across cultures: it is widely practised in Japan, where the size of the gift is codified according to the type of social exchange. But in other cultures gift-giving practices may be less frequent, based on the view that it will be necessary to reciprocate and the donor will just embarrass the recipient, and finally both participants may resent being obliged to participate in the ritual. Thus, a way to question consumer behaviour cross nationally is simply to examine motivation in each of these basic actions: own, spend, buy, consume, show, share and give.

Learning and memory: A French–Brazilian contrast

Let us finish this section with an example which shows how deep-rooted are consumer attitudes, making it sometimes meaningful to enquire into child-rearing practices and education systems (Karsaklian, 1995). It starts from a simple comparison between the French and Brazilian education systems: whereas Brazil offers each pupil 800 hours teaching per year, France gives 1,760 hours per year. Brazilian pupils spend only half a day at school, and their education is based on themes; they spend much more time watching TV than their French counterparts, who spend four full days and one half-day each week at school, with their formal education being based on disciplines (writing, calculation, history, geography). The process of learning to read follows two quite different routes: the Brazilian route is based on *associating* pictures of objects with their written form (see Figure 4.1 for the example of a 'hat'): it is based on the relationship between signifier and signified. The French route is strictly based on the *dissociation* of words into the basic units, syllables and letters. The traditional syllabic method is still widely used, since the semi-global and global methods which associate sounds with full words rather than letters and put words into the context of sentences, are considered in France a near-total failure, after a ten-year experiment.

Brazilian and French pupils were shown four advertisements for well-known products in the two countries (Fanta, Galak white chocolate from Nestlé, Lego, Coca-Cola). It has been shown that Brazilian children performed significantly better on the recognition of the design of an advertisement: their non-verbal and visual aptitudes being better than those of the French children. Conversely, the French children performed significantly better in the recognition of the verbal part (which story was recounted and which words were employed). Whereas Brazilian children remembered the advertisement globally, the French remembered parts of it (Karsaklian, 1995).

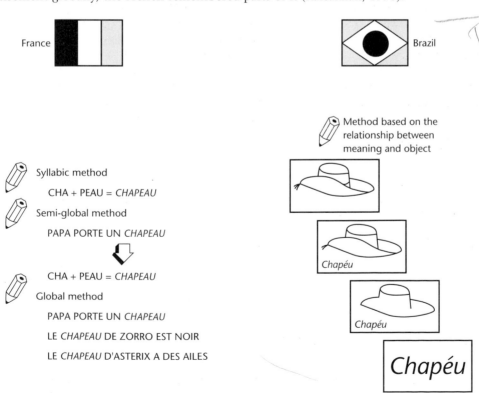

FIGURE 4.1   Two different ways of learning how to read.

Ethnicity as a thwarted ingroup orientation

The reality of ethnic consumption is a strong component of modern consumption culture. First, ethnic products have been popularized world-wide and ethnic food and restaurants are the fastest-growing segments in the food industry. Ethnicity reflects the internationalization of lifestyles in two respects: (1) because people move internationally through migrations and (2) doing this they introduce new consumption opportunities. Ethnic consumption has a great deal to do with mixing the home and host country consumption patterns. A very interesting description of the amalgamation of an immigrant culture's eating and consumption habits with those of the host country culture is given by Herbert Gans (1962) in his classic book *The Urban Villagers*, about the life of Italian-Americans in a New York neighbourhood, which he calls 'West End'.

> Their actual diet, however, bears little resemblance to that of their Italian ancestors, for they have adopted American items that can be integrated into the overall tradition. For example although their ancestors could not afford to eat meat, West Enders can, and thus spend considerable amounts for it. Typically American meats such as hot dogs, hamburger and steak are very popular indeed, but they are usually prepared with Italian spices, and accompanied by Italian side-dishes. The role of American culture is perhaps best illustrated by holiday fare. Turkey is eaten on Thanksgiving, but is preceded by a host of Italian antipastos, accompanied by Italian side-dishes, and followed by Italian desserts. This amalgamation of ethnic and American food is of course not distinctive to the West Enders, but can be found among all groups of foreign origin. (p. 184.)

Ethnic subcultures are based on shared beliefs and habits and the sense of belonging to a specific group of people, different from the society at large. Ingroup orientation is central in ethnicity, but, to a large extent, the sense of belonging to the subcultural community is thwarted, because it is simultaneously necessary (and difficult) to identify with the values and behaviour of the dominant ingroup, the nationals of the country of residence. Hispanics in the USA have to cope with this dilemma: they have to adjust to a predominantly WASP (White Anglo-Saxon Protestant) culture while their basic assumptions, interaction models and sense of belonging would drive them towards the Hispanic community. Ethnicity is a matter of shared belief about a common descent and Bouchet (1995) lists six main attributes of ethnic community: (1) a collective proper name; (2) a myth of common ancestry; (3) shared historical memories; (4) one or more differentiating elements of common culture (e.g. language); (5) an association with a specific homeland; and (6) a sense of solidarity. Since ethnic belonging in the immigration country is taken from the territory and people from where the culture originated, people often try to maintain the subculture by means of ethnic stereotyping. In marketing, this gives rise to opportunistic use where, for instance, 3M has used Scottish imagery to denote value in 'Scotch' tape, since the Scottish stereotype of supposed frugality is viewed favourably in the USA (Solomon, 1994).

The assimilation model

It may be wrong to equate consumers from a definite ethnic group to a specific market segment which seeks specific products or service benefits. For instance

Yankelovitch *et al.* (1982) found Hispanics to be more American than other Americans on a number of characteristics. Assimilation takes place when the relative influence of the culture of origin diminishes and immigrants hold faster to the values and behaviours of the country of residence. Assimilation is evidenced in the following areas: consumption patterns, employment, marriage with people originating from the host culture, participation in the political process as a candidate, acquaintances outside the ethnic community. The process of assimilation is a lengthy one, which may require several generations to be fully accomplished.

In the assimilation process two mechanisms are at work (Wallendorf and Reilly, 1983). The first is based on structural constraints: if people drive on the other side of the road, the individual will be obliged to adapt; compliance is compulsory, not voluntary. The second is based on the newcomer's willingness to adjust to the new culture's behaviour and rules; it fits with a certain enthusiasm for what the new culture brings, in terms of increased freedom and improved material status. This motivational component depicts the positive side of assimilation. But the negative side, structural constraints, may provoke a false adjustment. As Calantone *et al.* explain it (1985, p. 208):

lack of availability may force some immigrants to make changes in the foods they purchase. Thus, behavioural change may occur without a concomitant change in values or beliefs. In making empirical comparisons, therefore, it is crucial to include only those behavioural patterns that reflect free choices by immigrants and to exclude adaptation to structural constraints.

Ethnicity as identity

When assimilation has fully taken place, that is probably for people of the third or fourth generation, they may share much more with the society at large than with their subcultural group. However, there is a resurgence of ethnicity; as Bouchet (1995) remarks, ethnicity has more to do with the evolution of identity in general than with the origin of one's historical identity. Bell (1975, p. 171) explains the salience of ethnicity as a quest for identity:

ethnicity in this context, is best understood *not* as a primordial phenomenon in which deeply held identities have to reemerge, but as a strategic choice by individuals who, in other circumstances, would choose other group memberships as a mean of gaining some power and privilege. In short, it is the *salience* not the *persona* that has to be the axial line for explanation. And because salience may be the decisive variable, the attachment to ethnicity may flush or fade very quickly depending on political and economic circumstances.

Thus ethnic consumption should be considered as a complex and unstable reality, at which marketers need to look with a quite open mind. It gives birth to strange mixtures such as the Chino-Latino cuisine, a fusion of Asian and Cuban cuisine to be found in New York, which has its roots in the Chinese immigration to Cuba in the early 1900s (Straus, 1992). When dealing with ethnic consumption, the following points have to be constantly kept in mind:

1. Translation or spelling mistakes or inadequate wordings may be resented as offending the group's honour. For instance, a *burrito* was mistakenly called in Spanish a *burrada*, which means 'big mistake' (Solomon, 1994). This results in minority group people having a sense of being rejected because their language is not used properly, or at least not understood, that is *not respected*.

2. In ethnic behaviour the phantasm of membership, that is, the claim for being 'different', is central and may be pushed to its extreme. Smaller ingroups will be perceived as the best platforms for identification. Hispanics will therefore break further down into Mexicans, Puerto-Ricans, Cubans, etc.

3. The level of acculturation, that is, the degree to which people have learnt the ways of the host culture, and their age have an influence on ethnic consumption: older people and less acculturated people tend to display a stronger attitude as an ethnic consumer.

4. Identification needs are 'reversible', creating ambiguous and even contradictory demands. Most people belonging to ethnic communities strive for both integration into the society at large and maintenance of their specific cultural roots. In some areas of consumption, for instance housing and furnishing, they may express their belonging to the larger national ingroup and in another area, food for instance, they may maintain strong ethnic behaviour.

4.5   MARKETING AS AN EXCHANGE OF MEANINGS

As suggested by McCracken (1991, p. 5), 'We may see consumer goods as the vehicles of cultural meanings . . . consumers themselves as more or less sophisticated choosers and users of these cultural meanings.' But in doing this, we have to look with other eyes. Marketing may be seen primarily as a process of exchange where communication, broadly defined, is central. As Richard Bagozzi (1975, p. 35) states:

In order to satisfy human needs, people and organizations are compelled to engage in social and economic exchanges with other people and organizations. This is true for primitive as well as highly developed societies. Social actors obtain satisfaction of their needs by complying with, or influencing, the behaviour of other actors. They do this by communicating and controlling the media of exchange, which in turn, comprise the links between one individual and another. Significantly, marketing exchanges harbour meanings for individuals that go beyond the mere use of media for obtaining results in interactions.

Consumers buy meanings and marketers communicate meanings through products and advertisements. Many of these meanings are culture based: they are intersubjectively shared by a social group (D'Andrade, 1987). Intersubjective sharing of meanings means that each person in the group knows that everyone else knows the cognitive schema. Therefore in the process of exchange through buyer–seller relations, marketing communications or product consumption, interpretations are made spontaneously, as if they were obvious facts of the world, and a great deal of information in the process of marketing as exchange and communication need not be made explicit.

Culture may be considered as a sort of *meta-language* which is central in the marketing process when viewed as exchange and communication, as noted by Bagozzi. It works as a kind of *game rule*, implicitly indicating how people will interact in an exchange relationship, their constraints and their leeway in behaviour and decisions. The attitudinal differences toward market research between American and Japanese people (section 7.6) is a good example of this: what is the 'right' way (legitimate, appropriate) to communicate with the market? What is the market (actual buyers versus potential consumers)? In each case the objective is seemingly the same: to collect relevant information and market data, in order to decide on marketing strategies.

Two examples will help us illustrate the differences in marketing meta-communication: first, the role of emotions in Japanese marketing, and second, the emphasis on the symbolic relationship between person and object in the Italian style of marketing.

The role of emotions in Japanese marketing

There is wide range of books on Japanese marketing, which are unfortunately written only in Japanese *Kanji* and *Hiragana*, thereby limiting access for non-Japanese *(Gai-jin)* readers. But the Japanese provide details in English in the review of the largest Japanese advertising agency, *Dentsu Japan Marketing/Advertising*. Koichi Tanouchi, a professor of marketing at Hitotsubashi University, depicts the Japanese style of marketing as being fundamentally based on emotions and sensitivity. He first insists, as many authors do, that Japan is oriented towards rice production and is not a nation of hunters and gatherers. This means more collective organization and interpersonal sensitivity: the cultivation of rice needs the flooding of paddy fields, which cannot be decided by an isolated landowner; paddy fields have to be flooded simultaneously. This involves a strong collective solidarity, serious planning and individual tenaciousness. Tanouchi states that, in his opinion, 'masculine' values are less developed in Japan than 'feminine' values, which he illustrates by the example of marital relationships in household and personal spending (1983, p. 78):

In Japan, the husband is supposed to hand all his income over to his wife. If he doesn't, he is criticized by people around him. If she complains about this to his boss in his business company, the boss is very likely to take the wife's side, and advise him to give all his salary to his wife and add that that is the best way to keep peace at home and that everyone else is doing so. The wife has the right to decide how much money her husband can have for daily lunch and coffee. Regularly, about once in a half year, Japanese newspapers carry a research report about the average amount of the money the average husbands get from their wives. Wives decide about their husbands' lunch money watching these figures.

Tanouchi and other authors (Lazer *et al.*, 1985) argue that sensitivity and emotions permeate most aspects of Japanese marketing. This is evidenced by the high level of sensitivity and response to *actual* consumer needs and by the search for social harmony between producers and distributors (see section 12.1 on *Keiretsu* distribution). It is also prominent in Japanese sales force compensation arrangements, where collective reward systems are often used. They foster co-operation, avoid threatening individual competition and promote social harmony in the sales team (section 15.4).

The role of the symbolic link between object and person through the medium of design in Italian marketing

It can be said that a specific Italian marketing style is emerging. This style is characterized by heavy emphasis (and corresponding financial commitment) devoted to product appearance and design. The article sold is intended to act as a link between the producer–seller and the consumer–purchaser: both appreciate the aesthetic qualities of the object. The Italians concentrate on the style and functionality of the object, and its integration in the environment. With such premises, the symbolism of the object and its fit with the meaning attributed to it by consumers being considered as points of focus, increasing importance should be given to qualitative studies. Baudrillard (1968) and his 'system of objects', which was fairly successful in France, ultimately achieved real success in Italy, where he is a guru of marketing semiology (Box 4.4).

Dino Buzzati (1967), the author of *The Desert of the Tartars*, has written a short story entitled 'Suicide in the Park' which illustrates quite clearly the fusion between the person and the object through the medium of the imagination, leading to a passionate relationship. The narrator tells the story of one his friends, Stefano, who became mad about a very nice sports car, which he could not buy. The life of his wife Faustina was literally poisoned by the obsessive passion of Stefano for this car. One day, Stefano appeared driving a long, blue, brand new sports car. The narrator admired the car and asked what Faustina thought of the buy. Stefano, embarrassed, then explained that she had gone; he was vague about the reasons. A few years passed. The narrator asked for news from Faustina each time he saw Stefano, who replied that she was gone for ever. A few years later, Stefano, asked by the narrator about this car, said that it had been a good car but it was used now and had to be repaired constantly and no mechanic was able to service the foreign-made engine. At the end of the short story, the narrator reads a strange report in the newspaper about a blue car which started without a driver, ran through various streets and avenues, and finally threw itself against the ruins of the old Sforza palace. The old blue sports car caught fire and was completely burnt. He

---

BOX 4.4

The functional form of the cigarette lighter

The stylized fluidity of the 'functional forms' testifies to the connotation of mental dynamics, the semblance of a lost relationship, in an attempt to reconstruct a purpose through the accumulation of signs. For example, a lighter in the shape of a pebble was successfully launched by advertising some years ago. The oblong, elliptic and asymmetrical form is 'highly functional', not because it provides a better light than another lighter, but because it fits exactly into the palm of the hand. 'The seas have polished it into the shape of the hand': it is an accomplished form. Its function is not to give a light, but to be easy to handle. Its form is, so to speak, predetermined by Nature (the sea) to be handled by man. This new purpose is the sole rhetoric of the lighter. The connotations are here twofold: as an industrial object, the cigarette lighter is supposed to recall one of the qualities of the handicraft object, the shape of which furthers the gesture and the body of man. Moreover the allusion to the sea brings us to the myth of Nature, itself cultured by man, which follows all his desires: the sea plays the cultural role of a polisher; it is the sublime handicraft of nature. As the stone rolled by the sea, furthered by the hand producing light, the cigarette lighter becomes a wonderful flint, a whole prehistoric and artisanate purpose comes into play in the very practical essence of an industrial object.

(Source: Baudrillard, 1968, pp. 82–3. Author's translation.)

rushes to Stefano's house and finds him upset. Stefano admits: 'It was Faustina' and he explains how, absurd as it may seem, some nine years ago, when they were making love one night, she began to cry and to shiver, to swell and had just enough time to go out into the street.

It is of course unrealistic to claim that the Italians are alone in having an awareness of the symbolic meaning of possessions for consumers. But they incorporate it at a very high level and make it an essential element of their marketing communication.

4.6   CONCLUSION

The other side of the poster, mentioned at the start of this chapter, says *'Bei Mercedes bleibt alles anders'* (with Mercedes everything remains different). Looking at *different* consumer behaviour with *different* eyes is the attitude to be recommended in international marketing, whenever we know that a lot is *similar*. It provides a method of enquiry which favours the discovery of significant differences in consumer behaviour across cultures and offers insights into the way consumers invest meaning into their buys.

QUESTIONS

1.   What would you expect to be the link of *consumer loyalty* with the following cultural variables? Argue why, in your opinion, consumers having a certain cultural trait would be more, or conversely less, loyal:
     (a)   strong future orientation;
     (b)   strong ingroup orientation;
     (c)   high individualism;
     (d)   high uncertainty avoidance.
2.   Discuss how strong emphasis on group belonging in a particular culture may influence buying decisions.
3.   Discuss possible cross-cultural variability in the concept of 'status-seeking consumers'.
4.   Why can 'word-of-mouth communication' among people be considered as a fairly robust consumer behaviour concept cross-culturally?
5.   What is *ethnic consumption*?

APPENDIX 4: TEACHING MATERIALS

A4.1   Exercise 'Dichter's consumption motives'

QUESTION

Discuss the cross-cultural variability of the major motives for consumption as identified by Ernest Dichter (some thirty years ago). Choose five associations between motives and associated products for your discussion.

Motive	Associated products
Power, masculinity, virility	Power: Sugary products and large breakfasts, bowling, electric trains, pistols, power tools. Masculinity, virility: Coffee, red meat, heavy shoes, toy guns; buying fur coats for women, shaving with a razor.
Security	Ice-cream, full drawer of neatly ironed shirts, real plaster walls, home baking, hospital care.
Eroticism	Sweets, gloves, a man lighting a woman's cigarette.
Moral purity, cleanliness	White bread, cotton fabric, harsh household cleaning chemicals, bathing, oatmeal.
Social acceptance	Companionship: ice-cream (fun to share), coffee. Love and affection: toys, sugar and honey. Acceptance: soap, beauty products.
Individuality	Gourmet foods, foreign cars, cigarette holders, vodka, perfume, fountain pens.
Status	Scotch [whisky], ulcers, heart attacks, indigestion, carpets.
Femininity	Cakes and cookies, dolls, silk, tea, household curios.
Reward	Cigarettes, candy, alcohol, ice-cream, cookies.
Mastery over environment	Kitchen appliances, boats, sporting goods, cigarette lighters.
Disalienation (a desire to feel connectedness to things)	Home decorating, skiing, morning radio broadcasts.
Magic, mystery	Soups (have healing powers), paints (change the mood of a room), carbonated drinks (magical effervescent property), vodka (romantic history), unwrapping of gifts.

(Source: Solomon, 1994, p. 98.)

A4.2 Exercise: Investigating the cross-cultural transposability of a consumer complaint scale

You will find below a scale of consumer complaint behaviour (CCB) which has been developed by Singh (1988). US respondents were asked to express their degree of agreement or disagreement on a six-point Likert scale on the items listed below (possible behavioural responses to dissatisfaction with a consumption experience). Factor analysis allowed three dimensions to be distinguished for CCB.

1. *Voice CCB*

    (a) Forget about the incident and do nothing.

    (b) Definitely complain to the store manager on your next trip.

    (c) Go back or call the repair shop immediately and ask them to take care of your problem.

2. *Private CCB*

    (a) Decide not to use that repair shop again.

    (b) Speak to your friends and relatives about your bad experience.

(c)   Convince your friends and relatives not to use that repair shop.

3.   *Third party CCB*

(a)   Complain to a consumer agency and ask them to make the repair shop take care of your problem.

(b)   Write a letter to the local newspaper about your bad experience.

(c)   Report to the consumer agency so that they can warn other consumers.

(d)   Take some legal action against the repair shop/manufacturer.

QUESTION

Investigate the cross-cultural transposability of such a scale. Since you cannot do this with a full psychometric design, conduct your investigation mostly into the meaning, situations, institutions and behaviours depicted by the items.

A4.3   Case: Eliot Greeting Card Company (1)

The Eliot Company was established by Gregory Eliot in the early 1950s in St. Louis, Missouri. Although the company only had about 4 per cent of the US greeting card market, it had been profitable since its beginnings, and had shown modest growth in a market environment dominated by Hallmark Company (which maintained over 40 per cent of the market), American Greetings (about 30 per cent market share) and several smaller companies that had market shares of 5 to 15 per cent. Eliot had been successful largely by carving itself a niche, marketing lines of speciality cards for which the other firms seemed to have little interest.

Recently, however, the greeting card market had been experiencing a period of (at least temporary) flat sales. This was seen to be the result of both the relatively weak economy and a dramatic increase in telephone advertising, urging consumers to 'reach out and touch someone' at the expense of sending greeting cards. This has led to quite intense marketing efforts by the larger greeting card companies to gain percentage points of the relatively sluggish market. It was becoming obvious that the competition was turning its attention to the speciality lines that Eliot had been able to use to its advantage for so long (see Exhibit 1).

Exhibit 1 'Greetings, One and All!' Cardmakers Gear up for Mother's Day, and Every Day
Just in case anyone forgot, the greeting card industry is busy reminding people that Sunday is Mother's Day. Of course, everyone will want to pick up cards for Mom, wife, and Grandma. But what about sisters and favorite aunts? Sure. There are Mother's Day cards for them too, and a host of greetings for a mother-in-law. How about someone expecting a baby in July? No problem. Any number of companies make Mother's Day cards for mothers-to-be. And why should Pop feel left out and have to wait until June for his special day? Hallmark puts out a card that says 'You're a terrific parent, too, Dad!' Why in fact should Mother's Day be restricted to parents? It is not. A card by Recycled Paper Products of Chicago has this touching message: 'Although you're not my mother, your little motherlies mean a lot to me. Happy Motherish Day.'

No business is better than greeting cards at finding imaginative ways to package and promote an old product. The leading companies, Hallmark of Kansas City and American Greetings of

Cleveland, have roots that go back almost to the turn of the century, but they strive to be as innovative as fledgling Silicon Valley computer firms. The cardmakers are experimenting with different styles, coming up with novel reasons for people to buy their wares and using new technology that enables cards to play tunes or talk. Hallmark offers 1,200 varieties of cards for Mother's Day, the year's fourth biggest card day (after Christmas, Valentine's Day, and Easter), while American Greetings boasts of 1,300. The products range from a traditional card with a picture of flowers and syrupy poetry for $1 or less to a $7 electronic version that plays the tune of 'You Are the Sunshine of My Life.'

Hallmark holds about 42 per cent of the $3.2 billion-a-year greeting card business, followed by American Greetings' 30 per cent. The two leaders are now being challenged by Cincinnati-based Gibson Greetings, which has captured an estimated 10 per cent share, up from 5 per cent in 1978. Gibson scored a coup in February by striking a deal with Walt Disney Productions for the rights to use Mickey Mouse and his friends, who had previously been featured on Hallmark cards. Gibson had also signed up Garfield the Cat and the Sesame Street characters, but Hallmark's line of Peanuts cards is still one of the industry's most successful. American Greetings got a boost last year by reaching an agreement with Sears to be the exclusive cardseller in all its department stores. That more than matched a similar arrangement that Hallmark has with J. C. Penney.

As the top three cardmakers battle among themselves, they also keep an eye on about 300 smaller manufacturers, which are often daring and inventive. Says Hallmark Chairman Donald Hall, 'Industries that aren't competitive get stagnant after a while. Ours is very competitive, and the fever of creativity is at a high point.' One sign of the industry's brainstorming is the burgeoning number of occasions for which greetings are available. Card buyers can now congratulate a friend on getting a driver license, buying a new car, or completing a successful diet. Customers can use cards to announce a divorce, propose a tryst, or console a pal whose pet dog has died. Carrying that marketing strategy to an extreme, California Dreamers, a Chicago company, has put out an all-purpose generic greeting card. The message: 'Whatever.'

The card manufacturers have been alert to changes in the American family. Says Richard Connor, executive vice-president of American Greetings, 'The divorce rate has brought about new families, single fathers, and working mothers. These new relationships open up new avenues for card sending.' One of Hallmark's Mother's Day cards shows Mom at her office. Both American Greetings and Hallmark have cards with messages to 'Mom and Her Husband' or 'Dad and His Wife.'

Paper Moon Graphics, a small, fast-growing Los Angeles firm has won over customers with a combination of quirky humor and striking visual images. One of its cards shows a bride perched on the shoulders of her groom, who is standing precariously on a high wire. Inside, it says, 'So Far . . . So Good. Happy Anniversary!' Maine Line of Rockport, Maine, has found a profitable niche by specializing in cards that appeal to women. A sample message: 'A woman in the White House would feel right at home . . . She already knows how to clean up the mess men have made.' Maine Line even has a few cards that could be used by homosexuals. One says, 'Hip hip hooray, I'm glad you're gay.'

The industry leaders have responded to the competition by introducing their own yuppie-style cards. Hallmark has a new line called Modern Woman, with messages that might often seem risqué for the venerable 75-year-old firm. Example: 'You're such a totally together man. You're sensitive, kind, understanding and a good listener . . . Nice buns, too! Happy Birthday.'

One of the newest frontiers in the industry is talking cards. The voice comes from a minute speaker connected to a microchip, where the message is stored. One card by American Greetings has the words 'Open this birthday card fast' printed on the outside. When the card is opened, a relieved voice says, 'Thanks, it was really getting stuffy in here. Happy Birthday!' Priced as high as $10, the electronic cards are still a novelty item. But since the cost of microchips is coming down, the industry hopes that tuneful and talking cards may eventually become a mainstay of Mother's Day, and every other conceivable occasion.

(Source: 'Greetings, One and All,' *Time*, 13 May 1985, p. 54.)

For the first time in its history, Eliot Greeting was faced with a decline in its modest share, each point of which was worth several millions of dollars in sales. At a brainstorming session by the firm's board of directors, President Tom Eliot suggested that one possible solution to the problem would be to develop an export market for its products to avoid the high costs of head-to-head competition for US customers. He reasoned that it would be easier for the company to design and make cards for English-speaking consumers in countries like the United Kingdom and Australia than to continue to slug it out with the market leaders at home.

Bill Yates, vice president of Sales, had an alternative suggestion. He had recently returned from a vacation in the US Southwest where he had become aware of the large number of Hispanic Americans, who were, according to his sales representatives, beginning to improve their traditionally low economic status. Yates's idea was to create and market a line of greeting cards for this largely Spanish-speaking group of Americans for whom greeting card sending was at a relatively low level, compared with the general population. He argued that, rather than expand its efforts to approach foreign customers, the firm would be better able to take advantage of its existing production and distribution system to develop this relatively untapped market at home. An argument developed between Tom Eliot and Bill Yates as to which avenue would be the better source of growth for Eliot Greeting Card Company. Tom had recently seen an article in the local paper (see Exhibit 2) describing his competitors' moves in the US Hispanic market. He certainly did not want another slugfest with competition. Bill argued that the potential of the US Hispanic market was large enough for all greeting cards firms and that they would have to develop skills either now or later in marketing cards to this significant segment in the US market. They agreed to postpone a decision until they could get more information on each option.

Exhibit 2 'Greeting Card Firms Expand Hispanic Line'

Two major U.S. greeting card companies are expanding their lines of Spanish language cards and gift items in response to growing demand from the Hispanic market.

Hallmark Cards, Inc., and American Greetings Corp. have announced plans to publish more greeting cards written in standard, dialect-free Spanish incorporating new designs that eschew old-fashioned stereotypes in favor of popular characters such as Strawberry Shortcake.

Old views knocked

The U.S. Census Bureau says that Hispanics comprised 6.4 percent of the total population in 1980 and increased in number by 61 percent during the 1970s.

The U.S. Hispanic Chamber of Commerce, which meets in San Antonio later this week, has reported that the nation's 20 million Hispanics now have purchasing power worth $70 billion – a figure the chamber expects to more than double by the year 2000.

Recent marketing studies have knocked down some old views about Hispanic consumers and provided new data on buyers seeking high-quality goods and services.

Hallmark Cards, the industry leader with $1.5 billion in annual sales, expects to double its Spanish language line of everyday and seasonal cards by next May, said Nancy Matheny, manager of marketing and communications.

American Greetings has launched a new line of Spanish language cards, posters, and calendars featuring popular characters such as Ziggy and Strawberry Shortcake, and the 'classical romantic' expressions of its 'Soft Touch' series.

The 95 new designs, now available in San Antonio stores, will expand the company's current line of approximately 300 everyday and seasonal greeting cards, invitations, and gift tags in Spanish, said product manager Ross Bennett.

American Greetings, the largest publicly held greeting card publisher with $1 billion in annual sales, based its latest expansion on the results of focus group interviews with Hispanic women in Los Angeles and New York City, Bennett said.

Women predominate in both the Hispanic and Anglo card market, accounting for 90 percent of all card buyers and 85 percent of all dollars spent on greeting cards, Bennett said from his Cleveland office.

Bennett said the Hispanic women interviewed told American Greetings:

- Spanish language greeting cards are difficult to find, even in mostly Hispanic neighborhoods in large cities.

- Cards in Spanish are sent most frequently to older relatives and friends, especially those who still speak mostly Spanish, and to those living in Mexico, Puerto Rico, Cuba, and other foreign countries. Cards in English usually are preferred for young relatives, such as brothers and sisters, and for children, co-workers, and non-Hispanic friends. Exceptions to these general rules are religious observances, such as baptisms, weddings, name days, and fifteenth birthday days, when Spanish-language greetings are preferred.

- The industry's offerings in Spanish had been inferior to their English language counterparts. Among the criticisms: limited variety of designs, poor quality of photographs and paper, and overuse of loud, garish colors.

Bennett said the U.S. Hispanic population's growing affluence during the past ten year has created a need for Spanish cards of improved quality and variety. The old stereotypes of sombreros and burros do not work anymore, he added.

But simply translating an English language sentiment into Spanish and slapping on a new cover will not sell more cards to Hispanic customers, industry leaders say.

Both Hallmark and American Greetings employ linguistic consultants and bilingual editors to develop pithy verses in traditional, or Castillian, Spanish.

'We don't regurgitate English words or sentiments straight into Spanish,' Matheny said from Hallmark's Kansas City, Missouri, headquarters. Cultural and linguistic idiosyncrasies are incorporated in the company's line of Spanish cards, which was begun in 1982 with 100 designs.

Matheny predicted the firm will produce 500 to 600 everyday and seasonal designs in Spanish by May 1985. Hallmark and its Ambassador subsidiary publish cards and other items in 20 languages for sales in 100 countries, with 11 million cards produced daily.

Differences blur

Bennett pointed out that Spanish greeting cards should be written in a standard grammatically correct version of the language that does not reflect any regional dialect, just as English cards are written.

American Greetings' research showed that card senders preferred to write their own personal message on the card to incorporate any regionally distinct dialect, he said.

A recent survey of the U.S. Hispanic market by Yankelovich, Skelly & White, Inc., revealed a 'blurring of differences' among Spanish-speaking nationalities, leading the researchers to propose that all Hispanics be considered as one population segment or marketing purposes. 'Localized patterns of speech, slang, etc., are felt to be a lessening barrier between Hispanics of different national origins,' the report states.

Rousana Cards, a Hillside, N.J., company specializing in greeting cards aimed at Hispanics, blacks, and other ethnic groups, has been publishing cards in Spanish since 1947.

Rousana President Ira F. Rubin said although his firm's cards generally use vernacular Spanish, some idioms also are included. He cited one example: *yerno*, the standard Spanish word for son-in-law, becomes the feminine *yerna*, daughter-in-law, only in a Puerto Rico dialect. Rubin's company publishes cards for *yernas* and markets them in appropriate neighborhoods.

'We feel very bullish regarding greeting cards in Spanish,' Rubin said. 'People have told us that as Latins become more Anglicized, we would lose our market, but that just doesn't happen.'

(Source: 'Greeting Card Firms Expand Hispanic Line', *Express News* (San Antonio, TX), 18 September 1984.)

English-speaking export markets

The English-speaking export market was a potentially large one. Its major components were the United Kingdom (England, Scotland, Wales and Northern Ireland), Canada, Australia and New Zealand. These four markets comprised a total population of 96.2 million, broken down as follows:

United Kingdom	55,226,400
Canada	24,343,200
Australia	13,548,500
New Zealand	3,125,100
	96,243,200

In addition, the Republic of South Africa had a population speaking English as a first language of nearly one million. Several other former British colonies, such as Kenya, Hong Kong and Singapore, had English-speaking minorities, but the major English-speaking markets offered a greater immediate potential. All four of the English-speaking nations were economically developed. Canada had been classified by most experts as belonging to the small group of affluent nations even though it had been experiencing serious economic problems in the mid-1980s. The other three markets were clearly in the category of developed nations, having predominantly middle-class populations with considerable disposable income.

Culturally, the four markets share a common heritage with the United States, but each culture has evolved somewhat differently over the years. Although they all speak the English language, they exhibit varying degrees of difference in word usage. Since the Eliot Company's product is written communication, it would be dangerous for its management to assume that identically worded messages would have an identical meaning in each country. Much of the charm and appeal of greeting cards comes from subtle plays on words, and such messages might not be perceived in the same way in the other countries. Canada would present the least difficulty in this matter. Because Canada shares a long border with the United States and Canadians are exposed to large amounts of American media (television and magazines), word usage is very similar in the two nations – similar enough that identical messages would usually be successful. However, in the United Kingdom, where a 'closet' is a 'cupboard' and 'to schmooze' is 'to chat', the danger of miscommunication is very real. This is equally true of Australia and New Zealand. Eliot would have to test all messages with local experts and, in many instances, work out entirely different messages for each country.

A second major cultural difference between the United States and these other English-speaking countries may lie in the use and perception of greeting cards. Historically, in

English-speaking cultures, a personally written note or letter has been considered the polite and proper method of communicating with a friend. Standardized, pre-printed messages, such as are found on greeting cards, were considered to be less polite, less caring substitutes. Greeting cards may have complete acceptance in the United States, but before the Eliot Company decides to launch its products in any of these other countries, it must learn how their residents perceive greeting cards today.

The US Hispanic market

Some preliminary demographic data were gathered to support the feasibility of Yates's proposal to sell Spanish-language cards to the Hispanic market in the United States. The 1980 census estimated conservatively that Hispanics numbered nearly 15 million in the United States and that their growth rate was much higher than that of the population at large. It was speculated both because of immigration and high fertility rates that by the year 2000, Hispanics would surpass blacks in numbers in the United States and hence become the largest minority group. Yates was placed in charge of conducting secondary research into the idea and he hired the consulting firm of Lorca and Associates, specialists in the US Hispanic market. Yates requested that the firm provide recommendations concerning general customer behaviour of the Hispanic population so that decisions could be made about what the company would need to do to design and market greeting cards to the Spanish-speaking market in the United States.

The consultant's report

Jose Lorca, president of the consulting firm, presented Bill Yates with a review of the literature pertaining to the consumer behaviour characteristics of US Hispanics. He took some pains to point out that empirical data about this subpopulation were very meagre and that much of the information came from articles in trade periodicals. These sources reflect experience by firms which have been interested in the Hispanic market, but do not report much of the hard data which would normally be expected to support conclusions made about Hispanics. He expressed a desire for more extensive consumer research to verify the speculations used to characterize the Hispanic market. With this caution in mind, Lorca reported his interpretations. He extracted seven themes from these studies which to him summarized the traits attributed to Hispanic consumers:

1. A preference for locally owned, Spanish-speaking businesses as well as a preference for Spanish ethnic products.
2. A high degree of brand loyalty and susceptibility to brand influences.
3. A tendency for purchases to be influenced by pride in Hispanic heritage.
4. A high degree of price consciousness and careful shopping characteristics.
5. A high degree of influence from 'family' in making purchase decisions.
6. Preference for Spanish-language media, especially radio and television.
7. A tendency to become 'acculturated' with rising affluence.

Thus, Eliot Greeting was confronted with the prospect of developing the use of greeting cards among a relatively provincial and traditional group of potential customers who appeared to be heavily dependent upon their cultural background for purchase decisions. Moreover, as these individuals become more economically secure, they become more like typical American consumers.

Lorca pointed out several other problems with developing the Hispanic market. First, it could not be said that the consumers in the overall Hispanic market were homogeneous. In addition to the acculturation characteristic (Hispanics were not alike at different economic levels), US Hispanics represent a number of different ethnic subgroups, depending on their national origins. These include Mexican Americans (59 per cent), Puerto Ricans (15 per cent), and Cubans (6 per cent) as well as Hispanics with origins in other Central and South American countries and Europe (20 per cent). These groups differ widely in cultural traits, especially in the particular dialects of Spanish spoken. He also noted that nearly all these people speak a kind of Spanish that is considerably different from the classical Castillian Spanish typically taught in Spanish courses offered at US high schools and universities. This fact seemed particularly important to the creation of Spanish verses for greeting cards, especially in light of the uniquely personal nature of messages used.

Questions

1. Isolate the probable impact of culture on Hispanic preferences and purchasing pattern for greeting cards. Investigate the symbolic meaning of sending a greetings card – to whom, on which occasions, in which language?

2. What issues will have to be addressed prior to the development of the English-speaking export market?

3. What are the benefits of each strategy: Hispanic market in the United States versus English-speaking export market?

(Source: Adapted from a case prepared by Joel Saegaert, University of Texas at San Antonio, in Cundiff and Hilger, 1988, pp. 156–63.)

NOTES

1. *Potlach* still exists in modern societies, especially in the context of fund raising where appreciation banquets, kick-off luncheons and campaign parties present ritualized, symbolic gift giving which induces participants into the social dynamics of philanthropy (Hanson, 1997).

2. Rather than needs, which have a distinct rational and utilitarian connotation, consumer *desires* may be a more useful concept for cross-cultural consumer behaviour. Belk *et al.* (1997), based on projective research, evidence substantial convergence across American, Danish and Turkish subjects on three dimensions: (1) desires are interpersonal, (2) desire can be dangerous and (3) desires follows a cycle where emotions and feelings differ in the 'before', 'during' and 'after' stages, suggesting that 'the thrill lies more in the desire than in its realization' (p. 26).

3. See for instance: Kushner (1982), Laurent (1982), Redding (1982), Yau (1988), Yang (1989) and Robinson (1996).

4. A very large number of aspects of consumer behaviour are now being investigated in a cross-cultural perspective; see for instance Dawar *et al.* (1996), who investigate interpersonal infor-

mation exchange across eleven nationalities in the case of consumer electronics; they show that consumers from high uncertainty avoidance and power distance cultures tend to use more personal information sources, whereas opinion leadership appears as a more individual rather than culture-based consumer characteristic. See also McDonald (1995) on how Japanese and American consumers make decisions and Alden *et al.* (1994) on evaluation strategies of American and Thai consumers, especially when they face perceived risk.

5. Chapman and Jamal (1997) explain how the immigrant community in Bradford (UK) does not share with the local British community the same symbolism of space, especially that which concerns the garden. This is treated by 'Pakistani' immigrants as public, outer space whereas it was regarded by the native Britons as domestic space.

6. On the meaning of possessions across cultures, see Wallendorf and Arnould (1988); on cross-cultural differences in materialism see Ger and Belk (1996a) and Eastman *et al.* (1997); on gift-giving across cultures, see Sherry (1983), Beatty *et al.* (1991). Arunthanes *et al.* (1994) distinguish between high context cultures (to which Asian countries typically belong) where business gifts are imperative, accepted as a normal social practice and have reciprocal effects, and low context cultures (the prototype being the United States or Northern Europe) where they are optional, and even sometimes perceived as attempts at bribery. Some studies suggest major cultural differences between gift-giving behaviour in Oriental and Western cultures (Green and Alden, 1988; Beatty *et al.*, 1991). For instance, reciprocation and moral obligations are central in the Japanese gift-giving tradition. Japanese tourists travelling abroad must bring back home *omiyage*, that is, local specialities purchased as gifts for families and friends at home (Applbaum and Jordt, 1996). *Omiyage* are, for many Japanese tourists, Louis Vuitton luggage or other French luxury brands, of which they are major purchasers when they stay as tourists in Paris. As emphasized by Wong and Ahuvia (1995, p. 81): 'Unlike souvenirs which are purchased for the self, *omiyage* are tokens for others to share in one's travel experience.' Buying gifts for oneself is more often a pattern to be found in societies that value an independent self, a typical statement about such purchases being that it is 'a present from me to me' (Mick and DeMoss, 1990, p. 322).

7. For a detailed discussion of concepts of the self in western and Asian cultures (independent vs. interdependent) and how they impact on cognition, emotion and motivation, see Markus and Kitayama (1991). An empirical investigation of self concepts in Japan and the United States which has been undertaken by Abe *et al.* (1996) provides support for the idea that Markus and Kitayama's categories of the self have influence on consumer behaviour.

8. See for instance Olsen (1995), who explains how brand loyalty builds on memories, past experiences and consumer nostalgia, with personal and family histories being deeply enmeshed in the cultural biography of brands.

9. Watkins and Liu (1996) offer a complete discussion of how collectivism, individualism and ingroup membership can have an impact on consumer complaining behaviour. This may be of assistance for exercise A4.2.

REFERENCES

Abe, Shuzo, Richard P. Bagozzi, and Pradip Sadarangani (1996), 'An investigation of construct validity and generalizability of the self-concept: Self-consciousness in Japan and the United States', *Journal of International Consumer Marketing*, vol. 8, nos 3/4, pp. 97–123.

Alden, Dana L., Douglas M. Stayman and Wayne D. Hoyer (1994), 'Evaluation strategies of American and Thai consumers', *Psychology and Marketing*, vol. 11, no. 2, pp. 145–61.

Applbaum, Kalman and Ingrid Jordt (1996), 'Notes toward an application of McCracken's "cultural categories" for cross-cultural consumer research', *Journal of Consumer Research*, vol. 23 (December), pp. 204–18.

Arunthanes, Wiboon, Patriya Tansujah, and David J. Lemak (1994), 'Cross-cultural business gift giving: A new conceptualization and theoretical framework', *International Marketing Review*, vol. 11, no. 4, pp. 44–55.

Bagozzi, Richard P. (1975), 'Marketing as exchange', *Journal of Marketing*, vol. 39, no. 4, pp. 32–9.

Ballah, R.N. (1970), *Tokugawa Religion*, Bencon Press: Boston.

Baudrillard, Jean (1968), *Le Système des objets*, Gallimard: Paris.

Beatty, Sharon E., Lynn R. Kahle, and Pamela Homer (1991), 'Personal values and gift-giving behaviors: A study across cultures', *Journal of Business Research*, vol. 22, no. 2, pp. 149– 57.

Belk, Russell W. (1988), 'Third World consumer culture', in E. Kumçu and A. Fuat Firat (eds.), *Research in Marketing*, supplement 4, JAI Press: Greenwich, Connecticut.

Belk, Russell W., Güliz Ger and Søren Askegaard (1997), 'Consumer desires in three cultures: Results from projective research', in Merrie Brucks and Debbie McInnis (eds.), *Advances in Consumer Research*, vol. 24, Association for Consumer Research: Provo, UT, pp. 24–27.

Bell, D. (1975), 'Ethnicity and social change', in N. Glazer and D. P. Moynihan (eds.), *Ethnicity, Theory and Experience*, Harvard University Press: Cambridge, MA.

Bouchet, Dominique (1995), 'Marketing and the redefinition of ethnicity,' in Janeen Arnold Costa and Gary J. Bamossy (eds.), *Marketing in a Multicultural World*, Sage: Thousand Oaks, CA, pp. 68–105.

Buzzati, Dino (1967), *Le K*, Robert Laffont: Paris.

Calantone, R., M. Morris and J. Johar (1985), 'A cross-cultural benefit segmentation analysis to evaluate the traditional assimilation model', *International Journal of Research in Marketing*, vol. 2, pp. 207–17.

Cavusgil, S. Tamer and Erdener Kaynak (1984), 'Critical issues in the cross-cultural measurement of consumer dissatisfaction: Developed versus LDC practices', in Erdener Kaynak and Ronald Savitt (eds.), *Comparative Marketing Systems*, Praeger: New York, pp. 114–30.

Chapman, Malcolm and Ahmad Jamal (1997), 'Acculturation: Cross-cultural consumption and the symbolism of domestic space', in Merrie Brucks and Debbie McInnis (eds.), *Advances in Consumer Research*, vol. 24, Association for Consumer Research: Provo, UT, pp. 138–44.

Chien, M. (1979), *Chinese National Character and Chinese Culture: A historical perspective*, The Chinese University of Hong Kong Press: Shatin, Hong Kong (in Chinese).

Chiou, Jyh-Shen (1995), 'The process of social influences on new product adoption and retention in individualistic versus collectivistic cultural contexts', *Proceedings of the Second Conference on the Cultural Dimension of International Marketing*, Odense, pp. 107–27.

Cundiff, Eward and Marye Tharp Hilger, *Marketing in the International Environment*, 2nd edn, Prentice Hall: Englewood Cliffs, NJ.

D'Andrade, Roy G. (1987), 'A folk model of the mind', in Dorothy Quinn and Naomi Holland (eds), *Cultural Models in Language and Thought*, Cambridge University Press: Cambridge, pp. 112–48.

Dawar, Niraj, Philip M. Parker, and Lydia J. Price (1996), 'A cross-cultural study of interpersonal information exchange', *Journal of International Business Studies*, vol. 27, no. 3, pp. 497–516.

Dubois, Bernard (1987), 'Culture et marketing', *Recherche et Applications en Marketing*, vol 2, no. 3, pp. 37–64.

Eastman, Jacqueline K., Bill Fredenberger, David Campbell and Stephen Calvert (1997), 'The relationship between status consumption and materialism: A cross-cultural comparison of Chinese, Mexican and American students', *Journal of Marketing Theory & Practice*, vol. 5, no. 1, pp. 52–66.

Engel, James F., Roger D. Blackwell and Paul W. Miniard (1986), *Consumer Behavior*, 5th ed., Holt, Rhinehart & Winston: New York.

Fei, X. T. (1948), *Rural China*, Guancha She: Shangai (in Chinese).

Gans, Herbert (1962), *The Urban Villagers*, The Free Press: New York.

Ger, Guliz and Russell W. Belk (1996), 'Cross-cultural differences in materialism', *Journal of Economic Psychology*, vol. 17, no. 1, pp. 55–77.

Green, Robert T. and Alden, Dana L. (1988), 'Functional equivalence in cross-cultural consumer behavior: Gift giving in Japan and the United States', *Psychology and Marketing*, vol. 5, pp. 155–68.

Hanson, John H (1997), 'Power, philanthropy, and potlatch: What tribal exchange rituals can tell us about giving', *Fund Raising Management*, vol. 27, no. 12, pp. 16–9.

Hirschmann, Elisabeth C. (1985), 'Primitive aspects of consumption in modern American Society,' *Journal of Consumer Research*, vol. 12 (September), pp. 142–54.

Howard, J. and J. N. Sheth (1969), *The Theory of Buyer Behaviour*, John Wiley: New York.

Hsieh, Y. W. (1967), Filial piety and Chinese society, in C. A. Moore (ed.), *The Chinese Mind*, University of Hawaii Press: Honolulu, pp. 167–87.

Hsu, F. L. K. (1971), Philosophical homeostasis and jen: conceptual tools for advancing psychological anthropology, *American Anthropologist*, vol. 73, pp. 23–44.

Karsaklian, Eliane (1995), 'Mesure de la mémorisation des messages publicitaires par les enfants: l'Influence du système scolaire', Unpublished doctoral thesis, July, HEC: Jouy-en-Josas.

Kotler, Philip (1994), *Marketing Management*, 8th edn, Prentice Hall: Englewood Cliffs, NJ.

Kushner, J. M. (1982), 'Market research in a non-Western context: the Asian example', *Journal of the Market Research Society*, vol. 24, no. 2, pp. 116–22.

Laurent, Clint R. (1982), 'An investigation of the family life cycle in a modern Asian society', *Journal of the Market Research Society*, vol. 24, no. 2, pp. 140–50.

Lazer, William, Shoji Murata and Hiroshi Kosaka (1985), 'Japanese marketing: Towards a better understanding', *Journal of Marketing*, vol. 49 (Spring), pp. 69–81.

Levitt, Theodore (1983), 'The globalization of markets', *Harvard Business Review*, vol. 61 (May–June), pp. 92–102.

McCracken, Grant (1991), 'Culture and consumer behaviour: An anthropological perspective', *Journal of the Market Research Society*, vol. 32, no. 1, pp. 3–11.

McDonald, William, J. (1995), 'American versus Japanese consumer decision making: An exploratory cross-cultural content analysis', *Journal of International Consumer Marketing*, vol. 7, no. 3, pp. 81–93.

Markus, Hazel Rose and Shinobu Kitayama (1991), 'Culture and the self: Implications for cognition, emotion and motivation', *Psychological Review*, vol. 98, no. 2, pp. 224–53.

Maslow, Abraham H. (1954), *Motivation and Personality*, Harper & Row: New York.

Mendenhall, Mark, Betty Jane Punnett and David Ricks (1995), *Global Management*, Blackwell: Cambridge, Mass.

Mick, David Glen and Michelle DeMoss (1990), 'Self-gifts: Phenomenological insights from four contexts,' *Journal of Consumer Research*, vol. 17 (December), pp. 322–32.

Mitchell, V. W., M. Yamin, and B. Pichene (1996), 'A cross-cultural analysis of perceived risk in British and French CD purchasing', *Journal of Euromarketing*, vol. 6, no. 1, pp. 5–24.

Olsen, Barbara (1995), 'Brand loyalty and consumption patterns', in John F. Sherry, Jr. editor, *Contemporary Marketing and Consumer Behavior*, Thousand Oaks, CA: Sage Publications, pp. 245–81.

Redding, S. Gordon (1982).'Cultural effects on the marketing process in Southeast Asia', *Journal of the Market Research Society*, vol. 24, no. 2, pp. 98–114.

Richins, M. (1983), 'Negative word-of-mouth by dissatisfied consumers: A pilot study', *Journal of Marketing*, vol. 47 (Winter), pp. 68–78.

Richins, Marsha (1994), 'Valuing things: the public and private meaning of possessions', *Journal of Consumer Research*, vol. 21, no. 3 (December), 504–521.

Richins, M. and B. Verhage (1985), 'Cross-cultural differences in consumer attitudes and their implications for complaint management', *International Journal of Research in Marketing*, vol 2, pp. 197–205.

Robinson, Chris (1996), 'Asian cultures: the marketing consequences', *Journal of the Market Research Society*, vol. 38, no. 1, pp. 55–62.

Sherry, John S. (1983), 'Gift giving in anthropological perspective', *Journal of Consumer Research*, vol. 10 (September), pp. 157–67.

Singh, Jagdip (1988), 'Consumer complaint intentions and behavior: definitions and taxonomical issues', *Journal of Marketing*, vol. 52 (January), pp. 93–107.

Solomon, Michael R. (1994), *Consumer Behavior*, 2nd edn, Allyn and Bacon: Needham Heights.

Straus, Karen (1992), 'Go hog wild with Chino-Latino pork dishes', *Restaurants and Institutions*, vol. 102, no. 19, pp. 43–57.

Tanouchi, Koichi (1983), 'Japanese-style marketing based on sensitivity', *Dentsu Japan Marketing/Advertising*, vol. 23 (July), pp. 77–81.

Van Raaij, W. F. (1978), 'Cross-cultural methodology as a case of construct validity' in M. K. Hunt (ed.), *Advances in Consumer Research*, Association for Consumer Research: Ann Arbor, vol. 5, pp. 693–701.

Wallendorf, Melanie and Eric J. Arnould (1988), '"My favorite things": A cross-cultural inquiry into object attachment, possessiveness, and social linkage', *Journal of Consumer Research*, vol. 10 (December), pp. 531–47.

Wallendorf, Melanie and Michael D. Reilly (1983), Ethnic Migration, Assimilation and Consumption', *Journal of Consumer Research*, vol. 10 (December), pp. 292–302.

Watkins, Harry S. and Raymond Liu (1996), 'Collectivism, individualism, and in-group membership: Implications for consumer complaining behaviors in multicultural contexts', *Journal of International Consumer Marketing*, vol. 8, nos 3/4, pp. 69–96.

Wilk, Richard (1995), 'Real Belizean food: Building local identity in the transnational Caribbean', *Proceedings of the Second Conference on the Cultural Dimension of International Marketing*, Odense, pp. 372–91.

Wong, Nancy and Aaron Ahuvia (1995), 'From tofu to caviar: Conspicuous consumption, materialism and self-concepts in east-Asian and Western cultures', *Proceedings of the Second Conference on the Cultural Dimension of International Marketing*, Odense, pp. 68–89.

Yang, Chung-Fang (1989), 'Une conception du comportement du consommateur chinois', *Recherche et Applications en Marketing*, vol. IV, no.1, pp. 17–36.

Yang, M. C. (1972), 'Familism and Chinese national character', in Y. Y. Lee and K. S. Yang (eds.), *Symposium on the Character of the Chinese*, Institute of Ethnology, Academia Sinica (in Chinese), pp. 127–74.

Yankelovitch, Skelly and White (1982), *Spanish USA: A study of the Hispanic market in the U.S.*, for Spanish Television Networks.

Yau, Oliver H. M. (1988), 'Chinese cultural values: Their dimensions and marketing implications', *European Journal of Marketing*, vol. 22, no. 5, pp. 44–57.

5 Local consumers and the globalization of consumption

IKEA is often cited as an example of successful marketing strategy given the globalization of world markets. However, consumption habits and way of life as regards household equipment, furniture and related items remain significantly different, according to whether people sleep with duvets or with sheets, the size of pillowcases, or the kind of materials they use for their bath rooms. In Germany, for instance, most homes have no cupboards: when Germans are interviewed, the underlying assumption surfaces that only lower-class people have cupboards, because they cannot afford nice wardrobes. This traditional value in the Germanic world extends to Alsace but stops in France and the Latin countries, where cupboards are viewed as convenient alongside wardrobes, and there is no implied meaning in terms of perceived wealthiness of the household. There is clearly a paradox of globalization based on the rather harmonious coexistence of global and local patterns. Thus IKEA succeeds globally while maintaining a strong Swedish brand image, with waitresses in traditional Swedish costume serving *glögg* to its customers, and branding its items of furniture with names that sound strongly Nordic.

The central paradox of globalization is the encounter between companies that are increasingly global and consumers who remain largely local. The general line of argument developed by this chapter is that consumption styles converge only at a macroscopic level. Consumption patterns are a little bit like Russian dolls, building up from home to city, from community to region, and from nation to global (Bell and Valentine, 1997).[1] Paradoxically, it has never been so urgent to take a close look at differences, that is, unique elements of meaning invested by local consumers in the things and services they buy and in their consumption experiences. While a key issue for designing international marketing strategies, globalization is a difficult phenomenon to observe since demand is observed in actual markets and can never be fully separated from supply.

In order to dig deeper into the apparent trend toward homogenization, three aspects of globalization process must be distinguished. The first is the globalization of demand, that is, the convergence of (1) consumer behaviour (this chapter), and (2) marketing environments world-wide (next chapter). The second aspect is the global-ization of supply and competition, with the progressive shift from domestic industries operating in national markets protected by non-tariff barriers to global industries (Porter, 1986). Changes have been largely initiated through the successive rounds of the General Agreement on Tariffs and Trade (GATT), and are now implemented by the World Trade Organization, a full-fledged international organization and by regional market agreements such as the European Union (EU) or the North American Free Trade Agreement (NAFTA). The third aspect deals with the globalization of products and marketing offerings. Companies react to globalization partly by shaping new strategies and partly by refining their organizational design. They do this under cost constraints, given the potential for the experience effect of available technologies and the impact of transportation costs (Chapter 8).

The first section of this chapter explains how traditional models of international trade have been a strong driver for the partisans of globalization: the denial of local consumers' tastes and differences across products according to local ways of designing and manufacturing and a focus on merely utilitarian needs for undifferentiated generic products, have been a justification for those who argue in favour of world-wide similarity. Section 5.2 documents the global convergence of consumption patterns, arguing basically that, on the basis of broad, generic product categories, convergence at the quantitative level is indisputable, whereas it is much less obvious when one adopts a micro-level of analysis looking at specific products and the minutiae of con-sumer behaviour. Section 5.3 investigates what happens at the global level, where local/traditional consumption patterns are seemingly replaced and overwhelmed by new ones based on a world standard package of goods that every consumer on earth would be entitled to desire, resulting in the emergence of a global consumer culture built on the values of 'modern culture'. Section 5.4 dives back to the local level, and examines precisely how products are to various degrees culture bound, and how goods and services are integrated into local meanings and lived as unique consumption experiences. The next section documents the issue of consumers' resistance to global products and consumption patterns when these are resented as harmful to the local cultural or economic interests. The final section (5.6) tries to give an idea of the com-plex, kaleidoscopic patterns of local consumption in a globalizing world, that is, how consumers mix globalized products and local items in a grand *bricolage*.

5.1   FREE TRADE DOCTRINE AND THE DENIAL OF CULTURAL VARIETY IN CONSUMERS' TASTES

Ricardo's hypotheses

Traditional international trade doctrine has laid the foundations for a denial of culture in international marketing. One of the seminal texts on international trade is the sev-enth chapter of David Ricardo's *On the Principles of Political Economy and Taxation* (1817), which deals with foreign trade. This text basically explains why countries (and their traders) may derive benefits from developing international trade and trading their products internationally, instead of simply producing and trading within their own domestic market. Ricardo considers the case of two countries, England and Portugal, and two types of goods, wine and sheets. This law, which is called the law of comparative or relative advantage, conveys a very powerful message: a country which would be at a competitive disadvantage for both products would still benefit from participating in international trade. By trading internationally this country finds a better exchange ratio between the two goods than that which is provided by its domestic market. By concentrating efforts and resources on the product where they have a relative advantage, the countries, by exporting this product and importing the other, increase their national welfare (probably) and (certainly) global welfare. Many implicit assumptions are not clearly spelled out in Ricardo's text, which is both visionary and confused: (1) gains from trading internationally must offset transportation, customs duties and trading costs; (2) there are constant returns to scale; (3) products are identical, or at least are perceived as such by both consumers and merchants; (4) information must be easily available and efficient enough, so that merchants in the two countries may be aware of the potential gains to be derived from international trade; and (5) there must be no other financial or government restriction or market barrier that limits international trade for these products.

The implicit assumption that products and consumers' tastes, habits and preferences are perfectly identical in the two countries (and accordingly by logical extension throughout all the countries in the world) is a strong one. England was producing almost no wine at the time and it is doubtful that the British wine had the same physical characteristics, the same alcoholic content or the same taste as the Portuguese wine. Additionally, the preferences of the English and the Portuguese were probably distinct enough to enable them to recognize clearly which were 'their' sheets. They certainly had different fabrics and embroideries, and natives of the two countries would have been fully aware of the origin of the sheets on which they were sleeping. Furthermore in English pubs it is beer that is mostly drunk, whereas *vinho verde* or *porto* are the favourite drinks of the Portuguese while they listen to *fado*. This full negation of consumer culture, of non-utilitarian motives, is based on the assumption that products have no reality as cultural artefacts; therefore, consumers are considered as investing no meaning beyond the strictly utilitarian aspect of the product. Only quantity and price matter. Exchange is purely economic: goods and services are commoditized, generic and indefinitely marketable; they cease to be singularized and invested with cultural meaning by local consumers.

These 'wine and sleep' considerations probably appeared as rather anecdotal and naive. The cultural variable – related to national culture and local ways – has been neglected in international trade theory, which is almost purely economics based, whether on theoretical grounds or for practical purposes. Classical economists and their successors did not like national culture, which has an aura of inertia and resistance to change attached to it. Their theories favour commonalities, not differences. They were based on utility maximization rather than on identity building through non-utilitarian motives.

Ricardo's theory was contemporaneous with a major decision in Britain's economic policy: the Corn Laws. Ricardo demonstrated that England should reduce its customs duties, and thereby open up its domestic market to foreign agricultural commodities – especially those from the colonies which were more cost competitive – and specialize in certain manufactured goods that it should export world-wide. Nevertheless the rationale behind this type of decision appears rather simplistic when real people are facing its real-world consequences: rapid rural depopulation, lack of self-sufficiency in food supplies for the country as a whole, changes in the landscape, the emergence of new urban social strata and so on. The increase in global welfare predicted by the theorists of international trade has always served to designate as nationalistic and resistant to inevitable change those local population groups whose jobs were endangered by the progressive opening of the world economy over the last century.

From this initial assumption, it was apparently axiomatic that the defence of cultural identity was inextricably linked to protectionist attitudes in international trade. This is illustrated in France by the *Lois Méline* (at the end of the nineteenth century), introduced out of a desire to protect French food supplies and French farmers, even though this meant higher costs for the consumer. This was also true in Germany where the writings of Friedrich List promoted a nationalistic approach to economic growth. In practice it is difficult, except on the basis of questionable arguments, to make a sharp distinction between the protection of national/cultural interests (their own identity being largely enhanced by what people consume) and the interests of some industries which may deprive consumers of some bargains, or even of the opportunity to buy particular products.

Hence there is a natural tendency to ignore culture or to consider it as an anecdotal and residual explanatory variable, defending local, narrow interests rather than promoting global welfare. This tendency of international trade theory has been largely adopted/inherited by international business and international marketing, where culture remains a subsidiary explanation, with a weak explanatory power. This is exactly how partisans of the globalization of markets such as Levitt (1983) see the cultural variable: a reminder of the past, a vestige in a world where we all tend to adopt a sort of 'modern' lifestyle, at best a bunch of anecdotes and at worst useless constraints.

The dismal treatment of diversity in global marketing

Lack of consideration for what consumers invest locally, as meaning, in their consumption has been a major driver of the global products philosophy. This is because price is a fairly universal concern and low-cost arguments make sense. In this utilitarian view, things are commoditized in a world-wide sphere of exchange. As explained by Kopytoff (1986, p. 68): 'A commodity is a thing that has use value and that can be exchanged in a discrete transaction for a counterpart, the very fact of exchange indicating that the counterpart [most often, money] has, in the immediate context, an equivalent value.'

As advocated by Levitt, and continually repeated, rephrased and almost advertised by almost all authors in the area of international marketing, we might expect to see the emergence of global markets for standardized consumer products on a previously unimagined scale. In Levitt's words it would 'not [be] a matter of opinion but of necessity' (1983, p. 97). Traditional differences in national tastes would disappear, while local consumer preferences and national product standards would be 'vestiges of the past'. Consumers world-wide would look for good quality/low-cost products and the global competitor would seek to standardize his offering everywhere. Farewell diversity: we will not regret you!

This world-view, contains a number of assumptions which will be discussed in this chapter and others. The first concerns the strong ideology of 'standard' in the American mind. What dominates consumption is the utilitarian and materialistic side: people strive for a large quantity of fair-quality, low-cost products. Levitt rightly argues that low cost and high quality are not incompatible. The problem is his quantitative definition of product quality: it is based on statistical reliability, performance and durability, rather than on specific characteristics or attributes that distinguish one product from other products (that is, the first meaning of the word 'quality', see *Collins Dictionary* 1990, p. 810, while the sense of 'having or showing excellence or superiority' is only the ninth and last meaning of the word). Levitt's text incorporates a section entitled 'vindication of the model T', where he clearly explains his views of 'consumption fordism' as the only possible pattern. The second assumption deals with the continuum between traditional and modern societies:[2] traditional is associated with the past, which receives low value in the American tradition; the past is mostly seen as an impediment to effective action. This naive view of world diversity states that we are all converging towards a 'modern' lifestyle marked by standard products and consumption patterns world-wide. To be honest, the democratic aspects of fordist consumption are, however, positive.

The same kind of anti-diversity discourse can be found in international marketing texts while the inevitability of global preferences is presented as a simple fact, not to be discussed: 'No longer an alternative, global marketing has become an imperative for business' (Czinkota and Ronkainen, 1995, p. 3). The main result is that, in most international marketing textbooks, diversity is treated as an anecdotal constraint. There are, however, non-utilitarian reasons for consumer behaviour, and cultural diversity at the international level is a reality, as has already been shown in the previous chapters. Moreover, diversity offers an opportunity to companies which, far from adopting the 'consumption fordism' view of globalization, build on diversity to create differentiation and competitive advantage.

5.2 THE GLOBAL CONVERGENCE OF CONSUMPTION PATTERNS

General convergence at the macro-level

As will be argued in more detail in Chapter 8, supply is now largely globalized. This alone is enough to explain a large part of the globalization of consumption. For example, when examining sociodemographic trends for basic aspects of consumer behaviour in the European Union, Leeflang and Van Raaij (1995) note significant, rapid, demographic convergence: (1) the age distribution of the population comprises more and more older persons; (2) the size of households is constantly decreasing, with an EU average of 2.7 persons, ranging, however, from a low two persons in Denmark to a high 3.6 in Spain; (3) the proportion of immigrants is increasing and they are now a significant part of the population in most European countries, with higher concentrations in large cities. Convergence is also to be observed in the sociocultural environment in the form of growing equality between men and women and increasing percentages of working women, while all over the EU, health and environment concerns are on the rise. In Hofstede's terms, there is a trend towards more femininity. Convergence in consumer behaviour can be observed at a broad level: services tend to replace durables in household budgets and demand is growing for health-care, environmentally friendly, fun and convenience products.

Most of the empirical studies on globalization are synchronic in design; they study cross-national similarity in consumption patterns at a precise point in time. The most logical way to study the convergence process is, however, to examine how consumption changes over several time periods. A good example for illustrating long-term convergence in consumption figures is that of wine, traditionally a southern European drink, and beer, traditionally a northern European drink. Figure 5.1 presents annual consumption in litres per capita for wine for both southern and northern Europe over a 45-year period. Wine consumption has decreased steadily in the south whereas it has increased as steadily in the north of Europe. Convergence is somewhat different for beer: consumption has increased in northern Europe then stabilized, while being partly caught up by the south (Smith and Heede, 1996). The north/south ratio for annual per capita beer consumption has decreased from a high of 9 to a low of 2.2 over 45 years; even more strikingly, the south/north ratio for wine plummeted from 11.7 in 1950 to only 1.8 in 1995.

Clements and Chen (1996) provide evidence of increasing quantitative similarity in cross-national consumption patterns using a large body of data based on broad commodity groups. This is achieved at the very macro-level based on a utility-maximizing framework. Only actual consumption figures are examined, rather than consumer motives and involvement in the purchase.[3] Numerous detailed examples are cited in support of the globalization of consumption behaviour, if not of consumers themselves and their motivations. Thus, clothes-washing habits converge toward lower temperature (40°C) and higher frequency (Bartlett, 1983). Beef consumption in Japan, traditionally a fish-eating country, has developed considerably while there has been a rise in fish consumption in traditionally meat-eating countries; there have been similar changes in relation to rice and wheat between the West and the East, etc. (see Box 5.1). Rather than discuss quantitative globalization, which cannot be denied, it makes more sense, from an international marketing perspective, to try to understand the nature of this phenomenon. With decreasing barriers to international trade over the last century, and mostly in the last fifty years, more variety has been brought to consumers in most countries of the world. In this sense, globalization increases, not decreases, diversity in everyone's experience.

Evidence of consumers' globalization at a micro-level

Eshghi and Sheth (1985) have investigated the globalization of consumption patterns with data provided by the Leo Burnett Advertising Agency. They compare lifestyle variables across four countries (France, Brazil, Japan and the United States). Modern lifestyle and traditional life-style groups are contrasted in each country. Their hypothesis is that lifestyle contrast (within countries) would account for more variance in consumption behaviour than the national contrast (across countries). The dependent

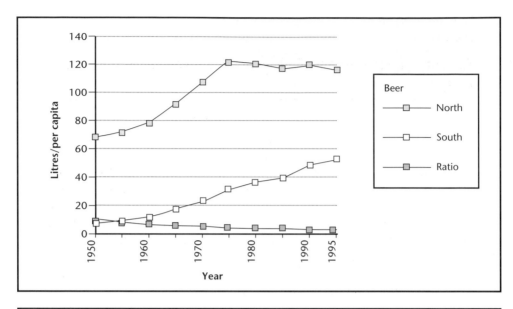

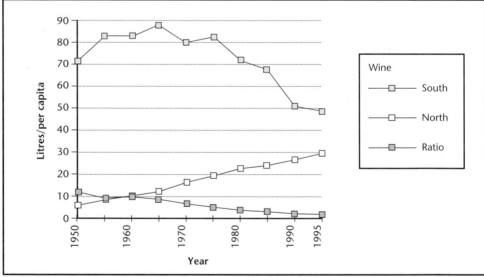

FIGURE 5.1   Beer and wine consumption in northern and southern Europe.

(Source: Smith and Heede, 1996, p. 1081) .

variables are six dichotomous consumption variables: users versus non-users and owners versus non-owners of stereo equipment, soft drinks, fruit juices, alcoholic beverages, cars and deodorants. Lifestyle influences significantly explain consumption behaviour, but not very strongly. National and cultural influences continue to determine the consumption patterns across the four countries. They emphasize that the inclusion of national identity as an independent variable in the analysis does not eliminate the effect of modern lifestyle (Eshghi and Sheth, 1985).

BOX 5.1

Savoury snacks and global law: Two different routes for globalization

Globalization can occur even when local patterns do not disappear. In the two examples below local patterns work either as an opportunity or as a constraint for the emergence of globalized product or service use.

Japan has a long tradition of savoury snacks based on local ingredients such as rice crackers (*arare* and *senbei*), dried seafood snacks (*kozakana*) and *edamame* (green soybeans lightly boiled in salt). Although these snacks still have high consumption rates among elderly people, they have lost ground to potato and corn-based western-style snacks: sales of traditional Japanese-style snacks decreased by 16.5 per cent between 1993 and 1997.

In a totally different field, legal practice, local legal systems have presented an opportunity for US and English law firms (Spar, 1997). Due to the political nature of law, most countries restrict the practice of law to their own nationals. However, US law firms have been following the globalization of US companies which took them along as they expanded abroad, in particular to arrange cross-border deals that maximized advantages under US tax law. By learning the intricacies of local systems of law, US law firms have adjusted to local contexts while maintaining their comparative advantage in terms of the common law (the prevailing legal tradition in the United Kingdom and the United States), by assisting foreign firms willing to enter the US market or drafting international business contracts based on the common law.

(Source: adapted from Spar, 1997 and *Euromonitor*, 1997.)

Zaichkowsky and Sood (1988) have looked at consumer involvement in 15 countries (Argentina, Barbados, Canada, the United States, Finland, Yugoslavia, Sweden, China, Austria, Colombia, Australia, Chile, England, Mexico, France) with eight 'potentially global' products/services (air travel, beer, jeans, eating at a restaurant, hair shampoo, going to the cinema, soft drinks and stereo sets). The same questionnaire, back-translated into each language, was administered to groups of approximately 50 students for each country. The independent variables were the 15 countries and the dependent variables were, first, a PII (personal involvement inventory), intended to measure the respondent's involvement level with the goods and services, and, second, the frequency of use of each product or service over a suitable time frame (self-reported).

Results indicate that the greatest variation in use due to the country effect is found in restaurants (22 per cent), air travel (31 per cent) and hair shampoo (45 per cent). The greatest variation in involvement levels due to the country effect (i.e. as a source of variance) was found in soft drinks (20 per cent) and going to the cinema (12 per cent). Stereo set product use is weakly influenced by the country effect (10 per cent) and involvement level is not related to country (1 per cent). It is difficult to draw simple conclusions about globalization as a whole from Zaichkowsky and Sood's findings. They nevertheless show clearly that the level of consumer globalization differs considerably, according to which product/service category is considered.

Huszagh *et al.* (1986) have approached the consumption globalization process empirically by investigating which products exhibit similar acceptance rates across national markets and whether fundamental product characteristics can explain acceptance rates. They first clustered 21 countries, choosing 16 variables such as urbanization, consumer price index, life expectancy and average working week. A subcluster of five countries (Belgium, the Netherlands, France, the United Kingdom and West Germany) was finally selected as a 'more homogeneous grouping in order to develop a more favourable empirical setting for a global marketing approach' (p. 35). Penetration/consumption rates for 27 products were collected for the five countries and a coefficient of variation was computed for each product's penetration rate across countries. The divergence in acceptance rates (coefficients of variation) is then plotted against three product perception scales: durable/non-durable, household/personal and sensory/functional. A rather counterintuitive result is drawn from this experimental design:

> In summary, the three plots indicate that the more nondurable/sensory/personal a product is, the more consistent the acceptance rate . . . However the relationships are not clearly defined . . . Nevertheless, to some extent, these patterns do support Levitt's promise that 'high touch' products are the most amenable to global marketing. (Huszagh *et al.*, 1986, p. 41.)

Woods *et al.* (1985) have investigated differences in consumer purpose for purchasing in what they term 'three global markets', namely, the United States, Canada and South Korea. The consumer purposes considered are maintenance (basic necessities, convenience), enjoyment, enhancement (satisfied self-image, improves appearance) and defence (protects health, avoids offending). Convenience samples of female shoppers in shopping centres in the United States and Canada and female workers at the workplace in Korea were chosen. Respondents were asked to indicate, for 16 products, one or more purposes out of 14 associated with the four major purposes indicated above.

There seems to be a larger use of products for maintenance purposes in Korea than in the United States or in Quebec, whereas US consumers are more hedonistically oriented. Both the Korean and the Quebecois female consumers are more defence oriented. Different patterns of use of products for enhancement purposes appear across the three national groups. Woods *et al.* (1985, p. 168) conclude that, taken as a whole, the findings indicate that the age of universal marketing is not yet upon us. Koreans are thinking about products in some of the same terms as are those in the United States and Quebec. Yet important differences are found in the reasons why they purchase products familiar to all three cultures. Women in Quebec also differ from those in the United States in the reasons they purchase products. Thus, aside from the economic difference and differences in purchasing power, cultural and psychological differences are pervasive enough to suggest differences in consumer behaviour.

Dawar and Parker (1994) study the use by consumers of four major quality signals (brand name, price, physical appearance and retailer reputation) for consumer electronics, by investigating the behaviour of a sample of about 700 MBA students from 38 nations, mostly industrialized countries. They do not find meaningful differences across cultures in the use of signals, which seem to be consistently used across all countries with the same rank order of importance: (1) brand, (2) price, (3) physical appearance and (4) retailer reputation. However, they report culture-specific behaviour especially as concerns the use of information sources and conclude cautiously that some behaviours are likely to be universal whereas others are not.

Evidence at a micro-level, that of specific products and aspects of consumer behaviour, is somewhat inconclusive about the globalization of consumer behaviour. Finding convincing proofs of this process is difficult, since testing for it would include such issues as the pace and process of globalization, the market segments involved and the geographically significant cultural areas (Jain, 1989). The trend towards globalization depends partly on which aspect of consumer behaviour is concerned, whether buying behaviour, shopping behaviour, lifestyle, values, psychometrics and underlying attitudes, influence processes (in the family, word-of-mouth communication). The use of culturally unique concepts and research instruments (roughly translated as 'American') compresses differences, even when cross-cultural precautions have been taken. Since the concepts and theories of marketing are mostly US-culture based, their full ability to capture local patterns of consumer behaviour is questionable.

5.3   THE EMERGENCE OF A GLOBAL CONSUMER CULTURE

Consumer culture derives from the capacity of consumption to generate cultural values and behaviours. It is defined by Belk as a culture in which the majority of consumers avidly desire, and therefore try to acquire and display, goods and services that are valued for non-utilitarian reasons such as status seeking, envy provocation and novelty seeking (Belk, 1988, p. 105). The rise of massive, democratized consumption as a legitimate and positively valued human activity (e.g. rather than war, monastic contemplation, or other) in most countries of the world has led to the emergence of a global consumer culture. Even in countries where purchasing power does not really allow access to goods and services, US movie films, with an approximate market share of 90 per cent world-wide[4] have been a major driver of desires and aspirations, fuelling consumers' needs and envy.

The standard world package and 'McDonaldized' consumption

A consumer culture guides people in defining their aspirations towards a certain set of possessions. The standard US package of goods has developed into a standard world package that includes an automobile and a home with electric lighting, a refrigerator and a television set. The same holds true for services since the fast-food restaurant has become part of the standard world package. Ritzer (1993, p. 5) describes it as follows:

Many people identify strongly with McDonald's; in fact to some it has become a sacred institution. On the opening of the McDonald's in Moscow, one journalist described it as 'the ultimate icon of Americana', while a worker spoke of it 'as if it were the Cathedral in Chartres . . . a place to experience "celestial joy"'. Kowinsky argues that shopping malls – which we will show to be crucial to McDonaldization – are the modern 'cathedrals of consumption' to which we go to practice our 'consumer religion'.

In the process called by Ritzer 'McDonaldization' of society, that is, the emergence of a global consumer culture, the word 'standard' is central; its meanings is threefold: (1) the same for everybody; (2) the same everywhere in the world; (3) the same for all time. The paradoxical success of the 'Classic' Coke as against the 'new Coke' is an illustration of the last point. Standard also means that product quality remains the same unless new technological developments allow improvements, which appear as additional to the previous attributes.

Ritzer (1993) distinguishes four elements in the McDonaldization process:

1. *Efficiency*: the McDonaldized product or service offers the optimum method for getting from one point (being hungry) to another (being fed). We are living in the 'Republic of technology' as Levitt (1983) says. In contrast to traditional solutions, fordist consumption values assembly-line organization and continuous processes: with parking areas adjacent to the fast-food restaurant, a short walk to counter, a limited menu and quick choice, finger food and speedy disposal of leftovers.

2. *Systematic quantification and calculation*: McDonald's offers more 'bang for the buck' and provides its customers with 'value' meals. Rational economic calculations based on the emphasis on price and the size/weight given for each ingredient extol the utilitarian view. In this model quantity becomes equivalent to quality: the view that larger quantities are a sign of better value is latent in such a conception.

3. *Predictability*: whether in Chicago, Los Angeles, Paris, Moscow or Tokyo, we find the same Big Mac and French fries. Consumers find great comfort in this predictability which offers no surprises, good or bad, and reduces perceived risk. There is not much surprise in the limited range of products offered, but we know that it will be consistent over time and place. Predictable food is based on predictable, often frozen ingredients and corporate guidelines that detail everything to be done in the fast-food outlet.

4. *Control through the substitution of non-human for human technology*: the system is operated so that there is limited human involvement in the whole production process: rules are fairly strict and automatic systems (e.g. soft drinks or ice-cream dispensers) control the exact quantity, in line with point 2. This also facilitates predictability by reassuring customers about the service to be obtained from McDonald's.

The globalized consumption experience is only one part of the real world of consumption but it plays a dominant role because it has been consistently and heavily advertised as 'useful' and 'good for people'. It is also advertised in a somewhat deceitful way since there is much more local adaptation, both in Coca-Cola and in McDonald's, than affirmed by these global marketers.

Globalization and 'modern' culture

The most disputable and debatable aspect of globalization is the implicit assumption that we are all converging towards a 'modern lifestyle'. This view of cross-cultural buyer behaviour has three main assumptions: (1) modernity is a given and technology is our path to a bigger and better future for all of us on our little planet; (2) even if they differ externally, all societies can be placed on a continuum of social change – from traditional to developed societies; and (3) the criterion for placing a society on the continuum is its degree of resistance to the changes brought about by modernity (Sheth and Sethi, 1977). Firat (1995, p. 106) explains that in modern culture the central idea is that scientific knowledge and technology could control nature and improve human existence: 'thus, modern culture was a driven one with its eyes on the future and its feet securely planted on the material ground, in reality. Reaching the goals . . . required commitment, order, and universal, valid principles'. Even though it may be argued that we have already entered the postmodern era (Bouchet, 1994), most people world-wide still live in a modern era, marked by a strong belief in the achievements of science, its unlimited problem-solving capacity through technology and its exclusive contribution to global welfare. The modern project is clear in Levitt's view of globalization, when, criticizing multinational companies for being medieval (by which he means pre-modern), he writes:

The multinational corporation knows a lot about a great many countries and congenially adapts to *supposed* differences. It willingly accepts vestigial national differences, not questioning the possibility of their transformation, not recognizing how the world is ready to and eager for the benefit of *modernity*, especially when the *price is right*. The multinational corporation accommodating mode to visible national differences is *medieval*. (Levitt, 1983, p. 97; my emphasis.)

The controversial claim that the 'American way of life' would have universal appeal and extend progressively to backward nations is typical of the binary thinking of modern thought: past/future, traditional/modern, true/false, rational/emotional, etc. (Firat, 1995). In fact, the true globalization of consumption patterns would occur if the 'globalization route' ceased to be one-way: if world consumers are to become really global, US consumers will have to import genuine, unpasteurized, French *foie gras* or crude milk cheese which contain some innocent bacteria but which also have real taste and consistency. Similarly, French consumers will have to try peanut butter, Canadian women wear kimonos, and American males adopt Bavarian *lederhosen* as summer wear, if the route to globalization is to be less unidirectional.

The global values in modern culture emerge because consumers throughout the world inevitably have fairly similar responses, in terms of their way of life, to new technologies and product innovations. 'Modern' culture is characterized by: (1) an individualist orientation which is supported by the exercise of purchasing power as a manifestation of individual freedom; (2) a strong emphasis on material achievements and materialistic values, that is, a *doing/having* rather than a *being* orientation; (3) a strongly economic, 'commoditized' time; (4) a tendency to discard the past in favour of a future orientation, while expressing some frustration at not living in the present as much as one would like; and (5) a fairly high degree of utilitarianism. Household equipment, for instance, tends to individualize tasks and people are more and more freed from both the constraints and the pleasures of communal life, in a mostly urban environment where families are nuclear and the extended family separated by huge distances. An increased awareness of a clock-bound and universal time, at the expense of a local and nature-bound time, accompanies enthusiasm for innovation and change. Modern culture posits a strong future orientation as a mere imperative: consumers dispose quickly of machines and products that are still recent but already obsolete. Environmental concerns, although varying in degree, are typical of modern cultures since the deterioration of the earth's environment through increased levels of pollution and depletion of the ozone layer are common to many countries. Chan (1996) shows, for instance, that both Canadian and Hong Kong consumers are more and more interested in purchasing environmentally-friendly products. Although Germany, with its *grüne punkt*, still largely leads the movement, the interest in 'green' products is shared world-wide.

The emergence of a global 'modern' culture is often confused with the convergence of local cultures, leading to an incorrect description of the globalization phenomenon. A frequent mistake is to equate 'modern' with 'American': while it is true that the United States and American multinational companies have been literally the champions and heralds of modern culture in consumer goods (consumption fordism) and services, globalization is not simply the world-wide extension of the 'American way of life'. The imitation of solutions 'Made in the United States' results mostly from the borrowing of answers to challenges that were largely common world-wide. American society values a pioneer spirit and has less resistance to change and fewer social impediments than more traditional societies. When the Japanese, French or Chinese change, it is not as a result of any American pressure; rather, since these societies are less innovative in terms of social adaptation to technological developments, they borrow part of their responses from the United States, while often making them the scapegoats for the drawbacks of modernity. Modern culture, with both high individualism and structured time patterns, implies a kind of social organization centred on peer-age groups, limited to people of strictly the same age. Girls give up their Barbie dolls between 12 and 13 because it would be inappropriate to play with doll – even sophisticated ones – when they reach adolescence. Each age class increasingly has its own identity, its own way of doing things, and membership is signalled through consumption, and the values and behaviour shared transcend national borders.

The increased adoption of modern culture cross-nationally is erroneously interpreted as a sign of full convergence – and as testimony to the progressive disappearance of local cultures. Significant elements of local cultures are still intact and quite visible in the global landscape such as language, writing systems, religions and relational patterns. Cultural differences seem to matter little because they rarely appear as the key explanation for behaviour. However, local cultures allow a deeper understanding of consumption in particular contexts. Interpretation must be close to the local reality: for instance white wine, served chilled and drunk as an aperitif (as is common in the USA), is a widely different wine-drinking experience from red wine, drunk with a meal (the dominant southern European consumption pattern). Local cultures do not really disappear; rather, a new, common culture is superimposed on them. The very fact that the Japanese and the Chinese are not willing to change their ideographic writing system, which from a purely utilitarian perspective makes little sense, is proof of the very deep roots of local cultures.

5.4   LOCAL PRODUCTS AND CONSUMPTION EXPERIENCES

Not surprisingly, globalized fordist consumption has a striking preference for culture-free products and consumption situations. The new perspective on consumer behaviour centred on the cultural meaning of things (McCracken, 1986), despite its limited use in international marketing books, can, however, prove highly relevant. Applbaum and Jordt (1996) suggest the need to centre on things, on how they are used in context; they argue that it will provide more insights on the complex patterns of local consumer behaviour than the national character approach, which is based on a limited number of universal variables and the design of cultural ideal types (i.e. high versus low scores on common dimensions). They observe, for instance, the services for dating and arranged marriages in Japan and note that a Japanese wedding ceremony would be practically incomprehensible to a westerner, apart from the (now shared) appearance of diamond rings and white wedding dresses. They describe the *pro nakôdo*, a commercial go-between for marriage services as follows:

Through personal contacts – that is, not through advertising – a *pro nakôdo* is introduced to a young man or young woman interested in being set up for arranged marriage dates . . . The *pro nakôdo* association meets once a month to exchange information on new registrants. At the meeting each *pro nakôdo*'s new contribution will be photocopied and distributed among the other *pro nakôdo* . . . the *pro nakôdos* bring home and place in their loose-leaf notebooks between 100 and 200 new pages each month. At the end of five years, or on marriage, whichever comes first, a person's sheet is removed from the notebook. At the time of this study, the association had slightly more than 6,500 registered clients.

If consumer culture matters, then it is likely that consumers will invest more meaning in products and services that are more bound to cultural interpretation. The question is therefore: what is more culture free and what more culture bound, in terms of product and service categories on the one hand, and consumer behaviour on the other?

Culture-bound products

Culture bonds arise in a number of situations, some being related to the consumption situation, others being related to product attributes, that is, because of *peculiar qualities in the encounter between things and people*. The first aspect to check is whether a rich (or a poor) cultural context surrounds the product: shopping for it, buying it and/or consuming it and disposing of it. Furniture, for instance, will be more culture bound than consumer electronics, because there is most often a local style and a local manufacturing tradition for these items. Furniture may not only be bought, but also inherited or restored, which makes little sense for a hi-fi set. Consumer electronics, on the other hand, are a typical culture-free product category because they are technology based, low in cultural context and universally used. It comes as no surprise, therefore, that cross-national similarity of consumer behaviour is very high for consumer electronics (Dawar and Parker, 1994). However, consumer electronics are culture free among industrialized countries. In developing economies, as is shown in the case of China (see Box 5.2), colour TV sets are vested with symbolic values that are rooted in the local context.

Products will be more culture-bound the more closely they relate to elements of the *physical* environment which influence the local material culture, and which are linked to climate, density of population, housing, flora and fauna, etc. The absence of visible cattle rearing on most Japanese islands, except Hokkaido, distances Japanese people from dairy products. Japanese people find cheese, the most sophisticated dairy product, quite a strange kind of food; cheese conveys little meaning except that of its

BOX 5.2

Colour television as a life statement

Television has made tremendous inroads into Chinese homes over the last ten years: penetration rates are reaching 80 per cent in rural areas and 98 per cent in cities. Television, more than any other good, represents freedom from oppression in the 'new China', and breaking with the past by access to information, in a country that has traditionally been wary of foreign influence. Ownership of a TV set plays an important role in establishing one's financial image and projects an image of personal success. Chinese people indicate that owning a colour television is a prerequisite to marriage and some couples indicate that they are willing to wait two years to be able to afford the best possible TV (a Japanese one, often several times more expensive than a Chinese colour TV). One respondent said: 'Buying a Chinese TV will give my marriage a poor start. I must wait until I can buy a Japanese TV to project the right image to my friends.'

(Source: Adapted from Doran, 1997.)

foreignness. Culture bonds are strong for a product or service when there is much investment of consumers' cultural and national background and identity in consumption. Consuming then becomes, consciously or unconsciously, more than a simple utilitarian purchase, resulting in a preference for products made in one's own country. In terms of product attributes, the use of local materials and production processes, recipes and craft techniques will reinforce the perception of ethnicity when they are known as such by consumers. Language content is also a major constituent of the cultural content of a product, whether it is genuinely a cultural product such as records, soap operas, movie films, novels, etc., or for that part of all products which displays written language (packaging, brand name). The instructions for assembling IKEA kit furniture rely on pictures alone, thus avoiding the complexity of multiple-language explanations. Pictures prove advantageous for decreasing the degree of culture-boundedness because visual elements are more easily culture free than written linguistic materials.

Products that involve a relationship to others, in terms of displaying/showing or giving/sharing, are likely to be culture bound, precisely because this relationship is culturally coded. Conspicuous-consumption items, and more generally goods having a high sign value, are culture bound; although many luxury products appear in the form of global brands, the nature of their consumption is largely local, depending at the least on concepts of the self and others (Wong and Ahuvia, 1995). Products that have been consumed and that have been part of life experiences since childhood are often marked by locality. Peanut butter, for instance, is not a global product; it cannot be found in many countries and many American expatriates have difficulty obtaining it when they are assigned abroad (Usunier, 1998b).

'Complex products', such as movie films, are logically culture bound, because they need high interpretation activities and a knowledge of the local context in order for the film to be fully understood and enjoyed. One of the reasons for the limited global success of most movie films, except American ones, is that they rely on local cues which are not easily understood by different local audiences. Conversely, the success of American movie films is based on their weak contextuality, simplified characters, reliance on the universal appeal of violence, love, and wealth, and their simple moral dichotomy, where good struggles against evil.

The very nature of the product naturally has some influence on the level of universality of needs. Non-durables seem to appeal more to tastes, habits and customs; therefore they are more culture bound (Douglas and Urban, 1977). Empirical evidence (Peterson *et al.*, 1985) seems to suggest that industrial and high-technology products (for instance, computer hardware, machine tools and heavy equipment) are considered the most appropriate for global strategies, whereas clothing, confectionery, food and household cleaners are considered less appropriate. Therefore, one could easily believe that industrial products are typically culture free. However, this view is largely mistaken because the context in which they are used, and the functionalities sought, depend on culture.

The construction industry, for instance, is highly influenced by local cultural traditions as well as the attitude towards time (short-term versus long-term orientation) and therefore the trade-off between the price and durability of equipment. In Europe, the difference between national markets is considerable; for instance, the market estimate for clay water pipes is 460,000 tons/year in Germany, whereas it is only 11,000 tons/year in France. In fact, clay water pipes are more expensive (two or three times) than cast-iron pipes; however, their durability extends way beyond the lifetime of those who decide on the investment; they may last possibly one century, in some cases several centuries. The German local authorities and/or standard-setting bodies prefer a high investment cost/extended lifetime trade-off whereas the French seem to consider this as too costly and a lifetime of a century beyond significance for public decision-makers. Futhermore, the major player in France for this kind of water pipe, Pont-à-Mousson uses ductile cast iron, a solution it has promoted widely with the water utilities. Box 5.3 provides a further illustration of how benefits sought of equipment goods depend on local culture.

Local ways of doing are generally based on the local availability of certain substitute materials (wood, cement, stones, etc.) and certain craft traditions (e.g. masonry versus carpentry) or constraints (e.g. earthquakes), explaining the local dominance of particular technical solutions. For instance, the use of steel in bridges and urban freeways is much higher in Japan than it is in Europe where bridges are mostly built with reinforced concrete. Similarly wood is frequently used as a basic construction material for housing in the United States whereas it is quite marginal in western Europe except in Scandinavia. Gorman *et al.* (1996) discuss the case of the market for laminated house logs manufactured from kiln-dried lumber which have a similar appearance to traditional solid house logs but with enhanced performance characteristics. For the 622,000 feet of logs produced in the United States in 1994, the market was primarily a domestic one, with 81.7 per cent sold in the USA. Pacific Rim countries accounted for 11.9 per cent, almost as much as the US east coast with 12.8 per cent, but European sales accounted for only 6.4 per cent. Although it is not clear whether European needs were not covered by local manufacturing, it is likely that this low figure reflects local differences in the choice of materials for housing.

BOX 5.3

Time to blood . . .

Market data were gathered for blood analysis equipment in several European countries (Germany, France, Italy, Spain, the United Kingdom) in hospital labs. Doctors were asked to rate the importance of time to results, a reason for adopting automatic blood analysis equipment which allows speedier outcomes. Responses reflect different degree of preoccupation with time, Germans being the most concerned with short time to results (86 per cent of German labs mentioned this as a major factor in their buying decision), followed by the British (72 per cent), the French (67 per cent), the Spaniards (55 per cent) and the Italians (37 per cent). Thus, even for organizational purchasing, underlying cultural values are different.

A framework for unravelling the degree and the nature of culture bonds for products is to undertake a 'cultural biography' of the goods surveyed (Kopytoff, 1986). Drawing on the analogy with the life of a person, the biography of an object allows one to understand how it ultimately nests itself within a cultural milieu.

The biography of a car in Africa would reveal a wealth of cultural data: the way it was acquired, how and from whom the money was assembled to pay for it, the relationship of the seller to the buyer, the uses to which the car is regularly put, the identity of its most frequent passengers and of those who borrow it, the frequency of borrowing, the garages to which it is taken and the owner's relation to the mechanics, the movement of the car from hand to hand over the years, and in the end, when the car collapses, the final disposition of its remains. All of these details would reveal an entirely different biography from that of a middle-class American, or Navajo, or French peasant car. (Kopytoff, 1986, p. 67.)

Unique consumption experiences

Consumption is still largely a local reality. Far from being uniquely culture related, this local reality also reflects climate and customs, and the mere fact that much of our lives is still experienced, shared, perceived and interpreted with persons nearby who share the same kind of 'local knowledge' in the Geertzian sense (Geertz, 1983). Consumption experiences remain local while much global influence is integrated, in shared cultural meaning (McCracken, 1991). As noted by Applbaum and Jordt (1996, p. 207): 'Globalizing influences have bored intercultural tunnels around the world, but core meaning systems such as those wrapped up in the idea of the family, continue to differ significantly'. There are, for instance, still huge differences in the pattern of household expenditures across EU countries.[5] Consumers attribute meaning to products and services in context, especially what it means to desire, to search, to evaluate, to purchase, to consume, to share, to give, to spend money and to dispose of. Consumption experiences are full social facts in interaction with other players in the market game, manufacturers, distributors, salespeople and also other consumers. Two illustrations are given below.

Consumption as disposal

Consumption as disposal involves our views of the legitimate relationship to the environment, of nature to culture, what is clean or dirty and where the cleaning effort should be allocated, etc. Many consumption acts lead to the final destruction of the good, even in the case of consumer durables, when they are obsolete or out of order. Paper-based products are a good case in point: filters for drip-coffee machines are white in France and yellow-brown in Germany *(naturbraun)*, paper handkerchiefs are generally white in France and yellow-brown in Germany and toilet paper is generally pink or white in France and greyish in Germany. The Germans express their willingness to be environmentally friendly *(umweltfreundlich)* by purchasing paper-based products whose colour exhibits their genuinely 'recycled' nature, that is, not bleached with chlorine-based chemicals that are used to whiten the paper. The same holds true for German writing and copying paper which, because of its greyish and irregular appearance, would be considered by most French as 'dirty' and of poor quality. The difference in consumer experience lies in the difference of *continuity* in the ecological concern. Germans feel all the more strongly the necessity to be nearer to nature because they live in a country about three times more densely populated than France and they insist on strong coherence between their words and their deeds. The two peoples seem in any case to have different ways of combining and reconciling nature and culture: the contrast has often been made between German culture, natural, deep and aggressive, and sophisticated French civilization. German culture finds its expression in love for nature and a preference for isolation, whereas French culture advocates social life and shows disdain for everything which is too nature oriented (Gephart, 1990).

Offering wine

Offering wine is a different experience in southern Europe from what it is in the United States, Japan or northern Europe. Hosts who receive wine from their guests have to decide whether to keep it for themselves or to open it immediately to share it with their guests. In France, unless the host states explicitly that the wine is not suitable to accompany the meal, the wine received will be drunk with the guests, because sharing is a must and keeping the wine for oneself would imply that it may be not good enough to be drunk now. In many other countries, it would be impolite to drink their present with the guest, since it would mean destroying immediately a present that must kept as a memory, at least for a time. The emphasis in each case is on different values: the sense of sharing, on the one hand, the sense of keeping a present as a memory of the donor, on the other hand.

Habits, habitus and shared meaning

Rather than as a value system, culture may be viewed simply as shared habits and customs, and as shared meaning about how particular experiences are to be interpreted in context. This system of shared habits and interpretation is often encompassed under the general heading 'common sense' (shared meaning), which translates into

French as 'good sense' *(bon sens)* with a clear value judgement, or into German as 'sound understanding' *(gesunder Menschenverstand)*, showing that it is the appropriate solution. Habits are central in local consumer behaviour because they reduce the universe of ways of doing, enable people to form attitudes, to select interpretations or solutions as if they were self-evident. Habits facilitate choices in a multitude of everyday life situations, where it would be exhausting to review all possible alternatives. Habits give us self-assurance. However, they receive little treatment in accounts of consumer behaviour, probably because they are tainted negatively as passive behaviour.

A Chinese proverb says that 'habit starts with the first time', a western proverb that 'habit is a second nature'. To become fully built into a person, habits need support in rearing practices, schooling and education systems and the whole reward–sanction system that goes with the social game: habits are ways of doing and behaving that have been reinforced by authorization and gratification, so that, once the programming is forgotten they appear as legitimate. I illustrate this below with three examples taken from diverse contexts.

Kaffeetrinken

The German *Kaffeetrinken* is a traditional German form of enjoyment, organized mostly at week-ends or holiday afternoons with family or friends, at home or in a *Konditorei* (pastry shop serving coffee and tea) or a restaurant, at about three or four o'clock. The special relationship of Germans to coffee, sweets and cakes *(Kuchen)* has much to do with happy hours experienced since childhood when people relax in a somewhat tight society where pressure for conforming to rules is deeply internalized.

British fire safety systems

The United Kingdom is one of the largest markets for fire safety equipment in the world; fire alarms outside buildings are intended to attract people's attention quickly in case of fire. The wealth of fire safety instructions in both public and private buildings is striking for many foreigners. The tradition of wood used in buildings, and the Great Fire of London, are probably historical and objective reasons for this British phobia about fires. The United Kingdom logically follows the European norm EN52 on fire safety equipment, which, although compulsory, is not at present respected by the Italians and the Spaniards: not only would the implementation of this regulation in all public buildings involve massive investment that Italian and Spanish state budgets cannot afford, but also in Latin countries stone predominates over wood in construction and the anguish caused by building fires has traditionally been much lower than in the United Kingdom.

Drinking a beer

Individuals invest meaning in their consumption experiences: even if figures seem to demonstrate broad convergence, quantitative convergence in fact conceals huge qualitative divergence as far as experiences, context, perceptions and interpretations are concerned. More beer is indeed consumed in southern Europe than in the past, but the very experience of beer drinking still has a different meaning from that attributed to it in the north of Europe: the meaning differential has not yet diminished in the same proportion as the volume differential.

Shared situations, habits and stories around beer differ: the product is reincorporated in a universe of shared meaning which surfaces mainly in details, the shape and size of the beer glass, for instance. The Bavarian *Krug* (a large jar) does not give the same 'taste' to beer as the French *demi* (a quarter-litre stemmed glass) or the English pint glass. Beer differs in terms of bitterness, froth, bubbles, sweetness and alcoholic content. Most British beers are high-fermentation beers with a lower alcoholic content than beers on the Continent. To drink a beer in Germany has a different meaning from what it has in the United Kingdom or in France. In Germany, beer is consumed in a *Kneipe* (tavern) or bought from a *Getränkeshop* (a side-store to a supermarket entirely dedicated to beverages, a nice combination of German and English). Local beers play a dominant role in the German beer scene. In the region of Cologne, for instance, the *Kölsch* beers, some ten high-fermentation brands of beer, are seen as a reference to the place, a little like wines in France. German half-litre bottles, returnable ones, suit a densely populated country, where people are concerned with recycling glass. German beers always refer to the purity law *(Reinheitsgebot)* of 1516.

In a pub, in the British Isles, drinking a pint (0.57 litres) or half-pint of beer is a different experience; the pub is a comfortable place which invites people to stay as if they were at home. If people are to drink more than a single pint of beer, it must be low in alcohol. Much beer can be drunk without 'getting plastered', especially if one stays for quite a long period of time. A pub is a totally different world from the French *café-bar*, with its tiled floor and its rather cold interior design; in France regular customers invest the place with their own sense of comfort and human warmth and do not really need to have it materially invested in the place. But non-regular customers will never find in a *café-bar* the immediate comfort which they find in most British pubs.

This trip around European beer drinking could be completed with Finland where, until recently, only low-alcohol beer has been allowed to be sold in supermarkets. For the sale of standard beer, and also any other kind of alcoholic drink, the state chain Alko had a monopoly. Alko stores, still the dominant player on the market, have limited opening hours and are generally remote from central shopping areas. To buy beer (apart from the low-alcohol type) requires one to go to a taboo store; it openly manifests a leaning which the society disapproves of.

5.5   LOCAL CONSUMER CULTURES AND RESISTANCE TO CHANGE

The Danes dominate the world market for blue cheese with their Blue Castello, a decontextualized (Anglo-Italian name), pasteurized, inoffensive, white soft cheese, palatable for every mouth scared by germs of all sorts: a good candidate for promotion as a global product, a typical product of fordist consumption. The British Stilton, the French Roquefort, or the Italian Gorgonzola, all traditional blue cheeses, may be, in the long run, under threat from this global alternative. One may wonder therefore how much autonomy consumers have in pushing or limiting the movement towards globalization. Naturally, they may or may not buy globalized products and services – to this extent they 'vote with their feet'. But they also buy what is available in stores, astutely brought to them by sophisticated merchants. In this respect there could be some resistance to change, not at the level of the individual buying decision, but at more of a macro-level: people asking to have their 'way of life' protected, especially through some kind of protectionist measures. Also, people may consider that they lose from globalization as citizens and workers even though they win as consumers, leading to a preference for buying locally made products.

Whenever products may be global, there are strong arguments against the existence of a global consumer *per se*. As shown above, consumers' motivations do not easily globalize. Account managers working for large international advertising agencies face the complex task of managing a brand's images across several countries and accumulate detailed experience of consumers' responses to global product offering. Harold Clark (1987) of J. Walter Thompson argues that: (1) consumers are not 'global' themselves; (2) they are not aware of buying 'global' brands or products and they do not care whether the brand is available elsewhere in the world; and (3) consumers value personal and individual expression in their purchases; they will naturally let their individuality affect the values they place on the brands they buy. They contribute actively in this way to the *persona* of the brand in their own situation (Clark, 1987). Consumers always 'construct' the identity of brands, even for 'global products' and they do so on a local culture and identity base. 'Global brands' in this sense are portfolios of local marketing assets, federated under a common, lexically identical name. Although the Blue Castello builds on both an American referential (blue cheese dressing) and an Italian image, it is doubtful whether people in all countries have the same kind of buying motives, product use and product image. False 'global' consumers buy false 'global' products, which they re-invest with their own culture-bound motivations and purposes. This suggests that most of the resistance will be hidden from global marketers. Box 5.4 illustrates this point.

Will consumers resist the globalization process?

An implicit assumption about the globalization of consumption is that consumers are pleased with it because it means cheap, good-quality products and, therefore, they do not resist the process. They may, none the less, be self-contradicting individuals – for instance, drinking Coke while complaining about the Americanization of society. They might resist as citizens, voting for protectionist governments, or as consumer lobbyists, supporting public action (against fast food, for instance) in order to maintain or re-create entry barriers that protect local consumption. Globalization obviously has some drawbacks: some have denounced the de-humanizing process in post-fordist consumption, and the possible decrease in consumption diversity which may result from the progressive replacement of local consumption by globalized offerings (Ritzer, 1993). Others have wondered whether globalization is not going too far: the continual opening up of national markets through the WTO may result in increased worldwide competition across countries that have widely different levels of social security and therefore cannot compete on a fair basis. Globalization makes it more and more difficult to provide social insurance because it raises the cost of goods subject to globalized competition. Globalization would favour the consumer, not the worker, and raise complex issues when they are one single citizen.

'Globalization' is exposing a deep fault line between groups that have the skills and mobility to flourish in global markets and those who either don't have these advantages or perceive the expansion of unregulated markets as inimical to social stability and deeply held norms. The result is severe tension between the market and social groups such as workers, pensioners, and environmentalists, with government stuck in the middle. (Rodrik, 1997, p. 30.)

There are two different issues here. The first is knowing whether there are intellectual, ethical and practical reasons for protecting local cultures and consumers from the globalization of consumption patterns (Ger and Belk, 1996b). The second issue is whether resistance mechanisms to globalization actually occur at the individual and/or social level. Global marketing is often presented as a powerful tool for promoting economic development. It would enhance the needs and desires of badly treated consumers who live in sellers' economies. Marketing would then favour the creation of local industries to produce consumer goods and meet their demands. However, Belk (1988) describes a Third World consumer culture and emphasizes the hedonistic attraction for conspicuous consumption, even when basic utilitarian needs have not been met. Thus a growing body of literature, relating to marketing and economic development, emphasizes a marketing system which 'must design, deliver, and legitimate products and services that increase the material welfare of the population by promoting equity, justice and self reliance without causing injury to tradition' (Dholakia *et al.*, 1988, pp. 141–2). This means clearly resisting some of the uglier consequences of globalization, such as the problems caused by Nestlé infant formula in developing countries (see section 15.5). Global consumer culture encourages individuals to interpret their needs exclusively as utilitarian needs for commodities, but people may well have non-utilitarian needs to consume culture which is more tailored and localized (Sherry, 1987), especially when it is embedded in local items, both local cultural products and products whose consumption process is part of the genuine local culture.[6]

In the case of Turkey, Ger (1992) explains that satisfaction depends on social comparison and is not an immediate response. Most of the modern packaged goods mostly reach two groups of higher socio-economic status, representing respectively 1 per cent and 4 per cent of the Turkish population, whereas international products such as Coca-Cola target a larger audience by including the lower-middle class (46 per cent). She describes the positive and negative effects of marketing on socio-economic development, pointing out that increased dynamism, optimism, aspirations, communications, employment and demand for education are observed, whereas marketing 'accelerates the change in the set of value . . . Rapid transmission of the consumption culture from the core to the periphery has increased the desirability of both products and anything "Western"' (Ger, 1992, p. 329). The emulation of the West leads to resource allocation in gadgets and appliances at the expense of the satisfaction of more basic needs.

Preference for national products

It has persistently been demonstrated that in most developed countries domestic products generally enjoy a more favourable evaluation than foreign-made products. This strong preference for domestic products has been clearly evidenced for US, British,

BOX 5.4

Consumer resistance to McDonald's?

McDonald's is expanding in France, where there is cultural resistance against fast food and hamburgers, as a matter of national pride. Having first achieved great success with a limited number of successful 'luxury' (high end of the market) fast-food stores located in the centre of major towns in France, McDonald's is now expanding in suburbs and trying to offer breakfast service. Anti-fast-food consumer associations have resisted the fast-food movement, and nutrition specialists have shown that traditional French meals (based on diverse foods, lasting one hour) are much better for the digestion and prevent cancer of the digestive tract. Despite that McDonald's is quite popular with the young generation, especially children who will be tomorrow's adults and parents. Some outlets are located at motorway junctions in the suburbs.

McDonald's has been responsive to criticisms of nutritionists in the United States. It has reduced fat, salt and sugar in its products and introduced a lean Deluxe burger with only 10 grammes of fat and 310 calories against 20 grammes of fat and 410 calories for the Quarter Pounder. McDonald's has also been under attack from environmentalists, the plastic foam hamburger box being accused of generating pollution both in production and and on disposal (Ritzer, 1993). This packaging has been eliminated. In Northern Europe, McDonald's now insists on sorting its refuse so that it can be appropriately recycled. The company president in Sweden, Mats Lederhausen, has recently sent a letter to 500 Swedish politicians whose perception was that service jobs were not 'real' jobs, proposing to them that they spend one day working at a McDonald's outlet. Resisted or beloved, fast food is now an institution.

French, European in general, as well as Japanese consumers.[7] In the case of Finland, Finnish consumers deemed their products to be better on almost every attribute than those of seven other countries: United Kingdom, France, West Germany, Japan, Sweden, the Soviet Union and the United States (Darling and Kraft, 1977). Conversely, in developing countries, national products are not preferred to imported goods. Iranian producers, for instance, were shown to prefer imported products (Bon and Ollivier, 1979). In Iran, a product was favourably rated when it had a foreign/imported label. Bon and Ollivier did, however, observe the emergence of a deep-rooted nationalistic feeling in purchasing situations. They noted that there was at the time of their study no 'Buy Iranian' campaign in the style of state-sponsored advertising campaigns for the purchase of national products, such as occur regularly in European countries and the United States, or as are permanently undertaken in India. Despite that, some Iranian buyers had a nationalistic tendency which consisted of buying primarily local products. They perceived imported products as unfair competition to Iranian products and considered the success of foreign-made products a potential brake on the social and economic development of Iran. This attitude, however, did not seem to be very widespread. In eastern European countries similar images related to nationality and brand-name attitudes exist: for instance, the Hungarians generally evaluate foreign products more positively than domestic products, although their image of the latter is not particularly unfavourable (Papadopoulos *et al.*, 1990).

Different explanations have been proposed to explain this preference for national products, observed mostly in developed countries. Graby (1980b) suggests that unemployment appears to be a prime argument for the preference for French-origin purchases by French customers. She notes that high scores of agreement on buying French products as a way of maintaining employment should be interpreted cautiously because they pertain more to the prominence of the unemployment problem than to a true purchasing motive. In the same vein, an attempt has been made in the United States to measure 'consumer ethnocentrism'. Customers may consider the purchase of foreign goods to be immoral, since it puts the national economy at risk and leads to job losses. Shimp and Sharma (1987) studied the level of consumer ethnocentrism in different regions within the United States which were affected to a greater or lesser extent by foreign competition: Detroit, Denver, Los Angeles, North and South Carolina. They observed that consumer ethnocentrism was much stronger where the threat was perceived by individuals whose quality of life was affected by foreign competition, for instance in Detroit where unemployment in the automotive industry is adversely affected by Asian competition.

A related idea is that of 'consumer patriotism' (Han, 1988) which largely influences the outcome of 'Buy American', 'Buy British', 'Achetez français' or even 'Buy Canadian' campaigns (Kaynak and Cavusgil, 1983). Min Han claims that not only do patriotic consumers prefer to buy domestic products on the basis of strictly nationalistic feelings, but they also consider their quality and the service which accompanies them to be better. Han shows that for two different products/services, 'consumer patriotism' has contrasting effects: whereas it significantly influences the quality perception for motor cars, it does not affect the quality perception of vehicle maintenance and repair. In the case of television sets and their maintenance, the effect of consumer patriotism is non-existent.

'Buy national' campaigns should therefore be very cautious. The best approach to adopt would be to play clearly on nationalistic feelings, and not to attempt to influence consumers in their product evaluation. Consumers will probably remain fairly rational in their product evaluations; therefore an attempt to reinforce the quality perception of locally made products artificially could prove ineffective. Ettenson *et al.* (1988) investigated the effectiveness of 'Buy national' advertising campaigns with the case of a 'Made in the USA' campaign carried out for American clothing manufacturers. It was forecast that in 1995, 65 per cent of clothing sold in the United States would be cheap imported products. The CWPC (Crafted with Pride in the USA Council) provided a budget of $40 million that initially funded a series of television commercials showing American stars praising the superiority of American clothing. Consumers were subsequently questioned to determine the audience for and the effect of the campaign. They proved reluctant to reveal themselves to be unpatriotic. Furthermore, their attitudes towards domestic products failed to correspond with their purchasing behaviour. The results of the campaign were unconvincing: 'retailers who have adopted the "Made in the USA" theme are promoting their merchandise in terms of an attribute that may have relatively little effect on consumers' decision making . . . patriotic promotion campaigns should be considered circumspectly by retailers' (Ettenson *et al.*, 1988, p. 96). Johansson and Nebenzahl (1987) confirmed this result by showing that a campaign appealing to people to 'Buy American' had to be based on a normative influence (social norm favouring patriotic behaviour) as opposed to a cognitive influence (trying to convince the consumer that the national product is objectively superior).

5.6   EMERGENT PATTERNS OF A MIXED LOCAL/GLOBAL CONSUMER BEHAVIOUR

What emerges from the confrontation of global and local consumption is a complex pattern where the variety of consumption experiences reaches unprecedented levels. Global consumption patterns are reflected in local kaleidoscopes where myriad pieces of coloured glass are constantly rearranged in innumerable pictures.

Positioning the local *vis-à-vis* the global: patchworks and kaleidoscopes

As Firat, describing the postmodern existence, rightly observes, 'In an overwhelmingly marketized existence, individuals experience practically all aspects of their lives as consumers' (1995, p. 111). Whereas consumption was not always highly regarded in modern consumption, the postmodernist consumer pursues, with little afterthought, the construction of their self-image.[8]

Because the postmodern consumer experience is not one of committing to a single way of being, a single form of existence, the same consumers are willing to sample the different, fragmented artifacts. The consumer is ready to have Italian for lunch and Chinese for dinner, to wear Levi's 501 blue jeans for the outdoor party in the afternoon and to try the Gucci suit at night – changing not only diets and clothes but also the personas and selves that are to be (re)represented at each function. (Firat, 1995, p. 115.)

Whether people really change their selves so quickly may be discussed. However, they assemble extremely diverse consumption items in a very opportunistic, fragmented and idiosyncratic way, not hesitating to mix local products and ways with global products and services. There is high pragmatism in postmodern consumption, in particular because budgetary constraints are still highly meaningful. Fordist consumption items have their place in the patchwork: they offer good value and are often shrewdly advertised so that the potentially negative aspects of standard offerings on the consumer's self-image are largely erased. High-touch products and luxury brands play a complementary role, being the shiniest and most colourful pieces of the harlequin tights of postmodern consumption. Local products are also present: they make up the bulk of the patchwork with more discreet and less shiny pieces of fabric. As shown by Box 5.5, with my favourite example (beers), local products are candidates for promotion at a higher level of image in other countries where they are opportunistically re-interpreted, precisely because their foreignness allows it.

BOX 5.5

'European' beers

Typical of the diversity of the European brewing industry is how different brands in their segments are viewed from country to country. Brands, which do not have their origin in a country, which are 'foreign', are invariably viewed as premium segment products. A good example of this is BSN's Kronenbourg 1664, which is sold in France as an ordinary segment beer, but is viewed in almost all other (European) markets as a premium product. As an Italian brewer puts it: 'Foreign brands command a premium price for their image of higher quality.' However, potential hazards exist for brewers in pursuing this policy: 'In Great Britain, (Belgian) Stella Artois is a premium beer, one of the most expensive beers you can get there, and people buy it because it is expensive. It is marketed and promoted that way. The British are travelling people, so now when they come to Belgium, they discover that Stella Artois is a cheap beer. So they ask themselves if it is justified to pay so much for it in Great Britain' (French brewing manager).

(Source: Steele, 1991, p. 58.)

A process of creolization takes place whereby foreign goods are assigned new meanings and uses by the culture of reception, even when they are transferred to it without change. In this sense one can oppose the creolization paradigm, where attention focuses on the reception and domestication process of global goods in local contexts, to the Coca-colonization paradigm, where emphasis is on uniformity (Howes, 1996). A good example of such localization of consumption is Disneyland Tokyo, a perfect replica of the American model which is, however, completely Japanized, that is, fully reinvested by local cultural codes (for this see the lively accounts of Tokyo Disneyland by Van Maanen and Laurent (1992) and Brannen (1992)).

Central and peripheral consumption contexts

In the emergent consumption patterns, the consumption context is an important aspect of how consumers combine global 'fordist' goods and services, high-touch luxury brands and local items. Consumption contexts involve a certain space (i.e. certain rooms in a home), as well as particular time periods and people. A family dinner in a British dining-room or a ski vacation in the French Alps are consumption contexts. Djursaa and Kragh (1998) have studied the fragmented nature of globalization by distinguishing central and peripheral consumption contexts, based on in-depth, direct observation for two highly culture-bound product categories: furnishings and food. The consumption contexts of furnishings were Britain and Denmark, and the consumption contexts of food were three Arab cities: Riyadh, Jedda and Dubai. Centrality for food is defined in terms of time of the day when a meal is consumed whereas centrality in the case of furnishings is defined in spatial terms as the room where traditional cultural values are respected because this room carries a strong culture-bound meaning. British informants clearly expressed the dining-room as a central consumption context and, when presented with modernist furniture for dining-rooms, indicated that:

they would be OK for kitchens or breakfast rooms but not for 'proper' dining rooms, which for the majority of English respondents had to be traditional to carry the proper cultural message of identity. In Denmark, by contrast, modernism is the cultural norm and carries out notions of identity perfectly adequately in central rooms as well as in main homes. (Djursaa and Kragh, 1998.)

In peripheral consumption contexts, it is easier for a consumer to innovate, to borrow from foreign cultural contexts. Informants from the three Arab cities noted that dinner, a peripheral meal as opposed to lunch as the 'central' meal, was increasingly taken in fast-food outlets. A common pattern for Emiris is to go out for dinner at Pizza Hut, McDonald's or Harvey's which have compartments for male and female members of the family to eat together, separated from other guests. In the case of dinner taken at home, 'global products also play a very significant part in the meal; as one respondent says, "Dinner is pizza and Pepsi"' (Djursaa and Kragh, 1998).

Kaleidoscopic borrowing and the assemblage of local and global items is only possible if marketers are flexible enough to introduce some adaptations to their offerings, ignoring the Levittian (1983) criticism of adjustment to local ways. They have to target, in priority, peripheral consumption contexts for successfully introducing foreign products that are not rooted in the local culture. Borrowing is then progressive: McDonald's has started in many countries without being open at breakfast time as it is in the United States. It is now trying world-wide to introduce breakfast offerings which will result – in a fordist perspective – in increased efficiency in terms of covering overhead costs. To be really efficient, the fast-food formula needs a fairly constant demand pattern over a 14-hour period or more. In the USA, where people stop at a fast-food restaurant any time they are hungry, in order to 'refuel', demand peaks tend to be less severe than in Europe and most countries of the world where people eat at quite regular hours and spend more time, socializing while eating. McDonald's and other fast-food outlets have succeeded well in extending fordist consumption throughout the world because they have been pragmatically adaptive, partly tailoring their offering to local habits.

Complexity and ambivalence in globalized consumption patterns

Consumers constantly search for and create meaning because they need constantly to re-build their self-image. Consequently, their search for identity through consumption must be a key concern for marketers. In a globalized world, consumers, in their search for identity, can pick up products from two different shelves: one that favours the locality and the in-group orientation and another that displays desirable values, meanings and signs offered by foreign, out-group cultures. How consumers combine local and global meanings is complex. There is much ambivalence in the search for identity in a radically modern world where local diversity based on linguistic and religious differences will not disappear for centuries.

Globalized consumption has a threefold pattern. The first component is based on modernity and on fordist consumption; it corresponds to low-cost/fair-quality, weakly differentiated, utilitarian products, embedded in fairly low-context consumption experiences. Its highest potential for success is reached when products and consumption experiences are culture-free or consumption contexts peripheral. Examples range from the movie film *Titanic* to Camay soap. Families, because they often face stricter budgetary constraints than singles, are likely to be adept in modern fordist consumption. Despite appearances and discourse, fordist marketers show major adaptations and flexibility in facing local consumption. They display much more sensitivity to local ways than is described in textbooks. Their success is not ideological but pragmatic.

The second element is a postmodernist type of consumption: fragmented, continually re-assembled and re-interpreted; this can be particularly true for big brands, conspicuous consumption, younger people and yuppies. The third element corresponds to people who are aware that consumption is now a key driver for culture and that their choices as consumers will influence their culture. This radically modern type of person (in Ritzer's (1993) terms) behaves both opportunistically and critically, with a willingness to display diversity in consumption. For these consumers McDonald's is an ethnic, American restaurant.

In concluding this chapter, one may wonder why, in fact, companies should try to ignore local diversity. It is for them a superb opportunity for building competitive advantages, based on differentiation, which are easier to defend against competitors than low-cost advantages.

QUESTIONS

1. Take mineral water as a product example and outline how 'global' mineral waters such as Perrier or Evian can coexist with quite local ones.

2. Is there a 'modern' lifestyle, common to many cultures around the world? How could it be described? What could be its principal *raisons d'être*?

3. 'Dating' is a very curious concept for many people. In any case it cannot be fully translated into many languages and simply means 'making an appointment'. Share with US natives their view of what to 'date' means in context and compare this with other contexts, deomonstrating how the complex process of finding a partner for life can be commercialized in different cultures.

4. List some arguments and evidence which tend to show that globalization of consumption and lifestyles is under way. Outline the limitations and discuss the counterarguments.

5. To what extent are 'modern culture' and individualism primary inputs in the process of globalization of consumer preferences and lifestyles?

6. Discuss to what extent 'Buy national' advertising campaigns are efficient. What can they achieve? What can they not achieve?

7. The FDA (US Food and Drug Administration) prohibits the import of traditionally prepared French *foie gras*. FDA inspectors visit French *foie gras* laboratories and

refuse most of them the right to export to the United States since hygiene standards are not met. For the French too much antiseptic would kill the taste and for the Americans such unpasteurized products are dangerous to health. Discuss the difference in understanding of what 'good food' is.

8. Compare a global movie film (e.g. *Jaws* or *Titanic*) and a local movie film on a number of aspects: story, characters, situations, atmosphere, key appeals for the viewer (action, love, violence, etc.), combination of music and sound, rhythm, type of ending, etc. Explain why local films are most often not good candidates for reaching a global audience.

APPENDIX 5: TEACHING MATERIALS

A5.1 Case: Disneyland Paris

The Walt Disney corporation completed its first overseas theme park, Tokyo Disneyland, in 1984. In the following years the site proved to be a profitable operation: in its first year of operation more than 10 million people visited the park and the average expenditure per visitor proved to be almost 50 per cent more than expected. On the basis of this success, Disney considered expansion in Europe and decided in 1986 to start a park at Marnes-La-Vallée, near Paris; it opened in 1992. The European experience proved to be more difficult than the Japanese one, despite the seemingly smaller cultural distance.

In setting up its Japanese theme park, in 1984, Disney did not provide the financing itself and dealt mostly through franchising and licensing arrangements; by contrast, when it set up EuroDisney near Paris it took a 49 per cent stake. The Paris location was chosen after due consideration of alternative locations in neighbouring countries. The decision was made to transfer the basic successful Disneyland recipe to France, the same amusements, themes, and policy guidelines, including the no-alcohol policy. Minor adaptations were made such as waiting lines protected from the weather and more indoor shows, given the colder Paris climate.

However, while the project was under way, from 1986 to 1992, heavy criticism from the French called EuroDisney *'un Tchernobyl culturel'* (a cultural Chernobyl) invoking the risk of cultural invasion (although Mickey Mouse and other Disney cartoons have been very popular in France for over sixty years). On the other hand, parts of the French population were in favour of EuroDisney, including opinion leaders such as film star Yves Montand who declared: 'T-shirts, jeans, hamburgers – nobody imposes these things on us. We like them.' Disney tried to counter the nationalist reaction by explaining that Walt Disney was of French descent. Furthermore, they Europeanized the park by adding a Discoveryland based on the science fiction novels of Jules Verne, the nineteenth-century French author, and emphasizing European characters such as Pinocchio (Italian), Cinderella (French) and Peter Pan (British), as well as European history.

Disney made adaptations designed to combat nationalistic feelings. However, in at least two areas, cultural differences between the USA and Europe have been grossly underestimated: consumer behaviour and human resource management. Consumer behaviour as regards vacations is quite different in Continental Europe, where people frequently have six weeks' paid holidays in a year, compared with the USA where they tend to have only two weeks', often unpaid, holidays. This results in different attitudes: Europeans cannot spend masses of money per day on their vacations. They tend also to follow a pattern where one-week skiing holidays during the winter and three weeks at the beach in the summer is standard. As a result of extended vacation periods, European households have to control expenses, especially recreational expenses. As Milhomme emphasizes: 'In short the theme park is a short duration recreational means, with a high density spending pattern at the opposite of the recreational European pattern which aims at long duration recreational means with low density spending pattern.' (Milhomme, 1993, p. 94).

The French employees, highly individualist like most French people, had difficulties in accepting the strict Disney dress code. The prohibition of moustaches and beards was reported in the French press as an example of Disney curtailing employees' 'normal' individual freedom. Also the 'hire and fire' pattern was not easily accepted and French trade unions quickly acted to impose longer employment contracts.

During the first two years of operations, attendance was significantly under the target (10 million compared to 12 million visitors) and average spending per person was far lower than expected. The park admission fee was initially fixed at about $40 (FFr. 225) and $27 for a child. In 1993, it was decided to lower the price by one-third from FFr. 225 to FFr. 150.

EuroDisney accumulated heavy losses during 1993 and 1994. The American general manager was replaced by a French person. The share price dropped from about FFr. 100 in 1992 to FFr. 8 in September 1994. A package deal was devised, by which Disney waived royalties for the next five years and the banks granted very favourable debt-rescheduling conditions. At the end of 1994, despite a slow-down in the Paris Stock Exchange, the future of the Park seemed to look better, with the share reaching FFr. 11 ($2). In 1997 the shares fell to US$1, and the park has been renamed Disneyland Paris. Latterly, Disney seems to have swapped its initial short-term attitude towards its investment in Europe in favour of a more long-term stance.

(Source: Adapted from Daniels and Radebaugh (1991), Milhomme (1993) and the author's own information.)

QUESTIONS

1. Has the top management of Disney been culturally insensitive?

2. Comment in more detail on the issue of holiday regulations in Europe, the United States and Japan (duration, paid versus unpaid holiday) and their impact on leisure consumption.

3. Based on the accounts about Tokyo Disneyland by Van Maanen and Laurent (1992) and Brannen (1992) or other information, compare the Paris with the Tokyo experience. Which contrasts do you see in terms of culture resistance and creolization patterns?

A5.2   Case: IKEA

IKEA in the world

IKEA, the world's largest home furnishings retail chain, was founded in Sweden in 1943 as a mail-order company and opened its first showroom ten years later. From its headquarters in Almhult, IKEA has since expanded to world-wide sales of $2.6 billion from 83 outlets in 20 countries (see Table 5.1). In fact, the second store that IKEA built was in Oslo, Norway. Today, IKEA operates large warehouse showrooms in Sweden, Norway, Denmark, Holland, France, Belgium, West Germany, Switzerland, Austria, Canada, the United States, Saudi Arabia, and the United Kingdom. It has smaller stores in Kuwait, Australia, Hong Kong, Singapore, the Canary Islands, and Iceland. A store near Budapest was expected to open by 1990, with others to follow in Poland and Yugoslavia. Even the Soviet Union is not considered out of bounds.

The international expansion of IKEA has progressed in three phases, all of them continuing at the present time: Scandinavian expansion, begun in 1963, West European expansion, begun in 1973; and North American expansion, begun in 1974. Of the individual markets, West Germany is the largest, accounting for 30 per cent of company sales. The phases of expansion are detectable in the world-wide sales shares depicted in Figure 5.2. 'We want to bring the IKEA concept to as many people as possible,' IKEA officials have said.

The IKEA concept

Ingvar Kamprad, the founder, formulated as IKEA's mission to 'offer a wide variety of home furnishings of good design and function at prices so low that the majority of people can afford to buy them.' The principal target market of IKEA, which is similar across countries and regions in which IKEA has a presence, is composed of people who are young, highly educated, liberal in their cultural values, white-collar workers, and especially concerned with status symbols.

TABLE 5.1   IKEA's international expansion

Year	Outlets	Countries	Coworkers	Catalog circulation	Turnover in Swedish crowns
1954	1	1	15	285,000	3,000,000
1964	2	2	250	1,200,000	79,000,000
1974	10	5	1,500	13,000,000	616,000,000
1984	66	17	8,300	45,000,000	6,770,000,000
1988	75 (83[a])	19 (20[a])	13,400[b]	50,535,000[c]	14,500,000,000[d]

Source: *IKEA Facts, 88/89.*

[a]Stores/countries being opened by the end of 1990.
[b]13,400 coworkers are equivalent to 10,700 full-time workers.
[c]14 languages, 27 editions.
[d]Corresponding to net sales of the IKEA group of companies.

IKEA follows a standardized product strategy with an identical assortment around the world. Today, IKEA carries an assortment of 12,000 different home furnishings that range from plants to pots, sofas to soup spoons, and wine glasses to wallpaper. The smaller items are carried to complement the bigger ones. IKEA does not have its own manufacturing facilities but designs all of its furniture. The network of subcontracted manufacturers numbers nearly 1,500 in 50 different countries. IKEA shoppers have to become 'prosumers' – half producers, half consumers – because most products must be assembled.

Manufacturers are responsible for shipping the components to large warehouses, for example, to the central one in Almhult. These warehouses then supply the various stores which are in effect mini warehouses. The final distribution is the customer's responsibility. IKEA does cooperate with car-rental companies to offer vans and small trucks at reasonable rates for customers needing delivery service.

Although IKEA has concentrated on company-owned, larger scale outlets, franchising has been used in areas in which the market is relatively small or where uncertainty may exist as to the response to the IKEA concept. IKEA uses mail order in Europe and Canada but has resisted expansion into it in the United States, mainly because of capacity constraints.

IKEA offers prices that are 30 to 50 percent lower than fully assembled competing products. This is a result of large-quantity purchasing, low-cost logistics, store location in suburban areas, and the do-it-yourself approach to marketing. IKEA's prices do vary from market to market, largely because of fluctuations in exchange rates and differences in taxation regimes, but price positioning is kept as standardized as possible.

IKEA's promotion is centered on the catalog. The IKEA catalog is printed in 14 languages and has a world-wide circulation of over 50 million copies (see Table 5.1). The catalogs are uniform in layout except for minor regional differences. The company's advertising goal is to generate word-of-mouth publicity through innovative approaches.

Local store managers have substantial leeway in promotional decision making (for example, in choosing an advertising agency) but have to adhere to certain guidelines to ensure a universal image.

The IKEA concept is summarized in Table 5.2.

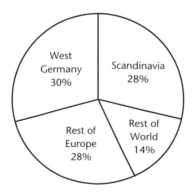

FIGURE 5.2   IKEA world-wide sales expressed as percentage of turnover.

TABLE 5.2   The IKEA concept

Target market:	'Young people of all ages'
Product:	IKEA offers the same products world-wide. The countries of origin of these products are: Scandinavia (52 percent), Western Europe (21 percent), Eastern Europe (20 percent), and others (7 percent). Most items have to be assembled by the customer. The furniture design is modern and light. Textiles and pastels.
Distribution:	IKEA has built its own distribution network. Outlets are outside the city limits of major metropolitan areas. Products are not delivered but IKEA cooperates with car rental companies that offer small trucks. IKEA offers mail order in Europe and Canada.
Pricing:	The IKEA concept is based on low price. The firm tries to keep its price image constant.
Promotion:	IKEA's promotional efforts are mainly through its catalogs. IKEA has developed a prototype communications model that must be followed by all stores. Its advertising is attention getting and provocative. Media choices vary by market.

IKEA in the competitive environment

IKEA's strategic positioning is unique. As Figure 5.3 illustrates, few furniture retailers anywhere have engaged in long-term planning or achieved scale economies in production. European furniture retailers, especially those in Sweden, Switzerland, West Germany, and Austria, are much smaller than IKEA. Even when companies have joined forces as buying groups, their heterogeneous operations have made it difficult

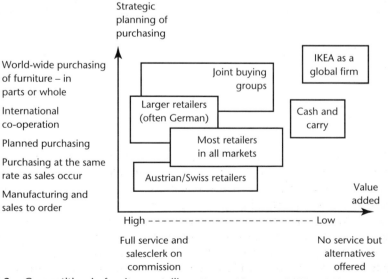

FIGURE 5.3   Competition in furniture retailing. (Source: Martenson, 1987, p. 14.)

for them to achieve the same degree of coordination and concentration as IKEA. Because customers are usually content to wait for the delivery of furniture, retailers have not been forced to take purchasing risks.

The value-added dimension differentiates IKEA from its competition. IKEA offers no customer assistance but creates opportunities for consumers to choose transport, and assemble units of furniture. The best summary of the competitive situation was provided by a manager at another firm: 'We can't do what IKEA does, and IKEA doesn't want to do what we do.'

IKEA in the United States

After careful study and assessment of its Canadian experience, IKEA decided to enter the US market in 1985 by establishing outlets on the East Coast. IKEA's three stores (Philadelphia, Woodbridge near Washington, D.C., and Baltimore) generated $93 million in 1988. The overwhelming level of success in 1987 led the company to invest in a warehousing facility near Philadelphia that receives goods from Sweden. Plans call for 60 additional stores over the next 25 years with only gradual expansion to the West Coast.

(Source: Czinkota and Ronkainen, 1990, pp. 203–7.)

QUESTIONS

1. Which features of the 'young people of all ages' are universal and can be exploited by a global/regional marketing strategy? How would you analyze them in terms of consumer behaviour?

2. What accounts for IKEA's success with a standardized product and marketing strategy in a business which is usually described as having some of the strongest cultural influences (styles of furniture, household items and, more generally, lifestyles at home are culture bound)? Consider, for instance, that an American buying IKEA beds will also have to buy IKEA sheets because the beds are in European sizes.

3. Is IKEA destined to succeed everywhere it cares to establish itself? What are the possible limitations of the IKEA concept?

A5.3 Case: Parker Pen

Parker Pen Company

Parker Pen Company, the manufacturer of writing instruments based in Janesville, Wisconsin, is one of the world's best known companies in its field. It sold its products in 154 countries and considered itself number one in 'quality writing instruments', a market that consists of pens selling for $3 or more.

In early 1984, the company launched a global marketing campaign in which everything was to have 'one look, one voice,' and with all planning to take place at headquarters. Everything connected with the selling effort was to be standardized. This was a grand experiment of a widely debated concept. A number of international companies were eager to learn from Parker's experiences.

Results became evident quickly. In February 1985, the globalization experiment was ended, and most of the masterminds of the strategy either left the company or were fired. In January 1986, the writing division of Parker Pen was sold for $100 million to a group of Parker's international managers and a London venture-capital company. The US division was given a year to fix its operation or close.

Globalization

Globalization is a business initiative based on the conviction that the world is becoming more homogeneous and that distinctions between national markets are not only fading but, for some products, they will eventually disappear. Some products, such as Coca-Cola and Levi's, have already proven the existence of universal appeal. Coke's 'one sight, one sound, one sell' approach is a legend in the world of global marketers. Other companies have some products that can be 'world products,' and some that cannot and should not be. For example, if cultural and competitive differences are less important than their similarities, a single advertising approach can exploit these similarities to stimulate sales everywhere, and at far lower cost than if campaigns were developed for each individual market.

Compared to the multidomestic approach, globalization differs in these three basic ways:

1. The global approach looks for similarities between markets. The multidomestic approach ignores similarities.

2. The global approach actively seeks homogeneity in products, image, marketing, and advertising message. The multidomestic approach produces unnecessary differences from market to market.

3. The global approach asks, 'Should this product or process be for world consumption? The multidomestic approach, relying solely on local autonomy, never asks the question.

Globalization requires many internal modifications as well. Changes in philosophy concerning local autonomy, concern for local operating results rather than corporate performance, local strategies designed for local – rather than global – competitors, are all delicate issues to be solved. By design, globalization calls for centralized decision making; therefore, the 'not invented here' syndrome becomes a problem. This can be solved by involving those having to implement the globalization strategy at every possible stage as well as keeping lines of communication open.

Globalization at Parker Pen Company

In January 1982, James R. Peterson became the president and CEO of Parker Pen. At that time, the company was struggling, and global marketing was one of the key measures to be used to revive the company. While at R. J. Reynolds, Peterson had been impressed with the industry's success with globalization. He wanted for Parker Pen nothing less than the writing-instrument equivalent of the Marlboro man.

For most of the 1960s and 1970s, a weak dollar had lulled Parker Pen into a false sense of security. About 80 percent of the company's sales were abroad, which meant that when local-currency profits were translated into dollars, big profits were recorded.

The market was changing, however. The Japanese had started marketing inexpensive disposable pens with considerable success through mass marketers. Brands such as Paper Mate, Bic, Pilot and Pentel each had greater sales, causing Parker's overall market share to plummet to 6 percent. Parker Pen, meanwhile, stayed with its previous strategy and continued marketing its top-of-the-line pens through department stores and stationery stores. Even in this segment Parker Pen's market share was eroding because of the efforts of A. T. Cross Company and Montblanc of West Germany.

Subsidiaries enjoyed a high degree of autonomy in marketing operations, which resulted in broad and diverse product lines and 40 different advertising agencies handling the Parker Pen account worldwide.

When the dollar's value skyrocketed in the 1980s, Parker's profits plunged and the loss of market share became painfully evident.

Peterson moved quickly upon his arrival. He trimmed the payroll, chopped the product line to 100 (from 500), consolidated manufacturing operations, and ordered an overhaul of the main plant to make it a state-of-the-art facility. Ogilvy & Mather was hired to take sole control of Parker Pen advertising worldwide. (Among the many agencies terminated was Lowe Howard-Spink in London, which had produced some of the best advertising for Parker Pen's most profitable subsidiary.)

A decision was also made to go aggressively after the low end of the market. The company would sell an upscale line called Premier, mainly as a positioning device. The biggest profits were to come from a rollerball pen called Vector, selling for $2.98. Plans were drawn to sell an even cheaper pen called Itala – a disposable pen never thought possible at Parker.

Three new managers, to be known as Group Marketing, were brought in. All three had extensive marketing experience, most of it in international markets. Richard Swart, who became marketing vice president for writing instruments, had handled 3M's image advertising worldwide and taught company managers the ins and outs of marketing planning. Jack Marks became head of writing instruments advertising. At Gillette he had orchestrated the worldwide marketing of Silkience hair-care products. Carlos Del Nero, brought in to be Parker's manager of global-marketing planning, had broad international experience at Fisher-Price. The concept of marketing by centralized direction was approved.

The idea of selling pens the same way everywhere did not sit well with many Parker subsidiaries and distributors. Pens were indeed the same, but markets, they believed, were different: France and Italy fancied expensive fountain pens; Scandinavia was a ballpoint market. In some markets, Parker could assume an above-the-fray stance; in others it had to get into the trenches and compete on price. Nonetheless, headquarters communicated to them all:

Advertising for Parker Pens (no matter model or mode) will be based on a common creative strategy and positioning. The worldwide advertising theme, 'Make Your Mark with Parker', has been adopted. It will utilize similar graphic layout and photography. It will utilize an agreed-upon typeface. It will utilize the approved Parker logo/design. It will be adapted from centrally supplied materials.

Swart insisted that the directives were to be used only as 'starting points' and that they allowed for ample local flexibility. The subsidiaries perceived them differently. The UK subsidiary, especially, fought the scheme all the way. Ogilvy & Mather

London strongly opposed the 'one world, one brand, one advertisement' dictum. Conflict arose, with Swart allegedly shouting at one of the meetings: 'Yours is not to reason why; yours to implement.' Local flexibility in advertising was out of the question.

The London-created 'Make Your Mark' campaign was launched in October 1984. Except for language, it was essentially the same: long copy, horizontal layout, illustrations in precisely the same place, the Parker logo at the bottom, and the tag line or local equivalent in the lower right-hand corner. Swart once went to the extreme of suggesting that Parker ads avoid long copy and use just one big picture.

Problems arose on the manufacturing side. The new $15 million plant broke down repeatedly. Costs soared and the factory turned out defective products in unacceptable numbers. In addition, the new marketing approach started causing problems as well. Although Parker never abandoned its high-end position in foreign markets, its concentration on low-price, mass-distribution products in the United States caused dilution of its image and ultimately losses of $22 million in 1985. Conflict was evident internally and the board of directors began to turn against the concept of globalization.

In January 1985, Peterson resigned. Del Nero left the company in April. Swart was fired in May, Marks in June.

(Source: This case was prepared for discussion purposes and not to exemplify correct or incorrect decision making, in Czinkota and Ronkainen, 1990, pp. 778–82.)

QUESTIONS

1. What marketing miscalculations were made by the advocates of the globalization effort at Parker Pen? (You should think in terms of product policy, target segments and competitive forces.)

2. Was the globalization strategy sound for writing instruments? If yes, what was wrong in the implementation? If not, why not?

3. Should the merits of global marketing be judged by what happened at Parker Pen Company?

NOTES

1. In their book entitled *Consuming Geographies*, Bell and Valentine (1997) explain how food consumption is understood at different levels, body–home–community–region–nation–global, and how culinary cultures map across space, with discourses and food practices being developed simultaneously at different levels.

2. Such a distinction is now abandoned in comparative management (Usunier, 1998a).

3. Clements and Chen study very broad consumption categories (food, clothing, housing, durables, medicine, transport, recreation, and 'other'), comparing the OECD countries and a group of less-developed countries (LDC). Income elasticities are fairly similar across groups of countries and consumption categories except for transport and food (broadly confirming Engel's law that food as a percentage of total budget decreases with increases in income). Differences in price elasticities are significant only for clothing and transport across the two groups, OECD and LDC. In its highly macroscopic approach, this article offers spurious support to the 'homogeneity of tastes' thesis which the authors partly acknowledge (p.750),

stating that 'first, we are only dealing with commodities that are broad aggregates and it might be reasonable to expect more idiosyncrasy and heterogeneity for goods which are more narrowly defined. Second, the analysis deals with *groups* of countries, rather than individual countries (let alone individual consumers), and, again heterogeneity may rise as the unit of analysis becomes smaller.' That is precisely what makes the huge difference between marketing and economics.

4.   In France, one of the few countries (with Japan and India) where the local film industry is still active, the market share of American movie films is generally between 55 and 60 per cent. In many countries of the world, with relatively small populations and their own language, the cost of making local movies is difficult to amortize on the basis of local audiences alone. Adding subtitles or dubbing foreign movie films is considerably less expensive. This explains why in many countries, for instance Scandinavian countries, the market share of American films is 90 per cent or more.

5.   Despite convergence, it is easy to find much evidence of remaining differences; see for instance *Euromonitor* (1997), or the special issue of the *International Journal of Research in Marketing* edited by Leeflang and Van Raaij (1995). The percentages spent by households in various EU countries on food in general, on vegetables, chocolate or cheese still widely differ. See also section 6.4.

6.   Sherry (1987, p. 189) states the culturally respectful marketing strategy as follows: 'the guiding rule of such a marketing strategy, as in any ethically invasive procedure, is *primum non nocere*: first do not harm. In the rush to globalization, the preservation of local culture has been considered primarily as an opportunity cost. If cultural integrity is epiphenomenal to business practice, splendid; if not, social disorganization is frequently the cost of progress.'

7.   Reierson, 1966; Gaedeke, 1973; Lillis and Narayana, 1974; Baumgartner and Jolibert, 1977; Morello, 1984; Heslop *et al.*, 1987. The preference for nationally made products in industrialized countries has been corroborated by several other studies (Nagashima, 1977 in the case of Japan; Bannister and Saunders, 1978, in the case of the UK; Graby, 1980a and 1980b, in the case of France; Cattin *et al.*, 1982, in the case of France and the United States. See also Samiee (1994). Schweiger *et al.* (1995) show that European consumers have a better evaluation of their domestic products ('Made in Europe') than products originating from both the United States and Japan on a wide range of items. See also section 10.2.

8.   For more about the postmodern consumer see Bouchet (1994).

REFERENCES

Applbaum, Kalman and Ingrid Jordt (1996), 'Notes toward an application of McCracken's "cultural categories" for cross-cultural consumer research', *Journal of Consumer Research*, vol. 23 (December), pp. 204–18.

Bannister, J. P. and J. A. Saunders (1978), 'UK consumers' attitudes toward imports: the measurement of national stereotype image', *European Journal of Marketing*, vol. 12, no. 8, pp. 562–70.

Bartlett, Christopher (1983), 'Procter & Gamble Europe: Vizir launch', *Harvard Business School Case* 9-384-139.

Baumgartner, Gary and Alain Jolibert (1977), 'The perception of foreign products in France', *Advances in Consumer Research*, vol. 16, pp. 103–5.

Belk, Russel W. (1988), 'Third World consumer culture', in E. Kumçu and A. Fuat Firat (eds.), *Marketing and Development: Toward broader dimensions*, JAI Press: Greenwich, CT, pp. 103–27.

Bell, David and Gill Valentine (1997), *Consuming Geographies*, London: Routledge.

Bon, Jérôme and Alain Ollivier (1979), 'L'influence de l'origine d'un produit sur son image à l'étranger', *Revue Française du Marketing*, 1979/2, Cahier 77, pp. 101–14.

Bouchet, Dominique (1994), 'Rails without ties: The social imaginary and postmodern culture: Can postmodern consumption replace modern questioning? *International Journal of Research in Marketing*, vol. 11, no. 4, pp. 405–22.

Brannen, Mary Yoko (1992), '"Bwana Mickey": Constructing cultural consumption at Tokyo Disneyland' in Jospeh J. Tobin (ed.), *Re-made In Japan*, New Haven: CT: Yale University Press, pp. 216–34.

Cattin, Philippe, Alain Jolibert and Colleen Lohnes (1982), 'A cross-cultural study of "made-in" concepts', *Journal of International Business Studies*, Winter, pp. 131–41.

Chan, T. S. (1996), 'Concerns for environmental issues and consumer purchase preferences: A two-country study', *Journal of International Consumer Marketing*, vol. 9, no. 1, pp. 43–55.

Clark, Harold F., Jr (1987), 'Consumer and corporate values: Yet another view on global marketing', *International Journal of Advertising*, vol. 6, pp. 29–42.

Clements, Kenneth W. and Dongling Chen (1996), 'Fundamental similarities in consumer behaviour', *Applied Economics*, vol. 28, no. 6, pp. 747–57.

Collins Dictionary and Thesaurus (1990), William T. McLeod (ed.), William Collins Sons & Co Ltd: Glasgow.

Czinkota, Michael R. and Illka A. Ronkainen (1990), *International Marketing*, 2nd edn, Dryden Press: Hinsdale, IL.

Czinkota, Michael R. and Illka A. Ronkainen (1995), 'Global Marketing 2000: A marketing survival guide', in Michael R. Czinkota and Illka A. Ronkainen (eds.), *Readings in Global Marketing*, Dryden Press: Hinsdale, IL.

Daniels, John D. and Lee H. Radebaugh (1991), 'Disneyland Abroad' in *International Business: Environments and Operations*, 6th edn, Reading, Mass.: Addison Wesley, pp. 31–3.

Darling, John B. and F. Kraft (1977), 'A competitive profile of products and associated marketing practices of selected European and non-European countries', *European Journal of Marketing*, vol 11, no. 7, pp. 519–37.

Dawar, Niraj and Philip M. Parker (1994), 'Marketing universals: Consumers' use of brand name, price, physical appearance, and retailer reputation as signals of product quality', *Journal of Marketing*, vol. 58, no. 2, pp. 81–95.

Dholakia, Ruby Roy, Mohammed Sharif and Labdhi Bhandari (1988), 'Consumption in the Third World: Challenges for marketing and economic development', in E. Kumçu and A. Fuat Firat (eds.), *Marketing and Development: Toward broader dimensions*, JAI Press: Greenwich, CT, pp. 129–47.

Djursaa, Malene and Simon Ulrik Kragh (1998), 'Central and peripheral consumption contexts: The uneven globalization of consumer behaviour', *International Business Review*, vol. 7, no. 1.

Doran, Kathleen Brewer (1997), 'Symbolic consumption in China: The color television as a life statement', in Merrie Brucks and Debbie McInnis (eds.), *Advances in Consumer Research*, vol. 24, Provo, UT: Association for consumer research, pp. 128–131.

Douglas, Susan P. and Christine D. Urban (1977), 'Life-style analysis to profile women in international markets', *Journal of Marketing*, vol. 41, no. 3 (July), pp. 46–54.

Eshghi, Abdolezra and Jagdish N. Sheth (1985), 'The globalization of consumption patterns: An empirical investigation', in Erdener Kaynak (ed.), *Global Perspectives in Marketing*, Praeger: New York, pp. 133–48.

Ettenson, R., J. Wagner and G. Gaeth (1988), 'Evaluating the effect of country-of-origin and the 'Made in the USA' campaign: A conjoint approach', *Journal of Retailing*, vol. 64, no. 1, pp. 85–100.

Euromonitor (1997), 'Market report Japan: Savoury snacks', Market Research International, December, vol. XXXVIII, pp. 111–3.

Firat, A. Fuat (1995), 'Consumer culture or culture consumed?', in Janeen Arnold Costa and Gary J. Bamossy (eds.), *Marketing in a Multicultural World*, Sage: Thousand Oaks, CA, pp. 105–25.

Gaedeke, Ralph (1973), 'Consumer attitudes towards products "made in" developing countries', *Journal of Retailing*, vol. 49 (Summer), pp. 13–24.

Geertz, Clifford (1983), *Local Knowledge*, Basic Books: New York.

Gephart, Werner (1990), 'Nature-environnement', in Jacques Leenhardt and Robert Picht (eds.), *Au Jardin des Malentendus, le Commerce Franco-Allemand des Idées*, Arles: Actes Sud, pp. 353–5.

Ger, Guliz (1992), 'The positive and negative effects of marketing on socioeconomic development', *Journal of Consumer Policy*, vol. 15, pp. 229–254.

Ger, Guliz and Russell W. Belk (1996), 'I'd like to buy the world a Coke: Consumptionscapes of the "less affluent world"', *Journal of Consumer Policy*, vol. 19, no. 3, pp. 271–305.

Gorman, Thomas M., Craig M. Hamanishi, and John R. Callison (1996), 'The laminated log industry: An overview of production and distribution', *Forest Products Journal*, vol. 46, no. 3, March, pp. 80–2.

Graby, Françoise (1980a), 'Consumérisme et produits étrangers' *Coopération-Distribution-Consommation*, no. 5, pp. 17–23.

Graby, Françoise (1980b), 'Le consommateur français et les produits étrangers' *Coopération-Distribution-Consommation*, no. 5, pp. 31–40.

Han, C. Min (1988), 'The role of consumer patriotism in the choice of domestic versus foreign products', *Journal of Advertising Research*, June–July, pp. 25–32.

Heslop, L., N. Papadopoulos, G. Avlonitis, G. Bamossy, J. Beracs, F. Bliemel, F. Graby, G. Hampton and P. Malliaris (1987), in Leeflang and Rice (eds.), 'A cross-national study of consumer views about domestic versus imported products', proceedings of the European Marketing Academy Conference, Toronto.

Howes, David (1996), 'Commodities and cultural borders', in David Howes (ed.), *Cross-cultural Consumption*, London: Routledge, pp. 1–18.

Huszagh, Sandra M., Richard J. Fox and Ellen Day (1986), 'Global marketing: An empirical investigation', *Columbia Journal of World Business*, vol. XX, no. 4, pp. 31–43.

Jain, Subhash C. (1989), 'Standardization of international marketing strategy: Some research hypotheses', *Journal of Marketing*, vol. 53, January, pp. 70–9.

Johansson, Johny K. and Israel D. Nebenzahl (1987), 'Country-of-origin, social norms and behavioral intentions', in S. Tamer Cavusgil (ed.), *Advances in International Marketing*, vol 2, JAI Press: Greenwich, CT, pp. 65–79.

Kaynak, Erdener and S. Tamer Cavusgil (1983), 'Consumer attitudes towards products of foreign origin: Do they vary across product classes?', *International Journal of Advertising*, vol. 2 (April–June), pp. 147–57.

Kopytoff, Igor (1986), 'The cultural biography of things: Commoditization as process', in Arjun Appadurai editor, *The Social Life of Things, Commodities in Cultural Perspective*, Cambridge, Cambridge University Press, pp. 64–91.

Leeflang, Peter S. H. and W. Fred Van Raaij (1995), 'The changing consumer in the European Union: A "meta-analysis"', *International Journal of Research in Marketing*, vol. 12, pp. 373–87.

Levitt, Theodore (1983), 'The globalization of markets', *Harvard Business Review*, vol. 61 (May–June), pp. 92–102.

Lillis, Charles M. and Chem L. Narayana (1974), 'Analysis of "made in" product images: An exploratory study', *Journal of International Business Studies* (Spring), pp. 119–27.

McCracken, Grant (1986), 'Culture and consumption : A theoretical account of the structure and movement of the cultural meaning of consumer goods', *Journal of Consumer Research*, vol. 13 (June), pp. 71–84.

McCracken, Grant (1991), 'Culture and consumer behaviour: An anthropological perspective', *Journal of the Market Research Society*, vol. 32, no. 1, pp. 3–11.

Martenson, Rita (1987), 'Is standardization of marketing feasible in culture-bound industries? A European case study', *International Marketing Review*, vol. 4 (Autumn), p. 14.

Milhomme, Albert J. (1993), 'Customized or global, the strategy may not work at Euro Disney' in Tom K. Massey, Jr. (ed.), *Marketing: Satisfying a diverse customerplace*, Proceedings of the Southern Marketing Association, New-Orleans, Louisiana, November, pp. 91–4.

Morello, G. (1984), 'The made-in issue: A comparative research on the image of domestic and foreign products', *European Research*, vol. 5, no. 21, pp. 68–74.

Nagashima, Akira (1977), 'A comparative "made in" product image survey among Japanese businessmen', *Journal of Marketing* (July), pp. 95–100.

Papadopoulos, Nicolas, Louise A. Heslop and Jozsef Beracs (1990), 'National stereotypes and product evaluations in a socialist country', *International Marketing Review*, vol. 7, no. 1, pp. 32–47.

Peterson, Blyth, Cato Associates Inc. and Cheskin Masten (1985), 'Survey on global brands and global marketing', Empirical Report, New York.

Porter, Michael E. (1986), 'Changing patterns of international competition', *California Management Review*, vol XXVIII, no. 2, pp. 9–39.

Reierson, Curtis (1966), 'Are foreign products seen as national stereotypes?', *Journal of Retailing*, Fall, pp. 33–40.

Ricardo, David (1817), *On the Principles of Political Economy and Taxation*, Chapter XXII, 'Bounties on Exportation and Prohibitions on Importation', in *The Works and Correspondence of David Ricardo*, edited by Piero Sraffa, Cambridge University Press, Cambridge, 1951.

Ritzer, George (1992), *The McDonaldization of Society*, Newbury Park, CA: Pine Forge Press.

Rodrik, Dani (1997), 'Has globalization gone too far?', *California Management Review*, vol. 39, no. 3, pp. 29–53.

Samiee, Saeed (1994), 'Customer evaluation of products in a global market', *Journal of International Business Studies*, vol. 25, no. 3, pp. 579–604.

Schweiger, Günther, Gerald Häubl and Geroen Friederes (1995), 'Consumers' evaluations of product labeled "Made in Europe"', *Marketing and research Today*, vol. 23, no. 1, pp. 25–34.

Sherry, John F. (1987), 'Cultural propriety in a global marketplace' in A. Fuat Firat, Nikhilesh Dholakhia and Richard P. Bagozzi (eds.), *Philosophical and Radical Thought in Marketing*, Lexington Books: Lexington, MA.

Sheth, Jagdish N. and S. Prakash Sethi (1977), 'A theory of cross-cultural buyer behavior', New York: North Holland Publishing.

Shimp, Terence A. and Subbash Sharma (1987), 'Consumer ethnocentrism: construction and validation of the CETSCALE', *Journal of Marketing Research*, vol. 26, August, pp. 280–9.

Smith, David E. and Søren Heede (1996), 'The North–South divide: Changing patterns in the consumption of alcoholic beverages in Europe', in Jozsef Beracs, Andras Bauer and Judit Simon (eds.), *Marketing for an Expanding Europe*, Proceedings of the 25th Annual Conference of the European Marketing Academy, Budapest, May, pp. 1065–84.

Spar, Deborah L. (1997), 'Lawyers abroad: The internationalization of legal practice', *California Management Review*, vol. 39, no. 3, pp. 8–28.

Steele, Murray (1991), 'European brewing industry', in Roland Calori and Peter Lawrence (eds), *The Business of Europe*, Sage: London.

Usunier, Jean-Claude (1998a), *International and Cross-Cultural Management Research*, London: Sage Publications.

Usunier, Jean-Claude (1998b), 'Oral pleasure and expatriate satisfaction: An empirical appraoach', *International Business Review*, vol. 7, no. 1.

Van Maanen, John, and André Laurent (1992), 'The flow of culture: Some notes on globalization and the multinational corporation', in S. Ghoshal and D. E. Westney (eds.), *Organization Theory and the Multinational Corporation*, New York: St Martin Press, pp. 275–312.

Wong, Nancy and Aaron Ahuvia (1995), 'From tofu to caviar: Conspicuous consumption, materialism and self-concepts in east-Asian and Western cultures', *Proceedings of the Second Conference on the Cultural Dimension of International Marketing*, Odense, pp. 68–89.

Woods, Walter A., Emmanuel J. Chéron and Dong Han Kim (1985), 'Strategic implications of differences in consumer purposes in three global markets', in Erdener Kaynak (ed.), *Global Perspectives in Marketing*, Praeger: New York, pp. 155–70.

Zaichkowsky, Judith L. and James H. Sood (1988), 'A global look at consumer involvement and use of products', *International Marketing Review*, vol. 6, no. 1, pp. 20–33.

6 The convergence of marketing environments world-wide

Consumers are immersed in local marketing environments that tend progressively to converge. There are three major levels in a local marketing environment that have more or less direct influence on how marketing strategy can be defined and implemented. The first level deals with the general aspects of an environment, its political, legal, social, cultural, and linguistic dimensions; their influence, although seemingly fuzzy and indirect, is pervasive. Many chapters deal with one or the other of these aspects of the international marketing environment, especially linguistic (Chapter 13).

The second level of the marketing environment is much nearer to actual marketing decisions; it deals with marketing institutions and infrastructures: professional associations (marketing, salespeople, advertisers, etc.), regulatory bodies and how marketing regulations are enforced (codes of conduct or the law). The first section of this chapter (6.1) deals with these aspects of the local marketing environment. The third level of the marketing environment, that of *local marketing knowledge*, is generally overlooked, if not blatantly ignored, by international marketing textbooks. Local knowledge indubitably does matter: if people, as employees, consumers or viewers, do not know, misunderstand and/or do not accept marketing concepts and practices, it is possible that policies will be hard to implement. Section 6.2 deals with the issue of how marketing concepts and practices have been imported locally, especially how marketing is treated in the education system and in higher education programmes.

The following sections of this chapter deal with the regionalization of marketing environments. Marketing environments converge regionally through regional integration in the GATT framework and now under the WTO (section 6.3). Section 6.4 focuses on diversity in a marketing environment and presents the regional environment of western Europe, the European Union, and shows how this seemingly unified marketing environment is still highly diverse and needs tailored approaches; at least, much caution is needed when considering Europe as a single market area. Section 6.5

treats the case of an unstable and changing environment, that of eastern Europe and the former USSR, when the marketing environment is undergoing fundamental changes at all levels and everything is unsettled and negotiable. Section 6.6 deals with challenges when an environment is both difficult to understand and needs much adaptation; it highlights the case of east Asian countries which, despite major diversity among them, share common traits when compared with the West. A concluding section (6.7) outlines some limitations to the world-wide convergence of marketing environments.

6.1   LOCAL MARKETING ENVIRONMENTS

When trying to understand local marketing environments, self-criticism is a necessary perspective because we understand it with our own ethnocentric biases. There is always a reference point which makes judgements implicitly comparative (Usunier, 1998a). If local people do not properly understand the interviewing process in market research, a value judgement would be to say that they are underdeveloped and need to be educated. An entirely different attitude is to try and understand critically that scientific methods are not necessarily the only way of collecting data on how products and services are used by people. F. A. Hayek phrases as follows the question of which knowledge should be used when we want to plan a complex set of interrelated decisions about resource allocation (e.g. an international marketing strategy):

the answer to our question will therefore largely turn on the relative importance of the different kinds of knowledge; those more likely to be at the disposal of particular individuals and those which we should with greater confidence expect to find in the possession of an authority made up of suitably chosen experts. If it is today so widely assumed that the latter will be in a better position, this is because one kind of knowledge, namely, scientific knowledge occupies now so prominent a place in public imagination that we tend to forget that it is not the only kind that is relevant . . . Today it is almost heresy to suggest that scientific knowledge is not the sum of all knowledge. But a little reflection will show that there is beyond question a body of very important but unorganized knowledge which cannot possibly be called scientific in the sense of knowledge of general rules: the knowledge of the particular circumstances of time and place. (Hayek, 1945, p. 521.)

From this perspective, local knowledge is important because it is operational, although at times it may be difficult to access because it is tacit rather than explicit. Taking note of local knowledge, as an outsider, produces a long list of caveats that may seem at times boring, but make much sense for implementing marketing decisions. High-context international marketing, infused as it is with local knowledge can be contrasted with low-context marketing strategies in foreign markets which use supposedly universal marketing knowledge and treat locality as constraint rather than as opportunity. Figure 6.1 shows how local marketing knowledge must be considered as a full-fledged dimension of a national marketing environment.

Economic and political aspects of the local marketing environment

Culture and language are only part of the marketing environment. A set of economic, political, legal, social and cultural characteristics has an influence on the implemen-

```
┌─────────────────────────────────────────────────────┐
│ The broader environment                             │
│                                                     │
│ • Economic                                          │
│ • Political                                         │
│ • Social and ethnic                                 │
│                                                     │
├─────────────────────────────────────────────────────┤
│ Marketing institutions and infrastructures         │
│                                                     │
│ • Research                                          │
│ • Communication                                     │
│ • Distribution                                      │
│ • Consumerism                                       │
│                                                     │
├─────────────────────────────────────────────────────┤
│ Local marketing knowledge                           │
│                                                     │
│ • in business                                       │
│ • in education                                      │
│ • consumers' marketing knowledge                    │
│ • in the society at large                           │
│                                                     │
└─────────────────────────────────────────────────────┘
```

FIGURE 6.1   Dimensions of a local marketing environment.

tation of marketing decisions, and on marketing decisions themselves because it is important to integrate decisions and their implementation. For this reason, marketers have to understand the local marketing environment before preparing strategy. A key economic feature of a marketing environment is the purchasing power per capita, because it sets the *average* level of budgetary constraints. United Nations or International Monetary Fund statistics give accurate data and most of the aggregate economic data for countries is available on the Internet and easy to access.[1] To a certain extent prices are adapted by global marketers so that they can fit with local purchasing power. However, there are some cases where low purchasing power simply excludes the sale of items felt locally to be unnecessary. Pet foods, for instance, remain largely dependent on per capita purchasing power: people in most countries where income per capita is low resent money spent on expensive pet foods for dogs and cats while part of the local population fights for its everyday ration. In North African countries, where European television is received via satellite dishes, people are quite shocked by pet food advertisements which they view as showing contempt for human beings, who should be given priority over animals. The strong affectional bond between an old lady and her beloved Yorkshire Terrier in a Parisian flat is beyond the bounds of their imagination.

Often more important than average income is the distribution of national income across social groups and individuals. Income and wealth inequalities are closely related to power distance, as explained in Chapter 3. In many developing countries such as

Brazil, Indonesia or Egypt, a fairly small segment of the population has high per capita purchasing power, but larger numbers are tending to move towards middle-class status. The well-off tend to develop similar consumer behaviour to that of the corresponding social class in more developed countries. This partly explains globalization. However, even among the poorer strata of the population, economic desires and achievements may be greater than they seem at first sight. Real estate development takes place in Brazilian *favellas*, even though the sale of housing units is obviously not conducted by Century 21 real estate agencies.

The unemployment rate requires careful consideration, and it is necessary to investigate well beyond the official statistics. The existence of a large informal sector in some economies, based on moonlighting and non-registered entrepreneurs, causes unemployment to be somewhat overestimated (Berger, 1991). For instance, the informal sector is important for car repair in Africa where, given the scarcity of resources and the high duties on imported cars, it makes sense to maintain cars over long periods of time, 25 years and more. Informal (unregistered) car repair shops are relevant when targeting customers for spare parts because officially registered garages do not make up the bulk of the market. Product substitution and more general substitution solutions (buy or repair, make or buy, acquire or rent, share or fully own) largely depend on the relative price and taxation levels of goods and services.

As far as political institutions are concerned, democracy is generally considered as *the* favourable marketing environment, the citizen's freedom of choice being implicitly associated with that of a consumer. However, although clearly associated with a favourable marketing environment, liberal democracy is not a full prerequisite. The example of the development of marketing in China shows that liberal democracy and full respect for individual human rights are not absolute prerequisites for the growth of a consumer and market-oriented society (Ho, 1997; Doran, 1997). Political aspects of the local environment are generally associated with political risk, a basic definition of which would be the negative consequences for foreign companies (nationalization, contract revocation, repatriation of funds, threats to expatriate personnel, etc.) of political events such as revolution, riots, coups, or, more generally, severe political instability in the host country. From a low power distance perspective, that of most international marketing textbooks, political risk is a major problem for foreign operations. However, from a high power distance perspective, the most important issue is to pragmatically develop relationships with those holding the power, provided that their expected time in power will be significant. Thus a major task in scanning an environment is to appreciate the racial, social and ethnic distinctions within a country and the relationships between diverse groups. The Malaysian marketing environment cannot be understood without reference to the Malay majority and the Chinese minority and the consensus between the two groups which gives political power to Malays and economic influence to the Chinese. Similarly, Sri Lanka cannot be understood without reference to the large Tamil minority in the northern part of the island which has been in constant struggle against the Singhalese majority for years. The outgroupist/low power distance assumption of international business and marketing knowledge is rather misleading in this respect. However, once again real-world global companies do not act as in textbook examples do. For some years, Procter & Gamble has defined a market environment, called 'Balkan' which embraces countries that, until recently, have had very difficult political relationships with one another (Bosnia, Bulgaria, Croatia, Makedonia, Romania, Serbia, Slovenia).

The legal environment is extremely important because sales and marketing are based on agreements, and especially formal contracts. Understanding a local legal environment begin with ascertaining to which main legal tradition it belongs. In Europe whether a country uses code law, starting from general principles, or common law, based on precedents, has much influence on a wide variety of laws relating to marketing, such as those dealing with advertising, sales promotion, labelling, product liability, sales contracts, contracts with agents and dealers (e.g. termination payments), etc. Section 6.4 explains some consequences of the legal diversity in European environments that explain the difficulties that hinder the development of a unified marketing environment in Europe. Ethics also are influenced by the legal tradition (see sections 15.6 and 15.7): common law countries do not generally like to regulate excessively and leave more room to people and companies, allowing for business self-discipline in the form of professional codes of conduct, in contrast to code law countries which like to legislate on many matters. In France, a typical code law country, contracts for work and rental leases are framed by law and people making contracts only fill in the blanks. Finally, contracts with consumers or between business partners may lead parties to litigation. It is not a universal conception in world cultures that a contract is the law of the parties and that litigation is the appropriate way to obtain redress from an *unfair* partner: contracts may also be understood as not binding to the letter, and litigation as evil, inasmuch as it shows that former business friends are now enemies and have proved unable to manage their relationship in harmony (see section 16.7).

Local marketing institutions and infrastructures

The whole marketing process is based on a series of steps, most of which need to be applied locally, either in preparing for decisions (market research) or for implementing them (e.g. advertising campaigns or placing the product in distribution channels); sometimes the feasibility of marketing decisions, and, more often, details of their execution are affected by local marketing institutions and infrastructures. Market research can naturally be undertaken in most countries of the world and international marketers will find subsidiaries of major international market research organizations, or local or regional companies, that offer good research services almost everywhere. However, quite apart from the technicalities of market research, which are explained at great length in specialist textbooks, market research is a human activity that generally involves interviewers/researchers and informants/respondents as human beings. The kind of neutral objective stance that is required from informants who must speak their true mind without any influence from the interviewing person is difficult enough to find in countries where market research, polls and panels are well established. It is all the more difficult to find in many local environments where willingness to answer, or more generally to deliver information, is low, since interviewers are seen to be hidden sellers or impolite intruders. Similarly, motivation to answer will be low when there is no local awareness that answering will finally benefit consumers as a community, because the feedback loop which links consumer research information to product improvement and to personal interest is complex and uncertain. Chapter 7 provides many examples which call for adaptation of market research methods in local environments.

How distribution channels are organized is a mix of national culture, legal requirements concerning store size and the opening of new stores, physical constraints and established social and economic practices between manufacturers and middlemen in the distribution channels. Section 12.1 presents the example of the Japanese distribution system, which is often misunderstood and criticized because its locality is misunderstood. Direct marketing, although its techniques are fairly consistent world-wide, needs access to mailing lists, provision of which may conflict with the protection of personal data and individual privacy. For instance, the German provisions concerning customer lists and their use are extremely strict: *Datenschutz*, as the Germans call it, may be an obstacle for foreign catalogue sales operators, if they do not adjust. Section 12.4 gives indications of how global direct marketing must be adjusted to local environments.

Advertising agencies are probably the most significant institutions in a local marketing environment. Local advertising agencies, whether subsidiaries of international groups or merely local companies, are likely to have much knowledge of local consumers and viewers, since communication is a 'code business' based on linguistic and visual cues that are interpreted/decoded on the basis of local cultures. Chapter 14 explains how both advertising strategy and execution need to be responsive to local conditions. The local advertising profession is likely to use a mix of universal knowledge about strategy and execution of advertisements and local knowledge based on a deep understanding of what attracts people as viewers and potential consumers. Taylor *et al.* (1996) explain how French advertising professionals work with two distinct models for developing campaigns, one labelled the American model and the other built on the French leaning for semiotics and linguistics, in fact two different knowledge bases, one relying on tests and the other on experience and intuitive decisions, the use of which depends on the client's background (Box 6.1). Similarly, Johansson (1994) explains that Japanese TV advertising is soft-sell oriented because of the uneasiness of the Japanese with the rough instrumentality of business transactions and direct messages; this prohibits being too obviously logical; moreover:

Another cultural factor related to the imposition that TV advertising makes on viewers' time. The polite advertiser needs at some level to justify to the audience why the commercials interrupt the program, and a hard-sell approach is not conducive to such an apology . . . It is not uncommon to hear 'gomen kudasai' ('I am sorry') in the audio of Japanese TV commercials. (1994, pp. 21–22.)

The last steps in the marketing chain are payment and (possibly) consumer complaints. How payment is effected is a significant characteristic of a marketing environment that needs to be studied, especially the availability of electronic payment, local customs in terms of payment dates and customer credit practices. As explained in Chapter 4, consumerism also varies greatly across contexts because of the degree of legitimacy of consumer complaints, the focus of the complaint, whether broad or narrow, and the expectations of the consumer as to the outcome of the complaint.

In addition to purely marketing institutions, product-specific infrastructures need to be surveyed in order to understand the local marketing environment, such as that of medical doctors and pharmacists for the marketing of drugs, that of libraries and book-

BOX 6.1

Comments by three French advertising professionals

'When you work with clients who have a very sophisticated marketing approach, it is outside the question to make abstractions . . . You never launch an advertising campaign without having a pre-test and afterwards a post-test . . . The marketing directors of French companies most often have studied formally in American colleges. They follow faithfully the roads of American marketing . . . not that it's good, but it's reality.'

'I respect research but generally it's experience that tells you if it will work in France. I would say that 80% of the time we do not need tests.'

'When I look at the way American people approach [planning], they investigate ten different ways of doing it, evaluating . . . and they enjoy it. In France we would rather say "We think this is the way to do it, and we try it".'

(Source: Taylor *et al.* 1996, pp. 6–7.)

stores for the marketing of books, etc. The marketing knowledge of local consumers is also a significant part of the marketing environment; it can be assessed by looking at various indicators: the courses taught in higher education, textbooks, student enrolment on marketing causes, television programmes dedicated to buying, consumption and advertising on TV channels (apart from TV spots and teleshopping), etc.

Learning local cues is in fact a key issue for companies marketing internationally because they have to develop a fit with local culture. A marketing environment must always be studied before choosing a marketing strategy because decision cannot be divorced from implementation: if a 'good' strategy proves difficult to implement, it is in fact a bad strategy.

6.2   MARKETING: BORROWED CONCEPTS AND PRACTICES

The first basic link between culture and marketing, which is almost never mentioned, is the initial entrenchment of marketing in one particular national culture: that of the USA. Marketing concepts and practices have been enthusiastically adopted in many other countries, even those that do not share the same cultural background. All countries have their traders and merchants, and since marketing is a powerful tool for developing and controlling existing and new businesses, they may rightfully borrow it. But in doing so, they transform it and then integrate it into their own culture.

Marketing: US-based vocabulary, information sources and concepts

Marketing concepts and practices were initially and for the most part developed in the USA and have continued to spread because of the success of large US-based multinational companies in world-wide consumer markets. They have been popular-ized by Philip Kotler's *Marketing Management* (1994) in its numerous translations and editions. Still, nowhere is their influence so strong as in the USA. In France, where much has been borrowed from the USA, about twenty thousand students attend a basic course in marketing each year. This compares with three hundred thousand in the USA. Since the population of the USA is four times that of France, the *marketing intensity* of the USA, on the figures mentioned, is still about four times that of France. The same ratios hold true for most developed countries outside the USA. In addition to quantitative differences in marketing intensity, there are also qualitative differences across countries, in content, style and practices.

The success of the word 'marketing' gave a new image to trade and sales activities, in many countries where it had often previously been socially and intellectually deval-ued, especially in Latin countries because of the relative lack of interest on the part of Catholicism in trade and business. In Ancient Greece, the god Hermes, messenger of the Olympian gods, was also the god of communication, exchange, trade and mer-chants (and also thieves). Despite the success and the seemingly general acceptance of the term 'marketing', many examples indicate that there have been some basic mis-conceptions of it in many countries, especially developing countries (Amine and Cavusgil, 1986). For instance, a survey of Egyptian business people indicates a clear lack of understanding of the meaning of marketing (El Haddad, 1985). Either man-agers do not understand what marketing is all about or, if they do, they tend to believe that it has no application to their business. In fact they see marketing as the mere fact of selling, or the promotion of sales. Although 'marketing' has been imported (as a word, and even as a sort of slogan), its former cultural roots and its precise meaning have been forgotten.

In Japan, most of the books on marketing management were borrowed from the United States and then translated directly without much adaptation. Moreover market survey techniques, the underlying concepts and the wording of questions, as well as questionnaire, interview and sampling techniques, were all widely imported. As Van Raaij says (1978, p. 699): 'Consumer research is largely "made in the U.S.A." with all the risks that Western American or middle-class biases pervade this type of research in the research questions we address, the concepts and theories we use and the interpre-tations we give.'

In fact it is more frequently the word itself, and not its whole sense and the social practices it involves, that has been imported. It is normal to find large gaps between the rhetoric of marketing and the actual selling practices adopted by companies. Marketing did not really replace long-established commercial practices in many coun-tries: it superimposed itself on local selling practices and merged with them.

The imported nature of marketing concepts and practices is clearly evidenced by the vocabulary, information and reference sources, and the origin of literature on the subject, all demarcating it as an area of knowledge. Marketing vocabulary is now used world-wide: 'mailing', 'media planning' and 'merchandising' have become familiar words. Even though efforts have been made in some countries to localize these words, they have generally failed. For instance in France hardly anyone uses the official word *la mercatique* (it sounds ugly). It is legitimate and indeed wise to retain an imported word in its original form until its total integration as a concept has been realized. This evidence of borrowing allows the foreign origin of the concept to be kept in mind and thereby, paradoxically, improves its chances of successful localization. The transplant has all the more chance of being successful because there is a strong fascination for what is made abroad.

Data and information sources (Nielsen panels, for instance) and consultancy businesses (advertising agencies, market consultants) are mostly of American origin, even if they are by no means all American. Last but not least, the marketing and academic journals, such as the *Journal of Marketing*, the *Journal of Marketing Research* and *Advertising Age*, came largely from the United States. In Europe (France, Germany, the United Kingdom, the Benelux and north European countries), as well as in Canada or Japan, many other journals exist. But research and new advances for practitioners as well as for scholars are made on the basis of imported materials. For instance, the percentage of US references in the bibliographies of British, German or French reviews of marketing is often as much as 90 per cent, on specialized topics. A similar situation currently prevails in Japan: as Lazer *et al.* point out (1985, p. 71): 'what has occurred [in Japan] is the modification and adaptation of selected American constructs, ideas and practices to adjust them to the Japanese culture, that remains intact'. They stress the importance of economic non-functionality which 'emphasizes that marketing actions consider individual human factors rather than merely economic efficiency and business profits'.

A progressive integration

In many countries marketing knowledge has been progressively imported, at first simply, as universal and explicit knowledge, then it has merged with local tacit knowledge and ways of doing. In the case of Japan Johansson and Nonaka (1996, p. 4) call the Japanese marketers 'professional non professionals', everybody in the organization being extremely concerned with the interaction with the outside world:

Japanese marketers are not professionals in a technical sense; they seem to consider marketing too important to leave to experts . . . The common Japanese practice of entry-level hiring and subsequent rotation of job positions is predicated on the lack of position-specific skills. These practices help account for the fact that many individuals with engineering backgrounds are involved in marketing in Japanese manufacturing firms . . . Even though a rising number of managers are educated in marketing abroad, and Japan is also developing business schools, the entry-level hiring practices and the development of company-specific skills have made MBAs difficult to assimilate, and they are mainly used as internationalization (*kokusaika*) catalysts, rather than as skilled professionals.

A similar situation is also to be found in France, where adaptation to the cultural context has now been broadly achieved. There are now several French textbooks – about ten on marketing management, and two to five on each major area of marketing such as advertising or sales management. Continuous efforts have been made to enable 'marketing' to appear as a *'rationalisation de la démarche commerciale'* ('rationalization of trade and sales practices'). It is seen as confronting the traditional *commercial* style with new concepts that are better suited to international competition (Dayan *et al.* 1988, p. 14):

In a [French] company, at the beginning of the industrial revolution . . . selling was not considered to be an honourable activity. The essence of trading – bargaining with the client – is seen as not being codifiable; it is an *art*, based on individual talents, intuitions and experience. Consequently commercial activities do not follow the standards of the company as a whole, which are based on rationality, logic, and organisation. With the advent of *marketing*, brand image activities have been improved, and they have been better integrated to the company as a whole. A full scale *direction de marketing* (marketing department) attracts significant areas of the human, intellectual, and financial resources of a company: it often has a critical influence on strategic decisions, it uses more and more sophisticated techniques, and it adopts a rational approach, which raises the *direction de marketing* to the level of other functional areas.

In this small passage (from the introduction to a French *marketing* textbook) several elements typify the importation process and its limits: the expression 'full scale' *(à part entière)* suggests that there are still many *directions de marketing* which cover only a part of the marketing function; the *power* of marketing within the organization is an important issue *per se*; the dialectic opposition of irrationality and art versus logic and rationalization. In French society, only Cartesian logic may give legitimacy and credibility to marketing.

In French companies one often finds a *directeur du marketing* (vice president, marketing) and a *directeur commercial* (v.p., sales) whereas in the USA a vice president, marketing would more commonly deal with marketing strategy but also with sales and advertising. The French *directeur commercial* is actually responsible for a large part of what Americans call 'marketing' as a functional area. The duties of a *directeur commercial* are primarily the supervision of sales, distribution outlets and sales representatives, as well as the management of customer relations; a *directeur du marketing* will most often be responsible for marketing surveys and/or communication. The organizational relationship between the *directeur du marketing* and the *directeur commercial*, whether parallel or hierarchical, will not encourage them to collaborate, especially when marketing is subordinate to the sales department. Many managers still tend to view marketing as somewhat 'intellectual', with little practical orientation, directed towards long-range targets and market strategy, or even confuse it with advertising as a rather 'indirect' method of influencing the market.

In a somewhat linguistically defensive country like France it was considered necessary to create a new word and rename the concept *la mercatique* despite the fact that the word 'marketing' contains no letter that does not exist in the French alphabet and is easy to pronounce in French. The word *mercatique*, a neologism, was created in 1973 by the Commission de Terminologie Française, established by the French Ministry of Economics and Finance. Despite this centrally inspired procedure, people in everyday life still use the original word 'marketing'. The argument in favour of *la mercatique* was as follows:

Not only did mercatique have a clear etymology (from the Latin mercatus the market) but also its definition, by its strictness, allowed for a more profound understanding of the concept and avoided the deviations, misinterpretations and misconceptions that the blurredness of the English expression entailed. These misconceptions were frequent: thus, for Pierre Hazebroucq, secretary of the Académie des Sciences Commerciales, the word 'marketing' designated 'everything related to influencing markets'; similarly P. Kotler wrote, in *Management Direction* in June 1974, that marketing management was the set of actions which aims at regulating the level, the pace and the nature of demand for one or several products of a company – this dragged up memories of the 1900–50 period, where the supply side was given higher priority, that is demand had to adapt to those products which were actually offered. How, under these conditions, was it possible to get young people interested in commercial action and entrepreneurship?

Whereas, with the French concept of *mercatique* young people passionately fond of trade action discovered an outlet for their enthusiasm; 'manipulative' commercial activities were rejected, as well as activities which were limited exclusively to the act of buying or solely to the act of selling, often with contempt for customers, or at least a definite lack of attention to their needs. (Darbelet and Lauginié, 1988, pp. 133–4.)

People who speak ordinary, everyday language have not adopted the word *mercatique*. Other French words created to replace a foreign word or concept have, however, been completely successful. For instance, *ordinateur* has replaced 'computer', which has been borrowed by many other languages from the United States, where computers were invented.

In order to assess how marketing has been integrated in a local environment it is advisable to use both quantitative and qualitative cues. The quantitative cues have been described above: student enrolment in marketing courses, the membership of professional and academic marketing associations, the number of marketing-related books published, the circulation of marketing journals, etc. The qualitative side of the integration process is more difficult to uncover because it deals with how broad cultural values and well-entrenched local practices conflict with some of the values underlying marketing (pragmatic, money oriented, expert knowledge, materialistic). They are reconciled by flatly ignoring certain dimensions (marketing as expert knowledge), by over-emphasizing some of its positive aspects (marketing can also serve non-profit operations) or by maintaining, somewhat schizophrenically, two systems, one based on explicit, official marketing, and the other based on tacit, local knowledge of the appropriate ways to interact with customers and markets.

6.3   REGIONAL CONVERGENCE

The GATT and regional integration

Regional integration is now under way, based mostly on trade agreements. The basic assumptions, interaction models and attitudes described in Chapters 2 and 3 are located at too deep a level to be taken into account in negotiation between nation states. Therefore, convergence is basically economic (as in the case of the North American Free Trade Agreement, NAFTA), more rarely political (as in the case of the EU, and this with obvious pains). Cultural convergence is a more difficult process: it certainly happens but over a very long period and with people unaware of it. Groups of countries can be identified for the purpose of marketing strategy on the basis of key elements in the regional environment – both similarities (which unite them against the rest of the world) and differences (which account for the intraregional diversity that needs to be taken into account).

The GATT treaty does not take into account the cultural variable. Its fundamental articles are based on quite opposite premises. Article 1 sets out the concept of 'general most favoured nation treatment', stating that, with respect to customs duties and similar charges, 'any advantage, favour, privilege or immunity granted by any contracting party to any product originating in or destined for any other country shall be accorded immediately and unconditionally to the like product originating in or destined for the territories of all other contracting parties' (GATT, 1986, p. 2). This is clearly a multilateral view, based on strong outgroup orientation, whereby the whole world is seen as being open to international trade and not covered by a dense network of bilateral trade agreements that would replace free markets by administered trade. However, it was necessary to make an exception for those countries which, by virtue of their geographical proximity, had a natural interest in establishing closer links, basically by setting to zero customs duties between them, instead of simply reducing progressively the average level of duties, as achieved in the multilateral GATT framework.

The GATT treaty represents clearly the view of the liberal/individualist/utilitarian UK and the Anglo-Saxon world. For long periods, its achievements have been considerable. It has now been succeeded by the WTO (World Trade Organization) which first met in January 1995. The GATT was a treaty with permanent staff, but not a fully fledged international organization. The WTO is now a full international organization with about 130 members. It has adopted the pragmatic stance of the GATT, and the basic treaty has largely been retained, including the philosophy of self-enforceable rules. There have been many bilateral trade agreements, but the GATT has kept them under control.

Article XXIV of the GATT treaty allows various forms of regional integration provided that the purpose 'should be to facilitate trade between the constituent territories and not to raise barriers to the trade of other contracting parties' (GATT, 1986, p. 41). There are various forms of regional integration, the simplest being that of a free trade area, where countries have abolished customs duties between members but maintain their own external tariffs and customs procedures *vis-à-vis* third countries. A much stronger form is the customs union, which adds to the former situation, a common external tariff and customs procedures. The EU (previously the European Community) has been a customs union since its inception, whereas NAFTA is a free trade area (as its name clearly states). NAFTA has limited scope, although it has been claimed to be a major evolution for regional trade on the whole of the American continent (there are talks about its extension to some South American countries). As shown in Table 6.1, Americans are fundamentally different from the Mexicans and the Canadians. Furthermore, the size of the US market makes it a region in its own right.

The strongest form of regional integration is the economic union, whereby the member countries of a customs union commit themselves to co-ordinate and even integrate their economic policy. The EU has been an economic union since the Maastricht Treaty came into force, in January 1994, with the prospect of a single currency in the year 2001. In the GATT arena, now the WTO, no individual EU country is represented. Since the enactment of the Treaty of Rome in 1958, the EU itself has negotiated the GATT agreements, after a discussion between member states has produced a common position.

Comparison across regional areas

There is obviously convergence in regional areas of the world; as argued above it is economic rather than cultural. But the process is complex: whereas non-tariff barriers are

TABLE 6.1   Contrasts across large regional areas

Variable/Region	European Union (EU)	Eastern Europe (EE)	ASEAN[a]	NAFTA
Type of regional agreement	Customs & economic union	Absence of any real agreement after Comecon[b]	Informal group of nations	Free trade area
Linguistic diversity	Very large (12 different official languages)	Medium (all Slavic languages except Hungary and Romania)	Medium	Bi-polar (English + Spanish/ French), with a predominance of English
Legal style	Legal statutory	'Weak legality'	Informal/relational	Legal-contractual
Political system	Bureaucratic democracy	Chaotic transition to democracy	Authoritarian pluralism	Liberal democracy
Time orientation	Past orientation + linear time	Present time orientation	Cyclical/integrated/ arrowed time	Economic time dominant
Individualism/ collectivism	Individualist	Collectivist individualism	Collectivist	Individualist except in Mexico
Power distance	Low: Northern EU High: Southern EU	High	High	Low except in Mexico
Masculinity/ Femininity	Predominantly feminine	—	Neutral	Masculine
Uncertainty avoidance	High: Roman Germanic nations Low: Britain and Nordic countries	High	Weak	Weak
Dominant type of organization (Hofstede, 1991)	A mix of pyramids, machines, markets. No cross-national organizational consensus	'Egyptian Pyramids' (ruins of a centrally planned system, now privately exploited)	'Families'	Markets

[a]ASEAN, free trade Association of South East Asian Nations.
[b]Comecon, former economic association of communist countries.

progressively relaxed, market barriers – based on cultural differences rather than legal dispositions – remain. Table 6.1 gives an idea of the significant differences that exist across regional areas. In the next three sections, discuss some features of the regional environment in the European Union, eastern European (including the former USSR) countries and East Asian countries.

6.4   A DIVERSE MARKETING ENVIRONMENT: THE EUROPEAN UNION

The European Union is converging quickly, in terms of the economic environment, especially with the planned introduction of a single currency which should be effective by the year 2001 in conformity with the Treaty of Amsterdam, and despite limited support from the populations of some member states. Linguistic and cultural diversity in the EU remains very high. Companies have developed considerable cross-border operations over the past twenty years and Leeflang and Van Raaij (1995) refer to the following elements of macro-economic convergence: (1) most European countries have reduced and kept inflation under control since the end of the 1980s; (2) the average unemployment rate is high in all EU member states; (3) GNP growth is weak; (4) household income tends to be more unequally distributed and the gap between the most affluent consumers and those with lower purchasing power tends to widen.

The institutional basis of the European Union

The EU is based on the Treaty of Rome, which was signed by the six original member countries, Belgium, France, Italy, Germany, Luxembourg and the Netherlands, all of which belonged to the Roman-Germanic legal tradition (also called the *code law* or *civil law* tradition). There are four basic principles in the Treaty of Rome: the free movement of goods, the free movement of capital, the free movement of persons and the free movement of services. Understandably, such broad statements needed to be clarified, as has been done by issuing 22,000 regulations in about 35 years! Furthermore the European Court of Justice issued about 4,000 rulings that have, to a certain extent, clarified the implementation of rules in precise cases. For countries such as the UK and Denmark, which entered in 1973, it has never been easy to accept this strong legislative orientation. They are low power distance societies, which favour more pragmatic and 'near-to-the-people' ways of solving problems.

The state interventionism tradition has historically been strong everywhere in Europe: even in northern Europe and Britain, although it is even larger in Latin Europe than in Germany (see Lessem and Neubauer, 1994). This tradition is challenged by a general trend towards the disinvolvement of the state and public authorities in money-losing businesses which do not necessarily fall under their obvious competence. EU policies have a very wide impact on companies, in areas such as: industrial standards policy, taxation policy, antitrust policy (Articles 85 and 86 of the Treaty), monitoring of public subsidies to industry, R&D policy, EU legislation on public procurement (EC Committee of the American Chamber of Commerce in Belgium, 1994).

But contrary to what is often said, the EU is not a large bureaucracy; it has a staff of some 20,000. It is rather a small bureaucracy which has incomplete control over the enormous amount of money of the European budget (Euros 500 billion). Given the number of European civil servants really in charge of policy (about 5,000), each has to control an average amount of Euros 100 million (about $100 million) which partly explains the lack of control over the use of European funds. The decision system works on the basis of weighted votes per country (ten for large countries and between two and five for smaller countries) and qualified majority voting in the Council of

Ministers. In terms of the differences (explained in section 3.4) between code law and common law, the legal approach in the EU is completely based on code law. The Roman-Germanic legal tradition was fully shared by the six original members, but not by all of the member states which have since joined. Box 6.2 provides evidence of such divergence in the case of European company law, a sensitive issue for companies.

BOX 6.2

Twenty-five years of discussion and still no agreement

Company laws in Europe differ widely in their inspiration. Briefly stated, there are three main traditions: German, English and French/Latin. Let us start with the German tradition, that of the AG (*Aktien Gesellschaft*). It leaves little room for the shareholders to define their own 'company contract'. The rules are quite strict. A way of characterizing German company law could be *'Alles was nicht erlaubt ist, ist streng verboten'* (all that is not explicitly permitted is strictly forbidden). As a result, in discussing matters concerning SE (*Societas Europea*) with the EU Commission, the Germans always ask for a list (*'Eine Liste'*) of what is permitted, for instance in defining the scope of the decisions of a general meeting of shareholders. By contrast, French company law provides for any decision that is not explicitly given to a particular organ in the company to be taken by the general meeting. The German model of a public limited company is that of an institution (in which the parties adhere to a system which is entirely fixed) rather than of a contract (where the parties have a wide range of 'blank lines' and 'free paragraphs' in the company statute, which allows them to design 'their' company statute as a contract). In the legislation of EU countries, with the exception of Germany, parties are allowed to envisage any arrangement which is not explicitly imposed or forbidden by the legal framework.

The Anglo-Saxon system is much more liberal than the German system. Shareholders are supposed to design their future relations within the company on a fairly contractual basis. Unlike German law, which tries as far as possible to protect third parties, workers and minority shareholders by means of a compulsory and detailed legal company statute, the UK legal tradition solves these problems in different ways. Workers are seen as being tied to the company by work contracts, which they have negotiated in the general framework of labour laws. It is not the function of company law to regulate employee/employer relationships. As concerns third parties, especially suppliers and customers, they are protected through contract law governing bonds, bills of exchange, claims and debentures, securities, etc.

The liberal orientation of the UK goes so far as to propose that the German dualist system may be offered to SEs registered in the UK, even if it does not exist for British public limited companies.

An example of EU policy: The free movement of goods

Among the numerous EU policies, one deserves special attention, because it is aimed at the free movement of goods. There were many obstacles at the beginning of the 1980s on the road to a real 'common market', especially fiscal barriers, related to different indirect tax rates, and technical barriers due to different industrial standards in the EU. This made the elimination of physical borders problematic (Cecchini, 1988). Fragmented national markets resulted in smaller volumes of production and cost inefficiencies at the European level, especially in comparison with the United States and Japan. The EC White Paper of 1985 set out a full programme of 300 European directives to be adopted by 1992. Many of them dealt with common industrial standards at the European level, for which specific standardization bodies were established in order to co-ordinate the setting of standards (e.g. Comité Européen de Normalisation (CEN), Comité Européen de Normalisation Electro-technique (CENELEC) and European Telecommunications Standards Institute (ETSI)). The process was based on several possible means of standardization: (1) approximation of regulations (for instance, EU countries design common legislation Europe-wide for car exhausts); (2) mutual recognition (member states recognize another member state's legislation on a bilateral and reciprocal basis); and (3) the 'home country rule', based on the *Cassis de Dijon* ruling of the European Court of Justice: products which had been manufactured according to the standards and regulations of a particular member state could not be barred from entering any other EU national market, unless the local regulation did not meet the minimal compulsory EU standards. Although much has been achieved in the area of common standards, there still remain some discrepancies owing to climate and industrial traditions (see Box 6.3).

European consumer?

More than thirty years ago Fournis (1962) remarked that there cannot be such an individual as a 'European consumer' since customs and traditions tend to persist. European countries, and cultures, are deeply rooted in the past. Furthermore a long history of wars and conflicts has ensured the persistence of strong feelings of national identity. Naturally European cultures share some common cultural values: the majority of them, to do with major life events (birth, marriage, death), share a set of values which differentiate them from Asian cultures. Patterns of displaying emotion, for instance, differ widely between European and Asians; and where Asians tend to prize group harmony, Europeans tend to favour self-esteem and respect for individuals.

   Nevertheless this apparent cultural homogeneity of Europe, when compared to Asia, ceases to be so clear when we look at cultural variance inside Europe. Stoetzel (1983) who has observed public opinion polls in Europe for many years (compiling a 'Eurobarometer'), shows that there are more 'European cultures' than a 'European culture' as such. Family relation patterns, religion, organization of everyday life – as regards meals, social, family and business life – tend to be quite heterogeneous. In the same vein, Wierenga *et al.* (1996, p. 52) show that there is much variation in the qualities considered important in the education of children in EU countries. While most countries value honesty, Spanish parents do not emphasize it; independence is valued

BOX 6.3

Concrete, yoghurts and sewage plates: The shock of cultures . . . and climates

The conditions of use of concrete vary according to climate. The Greeks have no interest in concrete specifications concerning frost except in a few mountain villages. The Finns need concrete which can endure –40 degrees Celsius, but they are not preoccupied with the number of frost–defrost cycles. The French will prefer a concrete which can resist at least twenty frost–defrost cycles. That is why the classes for each use cannot be seen as quality classes.

Similarly, there is no common European definition of what is a yoghurt. Latin countries require that they are produced with living micro-organisms, whereas the Anglo-Saxons favour their sterilisation. This lack of harmonisation is a hindrance for the producers' European marketing strategies.

The Germans wanted to impose a minimal weight for manhole covers. Pont-à-Mousson, a French producer, uses ductile cast-iron instead of grey cast-iron for the Germans, with the result that French manhole covers weigh 50 to 60 kilos (so that they can be manoeuvred by a sewer worker) instead of 100 to 120 kilos for the German (so that they are very steady on the roads). Different industrial traditions exist, corresponding to different functional benefits looked for by each country. The French company succeeded to have the minimal weight not mentioned in the European standard. It saved a billion dollar European business.

(Source: Esposito, 1994.)

by the Germans but not by the French; politeness is a French value while tolerance is highest with the British, etc.

In conclusion I believe that Marketing strategies for culture-bound products still need tailoring to each national market, or to groups of countries. Beer, for instance, is subject to differences in national tastes, in terms of being more or less bitter, frothy, bubbly, sugary, alcoholic, and other taste attributes, and the leading brewer in Europe, Heineken, continues to tailor its products and marketing policies since beer distribution systems vary across Europe. Whitelock (1987) shows that standard sizes for pillow-cases differ in the various European national markets: 60×75 cm in Great Britain, 65×65 cm in France, 60×70 cm in The Netherlands and 80×80 cm in West Germany. He interviewed textile companies which all agreed on the necessity to customize sizes, even after the creation of the Single Market. This had still not fully been achieved in 1998. Nivea skin care cream, produced by the German multinational company Beiersdorff (BDF) has a leading edge in each national market in Europe. Nevertheless its consistency has to be changed and its formula has to be adapted, depending on whether it is sold in northern or southern Europe (Mourier and Burgaud, 1989), and the Single Market has not changed this.

Wierenga *et al.* (1996) also argue in favour of largely customized strategies in Europe, given the dissimilarity of EU markets on a number of aspects of the marketing environment. Income allocation patterns across major domains of expenditure (food, clothing, energy, furniture and household equipment, health care, transport, leisure) vary significantly across member states according to Eurostats. Although converging, as noted in the previous chapter, the number of persons per household still ranges from a low of 2.3 in Denmark to a high of 4.09 in Ireland. The marketing infrastructure also still differs: the number of points of sale per 100 inhabitants ranges from a low of 0.75 in The Netherlands to a high of 4.01 in Portugal; distribution is highly concentrated in France where 9 per cent of all shops account for 89 per cent of the retail volume but it is not at all concentrated in Portugal, Italy or Spain. Although some have argued that convergence in Europe has already largely been achieved (Leeflang and Van Raaij, 1995), a close look at their data shows differences across EU countries in significant elements of the marketing environment such as the share of private labels in retail food stores, per-capita expenses on direct marketing, or the share of the print, TV, radio and other media in total advertising expenditures.

Is cultural convergence possible without a common language?

As Wolfe (1991, pp. 53–4) emphasized:

The most fundamental point of all is that there will eventually be a Euro-market, and there may be one day Euro-retailers, but there will be no European-consumers in the foreseeable future! . . . It is very easy for English business-people to see English as the language of Europe . . . But a pack printed only in English would be understood by at most 2 out of 5 consumers in the EU, and in other languages by even fewer.

An implicit, but extremely strong and enduring assumption underlying the treaties that created the European Union is the respect for national languages, cultures and identities. However, it is phrased in Article 128, section 1 of the Maastricht Treaty in terms which introduce a compromise in relation to the promotion of members' cultures or the common European culture: 'The Community shall contribute to the flowering of the cultures of the Member States, while respecting their national and regional diversity, and at the same time bringing the common cultural heritage to the fore' (Council of the European Communities, 1992, p. 48). A fundamental element of culture is language, as will be shown in Chapter 13. Language has a strong influence on our world-views and partly shapes our individual and collective behaviour. Even if this assumption in its strongest version (called the Whorfian hypothesis) has been challenged by linguists, it remains a useful metaphor for illustrating its influence on behaviours. Europeans are committed to their language as a social and cultural asset. In most European countries there is much stronger emphasis than in the United States on grammatical appropriateness, and correct pronunciation is often a social prerequisite for the holding of a number of posts.

The six founding countries had four different languages. From 1986 there were twelve countries with ten languages, and since January 1995, with the joining of Finland, Sweden and Austria, the fifteen EU member states have twelve different official languages. One of them, Gaelic, the original language of Ireland, is now little used in its home country. This 'Tower of Babel' situation makes communication difficult and an army of more than 3,000 full-time translators are employed on the EU staff. The issue of a common language for Europe has never been addressed, at least publicly. It is a taboo, even an absolute taboo. In the European Single Act of 1987, Article 34 states that: 'This act [is] drawn up in a single original in the Danish, Dutch, English, French, German, Greek, Irish, Italian, Portuguese and Spanish languages, the texts in each of these languages being equally authentic' (European Communities, 1987, p. 574). One of the main proponents of keeping taboo the common European language issue is France (see Box 6.4), but the Germans are also very keen to have their language spoken, since there are now almost 90 million German speakers in the EU, as a result of the reunification of East and West Germany and the addition of Austria to the EU.

BOX 6.4

French fears about English as the common European language

There is great pride in the French language in France. It is recognized as one of the two official languages of the United Nations, on a par with English. French people have a rather defensive attitude towards English, and since the 1970s the French authorities have regularly issued official decrees prohibiting the use of English words, especially business words, in French texts (Usunier, 1990).

French fears typify resistance to globalization, since it is believed that through consumption patterns the whole of French society and culture could be 'Americanized'. The French are fascinated by the 'American way of life' as an exotic item. But many French people, including politicians, would be horrified to have it 'at home'. If the fears are, perhaps, legitimate, the defensive measures are certainly inadequate. The example of northern European countries shows that it is quite feasible to have a double-language culture. One is the local culture; it corresponds to ways of life and consumption patterns which are not to be globalized. The other is in English; it corresponds to an international lifestyle and globalized consumption patterns. Television channels in English such as MTV, Sky Channel and Super Channel can be seen in many northern European countries, although not in France, where the development of cable television has been stringently restricted. A few years ago the number of householders with cable television in France was half that of Ireland, a country with a population one-fifteenth the size of that of France, and a much lower per capita purchasing power.

Most people believe that satellite TV in Europe, and other new communication technologies, will help to standardize the profile of the European consumer. But the conditions for achieving this will be much better if there is a common language through which to build a common European culture, sustaining new European consumption patterns.

However, it is clear that resistance to change will not suffice to prevent English from being the common language, not the first language, but the standard second language. This is already true for business all over Europe. Even in the publishing business where linguistic differences between countries were traditionally viewed as powerful barriers to internationalization, English is more and more considered the standard language, especially for scientific and technical publications. Sinatra and Dubini (1991, p. 99) quote an English publisher as saying, 'All is published in English. In general publishing, anything significant is published in English, regardless of the mother language of the author. Higher level academic journals, they will all be in English.' A Dutch publisher gives a slightly different view: 'I don't think language will be a problem in the near future. I do not adhere to the idea of a common language for all countries of the community, but I think that soon all European citizens will be able to read three or four different languages. People will be citizens of Europe in the next century.'

A good example of how English will spread over the whole community is given by the new ECTS, European Credit Transfer System, sponsored by the EU Commission and designed for facilitating cross-border higher education. The ECTS information package that each university must prepare has to be written in two languages (these are not specified). Naturally all of the universities involved have chosen their own national language plus English.

6.5   A CHANGING MARKETING ENVIRONMENT: EASTERN EUROPE AND THE CIS

The heritage

Communism meant collective ownership of the means of production. In most countries, except Poland, a large part of agriculture was state-owned and managed. The same was true for foreign trade, which was the monopoly of sectoral agencies. Administered trade was the rule in the Comecon where both production and trade were centrally organized. Ikarus buses were made in Hungary for the whole of eastern Europe and similarly Balkancar forklifts were made by the Bulgarians. As Naor (1986) emphasized in the case of Romania, distribution was as cost efficient as possible, that is, direct distribution from producer to retailers was advocated to the greatest extent possible. But distribution was very poor and parallel, informal distribution often replaced state-run retail outlets where people had to wait to find the few products available. Although the concept of marketing has long been known in countries such as Hungary and Poland, there was an absence of real marketing infrastructures, such as market research consultants, panels, advertising agencies, etc. Communism, having existed for between 40 and 70 years, and although a political system rather than a full culture, has left its mark. Consumers have been used to facing systematic undersupply moderated by queues rather than prices. In Bulgaria, for instance, people had to wait several years to obtain a car which they finally paid for, at a price so low that it could not be compared with a market price elsewhere. Managers, if taking any initiative, had to take into account political and ideological rather than management criteria.

In eastern Europe, despite the fact that most countries now have democratically elected governments that have privatized large sectors of the economy, government still plays a major role in the business sector. This role is even greater when a foreign company is involved. The most important difference between the West and eastern Europe is the fact that there exists a gap of at least two or three generations in terms of productivity and infrastructure. In the most advanced countries, Hungary, Poland and the Czech Republic, there has been some progress in maintaining property rights and removing some market imperfections, but this progress is far behind the West.

Although most countries in eastern Europe are committed to improving their economies, there are still too many interrelated obstacles to be dealt with in the path to growth. Issues such as trade barriers, the development of banking and loan systems, pricing mechanisms, property and contract law all need immediate attention. Privatization is considered a means to achieving market economies and growth, but there is no easy way to achieve privatization in eastern Europe. Over-optimistic estimates are now being revised and people have started realizing that it might take a decade or two before a privatized market economy is achieved.

The transition: Opportunism and misconceptions

Reactions from western companies to market developments in eastern Europe have been rather cautious. However, in spite of this reluctance, most multinationals have entered these markets. Companies such as McDonald's, Pepsi-Cola, Coca-Cola, Statoil, Ericsson, Ikea, Fiat, Nokia, Volkswagen, Estée Lauder, Philip Morris, almost all pharmaceutical firms and several small and medium-sized companies have already established operations in these markets. The governments are providing a number of incentives to foreign companies to invest in their countries. For example most of the western retailers, more specifically 77 in number, are active in Eastern Europe (Tietz, 1994). In spite of the reluctance from western companies to invest, there has been a considerable increase in registered joint ventures. By March 1992, there were 34,121 registered joint ventures between western companies and organizations from eastern Europe. This figure was 12,512 in 1989 and reached 106,295 in 1994 (Ghauri and Usunier, 1996).

Since 1989, with the de-communization of eastern European countries marketing infrastructures have been increasing (Domanski, 1992), the same being true to a lesser extent for Russia (Holden, 1995). Such a process is, however, a lengthy one. A fundamental condition for the development of markets and marketing is a change in the ownership structure. In 1992, 83 per cent of Polish production assets were still state or co-operative property (Dietl, 1992). Privatization programmes have therefore been a major challenge for the governments, with major problems related to their implementation such as valuing companies, establishing a stock exchange, creating notaries and specialized intermediaries for real estate. One of the trickiest problems was to find local shareholders in countries where capitalism had long been associated with exploitation. Private ownership presupposes rules and institutions such as contract law, bankruptcy law, or courts for settling business disputes. The absence of such infrastructure created massive opportunism, as in the case of the former Soviet Asian republics (Box 6.5).

The eastern European countries comprise two groups; the northern countries have formed an alliance called the Visegrad group (Hungary, the Czech Republic, Slovakia

BOX 6.5

Cotton story

In April 1994, a commodity trader was discussing the purchase of raw cotton in the former Soviet Asia (mainly Uzbekistan, Turkmenistan and Tadjikistan): 'For two years, the market for raw cotton has been tense, mainly for the three following reasons: (1) climatic hazards in certain producing regions which thus became net importers instead of net exporters, especially China; (2) reduction of cultivated zones in Uzbekistan; (3) to this, you must add that salespeople break their word in the former Soviet Asia. Last year, the Uzbeks sold their crops twice or thrice; this year, they seem to be a little more serious; but the worst is to be experienced in Turkmenistan. Last year, I signed several contracts for 20,000 tonnes, one of them for 4,000 tonnes, with an official export licence, a ministerial approval and a shipment certificate; I have never received anything!'

This failure appears all the more striking when one takes into account that in world-wide cotton trading it is a well-established custom that the professional who does not respect a contract not only must pay damages but also is blacklisted by the whole trading community.

(Source: M. O. Ancel, commodity trader at Louis Dreyfus & Co., Paris, 1994.)

and Poland). The value structure of consumers differs widely across the region: Lascu *et al.* (1996) have shown that Polish and Romanian people exhibit different value structures, and a regiocentric approach to marketing must be used cautiously, since the belief systems have been shaped by different environmental influences. Similarly, Poland and Hungary have a long tradition of marketing education which makes them more comparable in terms of local marketing knowledge to France or Germany than to Bulgaria or Romania. The Polish journal of marketing can be consulted on the World-Wide Web.

The group of southern Balkan states has traditionally been less developed and highly compartmentalized. National identity takes priority over co-operation in an area where ethnic and religious diversity has always been quite strong. The Bulgarians, for instance, have poor relations with all their neighbours except the Serbs. Eastern Europe, and more generally the ex-communist countries, are experiencing rapid changes. They started from a situation where people had no idea of what a contract, a price and delivery times were, and their countries are slowly moving towards a market economy. Holden (1995, pp. 36–7), for instance, comments on the two Russian marketing textbooks:

The one text *Contemporary Marketing* by Khrutskogo (1991), which stresses the importance of modern marketing knowledge to Russia, introduces marketing in ideological terms, citing both Marx and Engels. The second book, *Marketing – The Success Formula* by Zayavlov and Demidov (1991) focuses on marketing squarely in terms of 'how to operate effectively in foreign markets'.

BOX 6.6

Taking a taxi in Moscow

A Belgian engineer, with no particular knowledge of 1994 Russia, was due to go to a construction site in Siberia for the German contractor he worked for. When he arrived in Moscow, he was transferred from the international to the national airport by a chauffeur of the German company. After working on the site in Siberia, a much quieter area than Moscow, he decided to return on his own, and earlier than initially planned, because the job had been done more quickly. When in Moscow, he took a taxi to the local offices of the German company. Taking the first available car, he negotiated the fare at $50. At first, all seemed to be normal, but after a while, the taxi stopped in a fairly remote, deserted and unfriendly area. The driver then explained that he needed an additional $50 to continue to transport him. He paid without discussion and reached the company offices with no problem. He was lucky: it could have been much worse . . .

(Source: M. O. Ancel, commodity trader at Louis Dreyfus & Co., Paris, 1994.)

The differing orientations of these books shed useful light on the Russian approach to marketing knowledge. The Khrutskogo book emphasises a preference for presenting marketing knowledge in relatively intellectual terms, using discredited, yet still very familiar concepts for explaining the market. His approach reveals a Russian penchant for searching for laws that govern social and economic behaviour. The contribution of Zayavlov and Demidov reinforces the conviction that marketing knowledge is held by many Russians to be mainly applicable to foreign business interactions and not so much to home-market activities.

As understood in the local scene, the free market economy tends to be confused with mere business opportunities, as illustrated by Box 6.5. The absence of rules, which is stronger in the former USSR than in eastern European countries, further helps the development of corrupt behaviour in business. However, this is only a transitory situation. A major comparative advantage of the ex-communist countries is their good level of general education. Even if people in the ex-communist countries progressively build marketing infrastructures (Quelch *et al.*, 1991), an international marketer there still has to live a very adventurous life. Anecdotally western European business people who take their own cars to these countries are told to take the wipers with them each time they park their car so that they will not be stolen. If they have to take a taxi, some precautions must be taken, as evidenced by Box 6.6.

6.6   A CHALLENGING MARKETING ENVIRONMENT: EAST ASIA

East Asia is challenging for westerners because the values and mindsets are different. East Asians are perceived as economic rivals by westerners and their path to success has been often stereotypically attributed to imitative behaviour (at best) or counterfeiting (at worst). The challenge is to overcome stereotypes and misunderstandings. Despite the 1997 economic downturn in Asia (affecting, in particular, South Korea, Thailand and Indonesia), the achievements in the ASEAN countries and in far East Asia have been remarkable since the early 1980s. High rates of economic growth have been combined with increasing shares in world trade. Chinese GNP has grown at 13 per cent per annum and its exports at almost 30 per cent each year. However, in the mid-1960s, there was extensive pessimism about the future of Asia, considered to be overpopulated and unable to achieve proper development: a book published in 1968, on the basis of late-1960s data, by Gunnar Myrdal, a Nobel Prize winner, was entitled *Asian Drama, An Enquiry into the Poverty of Nations*. This pessimistic view has been largely denied by facts.

Asian commonalities, in contrast to those of 'westerners', were viewed as a drawback, as not conducive to business initiative; such characteristics included the lack of individualism. Hofstede (1980) established a correlation between individualism and GNP per capita which seemed to suggest that individualism was a precondition for high levels of economic development. Now the perspective has been totally reversed. The issue is now for the West to understand why the collectivist values of many Asian nations help them to achieve much more than individualistic European countries which have lower rates of economic growth and higher unemployment rates over the same period of time.

The Confucian values have been said to be an essential driving force behind such dynamism (see Box 6.7). Some have argued that, at the society level, they are backed by a system of *authoritarian pluralism* (Pohl, 1995) quite different from the liberal democracies in the West. Drug trafficking, for instance, is heavily sanctioned in countries such as Singapore, Malaysia and Thailand. A Dutch prime minister who recently travelled to one of these countries to plead for one of his countrymen who had been sentenced to death for drug trafficking, discovered that the rules were applied with much less leniency than in the United States or in Europe: he did not obtain mercy for the condemned man.

The components of authoritarian pluralism are as follows:

1. A negation of individualism: group belonging and consequent obligations are more important than individual human rights; persons try to be in unison rather than in discordance with society.

2. Family, as already emphasized in Chapter 4, is the basic building block. Divorce rates are much lower than in the West; family is a form of social insurance which efficiently replaces the costly impersonal welfare systems of western countries.

3. Education is highly valued and people are ready to make financial sacrifices and efforts to obtain it.

4. Thrift, modesty and renunciation are the rule *until* somebody can show through conspicuous consumption that he or she has really deserved personal enjoyment (Asia is the dominant market for French XO cognac at $80 per bottle).

5. The strong work orientation is facilitated by the collective ambience of effort.

6. A 'national teamwork' orientation: trade unions, businesses and the government strive more in the same direction than in the West, although conflicts of interests also exist.

7.   The Asian form of *contrat social*: the role of the state is mostly to provide law and order, as in Singapore. Citizens follow the rules in as far as the state is fair and humane.

8.   The state is a company and the citizens its shareholders.

9.   An orientation towards a 'morally clean environment': unbridled representations of sex and crime are not tolerated; attacks on other beliefs are inexorably pursued, since most of the societies comprise several religions.

10.   The press is free, but is not a 'fourth power'. Asian states believe in the necessity of a free press as a condition of good governance. But the press has no absolute right and must blend with the national consensus.

However, Asian diversity remains very strong, at least in terms of perceived inter-Asian differences. The Chinese perceive themselves as totally different from the Japanese, the Vietnamese or the Koreans. The Chinese Diaspora is present in several countries, with extended economic power and sometimes with difficult relationships with the native populations. The consensus is at society level: some strong conflicts between ingroups, for instance between Chinese and Malays in Malaysia, although

---

BOX 6.7

The fifth dimension: Confucian dynamism

A new dimension has been added to Hofstede's four dimensions described in Chapter 3. Michael Bond, a researcher based in Hong Kong, has designed a questionnaire called CVS, the Chinese Value Survey, which has been administered in 23 countries. It is based on basic values as seen by native Chinese social scientists. A new dimension was discovered through the CVS. Bond coined the term 'Confucian dynamism' to emphasize the importance of Confucian practical ethics, based on the following principles:

1.   The stability of society is based on unequal relationships, expressing mutual and complementary obligations as between father and son, older brother and younger brother, ruler and subject.

2.   The family is the prototype of all social organizations; individuality has to be repressed if it threatens harmony, but everybody's face must be maintained by preserving others' dignity.

3.   'Virtuous behaviour' towards others consists of not treating others as one would not like to be treated oneself.

4.   Virtue with regard to one's tasks in life consists of trying to acquire skills and education, working hard, not spending more than necessary, being patient and persevering.

(Source: Adapted from Hofstede and Bond, 1988, and Hofstede, 1991, p. 165.)

still very present, have been overcome in favour of co-operation. To illustrate the different attitudes and values of east Asians, Rosalie Tung (1996, pp. 369–70) recounts the following hypothetical situation presented to her by a Korean professor: two cars, driven by two Korean males, approach each other from the opposite ends of a narrow bridge; only one vehicle can pass at a time. He asks her what the two Koreans would do, and what two Japanese or two Chinese drivers would do in their place.

My response was as follows: 'the two Koreans would most probably step out of their cars and fight it out'. 'Correct', said my Korean colleague. 'In the case of the two Japanese drivers, each person would most probably ask the other to go first', I continued. 'Right you are again', nodded the Korean professor. I hesitated about the response to the possible reaction of the Chinese because China is a much larger country and there can be lots of regional differences. I told my Korean friend that I will venture an answer which is more characteristic of inhabitants in southern China. 'Each driver will most probably pull out the newspaper and start reading.' 'Correct again', my Korean friend said.

The formidable rise of China as a marketing environment is a special case in many respects because it is both an East Asian and a former communist country, while also a continent. Ho (1997) commenting on the emergence of consumer power in China, explains that a DRI/McGraw Hill report forecasts an average annual growth of 7.5 per cent for the Chinese consumer market over the decade. Now the eighth-largest country in the world in term of total advertising expenses, China has more than 25,000 official advertising agencies employing more than half a billion people *(Advertising Age International*, 1997; see Chapter 14). How China will import and develop marketing knowledge over the coming years is probably the greatest challenge faced by international marketers in the East Asian region.

6.7   LIMITATIONS TO THE WORLD-WIDE CONVERGENCE OF MARKETING ENVIRONMENTS

The political environment world-wide has clearly converged, with the steady decline of communist regimes. It is more and more difficult, given the powerful means of telecommunications, including satellite television and the Internet, to block the access of citizens to information on what is happening in their own country and in the world. Only a very few countries deny their citizens access to the Internet while some, like China and Tunisia, try to control access. The general economic environment is to a certain extent converging, but there are major limitations in a number of areas that are important for marketing. While economic systems are converging towards a market economy, the degree of poverty of a significant group of developing countries has been increasing over the years. Legal integration has limits since legal traditions continue to differ greatly. Some legal materials are duplicated and become complex, as in the European Union where laws pertaining to marketing are regulated both at EU level and at the level of member states, resulting sometimes in discrepancies, even if local regulations are supposed to comply with Europe-wide directives.

Marketing infrastructures are converging, because the standards of the marketing profession are fairly consistent world-wide. Multinational companies have heavily influenced the widespread adoption of similar practices even if to some extent tailored to local environments. Marketing knowledge is probably the most controversial issue. It is based on Anglo-American cultural premises and seems to have been widely adopted world-wide. However, a multitude of differences, both local and cultural, reflect how marketing knowledge has been understood, sometimes misunderstood, and often transformed. Hence, management expectations about both consumers' responses and the performance of marketing tasks can be partly disproved, even in an environment to which they are apparently suited, because there has not been enough awareness and understanding of the local marketing environment.

QUESTIONS

1. Why is local marketing knowledge important for designing marketing strategies?

2. In Sweden, the consumerist movement is particularly strong, as compared with France, Italy and Spain. Discuss why in the light of Hofstede's four dimensions (see Table 3.3).

3. What are the common values shared by people in the European Union? Conversely, what may be the differences?

4. To what extent does 'Confucian dynamism' explain the economic success of South-East Asian countries?

5. Based on the case of eastern European, and more generally the ex-communist, countries, explain what is a 'transition culture'.

6. What are the values shared by US, Mexican and Canadian societies? Conversely, on which aspects do they differ?

7. Discuss the limitations of the following statement: 'In the future there will be three major trading blocs: North America, western Europe and East Asia'.

APPENDIX 6: TEACHING MATERIALS

A6.1 Exercise: Clustering African countries

Relying on basic criteria (e.g. language, religion, political system, purchasing power per capita) define on a political map of Africa the main groupings of countries and their overlaps. Maps may be compared across students in the class in order to find a common division of the African continent into regional zones.

A6.2 Case: Odol

When Manfred Hansen took over as marketing director of Lingner and Fischer in 1985, the company held a meagre 15 per cent of the oral care market in Germany – half of what the leader, Procter & Gamble, could claim. Known since 1997 as SmithKline Beecham, the company now commands a 30.4 per cent share of oral care while P&G's slice has shrunk to 13.8 per cent according to AC Nielsen. And Mr Hansen has kept his promise to be the leading oral care company in Germany, while becoming No. 1 in Switzerland and Austria as well.

SmithKline managed this turnaround through savvy marketing, including extending the familiar Odol and Dr Best brand names, bringing a fresh positioning to whitening products and paying close attention to consumer needs in areas such as packaging, where it eliminated wasteful wrapping entirely. The company also achieved its success in Germany by keeping an eye on global strategies while giving local managers some autonomy. 'SmithKline Beecham is acting much faster and takes greater risks than P&G,' said a marketing manager at the now pacesetting company. 'We are in constant touch with headquarters in order to understand market situations in other countries, [but] fortunately headquarters leaves us freedom to act in our market, taking into consideration the local situation.'

Becoming the market leader in toothpaste, a $545 million category in Germany and hotly contested by rivals P&G, Colgate-Palmolive Co. and Elidda-Gibbs hasn't been easy. Newcomers barely get a chance to survive; Henkel's thera-med, launched in 1979 is a rare exception. So SmithKline and Mr Hansen proceeded cautiously, testing its toothpaste in a year-long test in two German cities, Bad Kreuznach and Buxtehude, of the names Odol med 3, Aquafresh med 3 and – extending the name of its existing toothbrush line – Dr Best med 3. It soon became evident that consumers favoured Odol med 3, a brand name under which the company had marketed a mouthwash concentrate since 1893. Not coincidentally, Odol is category leader in mouthwash with a 70 per cent share in Germany, 80 per cent in Austria, and 60 per cent in Switzerland. 'Odol's brand name is extremely strong; consumers have had confidence in the product for 100 years,' Mr Hansen said. 'We used this name because of the brand capital it has. Our headquarters ensures that each subsidiary uses international experience, but if we can be more successful with a local brand name, we use it.' For example, in Spain, the Aquafresh brand is marketed under the name Binaca Med 3.

SmithKline's eventual success in toothpaste was an even harder-won fight considering Odol med 3's premium price. The toothpaste was marketed for 25 per cent more than the average in Germany, but the price was justified by its attributes, such as three-prong protection against cavities, plaque and periodontal disease. After notching a 4 per cent market share in 1989, its first year, Odol med 3 climbed to 6 per cent in 1990 with the introduction of a mint line extension. By 1993, share was still climbing despite the fact that SmithKline was spending only $8 million to $10 million on advertising – half of what P&G was laying out for its Blend-a-Med brand. Odol also got a boost from SmithKline's move in 1991 to strip away cumbersome packaging and sell the tubes without an outer box. 'We take our consumers very seriously,' Mr Hansen said. 'When we noticed that consumers were reacting to unnecessary packaging, we acted immediately.'

The stripped-down package was touted in an amusing campaign from Grey Advertising, Düsseldorf, SmithKline's agency of record in oral care for 15 years. The spot mimicked a strip-tease act with the toothpaste unburdening itself of its outer wrapper as an audience of animated teeth yelled out cheers and catcalls. Mr Hansen, in fact, said its close relationship with Grey was a major reason for its conquest of German-speaking countries. 'We are one team,' he said. 'We have integrated the agency – the account people as well as the creative team – totally in our marketing, and we discuss with them everything from product policy to marketing strategy, prices and distribution.'

Grey, then, was part of SmithKline's decision to create a special package shaped like a tooth for Odol med 3 in Germany. This development also helped the base brand reach its current 9 per cent market share in Germany neck-to-neck with Blend-a-Med. The package is being used as a template in other markets, Mr Hansen said.

What put SmithKline finally over the top was its whitening line extension, Odol med 3 samtweiss. At the time of its introduction, in 1996, whitening toothpastes were considered an also-ran in the category, used mainly by smokers and coffee and tea drinkers, and they claimed only a 5 per cent segment of the total toothpaste market in Germany. Mr Hansen and his team aimed to change that with advertising that argued against consumers' notions that whiteners damage teeth and are abrasive. Further, the message was that everyone with yellowing teeth should try Odol med 3 samtweiss. In a single year the strategy propelled the toothpaste's German share to 6.8 per cent share and rocketed SmithKline's overall toothpaste share to 15.8 per cent. That sent competitors, including Henkel and Colgate, scrambling to introduce whiteners, which are just now about to hit store shelves.

But SmithKline's wasn't finished yet. There were still toothbrushes to consider. Although the company had sold a toothbrush under the Dr Best name since 1953, the brand's share languished at 5 per cent of the German market in the mid-1980s, and Mr Hansen said the company was considering spinning it off. 'We even discussed selling the brand,' he revealed, 'but I fought for its survival because market research showed us the Dr Best name had a recognition level of over 70 per cent. What we needed was a product advantage.' The break came in 1988, in the form of a new brush with a floating neck and a flexible handle that massaged the gums without injuring them. Grey then set to work: the agency sought, and found, a real Dr Best, a dental professional from the United States who appeared in TV ads that showed the toothbrush working on a tomato without damaging its delicate skin.

Not surprisingly, P&G and Colgate followed with products of their own – but not until SmithKline had leapt into the leadership position in toothbrushes with a 39.8 per cent share, up from a mere 5 per cent in 1985 when Mr Hansen began his initial assault.

(Source: Adapted from Mussey, 1997.)

QUESTIONS

1. Which aspects of the German marketing environment explain the success of Odol med 3 in terms of consumer response to the brand's innovations?

2. Why can a market like Germany be a lead market for packaging innovation in general?

3. Discuss the issues involved in transferring part of Odol's recipe for success to near national markets (France, the United Kingdom), especially the toothlike packaging.

NOTES

1. See for instance the four volumes published by Philip Parker (1997a, 1997b, 1997c and 1997d) which give detailed statistical references for the religious, linguistic, ethnic and national cultures of the world.

REFERENCES

Advertising Age International (1997), 'China's media boom rewards those willing to endure growing pains', October, p. i6.

Amine, Lyn S. and S. Tamer Cavusgil (1986), 'Demand estimation in a developing country environment: Difficulties, and examples', *Journal of the Market Research Society*, vol. 28, no. 5, pp. 43–65.

Berger, Brigitte, editor (1991), *The Culture of Entrepreneurship*, San Francisco: ICS Press.

Cecchini, Paolo (1988), *The European Challenge 1992*, Wildwood House: Aldershot.

Council of the European Communities (1992), *Treaty on European Union*, Luxemburg: Office for Official Publications.

Darbelet, Michel and Jean-Marcel Lauginié (1988), *Economie d'Entreprise*, vol. 1, Editions Foucher: Paris.

Dayan, Armand, Jérôme Bon, Alain Cadix, Renaud de Maricourt, Christian Michon and Alain Ollivier (1988), *Marketing*, Collection PUF Fondamental, Presses Universitaires de France: Paris.

Dietl, Jerzy (1992), 'Determinants of private business activities in Poland', *Journal of Business Research*, vol. 24, pp. 27–35.

Domanski, Tomasz (1992), 'Development of small private companies and their marketing activities', *Journal of Business Research*, vol. 24, pp. 57–65.

Doran, Kathleen Brewer (1997), 'Symbolic consumption in China: The color television as a life statement', in Merrie Brucks and Debbie McInnis (eds.) *Advances in Consumer Research*, vol. 24, Provo, UT: Association for consumer research, pp. 128–131.

EC Committee of the American Chamber of Commerce in Belgium (1994), *Business Guide to EC Initiatives*, Brussels, Winter/Spring.

El Haddad, Awad B. (1985), 'An analysis of the current status of marketing in the Middle East', in Erdener Kaynak (ed.), *International Business in the Middle East*, de Gruyter: New York, pp. 177–97.

Esposito, Odile (1994), 'Concurrence: L'Arme des Normes', *L'Usine Nouvelle*, 25 August.

European Communities (1987), *Treaties Establishing the European Communities*, Office for Official Publications of the European Communities: Luxemburg.

Fournis, Y. (1962), 'The markets of Europe or the European market?' *Business Horizons*, vol. 5 (Winter), pp. 77–83.

GATT (1986), *Le Commerce International en 1985–1986*, GATT: Geneva.

Ghauri, Pervez N. and Jean-Claude Usunier (1996), *International Business Negotiations*, Oxford: Pergamon/Elsevier.

Hayek, F. A. (1945), 'The use of knowledge in society', *The American Economic Review*, vol. XXXV, no. 4, September, pp. 519–30.

Ho, Suk-Ching (1997), 'The emergence of consumer power in China', *Business Horizons*, vol. 40, no. 5, pp. 15–21.

Hofstede, Geert (1991), *Culture and Organizations: Software of the mind*, McGraw-Hill (UK): Maidenhead.

Hoftsede, Geert and Michael Harris Bond (1988), 'The Confucius connection: from cultural roots to economic growth', *Organizational Dynamics*, vol. 16, no. 4, pp. 4–21.

Holden, Nigel (1995), 'A diachronic view of Russian misconceptions of marketing', *Proceedings of the Second Conference on the Cultural Dimension of International Marketing*, Odense, May 27–31, pp. 30–52.

Johansson, Johny K. (1994), 'The sense of "Nonsense": Japanese TV advertising', *Journal of Advertising*, vol. XXIII, no. 1, pp. 17–26.

Johansson, Johny K. and Ikujiro Nonaka (1996), *Relentless: The Japanese Way of Marketing*, New York: HarperCollins.

Khrutskogo, V. E. (ed.) (1991), *Sovremennyi Marketing*, Financy i Statistika: Moscow.

Kotler, Philip (1994), *Marketing Management*, 8th edn, Prentice Hall: Englewood Cliffs, NJ.

Lascu, Dana-Nicoleta, Lalita A. Manrai and Ajay K. Manrai (1996) 'Value differences between Polish and Romanian consumers: A caution against using a regiocentric marketing orientation in Eastern Europe', *Journal of International Consumer Marketing*, vol. 8, nos 3/4, pp. 145–67.

Lazer, William, Shoji Murata and Hiroshi Kosaka (1985), 'Japanese marketing: Towards a better understanding', *Journal of Marketing*, vol. 49 (Spring), pp. 69–81.

Leeflang, Peter S. H. and W. Fred Van Raaij (1995), 'The changing consumer in the European Union: A "meta-analysis"', *International Journal of Research in Marketing*, vol. 12, pp. 373–87.

Lessem, Ronnie and Fred Neubauer (1994), *European Management Systems*, Maidenhead: McGraw-Hill.

Mourier, Pascal and Didier Burgaud (1989), *Euromarketing*, Les Editions d'Organisation: Paris.

Mussey, Dagmar (1997), 'Marketing director provides SmithKline reasons to smile', *Advertising Age International*, November, p. 24.

Myrdal, Gunnar (1968), *Asian Drama, An Enquiry into the Poverty of Nations*, New York: Pantheon Books.

Naor, Jacob (1986), 'Towards a socialist marketing concept – The case of Romania', *Journal of Marketing*, vol. 50 (January), pp. 28–39.

Parker, Philip (1997a), *Religious Cultures of the World*, London: Greenwood Publishing.

Parker, Philip (1997b), *Linguistic Cultures of the World*, London: Greenwood Publishing.

Parker, Philip (1997c), *Ethnic Cultures of the World*, London: Greenwood Publishing.

Parker, Philip (1997d), *National Cultures of the World*, London: Greenwood Publishing.

Pohl, Manfred (1995), 'Südostasien: Autoritärer Pluralismus und witschaftliche Dynamik', *Entwicklung und Zusammenarbeit*, vol. 36, no. 2, pp. 40–3.

Quelch, John A., Erich Joachimsthaler and Jose Luis Nueno (1991), 'After the wall: marketing guidelines for eastern Europe', *Sloan Management Review*, vol. 82 (Winter), pp. 82–93.

Sinatra, Alexandro and Paola Dubini (1991), 'Book publishing', in Roland Calori and Peter Lawrence (eds.), *The Business of Europe*, Sage: London, pp. 94–115.

Stoetzel, Jean (1983), *Les Valeurs du temps présent: une enquête européenne*, PUF: Paris.

Taylor, Ronald E., Mariea Grubbs Hoy and Eric Haley (1996), 'How French advertising professionals develop creative strategy', *Journal of Advertising*, vol. XXV, no. 1, pp. 1–14.

Tietz, B., (1994), The Opening up of Eastern Europe: The Implications for Western Businesses, in Buckley, P. and Ghauri, P. (eds.) *The Economics of change in East and Central Europe: Its Impact on International Business*, London: Academic Press.

Tung, Rosalie (1996), 'Negotiating with East Asians', in P. N. Ghauri and J.-C. Usunier (eds.), *International Business Negotiations*, Oxford: Pergamon/Elsevier, pp. 369–81.

Usunier, Jean-Claude (1990), 'Some contextual aspects of the French international business education system: A pessimistic view', *European Management Journal*, vol. 8, no. 3, pp. 388–93.

Usunier, Jean-Claude (1998), *International and Cross-Cultural Management Research*, London: Sage Publications.

Van Raaij, W. F. (1978), 'Cross-cultural methodology as a case of construct validity' in M. K. Hunt (ed.), *Advances in Consumer Research*, Association for Consumer Research: Ann Arbor, vol. 5, pp. 693–701.

Whitelock, J. M. (1987), 'Global marketing and the case for international product standardization', *European Journal of Marketing*, vol. 21, no. 9, pp. 32–44.

Wierenga, Berend, Ad Pruyn and Eric Waarts (1996), 'The key to successful Euromarketing: Standardization or customization?', *International Journal of Consumer Marketing*, vol. 8, nos 3/4, pp. 39–67.

Wolfe, Alan (1991), 'The single European market: National or Euro-brands', *International Journal of Advertising*, vol. 10, pp. 49–58.

Zayavlov, P. S. and Demidov, V. E (1991), *Formula Uspekha – Marketing*, Mezhdunarodniye Otnosheniya: Moscow.

7 Cross-cultural market research

A French syrup maker ordered a survey of the Swedish market from a large international market research company: syrup, a solution of sugar dissolved in water and flavoured with fruit juice, was incorrectly translated as *blandsaft*, a Swedish term for concentrated fruit juice, a local substitute for syrup with much less sugar. When the results came in, they were of no use, because it was a local product rather than the product category at large that had been surveyed. Some brief introductory examples will serve to explain the topic of this chapter, that is, the problems that are met when undertaking market research across national/cultural environments and their solutions. Typical research questions may be similar to the following:

1. How should one undertake a market survey for instant coffee in a traditionally tea-drinking country (i.e. the United Kingdom or Japan)? What information and data must be sought? How should the data be collected?

2. Which information-gathering technique should one use for personal care products in a country where, for instance, potential respondents resent interviews as an intrusion into their privacy?

3. Where the starting point is a questionnaire that was originally designed for a specific country/culture, how should it be translated and adapted to the cultural specificity of other countries in which it is to be administered?

This chapter aims to provide the reader with some basic insights, drawn mostly from cross-cultural methodology in the social sciences, on how to solve these problems. The simultaneous launch of new products on several different national markets is becoming more and more frequent; therefore research of these markets has to be undertaken simultaneously. Cultural differences are the main characteristic when contrasting national contexts, as non-tariff barriers are eased. Again taking instant coffee as an example, we find that there is a marked difference in the research perspective according to which research questions are addressed.

1. How does one recover the market share lost by instant coffee to ground coffee in a traditionally coffee-drinking country? This requires the investigation of consumption patterns in certain social and family situations, when people drink specific coffee-based beverages.[1]

2. How does one increase the market share for instant coffee (out of the total hot beverages market) in a traditionally tea-drinking country?

Research objectives when developed through differing cultural contexts cannot be the same as those for domestic market research: an understanding of the cross-cultural environment is a basic requirement of research-objective formulation. Given the multinationalization of business, establishing the quality of research instruments, the consistency of behavioural/attitudinal constructs and the equivalence of samples are of paramount concern to the marketer. This chapter presents the main limits to equivalence across national/cultural contexts when one undertakes cross-cultural market research, and in particular the issue of conceptual and functional equivalence (section 7.1), translation problems (section 7.2), measure equivalence related to different units being used cross culturally (section 7.3), the comparability of samples and sampling procedures (section 7.4) and the equivalence problems in data-collection procedures resulting from interviewers' and respondents' attitudes towards surveys (section 7.5). The last section (section 7.6) discusses whether international market research should use a different approach from traditional positivistic market research techniques.

7.1   EQUIVALENCE IN CROSS-CULTURAL RESEARCH

If the type of data sought and the research procedures implemented are considered to be of general application, the main difference between domestic and cross-cultural market research lies in the likely difficulties in establishing equivalence at the various stages of the research process.[2] It is not self-evident, as the Japanese style of market research shows (see section 7.6), that research procedures and the type of data sought are completely independent of the cultural context of the researcher. But this chapter first emphasizes dependence on the researched context.

1. The complexity of the research design is greatly increased when working in an international, multicultural and multilinguistic environment (Douglas and Craig, 1983), not to mention the difficulties in establishing comparability and equivalence of data.

2. Even larger problems may arise when differences in sociocultural or psychographic variables imply different attitudes and behaviour when using particular types of product.

For instance, Plummer (1977) compared the attitudes of women from the United States, Europe and several Commonwealth countries, including Canada, regarding housework, child care and the use of deodorants, and demonstrated a wide range of results due to cultural differences. He showed, for example, that the US housewife does not consider house cleaning as important as her Italian counterpart. The benefits expected from cleaning products are more functional for Americans and more symbolic for the Italians, since Italian housewives regard their role in a more traditional way. Therefore the list of benefits shown on cards to potential interviewees should be changed according to each country (see the hair shampoo exercise in section A7.2).

Research approaches: emic versus etic

The classic distinction in cross-cultural research approaches, between emic and etic, was originated by Sapir (1929) and further developed by Pike (1966). The emic approach holds that attitudinal or behavioural phenomena are expressed in a unique way in each culture. Taken to its extreme, this approach states that no comparisons are possible. The etic approach, on the other hand, is primarily concerned with identifying universals. The difference arises from linguistics where phon*etic* is universal and depicts universal sounds which are common to several languages, and phon*emic* stresses unique sound patterns in languages.

In general, market research measurement instruments adapted to each national culture (the emic approach) offer more reliability and provide data with greater internal validity than tests applicable to several cultures (the etic approach, or 'culture-free tests'). But use of such instruments is at the expense of cross-national comparability and external validity: results are not transposable to other cultural contexts. This is why we will look now at establishing cross-national equivalence, which is inspired by the etic rather than the emic perspective.[3] In terms of Table 4.1 the issue would be very much at the centre of the four cells; it lies somewhere between looking with the same eye at an object which is supposed to be different and changing to a slightly different eye in order to have a better look.

Levels of cross-cultural equivalence

Management must provide guidelines for data collection. Consequently the systematic collection of data is vital, either domestic or international. It is important to follow a precise plan which outlines the various steps of the research process (Green *et al.*, 1988), starting with a clear and concise statement of the research problem. The relevant literature comprises several studies which explore the issue of cross-cultural equivalence (Green and Langeard, 1979; Leung, 1989, Poortinga, 1989, Van Herk and Verhallen, 1995; Cavusgil and Das, 1997). In one of the most exhaustive reviews of equivalence levels, Douglas and Craig (1984) identify thirteen areas where non-equivalence, causing non-comparability, may arise in comparative consumer research. The various levels of cross-cultural equivalence displayed in Table 7.1 are explained in the text of the chapter, with six main categories and sixteen subcategories that are further discussed in this text.

Conceptual equivalence

A basic issue in cross-cultural research is the determination of whether the concepts used have similar meaning across the social units studied. Problems of *conceptual*

TABLE 7.1   Categories of cross-cultural equivalence

A. Conceptual equivalence	**B. Functional equivalence**
C. Translation equivalence • Lexical equivalence • Idiomatic equivalence • Grammatical–syntactical equivalence • Experiential equivalence	**D. Measure equivalence** • Perceptual equivalence • Metric equivalence • Calibration equivalence • Temporal equivalence
E. Sample equivalence • Sampling unit equivalence • Frame equivalence • Sample selection equivalence	**F. Data collection equivalence** • Respondents' co-operation equivalence • Data collection context equivalence • Response style equivalence

Source: Partly from Douglas and Craig (1984, p. 95).

equivalence are more frequent when testing the influence of certain constructs on consumer behaviour, for example when a uniform cognitive theory is used in several countries (Green and White, 1976). For instance, the hypothesis of the cognitive theory that people do not willingly behave inconsistently may hold true in the United States while not being applicable to some other countries (conceptual equivalence).

The following statement from the anthropologist Clifford Geertz (1983, p. 59) gives a slight feeling of how difficult it may be to reach true conceptual equivalence between cultures:

The Western conception of a person as a bounded, unique, more or less integrated, motivational and cognitive universe, a dynamic center of awareness, emotions, judgement and action, organized in a distinctive whole . . . is, however incorrigible it may seem, a rather peculiar idea, within the context of world's cultures.

Such basic concepts as beauty, youth, friendliness, wealth, well-being, sex appeal and so on are often used in market research questionnaires where motivation for buying many products is related to self-image, interaction with other people in a particular society and social values. They are seemingly universal. However, it is always advisable to question the conceptual equivalence of all these basic words when designing a cross-cultural questionnaire survey. Even the very concept of 'household' (widely used in market research) is subject to possible inequivalence: Mytton (1996) cites the case of Northern Nigeria where people often live in large extended family compounds or *gida* which are difficult to compare with the prevalent concept of household which reflects the living unit of a nuclear family.

Many examples in previous chapters illustrate the practical difficulties in dealing with the conceptual equivalence of constructs used in a survey. When looking at the underlying dimensions across countries, one often realizes that they are not equivalently weighted or articulated in the total construct. For instance, in the construct 'waiting in line' (to be served), the dimension of 'losing one's time' may be emphasized in a time-conscious culture whereas it may be almost non-existent in one that is not economically time minded. When 'waiting in line', the dimension of 'guilt for pushing in' is more developed in guilt-oriented societies. Often the conceptual equivalence of several basic interrelated constructs has to be questioned, inasmuch as they relate to consumer behaviour idiosyncrasies for the specific type of product or service surveyed. Box 7.1 shows some construct equivalence problems in the case of life insurance policies.

BOX 7.1

A multinational survey on life insurance: Conceptual equivalence problems in Islamic countries

In Islam it is considered evil to talk about death. Nevertheless Muslim people do not fear death. On the contrary, they are probably much less frightened by the prospect of death than most people in western/Christian countries. But the notion of destiny is of the utmost importance: humans may not decide about their own death, nor are they entitled to control the process of it. One is not allowed to challenge the course of destiny, and therefore one should not speculate on one's own life and death. A verse of the Koran says approximately this: 'Behave each day as if your life will be very long, and for your after life, behave as if you will die tomorrow.' In Saudi Arabia, life insurance is forbidden. But some high-risk industries, such as oil production, bypass this prohibition by insuring their local employees through foreign life-insurance companies, with policies located abroad.

In the Islamic world people do not like to invest and bet on the long term. Effort must be rewarded quickly if it is to be maintained. The concept of a financial product such as life insurance needs a long-term orientation and a strong individual capacity to imagine the future. Projection towards the future is a culture-related trait (see section 2.2). In Islam, you may certainly imagine how you will be tomorrow, but not at a particular place or moment. The future tense exists, but it is certainly not as accurate or meticulous as that of the English or European languages. Moreover, protection of the family and solidarity within the extended family are highly valued and work effectively. If a man dies, his brother will care for his wife and children.

The concept of life insurance is related to culture in at least the following four aspects: protection of the family and/or the individual; future orientation; betting on one's own life and death; the degree of solidarity in the family and extended family group. In Islamic countries it is important not to offend interviewees at first contact. It is better to rely on in-depth non-directive interviews and focus groups carried out principally by briefed local researchers who have a thorough personal knowledge of Islam and the local culture (the Islamic world spreads from black Africa to China). Some research questions will have to be addressed in order to

BOX 7.1 *CONTINUED*

prepare an adequate marketing strategy. Which is the appropriate mix, for the design of the life insurance policies offered to potential consumers, in terms of death benefit (amount of money to be paid when a person under a life insurance policy dies) and annuities (a series of payments made at regular intervals on the basis of the premiums previously paid)? Which term(s) should be proposed for people before they receive the benefits of their life insurance policy? How should the beneficiaries be designated? How should this offer be communicated to potential consumers through advertisement: which brand name should be adopted and which themes and advertising style should be favoured in the advertising campaign?

Many popular marketing constructs have been used in cross-cultural research settings (perceived risk, brand loyalty, Rokeach value survey, lifestyles, etc.). Generally speaking, conceptual equivalence is an obstacle to the direct use of constructs which have been specifically designed for the US culture. The perceived risk construct, for instance, may differ in its components across cultures. It may be broken down into several subdimensions: social risk, physical risk, financial risk (Van Raaij, 1978). The emphasis placed on these subdimensions may vary across cultures: when buying cars, for example, people in some cultures may give more value to social risk (because their purchase and use of car is mostly status oriented) whereas in other cultures people may be more concerned with physical safety (because death in accidents is greatly feared).

Therefore it is necessary to investigate, far more frequently than is actually done, the construct validity in each culture where a cross-cultural consumer behaviour study is undertaken. This should be done by following recognized procedures to assess the validity of the underlying constructs at the conceptual level and reliability at the empirical/measurement instrument level (Grunert *et al.*, 1993).[4]

Similar products and activities performing different functions: Functional equivalence

If similar activities perform different functions in different societies, their measures cannot be used for the purpose of comparison (Frijda and Jahoda, 1966). Concepts frequently used in market surveys, such as preparing a meal, are not necessarily functionally equivalent across countries. When asked: 'What dishes do you cook, or prepare with tomato juice?', Italians and Danes will not think of the same. A similar product may perform different functions (Green and White, 1976): for example, a bicycle in one country may be considered a transportation vehicle (in The Netherlands for instance) whereas in other countries it may be only a leisure item. Stanton *et al.* (1982) illustrate this functional equivalence problem by taking the example of hot milk-based chocolate drinks. Whereas in the USA and the UK they are considered an evening drink, best before going to sleep, in much of Latin America a 'Chocolate Caliente' is a morning drink. Functional equivalence is reached neither in the consumption time period nor in the purpose for use (waking/energizer versus sleep/relaxer).

A watch may be used as wrist jewellery or an instrument for handling time and daily schedules. The same holds true for a fountain pen. In some countries its function may be as a simple general-purpose writing instrument; in others it may be regarded mostly as an instrument for signing documents. Elsewhere it may be considered purely non-functional since it needs time and care to refill it, and often leaks over one's fingers. Many other examples could be given, such as wine (everyday beverage accompanying meals versus beverage for special occasions), beer (summer refresher versus all-year standard 'non-water' beverage) and perfumes (masking bodily odours versus adding a pleasant smell after a shower).

The simple word 'coffee' covers a whole range of beverages which are enjoyed in very different social settings (at home, at the workplace, during leisure time, in the morning, or at particular times during the day), in quite different forms (in terms of quantity, concentration, with or without milk, cold or hot), prepared from different forms of coffee base (beans, ground beans, instant). The function of the Brazilian *cafezinho*, very small cups of coffee, rather strong and drunk every hour in informal exchanges with colleagues, cannot be compared with that of the US *coffee* which is very light and drunk mostly at home and in restaurants. One of the best ways to investigate functional equivalence is to examine the social settings in which a product is consumed.

7.2   TRANSLATION EQUIVALENCE

For many reasons which are outlined principally in Chapter 13 on language, culture and communication, translation techniques, even sophisticated ones, might prove incapable of achieving full comparability of data. Let us first make a small review of translation equivalence problems.

Categories of translation equivalence

Translation equivalence may be divided into the following subcategories: lexical equivalence, idiomatic equivalence, grammatical–syntactical equivalence and experiential equivalence (Sechrest *et al.*, 1972). Lexical equivalence is that which is provided by dictionaries: for instance, one may discover that the English adjective 'warm' translates into the French '*chaud*'. The problem of idiomatic equivalence comes when you try to translate a sentence such as 'it's warm': French has two expressions for it, either '*il fait chaud*' (literally, 'it makes warm' meaning 'it's warm [today]') or '*c'est chaud*' (meaning 'it [this object] is warm'). An idiom is a linguistic usage that is natural to native speakers. Idioms are most often non-equivalent: the present continuous (i.e. I am *doing*) has no equivalent in French, except '*je suis en train de . . .*' which is highly colloquial, not to be used in correct French written language.

Grammatical–syntactical equivalence deals with how in a language words are ordered, sentences are constructed and meaning is expressed. English generally proceeds in an active way, starting with the subject followed by the verb and then the complement, avoiding abstractions as well as convoluted sentences. Many languages, including German and French, start by explaining the circumstances in relative clauses, before they proceed into the action. This makes for complex sentences (as you may find in this book!) starting with relative clauses based on when, where, even though, although and so on. The Japanese language has a quite different ordering of words from western languages: verbs are always at the end of the sentence: '*Gurunoburu no daigaku no sensei desu*' means: 'Grenoble of [the] university of professor [I] am', that is, 'I am a professor at the university of Grenoble'.

Experiential equivalence is about what words and sentences mean for people in their everyday experience. Coming back to '*chaud*', it translates into two English words 'warm' and 'hot': the French do not experience 'warmth' with two concepts as the English, the Germans and many others do. Similarly the special experience of coldness in the word 'chilly' cannot be adequately rendered in French. Translated terms must refer to real items and real experiences, which are familiar in the source as well as the target cultures. An expression such as 'dish-washing machine' may face experiential equivalence problems when people, even if they know what it is, have never actually seen this type of household appliance nor experienced it.

Another example of experiential non-equivalence is given by the Japanese numbering system which reflects a special experience of counting, where the numbers cannot be fully abstracted from the object being counted. Most often the Japanese add a particle indicating which objects are counted. *Nin* for instance is used to count human beings: *yo-nin* is four (persons). *Hiki* is used for counting animals, except birds for which *wa* is used (meaning 'feather'), *satsu* for books, *hon* for round and long objects, *mai* for flat things such as a sheet of paper, textiles, coins, etc., and *hai* for cups and bowls and liquid containers in general. As a vivid illustration of translation problems, Box 7.2 shows the translation errors in the case of a major concept, 'reproductive health', for the UN World Conference on Population Development, held in Cairo in 1994.

BOX 7.2
'Reproductive health'

Cultural discrepancies are not only evidenced in factual themes, they also manifest themselves in translation difficulties: the concept of 'reproductive health' was translated into German as '*Gesundheit der Fortpflanzung*' (health of propagation). The Arabic translators invented the formula: 'spouses take a break from each other after childbirth', the Russian translators worded this in despair as 'The whole family goes on holiday' and the Chinese translators elevated themselves to the almost brilliant formula 'a holiday at the farm'. This shows that the new word-monsters, elegantly coined by the Americans, are almost non-translatable worldwide; on the other hand, they infuse international conferences with a lot of humour.

(Source: Bohnet, 1994.)

Back-translation and related techniques

The back-translation technique (Campbell and Werner, 1970) is the most widely employed method for reaching translation equivalence (mainly lexical and idiomatic) in cross-cultural research. This procedure helps to identify probable translation errors. One translator translates from the source language (S) into a target language (T). Then another translator, ignorant of the source-language text, translates the first translator's target language text back into the source language (S'). Then the two source-language versions, S and S', are compared.

For instance, when translating *'un repas d'affaires'* ('a business meal' in English) from French to Portuguese in the preparation of a questionnaire for Brazil, it is translated as *'jantar de negocios'*. When back-translated, it becomes a *'dîner d'affaires'* ('business dinner'). In Brazilian Portuguese, there is no specific expression for *'repas d'affaires'*. It is either a 'business lunch' (*'almoço de negocios'*) or a 'business dinner'. One has to choose which situation to elicit in the Brazilian questionnaire (as would be the case in English): the 'business meal' has to be either at noon or in the evening in the Portuguese version. When back-translating, discrepancies may arise from translation mistakes in either of the two directions or they may derive from real translation equivalence problems which are then uncovered. Then a final target-language questionnaire (T$_f$) is discussed and prepared by the researcher (who speaks the source language) and the two translators. In practice it is advisable to have one translator who is a native speaker of the target language and the other one a native speaker of the source language. It means that they are translating *into* their native language rather than *from* it, which is always more difficult and less reliable.

However, back-translation can also instil a false sense of security in the investigator by demonstrating a spurious lexical equivalence (Deutscher, 1973). Simply knowing that words are equivalent is not enough. It is necessary to know to what extent those literally equivalent words and phrases convey equivalent meanings in the two languages or cultures. Another technique, blind parallel translation (Mayer, 1978), consists of having several translators translate simultaneously and independently, from the source language into the target language. The different versions are then compared and a final version is written.

Combined translation techniques, limits of translation

Parallel and back-translation can be merged, as shown in Figure 7.1. When two languages and cultures present wide variations, such as Korean and French, combining parallel and back-translation provides a higher level of equivalence (Marchetti and Usunier, 1990).

For example, two Koreans translate the same French questionnaire F into two Korean versions, K1 and K2. A third Korean translator, who is unfamiliar with the original French text F, translates K1 and K2 into F1 and F2. A final Korean questionnaire, K3, is then prepared by comparing the two back-translated French versions F1 and F2. English is used to help compare them as it is widely used and more precise than either French or Korean. This example could be refined: the number of parallel translations may be increased, or back-translation processes may be independently performed (Usunier, 1991).

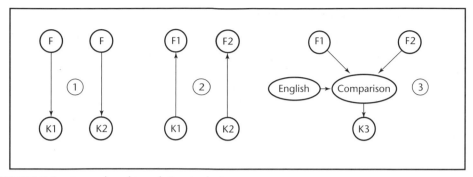

FIGURE 7.1   Examples of translation techniques.

(Source: Marchetti and Usunier, 1990.)

A more sophisticated solution to the problem of translation has been suggested by Campbell and Werner (1970). Research instruments should be developed by collaborators in the two cultures, and items, questions or other survey materials should be generated jointly in the two cultures. After back-translation, or after any initial translation process has been performed, there is an opportunity to change the source-language wording. This technique, called *decentring*, not only changes the target language, as in the previous techniques, but also allows the words in the source language to be changed, if this provides enhanced accuracy. The ultimate words and phrases employed will depend on which common/similar meaning is sought in both languages simultaneously, without regard to whether words and phrases originate in the source or the target languages. In the above example of the business meal, choosing

TABLE 7.2   Advantages and drawbacks of translation techniques

Technique ⇨	Direct translation	Back-translation	Parallel translation	Combined techniques
Process	S ⇨ T	S ⇨ T; T ⇨ S' comparison S to S' ⇨ final version T_f	S ⇨ T; S ⇨ T' comparison T to T' ⇨ final version T_f	S ⇨ T; S ⇨ T' T ⇨ S'; T' ⇨ S" comparison S' and S", decentring of S ⇨ final version T_f
Advantages	Easy to implement	Ensures the discovery of most inadequacies	Easier to implement in S country with T translators	Ensures the best fit between source and target versions
Drawbacks/ Constraints	Leads to translation errors and discrepancies between S and T	Requires the availability of two translators, one native in S and one native in T languages	Leads to good wording in T, but does not ensure that specific meaning in S is fully rendered	Costly to implement Difficult to find the translators Implies readiness to change source-language version

Key: S = source language, T = target language (translators or versions).

the decentring method would imply changing the words in the source questionnaire to 'business lunch'. In any case, it remains absolutely necessary to pre-test the translated research instrument in the target culture until satisfactory levels of reliability on conceptual and measurement equivalences are attained (Sood, 1990). Table 7.2 presents a synthesis of translation techniques as well as their advantages and drawbacks.

7.3   MEASURE EQUIVALENCE

Variations in the reliability of research instruments

Variation in cross-cultural reliability of underlying instruments has already been assessed, and Davis *et al.* (1981) claim that measurement unreliability is a threat to cross-national comparability. They investigated the problem of measurement reliability in cross-cultural marketing research for three types of consumer behaviour measures (demographics, household decision involvement and psychographics) across five country-markets, utilizing three different reliability assessment methods. Their findings show that it is easier to obtain measurement equivalence between demographic variables than between psychographic variables such as lifestyles. The assessment method and the nature of the construct may be two causes of measurement unreliability across countries.

Variations in knowledge and familiarity with products, concepts or attitudes, evoked in the section above, have a deep impact on the equivalence of measures. Parameswaran and Yaprak (1987) have compared the attitudes of respondents in two countries (the United States and Turkey) towards the people and products from three countries of origin (West Germany, Japan and Italy) using three products (cars, cameras and electronic calculators). They demonstrate that the same scale may have differing reliabilities when used by the same individual in evaluating products from differing cultures. The cars reviewed are the Volkswagen Golf (VW Rabbit, West Germany), the Honda Civic (Japan) and the Fiat 128 (Italy). Cameras considered are Leica (West Germany), Canon (Japan) and Ferrania (Italy). The brands of electronic calculator used are Royal (West Germany), Canon (Japan) and Olivetti (Italy).

differing levels of awareness, knowledge, familiarity and affect with the peoples, products in general, and specific brands from a chosen country-of-origin may result in differentials in the reliability of similar scales when used in multiple national markets . . . Two alternative courses of action may alleviate this problem. Measures to be used in cross-national market comparisons may be pre-tested in each of the markets of interest until they elicit similar (and high) levels of reliability . . . Alternatively, one might devise a method to develop confidence interval (akin to statistical spreads based on sample sizes) around the value of the measure based on its reliability. (Parameswaran and Yaprak, 1987, pp. 45–6.)

Therefore, comparison of results across countries should be made while simultaneously analyzing and checking for the reliability measures of the rating scales.

Perceptual equivalence

As emphasized in sections 1.4 and 9.4 perception varies across cultures. Colours are perceived differently according to cultures, that is cultures do not have equivalent

sensitivity to the various parts of the colour spectrum, and the corresponding languages do not qualify colours in exactly the same way. The next step (after colour identification) is the symbolic interpretation of colour, which varies widely (Box 9.5).The
same is true for smells: the first issue in equivalence is whether people perceive them
physically and mentally, related to the training of their olfactory apparatus; the
second issue deals with the kind of interpretation they vest in these smells. When
conducting research about packaging, perfumes for washing liquids or other products
where perceptive clues are important for product evaluation, it is a key research issue
to formulate questions so that interviewees can express their native views on the smell
or the colours. Rather than ask them whether they like a lavender smell, it is better to
ask them first to recognize the smell, then to comment on what it evokes.

Metric equivalence

The validity of a rating scale in a cross-cultural study is affected by the metric equivalence of the scales and by the homogeneity of meanings. Pras and Angelmar (1978)
did a comparison of verbal rating scales (semantic differentials) in French and English.
They showed that difficulties can occur in determining lexical equivalents in different
languages of verbal descriptions for the scale (see Table 7.3). It is also difficult to ensure
that the distances between scale points (adjectives, for instance) are equivalent in the
two languages (metric equivalence). In this case the standard deviation for French
respondents was significantly smaller than for US respondents, this being due to a
greater cultural homogeneity in France.

The method suggested by Pras and Angelmar leads to the rejection of definitional
equivalence of concepts with source language measurement instruments: in other

**TABLE 7.3   Adjectives which have the same level of meaning in two
languages and provide similar distances between the point
of the scale**

Colloquial rating scale				Formal rating scale			
US adjectives			French adjectives	US adjectives			French adjectives
Fantastic	20	20	Extraordinaire	Remarkably good	17	17	Très bon
Delightful	17	17	Superbe	Good	14	14	Bon
Pleasant	14	14	Très correct	Neutral	10	10	Moyen
Neutral	10	10	Moyen	Reasonably poor	6	6	Faible
Moderately poor	7	7	Assez faible	Extremely poor	3	3	Très mauvais
Bad	4	4	Remarquablement faible				
Horrible	2	2	Terriblement mauvais				

(Source: Pras and Anglemar, 1978, p. 76.)

words, it is naive to use a differential semantic scale originally written in English, French or any other language and translate it lexically (simply with dictionary-equivalent words) into other languages. Pras and Angelmar favour decentred measurement which means constructing reliable and valid scales for all the countries under survey. In this case the original wording of the scale may be changed if it provides better measurement equivalence across countries/cultures.

Sood (1990) studied the metric equivalence of nine scale terms (from 'excellent' to 'very bad') across eight languages (English, Arabic, Chinese, Farsi, French, German, Korean and Spanish). He evidences two facts: (1) some languages have fewer terms to express gradation in evaluation (e.g. Korean), whereas others have a multitude (French); and (2) there are large discrepancies in the 'value' of these adjectives, measured on a scale from 0 to 100: for instance, the Spanish *'muy malo'* was 58 per cent higher than its supposed English equivalent of 'very bad'. Therefore the best solution is not to try and translate scale terms but rather to start from local wordings based on scales used by local researchers.

One of the promising avenues for cross-cultural research is the use of purely visual scales that avoid the verbocentric nature of most market research instruments, which are based on words and sentences that never translate perfectly. Zaltman (1997) argues in favour of 'putting people back in': most communication relies on images and is non-verbal, whereas thinking processes rely on metaphors which are important in eliciting hidden knowledge. That is the reason for using instruments that allow respondents to express the mix between emotions and reason. The use of 'smiling faces' as scales should not be necessarily limited to children, on the basis of the (unconscious) view that adults should use words, not pictures, and should not express their views metaphorically. More sophisticated visually oriented scales, such as the self-assessment manikin (SAM), allow cross-cultural measurement with less biases than verbal scales; they further enable a better apprehension of the respondents' emotions (Morris, 1995).

Calibration equivalence

To calibrate is to mark the scale of a measuring instrument so that readings can be made in appropriate units. A typical calibration equivalence problem relates to differences in monetary units; this is especially true in high-inflation contexts where daily prices over a year cannot be directly compared with those of a low-inflation country. Naturally, exchange rates and units of weight, distance and volume cause calibration equivalence problems. Calibration equivalence mixes with perceptual equivalence: for instance, how many colour classes are recognized by people from a particular country? This might prove useful for a packaging test or a product test. Western subjects, for example, have more colour classes than African subjects, and some primitive people have only a two-term colour language. The Bantu of South Africa, for example, do not distinguish between blue and green. Consequently they do not discriminate between objects or symbols in these colours (Douglas and Craig, 1984, p. 100).

Calibration equivalence problems arise from different *basic* units being used as well as from *compound* units when they are based on different computation systems (see Box 7.3).

BOX 7.3

Measuring fuel efficiency across cultures

Most Europeans use the metric system, an international standard. They measure distances in kilometres and liquid volumes in litres (one cubic decimetre). When looking at fuel consumption, they reckon how many litres are necessary for driving a hundred kilometres, at a particular average speed. Fuel consumption is measured in litres/100 km. In the USA, 'gas mileage' is based on a reverse concept: given a definite fuel volume, namely a gallon, how many miles can one drive with it? For Europeans trying to understand what 'miles per gallon' means is somewhat nightmarish. First, they have to know which gallon it is: the British or Imperial gallon (4.55 litres) or the US gallon (3.79 litres) and whether it is a statute mile (1.609 kilometres) or a nautical mile. When they understand that it is a US gallon and a statute mile, they still have to make an inverse calculation and try to finish with 100 kilometres in the denominator in order to know whether the car has high petrol consumption or poor gas mileage. Fortunately, gasoline is cheap in the United States.

Temporal equivalence

Temporal equivalence is near to calibration equivalence, in terms of calibrating dates and time periods. Information, for instance, ages at different speeds across countries: in a country where the annual inflation rate is 1 per cent, income and price data are comparable across years; whereas in a Latin American country with a 2,000 per cent annual inflation rate, it is necessary to indicate on which exact day the data were collected and what the price indexes and exchange rates were at that exact date. Temporal equivalence also deals with differences in development levels and technological advancement: certain countries are 'equivalent' to what others were 20 years ago. Assessing time lags may be useful for making analogies: such a market may develop in South Africa now as did in the United States 15 or 20 years ago and the product life cycle may be similar even though the two countries are at different points on the curve.

7.4   COMPARABILITY OF SAMPLES

When secondary data – especially published statistical data – are sought, there may be some difficulties in comparing these data across countries:

1. Differences in categories: for instance, for age brackets, income brackets or professions.

2. Difference in base years, when some countries have no recent data.

3. Unavailable or unreliable data, the data collection procedure by the local census bureau being biased for certain reasons (non-exhaustive census, inadequate sampling procedure).

4. Sampling unit (who should the respondent be?).

Choice of respondents (sampling unit equivalence)

An important criterion for sampling is the choice of respondents. Selecting a unit of analysis is a key issue in the conceptualization of comparative research design. The role of respondents in the buying decision process (organizational buying, family buying, information and influence patterns, etc.) may vary across countries. This statement is as relevant for industrial markets as for consumer goods markets. In the United States, for instance, it is not uncommon for children to have a strong influence when buying cereals, desserts, toys or other items, whereas in countries that are less child oriented, children's influence on the buying decision will be much smaller (Douglas and Craig, 1984). The same holds true for the extended-family pattern in South East Asia, which heavily influences individual buying decisions. It is therefore of primary interest to assess, first, the basic equivalent sampling units: for instance, when researching industrial products, to compare the position, role and responsibility of industrial buyers throughout different countries.

Representativeness and comparability of national/cultural samples

Sampling is a basic step in most market surveys. A complete census, where the whole population of interest is researched, generally proves too costly. Therefore it is advisable to infer the characteristics of the whole population from a limited sample. In this process the following tasks must be carried out:

1. Finding a sampling frame, the basic characteristics of which are known (a telephone directory, an electoral list, etc.).

2. Drawing a sample from this frame, by a method which may be either probabilistic or non-probabilistic.

3. Checking that the selected sample is representative of the population under study.

The main problem in the cross-cultural sampling process is the selection of samples that can be considered comparable across countries. According to Green and White (1976), reaching perfect comparability is very difficult, in fact almost impossible. These limitations should be considered when interpreting research findings. An initial issue to be addressed is the two-level type of sampling where the first level is a sample of countries or cultures and the second level is based on samples of individuals within these countries or cultures, that is, within each national sample.

At the first level, the research question is directly comparative. Hofstede clearly explains that samples of cultures should not be confused with samples of individuals. He draws attention to the risk of abusive stereotyping, whereby country characteristics are considered as individual characteristics: 'Mean values are calculated from the scores on each question for the respondents from each country. We do not compare individuals, but we compare what is called central tendencies in the answers from each country' (Hofstede, 1991, p. 253). Samples of countries can be used to compute the average influence of cultural values on certain consumption patterns. For instance, what are the main cultural variables which, in combination with sociodemographic and economic variables, determine the per capita consumption of a particular product or service: motor insurance, telephones, milk powder, etc? Strategic marketing decision making often needs such research for selecting target national markets and markets with low actual demand but high growth potential, and for deciding where to locate efforts for the future. A cross-cultural/cross-national design may also be useful when one tries to derive an estimated market demand figure in a country where statistical sources are scarce and unreliable. Amine and Cavusgil (1986) give examples of methods for estimating market potential, when limited data are available. They take the case of the Moroccan demand for wallpaper. For instance, it is possible to estimate a regression equation explaining per capita annual wallpaper consumption, with explanatory variables such as income per capita, percentage of home ownership, frequency of use of other wall-covering materials, etc. To estimate the parameters it is possible to use a cross-section sample (data for a sample of countries, for the same year), or a pooled cross-section/time series sample, when the countries' data are available for several years. For a country where wallpaper consumption is unknown, it is then possible to compute it with the values of the explanatory variables.

A second issue is the representativeness of each sample in each unit of analysis, which may be a country, a culture, or a common language group which shares similar patterns of social interaction and communication (Douglas, 1980; Douglas and Craig, 1997). Countries are generally the least bad proxies for cultural units. In cross-cultural research it seems *a priori* relevant to follow a systematic procedure, the same in every country, to achieve reliability and comparability of data. Unfortunately, demographic definitions do not correspond exactly from one country to another. Age does, of course, as long as people know their birth dates, but occupation, education and socioeconomic status usually do not. If data are presented in categories, say for income or age bracket, these categories will most likely not correspond exactly across countries (category equivalence). Religion and tribal membership will also have to be added to traditional demographics as they are of the utmost importance in some less developed countries (Goodyear, 1982).

A representative sample?

The researcher then constructs a sample which represents the population of interest. However, a sample split into 50 per cent men and 50 per cent women conveys a different meaning in a country where women's rights are recognized from that in more traditional countries where women's status is lower. The expression 'representative sample' therefore makes little sense if one does not clarify which traits and characteristic this sample actually represents. For instance, shopping behaviour is very different world-wide: in some places men tend to do most of the shopping, in other countries it is mostly women; this also depends on various other factors (income level, type of product, etc.). In this case the samples must represent actual shoppers, rather than men and women as they are in the general population of potential shoppers.

In order to define a sampling procedure for cross-cultural research, one must select a method that is based on several national samples, each of them being fully representative of the population of the country which it attempts to represent, and which furthermore provides comparable data across countries. Douglas and Craig (1983) stress the limited availability of an exhaustive sampling framework which corresponds exactly to the characteristics of the population at a global (multi-country) level.

Sampling frames are often biased. Mytton (1996), doing audience research for the BBC world-wide, stresses the frequent lack of reliable or recent census data in many developing countries, in the former Soviet Union and in eastern Europe. A sample drawn from the electoral list in Bolivia may over-represent men since women are not as likely to vote (Stanton *et al.*, 1982). Tuncalp (1988) states that most sampling frames in Saudi Arabia are inadequate: there is no official census of the population, no elections and therefore no voter registration records, and telephone directories tend to be incomplete. Tuncalp suggests further that non-probability sampling is a necessary evil.

Douglas and Craig (1983) also suggest that an empirical method (non-probability sampling procedures) may prove as efficient as probability sampling, when researching cross culturally. Data can be collected at a reasonable cost, compatible with the objectives of the survey. Therefore the basic criterion for selecting the sampling procedure(s) will remain the comparability of results across countries. Taylor (1995) explains how survey firms in different countries measure public opinion and survey markets with different methods; he shows for instance that quota sampling, considered as unacceptable since the 1950s in the United States, is used in most of Europe. Similarly the use of RDD (random digit dialling) to construct phone samples, which is standard practice in the United States for telephone surveys, in order to include both unlisted people and recent movers, is not used in phone samples in most countries of the world.

Estimating sample size is also a critical step. The use of traditional statistical procedures, such as constructing confidence intervals around sample means, or hypothesis testing, is difficult to implement inasmuch as such procedures require precise estimates of the variance of the population. This variance estimate is often unavailable in countries which have poor census data.[5] The most frequently used procedure is therefore the selection of sample size, country by country, taking into account their respective peculiarities (Douglas and Craig, 1983).

If research starts from a domestic survey, where the home country representativeness has been emphasized, and is then extended to other countries, it may be difficult to achieve comparability. Although true random sampling is necessary for the successful completion of research projects, studies using non-random samples can also be valuable, if they include all the characteristics of the subjects and environment that could potentially influence the results or their interpretation.

Finally one may conclude that representativeness and comparability of cross-cultural samples can be better achieved by using different samples and sampling techniques which produce equivalent levels of reliability, than by using the same procedure with all samples. The main problem (before any statistical procedure is implemented) is to secure equivalence in meaning: does it make sense to represent the same populations across various countries? Do the samples actually represent these populations in the same way?

7.5   DATA-COLLECTION EQUIVALENCE

Where primary data are concerned, discrepancies in response patterns across countries may cause data unreliability and so limit direct comparison. Let us assume that through any of the translation procedures described above we are able to develop equivalent national versions of a common questionnaire for a cross-cultural market research study, and we have consistent and equivalent samples. Response equivalence problems may, however, appear, such as the following:

1.   Secrecy/unwillingness to answer (respondents' co-operation equivalence).

2.   Response biases (data-collection context equivalence).

3.   Differences in response style (response-style equivalence).

Sources of error measurement related to response styles are multiple and may directly create discrepancies between observed measurement and true measurement. Some basic precautions may help to avoid the generation of data with a great deal of measurement error.

Reluctance to answer: Respondents' co-operation equivalence

Respondents sometimes feel that the interviewer is intruding into their privacy. They prefer not to answer, or they consciously bias their answers, fearing that their opinion could later be used against them (Stanton *et al.*, 1982). Many countries have strong privacy/intimacy patterns, where the family group is protected from external, impersonal interference. Tuncalp (1988) explains that the very private and reserved nature of Saudis is not conducive to personal interviews. Being independent, Saudis do not want to be possibly exposed to justifying or explaining their actions when answering a barrage of questions. In the case of Afghanistan and Mozambique, Mytton (1995, p. 26) explains that:

Protocol demands that the most senior woman of the house should be interviewed before any other female . . . In some areas of Afghanistan, [women] cannot be used as interviewers. In others the reverse is the case; a male stranger coming to a house would be regarded as a possible threat . . . As in Afghanistan, many respondents in Mozambique did not know their own age or that of other members of the household . . . In several areas the presence of strangers writing down information on pieces of paper while talking to people, started rumours. One rumour suggested that the survey team was registering the number of children in each household with the intention to return later and kidnap them. Research had to be delayed for meetings to be held with the local authorities in order for them to reassure people living in the area.

Context equivalence of data collection

There is inevitably a social and cultural context of questions; questions are never culture-free. Contextual equivalence relates to elements in the context of the data-collection process that have an influence on responses. As Douglas and Craig explain (1984, p. 109): 'In the Scandinavian countries, for example, respondents are considerably more willing to admit overdrinking than in Latin America. In India, sex tends to be a taboo topic.' Any question that deals, directly or indirectly, with social prescription needs to be worded so that people can elaborate a response without feeling too embarrassed, and responses have to be screened in order to know if the responses reflect actual reality or a view of what is socially desirable. Some well-disposed and open-minded interviewees may be questioned further to deliver their true view on the question.

Biases resulting from the relationship with the interviewer

Sexual biases between interviewer and respondent are also an important source of the reluctance to grant interviews (Kracmar, 1971). In many traditional countries, house-wives are reluctant to grant interviews to male interviewers. Ethnic bias may also exist between the interviewer and the respondent: a Chinese person may feel uncomfort-able when interviewed by a Malay (Kushner, 1982). Much response bias may result from the interviewees not understanding that the process of interviewing them is in order to generate objective data. Informants may perceive the purpose of research as a very long-winded form of selling, especially in developing countries (Goodyear, 1982). The objective and the process of the interview must often be explained at the begin-ning. When briefing native interviewers (management students) in Mauritania, I was asked the following question: 'What do you want us to tell the interviewee to answer?' It was necessary to explain to the interviewers that interviewing was a distanced and objective process, where interviewees had complete freedom of response. The idea of objective truth, external to personal relations, is unfamiliar to Mauritanians (Box 7.4). Furthermore, among the Mauritanian interviewers, the Maures, of Arabic descent, clearly explained that they would not interview black Africans. Fortunately, there were some black Africans who were potential interviewers for their own ethnic group. Strong ingroup orientation implies that group membership has to be shared between interviewer and interviewee for the process to take place. Maruyama (1990) explains in the same vein that Japanese managers in Indonesia tend to recruit Bataks, because their characteristics resemble those of the Japanese, although they are not necessarily liked by other Indonesians and they may perform poorly as data collectors. This ethnicity-of-interviewer bias has been shown to exist even within the United States, where both Hispanic and Anglo-American respondents significantly bias their responses to items pertaining to the interviewer's culture; therefore it seems more appropriate to match respondent's and interviewer's ethnicity, especially for Anglo-Americans (Webster, 1996).

Some respondents, especially in Latin-American countries (Stanton *et al.*, 1982) tend to present a 'courtesy bias' by answering in order to please the interviewer. Respondents tend to tell the interviewer what they think the interviewer would like to hear. This response pattern probably takes place in countries where people tend to have difficulty in answering opinion surveys and market research questionnaires. When they agree to participate, it can be from a personal feeling of goodwill towards the interviewer.

Response-style equivalence

Response-style equivalence is the final step (all the rest may be equivalent; yet our respondents may offer non-equivalent responses). The three main concerns in relation to response-style equivalence are:

BOX 7.4

The weaknesses and strengths of the 'local researcher'

1. Weaknesses.
   (a) Often of lower intellectual ability and research experience than his or her equivalent in developed countries.
   (b) Often finds it difficult to adopt neutral, objective stance with reference to informants or clients. May want to be didactic in groups and may well prefer to distort findings to reflect a more educated picture of his countrymen than exists in reality. Alternatively, may seek to distance himself from the 'average consumer' by exaggerating their foibles and lack of sophistication. He himself, especially if he is from an educated family, may be out of touch with his countrymen.
   (c) He may be unwilling or unable, even for business reasons, to cross traditional barriers of class, religion or tribe.
   (d) He rarely has the Puritan work ethic and does not always see the value of objective truth. Delays, shortcuts and distortion are likely.

2. Strengths.
   (a) He knows the country and its people. He can usually establish rapport easily and understands what is said. If he knows the Western country he can also interpret the significance of what is said, to explain differences.
   (b) He knows the language. Language can be an enormous barrier, as anyone who has tried to interview through interpreters must recognise.
   (c) He is immune to local ailments and is physically comfortable in the (research) environment. He can cope, through familiarity, with common problems.

(Goodyear, 1982, pp. 90–1.)

1. Yea-saying pattern (and, conversely, a nay-saying pattern).
2. Item non-response pattern.
3. Extreme response style.

Douglas and Craig (1983) describe this response-style as introducing a 'yea-saying' pattern. Response scores tend to be inflated and the mean score of the respondents are biased towards the positive end of the scale. If the 'courtesy bias' is generally high such a bias may be found. Van Herk and Verhallen (1995) evidence such a bias when interviewing Greek and Italian housewives on their cooking behaviour: there is systematic tendency in the Greek sample to give more positive answers in psychographics as well as in product-related questions, than in the Italian sample. The yea-saying bias translates into a higher mean score on almost all questions. Standardizing scores across cultures allows the 'yea-saying' pattern to be eliminated, although it is fairly difficult to differentiate whether people were generally striving to give answers towards the positive end of the scale or were agreeing strongly with a particular item. Thus the 'yea-saying' pattern is diagnosed only when it is consistent across almost all the questions.

Item non-response is an important source of bias in cross-national surveys. Respondents may be unwilling to respond to some questions, such as those relating to income or age. Douglas and Shoemaker (1981), studying non-response to different items in a public opinion survey in eight European countries, found evidence of non-response in relation to income being higher in the United Kingdom and Ireland, whereas the willingness to respond to political questions was highest in Germany and Italy.

Another potential bias may also be introduced by significant differences in extreme response style patterns across countries. The overall response pattern is systematically marked by higher standard deviation. US people tend to respond with more enthusiasm, and therefore present a more extreme response style in answering, than the Japanese (Zax and Takashi, 1967) or Koreans (Chun et al., 1974). This could produce a bias in the standard deviation of data, increasing it artificially in cultures where people tend to overreact to questions, compared to other cultures where people may tend to suppress their opinions, either positive or negative.

7.6   RESEARCHING INTERNATIONALLY

For various reasons, apart from the equivalence issues reviewed previously, international research is different from domestic research: (1) it is more difficult and more costly to implement, and the stakes are often smaller than those in the domestic market; and (2) information often needs to be fed more directly into action, thus a 'hands-on' approach is to be recommended.

The Japanese style of market research

Johansson and Nonaka (1987) show that Japanese firms use market survey techniques that are quite distinct from those used by US companies. Japanese do survey markets, but decide what to do afterwards fairly independently of the survey conclusions. For example, research was presented to Akio Morita, founder and president of the Sony corporation, which suggested that the Walkman would not be bought by consumers: they would not buy a tape player that does not record, even a portable one. Trusting his intuition, though undoubtedly after fairly wide consultation, Akio Morita and Sony took the decision to launch the Walkman, with the success we all know. It is likely that an American boss would not have taken such a decision.

In fact Japanese firms take a direct interest in the realities of the market-place and outlets. They look for information from the actual *buyers* (not the potential consumers), who are interviewed about the products they want, and how the products themselves could be better tailored to consumers' needs. Johansson and Nonaka cite the example of the chief executive officer of Canon USA. He spent six weeks visiting Canon distribution networks, chatting to sales executives, customers and store managers, in order to find out why Canon cameras were not selling as well as the competition.

This attitude is quite different from the prescriptions of traditional market research, which are as follows:

1. Market research has to be representative, therefore a representative sample must be used.

2. Market research must be scientifically objective. A questionnaire (that is, a systematic but not necessarily *open-ended* information retrieval instrument) should be administered by non-participating researchers (they should not be personally involved in the consequences of the responses given by interviewees).

3. Research has to study the *potential* market, not the actual market (that is, real buyers and real users).

4. As far as possible, the people who undertake market research should not be the same people who ultimately decide on the marketing strategy to be adopted. There is a potential danger that the boss of Canon USA could be manipulated by customers and distributors, who might take the opportunity to demand lower prices or other benefits by overstating competitors' strengths. There is also the risk that by focusing on the actual market, as yet untargeted market segments could be ignored or neglected.

As Johansson and Nonaka emphasize (1987, p. 16):

Japanese-style market research relies heavily on two kinds of information: 'soft data' obtained from visits to dealers and other channel members, and 'hard data' about shipments, inventory levels, and retail sales. Japanese managers believe that these data better reflect the behaviour and intentions of flesh-and-blood consumers. Japanese companies want information that is context specific rather than context free – that is, data directly relevant to consumer attitudes about the product, or to the way buyers have used or will use specific products, rather than research results that are too remote from the actual consumer to be useful.[6]

Market research as images of reality: Atomistic versus organic views

In fact, market surveys are, at best, 'photographs' of the market; they are not the market itself. At the Los Angeles County Museum of Art there is a painting by the Belgian Painter René Magritte, called 'La pipe'. It simply shows a pipe, with a thin trail of smoke going out of it. That is (almost) all. Then: there is a short subtitle at the bottom of the painting, saying *'ceci n'est pas une pipe'* (this is not a pipe): a very 'down to earth' way of reminding us that *images of reality* should not be confused with reality itself. We may create images of reality, especially through the media (for instance, a war reported on a TV screen) but we may also ignore large chunks of reality (especially its experiential elements).

On the other hand, we should not underestimate the power of the process of designing images of reality, especially for decision-making purposes. Scientific market research provides marketing decision makers with an image of the actual and/or potential market, consumer behaviour and the competition. Large parts of reality are beyond our limited perceptual apparatus. Let us take another example: at the Mount

Wilson observatory in California, there are photographs of the stars taken with a special quality of film, with a shutter exposure of four hours. The stars in the sky are far more numerous than we will ever see with our limited eyes. The same holds true for market research: from panels, or more generally, from a large and representative sample of consumers, we may derive images of the market, which we will never match simply by talking with anyone who is around.

Our argument is that, across countries, marketing decision makers do not use exactly the same information for a similar decision process, and that, to a certain extent, culture influences the scope and nature of researched information, and the use of the results in the process of marketing decision making. Two basic approaches to reality may be contrasted, as ideal types, the atomistic and the organic approaches (Table 7.4), which we all share, across individuals and cultures. In terms of research traditions, the atomistic view is close to distanced positivistic research, the organic view is nearer to humanistic inquiry (Hirschmann, 1986) and action research.[7] First, we can consider ourselves as being outside the real world, as observers, able to depict with a certain degree of precision workable images of the real world (atomistic), and then to use them to interact with this external world. Conversely, one may emphasize that we are an integral part of this reality, to which we belong so inextricably that it is not really possible to separate oneself from the reality. We are so deeply immersed in it that it would make no sense. These two approaches are complementary rather than simply antagonistic. But one approach can be dominant among a group of people or, a culture, or in an individual or an area of knowledge (Usunier, 1997).[8]

The atomistic approach leads us to consider reality as fundamentally divisible into units which display enough independence that, operationally, we can ignore the interrelations between pieces of reality. In contrast, the organic approach assumes the indivisible nature of reality, its elements (if there are any) being fundamentally interdependent. Reality is global rather than piecemeal. Table 7.4, which builds on Tables 2.1 to 3.5, shows how these approaches are linked to major categories of cultural differences, although the difference between atomism and organism is not a cultural difference. The atomistic belief in *divisibility* favours the view that time is divisible, that the basic unit of interpersonal relations is the individual, and that communication can and must be explicit (that is, clearly separated, 'divided' from surrounding issues, topics and preoccupations). Separating emotions from actions, friendship from business, is typically an atomistic attitude towards reality, seen as divisible. Very naturally, the atomistic approach favours the perception that data orientation and measurement are the proof that a piece of reality is divisible and (therefore) exists. To illustrate the importance of measurement in the atomistic approach, let us take the case of a company which is trying to improve service *within* the company, so that it is not only front-line service providers who are concerned with service to customers. In addressing such an issue, a typical atomistic statement would be: 'To arrive at a position where excellent service is achieved will be a difficult enterprise. This primarily results from the lack of service measurement knowledge *within* the company.' In fact, scales exist only to measure service quality *vis-à-vis* customers, so that the atomistic solution is to try and develop a measurement instrument, because the reality of within-company service cannot be tackled in the absence of measurement instruments. The organistic approach holds the contrary assumption:

it is precisely because measurement is difficult that the two issues are considered as non-separate and to be treated as a joint piece of reality. The research approach will be quite different.

On the other hand, the organic approach is tightly linked to collectivism in its strongest sense: people do not consider themselves as being separate from the group to which they belong. Their sense of belonging includes the implicit view that they are not really separable from their group. The communication style is more implicit and contextual, because the sense of the interdependence of pieces of reality is much stronger. In interpersonal relationships, loyalty is characteristic of the organic approach, whereas reciprocity, based on tabulated favours on each side (time, amount and persons being clearly defined), is linked to the atomistic approach. To this list can be added that proof (in the sense of making it work, be accepted and be considered as a necessary piece of reality) is based on validated theory, for the atomistic approach, and on arguments favouring conviction and virtue, for the organic approach.

With divisible reality, linear time and individual emphasis, the atomistic approach conceives of decision making as a highly formalized process, followed by implementation, control and feedback. It is a time sequence such as we see in many managerial textbooks. Conversely, the organic approach emphasizes circularity in time and the integration of time horizons. Preparing, making decisions and implementing them are not easily seen as completely separated pieces of time reality, leading to a fairly unstructured decision-making process. Finally, the organic approach does favour 'localism', local solutions, because solutions are built in the context and there is a difficulty in conceiving universal solutions. Conversely, the data and theory orientation in the atomistic approach favours universalism, because reality, when reduced to figures, shows a fairly high degree of universality.[9]

The case of research on international markets: Doing research with limited data availability and limited resources

More than twenty years ago Keegan (1974) pointed out in a study of multinational scanning by US firms that information sought for international market research is rather different in focus and type from domestic research. His study documented

TABLE 7.4   Atomistic versus organic approaches

Approach to reality	Atomistic	Organic
Nature of reality	Divisibility/independence	Global/indivisible/dependent
Time	Linear/divisible	Cyclical/integrative
Communication style	Explicit/low context	Implicit/high context
Interpersonal relations	Individualist/reciprocal	Collectivist/loyal
Intellectual style	Data/measurement oriented	Intellectual modesty
Proof	Validated theory (truth)	Virtue/conviction
Space	Universalist	Localist
Decision making	Formalized	Weakly structured

marketing decisions made on the basis of several information sources. In 60 per cent of the instances, survey-based information, often highly subjective, constituted approximately two-thirds of the information package. As explained in the sections above, when research is conducted internationally, the basic conditions of market research are different from those prevailing in the domestic market. Market experience, market share and availability of people and resources are generally much higher in the domestic environment than in international markets (Grønhaug and Graham, 1987). Cavusgil and Godiwalla (1982) stress the high level of uncertainty in international markets and the limited availability of objective information, both in quantity and in quality. This may explain why international marketing decisions are dominated by the influence of subjective and perceptual factors.

The less sophisticated nature of international marketing research is also evidenced by Cavusgil (1984). Officials of 70 companies from Wisconsin and Illinois, involved in international business, were interviewed. Mostly simple survey techniques were used: foreign market research is generally informal, with no standard procedures. Furthermore, the frequency of identifying and analyzing foreign markets is much less than once a year. Sophistication increases with the higher degree of involvement in foreign markets, as measured by the percentage of export profits to total company profits. A study by Koh (1991) confirms these findings: a large proportion of US exporters, approximately two-thirds of the companies surveyed, do not adopt a formalized marketing plan. But when they do, they tend to focus on issues similar to those researched domestically and to neglect 'strategic issues relating to risks appraisal, environmental issues, cultural considerations . . . which require close contact with the foreign environment' (Koh, 1991, p. 17).

The acceptance of intuition in the decision-making process is a key element of those differences. Should we continue with very in-depth research, if the final decision is taken by somebody who may or may not follow the conclusions of the research? Should the researcher and the decision maker be different people or the same? These questions are raised by the cross-cultural comparison of marketing research practices.

Encouraging feedback from the informant on cultural adequacy

As Maruyama (1990) emphasized, humans are not simple response machines. Maruyama cites 'criticality dissonance', where respondents disguise and transform responses because they fear that information may be misused. As shown above, international market research is full of criticality dissonance. The basic process affecting the truthfulness of responses is 'relevance dissonance': 'the purpose of the questionnaire survey as perceived by the respondent differs from the respondent's own purpose. The questionnaire is perceived as irrelevant and useless. In such a case counter-exploitation takes place. The respondent looks for a way to manipulate the survey or interview to produce some benefit' (1990, p. 30).

For these reasons, it seems necessary to design research procedures where feedback from the informant is possible: for instance focus groups, in-depth interviews and open-ended questions. Unique features of cultural behaviour cause non-equivalence. It is impossible to uncover these levels of non-equivalence if the instrument and methodology prevent them from appearing. A pragmatic solution is to ask interviewees their opinion of the relevance of questions, words and concepts used in the questionnaire at the end of the normal interview process (post-test). A pre-test of questionnaires is also necessary.

A questionnaire forced upon interviewees does not elicit information (see the hair shampoo exercise in section A7.2). If emic feedback is to be introduced, both interviewers (especially when they have not been personally involved in compiling the questionnaire) and interviewees must be put in a situation where they may comment on the questions themselves and explain what is culturally meaningful in their own context and what is not. Interviewees should be given the opportunity after the normal answering process to elaborate freely on what they think of the questions, the situations described and so on. This orientation is slightly different from the traditional one where interviewed people are simply required to answer, not to 'criticize' the questions. Emic feedback allows an improvement in the adequacy of the source culture's constructs and instruments.[10]

Informants should be neither overestimated nor underestimated. They cannot respond to a barrage of questions alien to their knowledge and frame of reference. Therefore the content of the research must somehow be strictly controlled and must focus on really significant issues; surveys should be parsimonious and should not ask too much from informants. On the other hand, informants need to be carefully listened to because it is they who, as insiders, have the relevant pieces of information. The same care has to be taken with interviewers: they must be properly controlled (some – not all – may cheat by guessing responses or even filling in questionnaires themselves), and adequately briefed (professional interviewers may not be found everywhere – see Box 7.4).

7.7   CONCLUSION

It is dangerous to prepare an international market survey by simply transposing domestic research. The nature and scope of researched market information, the ways of collecting it, the accuracy of the data as well as the criteria of reliability of the data present cross-cultural variance. This holds true even when these factors are perceived as normatively quite universal. International market researchers have to reveal their own ethnocentric biases, by giving feedback opportunities to their informants or to local collaborators. From this point on, a systematic search for formal equivalence may appear dangerous. Equivalence of constructs and instruments has to be established first. The final recommendation is to search for the meaning, bearing in mind the following advice:

1. Scientific methods provide pictures which otherwise would not be available (the 'Mount Wilson' argument),

2. But images of reality are not reality itself (the '*la pipe*' argument).

3. Address the relevant questions (only those that can be articulated into decision and action).

4. Respect your informants and consider their competence as insiders as superior to yours as an outsider; but interview only those people who have something to say.

5. Keep a 'hands-on' approach to market research.

6. Culture must be examined at each step of the research process: questions, survey methods, interviews and questionnaires, informants.

QUESTIONS

1. Define the following terms:
    (a) conceptual equivalence;
    (b) temporal equivalence;
    (c) sexual biases.

2. Discuss the functional equivalence of the following products or consumption experiences. For this, choose countries/culture with which you have familiarity and experience and think in terms of benefits and those which are particularly emphasized in certain cultures:
    (a) a bicycle;
    (b) drinking a beer;
    (c) red wine;
    (d) a watch.

3. What are the obstacles in the way of a sample of consumers being cross culturally representative?

4. Discuss how market size can be estimated in a country where there is little or poor statistical data available.

5. List possible benefits for a washing powder or liquid and suggest possible cross-cultural variability in the dominance of certain benefits as compared with others.

6. Suggest ways of obtaining relevant market and consumer behaviour information where potential informants are not used to questionnaires and interviews.

7. How does the individualism/collectivism difference have an impact on the drafting of market research questionnaires?

8. Which constraints does strong ingroup orientation put on the data-collection process?

APPENDIX 7: TEACHING MATERIALS

A7.1   Case: Eliot Greeting Card Company (2)

QUESTIONS

Using the same text as in Chapter 4 (see A4.3), answer the following questions:

1. Assuming that Eliot Greeting Card Company has decided to undertake an in-depth market survey in order to decide whether to develop the Hispanic market, how would you design such a survey?

2. What information is needed?

3. How would you collect it?

A7.2   Exercise: Hair shampoo questionnaire

You will find below a market survey questionnaire, administered by interviewers to women interviewees between the ages of 18 and 30. It was originally designed for the US market. A similar market survey, as far as the objectives are concerned, will be undertaken in other countries. Suggest cross-cultural adaptations to this instrument. In particular,

1. Review the possible problems related to the translation of the questionnaire. Suggest solutions and translate it into . . .[11]

2. Review the data-collection procedure, from the point of view of the interviewer as well as that of the interviewee.

3. Suggest changes in the questionnaire design and/or wording, and/or modification in survey methods, if:
    (a) the information sought is meaningless in the local context;
    (b) the required information is meaningful but the data-collection procedures are inadequate; either they will not enable you to collect the information, or else this information will be biased.
    •   You must do this for each of the following countries: Algeria, Brazil, France, Germany, Thailand.
    •   You should then propose a 'central' version of the questionnaire, that is, a survey instrument which enables you to collect the maximum amount of information, which could be retrieved in a reliable manner, in the largest possible number of countries. This questionnaire would then help the meaningful comparison of countries.

Questionnaire used in hair shampoo study

Time Interview   Started _____
                 Ended _____

Respondent Name _____   Respondent No. _____
Address _____
City _____   State _____
Telephone No _____
Interviewer _____
Name _____
Interview Date _____

Screening Questions (Part S)
Hello, I'm _____ of the Wharton School, University of Pennsylvania. We're conducting a survey on women's attitudes and opinions about hair care products.

1. On the average, how often do you shampoo your hair at home?
    More than twice a week   _____
    Once or twice a week   _____
    Once or twice every two weeks   _____
    Once or twice every three weeks _____

Twice a month

Less than twice a month

....

....

IF LESS THAN TWICE
A MONTH, TERMINATE

2.   What is your age?   ....
        (IF UNDER 18 OR OVER 30 TERMINATE)

PART A

First I'm going to show you a set of 16 cards. Each card contains the name of a bene-fit that a hair shampoo might provide. (PLACE SET OF WHITE CARDS ON TABLE IN FRONT OF RESPONDENT.) Please take a few moments to look over these benefits. (ALLOW TIME FOR RESPONDENT TO STUDY THE CARDS.)

Now, thinking about various brands of hair shampoo that you have tried or heard about, pick out those benefits that you think are most likely to be found in almost any hair shampoo that one could buy today. (RECORD CARD NUMBERS IN FIRST COL-UMN OF RESPONSE FORM A AND TURN SELECTED CARDS FACE DOWN.)

Next, select all of those remaining benefits that you think are available in at least some hair shampoo – but not necessarily all in a single brand – that's currently on the market. (RECORD CARD NUMBERS IN SECOND COLUMN OF RESPONSE FORM A. RECORD REMAINING CARD NUMBERS IN THIRD COLUMN. THEN RETURN ALL CARDS TO TABLE.)

Next, imagine that you could make up an ideal type of shampoo – one that might not be available on today's market. Suppose, however, that you were restricted to only four of the sixteen benefits shown on the cards in front of you. Which four of the six-teen benefits would you most like to have? (RECORD CARD NUMBERS IN FOURTH COLUMN OF RESPONSE FORM A.)

RESPONSE FORM A

(1)	(2)	(3)	(4)
Benefits Most Likely to be Found in Almost Any Hair Shampoo – Card Numbers	Benefits Available in Some Shampoo – Card Numbers	Remaining Benefits – Card Numbers	Four Benefit Ideal Set – Card Numbers

PART B

Now, let's again return to some of the shampoo benefits you have already dealt with. (SELECT WHITE CARD NUMBERS 1 THROUGH 10: PULL OUT CARD 4 AND PLACE IT IN FRONT OF RESPONDENT.)

Suppose a shampoo were on the market that primarily stressed this benefit – 'Produces Hair that Has Body.' If you could get a shampoo that made good on this claim, which one of the remaining nine benefits would you most like to have as well?

(RECORD NUMBER IN RESPONSE FORM B.) Which next most? (RECORD.) Please continue until all of the nine benefits have been ranked.

RESPONSE FORM B

(Enter Card Numbers 1 Through 10 Excluding Card #4)

( ) Most Like to Have   ( )

( ) Next Most   ( )

( )   ( )

( )   ( )

( )   ( ) Least Most

PART C

Now, I am going to read to you some short phrases about hair. Listen to each phrase carefully and then tell me what single words first come to your mind when you hear each phrase? (RECORD UP TO THE FIRST THREE 'ASSOCIATIVE-TYPE' WORDS THE RESPONDENT SAYS AFTER EACH PHRASE IN RESPONSE FORM C.)

RESPONSE FORM C

(a)   Hair that has body

_____   _____   _____

(b)   Hair with fullness

_____   _____   _____

(c)   Hair that holds a set

_____   _____   _____

(d)   Bouncy hair

_____   _____   _____

(e)   Hair that's not limp

_____   _____   _____

(f)   Manageable hair

_____   _____   _____

(g)   Zesty hair

_____   _____   _____

(h)   Natural hair

_____   _____   _____

PART D

At this point I would like to ask you a few questions about your hair

1. Does your hair have enough body?
   Yes _____ No _____

2. Do you have any special problems with your hair?
   Yes _____ No _____
   If yes, what types of problems?

   _____

   _____

3. How would you describe your hair?
    My hair type is:
    Dry _____   Normal _____   Oily _____

4. The texture of my hair is:
    Fine _____   Normal _____   Coarse _____

5. My hair style (the way I wear my hair) is:
    Straight _____
    Slightly wavy or curly _____
    Very wavy or curly _____

6. The length of my hair is:
    Short (to ear lobes) _____
    Medium (ear lobes to shoulder) _____
    Long (below shoulder) _____

7. How would you describe the thickness of your hair?
    Thick _____   Medium _____   Thin _____

PART E

Now I would like to ask you a few background questions.

1. Are you working (at least twenty hours per week, for compensation)?
    Yes _____   No _____

2. Are you married?
    Yes _____   No _____

3. What is your level of education?
    Some high school _____
    Completed high school _____
    Some college _____
    Completed college _____

4. (HAND RESPONDENT INCOME CARD.) Which letter on this card comes closest
    to describing your total annual family income before taxes? (CIRCLE APPROPRI-
    ATE LETTER.)
    A. Under $9,000   E. $30,001–45,000
    B. $9,001–15,000   F. $45,001–60,000
    C. $15,001–20,000   G. Over $60,000
    D. $20,001–30,000
    (THANKS VERY MUCH FOR YOUR HELP)

Appendix

Text of the 16 benefits cards (original text in English + my translation into French):

1. Hair Stays Clean a Long Time

2. Hair Stays Free of Dandruff or Flaking

3. Hair That Looks and Feels Natural

4. Hair That Has Body

5. Manageable Hair That Goes Where You Want It

6. Hair With Sheen or Luster

7. Hair With No Split Ends

8. Hair With Enough Protein

9. Hair That Doesn't Get Oily Fast

10. Hair That's Not Too Dry

11. Hair With Fullness

12. Hair That's Not Frizzy

13. Hair That Holds A Set

14. Hair With Texture

15. Hair That's Easy to Comb When It Dries

16. Hair That Looks Free and Casual

Example of a translation into French. Below are my suggestions:

1. *Des Cheveux qui restent propre longtemps*

2. *Des Cheveux sans pellicules ni noeuds*

3. *Des Cheveux respirant le naturel*

4. *Des Cheveux qui ont du volume*

5. *Des Cheveux souples que l'on peut coiffer à son gré*

6. *Des Cheveux brillants et chatoyants*

7. *Des Cheveux qui ne se cassent pas*

8. *Des Cheveux assez riches en protéines*

9. *Des Cheveux ne devenant pas gras trop vite*

10. *Des Cheveux pas trop secs*

11. *Des Cheveux qui ont de la plénitude*

12. *Des Cheveux qui ne sont pas frisottés*

13. *Des Cheveux tenant la mise en plis*

14. *Des Cheveux ayant une bonne texture*

15. *Des Cheveux faciles à coiffer lorsqu'ils sèchent*

16. *Des Cheveux naturels, en liberté*

(Source: Adapted from Green *et al.*, 1988, pp. 359–62.)

NOTES

1. See for this Weiss (1996) who compares European coffee experiences to that of the Haya community in Tanzania, a coffee-producing country. He explores the meaning of coffee for Haya people who produce it and consume it in ways which remain largely distinct from the meanings attributed to coffee in the global economy.

2. The issue of cross-cultural equivalence was initially developed in psychology (see Frijda and Jahoda, 1966; Poortinga, 1989) and was later borrowed by international market research.

3. Wind and Douglas (1982) propose a hybrid approach which they define in the following way: 'The proposed approach develops country, culture or sub-culture specific concepts and measures. These are compared, combined or modified, and wherever possible common "pan-cultural" concepts, which do not have a specific cultural bias, and which reflect the idiosyncratic characteristics of each country, culture or sub-culture are identified. Country-specific measures of the "pan-cultural" and country idiosyncratic concepts are developed and compared. To the extent possible they are combined and country-specific measures are administered, generating the secondary data for the comparison.'

4. Green *et al.* (1988) give the following definitions of validity and reliability of measurement: 'By validity the behavioural scientist means that the data must be unbiased and relevant to the characteristic being measured . . .'. By reliability 'the behavioural scientist means the extent to which scaling results are free from experimental error' (pp. 249 and 253). Validity is then broken down into content, criterion and construct validation: see Green *et al.* (1988, Ch. 7, 'Measurement in marketing research', pp. 240–79).

5. Sentell and Philpot (1984) propose a method for evaluating the representativeness of samples taken from imperfectly known parent populations. Their method is based on the comparison of proportions estimated from two independent samples, focusing on situations where the larger sample size is unknown. Their method is implemented by testing two sets of sample statistics of Thai households.

6. Naumann *et al.* (1994) provide somewhat contrary evidence to that of Johansson and Nonaka (1996) when they compare the practices of United States and Japanese market research firms. Based on mail surveys sent to research firms in both countries, they show that in most areas Japanese and American market research practices seem to be similar. Research firms in both countries survey similar research issues, with the exception of competitor analysis and distribution where Japanese research is more intense. There appears to be no difference in the use of quantitative versus qualitative research between the two countries. However information is based on self-reports by respondents, who may be concerned with the image of professionalism; this may bias Japanese answers towards the positive response style, which could explain why there systematically appears to be a higher percentage of Japanese firms than US firms using any type of quantitative data analysis techniques. Johannson and Nonaka's views are based on insiders' views and backed by ch. 3 in their recent book, *Relentless: The Japanese Way of Marketing* (Johansson and Nonaka, 1996).

7. For a clarification of these terms see Easterby-Smith *et al.* (1993).

8. The distinction I make here is ideal typical and can cross the borders of the two national groups which I use probably with some exaggeration and some simplification, as archetypes. Let me quote a keynote address, given by the chairman of Heineken, at an ESOMAR (European Society for Opinion and Marketing Research) meeting: 'Decision making itself is about making choices, about taking risks, about looking ahead . . . Research is about describing, about facts, about analysing . . . I believe that the rational paradigm of collecting data, analysing them and acting upon them is not sufficient for the issues decision makers are confronted with . . . I am trying to make an argument for a more responsible use of research. A less absolute and more relative approach to its findings, one that leaves room for the more undefined factor in decision making. That of personal insight, judgement and intuition. And I think we should give a somewhat higher priority to this factor.' (Vuursten, 1996, p. 44.)

9. It is tempting to say that a typical atomistic culture is the United States and that Japan is a typical organistic culture. This is possible, but only as a modal characteristic, since the organistic approach also exists in the United States.

10. Badhuri *et al.* (1993) provide a quite interesting and lively review of how local market research agencies can co-operate, in the conduct of qualitative research, with client companies who undertake research from the United States in several European countries, with co-ordination being done by a European research company. They distinguish six approaches ('the hands-on approach', 'client as expert', 'we know best', 'the democratic approach', 'the colonial approach', 'cheap and cheerful approach') and show to what extent the client's ethnocentric views and the world-views of the local informants find their expression in the research process undertaken in each approach.

11. Language of translation is optional. Instructors will decide this according to their teaching objectives and to the language competencies of students. Cultural and linguistic contexts may be varied *ad libitum*, in relation to the participants themselves (nationalities, language skills, personal experiences in various countries, etc.). The participants are one of the main resources as far as cultural and language expertise is concerned. Students may also try to obtain information on foreign cultural contexts either by using secondary data, or by interviewing members of a particular group.

REFERENCES

Amine, Lyn S. and S. Tamer Cavusgil (1986), 'Demand estimation in a developing country environment: Difficulties, and examples', *Journal of the Market Research Society*, vol. 28, no. 5, pp. 43–65.

Badhuri, Monika, Marianne de Souza, and Tim Sweeney (1993), 'International qualitative research: A critical review of different approaches', *Marketing and Research Today*, vol. 21, no. 3, pp. 171–8.

Bohnet, Michael (1994), 'Was wurde in Kairo wirklich beschlossen', BMZ, Bonn, October.

Campbell, D. T. and O. Werner (1970), 'Translating, working through interpreters and the problem of decentering', in R. Naroll and R. Cohen (eds.), *A Handbook of Method in Cultural Anthropology*, The Natural History Press: New York, pp. 398–420.

Cavusgil, S. Tamer (1984), 'International marketing research: Insights into company practices' in *Research in Marketing*, Vol. 7, the JAI Press: Greenwich, CT, pp. 261–88.

Cavusgil, S. Tamer and Ajay Das (1997), 'Methodological issues in empirical cross-cultural research: A survey of the management literature and a framework', *Management International Review*, vol. 37, no. 1, pp. 71–96.

Cavusgil, S. Tamer, and Yezdi M. Godiwalla (1982), 'Decision-making for international marketing: A comparative review', *Management Decision*, vol. 20, no. 4, 47–54.

Chun, K. T., J. B. Campbell and J. Hao (1974), 'Extreme response style in cross-cultural research: A reminder', *Journal of Cross-Cultural Psychology*, vol. 5, pp. 464–80.

Davis, H. L., S. P. Douglas and A. J. Silk (1981), 'Measure unreliability: A hidden threat to cross-national research?', *American Marketing Association Attitude Research Conference*, March, Carlsbad, CA, pp. 1–40.

Deutscher, I. (1973), 'Asking questions cross culturally: Some problems of linguistic comparability', in Donald P. Warwick and Samuel Osherson (eds.), *Comparative Research Methods*, Prentice Hall: Englewood Cliffs, NJ, pp. 163–86.

Douglas, Susan P. (1980), 'Examining the impact of sampling characteristics in multi-country survey research', Proceedings of the 9th Annual Meeting of the European Academy for Advanced Research in Marketing, Edinburgh.

Douglas, Susan P. and C. Samuel Craig (1983), *International Marketing Research*, Prentice Hall: Englewood Cliffs, NJ.

Douglas, Susan P. and C. S. Craig (1984), 'Establishing equivalence in comparative consumer research', in Erdener Kaynak and Ronald Savitt (eds.), *Comparative Marketing Systems*, Praeger: New York, pp. 93–113.

Douglas, Susan P. and C. S. Craig (1997), 'The changing nature of consumer behavior: implications for cross-cultural research', *International Journal of Research in Marketing*, 14(4), pp. 379–95.

Douglas, Susan P. and Robert Shoemaker (1981), 'Item non-response in cross-national surveys', *European Research*, vol. 9 (July), pp. 124–32.

Easterby-Smith, Mark, Richard Thorpe and Andy Lowe (1993), *Management Research: An Introduction*, Sage: London.

Frijda, N. and G. Jahoda (1966), 'On the scope and methods of cross-cultural research', *International Journal of Psychology*, vol. 1, no. 2, pp. 109–127.

Geertz, Clifford (1983), *Local Knowledge*, Basic Books: New York.

Goodyear, Mary (1982), 'Qualitative research in developing countries', *Journal of the Market Research Society*, vol. 24, no. 2, pp. 86–96.

Green, Robert T. and Eric Langeard (1979), 'Comments and recommendations on the practice of cross-cultural marketing research', paper presented at the International Marketing Workshop, *E.I.A.S.M.*, Brussels, November, pp. 1–16.

Green, Paul E., Donald S. Tull and Gerald Albaum (1988), *Research for Marketing Decisions*, 5th edn, Prentice Hall: Englewood Cliffs, NJ.

Green, R. T. and P. D. White (1976), 'Methodological considerations in cross-national consumer research', *Journal of International Business Studies*, Fall-Winter, pp. 81–7.

Grønhaug, Kjell and John L. Graham (1987), 'International market research revisited' in S. Tamer Cavusgil (ed.), *Advances in International Marketing*, Greenwich, CT: JAI Press, pp. 121–37.

Grunert, Suzanne C., Klaus G. Grunert and Kai Kristensen (1993), 'Une méthode d'estimation de la validité interculturelle des instruments de mesure: Le cas de la mesure des valeurs des consommateurs par la liste des valeurs LOV', *Recherche et Applications en Marketing*, vol. 8, no. 4, pp. 5–28.

Hirschmann, Elisabeth (1986), 'Humanistic inquiry in marketing research: Philosophy, method and criteria', *Journal of Marketing Research*, vol. 13 (August), pp. 237–49

Johansson, Johny K. and Ikujiro Nonaka (1987), 'Market research the Japanese way', *Harvard Business Review*, May–June, pp. 16–22.

Johansson, Johny K. and Ikujiro Nonaka (1996), *Relentless: The Japanese Way of Marketing*, New York: HarperCollins.

Keegan, Warren G. (1974), 'Multinational scanning: A study of the information sources utilized by headquarters executives in multinational companies', *Administrative Science Quarterly*, September, pp. 411–21.

Koh, Anthony C. (1991), 'An evaluation of international marketing research planning in United States export firms', *Journal of Global Marketing*, vol. 4, no. 3, pp. 7–25.

Kracmar, J. Z. (1971), *Marketing Research in Developing Countries: A handbook*, Praeger: New York.

Kushner, J. M. (1982), 'Market research in a non-Western context: The Asian example', *Journal of the Market Research Society*, vol. 24, no. 2, pp. 116–22.

Leung, K. (1989), 'Cross-cultural differences: Individual level vs culture-level analysis', *International Journal of Psychology*, vol. 24, pp. 703–19.

Marchetti, Renato and Jean-Claude Usunier (1990), 'Les problèmes de l'étude de marché dans un contexte interculturel', *Revue Française du Marketing*, no. 130, 1990/5, pp. 167–84.

Maruyama, Magoroh (1990), 'International meta-marketing: Strategic judo, foreign user habits and interactive invention', *Human Systems Management*, vol. 9, pp. 29–42.

Mayer, Charles S. (1978), 'Multinational marketing research: The magnifying glass of methodological problems', *European Research*, March, pp. 77–84.

Morris, Jon D. (1995), 'SAM: The self-assessment manikin, an efficient cross-cultural measurement of emotional response', *Journal of Advertising Research*, vol. 35, no. 6, pp. 63–8.

Mytton, Graham (1996), 'Research in new fields', *Journal of the Market Research Society*, vol. 38, no. 1, pp. 19–32.

Naumann, Earl, Donald W. Jackson Jr. and William G. Wolfe (1994), 'Examining the practices of United States and Japanese market research firms', *California Management Review*, vol. 36, no. 4, pp. 49–69.

Parameswaran, Ravi and Attila Yaprak (1987), 'A cross-national comparison of consumer research measures', *Journal of International Business Studies*, Spring, pp. 35–49.

Pike, Kenneth (1966), *Language in Relation To a Unified Theory of the Structure of Human Behavior*, Mouton: The Hague.

Plummer, Joseph (1977), 'Consumer focus in cross-national research', *Journal of Advertising Research*, vol. 6, Spring, pp. 5–15.

Poortinga, Ype H. (1989), 'Equivalence in cross-cultural data: An overview of basic issues', *International Journal of Psychology*, vol. 24, pp. 737–56.

Pras, Bernard and Reinhard Angelmar (1978), 'Verbal rating scales for multinational research', *European Research*, March, pp. 62–7.

Sapir, Edward (1929), 'The status of linguistics as a science' *Language*, vol. 5, pp. 207–14.

Sechrest, L., T. Fay and S. M. Zaidi (1972), 'Problems of translation in cross-cultural research', *Journal of Cross-cultural Psychology*, vol. 3, no. 1, pp. 41–56.

Sentell, G. D., and J. W. Philpot (1984), 'A note on evaluating the representativity of samples taken in less developed countries', *International Journal of Research in Marketing*, vol. 1, pp. 81–4.

Sood, James H. (1990), 'Equivalent measurement in international market research: Is it really a problem?', *Journal of International Consumer Marketing*, vol. 2, no. 2, pp. 25–41.

Stanton, J. L., R. Chandran and S. Hernandez (1982), 'Marketing research problems in Latin America', *Journal of the Market Research Society*, vol. 24, no. 2, pp. 124–39.

Taylor, Humphrey (1995), 'Horses for courses: How survey firms in differents countries measure public opinion with different methods', *Journal of the Market Research Society*, vol. 37, no. 3.

Tuncalp, Secil (1988), 'The marketing research scene in Saudi Arabia', *European Journal of Marketing*, vol. 22, no. 5, pp. 15–22.

Usunier, Jean-Claude (1991), 'Business time perceptions and national cultures: A comparative survey', *Management International Review*, vol. 31, no. 3, pp. 197–217.

Usunier, Jean-Claude (1997), 'Atomistic versus organistic approaches: An illustration through cross-national differences in market research', *International Studies of Management & Organization*, vol. 26, no. 4, pp. 90–112.

Van Herk, Hester and Theo M. Verhallen (1995), 'Equivalence in empirical international research in the food area', *Proceedings of the Second Conference on the Cultural Dimension of International Marketing*, Odense, pp. 392–402.

Van Raaij, W. F. (1978), 'Cross-cultural research methodology as a case of construct validity', in H. K. Hunt (ed.), *Advances in Consumer Research*, vol. 5, Association for Consumer Research, Ann Arbor, pp. 693–701.

Vuursten, Karel (1996), 'Decision making at Heineken', *Marketing and Research Today*, vol. 24, no. 1, pp. 42–5.

Webster, Cynthia (1996), 'Hispanic and Anglo interviewer and respondent ethnicity and gender: The impact on survey response quality', *Journal of Marketing Research*, vol. XXXIII (February), pp. 62–72.

Weiss, Brad (1996), 'Coffee breaks and connections: The lived experience of a commodity in Tanzanian and European world', in David Howes (ed.), *Cross-cultural Consumption*, London: Routledge, pp. 93–123.

Wind, Yoram and Susan P. Douglas (1982), 'Comparative consumer research: The next frontier', *Management Decision*, vol. 20, no. 4, pp. 24–35.

Zaltman, Gerald (1997), 'Rethinking market research: Putting people back in', *Journal of Marketing Research*, vol. XXXIV (November), pp. 424–37.

Zax, M. and S. Takashi (1967), 'Cultural influences on response style: Comparison of Japanese and American college students', *Journal of Social Psychology*, vol. 71, pp. 3–10.

Marketing decisions for the intercultural environment

Introduction to Part 3

MARKETING DECISIONS FOR THE INTERCULTURAL ENVIRONMENT

For some decades, the '4Ps' model of marketing management has been widely used for designing marketing strategies and, to a lesser extent, for implementing them. Like most international marketing textbooks, this book follows the '4Ps' model. The last 'P', promotion, is largely treated in Part 4 since marketing communications deserve special treatment in an international context where communication needs to be tailored because of language differences. Part 3 explains how the first three Ps, that is, product, price and place, should be managed internationally with a view to generating the best possible compromise between large-scale operations and adaptation to local markets.

Multinational companies respond to the globalization of competition by designing international marketing strategies that try to create experience effects within the constraint of transport costs. They also use a number of production systems, such as flexible manufacturing, in order to gain differentiation advantages that are related to the customization of product offerings to local market needs. Chapter 8 deals first with the supply side by examining how cost arguments explain the emergence of global strategies and the globalization of competition. On the demand side, cross-border segments can be targeted in order to generate larger-scale operations;

Chapter 8 explains how geographical and demographic segmentation criteria can be combined in order to segment international markets optimally.

Chapter 9 documents the strategic choice between adaptation or standardization of products across national markets. It starts therefore with a review of key arguments in favour of the standardization or the adaptation of physical attributes. Physical attributes are the most sensitive to scale economies and at the same time those which require customization because of climate and other objective features of local markets. Service attributes need also to be tailored because consumers' expectations regarding service quality and service performance vary across national contexts. Finally, symbolic attributes linked to product design and packaging are examined in a cross-cultural perspective which highlights the diversity of cultural interpretations of symbols – looking at attributes such as colour, figure, shape, etc.

Among the symbolic attributes that diffuse meaning, two of great importance are the country of origin of products and their brand names. Chapter 10 deals therefore with the management of images diffused by these attributes. It reviews how consumers evaluate products according to their country of origin, taking into account perceived risk related to goods produced in other countries which may be cheaper or seen as less prestigious in terms of design and/or manufacture. The final section deals with the linguistic constraints of transferring national brand names on to the international scene and outlines the managerial limitations involved in the development of global brands.

Rather than seeing price merely as *the* objective factor in the economics of international marketing, Chapter 11 examines the role of price as a central element of relational exchange, that is, as a signal conveying meaning between buyer and seller, marketers and consumers, and between companies and their middlemen. It also presents and documents the main pricing decisions that a company has to face when it sells internationally. The first perspective developed is that of bargaining which is still widely in use in many markets and remains a key ritual in buyer–seller relationships because it mixes economics and human intercourse in a subtle way. Then cross-cultural variation in the use of price by consumers to evaluate and choose products is discussed. The three last sections of the chapter are devoted to managerial issues in international price policy, that is, how multinational companies may use price policy to conquer new markets, how to enter markets where competition is avoided through cartels and price agreements, how to fight against parallel imports by unauthorized dealers, and how prices should be managed in unstable environments which often combine high inflation, administered prices and strict foreign exchange control.

Chapter 12 is concerned mostly with the 'place' variable in the 4Ps model and deals consequently with international distribution. The case of Japanese *Keiretsus* distribution is used to exemplify the cultural embedding of distribution channels and the difficulty of entering foreign channels as a 'cultural outsider'. It shows how relationships between channel members are deeply rooted in local patterns of human and economic relationships and highlights the role of distribution as a 'cultural filter', which must be carefully considered (along with other criteria) before choosing a foreign distribution channel. Direct marketing world-wide, especially through catalogue sales and through the Internet, is developing fast: the section dealing with direct marketing explains which products best suit direct overseas distribution and outlines some linguistic and cultural limitations which must be carefully considered before design-ing and implementing cross-border direct marketing. The final section examines cross-national variations in sales promotion methods and explains which aspects need to be customized when transferring promotional techniques across borders.

8 Intercultural marketing strategy

Globalization is a process that occurs mostly at the level of competition. Regional agreements world-wide and the GATT framework allow for tariff and non-tariff barriers to be progressively replaced by entry barriers related to scale and experience. As far as consumer behaviour and marketing environments are concerned, natural entry barriers related to culture will diminish very gradually and only over a long period: there are still many very different marketing 'villages', not a global one. This chapter defends the ideas that strategic management has to be 'global', whereas marketing management largely needs to be tailored to local contexts; therefore, an intercultural orientation to international marketing best serves a global strategic view.

The strategic dilemma for international marketers is to achieve both low cost and differentiation in the minds of consumers *vis-à-vis* competitors. While differentiation, a key tenet of this book, may result in cost increases, there are possible compromises. I do not overlook the necessity for cost efficiency in three major areas: production, transport and marketing. In order to minimize both costs and unnecessary differentiation, and to maximize relevant differentiation, customers should be clustered in groups sharing common characteristics. Culture is naturally one of the main cues for clustering, but not the only one; sociodemographic criteria are also significant in an international perspective.

The first section of this chapter concentrates on cost arguments and shows that global strategies are very significant from a pure cost perspective. The second section discusses how global competition has progressively become the rule, due to the liberalization of world trade. The third section shows how companies have reacted to these major changes during the last twenty years and how they were forced by the pressure of world-wide competition to standardize their marketing strategies while keeping an eye on very dissimilar consumer environments. The final section deals with the segmentation of world markets and discusses the respective place of cross-border segments based on sociodemographics and lifestyles and geography-based cultural segments.

8.1   COST ARGUMENTS AND GLOBAL STRATEGIES

Multidomestic and global markets

The distinction between the multidomestic and the global market, identified by Michael Porter, has been widely applied since the beginning of the 1980s. At the industry level, there is a shift from multidomestic competition patterns to global ones. According to Porter, competition becomes global when 'a firm's competitive position is significantly affected by its position in other countries and vice-versa' (1986, p. 18). When an industry is multidomestic, separate strategies are pursued in different national markets, and the competitive scene remains basically a domestic one. There are some fundamental reasons for industries to remain multidomestic, including wide differences in consumer needs and attitudes across markets, legal barriers resulting from domestic regulations (which have long been in place in the case of banking and insurance), and non-tariff barriers which artificially maintain competition between purely national competitors (food and drug health regulations, for instance). Accordingly, the basic preoccupation of a global strategy is (very briefly defined) the configuration and co-ordination of activities, including marketing, across national markets.

Trends towards global (competitive) markets

The trends towards global markets differ fairly widely depending on the industry. First, the influence of national regulations and non-tariff barriers largely varies across product categories. The potential for experience effects also differs across product categories: for example, there is less potential for cost reduction due to volume increase in the case of cheeses than for microchips. Third, there are different degrees of international 'transportability', that is, the extent to which transportation costs impinge on the degree and patterns of globalization of an industry; exporting may be the dominant internationalization pattern for easily transportable products such as semiconductors. Foreign direct investment may be the prevailing pattern for industries whose products are expensive to transport long distance (e.g. cement). Fourth, the trend towards globalization may be curbed in the case of culture-bound products: the trend towards globalization in the cheese industry is slower, although clearly existing, than in the microchip industry.

Experience effects

The potential for experience effects differs widely across product categories. The Boston Consulting Group has isolated one of the main reasons for this through research into the success of various companies, including companies Japanese, in global markets. Experience effects provide companies with the ability to reduce units costs dramatically through an increase in product quantity. The experience effects determine the relationship of unit cost to cumulated production volume according to the following formula:

$$C_n = C_1 n^{-\lambda}$$

Where C_n is the cost of the nth unit; C_1 is the cost of the first unit; n is the cumulated number of units produced; and λ is the elasticity of the unit cost with respect to the cumulated production volume.

The form of the function reflects a constant elasticity. Let us call k the effect of elasticity. When production is doubled, the cost (and therefore, to a certain extent, the price) will decrease by $1 - k = 1-2^{-\lambda}$ per cent each time the experience doubles. If, for example, k equals 70 per cent, the cost will decrease by 30 per cent on a doubling of the cumulated production ($1 - 70\% = 30\%$). Experience effects theory has been supported by empirical verification (Day and Montgomery, 1983). Experience effects have been estimated for such diverse products and services as long-distance telephone calls in the United States, bottle tops in West Germany, refrigerators in Great Britain and Japanese motorcycles.

The source of experience effects is fourfold:

1. The effects of *learning by doing*. The more times one carries out a task or manufactures a component or a product, the more efficiently it is done or, alternatively, the less time is taken to do so.

2. *Scale effects*. By increasing the scale of production, the average cost can be reduced. Many industrial products require a large amount of research and development for product design, yet only a small quantity of raw materials for their manufacture (e.g. pocket calculators).

3. *Technological advances*. The increase in cumulated production offers a dual possibility of technological improvements. On one hand, production equipment may be refined; on the other hand, the product itself can be simplified and rendered cheaper to produce. These product simplifications usually result from a decrease in the number of parts, and not from a reduction in the number of functions and the degree of sophistication which would adversely affect the consumer.

4. *Economies of scope*. Component parts may be shared by different products. For instance, the same basic diesel engine may be used for a fork-lift truck, a small truck, a van, a car, or as an inboard motor for a boat, with a few slight adaptations. The increase in the production scale of shared components (or shared overhead costs, or any kind of shared common inputs) results in economies of scope.

Not every product has the same potential for experience effects. The potential is clearly smaller for cheese or books than for hi-fi systems or microcomputers. An examination of Japanese successes in world markets demonstrates that the Japanese have concentrated on goods that have very high experience effects, such as motorcycles, motor cars, photocopiers, video equipment, hi-fi systems, television sets, outboard motors, musical instruments and cameras. Right from the start, Japanese companies opted for global markets, even though their domestic market for such products was itself very substantial. Competitors have struggled to resist the competitive pressure of Japanese companies. The motorcycle industry is typical of the lack of experience effects amongst European manufacturers. In an attempt to compete with the Japanese (Honda, Yamaha, Suzuki, Kawazaki), Motobécane, a French manufacturer, launched a 125cc motorcycle twenty years ago. This model had a two-stroke engine that operated on a mixture of petrol and oil, since Motobécane was unable to make a four-stroke engine, like Honda, or an 'oil lube' (a device for mixing oil and petrol automatically), like Yamaha, Suzuki and Kawazaki. This motorcycle emitted a thick cloud of white smoke through its exhaust. The range of models offered has remained very limited, as with other French motorcycles. The 350cc Motobécane, which could have enjoyed a lucrative market by supplying the French police, was not fast or reliable enough. Both the 125cc and the 350cc were complete flops. Motobécane remained a company operating mainly in the French domestic market and as a result the company was undersized. The lack of experience effects in the company was a barrier to technological improvements. Motobécane is now renamed MBK and is a subsidiary of Yamaha.

International transportability

The unit weight, that is, dollar price per kilogram or per pound, differs widely across categories of goods, and therefore across the industries that manufacture them. The price of cement or basic ordinary steel products ranges from 50 cents per kilogram to several dollars per kilogram, whereas that of cars ranges from 10 dollars per kilogram (for example, a small family car at the bottom end of the market) to 60 or 70 dollars per kilogram for luxury cars at the top end of the market (large Mercedes, BMWs or Jaguars). A portable computer may reach a price of 750 dollars per kilogram (or even more), not to mention its component chips which may climb to several thousand dollars per kilogram.

In the international transportation system, shipping charges do not follow a simple tariff, which would be directly proportional to weight. They are calculated on the basis of a mix of criteria, depending on the nature of goods to be shipped and on the shipping line. Shipping lines are also subject to economies of scale. Transportation cost factors are influenced by the forces of competition between transportation companies, and also by the method of transportation (ship, aeroplane, truck or train). The mix of criteria includes weight, volume, dimensions, ease of loading and unloading, perishability, packaging and speed of delivery. However, weight, volume and perishability are clearly the most detrimental factors to international transportation.

Some markets will remain almost exclusively multidomestic, because goods and services cannot be transported – hairdressing services, for instance. Although transportability may have a negative influence on cross-border transactions of goods and services, it does not hamper the globalization of an industry where cross-border investments are possible. In the cement industry, markets are regionally segmented within countries because of the high cost of transportation in proportion to basic unit price. The cement industry still competes on a global basis through foreign direct investment and the sale and licensing of technology.

Transportability relates also to consumers, who may be more 'transportable' than the products or services which are offered to them. Ski resorts are a good example: ski slopes, buildings and equipment are not transportable, nor is snow. But potential skiers may be transported at low cost on charter flights, from countries without mountains, snow or ski resorts (but with some purchasing power). Thus we may observe in the international ski-resorts industry a twofold pattern of globalization. On the one hand, some world-famous ski resorts, such as Val d'Isère in France, Kitzbühl in Austria and Zermatt in Switzerland, enjoy a global market. People arrive from many parts of the world, often on package holidays sold by tour operators or travel agencies. On the other hand, there remains in most ski-oriented countries a large number of purely local ski resorts ('ski villages') which compete on a more domestic basis. This part of the industry is multidomestic. Between these two segments, one globalized, one multidomestic, there are in fact many intermediate ski resorts which compete on a regionally globalized basis. This is the case with most medium-size ski resorts in the European Alps: in Austria, France, Germany, Italy, Switzerland and some eastern European countries, which compete for European skiers.

The disconnection between sourcing and marketing

The countries where sourcing and marketing take place may be highly disconnected in industries which compete on a global basis. The sites of most cost-efficient production are often export processing zones in newly industrialized countries. Consumer markets may be located in very remote places. The same brand may be 'made in' various countries which generate different country-of-origin images (see section 10.2). Consumers, who use country of origin as an information cue for comparing brands, are now becoming more and more aware of the actual disconnection between sourcing and marketing.

A world view versus a local view

A 'global strategy' clearly implies a world view of competition and competitive advantage, not simply a belief that consumers and markets are themselves global. The issue of global strategies has been extensively documented in the strategic management literature; it is clearly beyond the scope of this book, which emphasizes the cultural dimensions of international marketing, to discuss in detail the specific issues related to global strategies.

In cultural terms, the ethnocentrism of the managing team of any company is shown by the way in which it treats the domestic/national market on the one hand and 'foreign' markets on the other. This issue is not purely academic; it permeates the ways in which a company organizes its international activities and the nationalities of its top executives as well as other more practical considerations such as the choice of the language(s) to be spoken between subsidiaries and head office.

Once the company has achieved a certain level of development in foreign markets, the 'export' view and the 'international development' view can no longer coexist effectively. They are dependent on four different perspectives: ethnocentrism, polycentrism, regiocentrism and geocentrism (Wind et al., 1973), two of these (ethno- and geocentrism) being somewhat irreconcilable. In terms of set theory, the domestic market is perceived as disjointed from foreign markets, whereas, in the geocentric view, the domestic market is seen as belonging to the world market in the same way as any other domestic market. Ethnocentric companies view international operations as secondary to their domestic operations. A company that considers its national base as its top priority will impose its own language on its foreign subsidiaries. It will supply the domestic market first when production capacity is overstretched. It will never invite a non-national on to the board of directors unless this person shares the company's native language and culture. Conversely, the firm that considers its national base as just one of many, a geocentric company, will make the opposite choices. This is in line with the distinction made by Wind *et al.* (1973) in the EPRG model (ethnocentric, polycentric, regiocentric, geocentric) of behaviour of international companies. Polycentrism results from the recognition of differences that occur in overseas markets. Each country is accepted as one of many ethnocentric places which may have their own marketing policies and programmes. Regiocentrism reflects the change by a company towards a more open understanding or towards world marketing, where regional marketing strategies are designed.

When companies distance themselves from an ethnocentric attitude by virtue of their management style and corporate culture, they develop genuinely offensive and defensive marketing strategies in foreign markets. Such a strategy manifests itself in flexible reallocation of resources from one market to another. For instance, a company will relocate into market Y, where it holds a solid position, as a reaction to one large competitor launching a price offensive in country X. This type of situation is conceivable in strongly oligopolistic markets where several (five to ten) large multinationals control the world market, as happens in the food industry or the liquefied gases industry.

Nevertheless it seems that stiff competition may give way to forms of co-operation between large companies from developed countries. The theory developed by Kenichi Ohmae, head of the Tokyo office of McKinsey Consultants, in his book *Triad Power: The coming shape of global competition* (1985), emphasizes the need for companies that want to survive international competition to have a solid base in the market area of each of the three major industrialized regions: North America, Japan and Europe, called the 'triad'. Ohmae further suggests that in each of these regions, companies should establish links of international division of labour with neighbouring developing countries. Companies in Latin American countries are natural subcontractors for North American companies. South East Asian countries subcontract for Japanese firms. The same co-operation pattern should occur between African countries and European companies. To ensure this necessary tripolar presence, Ohmae advocates that alliances should be built between companies belonging to one of the developed market areas. Most of these companies, even large ones, cannot individually afford to make the necessary investment that would ensure a full presence in each of the three regions.

Prioritized market(s) often remain undiscussed. To avoid this kind of 'collective unconsciousness', companies must reflect on how prioritized markets relate to corporate culture, to the search for market and business opportunities and to the decision-making process. Some European companies still supply their domestic market as a priority, on the basis that this market is the 'home base'. This attitude has two dangerous consequences:

1. It leads to a bias in *product design*. The modest sales records of certain European cars, mainly French and Italian, in the North American, principally the US, market is, at least partly, attributable to local French and Italian motor regulations

which bias the design of cars, and make them inappropriate for use in America. In France, the speed restrictions on motorways and a high road tax that largely increases with the size of the engine, has discouraged the production of large cars and sports cars. The same holds true in Italy, where the high cost of petrol has encouraged the production of small cars, too small in fact for US consumers. This has dissuaded car manufacturers in those countries from building high-speed luxury saloons, a gap in the market which was mostly filled by the Germans and the Swedes, before the Japanese came with their Lexus and Acuras.

2. Home-base-oriented companies often suffer the unfortunate reputation abroad of unreliability with respect to *delivery dates*. This is due to a 'marginal' conception of foreign markets, which are considered as a provisional outlet to be approached when the home market is depressed. It leads to a consistent preference for supplying a domestic customer rather than a foreign customer. Even though such foreign customers may have ordered earlier, they will be forced to wait and will only receive delivery after domestic customers have been satisfied. A genuine respect for delivery dates should have led to a different outcome.

As soon as domestic demand increases, such prioritization of national markets implies that production capacity will cease to be used for supplying foreign customers. As a consequence, there is a general risk that attempts to set up stable business relationships with customers and intermediaries in foreign markets will be hampered. Typically, foreign agents will only be visited when business at home is slack, and will be let down (as will foreign customers) as soon as the home market situation improves. This attitude fails to satisfy the essential precondition for effective international development.

The world market share concept: Global size and the diagnosis of economic market share

Calculating its world market share helps to prevent a company from being ethnocentric when defining its position *vis-à-vis* the competition. Competition is seen from the outset as global. Box 8.1 illustrates the dangers of overemphasizing domestic market share.

A diagnosis of a particular company's situation within world markets requires the following evaluations (even though estimates may be only approximate):

1. What is the size of the world market (volume, units, sales figures)?
2. What is the company's production size?
3. What is the company's share of the world market?
4. What is the minimum world market share necessary to remain competitive, considering potential experience effects?

The world market for fork-lift trucks was roughly 200,000 units per year. Fenwick held only 2 per cent of this market. 'Competitive' market share could be estimated to have been 10 per cent, or 20,000 trucks a year. Fenwick was therefore well below the required global size. In view of this, it should have reduced its range to either diesel or electric fork-lifts and to a limited range of sizes so that production could have been much greater in a more specialized world market.

BOX 8.1

Fenwick, a synonym for fork-lift

Fenwick, the leading company for fork-lift trucks in France, is also a word used in everyday speech as a synonym for fork-lift trucks. A few years ago the company controlled 40–50 per cent of the French market and nearly went bankrupt because it lacked international size. This company only produced 4,000 fork-lift trucks per year, whereas its western competitor, Toyota, produced 35,000 and its main East European competitor, Balkankar (a Bulgarian company), 70,000. This had a negative effect on Fenwick's unit costs. Fenwick should have adapted its marketing strategy, by reducing the depth of its product range, thereby increasing production size within this narrower product range. Toyota was in a position to offer a very wide product range (diesel or electric, with varying loading capacities, etc.). Fenwick, on the other hand, should have restricted its range – albeit at the risk of losing customers who expect to find a single supplier capable of dealing with all their requirements.

There is no precise rule for estimating the 'competitive' world market share. This figure depends on the optimum size of production, which in turn depends on the potential for experience effects for a specific product or service. Experience effects are, though, much stronger under the following conditions:

1. When the product/service is mass produced.
2. When the product/service involves a production process with large initial fixed costs (in R & D, and/or in production facilities investment, and/or in initial marketing costs).
3. When the added value of the product/service is high in relation to the whole production cycle.
4. When the product/service is in a fairly open international market; any producer may sell throughout the world without facing prohibitive transport costs, customs barriers, statutory restrictions or market barriers (e.g. differences in taste).

Limitations on international size arise in various areas; for example cement (very high transport costs compared to its price), pharmaceuticals (statutory restrictions), foodstuffs (taste differences), etc. As far as services are concerned, the potential for experience effects is much smaller, since in many cases services must be performed in a direct relationship with the consumer, are often intangible and therefore cannot be held in stock. In addition their market area is often fairly localized and they are subject to local customs and ways of life, such as the type of food and service found in a restaurant or the kind of treat offered by hotels. The easiest empirical solution for the evaluation of 'competitive' market share is to examine the size of competitors, and to determine the size of those competitors who operate most effectively.

Global markets as learning opportunities

Global markets work as a set of coherent opportunities, through markets being at different product life-cycle (PLC) stages and through experience cumulated across national markets. According to PLC theory (Vernon, 1966), national markets at different development stages offer different kinds of opportunities. If, for instance, the market for wallpaper is saturated in developed economies, it may be opening up in newly industrialized countries. PLC theory clearly indicates the way in which sourcing and marketing activities should be disconnected. PLC theory, in conjunction with the world market share concept, assists in the identification of what to supply and from where, and in which countries to market.

Global markets are also full of learning opportunities; the internationalization process has been presented mostly as a learning and experiencing process (Johanson and Vahlne, 1977). Since the cultural variable is fundamental to this learning process, some markets may be used almost purely as learning opportunities. When Procter & Gamble attacked the Japanese market for baby nappies (diapers) it initially achieved great success. Its market share subsequently dropped sharply against the main Japanese competitor Kao. P & G did its best to survive in the face of harsh competition from Kao and other Japanese producers, to satisfy the exigent Japanese consumers and to make its way through the Japanese Keiretsu distribution system (see Chapter 12). P & G's experience in Japan has made it aware of the competitive threat of the Japanese producers. P & G realized that it would face harsh competition if Japanese producers were to decide to expand in world markets. This has already helped P & G resist the internationalization of Kao which, to date, has not succeeded in becoming a global competitor to P & G.

Global markets may also be seen as partnership opportunities: with local consumers, with distributors and (why not?) with competitors (Box 8.2).

BOX 8.2

Stimorol and Hollywood

A Danish chewing-gum company, Dandy A/S, which produces Stimorol, encountered difficulties in selling its products in France. Dandy was particularly successful at producing chewing gum *dragée*. Hollywood France (owned by the US company General Foods/Kraft) was less successful in the production of this type of product, but had better access to the major distribution outlets (hypermarkets). In fact, only large companies are able to have their products referenced, that is, registered as products accepted for sale by the channel. Referencing requires the payment of large 'entry fees' to the hypermarkets, which are only semi-legitimate. Dandy of Denmark and Hollywood ended up forging a cross-competence alliance whereby Dandy produces Hollywood *dragée* products and markets Hollywood products through Dandy's international sales organization, and Hollywood markets Dandy's Stimorol brand in France and produces the Dandy stick products.

(Source: Hollensen, 1991, p. 736.)

8.2 THE GLOBALIZATION OF COMPETITION

Evidence from macroeconomic data on long periods of time

There is little doubt about the globalization of competition. Market areas do not depend mainly on consumer preferences. Their reach is influenced much more by potential supply and by trade barriers, whether tariff or non-tariff, and also by the opportunities of economies of scale and experience effects. Clear evidence from macroeconomic figures shows that competition is globalizing both at a world-wide level and at a regional level.

Over the past forty years, international trade has expanded steadily, and significantly more quickly than the sum of the gross national product (GNP) of the nations involved in international trade. From a base of 100 in 1970, the index volume of world exports was 180 in 1984 compared with only 154 for total world output. Even more significantly, the index of total world exports of manufactured goods was 238 in 1984 and only 171 for the total world output of manufacturing industries (GATT, 1986). From 1984 to 1994, the annual rate of increase for world trade has been 5.8 per cent, compared with 2.7 per cent for world production (*Focus*, 1995). This points to a long-term trend: an increase in the scale of production. Industrial productivity accompanies the freeing of international markets and the growth of international trade. Thus in a simple regression equation, general world-wide industrial productivity is a very good explanatory variable of the ratio of world exports to world total output over a long period, that is from 1955 to 1976 (Usunier, 1980).

This rule also holds true in very recent times (Ludlow, 1990): in the six years from 1983 to 1988 (inclusive) trade growth exceeded the increase in world output, generally by two or three percentage points in annual growth rate. The economic linkage between countries and therefore competition between companies has continued to grow. A comparable evolution may be observed, at an even greater pace, at the regional level. Distances are becoming less important and the move to world-wide globalization has its roots at regional level. In Europe the growth of intra-regional international trade was much faster than the overall world trade growth during the 1960s and 1970s (Usunier, 1980). But also trade within the Western Pacific area grew significantly more (32 per cent p.a.) from 1980 to 1988, compared to 14 per cent p.a. for the intra-western-European trade and 16 per cent p.a. for the intra-North-American trade, for the same period (Ludlow, 1990).

In recent years, from 1992 to 1994, Asia has been doing much better than Europe as an exporting region: 10.6 per cent average annual rate of increase in the value of its exports (19.4 per cent for China), against 3.4 per cent for the European Union (*Focus*, 1995). This shows a relative slowdown of the globalization of competition in Europe during the 1980s and 1990s and, as a consequence, a deterioration of its competitive position world-wide. This could change with the implementation of the European Union (EU) programme in 1992 and the progressive removal of physical borders which started on 1 January 1993 (see Box 8.3).

Globalization of competition: Evidence from business and industries

Many companies have been compelled to globalize their business, one example being Black & Decker, because of fierce competition with the Japanese power-tool maker

---

BOX 8.3

Europe 1992 agenda: Globalizing competition

From the Treaty of Rome to the Single European Act, the main European treaties have always had one main focus: to increase the size of fragmented national European markets. Customs duties have been abolished between the six founding member-states in July 1968. But the pace of integration has slowed down with the entry of new members.

Increased world-wide competition, especially coming from the Japanese and south-east Asian nations, resulted in an enhancement of awareness about the necessity to really build a large internal market (EC's White Paper, Completing the Internal Market, 1985).

The logic which lies behind the 1992 agenda, which is an appendix of the EC's 1985 White Paper, is clearly presented by the authors of the survey on the cost of non-Europe (Cecchini, 1988, p. xx, our italics):

For business and government, *the two main actors*, the road to market integration will be paved with tough adjustments, and the need for new strategies. For business, removing protective barriers creates a permanent opportunity, but signals a *definitive end to national soft options* . . . profits which derive from cashing in on monopoly or protected positions will tend to be squeezed. The situation will be one of *constant competitive renewal*.

(Source: Usunier, 1991, p. 73. Reproduced with the kind permission of the publisher)

Makita. The reasons for this are stated by *Fortune* magazine, reporting the strategic move of Black & Decker towards globalization: 'Makita is Black & Decker's first competitor with a global strategy. It doesn't care that Germans prefer high powered, heavy-duty drills, and that Yanks want everything lighter. Make a good drill at a low price, the company reasons, and it will sell from Baden-Baden to Brooklyn' (Saporito, 1984, p. 24).

This trend towards globalization of competition has been clearly noted, almost advertised, in business journals ('Your new global market: how to win the world war for profits and sales', cover page of *Fortune*, 14 March 1988). In most of these articles, which generally relate to the dynamics of competition in a specific industry, the vocabulary is often borrowed from the military: war, battlecries, strategic weapons, etc. Naturally this is not seen so clearly in company brochures, where companies promote an image of themselves as dedicated more to customer service and to product/service integrity. Sumitomo Trading Company (Sumitomo Corporation, 1988) emphasizes that:

the survival of the Sumitomo name for almost four centuries is testimony to the soundness of [our] business philosophy . . . That is why we have the confidence to call ourselves Global Market Makers. Being global implies the worldwide, long term perspective from which we build relationships and undertake business.

Michael Porter (1986) has analyzed the change in patterns of international competition. At the industry level, where competitive advantage is won or lost, there is a shift from multidomestic industries to global ones. Porter is not referring to consumer-led globalization but to a strategic move by companies trying to integrate activities on a world-wide basis, to gain competitive advantage over their competitors at various levels of the value chain. Nevertheless this process remains conditional on the maintenance of the freeing of trade barriers, for example, discussions in the GATT framework between nation states. The recently established WTO (World Trade Organization) is a major move towards consolidating the GATT's advances while at the same time offering improved institutional mechanisms for solving trade disputes between countries and an extension of the GATT's principles to services. No companies, not even large multinationals, are parties to the GATT multilateral trade talks. The globalization of the Japanese economy and of other Asian countries has posed some real threats to both the United States and Europe. Therefore free trade can be maintained and expanded only if a certain equilibrium of the balance of trade between nation states permits the maintenance of a low-trade-barriers environment which favours globalization at the industry level. The establishment of the WTO at the beginning of 1995 appears, in this respect, as an organizing framework for international competition, building on the rules of the GATT treaty, rather than a major breakthrough towards free trade world-wide. It will provide increased competition in the area of services, by relaxing national barriers in a number of service industries (telecommunications, insurance, banking, etc.). It will also provide more homogeneous rules concerning industrial property (patents and trade marks), thereby making it easier for brands to achieve global coverage.

8.3 INTERNATIONAL MARKETING STRATEGIES ARE BECOMING GLOBAL

Competition is becoming global and artificial entry barriers are tending to disappear. But global markets remain more apparent than real when one looks at consumption patterns (Sheth, 1986). So how can products and marketing strategies be globalized in the face of the fierce pressure of the globalization of competition and also under the constraint of consumers who tend to resist, at least partly, the globalization movement? With respect to this question, two major issues have to be considered:

1. The standardization of marketing programmes: what should be the degree of similarity in marketing strategies from one country to another?

2. Organizational issues: what is required to implement a standardized marketing strategy successfully?

Standardization of international marketing programmes

Before the classic article of Buzzell (1968), 'Can you standardize multinational marketing?', natural entry barriers related to culture were seen as very high, requiring adaptation to national markets and offsetting the potential advantages of scale economies. Buzzell showed clearly that, with the decrease of purely artificial trade bar-riers, large international companies could create natural entry barriers unrelated to culture through economies of scale. Since then there have been numerous texts which have sought to advise business people how to make the best choices between stan-dardization and adaptation of marketing policies to foreign markets (for instance: Hout *et al.*, 1982; Hamel and Prahalad, 1985; Quelch and Hoff, 1986; Ghoshal, 1987). This literature advocates either 'hard' or 'soft' globalization:

1. 'Hard globalizers' see globalization as a new 'paradigm' for international market-ing (Hampton and Buske, 1987). 'Consumers in increasing numbers demonstrate that they are willing to sacrifice specific preferences in product features, function and design for a globally standardized product that carries a lower price' (p. 263). According to Hampton and Buske there is a shift to the global marketing para-digm since the process of adapting products to national wants and needs contra-dicts their global convergence.

2. 'Soft' partisans of globalization see it as a necessary trend, but constrained by the environment. The physical conditions of a country as well as the laws relating to product standards, sales promotion, taxes or other aspects may affect standardi-zation of marketing programmes, especially in developing countries (Hill and Still, 1984a).

In both cases, what consumers actually want in various national markets is not really considered: differences are either denied or treated as an external constraint. This constraint should be taken into account only when ignoring critical differences in consumer behaviour and marketing environment could lead to market failures (Ricks, 1983). However, many examples show that it is rarely the whole of the mar-keting strategy that is globalized: many global brands have marketing strategies which are significantly tailored to local markets. As stated by Van Mesdag (1987, p. 73):

Some products that were deliberately developed to sell in global markets are margarine (though the originators of the product curiously never adopted a global brand strategy for it), IDV's Bailey's Irish Cream liqueur, Ferrero's Tic Tac candy, and Rocher chocolates. Some global brands have global strategies. Others – Coca-Cola, Kellogg's corn flakes, Heineken beer, and McDonald's ham-burgers – have not. In the food and drink arena brands that succeed in using the global market-ing approach are few and far between. The reasons are the low international convertibility of food and drink products and the increasing difficulty of finding brand names for international use.

Behind the globalization debate there is a quite practical issue in terms of the every-day life of companies: the traditional dilemma between production flexibility and marketing's tendency to customize products to diversified needs. Factory managers prefer to be inflexible, for low-cost purposes, whereas marketing managers favour as much tailoring to customers' needs as possible.

Developments in factory automation nowadays allow product customization with-out major cost implications (Wind, 1986). New strategies have been found to serve diversified needs, to customize products and at the same time to maintain low costs owing to economies of scale and experience effects. A modular conception of products permits shared economies of scale at the components level, whereas lagged differenti-ation maintains a high scale of production as long as possible in the production process and organizes cheap final customization either in the factory or in the distribution network (Stobaugh and Telesio, 1983; Deher, 1986; Gilmore and Pine, 1997; see Box 8.4). So why maintain such a strong 'paradigm for action' emphasis on globalization if consumption patterns are not clearly globalizing and if adjusting to global competition is reconcilable with tailoring products and marketing strategies to national markets?

BOX 8.4

Standardized components and mass customization

In the same way as the modular design of products, the use of standardized components in the production process enables manufacturers to postpone final product differentiation. Identical components may be shared by diverse end-consumer products: for example the same plug will fit various appliances. 'Modules' are standardized components designed to be suitable for a wide variety of possible uses, allowing a significant reduction in the numbers of components.

Lagged differentiation is illustrated by the crystal glassworks at Saint Louis which have only a limited number of basic moulds for producing all their glassware while finishes (size, engraving, decoration, etc.) are applied at the end of the line to plain glasses. Unfinished glasses of different sizes and shapes are mass produced.

Similarly, the same basic cream cheese Tartare is packaged in different ways, right at the end of the production line: packed in aluminium foil in individual servings, in a plastic tub, canned or wrapped. In other cases, a basic cheese will be flavoured differently (cherry, walnut, port wine, rose or other flower perfumes, etc.). Some packagings are standardized such as plastic containers which can be used for melted cheese as well as various types of fresh cheese.

Canson & Montgolfier manufacture papers of different weights on rolls 2.20 metres wide and several hundred metres long. This 'upstream' operation requires large-scale investment and a high level of technology, and has limited flexibility. As far as possible, each type of roll is manufactured in batches (several times a year) and stored before its final processing. Cutting, shaping and finishing is carried out on standard rolls, which are then customized to the required formats and styles of each country. At Petit-Bateau, which manufactures traditional knitwear, the knitting is done on unbleached yarn. Dying is applied to the yarn subsequently. Likewise, standardized patterns permit the creation of a large number of different clothes. At Dim, a lingerie manufacturer, tights are produced undyed. The dye, which is subcontracted, is applied at the last possible opportunity on untreated standard tights. This allows flexible tailoring to the different shades sought by consumers. Irons by SEB-Calor are all manufactured on the same

BOX 8.4 *CONTINUED*

moulding, which gives rise to 100 different models, according to function, colour, casing, voltage and brand name. Christofle's Arab cafetières, designed exclusively for the Middle East, are manufactured with the same stamping moulds as other cafetières.*

The Planter's Company, a unit of Nabisco chose cosmetic customization when it retooled its old plant in Suffolk, Virginia, in order to satisfy the increasingly diverse demand of its retail customers. Wal-Mart wanted to sell peanuts and mixed nuts in larger quantities than Safeway or 7-Eleven did, and Jewel wanted different promotional packages than Dominick's did. In the past, Planter's could produce only long batches of small, medium, and large cans; as a result, customers had to choose from a few standard packages to find the one that most closely met their requirements. Today the company can switch quickly between different sizes.**

(Sources: *Deher, 1986, p. 66 and **Gilmore and Pine, 1997, p. 94. Reproduced with permission.)

Globalization as a way to change the organizational design of international marketing activities

The reasons for globalizing marketing activities are largely organizational ones. Although there is evidence of some savings at the level of manufacturing costs, the financial pay-offs for hard globalization have been at best dubious when one considers the financial performance of companies as a whole (Samiee and Roth, 1992; Whitelock and Pimblett, 1997; see also Case A5.3). MNCs which grew fast world-wide in the 1960s and 1970s did so by granting a large degree of decision-making autonomy to their subsidiaries in their home markets. Subsidiaries were asked to replicate the corporate values and organizational practices of the parent company and also encouraged to adjust completely to the local market. Later on, subsidiary managers used the message of 'our market is unique' to defend specific, nationally designed marketing policies. Hence they defended their autonomy even at the expense of sometimes rather fallacious arguments. MNCs probably needed at the beginning of the 1980s to shift their organizational design towards more centralization. Parent companies wanted to have a more unified implementation scheme of new, more centrally designed international marketing strategies, responding to the globalization of competition. Procter & Gamble did this in Europe by introducing the Eurobrand concept, consisting of a common brand name and a basic marketing strategy for most western European countries (see Box 8.5).

Global companies willing to recentralize their operations tend since the 1980s towards some authoritarianism from headquarters, especially when they adopt the 'hard' version of the globalization creed. Often the globalization of consumption is presented as an unquestionable postulate, because it is much easier to 'sell' the

BOX 8.5

Reactions from European managers of Procter & Gamble to eurobrands

'We have to listen to the consumer. In blind tests in my market that perfume cannot even achieve breakeven.'

'The whole detergent market is in 2-kilo packs in Holland. To go to a European standard of 3 kg and 5 kg sizes would be a disaster for us.'

'We have low phosphate in Italy that constrains our product formula. And we just don't have hypermarkets like France and Germany where you can drop off pallet loads.'

(Comments of some managers in national subsidiaries)

'There is no such thing as a Eurocustomer so it makes no sense to talk about Eurobrands. We have an English housewife whose needs are different from a German Hausfrau. If we move to a system that allows us to blur our thinking, we will have big problems.

Product standardisation sets up pressures to try to meet everybody's needs (in which case you build a Rolls-Royce that nobody can afford) and countervailing pressures to find the lowest common denominator product (in which case you make a product that satisfies nobody and which cannot compete in any market). These decisions probably result in the foul middle compromise that is so often the outcome of committee decision.'

(Comments of a general manager to P & G European headquarters)

(Source: Bartlett, 1983. Reproduced with permission.)

recentralization policy within the organization. Kashani (1989) gives the example of Lego, the Danish toy company which was facing a leading competitor in the US, Tyco, which sold its toys in plastic buckets instead of Lego's elegant see-through cartons, standardized world-wide. When asked by the management of the US subsidiary to package in buckets as did the competitor, which was gaining market share, the head office rejected the request. After two years and a massive loss of share of the US market, Lego's headquarters in Billund (Denmark) decided to create a newly designed bucket. Not only was the share erosion in the US stopped, but the bucket was introduced world-wide and proved to be a great success.

The relationship between headquarters and subsidiaries in the defining of marketing strategy is complex. Too much autonomy results in purely local solutions with few economies of scale and an absence of world-wide co-ordination; then strong action is needed. This was the case in Black & Decker's gamble on globalization (Saporito, 1984, p. 26):

Globalization did not go down well in Europe for one good reason: Black & Decker owned half the market on the continent, and an astounding 80% in the U.K. European managers asked:

'Why tamper with success?' But Farley (B & D new chairman) believed that the company was treading water in Europe – sales failed to grow last year – and that Makita's strategy made globalization inevitable . . . Those who don't share Farley's vision usually don't stay around long. Last year he fired all of his European managers.

This was combined with a complete turnaround: Black & Decker acquired the GE small appliance division and a Swedish company producing woodworking tools, and changed the company name to B&D as well as the logo. B&D recentred a large part of its business on self-powered tools with built-in batteries; finally it achieved a strong comeback (Li, 1990).

The globalization of consumption patterns only partly explains the standardization of international marketing programmes; it is rather the patterns of globalization of competition which impose changes in organizational design (recentralization). In this process, negotiations and compromises between headquarters and subsidiaries are constant. As Kashani emphasized (1989, p. 92): 'the way global decisions are conceptualized, refined, internally communicated, and, finally implemented in the company's international network have a great deal to do with their performance'. Local managers naturally tend to emphasize the uniqueness of local consumption patterns and marketing environment (legal, distribution networks, sales promotion methods and so on). The headquarters of successful global companies are flexible rather than authoritarian in dealing with their subsidiaries' assumed or real uniqueness; for instance, they commission research rather than flatly ignore a subsidiary's arguments; they take new ideas and suggestions from the most talented and dynamic subsidiaries, rather than outrightly reject their advice.

In fact, international marketing programmes have experienced a trend towards greater standardization, but this needs to be differentiated, according to: (1) the elements of the marketing mix considered; (2) the type of market, whether it is a developed or undeveloped country; (3) the type of product: consumer or industrial goods; and (4) the control exerted over the subsidiary, whether it is wholly owned or a joint venture.

Picard *et al.* (1989) replicated a 1973 survey by Hansen and Boddewyn (1976) of the level of standardization of the European marketing policies of US multinational companies operating in Europe (50 usable answers in 1973, and 71 in 1983). This diachronic approach reveals mixed evolution: in consumer durables there was a decrease across the board in the degree of standardization of marketing policies, apart from product policy. In consumer non-durables, with the exception of branding, the percentage of respondents with standardized marketing policies in all EU countries was much higher in 1983 than in 1973. Surprisingly, they note a significant trend away from standardization of products for industrial goods. This trend towards adaptation to national context is also true for other elements of the marketing mix (advertising, branding, after-sales service).

Hill and Still (1984a) examined the international marketing policies of 19 MNCs that sell to LDC (less developed countries) markets. Out of 2,200 products sold by the subsidiaries in the sample, 1,200 had originated in either the United States or the United Kingdom. Their findings show that 'nearly seven changes (product adaptation) out of ten (69.4 per cent) are marketing oriented . . . for most products, the process of managing product adaptation is critical' (p. 94). They also found that greater product adaptation was required from MNCs in rural areas than in urban areas in the LDCs (Hill and Still, 1984b).

In many cases, standardization is often done incrementally by transferring existing products at headquarters level or in important subsidiaries: Hill and James (1991) show that there remains a considerable degree of power at subsidiary level in relation to product and promotion transfer in consumer goods multinationals. In most cases market needs are assessed by the subsidiary itself which then uses the world-wide product portfolio as a resource base. In developing countries, subsidiaries initiate product transfer in 85 per cent of the cases, whereas in developed markets they do it in only 63 per cent of the cases. This suggests that world or regional headquarters exert more authoritative pressure for standardization across developed markets, especially in Europe. In the transfer process some adaptation is made to local requirements (see Chapter 9 on this issue): the degree of adaptation varies according to marketing mix elements. Ozsomer *et al.* (1991) have investigated the degree of marketing standardization for 33 multinationals operating in Turkey: product characteristics, brand name, positioning and packaging are the least adapted elements; price, promotion and distribution are more tailored to the local environment. Furthermore, they show that the degree of standardization is larger in wholly-owned subsidiaries than in joint ventures.

Globalization is a process which occurs mostly at the competition level. Artificial entry barriers, related to duties and standards, are now being progressively replaced by natural entry barriers related to scale and experience. For international marketing, culture-related experience is all the more important since the natural entry barriers relating to consumer behaviour and marketing environments will diminish very gradually and only in the long term. Language-related differences, for instance, will remain. Therefore, global marketing strategies must be implemented cautiously, especially in culture-bound industries: local knowledge has to be generated, by research, by organizational learning, by hiring 'cultural' insiders or by acquiring local companies which have culture-specific business experience.

Globalization belongs to the realm of organizational discourse rather than to actual international marketing. Rather than a 'hard' global marketing strategy it is possible to adopt an intercultural marketing strategy which has basically the same goals but is more respectful of local culture and attempts to serve purely national as well as transnational market segments.

8.4   MARKET SEGMENTS: GEOGRAPHIC VERSUS DEMOGRAPHIC

Intercultural marketing is about localizing as much as globalizing; it aims to customize product and marketing strategies to customer needs within the framework of a global strategy. Intercultural marketing tries to balance cross-national differences requiring mandatory local adaptation and cross-national commonalities which enable the building of size and experience effects. To do this, the international marketer needs to define country clusters where similar marketing policies can be followed (for a review of country clustering, see Holzmüller and Stöllnberger, 1994). Many examples in this section derive from cultural products, in particular recordings of music which combine both local and global appeal.

Taking advantage of the desire for assimilation and cultural identification: The case of cultural products

Cultural products such as music, literature and movie films are strongly suffused with local particularism. Books, records and films are, however, three products where global marketing has been successfully employed. The success of Harlequin romantic novels, Michael Jackson records and Indiana Jones films has been remarkable: profound attraction has bypassed the filter of national cultures. The romantic and melodramatic adventures of Harlequin heroes found a lonely female public eager for tenderness in the majority of urban centres. Similarly, the meaning conveyed by the music of Michael Jackson extends far beyond American culture. The character of Michael Jackson touches deep layers of individual character in his admirers, that is, sexual ambiguity, in fact a very old theme in the cultural history of mankind.

Cultural products which build on fairly universal feelings and ways of being are the ones to which standardized marketing policy can be applied. In the record industry, particularly for as regards collections of popular music, marketing techniques have generally evolved similarly in industrialized nations, with increased large-scale distribution or specialized chains, similar promotion channels and advertising, and a global standardization of product presentation. The recipe for global success is, however, less easily applicable than it seems: American country music has failed in its attempt to achieve major success in continental Europe. Its only real international development occurred in Australia despite some success in the United Kingdom. A reason for this is the absence of a significant segment of the European population which can identify itself with the images evoked by the music of the American West and the symbols of a tradition of pioneers. The Australian bush, on the other hand, similar in many respects to the American Midwest, has given birth to an Australian musical tradition whose roots are in country music.

Intercultural marketing is facilitated when the conditions for product identification are present in the target market. Consumers buy the meaning that they find in products for the purpose of cultural identification, based on the desire for assimilation in a certain civilization – as in the case of ethnic consumption (see section 4.4). Such identification was the reason that record companies began to market classical music on a large scale in the form of collections. In the 1980s, market surveys showed that possession of records of classical music, combined with a superficial knowledge of the most famous pieces, promoted a personal image of stability and respectability for people between 25 and 40, projecting an image of successful integration in professional and social lives. As a result, certain record companies launched mass-market collections of classical music, the marketing strategy for which has been a strict implementation of the rules of global marketing: same product, same packaging, same price and same type of communication. These collections, however, became less successful when classical music ceased to be a major element in the acquisition of respectability in the 1990s.

Apart from their utilitarian aspects, McDonald's Big Mac and Coca-Cola are sources of meanings that provide their buyers with fantasized cultural adaptation to a desired way of life. Rock music represents a tolerant and leisurely way of life for many young Europeans and Asians. Identification with these symbols is one of the necessary conditions for being *trendy*. The international marketing of rock music achieves even greater success where certain values (e.g. individualism, strong desire for equality) are already present in the market segment to be conquered, in this case young people between the ages of 10 and 25.

The process of cultural identification functions in two ways: that of *identity* (the reproduction of national culture as it used to be, the desire to be 'at home'), and that of *exoticism* (the desire to escape from one's own culture, to experience different values and ways of life). These two ways are intermingled in a quite ambivalent fashion in the process of cultural identification. This ambivalence prohibits any simplistic approach; it is therefore necessary to cluster countries or consumers who share certain meaningful cultural characteristics. Such clusters form cultural affinity zones and cultural affinity classes.

Cultural affinity classes and cultural affinity zones

The intercultural marketing approach not only concentrates on geography- and nationality-based criteria but also takes into account consumer attitudes, preferences and lifestyles that are linked to age, class and ethnicity, or occupation. This does not, however, exclude other possible criteria for segmentation. Cultural affinity zones correspond to a large extent to national cultural groups. Cultural affinity classes exist in terms of age brackets or, more generally, across sociodemographic categories, for example people between the ages of 15 and 20 in Japan, Europe and the United States. People within a cultural affinity class share common values, behaviour and interests, and tend to present common traits as a consumer segment; their lifestyles converge world-wide irrespective of national borders. Lifestyle convergence can be observed for similar age classes in Europe, for instance teenagers who spend time watching MTV. Similarly, lifestyle convergence can be observed for gender-based segments on a world-wide basis; Tai and Tam (1997) review the change in lifestyles of female consumers in Hong Kong, Taiwan and China on a number of issues such as women's role and perception, family and home orientation, health and environment. They find that women in the People's Republic of China tend to be quickly influenced by western values and are increasingly becoming similar to both Hong Kong and Taiwanese female consumers. Similarly, Carey *et al.* (1997) report about a survey of 7-to-12-year-olds around the world, the ABC Global Kids Study, which aimed at tracking their lifestyle and consumption patterns. A pictorial response scale was used when interviewing children on emotions and preferences while product usage was reported more frequently by mothers, rather than children. World-wide, children basically seem to share many common dreams and aspirations; they tend to have significant purchasing power and participate actively in family decision making for a number of product categories.

De Mooij and Keegan (1991) review comparative lifestyle research in Europe and in Asia. Attempts at monitoring cross-border changes in lifestyles are made in Asia by the Survey Research Group (SRG), which conducts lifestyle surveys in Hong Kong, Malaysia, the Philippines, Singapore, Thailand and Taiwan. Similarly, changes in lifestyles across social milieus in European countries are monitored through extensive surveys, such as the ACE (Anticipating Change in Europe) study, CCA (Centre de Communication Avancée) Eurostyles and Sinus Gmbh 'Social Milieus'.

By making a systematic comparison of values, attitudes and beliefs in each social milieu across the four countries [the United Kingdom, France, Italy and Germany], a map of multinational target groups was obtained. Each of these target groups represents a distinctive segment across the different nations. Members of the social milieus within a multinational target group sometimes have more in common than with many of their fellow countrymen. In spite of these similarities, there are of course, differences. Similar values may translate differently at the local level. (De Mooij and Keegan, 1991, pp. 118–19.)

The practical difficulty is in combining geography-based cultural affinity zones and demographics and lifestyle segmentation criteria (cultural affinity classes). One may wonder for instance, in relation to a specific product or service, whether consumption behaviour, values and lifestyles among the 15-to-20-year-olds are more homogeneous across Europe or Asia than among the 30-to-40-year-olds in the same zones. Cultural affinity classes, in so far as they create a sense of belonging to a common age, gender or income group across different countries, are probably an ideal means of defining an international target for standardized products. Furthermore, the development of new media such as satellite television channels will help the international launch of products targeted at the same cultural affinity classes across different countries. Accordingly, market research should survey consumer segments as cells in a matrix, with countries in columns and cultural affinity classes in rows.

If similar behaviour is observed by market researchers for a particular row across the different cells of the matrix with regard to key consumer behaviour figures (e.g. consumption of soft drinks, organization of personal time, time spent listening to the radio or watching television, etc.), the emergence of a common consumption culture and a cross-national segment can be detected. If, on the other hand, different cultural affinity classes in different countries adopt similar behaviour at the international level, marketing communication will have to be modified to facilitate the process of diffusion from one country to another. If a drink, for example, is popular among 25-to-30-year-olds in one country and among 50-to-60-year-olds in another country, this indicates a weak affinity of national cultures.

Attempts to market products on a global level also highlight cultural affinity zones in which the same marketing strategy with the same type of products can be successfully implemented. In Europe, for example, two of these zones are quite separate (see Figure 8.1) – Scandinavia and the Mediterranean countries. A third zone encompasses the central European countries and Great Britain which serve as a bridge between northern and southern Europe, while retaining their own distinct personality. Despite the traditional isolation of the United Kingdom, there are fewer differences between the United Kingdom and Denmark or Sweden than between the UK and Italy or Spain. Accordingly an item successfully marketed in the United Kingdom is more likely to repeat this success in The Netherlands or Denmark than in southern Europe. The long-established differences between Anglo-Saxon and Latin culture are reinforced by the religious divide between Protestants and Catholics. Cultural affinity zones display similar characteristics for easily identifiable criteria such as language, religion, family-life patterns, work relations and consumption patterns. Intercultural marketing begins by choosing one of the main countries from a cultural affinity zone as a 'lead country' which will be used as a base for market entry and diffusion of strategy, with only minor adaptation for other countries throughout the zone. Marketing teams can interact with each other across zones within a regional area, especially when countries lie at the border of two zones. As an example, Figure 8.1 offers a *hypothetical map* of the zones of cultural affinities for western Europe.

The operational mapping of cultural affinity zones can be based on cultural as well as marketing criteria related to the product category, such as consumer behaviour, price levels, attitude towards innovation, opening hours in distribution outlets, etc. When a product is launched·internationally, the new product will be launched first in lead countries and subsequently marketed in other countries in the zones. For instance, a record successful in Latin countries during the summer, when waves of holiday-makers come from all over Europe, will have a greater chance of spreading into Nordic countries once people return home and go into record shops to buy the songs they have heard on holiday. Equally, a band may be so successful in a single country such as Germany that its music spreads into neighbouring countries. It spreads rapidly in the border regions, for example in Belgium, because of media over-lap. The launch of a new product through cultural affinity zones can take from eighteen months to two years, which is a relatively long period of time compared with the standard life cycle of a song, generally a few months (Usunier and Sissmann, 1986). The concept of 'lead country' has been used successfully by multinational companies such as Procter & Gamble when they developed the Eurobrand concept in the mid-1980s.

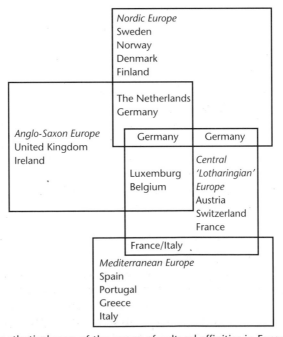

FIGURE 8.1   A hypothetical map of the zones of cultural affinities in Europe.
(*Source:* Usunier and Sissmann, 1986, p. 85. Reproduced with permission.)

What is the relevant geographical segmentation? National versus regional differences

Sovereign states have very dissimilar sizes: China (9,600,000 km²) is more than 232 times the size of Switzerland (49,293 km²), even though both countries are significant international players on the world scene. Geographical location has a relation to culture: for instance, on average, islands tend to develop more homogeneity than continental countries. A special case is that of mega-countries such as the United States, Canada, Brazil, China and India because their internal diversity is fairly large. Even smaller countries, such as the United Kingdom, Spain, Italy, Sweden and France, exhibit a strong North/South paradigm which is reversed in the southern hemisphere for countries such as Argentina or New Zealand. Tiny Switzerland also displays significant internal diversity especially between the French- and the German-speaking communities, which respectively account for 20 per cent and 75 per cent of the population. Therefore, national differences are not the only source of variance in consumer behaviour across different geographical locations.

Any geographical division may be taken as a base for segmenting marketing variables, for instance psychographics, and looking at their generality across different geographic locations (Lesser and Hughes, 1986). The case of the United States is one of the best documented. As Garreau (1981) emphasized, describing the 'nine nations of North America', regional differences in large countries with multi-ethnic and multicultural backgrounds can explain differences in consumer behaviour. Kahle (1986) shows that geographical segmentation is a basis for finding differences in values, whereas Gentry *et al.* (1987) show that geographical subcultures in the United States vary culturally. In administering a questionnaire in four regions of the United States – west (Washington), north central (Wisconsin), south west (Oklahoma) and north east (Massachusetts) – Gentry *et al.* (1987, p. 415) show that 'geographic regions vary in terms of innovativeness and perceived risk. Further differences exist across regions in terms of cultural adherence, religious commitment, and fate-orientation . . . Residents in those areas with more adherence to traditional values are less likely to try new products.'

But regional differences within countries, even if perceived more clearly by nationals than by foreigners, are most often much smaller than international differences. For instance, Saegaert *et al.* (1978) do not find significant differences in 'fad food' use among Anglo- and Mexican-Americans. Similarly, Calantone *et al.* (1985) find English Quebecois women to be more similar to French Quebecois women than to Ontario English women (all of these people being Canadians) in the benefits they seek from a brassiere. Their findings support the idea of the assimilation model, where the cultural values of the immigrants tend to merge with those of the locally dominant cultural group. This supports geography as an operational basis for international marketing segmentation.

8.5   CONCLUSION

When building clusters of countries ('cultural affinity zones') that can be approached with a regionally standardized marketing strategy, marketing professionals have to take into account basic cultural variables such as language, institutions, membership in a regional grouping and basic cultural traits as described in Chapters 2 and 3. However, some sociodemographic characteristics such as sex, age and income also provide a sound basis for transnational marketing strategies in terms of 'cultural affinity classes'. Thus international marketing segments must be defined in order to allow for the best possible compromise between national/cultural and sociodemographic characteristics.

QUESTIONS

1. Describe how experience effects induce firms to standardize products. Give examples.
2. Select a multinational company annual report and find evidence of globalization (global decisions, global products, globalization of competition, consumption patterns, management procedures, etc.).
3. Why is globalization taking place more clearly on the supply side than on the demand side?
4. For the following industries/products discuss to what extent: (a) a world consumer exists; (b) the product or services offered are themselves global (similar worldwide); and (c) the industry itself can be considered as global:
    *   Airlines
    *   Tobacco
    *   Meat-based foods
    *   Sheets and pillows
    *   Pharmaceuticals
5. What are zones of cultural affinity?
6. Discuss the relative importance for segmentation purposes of sociodemographic variables, such as age, sex, income, habitat, etc., in comparison with cultural variables based either on nationality or values.

APPENDIX 8: TEACHING MATERIALS

A8.1 Case: Lakewood Forest Products

Since the 1970s the United States has had a merchandise trade deficit with the rest of the world. Up to 1982, this deficit mattered little because it was relatively small. As of 1983, however, the trade deficit increased rapidly and became, because of its size and future implications, an issue of major national concern. Suddenly, trade moved to the forefront of national debate. Concurrently, a debate ensued on the issue of the international competitiveness of US firms. The onerous question here was whether US firms could and would achieve sufficient improvements in areas such as productivity, quality and price to remain long-term successful international marketing players.

The USA–Japanese trade relation took on particular significance, because it was between those two countries that the largest bilateral trade deficit existed. In spite of trade negotiations, market-opening measures, trade legislation and other government efforts, it was clear that the impetus for a reversal of the deficit through more US exports to Japan had to come from the private sector. Therefore, the activities of any US firm that appeared successful in penetrating the Japanese market were widely hailed. One company whose effort to market in Japan aroused particular interest was Lakewood Forest Products of Hibbing, Minnesota.

Company background

In 1988, Ian J. Ward was an export merchant in difficulty. Throughout the 1970s and 1980s his company, Ward Bedas Canadian Ltd, had successfully sold Canadian lumber and salmon to countries in the Persian Gulf. Over time, the company had opened four offices world-wide. However, when the Iran–Iraq war erupted most of Ward's long-term trading relationships disappeared within a matter of months. In addition, the international lumber market began to collapse. As a result, Ward Bedas Canadian Ltd went into a survivalist mode and sent employees all over the world to look for new markets and business opportunities. Late that year, the company received an interesting order. A firm in Korea urgently needed to purchase lumber for the production of chopsticks.

Learning about the chopstick market

In discussing the wood deal with the Koreans, Ward learned that in order to produce good chopsticks more than 60 per cent of the wood fiber would be wasted. Given the high transportation cost involved, the large degree of wasted materials, and his need for new business, Ward decided to explore the Korean and Japanese chopstick industry in more detail. He quickly determined that chopstick making in the Far East is a fragmented industry, working with old technology and suffering from a lack of natural resources. In Asia, chopsticks are produced in very small quantities, often by family organizations. Even the largest of the 450 chopstick factories in Japan turns out only 5 million chopsticks a month. This compares to an overall market size of 130 million pairs of disposable chopsticks a day. In addition, chopsticks represent a growing market. With increased wealth in Asia, people eat out more often and therefore have a greater demand for disposable chopsticks. The fear of communicable diseases has greatly reduced the utilization of reusable chopsticks. Reusable plastic chopsticks have been attacked by many groups as too newfangled and as causing future ecological problems.

From his research, Ward concluded that a competitive niche existed in the world chopstick market. He believed that, if he could use low-cost raw materials and ensure that the labour cost component would remain small, he could successfully compete in the world market.

The founding of Lakewood Forest Products

In exploring opportunities afforded by the newly identified international marketing niche for chopsticks, Ward set four criteria for plant location:

1. Access to raw materials.
2. Proximity of other wood product users who could make use of the 60 per cent waste for their production purposes.

3. Proximity to a port that would facilitate shipment to the Far East.

4. Availability of labour.

In addition, Ward was aware of the importance of product quality. Because people use chopsticks on a daily basis and are accustomed to products that are visually inspected one by one, he would have to live up to high quality expectations in order to compete successfully. Chopsticks could not be bowed or misshapen, have blemishes in the wood or splinter.

In order to implement his plan, Ward needed financing. Private lenders were sceptical and slow to provide funds. This scepticism resulted from the unusual direction of Ward's proposal. Far Eastern companies have generally held the cost advantage in a variety of industries, especially those as labour-intensive as chopstick manufacturing. US companies rarely have an advantage in producing low-cost items. Further, only a very small domestic market exists for chopsticks.

However, Ward found that the state of Minnesota was willing to participate in his new venture. Since the decline of the mining industry, regional unemployment had been rising rapidly in the state. In 1988, unemployment in Minnesota's Iron Range peaked at 22 per cent. Therefore, state and local officials were anxious to attract new industries that would be independent of mining activities. They were excited about Ward's plans, which called for the creation of over 100 new jobs within a year.

Hibbing, Minnesota, turned out to be an ideal location for Ward's project. The area had an abundance of supply of aspen wood, which, because it grows in clay soil, tends to be unmarred. In addition, Hibbing boasted an excellent labour pool, and both the city and the state were willing to make loans totalling $500,000. Further, the Iron Range Resources Rehabilitation Board was willing to sell $3.4 million in industrial revenue bonds for the project. Together with jobs and training wage subsidies, enterprise zone credits and tax increment financing benefits, the initial public support for the project added up to about 30 per cent of its start-up costs. The potential benefit of the new venture to the region was quite clear. When Lakewood Forest Products advertised its first 30 jobs, more than 3,000 people showed up to apply.

The production and sale of chopsticks

Ward insisted that in order to penetrate the international market properly, he would need to keep his labour cost low. As a result, he decided to automate as much of the production as possible. However, no equipment was readily available to produce chopsticks, because no one had automated the process before.

After much searching, Ward identified a European equipment manufacturer who produced machinery for making popsicle sticks. He purchased equipment from this Danish firm in order to carry out the sorting and finishing processes better. However, because aspen wood was quite different from the wood the machine was designed for, as was the final product, substantial design adjustments had to be made. Sophisticated equipment was also purchased to strip the bark from the wood and peel it into long thin sheets. Finally, a computer vision system was acquired to detect defects in the chopsticks. The system rejected over 20 per cent of the production, and yet some of the chopsticks that passed inspection were splintering. However, Ward firmly believed that further fine-tuning of the equipment and training of the new work force would gradually take care of the problem.

Given this fully automated process, Lakewood Forest Products was able to develop capacity for up to seven million chopsticks a day. With a unit manufacturing cost of $0.03 and an anticipated unit selling price of $0.057, Ward expected to earn a pretax profit of $4.7 million in 1993.

By means of intense marketing efforts in Japan and because Japanese customers were struggling to obtain sufficient supplies of disposable chopsticks, Ward was able to presell the first five years of production quite quickly. By late 1992, Lakewood Forest Products was ready to enter the international market. With an ample supply of raw materials and an almost totally automated plant, Lakewood was positioned as the world's largest and least labour-intensive manufacturer of chopsticks. The first shipment of six containers with a load of 12 million pairs of chopsticks to Japan was made in October 1992.

(Source: Adapted from Michael R. Czinkota, in Czinkota and Ronkainen, 1990, pp. 472–5.)

QUESTIONS

1. Why haven't Japanese firms thought of automating the chopstick production process?

2. What are the important variables for the international marketing success of chopsticks?

3. Rank, in order, the variables in Question 2 according to the priority you believe they have for foreign customers, especially Japanese and Korean consumers.

4. How long will Lakewood Forest Products be able to maintain its competitive advantage?

A8.2 Exercise: *Dangerous Enchantment*

First read the short extract from *Dangerous Enchantment*, the evocative title of the novel by Anne Mather (1966). Harlequin books are a world-wide success. They are translated into fifteen languages and read in many countries. Therefore they can be considered as a truly 'global' cultural product. This short extract has been chosen for its capacity to illustrate the style of Harlequin books.

The next day Julie had collected herself. She was glad in a way that she had seen the woman with Manuel. At least it brought home to her more strongly than any words could have done the completely amoral attitude he possessed.

Marilyn had seen the television as well, however, and said: 'I say, Julie, did you see that Manuel Cortez is back in England?'

Julie managed a casual shrug. 'So what?'

'Darling, really!' Marilyn gave her an old-fashioned look. 'Surely you aren't as indifferent as all that! I know you refused a date with him, but I'm sure that was more because of Paul Bannister than anything else.'

Julie tossed her head. 'I really can't see what all the fuss is about. Paul would make four of him!'

'You must be joking!' Marilyn giggled. 'Get you! I didn't know Paul was becoming such a dish all of a sudden. Why? What's changed him?'

Julie refrained from replying. She had no desire to get involved in an argument about Paul when it meant her stating things that in actual fact were not true. It was no use pretending about Paul's attractions; he was handsome, yes, and tall, yes, and young; but there was nothing particularly exciting about him and Julie could never understand girls who thought men's looks were enough. She had known many men, and in her small experience personality mattered far more than mere good looks.

However, during her lunch break she did borrow a newspaper from Miss Fatherstone in the hope that there might be more particulars about the woman with Manuel, but there was not. There was a picture of him at the airport, and a small article, and that was all.

When they left the building that evening it was snowing, and an icy wind was blowing, chilling them to the bone. Julie, wrapped in a loose dark blue mohair coat, hugged her handbag to her as she started along towards the main thoroughfare accompanied by Donna and Marilyn. She wore knee-length white boots, but between the place where her boots ended and the place where her skirt began she felt frozen, and she wondered whether for the winter at least she should go back to normal-length skirts.

Her hair was blowing about her face, for she was wearing no hat, and she walked straight into the man who stood purposely in her way.

'I'm sorry . . .' she began hastily, a smile lightening her face, and then: 'You!'

Manuel smiled, and her heart leapt treacherously into her throat. She had let go of Donna's arm in her confusion, but both Marilyn and Donna were staring open-mouthed. Manuel took Julie's arm, and said smoothly: 'You will excuse me, ladies,' in a mocking tone, and drew Julie across the pavement to the familiar green Ferrari.

'No, wait!' began Julie, but it was no use. Manuel had the car door open and was propelling her inside, his hard fingers biting cruelly into her arm.

'Don't argue,' he said, for all the world as though it was a natural occurrence that he should meet her from work.

Julie did not want to create a scene in the street, so she climbed into the luxurious warmth of the car and sliding across out of the driver's seat, she allowed him to slide in beside her. He slammed the door, flicked the ignition, and the car moved silently forward, purring like a sated panther.

She stole a glance at him as they turned into the main thoroughfare, and saw, with a sense of inevitability, that far from changing he was much more attractive than she remembered. He turned for a moment to look at her as they stopped at some traffic lights, and said: 'How have you been?'

Julie contemplated her fingernails. 'Fine. And you?'

He shrugged, and did not reply, and she felt like hitting him. How dared he sit there knowing that she must have seen him with that girl yesterday! She looked out of the car window, suddenly realizing that she was allowing him to drive her heaven knows where, and she was making no comment.

'Where are you taking me?' she asked in a tight little voice.

'Home,' he said lazily. 'Where do you think? I thought I would save you the journey on such a ghastly night. Tell me, how do you stand this climate? It's terrible. Me, I like the sun, and the sea, and warm water to swim in.'

'Don't we all?' remarked Julie dryly. 'This will do.' They had reached the end of Faulkner Road. Manuel shook his head. 'What number?'

'Forty-seven. But please, I'd rather you didn't drive along there. It would only cause speculation, and if you should be recognized . . .' Her voice trailed away.

'That's hardly likely tonight,' remarked Manuel coolly, and drove smoothly to her gate where he halted the car.

'Thank you, señor.' Julie gave a slight bow of her head, and made to get out, but Manuel stopped her, his fingers biting into her arm.

'Aren't you pleased to see me?' he asked mockingly.

Julie looked at him fully. 'No, not really.'

'Why'?'

'Surely that's obvious. We have nothing to say to one another.'

'No?'

'No.' Julie brushed back her hair as it fell in waves over her eyes. It glistened with tiny drops of melted snow and she was unaware of how lovely she was looking.

Manuel shrugged, and lay back in his seat. 'Go, then.'

Julie felt furious. It always ended this way, with herself feeling the guilty one. Well, he wasn't going to get away with it! She swung round on him.

'Don't imagine for one moment that I've been brought home believing your little tales,' she cried angrily. 'I know perfectly well that the reason you have brought me home is because you could hardly take me to the apartment when you already have one female in residence!'

Manuel stared at her, a dull flush just visible in the muted light of the car rising up his cheeks.

(Source: Mather, 1966, *Dangerous Enchantment*, pp. 89–92. Reproduced with permission.)

QUESTIONS

1. Identify the main sociodemographic characteristics of the target audience of such books.

2. Identify from the text (situation, characters and the relations between them) how, and to what extent, this text moves people in such a way as to touch feelings and emotions that are widely shared in the world population.

3. Define the target audience of Harlequin books, in terms of cultural affinity class(es).

REFERENCES

Bartlett, Christopher (1983), 'Procter & Gamble Europe: Vizir launch', *Harvard Business School Case* 9-384-139.

Buzzell, Robert D. (1968), 'Can you standardize multinational marketing?', *Harvard Business Review*, November–December, pp. 102–13.

Calantone, R., M. Morris and J. Johar (1985), 'A cross-cultural benefit segmentation analysis to evaluate the traditional assimilation model', *International Journal of Research in Marketing*, vol. 2, pp. 207–17.

Carey, George, Xiaoyan Zhao, Joan Chiaramonte and David Eden (1997), 'Is there one global village for our future generation? Talking to 7–12-year-olds around the world', *Marketing & Research Today*, vol. 25, no. 1, pp. 12–6.

Czinkota, Michael R. and Illka A. Ronkainen (1990), *International Marketing*, 2nd edn, Dryden Press: Hinsdale, IL.

Day, George S. and David B. Montgomery (1983), 'Diagnosing the experience curve', *Journal of Marketing*, Spring, pp. 44–58.

Deher, Odile (1986), 'Quelques facteurs de succès pour la politique de produits de l'entreprise exportatrice: Les liens entre marketing et production', *Recherche et applications en marketing*, vol. 1, no. 3, pp. 55–74.

De Mooij, Marieke K. and Warren Keegan (1991), *Advertising Worldwide*, Prentice Hall: Hemel Hempstead.

Focus (1995), Information bulletin of the World Trade Organization, January–February, no. 1, pp. 4–5.

Garreau, J. (1981), *The Nine Nations of North America*, Houghton Mifflin: Boston, MA.

GATT (1986), *Le Commerce International en 1985–1986*, GATT: Geneva.

Gentry, J. W., P. Tansujah, L. Lee Manzer and J. John (1987), 'Do geographic subcultures vary culturally?', in Michael J. Houston (ed.), *Advances in Consumer Research*, vol. 15, Association for Consumer Research: Provo, UT.

Ghoshal, Sumantra (1987), 'Global strategy: An organizing framework', *Strategic Management Journal*, vol. 8, pp. 425–40.

Gilmore, James H. and B. Joseph Pine II (1997), 'The four faces of mass customization', *Harvard Business Review*, vol. 75, no. 1, January–February, pp. 91–101.

Hamel, Gary and C. K. Prahalad (1985), 'Do you really have a global strategy?', *Harvard Business Review*, vol. 63, July–August, pp. 139–48.

Hampton, Gerald M. and Erwin Buske (1987), 'The global marketing perspective', in S. Tamer Cavusgil (ed.), *Advances in International Marketing*, JAI Press: Greenwich, CT, vol. 2, pp. 259–77.

Hansen, Dominique M. and Jean-Jacques Boddewyn (1976), *American Marketing in the European Common Market, 1963–1973*, Marketing Science Institute: Cambridge, MA, report no. 76–107.

Hill, John S. and William L. James (1991), 'Product and promotion transfers in consumer goods multinationals', *International Marketing Review*, vol. 8, no. 4, pp. 6–17.

Hill, John S. and Richard R. Still (1984a), 'Adapting products to L.D.C. tastes', *Harvard Business Review*, March–April, pp. 92–101.

Hill, John S. and Richard R. Still (1984b), 'Effects of urbanization on multinational product planning: Markets in L.D.C.s', *Columbia Journal of World Business*, vol. 19 (Summer), pp. 62–7.

Hollensen, Svend (1991), 'Shift of market servicing organization in international markets: A Danish case study', in Harald Vestergaard (ed.), *An Enlarged Europe in the Global Economy*, proceedings of the 17th Annual Conference of the European International Business Association, Copenhagen Business School: Copenhagen, pp. 732–42.

Holzmüller, Hartmut H. and Barbara Stöllnberger (1994), 'A conceptual framework for country selection in cross-national export studies', *Advances in International Marketing*, vol. 6, pp. 3–24.

Hout, Thomas, Michael E. Porter and Eileen Rudden (1982), 'How global companies win out', *Harvard Business Review*, vol. 60, September–October, pp. 98–105.

Johanson, Jan and Jan-Erik Vahlne (1977), 'The internationalisation process of the firm: A model of knowledge development and increased market commitments,' *Journal of International Business Studies*, vol. 8, no. 1, pp. 23–32.

Kahle, Lyn R. (1986), 'The nine nations of North America and the value basis of geographic segmentation', *Journal of Marketing*, vol. 50 (April), pp. 37–47.

Kashani, Kamran (1989), 'Beware the pitfalls of global marketing', *Harvard Business Review*, vol. 67 (September–October), pp. 91–8.

Lesser, J. A. and M. A. Hughes (1986), 'The generalizability of psychographic market segments across geographic locations', *Journal of Marketing*, vol. 50 (January), pp. 18–27.

Li, Tiger (1990), 'Black and Decker's turnaround strategy,' in Hans B. Thorelli and S. Tamer Cavusgil (eds.), *International Marketing Strategy*, Pergamon Press: Oxford, pp. 495–8.

Ludlow, Peter W. (1990), 'Global challenges of the 1990s: Future of the international trading system', *Economic Impact*, 1990/1, pp. 4–10.

Mather, Anne (1966), *Dangerous Enchantment*, Harlequin: London.

Ohmae, Kenichi (1985), *Triad Power: The coming shape of global competition*, Free Press: New York.

Ozsomer, Aysegul, Muzzafer Bodur and S. Tamer Cavusgil (1991), 'Marketing standardisation by multinationals in an emerging market,' *European Journal of Marketing*, vol. 25, no. 12, pp. 50–64.

Picard Jacques, Jean-Jacques Boddewyn and Robin Soehl (1989), 'U.S. marketing policies in the European Economic Community: A longitudinal study, 1973–1983', in Reijo Luostarinen (ed.), *Dynamics of International Business*, Proceedings of the 15th Annual Conference of the European International Business Association, Helsinki, vol. 1, pp. 551–79.

Porter, Michael E. (1986), 'Changing patterns of international competition', *California Management Review*, vol XXVIII, no. 2, pp. 9–39.

Quelch, John A. and Edward J. Hoff (1986), 'Customizing global marketing', *Harvard Business Review*, vol. 64, May–June, pp. 59–68.

Ricks, David A. (1983), *Big Business Blunders: Mistakes in multinational marketing*: Dow Jones-Irwin: Homewood, IL.

Saegaert, J., E. Young and M. Wayne Saegaert (1978), 'Fad food consumption among Anglo and Mexican consumers: An example of research in consumer behavior and home economics', in H. Keith Hunt (ed.), *Advances in Consumer Research*, proceedings of the 8th Annual Conference, Association for Consumer Research, Ann Arbor, Michigan, USA, pp. 730–3.

Samiee, Saeed and Kendall Roth (1992), 'The influence of global marketing standardization on performance', *Journal of Marketing*, vol. 56, April, pp. 1–17.

Saporito, William (1984), 'Black & Decker's gamble on globalization', *Fortune*, 14 May, pp. 24–32.

Sheth, Jagdish N. (1986), 'Global markets or global competition?', *Journal of Consumer Marketing*, vol. 3 (Spring), pp. 9–11.

Stobaugh, Robert and Piero Telesio (1983), 'Assortir la politique de fabrication à la stratégie des produits', *Harvard-L'Expansion*, Summer, pp. 77–85.

Sumitomo Corporation (1988), *Global Market Makers*, Sumitomo Shoji Kaisha: Tokyo.

Tai, Susan H. C. and Jackie L. M. Tam (1997), 'A lifestyle analysis of female consumers in greater China', *Psychology and Marketing*, vol. 14, no. 3, pp. 287–307.

Usunier, Jean-Claude (1980), 'Les Lois de déformation des réseaux du commerce international', unpublished doctoral thesis, University of Paris II.

Usunier, Jean-Claude (1991), 'The "European consumer": Globalizer or globalized?', in Alan Rugman and Alain Verbeke (eds.), *Research in Global Strategic Management*, vol. 2, JAI Press: Greenwich, CT, pp. 57–78.

Usunier, Jean-Claude and Pierre Sissmann (1986), 'L'interculturel au service du marketing', *Harvard-L'Expansion*, no. 40, Spring, pp. 80–92.

Van Mesdag, Martin (1987), 'Winging it in foreign markets', *Harvard Business Review*, vol. 65, no.1, January–February, pp. 71–4.

Vernon, Raymond P. (1966), 'International investment and international trade in the product life cycle', *Quarterly Journal of Economics*, vol. 80, no. 2, pp. 191–207.

Whitelock, Jeryl and Carole Pimblett (1997), 'The standardization debate in international marketing', *Journal of Global Marketing*, vol. 10, no. 3, pp. 45–65.

Wind, Yoram (1986), 'The myth of globalization', *Journal of Consumer Marketing*, vol. 3 (Spring), pp. 23–6.

Wind, Yoram, Susan P. Douglas and Howard V. Perlmutter (1973), 'Guidelines for developing international marketing strategies', *Journal of Marketing*, vol. 37 (April), pp. 14–23.

9 Product policy 1: Physical, service and symbolic attributes

A central issue in international marketing strategy is the decision whether to adapt products for foreign markets after the consumer, the national markets and their particular characteristics have been surveyed, or to standardize products, which is a simplified strategy based on experience effects and cost reduction. For instance, part of the UK's loss of dominant position in the Arabian Gulf countries to the Japanese during the 1960s was due to a lack of product adaptation. In contrast to the British, the Japanese were reported by local consumers to have adapted their products to the needs of local markets, after careful research into demographic, economic, sociocultural, political-legal and physical environments (Tuncalp, 1990).

The real issue is not a dichotomous choice, whether to adapt or to standardize completely. Export performance has been shown to be a combination of both adaptation and standardization strategies (Shoham, 1996) and to depend on a large number of factors related to the four components of the marketing mix (Baalbaki and Malhotra, 1995). Around a core product offering that is standard world-wide, most global companies such as Coca-Cola or McDonald's customize when needed. It has been shown that the industry's potential for standardization dictates a company's strategy: in global industries with more opportunities for high standardization, firms that respond by standardizing show superior performance; conversely, within a particular industry, that is, across firms which face similar world markets and standardization opportunities, firms that customize the most have the best performance (Samiee and Roth, 1992). Product customization may also result in market differentiation, thus creating a competitive advantage *vis-à-vis* actual competitors and raising the height of entry barriers for potential competitors. Therefore the message is: standardize as much as feasible and customize as much as needed.

This chapter and the next (which is devoted to the product's brand name and national image) propose a decision-making framework for the adaptation/standardization of various product attributes: physical characteristics, design, form, colour, functions, packaging, brand name and 'made-in' label. An assessment will be made of the adaptation and international standardization of different levels of product attributes: physical attributes, service attributes and symbolic attributes. The product conveys symbolic meanings through its colour, shape, country of origin, brand name and so on.

The first section of this chapter sets out a systematic model for the choice between adaptation and standardization of product policy. It can be applied successively to each existing national market as well as to markets where a company intends to set up new business. The second section is devoted to the physical attributes of the product. The third section deals with the standardization/adaptation of service attributes. The fourth section relates to symbolic attributes.

The etymology of the word 'symbol' comes from Ancient Greece, where the symbol was originally an object cut into two. The two halves were retained by the host and the guest and later passed on to their children. When these two halves were reunited, this enabled the owners to be recognized and served as proof of the bond of hospitality previously created. The symbol therefore replaces, represents and denotes some other entity by means of a conventional relationship or a suggestion, the evidence of which has usually been lost. The meanings that symbols diffuse are, of course, culture based. They are interpreted differently across countries.

Other important symbolic attributes are the brand name and the national images linked to the product and its country of manufacture. The conversion of a national brand into an international one, and the linguistic problems that may occur, are dealt with in Chapter 10. The issue of global brands, either world-wide or regional ones, is also considered in Chapter 10.

9.1   ADAPTATION OR STANDARDIZATION OF PRODUCT ATTRIBUTES

One may provocatively state that the public are not buying the product itself, but the benefits they hope to derive from the product. A product can be defined as a set of attributes which provide the purchaser/user with actual benefits. Consumers from different countries may assign different weights to similar product attributes: in the case of cars, for instance, German consumers give more importance to ecological attributes than do British consumers (Diamantopoulos, *et al.*, 1995). There are three layers of attributes:

1. The physical attributes (size, weight, colour, etc.). Standardization of these attributes affords the greatest potential for cost benefits since economies of scale are made principally at the manufacturing stage.

2. Service attributes (maintenance, after-sales service, spare parts availability, etc.). These attributes are fairly difficult to standardize, as circumstances for service delivery differ widely from one country to another. It should further be emphasized that most services are performed in direct relation to *local* customers. Service attributes are more dependent on culture.

3. Symbolic attributes are often the interpretive element of the physical attributes. A colour is simultaneously a chemical formula for a painting or a coat, and also the symbolic meaning conveyed by the material. Symbolic attributes affect the choice

TABLE 9.1   Factors influencing adaptation or standardization of product attributes

Product attributes	Arguments in favour of adaptation	Arguments in favour of standardization
Physical attributes	1 Cost-reducing adaptations Local standards, hygiene and safety regulations, consumer behaviour, marketing and physical environments	2 Experience effects Economies of scale International standards International product use
Services attributes	3 Limited savings related to scale Local peculiarities in service, maintenance and distribution	4 Significant learning effects 'Mobile' clientele
Symbolic attributes	5 Unfavourable image of imported products, company, nationality or brand name Inadequate meaning conveyed by colour, shape, etc.	6 Favourable image of imported products, company, nationality or brand Exotic or ethnic appeal Demands for 'universals'

between adaptation and standardization in a fairly ambiguous manner. Consumers have confused attitudes: a liking for domestic goods based on nationalism will often coexist with a penchant and even fascination for foreign cultures and their goods. Therefore, when adapting or standardizing symbolic attributes, the requirements for national identity symbols will intermingle with those for symbols of exoticism.

Table 9.1 proposes a systematic description of the arguments in favour of adaptation on the one hand and standardization on the other. Distinctions can be made according to the different levels of physical, service and symbolic attributes. Some arguments in favour of either adaptation or standardization originate from within the company, which can benefit from changing its way of operating. Other arguments are related to external constraints imposed by the environment, consumer behaviour and regulations: they imply company adaptation to demand, either by adapting or standardizing its offering. The numbering of the cells in Table 9.1 is used further in the text.

9.2   PHYSICAL ATTRIBUTES

As we saw in Chapter 8, experience effects, and accordingly the cost reductions related to cumulated production, clearly weigh in favour of standardization (cell 2). However one should investigate the opportunity of supplying an adapted product, corresponding to the local demand, in which the adaptation would lead to a sufficient reduction in costs to compensate for the loss in cumulated volume (cell 1). This situation is rare: the success of Japanese pick-up trucks in developing countries is to a certain extent a suitable illustration of this situation. Through adaptation involving product simplification in suspension, engine and gearbox, the Japanese have achieved a low cost level. Historically, there are some examples of 'simplified' cars or 'simplified' computers designed for developing countries. For instance, Ford and General Motors developed a 'bare bones' model T type of vehicle to sell in developing countries, both of which were failures. Similarly, a computer specially designed for developing countries was developed in the 1980s by Jean-Jacques Servan-Schreiber with French government funding. It was a total failure. In these cases, the advantages resulting from 'simplifications' were not offset by a decrease in economies of scale (increased unit costs), the losses in product functionality, or the resentment of local consumers at being offered simplified products and thus being treated as unsophisticated consumers. Since simplified products are not advantageous in terms of cost, it is the learning process of local consumers and how the local context affects this learning process which may become the central concerns for the international marketer (Wills *et al.*, 1991; Amine, 1993).

Compulsory adaptation

Compulsory adaptation of physical attributes is often related to national regulations and standards. Thus (cell 1):

1. *The industrial standards for the electricity supply*, for example the voltage, the frequency of the alternating current (50 versus 60 Hz), the shape of plugs, etc. Certain countries use standards which seem to operate as non-tariff trade barriers. Germany is known for its use of an exhaustive system of over 30,000 industrial standards (DIN) which are determined by standard-setting committees. German manufacturers are strongly represented on the boards of these committees. Nevertheless DIN standards are by no means intended as non-tariff barriers; for instance, German bicycles use drum brakes on the rear wheels which are operated by pedalling backwards, whereas British and French bicycles use brake pads. The German standard, which may at first sight appear safer, is in fact dangerous for other European cyclists because of the risk of skidding on corners by spurious back-pedalling.

2. *Safety standards*: in the motor industry for example, in relation to lighting, brake systems and vehicle safety. A few years ago Peugeot had to produce more than 500 versions of its 505 range, corresponding to the different engine types and equipment available, adapted for various countries targeted for export. This obviously had an adverse effect on costs. In addition to increased production costs, there was an increase in the requirements for documentation and country-specific spare parts. Control of the marketing management of the 505 around the world was adversely affected.

3. *Hygiene regulations*: the food processing, chemicals and pharmaceutical industries must carry out adaptations to comply with hygiene legislation. The producers of *foie gras* which is exported to the United States have to obtain FDA (Food and Drug Administration) hygiene certification. For this they have to allow the FDA to inspect their laboratories for bacteria as well as their methods of production. FDA inspectors often require *foie gras* to be pasteurized and the laboratories disinfected with an antiseptic detergent. This inevitably affects the taste and conflicts

with the traditional image of a home-made quality product. Many of the French *foie gras* producers have set up laboratories in the USA where the product is prepared according to US hygiene standards.

A huge variety of regulations influences the need for adaptation (marking, labelling, locally permitted standard sizes, sales promotion laws, etc.). In many countries, public or mutual bodies offer to assist companies by examining the problems of conforming to the technical aspects of foreign standards, right from the very conception of the product. A good number of companies, through a wholly understandable ethnocentrism, fail to consider the problem of adaptation of products for foreign markets. Newcomers to the export business often consider the problem only from the perspective of adaptation to technical standards and are only concerned with obligatory adaptation; at first they tend not to consider the loss of standardization.

In fact, obligatory adaptations are often minor in comparison to the required adaptations to differences in consumer behaviour and in the national marketing environment. Three main issues should be considered:

1. *Consumption patterns*: consumer tastes, frequency of consumption, the amount consumed per helping, etc. The required size of a cereal box and the ability of the packaging to preserve the product will not necessarily be the same for a country in which the average consumer eats 50 grams of cereal daily for breakfast and for a different country where the quantity consumed is higher but the frequency lower. Even products which are supposed to be the epitome of international standardization are subject to customization to local tastes (see Box 9.1).

BOX 9.1

'Pizza relativity'

There is, in the real world, a lot of 'pizza relativity'. During in-depth interviews at Hewlett-Packard in France, some American expatriates told me that they had travelled to Geneva, Switzerland, 100 miles (160 km) from the site where they were located, in order to have a meal at Pizza Hut. Although in Grenoble there are a large number of 'authentic' pizzerias (the town has a very large Italian presence), some Hewlett-Packard American expatriates preferred the taste, crustiness, toppings and cooking style of the American pizza. When attending a congress in Milan, I discovered that the Italian pizza (at least at the restaurant where I ate it) was not at all like those I am used to eating in Grenoble (made by cooks of Italian origin): the crust was much thicker and there was less topping. My last memory is of the oily Brazilian pizzas (which I tried only twice).

Conclusion: pizzas, like 'Chinese' food, are largely localized, often because of the lack of genuine ingredients, but also because taste is localized. Local views of what is 'genuine' are mostly based on phantasies about the 'true' pizza or the 'genuine' Peking duck.

2.   *Climate and the physical environment* in general are important, and sometimes neg-
     lected, factors behind further obligatory adaptation (cell 1). Motor vehicles must
     be specifically designed to withstand the harsh Scandinavian winters or the
     warmth and humidity of the Ivory Coast. The possible range of physical environ-
     ments where the product will be used must be taken into account: for example,
     the quality of road surfaces and the existence of tracks suitable for vehicles. The
     diversity of physical environments is often the source of later shocks and the
     cause of unexpected failure (Box 9.2). One should take into account in advance
     the range of elements that constitute potential demands for adaptation. This is
     not always such an obvious step to take. Ethnocentrism is often the rule in prod-
     uct design. In the case of a sheet-glass factory, the high temperature in the work-
     shops proved to be intolerable for Saudi workers when the factory was set up in
     Saudi Arabia on the basis of European parameters (Tiano, 1981).

3.   *Adapting products to local product usage.* A number of variables have to be consid-
     ered in order to ensure that buyers use the product properly, such as: level of
     literacy, technical knowledge and ability to use written information (such as

BOX 9.2

Adaptations to the physical environment

A European drinks manufacturer decided to widen the range of one of its
product lines with a giant-size version, with the purpose of its active promotion
in several markets, the United States in particular. After completion of production
facilities, the new model was launched. The company then realized to its horror
that it had forgotten one small detail: the giant-size bottle was a couple of inches
too tall for the shelves in the vast majority of the American stores. You can imagine the result: the sales promotion activities that were planned had to be
cancelled, there was discontent among the distributors and the sales force lost a
great deal of motivation while a new mould was hastily manufactured.*

   Quaker Oats has an established share of the Cameroon market: it has been
carefully adapted in line with consumption habits. It is easily made into the gruel
that the Cameroons call *paf* or *pap*. It is usually eaten with maize or tapioca. In
addition, Quaker uses metallic packaging which is perfectly suited to the preservation of the product in the Cameroon climate. The shelf life of the box is about
ten years, even in a tropical country. Cameroon itself is not a wholly typical tropical country since in Douala, for instance, there is an annual rainfall of 7 metres.
The metallic box ensures that the product is preserved despite the humidity. It
does, however, rust, and even though the product itself is not affected, certain
retailers refuse to repurchase Quaker Oats because their previous stock rusted.**

(Sources: * Adapted from Giordan, 1988, p. 110; **adapted from Camphuis, 1984.)

ingredients list or instructions for use). Lack of attention to such variables caused problems for Nestlé in the Third World with its infant formula: the addition of impure water and the failure to boil the water made the product dangerous for babies, even though the powder that left Nestlé's factories was perfect. Consumers, on average, tend not to read instructions for use sufficiently thoroughly and to try to use items especially consumer durables, too quickly, before they have learnt the basics of how to operate them. The Germans make special adaptations designed to guard against misuse by consumers; for instance, when the knob of a dish-washing machine is turned anti-clockwise, whereas it should be turned only clockwise, or when the machine is switched on when the water tap is off. In Germany, where the sense of uncertainty avoidance is quite strong (section 3.2), a product is called *idiotensicher* ('idiot proof') when all possible product design adaptations have been made to avoid the negative consequences of any imaginable misuse. Adaptation to possible misuses is related to the issue of product liability, where quite different legal solutions are found from one country to another. Windshield sun protectors made in Spain and sold there do not need to bear a special warning, reminding the user not to drive with the protector in place, because it is supposed that Spanish drivers are not fools. For export, especially to the United States, they must display such an explicit warning: in the case of an incident, the manufacturer could be held liable.

Requirements for international standardization

Yet national requirements sometimes lean toward international standardization (cell 2). This may occur in four situations:

1. Although technical standards largely originate in individual countries there are industries where international standards tend to develop. They can even become the dominant national standard. Thus in the field of oil drilling, the API (American Petroleum Institute) standards are in force world-wide. Every oil company, whether American or not, must follow the API standards. Oil-drilling equipment manufacturers are also obliged to standardize their products in accordance with these standards. However, the number of industries with world-wide standards remains limited. The adoption of foreign/international standards can even prove to be problematic for selling in the country of origin. For instance, a European iron and steel company obtained certification from ASME (the American Society of Mechanical Engineers) for the very thick steel plate used in nuclear and petrochemical plants. In this small industry, they had a quite substantial world market share. ASME certification was recognized world-wide since most nuclear plants use licensed American technology. When they subsequently came to sell their heavy steel plates for plants intended for German and French electricity utilities, the US standards were not considered acceptable and they were forced to adopt German and French standards.

2. Some products achieve 'international usage': aircraft suitcases (Samsonite of Belgium, and Delsey of France), portable computers, duty-free articles, etc.

3. Innovative products often experience an international diffusion process (Rogers, 1983). Large R & D expenses are initially incurred for many innovative products, and such products are not greatly affected by culture (VCRs, laser discs). The pace of the diffusion of innovations is largely enhanced by the strength of the groups of 'early adopters'. Presumably, these groups correspond to people who have a high level of exposure to international travel and to new products in the countries where they are first launched. By word-of-mouth communication, they transfer knowledge of the product to their non-travelling compatriots. These international travellers eventually introduce such products into their native country. They facilitate positive reactions from other consumers without exposure to these new products, in the first phases of the adoption process: awareness, interest, evaluation, testing. More generally, international travel accelerates the process of diffusion of standardized innovations.

4. The final point in cell 2 encompasses the basis of Levitt's assertions about the globalization of markets (1983). According to Levitt, certain aspects of ways of life would tend towards uniformity: differences in cultural preferences, national taste, standards and the institutional business environment are remnants of the past. Levitt argues that the so-called ethnic markets are a good example: Chinese food, country music, pizzas and jazz now tend to be found world-wide. Although Levitt claims that he is not advocating systematic disregard for local or national differences, he overestimates the world-wide convergence of taste for global products, as emphasized in Chapters 5 and 6. Whatever value judgements are made about the all-inclusive tendency towards homogenization of world cultures, that is, across countries, consumer segments and product categories, this issue must be raised for each company, on the basis of careful research on its product, consumers and markets.

The trend towards international standards

The costs required for adapting to national standards are very high since adaptation implies the replication of test and certification procedures in many countries. In the pharmaceuticals industry, the cost of bringing a new drug on to the market is estimated at US$230 million in the United States, $150 million in Europe, and $125 million in Japan. Countries still follow somewhat different routes for granting market entry to new pharmaceuticals. For instance Japan, with only 18 months, appears liberal in contrast with the US Food and Drug Administration; given the relative brevity of initial trials in Japan, approval covers only the first six years and the manufacturer must then reapply (Pahud de Mortanges *et al.*, 1997).

There is fortunately a definite trend towards common standardization world-wide, especially with ISO (International Organization for Standardization) standards; some of these are now widely applied, such as the standards on quality, the ISO 9000 family. European technical standardization is participating in this movement, which stems from the EC Treaty, especially Article 30, which prohibits quantitative restrictions on imports from other member states and measures having an equivalent effect (that is, this is mainly a form of protectionist standardization). As explained in Chapter 6, the *Cassis de Dijon* ruling firmly established the 'home country rule', whereby a product should not be barred from importation into an EU country when it conforms to the standards of the EU country in which it is produced. The EU countries, in conjunction with the six EFTA (European Free Trade Association) countries, are engaged in a European standardization process, through three Brussels-based organizations: CEN, CENELEC and ETSI. This largely stems from the 1985 EC White Paper, which identified technical barriers as one of the main obstacles to the achievement of a single market in Europe (see section 6.4).

Product standards are in fact a very complex strategic issue (much more so than depicted here), since they have a definite influence on the competitive strategy of the firm. In high-technology industries, for instance computers, consumer electronics and telecommunications, the issue of compatibility of standards over time (multi-vintage compatibility) and across competitors is a very important one. There are examples where promoting a standard and licensing it to competitors (the VHS of Matsushita) proved a better strategy than keeping a monopoly on one's own standard (the Betamax VCR of Sony). Other examples show that it was more efficient to keep the technology under total control, as Xerox did for its proprietary electrostatic photo-copying technology for many years before the patent expired.

9.3   SERVICE ATTRIBUTES

Service attributes may include the following (the list is not exhaustive):

1. Repair and maintenance, after-sales service.
2. Installation.
3. Instruction manuals, information and guidance on how to use the item.
4. Other related services (demonstrations, technical assistance).
5. Waiting time, delivery dates (and respect for them).
6. Guarantees (repair or replacement of goods).
7. Spare parts availability.
8. Return of goods, whether defective or not.

Adaptation of service in the light of local conditions

The extent of service attributes differs according to the type of good to be serviced. Service attributes are essential for industrial equipment and many consumer durables. Although it might not seem so, they also have a significant role to play in the field of consumer non-durables. Service requirements differ widely from country to country (cell 3) because they are related to environmental factors such as the following:

1. The level of technical expertise.
2. The level of labour costs, which is decisive in the balance between durability and reparability. Africans are experts at repairing and even revamping totally worn-out cars. Anywhere else, these cars would be scrapped.
3. The level of literacy (this may render instruction manuals useless).

4. Climatic differences: certain climates increase the difficulty of performing main-
    tenance operations because of temperature, humidity, etc.

5. The remoteness of locations – which can render services difficult and costly to per-
    form (e.g. servicing a gas turbine in the middle of the Amazonian forest).

6. Different ways of performing a seemingly identical service (see Box 9.3).

Actual services in developing countries are traditional ones and are of a limited
technical level, at least when viewed from technologically developed countries. In
societies where shortages are common, recycling is essential: African shoemakers, for
instance, are experts at making shoe soles from used tyres; technical expertise and

BOX 9.3

Who's afraid of injections?

What is more standard in appearance than a syringe and an injection? There are,
however, significant differences in the methods used to avoid causing pain to the
patient. For intra-muscular syringes, there are two different ways of administering
an injection. They correspond to two basic service attributes (correct injection of
the substance, avoidance of pain), but are performed in two different ways:

1. Only the needle itself is stuck in, then the body of the syringe (the cylinder
    containing the substance and the plunger driving it) is fixed into the base of
    the needle, in accordance with a technique known as *luerslip* (this method is
    used in America). The first question asked by an American nurse is: does it
    unscrew? (Service attribute.)

2. French, Italian and Spanish doctors and nurses prefer (and are used to) using
    the fully assembled syringe. The American method would probably involve
    the risk of 'slashing' their patient when connecting the two parts of the
    syringe once the needle has been implanted (an operation they are not used
    to doing). The service attribute required of the syringe is therefore based on
    its lightness and being in one piece, which is provided by a bolt system (*luer-
    lock*). The first question asked by a French, Italian or Spanish nurse is: does it
    hold tight?

Further service attributes relate to who is legally permitted and professionally
qualified to administer an injection and where it is possible to buy syringes. In
Italy – in contrast to other European countries – syringes are on general sale, even
in corner shops. They are available in blister packaging at the supermarket.
Traditionally, many housewives actually give injections to members of their
family.

(Source: Excerpt from a discussion with Beckton Dickinson, a world leader in single-use medical
items–consumables.)

craftsmanship is not lacking in developing countries; it is expressed differently, and relates to the prevailing economic conditions. In many African countries for instance, a lot of maintenance is done by small mechanical workshops, which succeed in repairing cars but take a long time to do so; although not orthodox, their repair methods work. Service instructions issued by car manufacturers naturally need some adaptation: it is better to show mechanics how to do a job than to send them a free 800-page book on maintenance operations. Services are generally delegated to distribution channels. The shortage of available and/or adequate channels and the small size of distribution outlets are obstacles to services, particularly in developing countries.

Even across developed countries, differences in the service offered by distribution channels are much greater than one might expect. The daily and weekly shop-opening hours vary widely between northern and southern Europe. They may range from less than 60 hours per week total opening time in northern Europe to more than 100 hours per week in southern Europe. This affects attitudes towards distribution services; for example, where weekly store-opening hours are limited, people tend to turn to mail order; they can look at a catalogue at home with no hurry, and pay without wasting their shopping time waiting at a cashier's desk. Where a husband and wife are at work during shop-opening hours, an elderly parent with different service requirements may have to do the shopping for them.

A number of dimensions of the service encounter are common cross culturally, but the way in which they are valued and interpreted by customers varies. Frazer Winsted (1997) highlights common dimensions explaining satisfaction with two types of service encounter (restaurants and doctors) in the part of American and Japanese people: civility of the service personnel, personalization of the encounter (asking and using the customer's name) and conversation (i.e. whether personnel are talkative and humorous). There are, however, a number of nuances: the overriding theme in Japan is caring for the customer and the Japanese introduce formality (proper dress and language) as a separate dimension whereas the Americans put emphasis on authenticity, use and remembering of customer's name, promptness of service personnel, and congeniality (personnel being friendly, happy, personal, pleasant, smiling, etc.). In the context of museum visits and in the case of two much closer cultures, Sweden and The Netherlands, De Ruyter *et al.* (1997) find few differences in the value dimensions of satisfaction in both countries. Visitors from both nations place emotional value on pleasant treatment at the museum entrance, and attribute logical value to the museum restaurant (value for money); however, they differ noticeably in their valuation of the permanent collection: emotional value is the most important determinant of satisfaction for the Swedes (a good atmosphere) and logical value (satisfactory information) for the Dutch.

Culture and the waiting experience

An important aspect of service is waiting to be served (to obtain maintenance or spare parts, to receive cash in a bank or to be served in a restaurant). In waiting, people have to deal with time, rules and power. The cultural assumptions concerning time are central in the waiting experience: people with a strong economic time pattern (see section 2.2) may experience waiting as a waste of time, a painful moment with negative emotions. Waiting is organized in queues to varying degrees and the rules concerning the waiting process are more or less respected according to culture (see section 3.6). Another important aspect of waiting is power: where power distance is strong, it seems almost legitimate to let the least powerful wait, whereas jumping the queue is standard behaviour for the most powerful. In fact, rather than jumped, the waiting line is bypassed: important consumers have a direct access to the service. On the contrary, in the United States, where low power distance and strong economic time prevail, waiting lines are well organized and everybody is treated fairly, following the principle of 'first come, first served'. Box 9.4 presents the Japanese attitude towards waiting in various service situations.

BOX 9.4

Sabisu (the Japanese concept of service)

Misako Kamamoto, chief conductor of the Japan Travel bureau recounts her experience guiding Japanese tourists overseas:

'When I take a group of Japanese tourists to a restaurant in Europe for the first time, I make a point to advise them in advance as follows: "Quite apart from the problem of whether the food suits the Japanese palate, you must be resigned to the fact that it takes a good deal of time to have a meal in a European restaurant."... some members of the party are bound to start complaining despite the warning that I have given them. "Why are European restaurants so slow in serving us? Please ask them to speed up the service." Some get so impatient that they stand up and leave, saying, "I don't want to wait for dessert or coffee. I can't stand a restaurant which gives such bad service." In a European restaurant, the essence of good service is to give the guests plenty of time to enjoy conversation together with the meal. So it makes sense that dishes are served with long intervals in between.

Japanese tourists who go shopping in Paris invariably return full of complaints because they were not treated like "gods" as in Japan. "The sales clerks take the attitude that they are doing you a favor by 'allowing you to buy'. They are so curt. What do they think customers are, anyway? The sales clerks have absolutely no interest in doing business. When I asked a clerk to show me something of a different color or different size, she acted annoyed and said brusquely, 'We have none.' She didn't even try to search."

In a Japanese bank, the clerk counts the notes by himself and puts them all together in a tray for the client, . . . few Japanese take the trouble of counting the notes on the spot . . . The Japanese usually consider that it is impolite to distrust anyone and believe that the other party will most naturally live up to the trust placed in him. In restaurants and hotels, Westerners do not make payment until they have thoroughly examined the bill, item by item and make sure that the sum

BOX 9.4 *CONTINUED*

is correctly totalled. In contrast the Japanese have always believed that restaurant and hotel bills are correct. Therefore, even when they are overseas, they assume the same and make payment without examining the bill. This habit sometimes becomes a trouble.

When they travel by train in Europe, the Japanese are struck by the quietness of the stations which are so unlike the noisy Japanese stations. There is no bell or loudspeaker signaling the departure of a train. Their first reaction is, "It's so nice and quiet." But this soon gives way to anxiety. "Why is it that there is no bell notifying us of the departure? It would be a lot of trouble if we missed the train," some say. . . . Whereas European railways give priority to silence and their rule is to have travelers enjoy a quiet journey, Japanese railways seem to think that their mission is to provide passengers with all kinds of information via blaring loudspeakers.'

(Source: Kamamoto, 1984, pp. 26–7. Reproduced with permission.)

Waiting time can be reduced or increased according to the level of service personnel available; it can therefore be adapted according to the locally prevailing assumptions about time. In Europe, where time is, on average, slightly less economic than in North America, the fast food outlets are not so quick as they are in America (where the formula was invented). People are not so preoccupied with the waiting time: in the USA Pizza Hut gives a free pizza to customers who have waited more than ten minutes; in most European countries this practice does not need to be transferred, because people do not resent waiting and may even value waiting time in a restaurant as a sign of careful preparation.

Another service attribute is the type of waiting rule and the degree to which the waiting lines are organized. In many countries, waiting is not organized at all and the principle 'first come, first served' finds no translation. Since people are used to unorganized waiting they know that they will have to fight those who will jump the queue, by shouting, threatening them or themselves jumping the queue. For instance, the contrast between French and Swiss ski resorts, especially at peak time is striking: whereas in France the absence of waiting corridors results in messy crowds, in Switzerland the waiting process remains fairly peaceful and organized even if the waiting time is slightly longer. It comes as no surprise that for American tourists travelling to Europe the service quality image of French ski resorts appears significantly lower than that of the Swiss and Austrian ski resorts, particularly as concerns honesty and friendliness (Ofir and Lehmann, 1986).

Cultural assumptions and the service encounter

The service encounter implies a person-to-person relationship, in maintenance as well as in restaurant or other services. To this extent, the prevailing cultural norms will apply in service encounters as they apply in any social interaction. Even though much is shared, especially from a normative point of view (availability, courtesy, willingness to give information), social codes concerning adequate service vary according to culture. Edward Hall (1976, pp. 58–9), for instance, explains how, when staying in a hotel in downtown Tokyo, he was completely mystified by a problem with his room:

I had been a guest for about ten days and was returning to my room in the middle of an afternoon. Entering the room I immediately sensed that something was wrong. Out of place. Different. I was in the wrong room. Someone else's things were distributed around the head of the bed and the table . . . I checked my key again. Yes, it really was mine . . . At the desk, I was told by the clerk, as he sucked in his breath in deference (and embarrassment?) that indeed they had moved me. My particular room had been reserved in advance by somebody else. I was given the key to my new room and discovered that all my personal effects were distributed around the new room almost as though I had done it myself.

Later Hall was to discover that, in contrast to the United States where being moved in such a way is almost an insult, in Japan it was tangible evidence that, after some days, he was treated as a family member, somebody belonging to the group of familiar clients, who can be treated in a relaxed and unceremonious way.

There are many situations where 'good' service is not self-evident. A case in point is when people are asleep on a plane when a meal is served. Kamamoto (1984) explains that, as far as the Japanese are concerned, the steward must wake those who are asleep so that they do not miss the meal, whereas westerners prefer not to be disturbed in their sleep. Naturally, the best solution, whatever the culture, would be for the steward to wait and serve the sleeping person as soon as he or she awakes; but such treatment is rarely possible because of schedule constraints. An important cultural aspect of the service encounter is the doing/being divide. Hall (1976, p. 109), contrasting the French and the Americans, phrases it in the following way: 'The French as a rule are much more involved [than the Americans] with their employees and with their customers and clients as well. They do not feel they can serve them adequately unless they know them well.' I do not agree with Hall's first sentence: to many foreigners, service quality in France (as in other Latin countries) appears poor in comparison with the United States. Many American visitors perceive the commitment of French service providers towards their clients as quite small. The real key is in Hall's second sentence: 'unless they know them well'. In societies where doing is strongly emphasized, as in the United States, waiters and other service providers are task centred rather than person or relationship centred. It is no real problem for them to serve *unknown* people. To many French or Latin eyes, North American service appears the exact opposite of Hall's judgement, more friendly, more attentive and more dedicated than in European countries, especially in southern Europe. Stereotypically stated, in a being-oriented society, the situation in service encounters is dichotomic: dedication and friendliness towards known customers, absence of real commitment towards customers when they *are unknown*.

Another interesting question is whether customers prefer automated service, which is widely expanding (e.g. automatic teller machines, ticket machines, etc.), or to be served by real, flesh-and-blood people. There is no research available on this issue. But one can hypothesize that the being orientation implies a preference for personnel in contact whereas the doing orientation favours automated service, which is purely task

TABLE 9.2   Cultural dimensions and automated service

Dimensions	High			
	Being		**Doing**	
Affectivity	1.	Strong preference for personnel in contact	3.	Like the machine but would like personnel also
Neutrality	2.	Do not like the machine but do not like people either	4.	Strongest preference for purely automated service

oriented. The dimension of affectivity versus neutrality (see section 3.5), an important aspect of Trompenaars' relational orientation (Trompenaars, 1993), can be combined with the doing–being divide for describing possible preferences, as in Table 9.2: affectivity will create a preference for personnel in contact, because human relationships in the service encounter are preferred to service automation. Naturally, all this is based on cultural ideal types; other factors, such as age and level of education, have a strong influence on individual acceptance of automated service; older people and less educated persons have difficulties in dealing with automated service devices, which they consider user unfriendly.

Factors in favour of service standardization

The decision to adapt services to diversified international requirements implies little cost in terms of economies of scale (cell 3), since it is far easier to reach increasing returns to scale for the physical attributes than for the service attributes of a product. On the other hand, there can be substantial learning effects with service attributes. For example, various management procedures such as the stocking of spare parts or hotel laundering may be standardized.

In certain cases (cell 3) the adaptation of service attributes will lead to cost savings because locally supplied services will be far less comprehensive than in the country of origin. This is feasible either when local service requirements are less demanding or when the product has been expressly constructed to be almost maintenance free. In this case it will also be designed to stand up to 'untrained' users. Physical attributes will then interact with service attributes within the product as a whole.

However, service standardization (cell 4) will be required when the clientele are internationally 'mobile'. Customers move with their service requirements. The global success of truck manufacturers from northern Europe (DAF, Volvo, Scania, Mercedes) is due in part to their ability to offer a standardized service in a range of countries and on sites along the routes that are most commonly taken by international lorry drivers. For instance, an engine or a gearbox can be completely overhauled within a specified period of time at any location on the route. The same holds true for McDonald's restaurants where service is to a large extent standardized world-wide: customers know what they will find in terms of service; bad surprises are avoided, whether they enter a McDonald's in Tampere, Finland, Osaka, Japan or Montauban, France.

9.4   SYMBOLIC ATTRIBUTES

The symbol can be defined linguistically as the sign that operates a relationship which is non-causal (as opposed to the *indicator*) and non-analogous (as opposed to the *icon*). The *Collins Dictionary and Thesaurus* (1987, p. 1018) defines symbol as 'something that represents or stands for something else, usually by convention or association, especially a material object used to represent something abstract'. Any animate or inanimate object may be a basis for making a symbolic association. A fox may be a symbol of cunning, whereas an oak may be a symbol of strength. The use of the words 'may be' recognizes the fact that not every culture makes such associations. Either there are no foxes or oaks, or other interpretative meanings are applied. Symbols work as a powerful means of suggestion and evocation. The symbolic aspects of consumption are important to consumers: the social meaning of many products is more important than their functional utility, or at least as important, clothes or perfumes for instance. As Solomon emphasized (1983, p. 320): 'Symbolic interactionism focuses on the process by which individuals understand their world. It assumes that people interpret the actions of others rather than simply react to them.' Most symbols are not universal; they may be understood and used by a large part, but not all, of the world population. One of the rare symbols to transcend cross-cultural boundaries is that of left and right, with a positive value put on the 'right' side, which is seen as the adequate way, as correct and true, or as being in accordance with moral or legal behaviour (Cohen, 1996). In French *(droit)* or German *(Recht)* the same word is used for designating both the right side and law.

In terms of adaptation/standardization, two different issues will be addressed:

1. The relationship between symbolic attitudes and national product images, with respect to product category, company and brand names and country of manufacture (see Chapter 10).

2. Cultural differences sometimes entail divergent symbolic interpretations. Meanings are principally conveyed by the packaging and outward appearance of a product. If a symbolic attribute which was ethnocentrically conceived has a very different and highly negative interpretation in the target culture, adaptation is required (cell 5). For instance, symbolic associations linked to objects or colours may vary considerably across countries and cultures. Carlsberg had to add a third elephant to its label in Africa, since two elephants seen together are considered an ominous sign (McCornell, 1971).

The link between symbols and culture

The link between symbols and culture comprises seven successive steps. The starting point is a conceptual one: colours, for example, are wavelengths of light reflected by objects; a set of waves of different frequencies produces a colour spectrum. If it is stated that an object is red, this means the following:

1. It soaks up all received light except red.

2. The language has the term called 'red', which designates a certain part of the spectrum that reflects the object (which has no colour as such).

3. Our perceptual apparatus – eyes, retinas, optical nerves, brains – are capable of identifying the wavelengths.

4. Through a learning mechanism, both linguistic and visual, we have learnt to recognize this colour as 'red' since early childhood; that is, to qualify it by imitation of all the other people who also designate this colour as 'red'.

Perception results from a culture-based adaptive process (points 2 and 4 above). Numerous experimental studies have shown that certain peoples have a less discriminating perception of colour (their vocabulary and identification is more restricted). They 'mix up' certain 'colours' that other peoples can distinguish. It has also been shown that sensitivity to visual illusions (shapes and length) varies according to culture, particularly as a result of the effects of syncretism. Suggestive visual associations result from our daily environment. Our native physical environment shapes our perceptual universe (see section 1.4). In the case of pictorial perception, Cohen (1995) distinguishes two questions: (1) 'What do people see when they look at this picture?' and (2) 'What does the picture mean?' The second question refers to meaning, interpretation and symbolism, but the first question, which has to be answered first, refers to what people *actually see*. Western pictorial conventions representing three dimensionality on a plane, for instance, are based on arbitrary codes: smaller objects, and higher objects in the picture plane, are meant to be farther away; an overlapped object is supposed to be farther away, and the rules of 'perspective' are applied in the form of convergence of lines. As explained by Cohen (1995, p. 219):

A picture of an empty bowl in front of a child was supposed to show that the child was hungry and malnourished. The two cues which should have indicated three-dimensionality were overlap and size. But when individuals in the target market were shown the picture, they thought the bowl was an empty washbowl. This was because the bowl was in the foreground and was large in size compared with the child.

In order to move on from the *percept* (i.e. the subjects are able to formulate verbally what has been shown to them) to the *symbolic image*, three steps must be added to the four previously set out. The cultural process intervenes at each of these three final steps:

5. An association has been established between a certain colour, form, smell, shape, etc. and a suggested meaning, as in the two parts of the Greek symbol (see the etymological definition of the symbol given in the introduction). Initially there can be a highly tangible link: for example, the colour brown may be tainted by a negative sense in the connotation of waste, since it may be concretely associated with excrement.

6. This link is ignored; there are two complementary parts but the way they are related has been forgotten: why in most western countries is blue the colour for little boys and pink for little girls (important for choices in baby-related markets)?

7. Then there is social overspill through education, advertising, the mass media, literature, magazines – in short, throughout society and indeed even to packaging and marketing communication in general. The symbol shares the characteristics of a language. It conveys rich and diversified meanings, full of nuances, and its messages are often implicit. It conjures up a set of evocations, suggestions and

interpretations which are almost subconscious yet still very real in the minds of consumers. Indeed this set of interpretations is to a large extent specific to each national culture. For example, does orange juice have to be yellow, orange or slightly red, full of pulp or clear, thick or very fluid, in order to evoke different product attributes: the sense of its being a nature-based/non-artificial drink, its dietary qualities, an image of refreshment, healthy for children as opposed to being intended for adults?

Images diffused by symbolic attributes

Symbols, in their capacity as signs with suggestive power that is non-causal and non-analogous, rely on natural elements: colours, shapes, locations, materials, everyday objects, animals, countryside and elements of nature, famous characters, etc. In certain cultures the lake is a symbol of love, the blue of virginity. Most commonly the 'natural' backgrounds of symbols appear fairly arbitrary, in so far as the original link has often been lost or transformed, as and when the symbol became widely used. The interpretation of symbolic messages conveyed by attributes, such as colour, shape and consistency, may differ significantly between the marketer's culture and the consumer's culture. Williams and Longworth (1989) cite the case of the Coral Sea Tuna Fishery in Australia, where the government spent money to develop exports to Japan. The fishing operation was unable to obtain a high price for its fresh tuna air-freighted to Japan, because the Japanese had a problem with the meat colour. After investigations were conducted in the Tsukiji central wholesale market, it appeared that the negative interpretation was related to the meat colour which evidenced a non-Japanese origin; this resulted in the Australian tuna consistently being sold at a discount. It is obvious that, in such cases, other markets have to be targeted.

Ethnocentrism is instinctive in all symbolic thought. It is therefore quite inevitable, especially when it is present in the consumer's culture. In the case of ethnic products, it may even be of some use to marketers, in order to maintain genuineness. However, inappropriate (or just poor) use of backgrounds that diffuse symbolic images which are not adapted to the local consumer presents a danger for international marketers. Inappropriate use of symbolic meanings may be based on the best possible intentions on the part of the marketer and may result in the worst consequences for users: the skull and crossbones symbol, used in most western countries to represent lethal danger (electricity, poison, steam, etc.), represents in many African countries a symbol of potency.

The symbolism of colours, shapes, numbers, etc.

White is the colour of birth and in the West usually celebrates a happy life event, whereas in China it symbolizes mourning. Conversely black, which symbolizes death in the West (because of darkness and fears that the sun will not return?), is an everyday colour in China.

Hidden behind each symbol is one or more material support. Red, for example, is the colour of blood: it can evoke and suggest meanings that differ widely depending on the culture (see Figure 9.1). Every culture has an image of blood, which feeds part

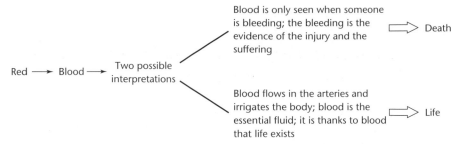

FIGURE 9.1   An example of diverging symbolic interpretations.

of the symbolic content of the colour red (see Box 9.5). Naturally, the colour red can be linked to substances other than blood – certain flowers, for instance. Use of red as the dominant colour on a product or its packaging must therefore be very carefully considered beforehand (cell 5 in Table 9.1).

Associating symbols

The following two examples illustrate symbolic associations. Symbols which are diffused by the design of a product or its packaging may be associated with the intrinsic qualities of the product itself.

The Italian company Olivetti produced a typewriter which was such a beautiful object that a New York museum displayed it in its modern art collection. This typewriter proved to be a commercial failure in the United States even though the Americans liked its appearance. Potential purchasers found that its design did not inspire an image of robustness (cell 5). Furthermore, in Anglo-Saxon societies there is often a puritanical attitude that work is an activity required by duty, which is sometimes arduous and should be more painful than enjoyable. This beautiful and enjoyable object was incompatible with such an attitude.

In many cases, symbolic associations may work even though, from a rational point of view, individual symbols are somewhat contradictory: consumers' interpretation of symbolic association take the form of an impressionistic halo rather than a detailed content analysis. An example is a German *Weissbier* (a beer brewed with wheat instead of barley), called Oberdorfer. It claims on one side of its label to be brewed according to the Bavarian purity law of the year 1516, whereas the other side of the label boasts 'ice-rifing' (sic), 'our new *coole* art to brew beer' (*coole* is a germanification of 'cool', which evokes positive values of quietness and relaxation in many non-English speaking cultures, and 'ice-rifing' probably evokes a late crop of hops which provides a more bitter taste). Associating (local) tradition and (foreign) modernity is in general no major problem: consumers themselves experience in their daily life the complex mix of modern and traditional, local and foreign values and behaviours.

A French company exported to West Germany a cheese from the Pyrénées. On the packaging was a shepherd surrounded by his sheep. This picture was directly related to what was shown in the television commercial. In France this image conveyed the idea of a natural manufacturing process and home-made qualities. A consumer test carried out in Germany, after the initial failure of the product, showed that the

BOX 9.5

Colours, things, numbers and even smbolic meanings . . . often not the ones you think!

Green, America's favorite color for suggesting freshness and good health is often associated with disease in countries with dense green jungles; it is a favorite color among Arabs but forbidden in portions of Indonesia. In Japan green is a good high-tech color, but Americans would shy away from green electronic equipment. Black is not universal for mourning: in many Asian countries it is white; in Brazil it is purple, yellow in Mexico, and dark red in the Ivory Coast. Americans think of blue as the most masculine color, but red is more manly in the United Kingdom or France. While pink is the most feminine color in America, yellow is more feminine in most of the world. Red suggests good fortune in China but death in Turkey. In America, a candy wrapped in blue or green is probably a mint; in Africa the same candy would be wrapped in red, our color for cinnamon . . . in every culture, things, numbers and even smells have meanings. Lemon scent in the United States suggests freshness; in the Philippines lemon scent is associated with illness. In Japan the number 4 is like our 13; and 7 is unlucky in Ghana, Kenya and Singapore. The owl in India is bad luck, like our black cat. In Japan a fox is associated with witches. In China a green hat is like a dunce cap; specifically it marks a man with an unfaithful wife. The stork symbolizes maternal death in Singapore, not the kind of message you want to send to a new mother.

(Source: Copeland and Griggs, 1986, p. 63. Reproduced with permission.)

shepherd was associated by the Germans with dirt. The shepherd was withdrawn and subsequently replaced with a picture of mountain scenery. The product was then able to undergo a successful relaunch. For the Germans, a mountain evokes the image of clean nature. In this example the problem stems from the association of symbolic opposites: country/mountain, dirty/clean, natural/artificial. Clearly in this case, the symbolic associations of the French and the Germans are very different.

Colours may also be associated with particular product categories or product attributes. Purple, for instance, is perceived as expensive in Asian cultures, but inexpensive in the United States. Black is perceived as demonstrating trustworthiness and high quality in China (Jacobs *et al.*, 1991). Colours may also be associated with countries, the products of which are supposed to be the most likely to have this colour dominant on their packaging. By gathering data in four countries (China, South Korea, Japan and the United States), Jacobs *et al.* (1991) show that Asian nations associate red with the United States, but US people do not associate their country with red; purple is associated with France, and the four cultures reviewed associate both France and Italy with the colour green.

Exotic, ethnic and universal appeals

Certain factors weigh in favour of the standardization of symbolic attributes (cell 6 in Table 9.1): favourable perception of imported products, positive association with the country of origin (perfume with France, fast food with the United States, etc.) and other factors which are examined in detail in the next chapter. Many people buy a small slice of American life when they enter a McDonald's restaurant, a touch of French romance when they buy a Cacharel perfume, or an instant of German *gemütlichkeit* when they drink a Löwenbräu beer. In these consumption experiences, ethnic product symbolism is associated with exotic appeal for the consumer; thus, symbolic attributes must be kept standardized even though the product or its surrounding services are to a certain extent adapted to local markets.

A good example of a purely standardized product is the 'Classic Christmas Cake' sold world-wide through mail order by Collin Street Bakery from Corsicana, Texas. The advertisement, sent by mail world-wide, emphasizes that they still bake the 'Deluxe cake true to the Old-World recipe brought to Corsicana, Texas from Wiesbaden, Germany in 1896, by master baker Gus Weidmann'; it boasts the richness of the ingredients ('a full 27% rich pecans') and claims to deliver in 196 countries. Associating symbols of tradition (Old World), genuineness and American richness, they have a full register of images which work world-wide (and claim to do so!). Some brands try also to build on universal symbols: Coca-Cola has always successfully avoided being associated too strongly with an American image, by creating a strong brand association with youth, sports and leisure situations, all universal themes. Packaging consistency is a solution for products that want to diffuse a universal image and build on a highly standardized offering: Coke uses the same red and white logo in each country, and its bottle design is consistent across markets. Similarly, McDonald's never strays from its yellow arches. The symbolic interpretation then shifts from the parts to the whole: rather than relating to interpretations of yellow and arches in particular cultures, it diffuses a message about McDonald's world-wide.

For the design of product attributes which convey appropriate symbolic meanings, the following recommendations can be made:

1. When conducting research on possible standardization before a product launch, it is preferable to choose symbols that have a universal or near-universal value (as far as they exist).

2. Since there is very great diversity in the interpretations and associations of symbols, product and packaging standardization must be systematically preceded by product and packaging tests carried out in each national market, using local informants.

QUESTIONS

1. List basic attributes of a perfume at the three levels (physical, service and symbolic). Indicate how the interpretation of symbolic attributes of perfumes may differ cross culturally.

2. What are basic attributes of Coca-Cola (physical, service and symbolic) in its original US context? Coca-Cola is adapted to suit local tastes and its advertising,

although based on core advertising themes and guidelines, is customized for local audiences. Why?

3. How can a company make compromises between world-wide product standardization and customization to local markets?

4. Why is service adaptation across markets necessary? Outline basic reasons.

5. People in a queue may be told how long they still have to wait before being served. What are the possible interpretations by consumers of such information?

6. You have to choose a colour and a design for a fire extinguisher. What are the standard colour and signs used in your native culture? Assess whether they are cross-culturally transferable. Answer the same question for a coffee package.

7. Are there universal, or near-universal, symbols? To what extent can they be used in a marketing strategy? Provide examples.

APPENDIX 9: TEACHING MATERIALS

A9.1 Case: Lestra Design

In May 1993 Mr Claude Léopold, President of Lestra Design, was wondering what action he should take regarding the Japanese market. For several years, Lestra Design had been trying to enter the Japanese market for duvets and eiderdowns. The Japanese market for these products was certainly the largest in the world, but Lestra Design had faced a number of obstacles that had cooled Claude Léopold's enthusiasm. Then recently, he had met again with Daniel Legrand, a French consultant in Tokyo who had been supervising Lestra Design activities in Japan for the last two years. Daniel Legrand had explained that despite the earlier difficulties experienced by Lestra Design, the company had several alternatives which could enable it to be successful in Japan.

Lestra Design was a subsidiary of Léopold & Fils, a family business established in Amboise, a medium-sized town about 250 kilometers south west of Paris (France). Claude Léopold's father had established the parent company in the early 1930s as a feather and down company. At first the company mainly traded in down and feathers, but Léopold & Fils soon became a major French manufacturer of feather and down-filled cushions, pillows, bolsters and eiderdowns. In 1979, when Claude Léopold took over the business from his father, he decided to establish two new companies: Lestra Design to produce and distribute feather and down duvets; and Lestra Sport to manufacture and distribute feather and down sleeping bags. By using more aggressive sales management and the talents of his wife Josette, a renowned French fashion designer, Lestra Design rapidly became the leading duvet company in France. Josette Léopold's creative ideas for using innovative fabric designs with attractive prints helped Lestra Design and Lestra Sport quickly establish an international reputation for high class, fashionable products. Although in 1993 Léopold & Fils, together with its two subsidiaries (Lestra Sport and Lestra Design), had only 128 employees for revenues of FFr.92 million (about $15 million) Claude Léopold believed that the prospect for growth in international markets was extremely promising.

Sales over the past five years had experienced double digit growth, and exports to England, West Germany and other European countries had recently started to boom, representing 20 per cent of Lestra Design's sales. A few years earlier, Lestra Design had also placed an order in Japan through Kanematsu-Gosho Ltd, a 'sogo shosha' (large trading company) affiliated with the Bank of Tokyo and traditionally strong in textiles. However, the Japanese trading company had not reordered any product from Lestra Design since 1987.

Lestra Design in Japan

In 1986 Georges Mekiès, General Manager, and Claude Léopold, President of Lestra Design, had met with Daniel Legrand, a French consultant established in Tokyo. That same year, Legrand had conducted a market survey for C. Léopold which clearly indicated that a major opportunity for growth existed in Japan. With close to 120 million inhabitants and half of the population using duvets, Japan was clearly the largest market for duvets in the world.

In 1986 and 1987 Claude Léopold had been preoccupied with developing Lestra Design's sales in Europe. As a result, he had not taken any immediate action to investigate further the potential of the Japanese market for Lestra Design products. C. Léopold first wanted to provide the French and other European markets with good service before addressing any other market in either the USA or Japan. In autumn 1987, during the ISPO exhibition in Frankfurt (West Germany), Claude Léopold and Georges Mekiès were approached by a manager from Ogitani Corporation, a Japanese trading company based in Nagoya. Mr Hiroshi Nakayama, the representative of Ogitani Corporation, wanted to import and distribute Lestra Design products in Japan. He especially liked the unique designs of Lestra Design's duvets and eiderdowns. He told Messrs Léopold and Mekiès that the innovative designs as well as the French image with the 'Made in France' label would be the two strongest selling points in Japan.

The trade-mark issue

In December 1987 Ogitani ordered 200 duvets to be delivered to Nagoya. However, after the goods were shipped, Georges Mekiès did not hear anything from his Japanese distributor. By chance, G. Mekiès discovered on a trip to Japan in April 1988 that Ogitani had registered the two trade marks, Lestra Sport and Lestra Design, under the Ogitani name. Mr Mekiès decided to call Mr H. Nakayama and request a meeting in Nagoya to discuss the trade-mark issue. Mr Nakayama responded that he was too busy. G. Mekiès then insisted that another executive from the trading company talk with him, but he received only a rebuff.

That same day, a furious Georges Mekiès called Yves Gasquères, the representative of the French Textile Manufacturers Association in Tokyo, for advice. Yves Gasquères who also represented the well-known Lacoste shirts in Japan, explained that Lestra Design was not the only such case. The best advice he could give G. Mekiès was to contact Koichi Sato, a Japanese lawyer specializing in trade-mark disputes.

Georges Mekiès also saw Daniel Legrand, who confirmed Y. Gasquères' advice. D. Legrand said that, although trade-mark disputes were rapidly disappearing in Japan, there had been some recent disputes between western and Japanese firms, especially those involving several big French fashion houses like Cartier, Chanel, Dior, etc.

D. Legrand also mentioned the recent example of Yoplait, a major French yoghurt producer. A few years ago, Yoplait had signed a licensing agreement with a major Japanese food company, to manufacture and distribute yoghurt in Japan. While negotiating the contract, executives at Yoplait discovered that the Yoplait name had been registered by another Japanese food company under various Japanese writing transcriptions. (The Japanese use three different types of transcription together with the occasional use of the Roman alphabet. In addition to Chinese ideograms ('kanji'), 'katakana' is used for the exclusive transcription of foreign words and names. 'Hiragana' is used for all other words not written in 'kanji'.) Although the French company decided to fight the case in court, Yoplait finally decided to use another name ('Yopuleito' using the Katakana transcription) for its products in Japan.

Before going back to France, Georges Mekiès arranged for Daniel Legrand to supervise the trade-mark dispute with Ogitani. A few weeks later, D. Legrand learned from Mr Nakayama at Ogitani that the Japanese firm had registered the Lestra Design and Lestra Sport brands under its own name only to prevent other Japanese competitors from doing so. Mr G. Mekiès was not fully convinced, however, about the sincerity of this answer. One month later, he learned from D. Legrand that the legal department of the French Embassy in Tokyo was going to intervene in Lestra Design's favour. Finally, at the end of 1990, D. Legrand informed Léopold & Fils that Ogitani had agreed to give up the two trade-marks in exchange for full reimbursement of the registration fees paid by Ogitani to the Tokyo Patent Office.

Looking for a new distributor

During his short stay in Japan, Georges Mekiès was able to size up the many business possibilities offered by the Japanese market. Despite the bad experience with Ogitani, Claude Léopold and Georges Mekiès felt that Lestra Design had a major opportunity for business development in Japan. The Lestra Design trade mark was now fully protected by Japanese law. In April 1991 Claude Léopold commissioned D. Legrand to search for and select a new Japanese partner. To shorten the traditional distribution chain and reduce costs, Daniel Legrand decided to use his personal contacts at some of the major Japanese department stores. Department stores such as Mitsukoshi, Takashimaya and Seibu, which sold luxurious products, enjoyed a reputation of considerable prestige in Japan. Moreover, department stores had branches all over Japan, which would enable Lestra Design to cover the whole Japanese market. Most of these department stores were already carrying competitive duvets from West Germany and France, including prestigious brands like Yves Saint Laurent and Pierre Cardin. D. Legrand thought that department stores would be the right outlet for Lestra Design to position its products in the upper segment of the Japanese duvet and eiderdown market. D. Legrand also went to various Japanese companies in the bed and furniture industry as well as to several large trading companies such as Mitsui & Co., Mitsubishi Corporation, and C. Itoh. He also visited Mr Inagawa, in charge of the Home and Interior Section of Kanematsu-Gosho, which used to import from Léopold & Fils. But Mr Inagawa said that his company did not intend to import any more duvets from Lestra Design because its products were too highly priced.

The general reaction from potential Japanese buyers was that Lestra Design's colours (red, green, white) were not appropriate for the Japanese market. However, most of these buyers agreed that, with some modifications to accommodate the Japanese market, the 'Made in France' image was a great asset for selling Lestra Design products in Japan. Duvets and eiderdowns under names like Yves Saint Laurent, Courrèges or Pierre Cardin were being manufactured in Japan under licence. They were being sold successfully because Japanese distributors and potential customers tended to view French interior textiles as another fashion product for which France was so famous.

To attract distributors, D. Legrand had advised Léopold & Fils to participate in the yearly Home Fashion Show held in Tokyo. However, C. Léopold and G. Mekiès had not responded to this suggestion. By June 1991, some potential distributors had already been identified, but most of them wanted to licence the design and then manufacture in Japan rather than import the final products from France. However, C. Léopold clearly preferred to export directly from France and thus create more jobs for his own employees.

Akira Arai

In July 1991 D. Legrand met with Akira Arai, President of Trans-Ec Co. Ltd, Japan, a firm specializing in importing and exporting down and feathers. A. Arai, 41 years old, had started his own company six years earlier, after working for a large trading company since his graduation from Keio University.

Akira Arai was enthusiastic about French duvets and quilts and the Lestra Design products mainly because of the 'Made in France' label and the prestige attached to French textiles. Like most of the potential distributors D. Legrand had talked to, A. Arai also perceived Lestra Design products as French fashion products similar to the duvets and quilts sold in Japan under prestigious names like Yves Saint Laurent, Cardin or Courrèges. Some French fashion designers almost unknown in France had built a very strong reputation in Japan. Both A. Arai and D. Legrand felt that there was room in Japan for Lestra Design to achieve a strong brand recognition. Akira Arai had had some experience working with other French firms. In the past, he had imported down and feathers from Topiol, a French company which was an indirect competitor of Léopold & Fils. D. Legrand thought that Mr Arai, who had already heard about Lestra Design, could be a potential partner for the French company. Arai knew the down and feather industry thoroughly, and he had good connections in the complex distribution system of the Japanese duvet industry. A. Arai had also been highly recommended by Mrs Eiko Gunjima, in charge of fashion items at the Commercial Section of the French Embassy in Tokyo.

Meeting Japanese tastes

In July 1991 Messrs Legrand and Arai met again in Roppongi, a fashionable district of Tokyo where Mr Arai's office was located. Akira Arai explained that it would be difficult to sell Lestra Design duvets in Japan as they appeared in the current Lestra Design catalogue. In his opinion, Lestra Design would have to adapt its products for the Japanese market. A. Arai proposed that Lestra Design send him a sample that would meet the market requirements (i.e., sizes, colours, fillings, etc.). In particular, he felt that the choice of colours was very important. Although A. Arai liked the innovative motifs and the colours of Lestra Design products, he told D. Legrand that Japanese customers would rarely buy a red, pink or black duvet. Most duvets sold in Japan were in soft colours with many flowers in the design. D. Legrand emphasized that Lestra Design was introducing something really new to the Japanese market, but A. Arai insisted that most Japanese customers would prefer floral motifs on their duvets. Indeed, Daniel Legrand had noticed that almost all the Japanese duvets displayed in Tokyo stores had designs with floral motifs.

Secondly, A. Arai recommended that Lestra Design duvets be smaller than French duvets and should be paving blocked (quilted) to prevent the down from moving too freely inside the duvet. A. Arai noted all these requirements, including all the technical detail needed to manufacture the duvet, so that Lestra Design could meet the Japanese trade expectations. A. Arai's product was quite different from those manufactured by Lestra Design, but D. Legrand was confident that the French company had the flexibility to adapt its products to the Japanese market. A. Arai also requested that Lestra Design deliver the sample within a month. D. Legrand had trouble explaining that Lestra Design, like most French firms, would be closed during the whole month of August for its summer holidays. A. Arai joked about the French taking so much holiday in summer, but he agreed to wait until the beginning of September.

The dust problem

At the beginning of October 1991, D. Legrand went to Arai's office with the sample that he had just received from France. With almost no hesitation, Georges Mekiès had agreed to completely redesign a duvet to meet the Japanese customer's expectations. The fabric was printed with floral motifs, paving blocked and exactly the requested size. Mr. Arai seemed pleased when he first saw the product. Then, as D. Legrand watched, A. Arai picked up the sample, carried it to the window, folded it under his arm and then slapped it vigorously with his hands. Both men were surprised to see a small cloud of white dust come from the duvet. Mr. Arai placed the sample on his desk, shook his head in disappointment and stated, 'This is not a good product. If Lestra Design wants to compete against the big Japanese, German and other French brands, the product must be perfect.'

D. Legrand immediately faxed Mr Arai's reaction to George Mekiès. In A. Arai's opinion, the problem had to do with washing the duvet. Although Mr Mekiès was surprised by the result of Mr Arai's test, he agreed to send a new sample very soon.

Just after New Year's Day D. Legrand arrived at Mr Arai's office with a new sample. Mr Naoto Morimoto, in charge of the Bedding and Interior section of Katakura Kogyo, a major textile trading company, had also been invited by Mr Arai to examine the new sample. In 1991, Katakura Kogyo had profits of US$5.5 million on sales of US$2.8 billion and employed 1,852 people. Naoto Morimoto was an old friend of A. Arai as well as a potential customer for Lestra Design products. After the ritual exchange of business cards between Messrs Legrand and Morimoto, A. Arai proceeded with the same test. Again, some dust came out although less than last time. Messrs. Arai and Morimoto decided to open the duvet and look inside for an explanation to the problem. In their opinion, the feathers had not been washed in the same way as in Japan. Mr Morimoto suspected that the chemicals used to wash the duvet were very different from those traditionally used in Japan. Moreover, Mr Arai found that the duvet was filled with both grey and white down. He asked D. Legrand to recommend that Lestra

Design use only new white down and no feathers at all, even very small ones. In front of Legrand, Akira Arai also demonstrated the same test with several Japanese and German duvets. No dust came out. As a result, D. Legrand and A. Arai decided to send Mr Mekiès samples of both a Japanese and a German duvet so that he could test the dust problem himself. With the two samples, Arai attached a note emphasizing that 'to compete successfully in Japan, Lestra Design products must be perfect, especially since the Japanese customer generally believes that textiles and fashion products from France are of high quality'.

At the end of March 1992 a third sample arrived in Tokyo. Mr Mekiès had phoned D. Legrand beforehand, emphasizing that the utmost care had been given to this sample. But again this time, the sample failed Mr Arai's test. D. Legrand immediately phoned G. Mekiès to inform him of the situation. Mr Arai was frustrated and, as he listened to Mr Mekiès' voice on the telephone, it sounded as if Léopold & Fils were about to give up on the Japanese market. Georges Mekiès could not fully understand Mr Arai's problem because in his whole career at Lestra Design he had never heard any complaint about dust coming out of Lestra Design duvets.

D. Legrand thought that the only way to save the Japanese business would be for Georges Mekiès to visit Tokyo. D. Legrand emphasized again the considerable opportunities offered by the Japanese market and thus convinced Mr Mekiès and Jacques Papillault, Lestra Design's Technical Director, to board the next flight for Tokyo. Mr Mekiès said they would only be able to stay 48 hours in order to meet with Mr Arai.

Mr Mekiès' trip to Tokyo

A few days later Messrs Mekiès and Papillault were in Tokyo. Mr Arai claimed that he was genuinely interested in selling Lestra Design products in Japan, but he explained that in order to compete with existing Japanese duvets, Lestra Design products had to meet the local standards of quality. Messrs Arai and Morimoto insisted that, since French textile products carried such a high image in Japan, they should be of the finest quality. Mr Arai also stressed that only new white goose down should be used to fill the duvet. In an aside conversation with Daniel Legrand, Georges Mekiès asked if this requirement came directly from the final customer. D. Legrand replied that it did not seem to be the case. He himself had interviewed Japanese customers in down and duvet shops and had found that the average customer did not know about the different qualities of down nor did customers seem to care whether the down was grey or white. Mr Mekiès was therefore a bit surprised by Mr Arai's requirement. In France, as in most European countries, the customer was usually only concerned about price and design. D. Legrand explained that A. Arai meant to use 'new white goose down only' as a major selling point to market Lestra Design duvets as a high quality product to the distributors and retailers. From previous conversations with both wholesalers and retailers, D. Legrand explained that 'new white goose down only' was indeed a reasonable expectation, consistent with the upper positioning of European products in Japan as well as with the high quality associated with French fashion items.

According to the trade, the 'new white goose down only' argument would also justify the premium price charged by the retailers for Lestra Design products. Retail prices for Lestra Design products in Japan were expected to range from ¥60,000 to ¥110,000 (in 1993, $250 to $450) and to be comparable with competitive high quality products imported from West Germany. However, prices varied greatly, from a retail price index of 100 to 300, depending on the quality of the down and feathers and their mixture inside the duvet. In fact, some stores, both in Japan and Europe, allowed customers to choose the filling for their duvets and eiderdowns, a policy which gave the customer a lot of pricing flexibility.

Retail prices for Lestra Design in Japan were more than two times higher than in France. Such a difference could be explained by the typically lengthy distribution system in Japan, which contributed to inflating the price of imported goods. For an ex-factory price index of 100, cost, insurance and freight would add 4 per cent, and duties an additional 6 per cent. Then, Mr Arai would price the goods so that he could gain a 12 per cent mark-up on his selling price to Mr Morimoto, who would receive a 10 per cent commission from the smaller wholesalers. In turn, the small wholesalers would put a 20 per cent mark-up on their selling price to the retailers, who would finally sell Lestra Design products at a price which would allow them a 40–60 per cent mark-up. On a retail price basis, Lestra Design products in Japan would be about 30–50 per cent more expensive than most local products of similar quality. Cheap models (either made locally or imported from China) would sell for ¥40,000. On the other hand, Nishikawa, the market leader, offered many models in Lestra Design's price range as well as a few prestigious models over ¥1,000,000. In selling competitive products from West Germany in Japan, the German tradition in making duvets was strongly emphasized. Advertising for these products would often carry the German flag, feature the 'Made in Germany' label and include a commercial slogan in German.

The conversation between Messrs Arai and Mekiès then moved to the dust problem. Mr Arai explained that, in his view, the problem lay with the composition of the chemical formula used to wash the down. Mr Arai had already made arrangements to visit a Japanese duvet and eiderdown manufacturer in the afternoon. To get this Japanese company to open their doors, he had simply told the plant manager that a group of French importers was interested in buying the company's products. As a result, the Japanese manufacturer was quite willing to let the French group visit the factory. Georges Mekiès and Daniel Legrand were impressed by the state-of-the-art equipment used by the Japanese firm. Jacques Papillault noticed that the Japanese were using microscopes and some very expensive machines that he had never seen in Europe to determine, for example, the greasiness of the down. Georges Mekiès was also amazed to observe three Japanese employees in white smocks separating down from small feathers with small tweezers. According to Jacques Papillault, not a single western manufacturer was as meticulous as this Japanese company. During the visit, Georges Mekiès also picked up some useful information about the chemical formula used by the Japanese manufacturer to wash the down and feathers.

The next day, George Mekiès and Jacques Papillault flew back to France fully aware that much remained to be done to crack the Japanese market. Before leaving, G. Mekiès told Mr Arai that this trip had been extremely useful, and that Léopold & Fils would work hard to make a new sample that would meet the Japanese quality standards. Mr Arai also promised Georges Mekiès that he would try to get more information about the chemical formula used by the Japanese company they had visited.

New challenges

Two weeks later, Mr Arai sent Léopold & Fils some additional information on the chemical formula. Georges Mekiès then contacted a large French chemical company that immediately produced an identical formulation for Lestra Design. At the end of April, Mr Arai told D. Legrand that Lestra Design should hurry with its new samples. Most wholesalers would be placing orders in May for late October delivery to the retail shops. Mr Arai also indicated that Mr Morimoto from Katakura Kogyo had already selected some designs and had basically agreed to order 200 duvets at the FOB price of FFr. 1,200 each, provided that Lestra Design solved the dust problem.

In late May 1992 three new duvet samples arrived in Japan. Mr Arai found them much better than the previous ones. However, he still felt that the dust problem was not completely solved. Messrs Arai and Morimoto decided to have the fabric inspected in the laboratories of the Japanese Textile Association in Osaka. They both explained to Daniel Legrand that the fabric used by Lestra Design did not have the same density of threads per square inch as most Japanese duvet fabrics had. D. Legrand reported this latest development to Georges Mekiès, who was obviously upset by this new complaint from the Japanese. D. Legrand was also worried that the time required to have the fabric inspected would further delay the manufacturing of the 200 duvets that Mr Morimoto was planning to order. In the meantime, Lestra Design had been obliged to order the fabric with the printed design selected by Mr Morimoto in order to get exclusivity with its French supplier.

'Gokai' (misunderstandings)

At the end of June 1992 Mr Takeshi Kuroda, an executive from Katakura Kogyo who was on a business trip in the southern part of France, visited Messrs Mekiès and Léopold in Amboise. Mr Mekiès had trouble communicating with the Japanese executive because of Mr Kuroda's limited ability in English. However, Mr Mekiès understood from Mr Kuroda that Lestra Design had the green light to manufacture 200 duvets using the fabric selected by Mr Morimoto. Mr Mekiès communicated the good news to D. Legrand who phoned N. Morimoto to thank him for the order. Mr Morimoto was surprised by D. Legrand's call because he personally had not taken any steps to confirm the order. Mr Morimoto had first wanted to have the results of the test being conducted in Osaka. Finally, in early July, the report from the Japanese Textile Association brought bad news for Lestra Design. The Japanese laboratories found that the density of Lestra Design's fabric was far below that of most Japanese duvet fabrics.

The test results confirmed the fears of Messrs Arai and Morimoto that the fabric problem created a major obstacle for selling Lestra Design duvets in Japan. Although the test could not legally prevent Lestra Design from selling on the Japanese market, A. Arai and N. Morimoto insisted that the French products had to be perfect to be sold in Japan. Thus, Naoto Morimoto told Daniel Legrand that he would not be able to proceed with importing the 200 duvets into Japan. Daniel Legrand tried to counter with the argument that the test was merely a non-tariff barrier for Lestra Design products in Japan. However, N. Morimoto answered that Lestra Design had to meet the market requirements to succeed in Japan.

When Daniel Legrand phoned the Lestra Design office in Amboise, Georges Mekiès was very upset. As far as he knew, the Japanese were the only ones in the world to conduct this kind of investigation, which he believed was a non-tariff barrier to prevent non-Japanese products from entering the Japanese market. Georges Mekiès' exasperation was increased because following Mr Kuroda's visit, the 200 duvets for Katakura Kogyo had already been manufactured. Because the duvets had been made to fit Japanese specifications, they could only be sold in Japan. Daniel Legrand replied that he would explain the situation to Mr Morimoto and that he would try to convince him to do something about it. During the following days, D. Legrand tried hard to persuade Naoto Morimoto to accept the order. It seemed to him that Mr Kuroda was directly responsible for the misunderstanding. But Mr Morimoto remained inflexible and said that he could not buy products inferior in quality to those sold by Japanese competitors.

During the latter half of 1992 little communication took place between the French and the Japanese. Claude Léopold and Georges Mekiès were upset by the attitude of the Japanese. On the Japanese side, Messrs Arai and Morimoto said that it was too late to meet with the distributors as most of their orders had already been placed in late July for the winter season. However, Daniel Legrand and Akira Arai had remained loosely in touch. At the end of February 1993, A. Arai said that he was still interested in importing Lestra Design's products. Both Daniel Legrand and Akira Arai were also convinced that, despite all the setbacks, there was still hope for Lestra Design to grasp a share of the huge Japanese market for duvets. Daniel Legrand had learned that Lestra Design's major French competitor had faced similar problems in Japan and had decided to give up the Japanese market. On the other hand, he knew that several German competitors were operating successfully in Japan.

In April 1993, Daniel Legrand took advantage of a business trip to France to visit Messrs Léopold and Mekiès in Amboise. He was aware that Lestra Design was making a successful start in the USA. In fact, Mr Léopold was just back from an exhibition in New York where a major order had been placed. Daniel Legrand emphasized again the great potential of the Japanese market and the need to take a long-term view of this market. Daniel Legrand recognized that, although Japan was a tough market to crack, persistence would eventually pay off. Claude Léopold said that he had already tried hard and confessed that he was still quite disappointed by the Japanese market. However, at the end of the meeting, Claude Léopold said that he would consider one last try.

The alternatives

In early May 1993 Daniel Legrand again met with Akira Arai and Naoto Morimoto. Mr Morimoto also mentioned that he would be interested in buying the original designs from Josette Léopold and then have the duvets manufactured in Japan under licence. Claude Léopold was not keen on this idea. He knew that Yves Saint Laurent, Lanvin and Courrèges duvets were manufactured this way in Japan. C. Léopold also knew that Lacoste shirts, although considered a universal product, had been completely adapted to suit the Japanese market. The colours, shape and even the cotton material of Lacoste shirts sold in Japan were different from the Lacoste products sold in the rest of the world. Bernard Lacoste, the son of the famous tennis player and a personal friend of Claude Léopold, ran the Lacoste business around the world. A few months earlier, Mr Léopold had heard from B. Lacoste himself that in the previous year, the Lacoste company had had trouble with its Japanese licensee. Yves Gasquères, the French consultant in Tokyo who was monitoring Lacoste's operations in Japan, had discovered that the licensee had at one point 'forgotten' to pay the full amount of royalties due to Lacoste in France. Claude Léopold was therefore wondering if licensing would be the best solution.

Mr Arai had also proposed that Lestra Design buy some Japanese fabric and manufacture the duvets in France. He argued that this would definitively solve the dust problem. Moreover, then Lestra Design products could still carry the 'Made in France' label which was so appealing to Japanese customers.

Another alternative recommended to Mr Mekiès was buying fabric for the duvets from West Germany where textile standards were similar to the ones in Japan. Lestra Design could then print Josette Léopold's designs on the German cloth and still manufacture the duvets in France. Because the Japanese insisted on floral motifs, Lestra Design could even buy fabric with floral prints in West Germany. Mr Arai had found that many Japanese companies like Nishikawa (the leading duvet manufacturer in Japan) were already buying a lot of German fabric for duvets. However, in order to be granted the design exclusivity, Mr Mekiès needed to buy a minimum amount of fabric, the equivalent of 300 duvets.

As he was reviewing these different alternatives for Lestra Design, Claude Léopold wondered if he should continue trying to gain a foothold in the Japanese market, or should he simply forget about Japan and focus more on Europe and the United States?

(This case was written by Dominique Turpin, IMD, Lausanne, Switzerland. Reproduced with his kind permission. Some names and dates have been disguised.)

QUESTIONS

1. Is the French concept of quality the same as the Japanese concept of quality? If it is not, how would you relate it to the differences between French culture and Japanese culture? If it is, why is quality a culturally universal concept?

2. How would you interpret the attitude of Lestra Design's Japanese partners?

3. What are the difficulties encountered by Lestra Design in the business relationships with its Japanese partners?

4. What reasons could push Lestra Design to continue to try to penetrate the Japanese market for duvets and eiderdowns? What financial results may be expected, and when?

5. Suggest to Messrs Léopold and Mekiès a strategic response concerning the Japanese market (go/no go, entry mode, producing locally or not, etc.).

A9.2   Case: Irish Cream O'Darby

Irish Cream is a typically Irish liqueur, prepared from a mix of whisky and cream, with a dash of chocolate. Irish Cream is very popular in Ireland. It conquered the US market in the 1960s and 1970s. Its success abroad has been so great that it is now no longer a negligible portion of total Irish exports.

The most famous brand is Bailey's. It holds a dominant market share, and the brand name tends to be used as a generic name. People speak of drinking Bailey's rather than Irish Cream. O'Darby is a challenger to Bailey's, and it competes for the second market share with Carolan's. A fourth brand, Royal Tara, and two small competitors, Waterford Cream and Emmets, share the rest of the market.

O'Darby, whose factory and headquarters are located in Cork, in the southern part of Ireland, was taken over at the beginning of the 1980s by Bacardi Rum, a leading multinational company in the spirits industry. Just a few months after the take-over, Bacardi undertook a large market survey, in the whole of the United States, to investigate how consumers perceived the generic product Irish Cream, and especially the O'Darby brand. It appeared that the green-coloured bottle was largely rejected by potential customers. New packaging was designed, where brown colour dominated, for the bottle as well as the label. It led to an astonishing growth of sales, not only in the United States, but also in other national markets.

At the beginning of 1991, the director for the marketing of O'Darby hired a young junior marketing executive, Peter Finch, to be in charge of promoting Irish Cream O'Darby in France. Peter Finch, who had just graduated from a continuing education programme for training young export executives, travelled to France to see what could be done to increase sales. The exclusive distributor of Irish Cream O'Darby was the Benedictine Group, a large liquor producer, which sold on the French market through a network of non-exclusive sales agents.

O'Darby was not the first company producing Irish Cream to try to penetrate the French market. In 1982 and 1983, Bailey's had spent a lot of money, especially on advertising, to launch Irish Cream. The results had been disappointing and sales margins had not been large enough to cover the marketing expenses. Bailey's had not withdrawn, but it had discontinued its costly marketing expenses. Bailey's had concentrated its sales coverage on Paris, the northern part of France, Normandy and Brittany. It appeared that Bailey's was unsuccessful in selling to customers in the southern part of France. When trying to explain this relative failure, sales agents had mainly questioned the price level which, according to them, was too high.

During his first stay in France from March to May 1990, Peter Finch had been involved in sales promotion operations, with the help of the Benedictine network. Shoppers in hypermarkets were asked to taste Irish Cream by giving them miniature bottles of O'Darby. It seemed to be difficult even to induce people to try the liquor.

However, this product was very popular in other developed markets for a variety of uses. For instance, in the United States consumers mixed it with Coca-Cola or orange juice, in cocktails. O'Darby was well placed for use in cocktails, compared to its competitors, because of a special formula that made it easy to mix with other beverages. In many markets, consumers used Irish Cream to coat ice-creams, cakes or strawberries. In Spain, where Irish Cream has achieved a good deal of product knowledge, Spanish consumers tend to call it Bailey's O'Darby.

In September 1991 the situation for Irish Cream O'Darby was as follows:

1. It was sold almost exclusively in very large food stores (hypermarkets); it achieved a low penetration rate as a bar drink; it was rarely to be found in restaurants.

2. The retail price was in the range of 45–50 francs for a bottle of 75 centilitres, compared to Bailey's which was priced in the bracket of 55–60 francs for a bottle of 70 centilitres.

3. The annual sales for 1990 were 24,000 cases of 12 bottles.

4. Sales coverage was limited to Paris, the northern part of France, Normandy and Brittany. The area where it sold best was the *département* of Finistère (Brest, Quimper), which is located in the most western part of France (a *département* is a French territorial unit where there are generally between half a million and one million inhabitants). Finistère is linked by ferries to Ireland. There, per capita consumption of Irish Cream was three times as much as in the Paris region.

5. There was no advertising. Sales promotion was done mostly by means of free sampling, in hypermarkets, disco bars or night clubs ('O'Darby party nights').

6. The promotional budget, which was 300,000 francs in 1989, was more than doubled in 1990 to 700,000 francs.

QUESTIONS

1. Discuss and, possibly, criticize the marketing strategy which was adopted by Irish Cream O'Darby in order to enter the French market. In doing this you should, in particular, take care to examine what kind of market research should have been undertaken: (a) prior to entering the market; and (b) after results had been achieved; and to question the coherence of the marketing mix. (You are not asked to prepare a marketing strategy as a whole, since the information available in this short case is not sufficient.)

2. Irish Cream O'Darby has to decide on the allocation of its total marketing budget to its various national markets. You are asked to outline the criteria and design of such an allocation method. The problem is allocation between national markets, not between local/regional markets within a particular country.

REFERENCES

Amine, Lyn S. (1993), 'Linking consumer behavior constructs to international marketing strategy: A comment on Wills, Samli, and Jacobs and an extension', *Journal of the Academy of Marketing Science*, vol. 21, no. 1, pp 71–7.

Baalbaki, Imad B. and Naresh K. Malhotra (1995), 'Standardization versus customization in international marketing: An investigation using bridging conjoint analysis', *Journal of the Academy of Marketing Science*, vol. 23, no. 3, pp 182–94.

Camphuis, Pierre-Arnold (1984), 'Launching a product on the Cameroon market', Internship report, Ecole Supérieure de Commerce de Paris.

Cohen, Judy (1995), 'Toward a theoretical understanding of the impact of culture on pictorial perception', *Proceedings of the Second Conference on the Cultural Dimension of International Marketing*, Odense, pp. 213–45.

Cohen, Judy (1996), 'The search for universal symbols: The case of right and left', *Journal of International Consumer Marketing*, vol. 8 , nos 3/4, pp. 187–210.

Copeland, Lennie and Lewis Griggs (1986), *Going International*, Plume Books/New American Library: New York.

De Ruyter, Ko, Martin Wetzels, Jos Lemmink and Jan Mattsson (1997), 'The dynamics of the service delivery process: A value-based approach, *International Journal of Research in Marketing*, vol. 14, no. 3, pp. 231–43.

Diamantopoulos, A., B. B. Schlegelmilch, and J. P. Du Preez (1995), 'Lessons for Pan-European Marketing? The role of consumer preferences in fine-tuning the product-market fit', *International Marketing Review*, vol. 12, no. 2, pp. 38–52.

Frazer Winsted, Kathleen (1997), 'The service experience in two cultures: A behavioral perspective', *Journal of Retailing*, vol. 73, no. 3, pp. 337–60.

Giordan, Alain-Eric (1988), *Exporter Plus 2*, Economica: Paris.

Hall, Edward T. (1976), *Beyond Culture*, Doubleday: New York.

Jacobs, Laurence, Charles Keown, Reginald Worthley and Ghymn Kyung-Il (1991), 'Cross-cultural colour comparisons: Global marketers beware!', *International Marketing Review*, vol. 8, no. 3, pp. 21–30.

Kamamoto, Mitsuko (1984), 'Japanese concept of service', *Dentsu Japan Marketing/Advertising*, January, pp. 26–9.

Levitt, Theodore (1983), 'The globalization of markets', *Harvard Business Review*, vol. 61, no. 3, May–June, pp. 92–102.

McCornell, J. D. (1971), 'The economics of behavioral factors in the multinational corporation', in Fred E. Allvine (ed.), *Combined Proceedings of the American Marketing Association*, p. 260.

Ofir, Chezy and Donald R. Lehmann (1986), 'Measuring images of foreign products', *Columbia Journal of World Business*, Summer, pp. 105–8.

Pahud de Mortanges, Charles, Jan-Willem Rietbroek and Cort MacLean Johns (1997), 'Marketing pharmaceuticals in Japan: Background and the experience of US firms', *European Journal of Marketing*, vol. 31, no. 8, pp. 561–82.

Rogers, Everett M. (1983), *Diffusion of Innovations*, 3rd edn, Free Press: New York.

Samiee, Saeed and Kendall Roth (1994), 'The influence of global marketing standardization on performance', *Journal of Marketing*, vol. 56, April, pp. 1–17.

Shoham, Aviv (1996) 'Marketing-mix standardization: Determinants of export performance', *Journal of Global Marketing*, vol. 10, no. 2, pp. 53–73.

Solomon, Michael R. (1983), 'The role of products as social stimuli: a symbolic interactionism perspective,' *Journal of Consumer Research*, vol. 10, December, pp. 319–29.

Tiano, A. (1981), *Transfert de Technologie Industrielle*, Editions Economica: Paris.

Trompenaars, Fons (1993), *Riding the Waves of Culture*, Nicholas Brealey: London.

Tuncalp, Secil (1990), 'Export marketing strategy to Saudi Arabia: the case of British exporters', *Quarterly Review of Marketing*, vol. 15, no. 2, pp. 13–18.

Williams, Stephen C. and John W. Longworth (1989), 'Factors influencing tuna prices in Japan and implications for the development of the coral sea tuna fishery', *European Journal of Marketing*, vol. 23, no. 4, pp. 5–24.

Wills, James, A. Coskun Samli and Laurence Jacobs (1991), 'Developing global products and marketing strategies: A construct and a research agenda', *Journal of the Academy of Marketing Science*, vol. 19, no. 1, pp 1–10.

10 Product policy 2: Managing meaning

A name can make substantial contributions to a brand equity, as Leclerc *et al.* (1994, p. 263) point out:

What do Klarbrunn waters, Giorgio di St Angelo design wear and Häagen-Dazs ice cream have in common? All three are successful brands, and all are not what they seem. Klarbrunn is not the clear mountain-spring mineral water from the German Alps that its brand name suggests; it is American water bottled in Wisconsin. Giorgio di St Angelo design wear is not the latest fashion from Milan but the product of U.S. designer Martin Price. And Häagen-Dazs is not Danish or Hungarian ice cream; it is American ice cream made by Pillsbury with headquarters in Minneapolis.

This chapter complements the preceding one directly: it deals with the symbolic attributes that are linked to brands and national images. These issues are particularly significant for a company which does not as yet have an established brand(s) on the international market. It is easy to avoid basic errors in relation to the choice of a brand name when starting from scratch. However, correcting mistakes once brand goodwill has been created can prove a costly and tricky operation. A brand, even one that has a poor impact, may be an asset because a marketing communication investment has been made. Consumers are often confused by changes in a brand name. Changes to brand names, if they are possible, risk wasting time and incurring expenditure.

This chapter begins by discussing the interplay of images – those of the product's country of origin, the company name and/or the brand name of its products. This complex interplay of images warrants closer analysis. When one starts without an established brand, there is the potential for the intentional diffusion of favourable images, suitable for the product category and the national segments targeted.

The evaluation of product quality by consumers has been documented by a great number of empirical studies. The perception of certain product attributes, according to their country of origin, has been experimentally assessed. The second section of this chapter reviews studies dealing with the country-of-origin paradigm. Consumers in different countries were questioned about their perceptions of their domestic products compared to foreign-made products from various other countries. These studies suggest consistent answers to such questions as the following: Which countries are best perceived, and on which attributes? Do countries' images change over time?

Section 10.3 addresses the issue of the conversion of national brands into international brands. The linguistic obstacles that are met in this conversion are examined. The question of the so-called 'global' brands is also documented since this is becoming a significant issue in international marketing.

10.1   NATIONAL IMAGES DIFFUSED BY THE PRODUCT'S ORIGIN AND BY ITS BRAND NAME

The complexity of national images diffused by the product

The purchasers of Swedish cars, who pay twice as much as for cars with comparable performance, acquire, at least to a certain extent, the symbolic label 'Made in Sweden' which, for them, suggests reliability and long life, thereby removing any fear of mechanical failure. There exists an important relation between images of products and the symbols diffused by their nationality. Relationships between product and nationality, in consumers' evaluations, were first studied with respect to the 'made in' label, that is the origin label put on products. But the 'made in' label is not the only element that contributes to consumer perception of product nationality. The following elements can be distinguished (Figure 10.1):

1. The image of imported products versus national products or the image of national products versus international products.
2. National images of generic products: yoghurt calls to mind the Balkans, perfume evokes France, a pair of jeans the United States, etc.
3. The national image of the manufacturing company.
4. The image diffused by the brand name.
5. The image of the 'made in' label in the sense of the manufacturing origin legally appended to the product; origin labelling is mandatory in international trade.

Leclerc *et al.* (1994) show that the French pronunciation of a brand name positively affects the perceived hedonism of the product and negatively affects its perceived utility. They further demonstrate that, in an actual product taste test where consumers have direct sensory experience of the product, foreign branding changes consumers' perceptions of the product (in this case yoghurt). In many cases, the product category is not clearly associated with only one country: wine is not associated with France only, but also with other European countries (Germany, Italy, Spain, Portugal) and with California, Australia, Argentina and Chile. There are also regional associations: furniture made of natural pine wood is often associated with Scandinavia as a whole. However, in an experiment looking at customer evaluations of advertisements, Harris *et al.* (1994) showed that the effect of foreign product names on country-of-origins attributions must be checked carefully. Their findings indicate that, contrary to what one might expect, German-named burger restaurants were preferred by US respon-

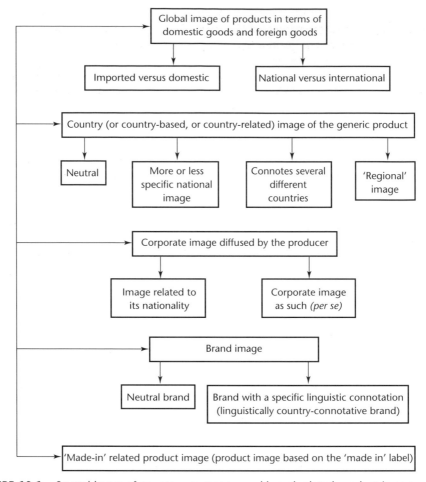

FIGURE 10.1 Several layers of country-, company- and brand-related product image.

dents over American ones. Beer, on the other hand, was associated with more than one nationality and a German-name beer was not necessarily preferred by consumers.

Japanese consumers associate countries with stereotypes (Nishina, 1990): Germany and France with long history and tradition, Switzerland and Australia with rich nature, California and Brazil with plentiful agricultural products, the United States and Germany with advanced industrial technology, and France with sense of design and high-class products.

Some examples will illustrate the levels on which national images can operate (see Table 10.1). The set of normative recommendations for management of a product's national image includes the following elements:

1. One should diffuse an image which corresponds in each country to what is locally valued (imported or national) in the product category concerned. This can lead to the adoption of a name from the target country, imposed by prevailing national-istic feelings.

TABLE 10.1   Some examples of the combined influence of brand name and country of origin on product image

Product	National image of the generic product	National image of the manufacturer	Country evoked by the brand name label	Country image diffused by the 'Made in' label
Shalimar (perfume by Guerlain)	French	French	India/Orient	French
Kinder (milk chocolate bars made by Ferrero)	Swiss and other countries	Italian (but the manufacturer's name, Ferrero, rarely appears)	German (means 'children' in German)	'Made in' hardly visible – often Italy
National (vacuum cleaner made by Matsushita)	Neutral	The manufacturer's name (Matsushita) does not appear	The National brand makes people believe that is a local product	'Made in' label hardly visible – different national origins
Coca-Cola	International	American	America	Neutral
Kremly (yoghurt by Chambourcy, part of Nestlé)	Balkan/ Bulgarian Slav	Looks French, but is a world-wide brand of the Swiss Nestlé	Kremly (name and graphics) evokes the Kremlin, a Slav image	The 'Made in' label is a local one
Brother (typewriters by Brother)	Neutral	English/American (in fact a Japanese company)	International	The 'Made in' label indicates the origin

2. If the generic product is generally associated with a specific country of origin, one should not hesitate to change the brand name. For example, a manufacturer of machine tools should not be reluctant to adopt a German name, because of the favourable association of German-sounding names with technical reliability.

3. It is often advisable to reduce the physical size of the 'made in' label if the perception of the country of origin proves negative for local consumers (provided such reduction is permitted, or ignored, by local regulations). On the other hand, one should enlarge it in cases where the opposite perception prevails.

4. The visibility of the company name, the brand name and the 'made in' label should be adjusted depending on their respective ability to convey the desired symbolic meanings.

10.2   CONSUMER PRODUCT EVALUATION ACCORDING TO COUNTRY OF ORIGIN

The use of the 'country of origin' attribute

Consumers use the manufacturer's country of origin (COO) on a symbolic level. In other words, they use it as an associative link: Germany – robustness, France – luxury,

Italy – beauty, etc. The cognitive processes that lead to these evaluations are therefore worth examination. Numerous studies have been devoted to the country-of-origin paradigm (Bilkey and Nes, 1982, Samiee, 1994). The simplistic approach which directly assimilates a country image with the image of a product originating from that country is gradually being disregarded in favour of an attempt to analyze the complex consumer evaluation processes that relate the image of the COO to perception of product attributes.

As Bilkey and Nes (1982) point out, the basic objective of these studies was to demonstrate that the country-of-origin cue actually influenced consumers' evaluations. Attempting to determine in which direction and why, was only a secondary objective in the first studies (Schooler, 1965; 1971; Reierson, 1966, Schooler and Sunoo, 1969; Etzel and Walker, 1974; Wang and Lamb, 1980). For instance Schooler and Wildt (1968) showed their subjects identical products (drinking glasses). Some drinking glasses were supposed to have been 'Made in USA' whereas the others claimed to be 'Made in Japan'. They clearly evidenced an evaluation bias due to the effect of the country of origin. But price discounts may lead the consumer to purchase the 'worst' product – the Japanese one in this case and at that time. However, considering the *country of origin* as the only criterion in consumer evaluation of quality leads to an exaggeration of the importance of the 'made in' label. Country of origin is now recognized as not being a single evaluation cue for consumers; they use it in combination with other product attributes such as price, perceived risk, etc. Peterson and Jolibert (1995), based on a meta-analysis of 52 COO studies, have shown that the average effect of COO was 0.30 in relation to quality/reliability, whereas its average effect for purchase intentions was 0.19; the latter figure was less reliable since it is computed on the basis of customers' intention to buy rather than actual purchasing behaviour.

A set of core standard images

Throughout COO studies one finds a limited number of stereotyped images. These fairly resistant stereotypes are consistent across nationalities of consumers: the image of the robustness of German products, the image of France as associated with luxury goods, the image of Korean products as being cheap. However, shared perceptual elements are restricted and unstable: for instance, the Italians do not have the same image of their products as do consumers from other countries, and the Korean image has changed over time.

Generally speaking, there are many elements of COO that are not shared by consumers of different national cultures. Often, minimal differences in relationships between countries (similarity of culture and language, past colonial links, etc.) lead to differences in the perception of one country across other countries (for example, Yaprak, 1978). Krishnakumar (1974) has, for instance, shown that Indian students evaluate British products more positively than do students from Taiwan, a difference attributable to the past colonial links between the United Kingdom and India. Yavas and Alpay (1986) have demonstrated that in two neighbouring countries, Saudi Arabia and Bahrain, consumers hold the same views of products originating from abroad.

Use by consumers of the image of the country of origin of goods for their evaluation

Country of origin is only one attribute among many that characterize a product. A product possesses intrinsic attributes (size, colour and quality, for example) as well as extrinsic attributes (such as price). COO is therefore only one criterion of evaluation (Erickson *et al.*, 1984). The influence of the COO evaluation cue is stronger where the consumer is unfamiliar with a product category. In this situation, the COO serves as a sort of proxy variable that facilitates evaluation in the absence of other criteria. It also serves to sum up diversified evaluation criteria within a sort of global evaluation (Morello, 1984). In the absence of other information cues, the consumer will use the COO to evaluate the product. It seems that knowledge and familiarity with the product category tends to decrease the use of the COO as an informational cue by consumers: expert consumers base their evaluation on the strength of actual product attributes whereas novices tend to rely more on the COO cue as such (Maheswaran, 1994). Similarly, it has been proposed that such situational characteristics as severe time limitations and limited product knowledge would lead consumers to make greater use of the COO stereotypical images (Swinder and Rao, 1997).

Various studies have insisted on the mediation of stereotypes concerning the country itself, by means of an association between product and country or country and attribute, in the effect of the COO on the evaluation of the product. For example, for the Iranians, 'The Germans are well-ordered and hard working, the French inventive and DiYers even in business matters, the Japanese copiers . . .' (Bon and Ollivier, 1979, p. 106).

For many reasons, aspects of the influence of COO on consumer evaluation have to be differentiated: (1) it is only one element in the evaluation, associated with other cues (price, store, brand, etc.); (2) it depends on the product category; (3) consumer knowledge of and familiarity with the product category have an influence; and (4) customer awareness of COO may be quite limited or even non-existent (Samiee, 1994), especially if the COO is neither advertised nor labelled. Schaefer (1997) has examined the influence of brand familiarity and consumer knowledge on the evaluation of COO by British consumers for lager beers imported from Australia, Belgium, the former Czechoslovakia, Denmark, Germany, The Netherlands in comparison to British brands. Objective product knowledge based on attribute information leads to an increased reliance on COO in product evaluations if the brand name is unfamiliar, but not if the brand is familiar.

The mediation of perceived risk

A sound hypothesis which has been proposed by several studies is the mediation of perceived risk to explain the influence of the COO on consumer evaluations. Either consumers perceive a lesser risk for national products, which would explain the preference for national products, or they perceive a lesser risk for the products of certain countries with a favourable image (see Box 10.1). Accordingly, consumers would tend to prefer certain sources because they perceive a reduced risk in purchasing that country's products (Lumpkin *et al.*, 1985).

Hampton (1977) considered the situation where American goods are manufactured either in the United States or abroad in selected countries. In the sample were some strong perceived risk countries (Algeria, Pakistan, Turkey), some moderate-perceived-risk countries (the Philippines, Hong Kong) and some weak-perceived-risk countries (Canada, Japan, West Germany). In the questionnaire these origins were combined with a sample of products that offered diverse levels of perceived risk. Overall the results confirmed that consumers perceived less risk for goods manufactured in the United States than for the same products when foreign made, whatever the level of perceived risk of the foreign country of manufacture. In several instances, product–country connections were clearly established in consumers' minds, such as the colour television and Japan, the calculator and Hong Kong, or even instant coffee and Brazil, thereby reducing the level of perceived risk of a country as a general place of manufacture. For these specific products, these were considered favourable manufacturing countries.

BOX 10.1

Confession of a purchaser of Italian products

When I consider the origins of my purchases I am fascinated by the number of Italian-made goods I have acquired. My Fiat Uno is the seventh Fiat I have bought. One of these Fiats (a 127) saved my life when I was in Paris. I was waiting at a red light when a Mercedes failed to brake and went into the back of me, sending me 30 metres forward. My Fiat had to be scrapped, but I was unharmed. At home, the washing machine and dryer are Zanussi, and the deep-freeze is a Hiberna. When I go trekking, my mountain shoes are from Trezetta. Like many Europeans, I like Barilla pasta and cakes. In fact, I am a price-minded consumer: Italian products are often the cheapest. Being somewhat price-averse (but not stingy), I believe that 'quality' and 'durability' will never match the price advantage. But price is not the only merit of Italian products. Italian products are much more reliable than stereotyped images would sometimes have you believe. Having successfully tried Italian products, my perceived risk is low when buying goods 'Made in Italy'. Italian goods are probably slightly less solid than German goods, but I very much like their design and function. Even though it is a small car, I like the style of the body and the interior of the Fiat Uno, as well as its sporty engine. If well maintained, Italian products are extremely durable. Their price–quality ratio is fairly reasonable in the long run. Paradoxically, Italian products often do not reach their ideal purchasers: many purchasers of Italian products belong to the price-minded segment but they tend not to spend the required time on maintenance Mercedes buyers, on the other hand, are much more likely to do so. The 'Made in Italy', label in my opinion, deserves greater appreciation.

In their study of the risk perceived by Americans for clothing – clothes and shoes made abroad versus those made in the United States – Lumpkin *et al.* (1985) confirm that the perceived risk is weaker for a product of national origin. They showed that perceived risk only has a strong influence when consumers are aware of the foreign origin of the clothes. They also detected differences according to the categories of products: certain countries (China, Korea) presented the same perceived risk whatever the product whereas Italy offered a weak perceived risk for shoe purchases and France offered a high perceived risk when buying jeans.

Also using clothing in their experimental setting, Baumgartner and Jolibert (1977) have proved that certain traits of a foreign country may reduce the perceived risk if the consumers (French, in this case) hold the belief that a foreign country, by virtue of its physical, climatic or social environment, is particularly suitable for the manufacture of a particular product: for instance, an English overcoat for the winter. Generally, the overall level of perceived risk for a specific national origin is less for its *ethnic* products.

Country of origin and brand perceptions: The effect of multinational production

As a result of the expansion of multinational firms, companies sell the same products under identical brand names in different countries throughout the world. These products actually have widely differing national origins, not necessarily that of the COO of the parent company. Sony products, for example, can be just as easily 'Made in France', 'Made in Germany' or 'Made in Britain' as 'Made in Japan'. In this sense, one must increasingly distinguish between COO and country of manufacture (Samiee, 1994), although the product design and brand name would originate from the COO (Ahmed *et al.*, 1994).

An attempt must therefore be made to distinguish consumer evaluations purely related to the brand (and its COO, when it is identifiable) from the particular effect of the country of production (Johansson and Thorelli, 1985). Johansson and Nebenzahl (1986) demonstrated that a change in the place of car production (e.g. for Chevrolet, Buick, Honda or Mazda) to West Germany is always positively perceived by American consumers. On the other hand, the status and quality image of these makes have suffered when a change has been envisioned in the place of their production to a country where low salaries are paid (e.g. Mexico, South Korea or the Philippines). This change clearly resulted in a loss of image in terms of social status and quality–price ratio.

Han and Terpstra (1988, p. 244) sought to determine which of the two effects had more influence, and their conclusion was unequivocal: 'the sourcing country has greater effects on consumer evaluations of product quality than does the brand name'. As for Eroglu and Machleit (1989), they concluded from their empirical study that consumers accord a similar influence to brand and country of manufacture respectively. Ahmed *et al.* (1994), in the case of industrial products, show that country of design is a more important cue in organizational purchase decisions than country of assembly and brand name. In the case of Russian, Hungarian and Polish consumers, that is, emerging market economies, brand name plays a limited role in comparison to COO (Ettenson, 1993).

The corollary question deserves consideration: what price reduction do consumers require to 'accept' a less favourable origin, in relation to a specific brand? Johansson and Nebenzahl (1986, p. 120) determined the levels of monetary discounts (dollar values) at which consumers were prepared to purchase products from a 'less favourable' COO. They were, for example, willing to buy a Buick manufactured in the United States for $10,258 rather than pay $7,351 for the same car made in the Philippines. Nebenzahl and Jaffé (1989) measured such elasticity of demand in the country of production with Israeli consumers (and Usunier *et al.*, 1993 did likewise, with French consumers), for three possible countries of production (South Korea, Japan and West Germany) and for three brands (Sanyo, Grundig and Sony). A discount of 30–40 per cent was necessary to sell Japanese or German brand products when they had been manufactured in South Korea. It was shown (Usunier, 1994) that consumers belonging to lower social classes (who are favourite targets for lower-priced goods) did not ask for a larger price discount than consumers of higher social status when it was proposed to shift production to a less favourable country of manufacture (South Korea). Furthermore, consumers from lower social classes evaluate Korea more positively as a COO than do higher social status consumers. Thus, it would be wise for the marketing strategy for 'cheap'-origin goods in highly developed markets to put emphasis on quality rather than price, especially when consumers with modest means and from lower socioeconomic classes are targeted.

Country image differences across product categories

Various studies have evidenced perceptual linkage between COO and product types; the relative influence of the COO cue varies according to product category and to the type of attribute considered (Eroglu and Machleit, 1989). Certain products are considered more 'ethnic', more typical of certain countries; consumers tend to associate countries and products: Italy and pizza, Germany and machine tools, Britain and puddings. Gaedeke (1973), for example, found that tinned meat produced in Brazil is much more highly regarded than televisions made there, and that video recorders that are 'Made in South Korea' were more highly regarded than shoes from the same country. Hooley *et al.* (1988) find clear associations in the minds of British consumers about fruit and vegetables with different origins: whereas grapes and tomatoes were associated with Italy, apples were associated with France, citrus fruit with Spain, and potatoes with Britain.

Different studies have been devoted to industrial purchasing (White and Cundiff, 1978; Jolibert, 1979; White, 1979; Perrin *et al.*, 1981; Cattin *et al.*, 1982). Industrial purchasers were asked about their perception of relevant attributes of the product: price, perceived quality and technological superiority. Germany consistently appears to have a substantial lead in product quality and reliability images, and also appears to be the most capable producer of heavy industrial equipment (Jolibert, 1979; Cattin *et al.*, 1982). This favourable image of German industrial products is to be found even in the United States, where American purchasers regard German industrial products as being of higher quality than their own. French and UK industrial products are regarded as being equivalent quality to US ones, and Italian industrial products as being of inferior quality to American products (White, 1979). A similar favourable image is found now for Japanese industrial products which receive better overall ratings from Korean importers than American products (Kraft and Chung, 1992).

Perrin *et al.* (1981) showed in a study of the International Marketing and Purchasing European group that different national markets across Europe are not equally demanding as a whole and furthermore do not emphasize the same requirements. German and Swedish industrial purchasers prove to be more demanding, whereas the Italian and British purchasers are less so. German and Swedish suppliers have the same image of good technical quality and punctual delivery across all European markets. It appears that French industrial companies are unique in respect of one achievement – the exceptional quality of the relationships they construct over time with their French clients: 'actually, in no other country do purchasers accord such an advantage on this point to their national suppliers' (Perrin *et al.*, 1981, p. 102).

Chang and Rim (1995) have examined the rating of import sources for industrial products in South Korea. There is a clear image domination of Japanese suppliers who display the highest scores on most attributes such as technological superiority, overall quality and reliability. There is no item on which US suppliers reach the highest score, whereas Germany has a median position between Japan and the USA, being close to Japan for about half of the product attributes revolving around quality and reliability. Korean industrial purchasers rate their own national suppliers at the lowest level on every attribute except price, communication and local knowledge. Thorelli and Glowacka (1995), who examined US industrial buyers sourcing internationally, contrast the willingness of these buyers to source from industrializing (e.g. Brazil, China, Mexico, Poland) as opposed to industrialized (e.g. Japan, Sweden, Taiwan, West Germany) countries. US purchasers were proven to be more willing to source from industrialized countries, except in the case of Mexico where buyers, having had more experience with this trade partner, the rating appeared much better than for other industrializing countries. US purchasers were also more ready to buy from foreign suppliers who had established warehouses or sales offices in the United States, irrespective of the COO. The very fact of having already done business with industrial suppliers from less favourably perceived COO, such as Latin American countries, causes experienced purchasers to hold a higher image of their products and quality than that held by inexperienced industrial importers (Saghafi *et al.*, 1991).

Influence of demographic variables on consumer attitudes towards the country of origin

The degree of consumer awareness and sensitivity to the COO attribute varies depending on the following:

1. *The effect of gender*: some studies have suggested a more favourable evaluation of foreign products by women than by men (Schooler, 1971; Dornoff *et al.*, 1974; Gopalakrishna *et al.*, 1989). Men are generally more influenced by 'Buy national' campaigns (Ettenson *et al.*, 1988). Nevertheless several other studies have shown that gender is not a discriminating factor (Anderson and Cunningham, 1972; Tongberg, 1972; Graby, 1982).

2. *Age group*: generally it would seem that the readiness to purchase foreign products decreases with age (Schooler, 1971; Tongberg, 1972; Dornoff *et al.*, 1974; Graby, 1982). Dogmatism, greater nationalism and stabilized consumption habits are

probably the result of ageing, and explain the reluctance to buy foreign goods. However, inconclusive results have been reached by other researchers, who have shown that age has no influence (Johansson *et al.*, 1985; Morganosky and Lazarde, 1987; Usunier, 1994).

3. *Education and income*: generally a more favourable evaluation of foreign products is made by consumers when they have a higher level of education (Anderson and Cunningham, 1972; Dornoff *et al.*, 1974; Wang, 1978) or a higher income level (Wang, 1978), or when they have travelled abroad and are therefore more familiar with the products of these foreign countries (Graby, 1982).

Country image and product image

Martin and Eroglu (1993) developed the construct of country image by showing that it can be divided into three subdimensions: (1) political; (2) economic; and (3) technological. Shimp *et al.* (1993) derive a concept of 'country equity' by allowing people freely to express thoughts about country and products for 11 possible COOs. They discovered two dimensions, price and quality, that account for almost three-quarters of the variance, each country displaying a certain equity based on its co-ordinates on the two axes.

However, country images may become partly divorced from the image of their products. Imagine, for instance, the case of a country under a non-democratic governing regime that nevertheless produces some excellent goods which are exported to democratic countries, as is the case with China. The image of a country, in political, economic, cultural and social terms, may influence the willingness of foreign consumers to purchase that country's products independently of their perceived quality. That was the case of the international boycott of French ethnic products during the French nuclear tests in the years 1995–6. Consumers may be unwilling to purchase products originating from a country under a dictatorship or one which acts in contravention of certain internationally recognized rules (i.e. child workers), even if these products fit their needs. One may wonder also whether the overall level of industrial development influences the evaluations of a particular COO and of its products by foreign consumers.

Wang and Lamb (1983) asked 94 people, all US nationals, about their readiness to purchase products from different countries (36 in all). They also asked them to identify the political, cultural and economic environment of each country. In this way they were able to demonstrate that variables related to the sociopolitical image of a country partially explained consumers' readiness to purchase products from that country. The American consumers were more prepared to buy products from politically democratic countries such as those in Europe, Australia and New Zealand.

This is in line with Crawford and Lamb's (1981) results: they sought to determine whether purchasers of industrial products were prepared to purchase foreign products and what their preferred sources were in terms of nationality. According to them, 'willingness to buy foreign products is influenced not only by the individual country, but also by the existing levels of economic development and political freedom' (Crawford and Lamb, 1981, pp. 30–1).

A study undertaken for industrial goods from eight South American countries (Crawford, 1985) showed that American industrial purchasers preferred national sources on the basis of their political freedom and stability: at the top they put Mexico and then Brazil, and at the bottom El Salvador and Cuba. The degree of industrial development (not only based on objective data, but also as perceived by partially unin-formed consumers) has an influence on the image of products. Khanna (1986) demon-strates that among the products of four countries from Asia (India, Japan, Taiwan and South Korea), evaluated by consumers from the same four countries, the Indian prod-ucts had the poorest image in terms of quality, creativity, design and technological level. Nevertheless it remains clear that vendors located in less favourable foreign environments may be cheap and reliable suppliers, so long as they are carefully eval-uated and given a fair opportunity to perform. That is, the cost of their *learning* should be shared with their customer, and afterwards both will benefit.

How does the image of products from certain countries change over time?

Another important issue in relation to COO images is whether there are changes in these images over time and, if there are, at what rate they occur. The response to this question seems to be yes, and the rate seems to be fairly rapid. This is particularly true for products originating from Japan and the new industrial countries of Asia, such as Korea and Taiwan (Jaffé and Nebenzahl, 1989). Dornoff *et al.* (1974) observed a change in American consumers' perception of imports from Asian countries over a few years towards a more favourable attitude.

By replicating a 1967 study eight years later, Nagashima (1970, 1977) showed that Japanese businessmen's perceptions of their own products had become more favourable and that their image of the Japanese 'made in' label had significantly improved. The Japanese stopped seeing their products modestly as simply 'cheap' and 'unreliable'. Many studies confirm the dramatic improvement of the image of Japan as a COO (Kraft and Chung, 1992; Kamins and Nagashima, 1995). This improvement has been confirmed in recent times in the case of Saudi consumers, who tend to rate Japanese products as the highest with respect to central product attributes, followed by American and German products, whereas products from the United Kingdom, France and Italy tend to be perceived as of lower quality (Bhuian, 1997).

According to Darling and Kraft (1977), the image that the Finnish consumers held of Japanese products was right in the process of changing in 1977. At the beginning of the 1970s, Japanese products were seen as being of dubious quality; they were backed by rather restricted guarantees and poor after-sales service. At the end of the 1970s they were seen by Finnish consumers as having improved significantly as far as quality was concerned. 'Thus penetration into the Finnish market with an exceptional effort to win over the confidence of the consumer by extensive guarantees based on a local network of approved retailers, could prove to be a real success' (Darling and Kraft, 1977, p. 528).

There was also a very clear improvement in the acceptance of South Korean prod-ucts in the United States in the space of just over two years. Khera (1986) has demon-strated this by comparing the results of a May 1982 study (Khera *et al.*, 1983) with those of a November 1984 replication (Khera *et al.*, 1985). Whereas in the first study only one-third of consumers declared themselves satisfied with Korean products, in the second the satisfied numbered almost two-thirds (65.3 per cent). The perception of the general level of Korea's industrial development (specifically in comparison with Taiwan and Brazil) improved similarly.

Nebenzahl *et al.* (1997) have provided a conceptual framework for accounting for the dynamic aspects of COO evaluations by consumers who revise their image according to the observed performance of product from a particular COO in comparison to the performance of products from competing COOs over the same period. The length of time required for image revision depends on the efforts made by a country and its manufacturers to improve image.

Issues related to the measurement of country of origin images

Many studies (though not all) have used samples of students to represent the overall population of consumers/evaluators, interviewing them about products of different origins. It has often been claimed that using student samples may limit the external validity of these studies. Students are not representative of the whole range of consumers. Furthermore the measurement instruments, such as questionnaires, psychometric scales, and the categories of products chosen or brands mentioned create problems of cross-cultural equivalence (Bamossy and Papadopoulos, 1987; Parameswaran and Yaprak, 1987). Cross-cultural equivalence issues for the measurement of COO effects are subject to the same solutions are explained in Chapter 7.

Jaffé and Nebenzahl (1984) tested the validity and accuracy of alternative questionnaire formats with the same respondents. They tested two formats of questionnaire (Q1 and Q2), which basically contained the same retrieved information but which were presented in two different ways: the scales in Q1 were listed according to attribute and in Q2 according to country. The scores were significantly different, which tends to suggest that images of COO are therefore not completely comparable across studies, but depend on the presentation of the questionnaire. In a similar vein, Han *et al.* (1994) show that the survey mode, whether personal interview, telephone survey or self-administered questionnaire, influences the ratings of COO. Personal interviews may be susceptible to demand artefacts (the subject distorts his answer in the direction intended to fulfil the researcher's expectations), and self-administered questionnaire to haloing biases (the lack of involvement results in all responses being based on a common stereotype). Social desirability biases (the subject responds in the same way as the 'average man' would) may be more likely to occur when interviews are conducted by telephone.

Combined effect of the image of the country of origin and evaluations as to the 'true' attributes of the product

The COO is not the only criterion consumers use when evaluating foreign products (Yaprak, 1987). It is often combined with other product attributes in the minds of the consumers. Some research has attempted to measure the relative impact of the COO, with respect to intrinsic attributes such as quality, or extrinsic attributes such as price. Two studies dealt with the relative effect of price and perceived quality in interaction with the country of manufacture (Peterson and Jolibert, 1976; White and Cundiff, 1978), but neither was able to establish truly meaningful links. The COO had no significant influence on the perceived quality.

Thorelli *et al.* (1989), by studying the interaction between store image, level of guarantee and COO, concluded that the effect of the COO on the perceived quality and the general attitude of the consumer is significantly less when the product is sold in an exclusive store and has effective guarantees. This seems to concur with Reierson's conclusions (1967) that the image of a product of a specific national origin can be improved (with respect to its previous image) by association with a prestigious distributor, in this case Neiman-Marcus. For the US market Morganosky and Lazarde (1987) have investigated the link between store image and the national origin of the products they offer (imported versus 'Made in the USA'). It appears that the quality rating of department stores and fashion boutiques was slightly enhanced by their association with American-made clothing, whereas it was negatively affected when their image was associated with that of foreign-made clothing. The quality image of discount stores was significantly improved when associated with American-made clothing, but not significantly hurt by association with foreign-made garments.

Erickson *et al.* (1984) and Johansson *et al.* (1985) introduce more complex consumer evaluation models, using the country of manufacture as an informative cue. They introduced other choice attributes and examined whether the true effects of the COO attribute were operating on attitudes or on beliefs. Consumer beliefs are located at a much deeper level in consumers' minds than attitudes, and are far more remote from actual buying behaviour. According to Erickson *et al.* (1984), the COO effect has an influence on the formation of beliefs, but not directly on attitudes towards the product (cars, in this case). The COO cue contributed just as much as the 'true' attributes themselves (objective ones such as price or gas mileage) to the formation of beliefs. Beliefs in turn have an influence on attitudes.

How the country of manufacture behaves on a cognitive level: As a halo effect or as (summary) global evaluation effect

Johansson *et al.* (1985) hypothesize that the COO cue works as a 'halo effect' when it influences consumer beliefs and attitudes. Johansson (1989) suggests two different interpretations of the cognitive effect of the COO:

1. Consumers use the COO in order to simplify the decision-making process. Consumers use it as a summary criterion, which provides them with a 'ready-made' global evaluation. It facilitates their choice, particularly when time is limited.

2. Consumers use the COO as a salient choice attribute when they have feelings towards and knowledge of a particular country.

According to Johansson, increased familiarity with a product category reinforces the use of the COO as a choice attribute, contrary to what had been previously claimed. Han (1990) has tested the 'halo effect', which affects consumers beliefs and (only indirectly) their evaluations, against the 'summary effect', where the COO cue directly influences consumers, in the form of a global evaluation. By testing these two different models on two products (television sets and cars), he has shown that the 'halo effect' is used more when consumers are unfamiliar with the product category, whereas the 'summary effect' is used once they have achieved familiarity.

Conclusion

Taken together, the results of COO research suggest some major guidelines which should be followed when trying to construct a 'national image' strategy for a country's products:

1. Consumers from developed countries have a preference for their domestic products, but campaigns in favour of buying national goods do not reinforce this preference (see section 5.5).

2. Consumers do not use the COO as an isolated choice attribute but within the overall purchasing context (product category, perceived risk, knowledge of the brand, knowledge of and beliefs about the manufacturing country, etc.). Furthermore, COO is used as an evaluation criterion in conjunction with actual attributes. Attempts to dissociate the image from the reality are therefore unlikely to be successful. There is no advantage to be gained from selling poor-quality products in combination with a good 'made in' label. Such choices could be very deceptive for consumers.

3. Images change fairly quickly over time. This is probably not the result of country or product image campaigns but rather because products of a particular national origin improve in quality, the industrial expertise of local producers has increased and guarantees offered to consumers are more extensive.

10.3   NATIONAL, INTERNATIONAL AND GLOBAL BRANDS

The majority of brands were originally conceived on a national level. Even among American brands, only a very limited number have achieved international recognition. In an empirical survey of US brands as global brands, Rosen *et al.* (1989) studied 650 US brands and their international scope (in how many countries, the age of the brand, etc.) and their general conclusion is that 'despite all the talk about the internationalisation of marketing efforts, the international diffusion of US brands is actually rather limited and . . . that most US brands are not marketed abroad' (p. 17). Most brands are related to a specific linguistic context. Their evocative power is dependent on the language of the country and markets where they were originally launched. In Europe, at least 99 per cent of all brands are still national, if not purely local, in their appeal (Wilsher, 1992).[1] However, certain brands were launched right from the start for their capacity to convey meaning internationally. The oil-refining and distribution brand name ELF was created at the time of the merger of the petroleum groups ERAP and SNPA. Similarly, the Toyota name was chosen at the beginning of the 1960s by the Japanese car manufacturer which previously had a completely different name deemed unsuitable for foreign markets; with increasing export sales, it was necessary to have a name suitable for international markets and Toyota, with its three syllables which can be pronounced in any language, was the name finally selected.

International companies face three situations in terms of international brand names:

1. The *ex nihilo* creation of a brand name, especially for new products with high global potential. The name must be pronounced and understood in a similar way across diverse linguistic and cultural contexts.

2. The management of a large brand portfolio resulting from both external growth by acquisitions of local players and multiple layers of branding (e.g. corporate names, category brands, product names). Such a brand portfolio is increasingly being managed by means of simplification, in order to avoid spreading brand advertising budgets too thinly over large a number of names; few of these names would become transnational brands. The appropriate course of action is then to nominate the best applicants in translinguistic terms, taking into account local brand equity and the attachment of both local consumers and local marketing teams to brands – which often have a rich history.

3. Assessment of the potential for an international extension of regional brands developed by a subsidiary based in the lead country for a region.

Transposition of a national brand name to an international level

Often the brand name of products is the name of the company which manufactures them. It is closely associated with the history of the company. Consequently, there is no question in the minds of consumers as to whether this brand name is a good one. Since the brand name is historically related to the founders of the company, symbolically it would be difficult to change it. Such companies as Procter & Gamble, a name which is difficult to pronounce in many languages, have followed a twofold brand strategy. Product brand names, such as Ivory, Camay, Pampers, Vizir and Tide, have been promoted almost independently from the Procter & Gamble company name (look at the respective sizes of the names on the packaging) and the Procter & Gamble name has been colloquially simplified so that it can be more easily memorized and verbalized, either to simply Procter or to P & G.

An example of lack of adaptation is offered by the leading French company for iron and steel and heavy mechanical equipment during the 1970s and 1980s, Creusot-Loire. It branded and sold its products under the company's name in many countries in the world, including the United States. Unfortunately American customers found this name difficult to pronounce, for the following reasons:

1. The hard 'CR' sound hardly exists in English.

2. 'EU' is a typically French diphthong, unpronounceable for Americans.

3. 'S' must be pronounced 'Z' because it is located between two vowels (French rule!).

4. 'O' is a very open sound.

5. 'T' is, here, a mute consonant and must therefore be ignored in pronunciation.

6. 'OI': once again a typically French diphthong (unknown in English).

7. 'R' is a hard 'r', almost unused in English.

8. 'E' is, at the end of the word, a mute vowel, and therefore must be ignored in pronunciation.

Naturally such a brand name is difficult to memorize for most customers in many countries. Moreover, such difficult brand names can be a serious obstacle to clear communication between buyer and seller; they may create confusion when discussing business on the phone. It is therefore necessary to be prepared to carry out the necessary modification.

As advocated by Onkvisit and Shaw (1989), standardized international branding offers more market efficiency, by reducing advertising and inventory costs and providing convenient identification for people travelling internationally. However, the diversity of national regulations and the rarity of brands with similar spellings in most national markets make it difficult to register a standardized brand across a large number of countries.

For the transposition of a brand name originally created for a specific national context, simple translation is never used because it would result in disasters in relation to meaning,[2] scattered brand image, and inability to create international brand recognition. *Transliteration* attempts to reconstitute in the target language the connotative meaning that exists in the source language (i.e. the language of the country of origin of the brand). In this way the American hair care product *Silkience* (Gillette) is sold under the same brand name in Germany, under the brand name *Soyance* in France and under the brand name *Sientel* in Italy (Czinkota and Ronkainen, 1990).

The best type of brand is the *transparent* brand, such as Sony, which is suitable everywhere. The name Sony arose from a real 'shooting down' of the company name by the brand name of its products (Yoshimori, 1989). The original name of the firm (Tokyo Tsuhin Kogyo – Tokyo Industrial Telecommunication Company) was changed to Sony as soon as the brand name of its products proved to be successful.

Linguistic aspects of the brand

Brands are signs based on sounds, written signs (letters or pictographs) and visual elements (logotype, brand design). The linguistic content of a brand name has an influence on its verbal, auditory and intellectual meaning, and its interpretation by consumers. The brand name is often associated with a copyrighted design. Visual elements comprise also how a brand is written (alphabet, syllabary, ideographs). Table 10.2 shows which branch of linguistics should be used to appreciate how the sound, spelling and design of a brand name travels from a source to a target linguistic context.[3] A brand name should generally be relatively easy to pronounce. A simple rule is that the brand name should not exceed three syllables, each composed of one consonant and one vowel. Chinese mostly has such simple successions of one consonant and one or two vowels (Huang and Chan, 1997), whereas German and Dutch often have many successive consonants (up to seven in a row in German) and French sometimes has long strings of vowels.

When considering the phonological aspects of an international brand, one should check that the sound pattern corresponds to phonemes that are pronounced in all major languages (phonetics) and that it does not use unique sound patterns of the source language (phonemics). Hewlett-Packard, for instance, is far from perfect and is better when shortened to HP. The English 'th' or the French nasalized triphthong 'oin' (don't try it!) are among such difficult combinations. Japanese, on the other hand, is a formidable language for international brands because it is exclusively composed of phonemes which are recognized by virtually all languages in the world, and it eschews successive consonants.[4] Denotative meaning, such as that of *Milka* chocolate which

TABLE 10.2   Brand cues and meaning transfer

Brand cue	Element of meaning		Branch of linguistics concerned
Sound		L	
– Assemblage (vowels and	⇨ Pure sound	I	Phonology
consonants)	⇨ Denotative meaning	N	(phonemics/
	⇨ Connotative meaning	G	phonetics)
– Tonality		U	Etymology
		I	Semantics/
		S	Rhetoric
Written name		T	
– Alphabetic letters ⇨ sounds	Sounds ⇨ words ⇨ ideas	I	Semantics
– Pictographic writing	Pictograph design ⇨ ideas	C	Semiology
	Pictograph design ⇨ symbols		
Design		F	
– Assemblage of words (brands and	– Descriptive	I	Grammar
slogans)	– Suggestive	L	Rhetoric
– Icons (causal and analogous sign)	– Humorous	T	Semantics
– Symbols (untraceable linkage)	– Claim supportive	E	Semiology
	– Oneiric	R	
	– Ethnic		

directly relates to milk, is lost in most other languages; understanding of this meaning is limited to Anglo-Saxon and Germanic languages which use this root (etymology) and to speakers of English as a second language. Similarly, connotative meaning is generally lost when a product crosses borders: the detergent *Tide* was once sold in France (the name being pronounced *teed*) but nobody had the slightest knowledge of the idea of powerful tidal waves washing clothes which was evoked by the brand in English-speaking markets.

Written brand names are generally based on the alphabet, that is, people first read sounds, then decode words and finish with ideas. A third of the consumers in the world use ideographic writing systems and they go directly from pictographs to ideas. Sounds for a definite written item vary: people in various parts of China and Japan use similar ideographs which they recognize as having the same meaning but they pronounce them quite differently.[5] However, even with the Roman alphabet, the use of identical letters may result in a brand sounding different, according to the linguistic context: the Danone brand of yoghurt is spelled Dannon in the United States because consistency of pronunciation is preferred to consistency of spelling (Colombat, 1997). Given the wide differences in tonicity across languages, a brand such as Coca-Cola cannot be considered global, in so far as sound patterns are concerned: when I order a Coke in Brazil in my flat French accent (there is very little tonicity in French) nobody understands and I am asked to say it again.

It is not only the purely linguistic content of a brand name that has an influence on its verbal, auditory and intellectual meaning. The design of a brand name also has extreme importance: Whiskas (a Mars brand) has a translinguistic iconic value because it uses a cat's head to suggest its favourite user; but the colours are probably interpreted differently across cultures. Brand names are usually associated with a copyright design and the graphic composition of a logo conveys as much meaning as the letters of the brand name. Accordingly Cabat (1989, p. 344) emphasizes that the IBM trade mark is inseparable from its graphics in its evocative ability to communicate with the consumer:

> The letters of the IBM logo are actually obtained by the superimposition of characters known as 'Mecanes' and of a 'blind' (alternate slats of coloured bands). The blind is in this case the informative image of the letters IBM, their morphological determinant . . . It thereby becomes the sign of computer language, binary-based. The 'Mecanes' are typesetting characters whose square serif evokes industrial production and rooting in the mechanical world.

The imagery of the IBM brand logo is translinguistic, and therefore offers a truly international ability to convey meaning. The link between brand and drawing is an intimate one. How, for instance, is the Coca-Cola brand name stored in consumers' minds? As eight letters, as the traditional design of the Coca-Cola words, of the Coke bottle, or as a combination of them? Trade-mark legislation around the world varies in this respect. In some countries trade marks can only be composed of alphabetic letters and their design must be separately registered under the design and pattern laws if they are to be effectively protected; in the United States a trade mark may be bereft of any linguistic content and can be registered solely under the trade-mark laws. There is no systematic need, in the United States and many other countries, for additional registration of a trade marks design.

Linguistic devices for brand names

Table 10.3 shows various linguistic devices that can be used in creating brand names. Whether by accident or design, advertisers and marketers strive to give some punch and evocative capacity to their brand names. Of course this is done, as far as possible, in line with the symbolic connotations that they intend to communicate in relation to product attributes and, inevitably, it is done in a particular source language. There are four main categories of linguistic device: phonetic devices (sound, perceived by the ears), orthographic devices (relating to writing, perceived by the eyes), morphological devices (adding morphemes to the brand-name root) and semantic devices (the figure produces meaning, perceived through culture-based interpretations).

The linguistic devices set out in Table 10.3 help one to understand what constitutes the pure linguistic capacity of a brand, independently of the established goodwill (brand recognition may be high for linguistically unadapted but long-standing brand names). The issue for brand marketers is whether these advantages are transposable into other linguistic contexts. The alliteration of Coca-Cola is, but the composition of the words Janitor-in-a-Drum or even the juxtaposition of opposites (Easy-Off) are not. This is because Coca-Cola does not require a basic comprehension of the words that make up the brand name. Where understanding of complex linguistic figures is

TABLE 10.3   Linguistic characteristics of brands

Characteristics	Definitions and/or examples
I Phonetic devices	
1. Alliteration	Consonant repetition (**Co**ca-**C**ola, **Co**coon)
2. Assonance	Vowel repetition (K**a**l K**a**n, V**i**z**i**r, **O**m**o**)
3. Consonance	Consonant repetition with intervening vowel changes (**W**eight **Wat**chers, Tic Tac)
4. Masculine rhyme	Rhyme with end of syllable stress (Max Pax)
5. Feminine rhyme	Unaccented syllable followed by accented syllable (A**meri**can **Air**lines)
6. Weak/imperfect/ slant rhyme	Vowels differ or consonants similar, not identical (Bl**ack** & De**ck**er)
7. Onomatopoeia	Use of syllable phonetics to resemble the object itself (Wisk, Cif, Wizzard)
8. Clipping	Product names shortened (*Chevy* for a Chevrolet, *Deuche* for a Citroen Deux Chevaux, *Rabbit* for a Volkswagen)
9. Blending	Morphemic combination, usually with elision (Aspergum, Duracell)
10. Initial plosives[a]	/b/, /c-hard/, /d/, /g-hard/, /k/, /q/, /t/, (Bic, Dash, Pliz, Pim's)
II Orthographic devices	
1. Unusual or incorrect spellings	Kool-Aid, Decap'Four
2. Abbreviations	7-Up for Seven-Up
3. Acronyms	Amoco, Amro, DB, Cofinoga, Lu, BSN
III Morphological devices	
1. Affixation	Jell-O, Tipp-Ex
2. Compounding	Janitor-in-a-Drum, Vache-qui-rit
IV Semantic devices	
1. Metaphor	Representing something as if it were something else (Arrid); simile was included with metaphor when a name described a likeness and not an equality (Aqua-Fresh, Longeurs et Pointes, Head and Shoulders, Tendres Promesses)
2. Metonymy	Application of one object or quality for another (Midas, Ajax, Uncle Ben's, Bounty)
3. Synecdoche	Substitution of a part for the whole (Red Lobster)
4. Personification/ pathetic fallacy	Humanizing the non-human or ascription of human emotions to the inanimate (Betty Crocker, Clio, Kinder)
5. Oxymoron	Conjunction of opposites (Easy-Off, Crème de peinture)
6. Paranomasia	Pun and word plays (Hawaiian Punch, Raid – insecticide, Fédor – orange juice)
7. Semantic appositeness	Fit of name with object (Bufferin, Nutella)

(Source: Adapted from Vanden Bergh *et al.*, 1987. Reproduced with the kind permission of the publisher.)

[a]An initial is said to be plosive if, to produce this sound, one needs first to stop the flow of air completely, then audibly release the air previously compressed.

required, brand names are difficult to translate and, more generally, to transpose. As a rule, the linguistic devices in categories I and II are the more 'translinguistic'. A good number of the devices in category IV are not at all translinguistic, especially nos 1, 4, 5, 6 and 7.

Semantic issues: Untranslated versus unintended meaning

As shown above, meaning can be lost when a brand crosses borders. Nestlé (*Nestele*: little nest in the Alemanic dialects of the southern German-speaking area) is lost in most of the world's languages and people probably cannot understand why the logo presents a bird in a nest. Beiersdorff's 'Uhu' brand for glue sticks is based on the German name for eagle owl. Most intended meaning does not extend much beyond the source language area. It is, however, not a major problem if consumers in other linguistic areas memorize the sound of brand names easily and invest them with new, positive meanings.

Unintended negative meaning is the most dangerous. The brand name should not have an unfortunate meaning in a different linguistic/cultural context. However, checking the translinguistic capacity of a brand name is by no means universal practice. There is no shortage of examples: the German hair spray Caby-Net launched on the French market (*cabinet* is a toilet in French); the Japanese gun, Miroku, the name of which has several meanings including 'look at your arse' in French, although ultimately the name was not changed. The examples of certain American cars in South American markets are also famous. The Chevrolet (Chevy) Nova (the intended meaning was 'new') translates into Spanish as 'does not work', which gave a poor image of the car's reliability. The American Motors Matador meant 'killer' in Spanish, in as far as it relates to the man who kills the bull in traditional Spanish *corridas*. Kellogg's renamed its *Frosted Flakes* as *Sucrilhos* for Brazil, and its *Cocoa Krispies* as *Crokinhos*; similarly it had to change its *Bran Buds* brand name in Sweden, so that Swedish people did not read that they were to be served 'grilled farmer' in their breakfast bowls (Giordan, 1988). The type of research that must be carried out is straightforward: it is necessary to interview a group of consumers from the target country about the perceptual effects of the intended names.

The case of Asian ideographic writing systems

We have stayed up to now within the limited framework of languages based on the Roman alphabet where letters correspond to sounds and sounds to ideas. Global brands wanting to reach the Chinese market face a difficult task. Even Coca-Cola is not known exactly by this name in China since the original name would have a negative connotation; Coca-Cola is transliterated as 'kekou kele' (in terms of approximate sound equivalence) and conveys the meaning of 'tasty and enjoyable/happy' (Wilke, 1994). In fact, Chinese characters are pronounced differently according to the dialect spoken (Mandarin, Cantonese, Hokkien, etc.), and there is a large number of homonyms (words written differently but with identical pronunciation). Thus there are many possibilities for the transposition of Roman-letter brand names into Chinese characters.

In East Asia and especially in China, calligraphy and meaning become much more important than in standard western branding. A brand name must have a positive connotation which is a combination of: (1) characters with favourable sounds, which can be pronounced in about the same way in as many regions as possible, while avoiding the pitfalls due to tonality; (2) characters which convey favourable meaning, if possible related to the brand's advertised qualities; (3) a balance between *yin* (even number of strokes) and *yang* characters (odd number of strokes); (4) a favourable content in terms of lucky numbers such as 8; (5) suitable calligraphy for the brand; the calligraphy must convey certain visual signs which fit with the brand imagery, such as in the case of the Volkswagen 'Cheep': a character was used that evoked an imaginary slope that the jeep had to climb (Schmitt and Pan, 1994). On the basis of the linguistic differences between Chinese and English, Pan and Schmitt (1995) show that spelling (i.e. characters) has more weight in forming brand attitudes among Chinese consumers whereas sound is more important for American people. People from both countries form strong associative links with the brand, but the linkage seems to be based more on auditory experience for the Americans and on visual experience for the Chinese.

Consequently, Pepsi-Cola is transposed into Chinese characters meaning 'hundred happy things' and Mercedes-Benz becomes 'Benchi', with two characters meaning 'striving forward fast'. However, such transposition is not possible for all brands: in some cases, when the transposition of sounds is preferred over the transposition of meaning, that is, when it is difficult to find a chain of characters that transliterate both sound and meaning (not to mention calligraphic elements), the brand name may sound very similar to the sound of the Western version, such as 'nifeya' for Nivea, but the meaning level may be very poor – in the latter case it is an assemblage of characters meaning 'girl-not/Africa-second rank/Asia' (Wilke, 1994).

In Japan the issue is both less and more complicated since the Japanese are familiar with the western alphabet (*romaji*) but they use also the Chinese characters (*Kanji*), and two syllabaries, the *hiragana* for Japanese words and the *katakana* for foreign loanwords (which uses the same syllables as the *hiragana*, but with a slightly different calligraphic style that signals the foreign origin). These alternative writing systems carry different associative meanings which must be carefully monitored in order to convey appropriate subliminal messages: (1) as to the origin of the product: *kanji* and *hiragana* will look more Japanese while *romaji* and *katakana* signal foreignness; (2) as to the product category: high-tech products will best be written in *katakana* which connote modernity, whereas traditional products are best served by *Kanji*; (3) as to the consumer universe implied by the writing style: *hiragana* have a feminine image and are used frequently for beauty products and cosmetics (Schmitt and Pan, 1994).

Functions of the brand according to national contexts

The trade name has a number of functions for the consumer such as *identity* (it guides consumers when making their choice), *practicality* (it works as a summary of information about product characteristics), *guarantee* ('signature of the manufacturer'), *personalization* (the brand name allows consumers to express their individuality through their purchases) and an *entertainment* function because the brand allows the exercise of free choice and enables consumers to satisfy their needs for freshness, arousal, and surprise (Lambin, 1989). For the producer, the brand fulfils two essential functions: the positioning within the competitive scene and the *capitalization* of image and advertising expenditure over the long term.

These functions are very differently valued across different countries, to the extent that some functions of the brand can be almost non-existent in certain national contexts. Accordingly, Contensou (1989) notes that in France there is a certain social mistrust of brands, especially by public authorities: they supposedly increase prices, constituting entry barriers to possible competitors and thereby limiting competition. Furthermore, being set up on the basis of large cumulative advertising expenditure, they are said to increase the price of the product to the detriment of the consumer. Contensou shows that in fact these fears are groundless and further points out that (1989, p. 246) 'inflationary tendencies have no connection to brand development and the multiplication of products sold under brand names'. Kapferer (1989), taking the same defensive attitude towards brand names, has shown that they support the actual intentions of the manufacturers, their achievements to the benefit of consumers and that without effective attempts to foster product quality, brand images cannot be sustained. In contrast to France, Japan seems to be a country where the brand is very highly valued. Yoshimori (1989, pp. 277–8) explains this:

In feudal Japan, the brand was not distinct from the name of the ancestral house itself. This name had great importance, to the extent that everything was done to protect its good image, and above all to perpetuate it. Anyone who tarnished that reputation even through mere carelessness was obliged to rectify the damage through dying . . . [Yoshimori then give examples of Japanese executives who have recently committed suicide because they believed that through their actions or negligence they had tarnished the reputation of their company] . . . a trading company, or any such firm, was not merely an economic entity; it also constituted a religious community which transcended the physical life of the family that controlled it. Ancestors occupied an almost divine place: it was therefore believed that the preservation and advancement of *kamei*, the name of the ancestral house, was an almost religious obligation since it (*kamei*) was the concrete translation of the presence of ancestors.

The brand in Japan is a real figurehead of competitive struggle. Abbeglen and Stalk (1986) show how, during the 1950s, the Honda brand name destroyed the Tohatsu brand (which today is completely unknown). They also describe in great detail the episodes in the Homeric quarrel between Honda and Yamaha at the start of the 1980s, which ended with a victory for Honda. In the United States, as in Japan, brands are central to competition. Brand marketing occupies a stable position in the strategies of US companies, but also one which is constantly changing, as are market shares. The vigour of the brand can only be built on 'tidal waves' of sales promotion and advertising as well as on consistent efforts towards improvement of product quality. Dupuy and Thoenig (1989) compared brand status in the United States, France and Japan. They noted that brands in France have a much weaker status than in Japan and the United States, where they have even stronger status.

When they refer to brands' 'weak status', they mean that brands are the stakes in an unstable and conflicting appropriation process conducted by economic agents. Large-scale retailers in France (hypermarkets) have created their own private labels over the last twenty years (*produits libres*). Distributors' brands do not need any product-related advertising expenditure and tend to compete with manufacturers' brands. Therefore brand competition between distributors and manufacturers constitutes a major stake at the retail level.

Differences in national distribution systems explain to a large extent the degree of brand-related competition. In Japan, the *Keiretsu* distribution system (see section 12.1) enables producers to control distribution channels and therefore to direct the brand name principally towards the relationship with the consumer. In France, where large-scale distribution is involved in conflicts with producers, the channels develop their own brands. This leads to an inflation of distributors' brands and private labels which compete against established manufacturers' brands.

International and global brands

International brands share a common trait of long-term orientation. The main objective of the brand is gradually to establish brand goodwill through consumer brand awareness and recognition. When products share very similar attributes and performance, a well-known brand may have the edge by virtue of its reputation and the consumer loyalty it has created. Accordingly, Procter & Gamble has retained brands for more than a century: Ivory soap, for example, is more than a hundred years old. Camay soap is claimed to be nearly seventy years old (the brand name that is, not the formula of the product, which has been regularly updated). International brands are therefore usually names whose public recognition has been based on *considerable cumulative advertising expenditure*. They are often supported by the history of a prestigious company (for cars, Mercedes, Jaguar, Ferrari, Cadillac, etc.). This brand goodwill was not 'built in a day'. These world-famous brands are obviously exceptions since, cognitively, there can only be a limited number of brands known by consumers in several countries throughout the world simultaneously (a few dozen, perhaps one or two hundred at most).

Many of these international brands have a *basic credibility which is based on a national image* (Shalofsky, 1987). Accordingly, Coca-Cola is a typical American drink; Marlboro (cigarettes) is in fact an American brand because of the Marlboro cowboy. Chanel No. 5 is based on the image of French *luxe* and *haute couture*, conveyed by the character of Gabrielle Chanel (Coco). Buitoni is understood as Italian pasta and Johnny Walker is a synonym for whisky from Scotland. Furthermore, as Clark (1987) argues, in each country, consumers 'repaint' the supposed international brand image with their own local images.

As noted in the introduction to this chapter, the interplay between brands and national images is a game of complex meanings (Table 10.1): one needs to be cautious before saying that a brand is universal. Coca-Cola's name is adapted in Chinese to avoid negative connotations. Low-calorie sugar-free Coke is called Diet Coke in the United States as well as in many other countries, but in some countries it is called Coca Light because the word *diète* conjures up the image of a strict diet of bread and water. Brand images combine with the product's origin and the manufacturer's name which is also a brand. A name like Brother offers a fairly good combination of interpretive meanings because the Brother name diffuses an English/international image which partially hides the Japanese origin of the manufacturer. Brother manufactures electronic typewriters and items with no 'ethnic' relation to a specific country. Finally, the concept of brotherhood supports the image of reliability, faithfulness and loyalty of an object with which people may work closely.

A basic condition for belonging to the very narrow club of global brands is to have built brand equity over a number of years by considerable advertising spending based on consistent core themes (consistent both over time and across countries). The value of a brand like Marlboro is estimated at \$31 billion, that of Coca-Cola at \$24 billion, and that of Kodak at \$13 billion (Kotler and Dubois, 1994). Advertising remains the key investment for developing brand awareness, although advertising spending has been claimed not to be an absolute necessity for creating brand equity, with such examples as the Body Shop or Haågen Dazs having developed their brands through events, sponsoring and retail shops (Joachimsthaler and Aaker, 1997). The second condition is that the brand's image must have been carefully monitored over time. This requires considerable sophistication in the management of meaning. Macrae (1991) explains that Coca-Cola, a world-class brand that celebrated its hundredth anniversary in 1986, had to be carefully monitored. It used the favourable image of American soldiers just after the Second World War but avoided having the brand's image damaged by the Vietnam war by launching, in 1971, the 'Hill top' advertising campaign world-wide. Young people of all nations and races, dressed in national costumes, were grouped together on a hillside and sang a song emphasizing peace and harmony between different peoples; the song became a hit at record stores.

Although some people try to defend the concept (Peebles, 1989), global brands are a somewhat blurred concept and probably even a deceptive one. As was pointed out in Chapter 5, global brands may only be portfolios of basically localized marketing assets (consumer franchise and goodwill based on images which are in fact heterogeneous), a mere collection of local brands, federated under a *lexically equivalent single name*. The brand name may not even be pronounced similarly in different linguistic areas, a factor which can be critical for radio advertising, for example.

The management of global brands is complex. In his overview of the topic, Peebles (1989, p. 76) notes the view of Marcio Moreira, New Products Director for McCann Erickson Worldwide, according to whom an advertiser should not pursue a global strategy to save money. The global brand, like the global campaign, requires a large amount of creative time and investment. A brand is a *sensitive asset of symbols*, suggested and maintained by diversified marketing communications: sponsoring, advertising, communication, public relations, communication through the product itself or even the style of outlets. This mix of marketing communications must be carefully managed, so that the public never feels betrayed in those beliefs that have been invested in the brand. Alain Etchegoyen (1990, p. 55, my emphasis) describes in the following way the brand image of Louis Vuitton:

> There is no mythology without gods or demi-gods. That is why one must not expect gods to collapse into the melting pot of the market. Some products have to keep at a distance so that other products appear to come from *somewhere else. The brand can only remain influential at the expense of maintaining a sacred fire.* The imaginary Eden of carefully tended [brand] images will not withstand the boorish hell of bar codes [products].

Furthermore, the complexity of trade-mark law must be considered on an international level. Although there are several international conventions, copyright and trade-mark regulations are still essentially based on national decrees. The 'Paris Union', an agreement which has been revised several times (the last in 1967 in Stockholm), provides that after a preliminary registration within a country of the Union, the beneficiaries have six months in which to apply for full registration. But full registrations are usually done by country, in accordance with locally prevailing regulations.[6]

The World Industrial Property Organization (WIPO), located in Geneva, centralizes the registration formalities for the more than twenty countries that have signed the Madrid Agreement. This does not constitute neglect of the principle of registration, but a simplification of the procedure across a limited number of countries. The EC directive on the harmonization of existing national legislation on trade marks in Europe was adopted in 1989 and was implemented in 1993. It was completed by the regulation on European trade marks which was adopted by the Council of the EU on 20 December 1993; implementation began on 15 March 1994. It permits the registration of trade marks by means of a new procedure and guarantees rights throughout the territory of the Union. The European office for trade marks is located in Alicante (Spain). The single application procedure will make it easier to register a community trade mark but will not reduce the costs of filing the trade mark or of searching for existing similar trade marks in the various countries of the EU.

In short, the costs and the legal complexity of managing a global brand remain extremely high. When one is starting from scratch, the creation of an international brand is an undertaking that should be considered as a long-term target. In this respect Yoshimori (1989, p. 279) quotes the reply of Sonys chairman, Akio Morita, in 1955 to an American client who was requesting Sony to manufacture for him as a subcontractor. Morita refused to manufacture 100,000 transistor radios in original equipment manufacturing and, allegedly, said:

Fifty years ago your brand name was probably as unknown as ours is today . . . Today I decide the first stage for the next fifty years of my company. In fifty years I can promise that our name [Sony] will be just as famous as your company's is today.

QUESTIONS

1. Discuss the international transferability of the following assemblages (product, company, country of manufacture, brand name).

Generic product	Company name	Brand name	Made in
Pizza	Dr Oetker	Pizza Rustica	Germany
Computer chip	Intel	Pentium	United States
Drilling tool	Bosch	Fuchsschwanz	Spain
Car	Daewoo	Daewoo/Nexia	South Korea
Tomato sauce	Mars	Dolmio	The Netherlands
Insecticide	Bayer	Baygon	Germany

2. A very large German food company, Dr Oetker, still sells its products in France under the name *Ancel* (the brand name of a French company taken over many years ago). Why?

3. Discuss the relationship between a country's image (through its people, its history, its political and social situation, etc.) and the image of products known to be made in this country.

4. Discuss the possible international extension of the following company and/or brand names:
    *   *Müller* (German yoghurts)
    *   *Barilla* (Italian pastas and cookies)
    *   *Procter & Gamble*
    *   *Teysseire* (French syrups)
    *   *Kuoni* (a Swiss tour operator)
    *   *Schimmelpenninck* (Dutch cigars and cigarillos)
    *   *Ishikawajima Harima Heavy Industries* (a Japanese industrial equipment company)
    *   *Roi des Montagnes* (French dried mushrooms)
    *   *Hewlett-Packard*
    *   *Douwe-Egberts* (a large Dutch food and tobacco company)
    *   *Club Méditerranée* (a French tour operator)

5. Given the increasing importance of China as a consumer market, Nestlé has decided to stop using the category brand name for milk-based products it has used world-wide, Chambourcy, a brand with great recognition in Europe and Latin America. The name was deemed too difficult to transfer in the Chinese linguistic context. Furthermore, Nestlé maintained advertising spending at three levels (corporate name, category name and product name) and decided to use the Nestlé name directly for all its milk-based products in addition to a brand name for the particular product in some cases. Discuss the marketing and management implications of such a decision.

APPENDIX 10: TEACHING MATERIALS

A10.1   Exercise: Interpreting symbolic attributes

For the following products, you are given possible physical attributes; try to imagine how they could be diversely interpreted at a symbolic level, in different cultures (you do not need to relate precisely a definite interpretation to a particular culture, but simply to emphasize probable divergence of interpretation across cultures in general).

*   A car/colour black
*   Orange juice/thick (with pulp)
*   Cheese/with traces of blue (*Penicillium glaucum*)
*   Beer/frothy
*   Orange juice/colour deep orange
*   Car/automatic gear-box
*   Apple juice/vitamins added

- Refrigerator/ice-cube distributor
- Cheese/packed in wooden case
- Car/diesel engine

For further guidance, see Zeithaml (1988), and also Solomon (1994, pp. 67–73).

A10.2   Case: Soshi Sumsin Ltd

Sammy Soshi's first assignment for his new job with Soshi Sumshin Ltd was to recom-mend a new name for the firm's line of electronic products. Sammy had completed his MBA at Emory University in May 1990 and had returned to Seoul, Korea, to work in his father's firm. Soshi Sumsin manufactured a line of electronic products, which included VCRs, stereos and televisions. The senior Mr Soshi got involved in electron-ics manufacturing when he agreed in 1980 to manufacture television components for an American manufacturer. Eventually, he was producing a full line of television sets, as well as VCRs and stereo equipment for three American firms. In addition, since 1987, he had been marketing his own line of products in the Korean market under the Sumsin brand name.

Mr Soshi felt that his firm was now ready, both in terms of manufacturing know-how and capital, to enter international markets under his own brand name. The American market was chosen as the first target because of its size and buying power, and an introduction date of April 1991 had been tentatively set. Having little famil-iarity with the American market, Mr Soshi was relying heavily on his son, Sammy, to help with marketing decisions.

The first problem to which Sammy addressed himself was the selection of a brand name for the line. His father had planned to use the Sumsin name in the American market. Sammy pointed out that a failure to give careful consideration to the effect of a brand name in a different culture could cause major marketing difficulties later. He cited the experience of Tatung as a case in point. Tatung was a Taiwanese maker of televisions, fans and computer terminals. When the company entered the American market it did not even consider changing its brand name. The Tatung company had a favourable connotation in Chinese and was known in the company's oriental markets. However, in the United States, not only was the name meaningless, but it was difficult to know how to pronounce it.

Because of these difficulties, Tatung's American advertising agency finally decided to emphasize the strangeness of the name, and it launched a campaign based on a play on words which might help customers to pronounce Tatung. Each ad carried the query, 'Cat Got Your Tatung?' Sammy believed that a lot of effort that should have been placed on the product itself had been expended to overcome a bad trade name.

Sammy cited a second example of problems resulting from a poorly chosen brand name. Another Taiwanese company, Kunnan Lo, introduced its own brand of tennis rackets in the American market in 1982. Recognizing that their own name would pres-ent problems in the American market, they decided to select an American name. Ultimately, they decided on the name Kennedy; it was quite similar to their company name, and it was certainly familiar in the United States. However, after initial promotional efforts, it quickly became apparent that Kennedy was not a neutral name. Many tennis players were Republicans, and for them the Kennedy name had negative connotations. As a result, the name was changed to Kennex, a neutral, artificial word that was still similar to the company name. However, Kennex also quickly proved to be unsatisfactory, because of some confusion with the name Kleenex. To eliminate this confusion, the name was finally changed to Pro-Kennex, which provided both a tennis tie-in and retention of a root similar to Kunnan Lo. The waste of resources in the series of name changes would have been better avoided.

Determined to avoid the mistakes of these other companies entering the American market, Sammy Soshi carefully evaluated the alternatives available to his company. The first was his fathers preference – to use a company family name. However, Sumsin was somewhat difficult for English-speaking people to pronounce and seemed meaningless and foreign. Soshi was equally unfamiliar and meaningless, but he was also afraid that Americans would confuse it with the Japanese raw fish, *sushi*.

A second alternative was to acquire ownership of an existing American brand name, preferably one with market recognition. After considerable research, he chose the name Monarch. The Monarch company had started manufacturing radios in Chicago in 1932 and Monarch radios had been nationally known in the 1940s. The company was badly hurt by television in the 1950s, which reduced the size of the radio market appreciably. The company was finally wiped out by the invasion of inexpensive transistor radios from Asia in the 1960s. The company filed for bankruptcy in 1972. Sammy found that he could buy the rights to the Monarch name for $50,000. The name was tied in with electronics products in the public's mind, but he wondered how many people still remembered or recognized the Monarch name. He also wondered whether this recognition might be more negative than positive because of the company's failure in the market.

A third alternative would be to select a new name and build market recognition through promotion. Such a name would need to be politically and socially neutral in the American market and ultimately in other foreign markets. It should be easy to pronounce and remember and have neutral meaning or favourable meaning to the public. The possibilities might be considered.

The first was Proteus, the name of an ancient Greek sea god. This name would be easy to pronounce in most European languages, but was almost too neutral to help sell the product. The other alternative was Blue Streak, again, an easy name in English, but not necessarily in other European languages. Sammy felt that the favourable connotation of speed and progress might provide a boost for the products to which it was applied.

(Source: Adapted from Cundiff and Hilger, 1988, pp. 440–2.)

QUESTIONS

1. Evaluate the alternative names being considered by Sammy Soshi. Which name would you recommend?

2. Whatever new name is chosen, should Soshi Sumsin adopt the same name in the Korean market?

3. What are the advantages of selecting different brand names, as appropriate, in each foreign market?

4. Enumerate the characteristics that should be possessed by a good international brand name.

A10.3   Case: Derivados de Leche SA

Derivados de Leche SA, founded in 1968, was the first firm to market yoghurt in Mexico. It distributed yoghurt under the brand name Delsa only in Mexico City, primarily in a limited number of upper-income areas. The company was family owned, and the capital was all local. For the first five years, Delsa was sold in food stores, particularly in the newly developing supermarkets, without any advertising or other promotion. Yoghurt was a new, unfamiliar food product in the Mexican market, but Delsa depended primarily on word of mouth to provide product recognition.

During the next four years, the structure of the yoghurt market changed dramatically with the entrance of three large multinational firms. In 1973, a number of laws regulating foreign investment in Mexico were modified under a single new 'regulation of foreign investment' law. According to this law foreign investors were welcome in Mexico on a joint labour basis so long as the foreign ownership share did not exceed 49 per cent. Labor-intensive industries that helped to decentralize population were particularly welcome. All three of the multinationals entering the yoghurt market operated on this joint venture basis.

The first new brand, Chambourcy, was introduced by a joint venture subsidiary of Nestlé which had operated in Mexico since 1935. This company, Industrias Alimentacias Club SA, was a major Mexican food producer with 7,000 employees. Chambourcy was launched with a strong promotional campaign and wide distribution. The following year, in 1974, a subsidiary of the French food firm, BSN-Gervais, launched their Danone yoghurt in the Mexican market. Danone was also heavily supported with promotion. Finally, in 1976, a third multinational entered the market. Productos de Leche SA was 51 per cent owned by Mexican capital and 49 per cent by the Borden Company of the United States; it entered the Mexican market with two brands of yoghurt, Darel and Bonafina.

By 1982, the management of Derivados de Leche SA was becoming concerned about its future position in the yoghurt market. All three of the multinational competitors were aggressive marketers and promoters and were strong financially. Although the foreign ownership was a minority (49 per cent), management was dominated in each case by the minority ownership, so that management was competent and professional. In the short term, Delsa benefited from the primary demand creation activities of the multinationals. In 1979, Delsa sales almost doubled to 800 tons, and by 1982, grew to 1,900 tons. But Delsa's market share had dropped from over 95 per cent in 1973 (there were some other, very small, Mexican-owned competitors) to only 21 per cent in 1982.

The three multinationals divided 77.5 per cent of the market among them. If the trend continued, it was feared that Delsa's share of the market might drop so low that it would provide very little product recognition. And it was possible that ultimately sales volume would stabilize and perhaps even decline.

By 1983, Delsa management was faced with the grim reality of competition from financially strong and aggressive, professionally managed multinationals. Delsa managers felt that pricing could not be blamed for this loss in market share; in 1982, the sales price of Delsa was slightly below that of its competitors. A major handicap for Delsa was its failure to promote recognition of its brand name. Although Delsa had been pulled along in the market by the initial marketing efforts which were designed to create a primary demand for yoghurt, the marketing efforts of the competitors were now focused almost entirely on selective brand-name promotion. Delsa management had concentrated its efforts on getting the product into retail outlets and maintaining good relationships with dealers; no effort had been made to create consumer recognition and franchises through advertising and other promotion. Management was made up of the family members who owned the company; they brought little professional training to the job.

Owner-managers of small and medium-sized firms in Mexico tended to run their businesses for quick, short-term profit rather than long-term development. New capital investment was needed to enlarge the production capacity, and serious consideration needed to be given to investing in a promotional campaign to build and maintain Delsa brand recognition.

Delsa was considering applying for a government-subsidized loan to double its production capacity from 2,000 tons per year to 4,000 tons. These loans were available only to 100 per cent Mexican-owned manufacturers, but were limited to the financing of manufacturing facilities. Delsa's marketing manager wanted to emphasize the local Mexican ownership of Delsa and to increase the firm's advertising budget from $20,000 to about $100,000. He also wanted to redesign the package so as to include some statement that indicated the brand was of pure Mexican origin. Delsa's owners wanted to put pressure on the Mexican government to limit the food processing industry to 100 per cent Mexican-owned firms. It was not known what the possibilities were of getting such legislation passed.

(Source: Adapted from Cundiff and Hilger, 1988, pp. 335–6.)

QUESTIONS

1. What are Delsa's strengths and weaknesses in competing with multinationals?
2. What is the impact of 'country of origin' on demand for yoghurt?
3. What recommendations can you make to strengthen Delsa's market position?

NOTES

1. For an examination of how companies can develop Eurobrands and the obstacles they face in such an endeavour, see Littler and Schlieper (1995).
2. Let us imagine the case of the detergent *Tide*, translated as *Marée* in French, a term which connotes strong smells and dirt rather than strength, washing power and cleanliness. Such examples are endless.
3. Definitions of the words used in Table 10.2: etymology: the study of the sources and development of words; grammar: the branch of linguistics that deals with syntax and morphology;

phonology: the study of the sound system of language(s); phonemics: aspects of phonology concerned with the classification and analysis of the phonemes of a language; phonetics: study of speech processes, including the production, perception and analysis of speech sounds; rhetoric: the art of using speech to persuade or influence; semantics: the branch of linguistics that deals with the study of meaning; semiotics: the study of signs and symbols, especially the relations between written or spoken signs and their referents in the physical world or the world of ideas.

4. When transcribed in the Roman alphabet (*romanji*), which is not their natural written form.
5. I remember travelling in Tokyo with a Chinese friend who was able to understand all the road signs but did not know how to pronounce them in Japanese.
6. Erickson (1996) provides a good description of how the Japanese patent system has been influenced by the local economic culture. This kind of information is useful for understanding the world-wide diversity in trade-mark, copyright and patent systems, which will not be eliminated in a day by the new trade-related industrial property rights (TRIPs) implemented within the WTO framework.

REFERENCES

Abegglen, James and George Stalk Jr (1986), 'The Japanese corporation as competitor', *California Management Review*, vol. XXVIII, no. 3 (Spring), pp. 9–7.

Ahmed, Sadrudin A., Alain d'Astous and Mostafa El Adraoui (1994), 'Country-of-origin effects on purchasing managers' product perceptions,' *Industrial Marketing Management*, vol. 23, no.4, pp. 323–32.

Anderson, William T., and William H. Cunningham (1972), 'Gauging foreign product promotion', *Journal of Advertising Research*, vol. 12, no. 1, pp. 29–34.

Bamossy, Gary J. and Nicholas G. Papadopoulos (1987), 'An assessment of reliability for product evaluations scales used in country-of-origin research', in Kenneth D. Bahn and M. Joseph Sirgy (eds.), *World Marketing Congress*, Academy of Marketing Science: Blacksburg, VA.

Baumgartner, Gary and Alain Jolibert (1977), 'The perception of foreign products in France', *Advances in Consumer Research*, vol. 7, pp. 103–5.

Bhuian, Shahid N. (1997), 'Saudi consumers' attitudes towards European, US and Japanese products and marketing practices', *European Journal of Marketing*, vol. 31, no. 7, pp. 467–86.

Bilkey, Warren J. and Erik Nes (1982), 'Country-of-origin effects on product evaluations', *Journal of International Business Studies*, Spring–Summer, pp. 89–99.

Bon, Jérôme and Alain Ollivier (1979), 'L'influence de l'origine d'un produit sur son image à l'étranger', *Revue Française du Marketing*, 1979/2, Cahier 77, pp. 101–14.

Cabat, Odilon (1989), 'Archéologie de la marque moderne', in Jean-Noel Kapferer and Jean-Claude Thoenig, (eds.), *La Marque*, McGraw-Hill: Paris, pp. 307–53.

Cattin, Philippe, Alain Jolibert and Colleen Lohnes (1982), 'A cross-cultural study of "made-in" concepts', *Journal of International Business Studies*, Winter, pp. 131–41.

Chang, Dae Ryun and Ik-Tae Rim (1995), 'A study on the rating of import sources for industrial products in a newly industrialized country: The case of South Korea', *Journal of Business Research*, vol. 32, pp. 31–39

Clark, Harold F. Jr (1987), 'Consumer and corporate values: Yet another view on global marketing', *International Journal of Advertising*, vol. 6, pp. 29–42.

Colombat, Catherine (1997), 'Danone imprime sa marque sur la planète', *L'Essentiel du Management*, April, pp. 74–80.

Contensou, François (1989), 'La Marque, l'efficience économique et la formation des prix', in Jean-Noel Kapferer and Jean-Claude Thoenig (eds.), *La Marque*, McGraw-Hill: Paris, pp. 231–73.

Crawford, John C. (1985), 'Attitudes toward Latin American products', in Erdener Kaynak (ed.), *Global Perspectives in Marketing*, Praeger: New York, pp. 149–54.

Crawford John C. and Charles W. Lamb Jr (1981), 'Source preferences for imported products', *Journal of Purchasing and Materials Management*, Winter, pp. 28–33.

Cundiff, Edward W. and Marye Tharp Hilger (1988), *Marketing in the International Environment*, 2nd edn, Prentice Hall: Englewood Cliffs, NJ.

Czinkota, Michael R. and Illka A. Ronkainen (1990), *International Marketing*, 2nd edn, Dryden Press: Hinsdale, IL.

Darling, John B. and F. Kraft (1977), 'A competitive profile of products and associated marketing practices of selected European and non-European countries', *European Journal of Marketing*, vol 11, no. 7, pp. 519–37.

Dornoff, Ronald J., Clint B. Tankersley and Gregory P. White (1974), 'Consumers' perceptions of imports', *Akron Business and Economic Review*, vol. 5 (Summer), pp. 26–9.

Dupuy, François and Jean-Claude Thoenig (1989), 'La Marque et l'échange', in Jean-Noel Kapferer and Jean-Claude Thoenig (eds.), *La Marque*, McGraw-Hill: Paris, pp. 159–89.

Erickson, G. Scott (1996), 'Patent systems and economic culture: The Japanese patent system', *Asian Journal of Marketing*, vol. 5, no. 1, pp. 7–22.

Erickson, Gary M., Johny K. Johansson and Paul Chao (1984), 'Images variables in multi-attribute product evaluations: Country of origin effects', *Journal of Consumer Research*, vol. 11 (September), pp. 694–99.

Eroglu, S. A., and K. A. Machleit (1989), 'Effects of individual and product specific variables on utilizing country of origin as a product quality cue', *International Marketing Review*, vol. 6, no. 6, pp. 27–41.

Etchegoyen, Alain (1990), *Les Entreprises ont-elles une âme?* Editions François Bourin: Paris.

Ettenson, Richard (1993), 'Brand name and country of origin effects in the emerging market economies of Russia, Poland and Hungary', *International Marketing Review*, vol. 10, no. 5, pp. 14–36.

Ettenson, R., J. Wagner and G. Gaeth (1988), 'Evaluating the effect of country-of-origin and the "Made in the USA" campaign: A conjoint approach', *Journal of Retailing*, vol. 64, no. 1, pp. 85–100.

Etzel, Michael J. and Bruce J. Walker (1974), 'Advertising strategy for foreign products', *Journal of Advertising Research*, vol. 14 (June), pp. 41–4.

Gaedeke, Ralph (1973), 'Consumer attitudes towards products "made in" developing countries', *Journal of Retailing*, vol. 49 (Summer), pp. 13–24.

Giordan, Alain Eric (1988), *Exporter plus 2*, Economica: Paris.

Gopalakrishna, P., B. L. Garland and J. C. Crawford (1989), 'Consumer satisfaction with foreign and domestic products: A cross-cultural comparison', Proceedings of the Annual Conference of the American Marketing Association.

Graby, Françoise (1982), 'Les consommateurs et les produits étrangers: application au marché français', Proceedings of the 7th Seminar on Research in Marketing, IAE: Aix en Provence, Lalonde des Maures.

Hampton, Gerald M. (1977), 'Perceived risk in buying products made abroad by American firms', *Baylor Business Studies*, October, pp. 53–64.

Han, C. Min (1990), 'Country image: Halo or summary construct?', *Journal of Marketing Research*, vol. XXVI (May), pp. 222–9.

Han, C. Min and Vern Terpstra (1988), 'Country of origin effects for uni-national and bi-national products,' *Journal of International Business Studies*, vol 19, no. 2 (Summer), pp. 235–55.

Han, C. Min, Byoung-Woo Lee and Kong-Kyun Ro (1994), 'The choice of a survey mode in country image studies', *Journal of Business Research*, vol. 29, no. 2, pp. 151–62.

Harris, Richard Jackson, Bettina Garner-Earl, Sara J. Sprick and Collette Carroll (1994), 'Effects of foreign product names and country-of-origin attributions on advertisement evaluations', *Psychology and Marketing*, vol. 11, no. 2 (March/April), pp. 129–44.

Hooley, Graham J., David Shipley and Nathalie Krieger (1988), 'A method for modelling consumer perceptions of country of origin', *International Marketing Review*, vol. 5, no. 3, pp. 67–76

Huang, Yue Yuan and Allan K. K. Chan (1997), 'Chinese branding name: From general principles to specific rules', *International Journal of Advertising*, vol. 16, no. 4, pp. 320–35.

Jaffé, Eugene D. and Israel D. Nebenzahl (1984), 'Alternative questionnaire formats for country image studies', *Journal of Marketing Research*, vol. 21, pp. 463–71.

Jaffé, Eugene D. and Israel D. Nebenzahl (1989), 'Global promotion of country image: the case of the 1988 Korean Olympic Games', in Reijo Luostarinen (ed.), *Dynamics of International Business*, vol. 1, proceedings of the 15th annual conference of the European International Business Asssociation, Helsinki, Finland, pp. 358–85.

Joachimsthaler, Erich, and David A. Aaker (1997), 'Building brands without mass media', *Harvard Business Review*, 75(1), January–February, pp. 39–50.

Johansson, Johny K. (1989), 'Determinants and effects of the use of "made in" labels', *International Marketing Review*, vol. 6, no. 1, pp. 47–58.

Johansson, Johny K. and Israel D. Nebenzahl (1986), 'Multinational production: Effect on brand value', *Journal of International Business Studies*, vol. 17, no. 3, pp. 101–26

Johansson, Johny K. and Hans B. Thorelli (1985), 'International product positioning', *Journal of International Business Studies*, vol. 16 (Fall), pp. 57–75.

Johansson, Johny K., Susan P. Douglas and Ikujiro Nonaka (1985), 'Assessing the impact of country of origin on product evaluations: A new methodological perspective', *Journal of Marketing Research*, vol. XXII (November), pp. 388–96.

Jolibert, Alain (1979), 'Quand les directeurs d'approvisionnement français et américains évaluent l'image des produits fabriqués dans cinq pays industriels', *Revue Française de Gestion*, January–February, pp. 94–101.

Kamins, Michael A. and Akira Nagashima (1995), 'Perceptions of products made in Japan versus those made in the United States among Japanese and American executives: A longitudinal perspective', *Asia Pacific Journal of Management*, vol. 12, no. 1, pp. 49–68.

Kapferer, Jean-Noel (1989), 'La face cachée des marques', in Jean-Noel Kapferer and Jean-Claude Thoenig, (eds.), *La Marque*, McGraw-Hill: Paris, pp. 9–44.

Khanna, Sri Ram (1986), 'Asian companies and the country stereotype paradox: An empirical study', *Columbia Journal of World Business*, Summer, pp. 29–38.

Khera, Inder (1986), 'A broadening base of US consumer acceptance of Korean products', in Kenneth D. Bahn and M. Joseph Sirgy (eds.), *World Marketing Congress*, Academy of Marketing Science, Blacksburg, VA, pp. 136–41.

Khera, I., B. Anderson and C. Y. Kim (1983), 'Made in India versus Hong-Kong/Korea/Taiwan', *Foreign Trade Review*, January–March, pp. 362–81.

Khera, Inder, David Karns and C. Y. Kim (1985), 'U.S. consumers' perceptions of Korean products and brands', Pan-Pacific Conference II, Seoul, Korea, 12–18 May.

Kotler, Philip and Bernard Dubois (1994), *Marketing Management*, 8th edn, Publi-Union, Paris.

Kraft, Frederick B. and Kae H. Chung (1992), 'Korean importer perceptions of US and Japanese industrial goods', *International Marketing Review*, vol. 9, no. 2, pp. 59–73.

Krishnakumar, Parameswar (1974), 'An exploratory study of the influence of country of origin on the product images of persons from selected countries', PhD Dissertation, University of Florida.

Lambin, Jean-Jacques (1989), 'La marque et le comportement de choix de l'acheteur', in Jean-Noel Kapferer and Jean-Claude Thoenig (eds.), *La Marque*, McGraw-Hill: Paris, pp. 125–58.

Leclerc, France, Bernd H. Schmitt and Laurette Dubé (1994), 'Foreign branding and its effects on product perceptions and attitudes,' *Journal of Marketing Research*, vol. 31, no. 2 (May), pp. 263–70.

Littler, Dale and Katrin Schlieper (1995), 'The development of the Eurobrand', *International Marketing Review*, vol. 12, no. 2, pp. 22–37.

Lumpkin, J. R, J. C Crawford and G. Kim (1985), 'Perceived risk as a factor in buying foreign clothes', *International Journal of Advertising*, vol. 4, pp. 157–71.

Macrae, Chris (1991), *World Class Brands*, Addison-Wesley: Wokingham.

Maheswaran, Durairaj (1994), 'Country of origin as a stereotype: effects of consumer expertise and attribute strength on product evaluations', *Journal of Consumer Research*, vol. 21 (September), pp. 354–65

Martin, Ingrid M. and Sevgin Eroglu (1993), 'Measuring a multi-dimensional construct: Country image', *Journal of Business Research*, vol. 28, pp. 191–210.

Morello, G. (1984), 'The made-in issue: A comparative research on the image of domestic and foreign products', *European Research*, vol. 5, no. 21, pp. 68–74.

Morganosky, Michelle A. and Michelle M. Lazarde (1987), 'Foreign made apparel: Influences on consumers' perceptions of brand and store quality', *International Journal of Advertising*, vol. 6, pp. 339–46.

Nagashima, Akira (1970), 'A comparison of Japanese and U.S. attitudes towards foreign products', *Journal of Marketing*, vol. 34, January, pp. 68–74.

Nagashima, Akira (1977), 'A comparative "made in" product image survey among Japanese businessmen', *Journal of Marketing*, July, pp. 95–100.

Nebenzahl, Israel D. and Eugene D. Jaffé (1989), 'A methodological approach to the estimation of demand functions from country-of-origin effects', in Reijo Luostarinien (ed.), *Dynamics of International Business*, vol. 1, proceedings of the 15th Annual Conference of the European International Business Association, Helsinki, Finland, pp. 386–414.

Nebenzahl, Israel D., Eugene D. Jaffé and Shlomo I. Lampert (1997), 'Towards a theory of country image effect on product evaluation', *Management International Review*, vol. 37, no. 1, pp. 27–49.

Nishina, Sadafumi (1990), 'Japanese consumers: Introducing foreign products/brands into the Japanese market', *Journal of Advertising Research*, vol. 30, no. 2, pp. 35–45.

Onkvisit, Sak and John J. Shaw (1989), 'The international dimension of branding: strategic considerations and decisions', *International Marketing Review*, vol. 6, no. 2, pp. 22–34.

Pan, Yigang and Bernd H. Schmitt (1995), 'What's in a name? An empirical comparison of Chinese and Western brand names', *Asian Journal of Marketing*, vol. 4, no. 1, pp. 7–16.

Parameswaran, Ravi and Attila Yaprak (1987), 'A cross-national investigation of consumers research measures', *Journal of International Business Studies*, Winter, pp. 35–49.

Peebles, Dean M. (1989), 'Don't write off global advertising: A commentary', *International Marketing Review*, vol. 6, no. 1, pp. 73–8.

Perrin, Michel, Claude Marcel, Robert Salles and Jean-Paul Valla (1981), 'L'image des biens industriels français en Europe', *Revue Française de Gestion*, January–February, pp. 97–107.

Peterson, Robert A. and Alain Jolibert (1976), 'A cross-national investigation of price and brand as determinants of perceived product quality', *Journal of Applied Psychology*, vol. 61, pp. 533–6.

Peterson, Robert A. and Alain Jolibert (1995), 'A meta-analysis of country-of-origin effects', *Journal of International Business Studies*, vol. 26, no. 4, pp. 883–900.

Reierson, Curtis (1966), 'Are foreign products seen as national stereotypes?', *Journal of Retailing*, Fall, pp. 33–40.

Reierson, Curtis (1967), 'Attitude changes toward foreign products', *Journal of Marketing Research*, November, pp. 385–7.

Rosen, Barry Nathan, Jean J. Boddewyn and Ernst A. Louis (1989), 'US brands abroad: an empirical study of global branding', *International Marketing Review*, vol. 6, no. 1, pp. 7–19.

Saghafi, Massoud M., Fanis Varvoglis and Tomas Vega (1991), 'Why US firms don't buy from Latin American companies', *Industrial Marketing Management*, 20, pp. 207–213.

Samiee, Saeed (1994), 'Customer evaluation of products in a global market', *Journal of International Business Studies*, vol. 25, no. 3, pp. 579–604.

Schaefer, Anja (1997), 'Consumer knowledge and country of origin effects', *European Journal of Marketing*, vol. 31, no. 1, pp. 56–72.

Schmitt, Bernd H. and Yigang Pan (1994), 'Managing corporate and brand identities in the Asia-Pacific region', *California Management Review*, vol. 36, no. 4, Summer, pp. 32–47.

Schooler, Robert D. (1965), 'Product bias in the Central American common market', *Journal of Marketing Research*, vol. 2, November, pp. 394–7.

Schooler, Robert D. (1971), 'Bias phenomena attendant to the marketing of foreign goods in the US', *Journal of International Business Studies*, Spring, pp. 71–80.

Schooler, Robert D. and D. H. Sunoo (1969), 'Consumer perceptions of international products: Regional versus national labeling', *Social Science Quarterly*, vol. 49, no. 4, pp. 886–90.

Schooler, Robert D. and A. R. Wildt (1968), 'Elasticity of product bias', *Journal of Marketing Research*, vol. 5, February, pp. 78–81.

Shalofsky, Ivor (1987), 'Research for global brands', *European Research*, May, pp. 88–93.

Shimp, Terence A., Saeed Samiee and Thomas J. Madden (1993), 'Countries and their products: A cognitive structure perspective', *Journal of the Academy of Marketing Science*, vol. 21, no. 4, pp. 321–30.

Solomon, Michael R. (1994), *Consumer Behavior*, 2nd edn, Allyn and Bacon: Needham Heights.

Swinder, Janda and C.P. Rao (1997), 'The effect of country-of-origin related stereotypes and personal beliefs on product evaluation', *Psychology and Marketing*, vol. 14, no. 7, pp. 689–702.

Thorelli, Hans B. and Aleksandra E. Glowacka (1995), 'Willingness of American industrial buyers to source internationally', *Journal of Business Research*, vol. 32, pp. 21–30.

Thorelli, Hans B., Jee-Su Lim and Jong Suk (1989), 'Relative importance of origin, warranty and retail store image on product evaluations', *International Marketing Review*, vol. 6, no. 1, pp. 35–46.

Tongberg, R. C. (1972), 'An empirical study of relationships between dogmatism and consumer attitudes toward foreign products', PhD. dissertation, Pennsylvania State University.

Usunier, Jean-Claude (1994), 'Social status and country-of-origin preferences,' *Journal of Marketing Management*, vol. 10, pp. 765–83.

Usunier, Jean-Claude, Israel D. Nebenzahl and Eugene D. Jaffé (1993), 'Pays d'origine et stratégie de prix', *Revue Française du Marketing*, 1993/1, no. 141, pp. 35–47.

Vanden Bergh, Bruce, Keith Adler and Lauren Oliver (1988), 'Linguistic distinction among top brand names', *Journal of Advertising Research*, vol. 27, no. 4, pp. 39–44.

Wang, Chih-Kang (1978), 'The effect of foreign economic, political and cultural environment on consumers' willingness to buy foreign products', PhD dissertation, Texas A & M University.

Wang, Chih-Kang and Charles W. Lamb Jr (1980), 'Foreign environmental factors influencing American consumers predispositions toward European products', *Journal of the Academy of Marketing Science*, vol. 8 (Fall), pp. 345–56.

Wang, Chih-Kang and Charles W. Lamb Jr (1983), 'The impact of selected environmental forces upon consumers' willingness to buy foreign products', *Journal of the Academy of Marketing Science*, vol. 11 (Winter), pp. 71–84.

White, Phillip D. (1979), 'Attitudes of U.S. purchasing managers toward industrial products manufactured in selected Western European nations', *Journal of International Business Studies*, Spring/Summer, pp. 81–90.

White Phillip D. and Edward W. Cundiff (1978), 'Assessing the quality of industrial products', *Journal of Marketing*, January, pp. 80–6.

Wilke, Margaritha (1994), 'Der Werte Name – Die Marke auf Chinesisch', *Der Neue China*, vol. 21, no. 3, September, pp. 15–6.

Wilsher, Peter (1992), 'Diverse and perverse', *Management Today*, July, pp. 32–5.

Yaprak, Attila (1978), 'Formulating a multinational strategy: A deductive cross-national consumer behavior model', PhD dissertation, Georgia State University, College of Business Administration.

Yaprak, Attila, (1987), 'The country of origin paradigm in cross-national consumer behavior: the state of the art', in Kenneth D. Bahn and M. Joseph Sirgy (eds.), *World Marketing Congress*, Academy of Marketing Science: Blacksburg, VA, pp. 142–5.

Yavas, Ugur and Guvenc Alpay (1986), 'Does an exporting nation enjoy the same cross-national image?', *International Journal of Advertising*, vol. 5, pp. 109–19.

Yoshimori, Masaru (1989), 'Concepts et stratégies de marques au Japon', in Jean-Noel Kapferer and Jean-Claude Thoenig (eds.), *La Marque*, McGraw-Hill: Paris, pp. 275–304.

Zeithaml, Valarie A. (1988), 'Consumer perceptions of price, quality and value: A means-end model and synthesis of evidence', *Journal of Marketing*, vol. 52, July, pp. 2–22.

11 The critical role of price in relational exchange

Price is, at first sight, anything but 'cultural'. That must be conceded. In fact it resembles an intrinsically objective element of exchange. It is usually a figure, a number, a unit – at least in appearance. It is therefore assumed that price determination is, in general, an issue reserved for rational economic factors. At this point in the book you are probably asking yourself what further evidence I have for insisting that everything is marked by culture. I wish to make three comments on this issue: (a) I am not denying (as I am myself an economist) that price is above all an objective element of exchange; (b) I am therefore insisting on human and subjective aspects of relational exchange where price is examined from a sociological and interactive point of view; (c) all authors, by definition, are the promoters of the ideas they choose to defend.

Price is a significant element of communication between buyer and seller, a short-term and/or long-term bond between them, and, for customers, a means of evaluating products in terms of social representations (Prus, 1989a) strongly akin to culture. Price is a decisive element in the social interaction between buyer and seller. It endorses their agreement. It shapes their relationship, immediately and in the long term.

This chapter does not consider the strictly economic aspects of price in international marketing: for instance, the relationship between price and costs in international marketing or the law of one price which states that, in the absence of transport, transaction-related costs and price discrimination, trade takes place in only one market and only one price prevails. Nor do I consider the incidence of exchange rate variance on price strategies in international marketing. It is the subjective and perceptual rather than the objective side of prices that is examined in this chapter; price is viewed as a signal conveying meaning (section 11.1).

Section 11.2 examines bargaining: this is a form of relationship between buyer and seller which is classical, primitive and normal, particularly in the absence of compulsory price labelling. In modern mass markets, the influence of the customer on prices fixed by anonymous sellers usually takes the form of a 'take it or leave it' bargain. This dichotomous attitude (choice/no choice) is contrary to the purpose of bargaining and relational exchange, where price is always supposed to be a 'friendly price', even a 'friend's price'. Each party wants to make a good deal: *human relations are practically inseparable from economic transactions*. In contrast to bargaining described in section 11.2, the third section of this chapter deals with the use of price in those situations where it is clearly marked and hence known by customers, so that they are in a position to appraise the price–quality ratio.

The last three sections of the chapter consider company attitudes in pricing decisions in international markets. This is a somewhat anthropomorphic approach since a company and its markets are considered as interacting parties to an exchange. Companies are led to distort and manipulate prices between domestic markets, either to increase consumer 'brand loyalty' in certain markets through offensive strategic pricing, or to avoid parallel imports which undermine their local distribution system (section 11.4). Price can also be used as a tactical weapon *vis-à-vis* competitors in particular national markets (section 11.5). Finally, price can be manipulated either because of a severe inflationary context or by over- or under-invoicing in order to make deals that otherwise would not be concluded (section 11.6).

11.1   PRICE AS A SIGNAL CONVEYING MEANING

In many cases, prices are fairly objective, especially in most consumer goods and consumer durables markets, where goods are sold to households in mass distribution outlets with extensive possibilities of price comparison across stores. Then the meaning conveyed by the price centres mostly on the value of the good and the money transfer which will be necessary for it to be acquired. Prices start to be a more central object in the relationship between buyer and seller, or the company and its customers, distributors or competitors, when: (1) price is not displayed; (2) it is not necessarily the seller who will announce the first price; (3) there is no clear market reference for what would be a 'fair price'; (4) a particular price is understood by both the seller and the buyer as taking place within a series of transactions, past, present and future; (5) prices for particular transactions are not necessarily meant to cover even marginal cost (manipulative prices); (6) prices may be distorted by inflation and government price regulation; and (7) the total price is a combination of direct and indirect prices (e.g. a product's price but also prices for its maintenance, spare parts, updates, etc.). Price is less strictly 'economic' and more 'relational' in a variety of situations which correspond to one or more of the seven conditions presented above, namely, in relation to industrial goods, in high inflation contexts, etc. As shown in Table 11.1, price can convey meaning and be an object of interaction between the various participants of the market situation (manufacturers, distributors, consumers, competitors).

TABLE 11.1   Price-based signals

Meaning conveyed by price in	by . . .	Section
Buyer–seller interactions	Bargaining rituals, price offers and relationship development	11.2
Consumer behaviour	Differences in consumer price-mindedness across cultures	11.3
Product evaluation	To what extent is quality inferred from price?	11.3
(Tough) competition	Signalling willingness to compete by dumping prices	11.4
Target market(s)	Showing commitment to customers in a target market by attractive prices	11.4
Distributors (grey markets)	Signalling willingness to avoid parallel imports from opportunistic distributors who disturb international price policy and risk damaging brand image	11.4
(Peaceful) competition	Signalling willingness to enter 'peacefully' in a cartellized market	11.5
Price increase policy	Meaning conveyed by price in high-inflation contexts	11.6
Relationship to suppliers	Overcoming the barriers for the supplier to receive the real price by using over- or under-invoicing.	11.6

11.2   BARGAINING

The limits of price as an element of social relation: Bargaining versus no bargaining

The importance of bargaining is often underestimated because as a rule prices are displayed and we have become accustomed to being informed about prices. If we do not find them satisfactory we will not buy the product. In many countries today, people no longer bargain; at least, they appear not to. Bargaining is either legally prohibited or strictly controlled in most developed countries. Most sales of consumer products take place within oligopolistic distribution channels which offer merchandise for sale from producers who are themselves organized in oligopolies. In direct relations with customers, prices are unilaterally set by vendors and are therefore non-negotiable. This price is either taken or left. Bargaining at the checkout in a supermarket is unheard of and, to be blunt, rather boorish. (This is without taking into consideration the various epithets that could be used by impatient customers still waiting in the queue.)

Yet, once the price of a product reaches a substantial level, people return to bargaining because of one of its irreplaceable functions: splitting a surplus between buyer and seller. In many markets exchange still takes place through bargaining, either legally or from necessity: for example, those for consumer durables and equipment for firms and households such as new cars, furniture, second-hand cars, property and industrial machinery.

In most developing countries, on the other hand, bargaining is still the rule, even for items of low value and products of little vital interest. A weak purchasing power considerably increases the importance of bargaining. In certain African markets, where sugar is sold by the lump and carrots by the slice (seen at the Nouakchott market in Mauritania in 1988), bargaining becomes essential for survival. Moreover, people are not pressed for time: the dividends from bargaining in relation to its cost are fundamentally different in developing and industrialized nations. Finally, bargaining has a fun dimension as well as a human one. The fun dimension exists because, in some ways, it is similar to a role play. The human dimension exists because the friendly/ unfriendly aspects of commerce and bargaining are contemplated with more seriousness in developing countries than in industrialized ones where commercial intercourse has been largely 'depersonalized' (at least for consumer goods – much less so for equipment and industrial goods).

This is in fact one of the major reasons that bargaining is either legally prohibited or socially restricted in developed countries. As stated by Allen (1971, p. 49):

it has conventionally been supposed that bargaining is socially disadvantageous, on the grounds that it breeds hostility, rivalry and distrust . . . While it is true that there is always an element of suspicion as to the real value of the commodity (and subsequently of the price), this suspicion never turns into an open conflict if the bargainers intend to conclude the sale. Any bargainer, whether seller or buyer, is careful not to offend his partner, for fear of putting an end to the transaction. Thus, though initiated by suspicion, bargaining tends rather to eliminate it, instituting instead an atmosphere of common interest and trust, which often leads to a lasting client relationship. In this way it cements community relations, rather than subverts them.

Ritual aspects of bargaining

Brand marketing is, by definition, not conducive to bargaining. Self-service and other non-personalized services do not allow people living in modern societies with advanced distribution systems to experience the rituals involved in bargaining. These rituals are a challenge in themselves. They are independent of the price negotiation, yet at the same time complementary. People who bargain more are no less rational; they are rational in a different way.

A Lebanese anthropologist (Khuri, 1968) describes the rituals involved in bargaining in the Middle East by emphasizing that such intercourse always begins with standard signs of respect, affection, common interest and trust. Words pertaining to parental relations are used in such circumstances to evoke affection and create an impression of friendliness and fraternity. As soon as a potential buyer shows interest in an item and requests information on the product, the seller replies vaguely:

Between us there is no difference; we share the same interest, price is not what pleases me, what pleases me is to find out what pleases you; pay as much as you want; brothers do not disagree on price; for you it is free; it is a gift.

Nothing in this speech should be taken literally. Not one potential customer would consider it as such. The opening incantation is a way of expressing a social bond of mutual interest and trust through allusions to a probable family tie in a metaphorical sense. The potential customer then insists that a price be indicated. The vendor hesitates and, perhaps, proposes a price after having presented and lauded the merits of his product at great length. In fact, a potential customer must never pretend to doubt the qualities of the proposed item, because that could make him seem ignorant and, as such, more vulnerable. The discussion continues, each party maintaining its price (a maximum price for the seller and a minimum price for the customer) below or above which no transaction can take place. The potential buyer suggests a price, but is not necessarily willing to pay it. After an agreement has been reached, the transaction then takes place, that is, the buyer decides to purchase the item for cash. The bargaining operation could have been primarily just to seek information on the price. This is one instance where the bargaining activity is partly, but only partly, disconnected from the sales activity. It could be disconcerting for people who are used to displayed prices and who, as a result, *do not envisage entering into any sort of pleasant economic intercourse* merely to obtain information. When prices are not displayed, it may be embarrassing for potential buyers to ask the price of an item, because it latently signals that they may experience difficulties in affording the purchase, and thus imply that they are lower-class people and have low purchasing power. Roeber (1994, p. 49) explains how asking the price is associated with class perception in the context of Zambia:

Working people, I was told, were 'sufferers'. The meaning of that word was best explained by the man who stated vehemently, 'If you have to ask the price of something, you are automatically a sufferer' . . . there was another category of people, the *apamwamba* or 'big shots', who did not have to ask for the price of commodities. They always had money to buy what they needed.

The relationship between bargaining and price display is obvious. Wherever the law forces the vendor to display prices clearly, the practice of bargaining will diminish. It is understandable that people who do not bargain every day, and who have therefore lost the habit of personalized commercial relations (if indeed they ever had it), should be rather embarrassed in these situations of implicit communication, where affection and economics, friendship and self-interest, are seemingly intermingled. The novice bargainer also risks provoking the seller's hostility if the seller gets the impression (or wishes to give the impression) of being 'taken for a ride' by the buyer. In fact, what remains of bargaining in western societies is disguised behind 'rational' arguments such as quantity discounts, stock liquidation operations and auctions of deleted items, etc. Moreover, bargaining could smear the image of the distribution channel as well as that of the goods it sells. Prus (1989b, p. 146) quotes certain remarks made by Canadian vendors:

'We're flexible, where if they're getting a larger order and they suggest it, we'll give a little . . . Some customers feel that they have to have a discount to buy it.' (Sales manageress, luggage.)

'You can dicker in furniture, appliances, carpeting, something like that, here. But not on the smaller things, like clothing, giftware, shoes.' (Department store salesman.)

'Normally I try not to dicker. I am quite firm on the prices. I've found that dickering can be rather awkward. It is awkward for the merchant and the customer. And it is especially awkward if other people are around. If you can stay away from dickering, you can also avoid an image as someone who will go down. I have been known to dicker, but it is something I try to avoid.' (Women's clothing.)

Declaring prices

Cavusgil (1990, p. 505) notes that international pricing is not a topic that lends itself to easy generalization and the setting of export prices must first address the unique nature of the individual firm or buyer with whom one is dealing; he takes the example of the Middle East where 'Regal Ware, a producer of kitchen appliances and cookware, uses a higher list price in such markets to leave a margin of discretion'. Indeed, proposing a price is a tug-of-war exercise. Who will give way, the seller or the customer? Who should be the first to make concessions, by virtue of the position of strength that is internalized within a particular society? At least four items play a major role in answering these questions:

1. The initial power situation of each party.
2. The degree of urgency for either the buyer or the seller to close the deal.
3. The importance of the negotiation margin from the start: whatever price is initially suggested, it must leave room for further discussion. It could be in the vendor's interest to exaggerate the first price in order to leave the customer some room

BOX 11.1

Price levels and the buyer/seller relationship

Scenario 1

The seller wishes to offer a fair price from the start, close to the final price, expecting that it will win the customer's loyalty. This should convince the buyer of the vendor's honesty, openness and genuine desire to do business. It so happens that the customer shares these (European and American) values and decides to co-operate. An agreement is quickly reached, and each party is satisfied.

Scenario 2

The same vendor suggests the same price, close to the final price, as a sign of goodwill towards the buyer. The buyer who comes from a different culture (say India or Pakistan) is embarrassed: rather than a low price, his boss expects him to obtain the greatest possible discount from the seller. His role centres on the price rebate rather than on the price level. The announced price, close to the final price, leaves almost no room for rebate negotiation. With no grounds to negotiate, buyer and seller will separate, dissatisfied.

Scenario 3

The vendor announces a much higher initial price. In doing so, he leaves room for negotiation right from the start so as to allow the buyer to demonstrate skill in a mutually beneficial bargaining exercise and to enable the two parties to increase the long-term value of their social relationship. The ultimate agreed price is very close to that of Scenario 1. The buyer being interested mostly in rebate and the seller in price level, both can achieve greater satisfaction than in Scenario 1.

for manoeuvre: when the vendor is dealing with a buyer whose performance is subject to confirmation by superiors, that buyer is supposed to obtain a discount. The buyer's job is to reduce the price: ironically, in such a case, the vendor would be doing the favour by opening the negotiations with an exaggerated price (see Box 11.1).

4. The kind of social process by which buyer and seller progressively adjust their price; for instance, in the case of competitive bidding situations, based on a tender offer, an excessively high price would eliminate that vendor from the short list of pre-selected candidates.

11.3 PRICE AND CONSUMER EVALUATIONS

Culture-based appraisal of quality and price

It is common knowledge that consumers use price as a surrogate indicator of quality, especially when other criteria are absent. Subjectivity plays a major role in such instances (Zeithaml, 1988), for various reasons:

1. It is very difficult to measure quality objectively. There is no generally accepted method of measuring the objective quality of a product (much less so a service).

2. Even more difficult to measure is the perceived quality of a product. The concept of quality is subjective but not irrational, in the sense that it is based on an evaluation of intrinsic product attributes (e.g. taste, physical characteristics) and extrinsic product attributes (e.g. advertisement, brand, price).

3. Perceived quality combines with other evaluation criteria (perceived monetary and non-monetary prices) to form a perceived value which shapes and determines the consumer's decision to buy or not to buy.

Perceived monetary price means that consumers may not recall the exact price, but may have framed in their minds a simplified, general impression ('it is expensive' or 'it is not so expensive after all'). This price impression should be sufficiently close to consumer expectations if they are to buy (Jacoby and Olson, 1978). With regard to perceived non-monetary price, consumer reactions may be better understood in terms of Becker's (1965) conclusions that an objective price is not the only sacrifice accepted by consumers when they buy a product. Other 'sacrifices', such as the time spent in shopping, cooking and sitting at table, should be included in the accepted price (perceived non-monetary price) before enjoying any satisfaction from the product.

Some elements of Becker's model, which has firm roots in American society and culture, are not cross-culturally equivalent: what is a costly 'sacrifice' in one country may be true enjoyment in another. Consumers do not build these subjective evaluations (of quality, monetary and non-monetary price) through irrational individual idiosyncrasies but through unconscious submission, in their everyday lives, to social representations dictated by their cultural upbringing. To cite a few examples of common aphorisms (the reverse of each aphorism is also defensible):

1. 'It is important to measure time, time is money' (see section 2.2): therefore, perceived non-monetary price will be higher in general for economic-time minded consumers.

2.   'Home-made food is the best': this maxim could, for instance, influence the perceived quality of frozen foods, even though there is no reason why their objective qualities (taste, dietary, conservation) should not be better.

3.   'Where there's pleasure, time doesn't count' (French proverb).

Certain representations directly influence the perceived non-monetary price of a product, particularly the desirability/non-desirability or the convenience/inconvenience of an activity forming a part of the perceived non-monetary price. To put this in a simpler way, the price of a nail for example is not easily separable from the non-monetary price involved in driving it in (i.e. the risk of hitting one's finger in the process). Non-monetary price is related to time costs, search costs and the psychic costs: these costs all enter into the consumer's perception of the sacrifice involved in the consumption experience in exchange for the satisfaction which is derived. Non-monetary price varies a great deal across cultures: a trip to buy a product, or the preparation of meals, may be perceived as enjoyable in certain cultures (no sacrifice; low non-monetary price) and as an inevitable and tedious task in other cultures. For instance, the rapid expansion of the 'do-it-yourself' market in France, in comparison to other neighbouring countries, is related to a marked preference for doing small jobs oneself instead of hiring the services of a tradesman. This behaviour can be traced to a social representation in a high-power distance society where being served is negatively valued: the French concept of *égalité* tends to associate service with servitude and humiliation. The French fiscal system has long corroborated this representation by offering tax rebates to people engaging in DIY, while restricting the opportunity of hiring domestics to the very upper classes.

Relationships between objective quality and price, and choice strategies

One might expect in a competitive market that price and objective quality strongly correlate. However, many studies show that the actual relationship between price and quality is fairly low, probably because consumers are imperfectly informed about both prices and quality of competitive products. Furthermore, quality is often revealed through product use, that is, with post-purchase rather than pre-purchase information cues. The weakness of the relationship between price and objective quality has been empirically assessed in many studies (for a review, see Fauld *et al.*, 1994). Objective quality is based on characteristics that can be measured by consumer tests such as durability, performance tests, safety features, etc. whereas measures of the price–quality relation are based on correlation between product evaluations carried out by consumer magazines such as *Consumer Reports* and their price.

In the United States, Oxenfeldt (1950), in the earliest study on the topic, found a rank correlation of only 0.25 for 35 comparative product tests in *Consumer Reports* between 1939 and 1949. Sproles (1977) found a positive correlation for 51 per cent of the 135 products retained in the study; in other words, in only a very slight majority of cases did a high price objectively correspond to higher quality. However, for 35 per cent of the products he found no correlation and for 14 per cent a negative correlation (lower quality products were priced higher). Similarly, Riesz (1978) found a positive rank correlation of only 26 per cent between price and objective quality among

685 categories of product. Curry and Riesz (1988) studied price quality over the product life cycle for 62 durable products; their findings indicate that when both low-quality/high-price and high-quality/low-price brands were introduced early in the product life cycle, the inconsistent relationship between price and quality tended to stabilize over time.

The same conclusion has been reached cross nationally: in Japan, the mean price–quality relationship reached –0.06 in the study of Yamada and Ackerman (1984), while it was –0.18 in the Japanese automobile industry studied by Johansson and Erickson (1985). In Canada, the correlation for durable products was 0.19 with a range between –0.82 and 0.93 according to product category. In the case of The Netherlands, Steenkamp (1988) reported a 0.29 correlation price–quality relationship with a range almost identical to that of Canada. In the case of consumer durables, Fauld *et al.* (1994), comparing Australia, Canada, New Zealand, the United Kingdom and the United States, find slightly positive price–quality correlations across the five countries, ranging from 0.18 to 0.35. All this confirms that there exists cross nationally a positive but weak correlation between objective price and objective quality.

To put it more concretely, it is not possible for consumers to assess clearly whether the Miele washing machine (from Northern Germany), three times more expensive than the Zanussi machine (from Italy, a subsidiary of the Swedish Electrolux group), lasts three times longer and is a considerably better performer in washing linen. The issue becomes that of how consumers perceive quality and use price as a cue to infer quality. When the consumption experience is immediate, which is often the case for non-durable consumer goods, quality can be assessed almost instantly and the price may not be a significant cue for inferring quality, all the more so when price differentials for non-durables are not large. Sjolander (1992), for instance, shows that when evaluating the quality of the same ice-cream, Polish and Swedish consumers do not differ in their evaluations: whether it is high, medium or low priced, they rate its quality at the same level.

In the case of consumer durables, specifically consumer electronics, Dawar and Parker (1994) have shown that price is a universal signal for quality. The formation of beliefs about price and quality may seem to be similar across nations and culture. In the case of urban Chinese consumers, Veeck and Burns (1995), show that the price–quality relationship is stronger for durables than for non-durables and inexperienced consumers tend to infer more quality from price than experienced ones. Yucelt and Firoz (1993), in the case of Turkey, showed that price is either a good or a fair indicator of quality for 75 per cent of the consumers they surveyed, a high price being relied upon as an indication of higher quality and as a protection against poor buys.

Thus consumers experience difficulties in establishing a clear price–quality relationship especially when quality is revealed by post-purchase experience and over a long period of time such as for household appliances and consumer durables in general. Furthermore, in order to form their perceptual evaluation of total price – monetary as well as non-monetary price – consumers need a better understanding of the costs involved in using the product (Zeithaml, 1988). Often, in the absence of information based on actual product use, they are forced to resort to simplified formulae to guide their choice.

Tellis and Gaeth (1990) depict three basic choice strategies when the consumer has a better knowledge of price than of quality, information on the latter tending to be sparser and more difficult to assess: The first strategy, called *Best value*, is used by people who, from a rational standpoint, choose the brand with the least overall cost in terms of price and expected quality (utility maximizing). In the second strategy, *Price seeking*, price is used as a proxy for the unknown quality (inference) and the consumer chooses the highest-price brand. In the third strategy, *Price aversion*, people choose the lowest-price brand, in order to minimize immediate costs (risk aversion). The significance of these three models varies according to the situation of the consumers – the amount of information they have, their capacity to establish price–quality relations and experience; Tellis and Gaeth show such relations for the United States. But we could also expect different attitudes in making a strategic choice, according to the consumer's national culture.

Cultural dimensions of price–quality evaluation and consumer choice strategies

That consumers are rational and attempt to evaluate, as objectively as they can, price–quality relations is a generally accepted idea. Yet this idea of the best price–quality relationship could be contested in various ways, for example by the introduction of the concept of minimum levels of quality and maximum levels of price, below or above which consumers will eliminate a product from their list of products to consider.

1. *North European consumers*: one may be surprised at the level of prices in northern European shops but also by the robustness and durability of products. A possible explanation is that these countries are Lutheran: this religion favours a certain austerity (in terms of material well-being) as a general way of life. Goods should be expensive in order to limit their consumption (see Box 11.2). On the other hand, people prefer lasting goods, in line with an austere, thrifty and utilitarian outlook on life. As a result, to furnish homes, for instance, they prefer sturdy, long-lasting furniture. This means looking for the best price–quality relation where the minimal level of quality is relatively high, thus eliminating a range of possibilities (even where the price is low enough to enhance the price–quality relationship). IKEA's strategy corresponds to this type of choice (see the case study (A5.2) at the end of Chapter 5).

2. *South European consumers*: purchasing power in southern Europe is somewhat lower than the north European average. People stay outdoors for longer because the climate is warmer; social life often takes place outdoors and is materially much less austere, hence the more pronounced taste for seasonal fashions and for appearance and show. In addition, the Catholic doctrine is rather ambiguous about money, and has little to say about the price–quality ratio. Moreover, the Catholic Church has never been preoccupied, either explicitly or implicitly, with the price and quality of material possessions. The Catholic religion is not a 'lover of money' and could be said therefore implicitly to support spending. Like all idealistic systems with a worldly dimension, the Catholic doctrine manages to sustain the paradox of being anti-money but not anti-expenditure. This is the complete opposite of the Protestant paradox of thrift which considers expenditure as a catalyst for poor morality but still favours the accumulation of wealth.

The difference exists in where the shame lies: for the Catholic, spending is not really shameful, but money is, and the religion rejects money while accepting its pleasures. For the Protestant (excessive) spending is shameful.

Max Weber (1958, p. 31) emphasizes the relative goodheartedness of the Catholic Church, 'punishing the heretic, but being lenient with the sinner', in contrast to the Reform Church which imposes stricter rules and regulation. The Catholic influence lacks the austerity and rigour of Protestantism. In a way, it accords free will to material choice, as in the famous dictum, 'Render therefore unto Caesar the things that belong to Caesar'. Consequently, the Latin (Catholic) consumer is more diverse, particularly in relation to displaying social class. In Latin society, social classes are more distinct and buying has the function of reinforcing one's social image. Given that there are marked differences in buying power, one would expect diversified choice strategies among consumers:

1. Snobbish consumers who, by definition, buy the most expensive foods (the Veblen effect of preferring high prices).

2. Consumers who are more concerned about price and who would automatically buy the least expensive items (price-averse consumers).

3. Consumers who use price–quality relations, in line with the Latin temperament which includes a propensity for intellectual logic and rationality.

BOX 11.2

The Puritan paradox

I fear, wherever riches have increased, the essence of religion has decreased in the same proportion. Therefore I do not see how it is possible, in the nature of things, for any revival of true religion to continue long. For religion must necessarily produce both industry and frugality, and these cannot but produce riches. But as riches increase, so will pride, anger, and love of the world in all its branches. How then is it possible that Methodism, that is, a religion of the heart, though it flourishes now as a green bay tree, should continue in this state? For the Methodists in every place grow diligent and frugal; consequently they increase in goods. Hence they proportionately increase in pride, in anger, in the desire of the flesh, the desire of the eyes, and the pride of life. So, although the form of religion remains, the spirit is swiftly vanishing away. Is there no way to prevent this – this continual decay of pure religion? *We ought not to prevent people from being diligent and frugal; we must exhort all Christians to gain all they can, and to save all they can; that is, in effect, to grow rich.*

(Source: Speech by the Methodist minister John Wesley at the end of the eighteenth century, a few years before the beginning of the Industrial Revolution in Britain. Quoted by Weber, 1958, last sentence italicized by Weber.)

11.4 INTERNATIONAL PRICE TACTICS

Price manipulation

Vendors may interact with customers in markets by using price, with diversified objectives. Pricing may serve three interrelated objectives, focusing on: (1) profits; (2) sales; and (3) market interactions, each being further subdivisible to give a total of 11 objectives. Profit is the most classical objective, and is pursued by trying either (a) to achieve maximum company profits or (b) to reach a target level of profits. The second category centres on the increase of (a) the unit volume of sales, (b) sales figures or (c) cash flows. The third category focuses on interaction with other market actors (customers, distributors, competitors, regulatory authorities) in order to:

1.   Set a price parity with competitors.

2.   Promote the image of the company and/or its products and/or brands.

3.   Achieve greater market stability.

4.   Develop new markets.

5.   Maintain customer loyalty.

6.   Eliminate competitors.

Price is a tactical variable in marketing and, quite often, a policy variable that can be used against competitors. Prices can be manipulated and distorted between (domestic) markets as long as customer or distributor arbitrage can be avoided. In fact, consumers cannot always arbitrate, because of transaction costs, complexities of international trade operations for private people, customs regulations and technical standards; but agents are often tempted to do it for them. Agents can reduce the transaction costs and rapidly gain experience in such practice. For example, certain agents may specialize in re-importing into a country products sold at lower prices in a neighbouring market. Price is both a tactical tool, in local markets, and a strategic tool in face of global competition: price tactics on domestic markets must take their place within a global strategy of cost domination (based on the search for economies of scale and experience effects; see Chapter 8) or differentiation (obtained by designing a product offering differentiated from competitors or tailored to local markets; see Chapter 9). Keegan (1984, pp. 359–60) describes three possible positions for international strategic pricing:

1.   *The extension/ethnocentric position*: a single global price based on the factory price of the goods, the customer being charged for insurance, freight and customs costs.

2.   *The polycentric adaptation position*: local subsidiaries fix their own prices according to local market conditions.

3.   *The intermediate geocentric inventive position*: the subsidiary takes into account local competition and seeks to maximize the firm's total income through international co-ordination of tactical pricing.

There follows an examination of examples of the tactical use of price in international markets.

Signalling willingness to compete: Domestic markets, export markets and dumping

Who gets the lowest prices? This question requires consideration when a company operates on different national markets, in which the opportunity exists to increase profits through price discrimination. It naturally presupposes that buyers or distributors do not have the possibility of arbitrage, buying where cheapest, either for themselves or for resale at a higher price in another national market. Other reasons for price discrimination across national markets may also be found among the 11 pricing objectives cited above.

A basic issue in international pricing is price discrimination between the domestic market and foreign markets which depends on the position of the domestic market *vis-à-vis* the export market on the company's cost curve. Basic microeconomic theory teaches that for a firm to maximize its profit, it must sell its products at a price greater than or equal to the marginal cost (the expenses incurred in the production of the last unit, that is, the direct cost of additional production). In practice, people refer more often to the cost price (the cost price based on the total costs) and may discard it in favour of direct costing (the variable costs directly engaged in production) in industries where overheads are high (aerospace, aircraft, chemicals, steel, etc.).

When a completely new model of aircraft is launched on to the market with initial fixed expenses of US$5 billion, or a new model of car with overhead costs of US$1 billion, is the domestic market or the export market supposed to 'pay' for the depreciation of these sunk costs? This is a very important question. Nevertheless, it calls for a number of subjective considerations. Should the domestic market (or other exclusive markets) pay for their loyalty or, on the contrary, should they benefit from price cuts as compensation and encouragement for their loyalty? If potential car purchasers in Britain, France and Italy were aware of the surcharge they pay (between 10 and 15 per cent) in comparison to, say, Belgian purchasers, perhaps they would show less loyalty.

Figure 11.1 addresses the problem of where to situate the domestic and export markets respectively on the horizontal axis of the cost curve. Since sales (whether domestic or export) usually take place simultaneously, the problem is one of subjective (but stable) conceptualization of the base of the cost curve, as it corresponds to exported quantities. It is this concept that leads directly to the practice of dumping. Dumping is prohibited by Article VI of the General Agreement on Tariffs and Trade (GATT) where it prejudices the production of one of the contracting parties. It allows certain countries to impose anti-dumping taxes on dumping prices. The United States regularly exercises this clause, especially on European and Japanese steel exports. Dumping is based on the following assumptions:

1. The role of the domestic market (or other exclusive markets) is to contribute to the recovery of sunk costs. These markets should therefore be situated on the ascending part of the cost curve in relation to the x-axis (quantities).

2. In placing the home market on this zone, the remaining zone where marginal costs decrease would be reserved for foreign markets where competition is supposed to be more open or where more attractive prices are offered. It should, however, be remembered that one company's home market is its competitors' foreign market.

3. Dumping assumes that foreign markets are considered as rubbish bins. This is true except in the situation where the aim is to assume the role of a predator, momentarily flooding the market with the deliberate intention of raising prices after a sizeable market share has been secured.

Showing commitment in a target market: Gaining market share through pricing

Slashing prices in the short term may appear an attractive strategy for obtaining new clients, building customer loyalty and finally increasing market share. This could even result in the consumer being trapped if prices are subsequently raised and if competitors, who have lost market share, are not prepared to engage in a price war to regain their previous share. Competitors will therefore accept the new *status quo* and products will be priced high.

Slashing prices is a price tactic when viewed from the perspective of a single market. Across markets, however, it is the implementation of a global strategy. The Japanese are unsurpassed in the art of initially penetrating a market through price rebates in order to obtain a sizeable share in it. Johansson and Nonaka (1990, p. 592) describe the pricing strategies of Japanese firms as follows:

The general theme was one of seeing the entry into a market as a long-term 'investment' and market penetration was accordingly a much more important pricing objective than quick profit taking with a skimming approach. Several of the firms employed a version of the 'experience curve pricing strategy' where a relatively low price was expected to lead to large volume and future cost savings. It became rather clear that individual markets were not seen as 'profit centers' but rather as pieces in one large global puzzle. By generating sufficient funds at home and in selected country markets where the share positions were strong, the lower returns emanating from a low price penetration strategy in newer markets could be sustained over a relatively long period.

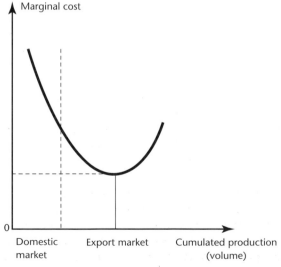

FIGURE 11.1 Dumping and the relationship between unit costs and cumulated production.

Thus, in many African countries, Japanese car manufacturers entered the market twenty years ago offering cheap, reliable, air-conditioned cars (in comparison to the European cars available). Since their objective was not to eliminate competitors, the Japanese left room for European cars after having acquired the lion's share of the market. They did this by raising prices. The benefits of this were threefold: they calmed hard-pressed rivals, raised their profit margins and finally avoided the risk that their relatively low pricing would lead to a lasting unfavourable image of their products.

Avoiding parallel imports: Combating grey markets and opportunistic distributors

A grey market occurs when 'an exporter knowingly or unknowing sells to an unauthorized agent who competes directly with the sole agent appointed by the exporter within the same territory' (Palia and Keown, 1991, p. 47). Grey markets are based on parallel imports that hamper the effectiveness of a marketing strategy across various national markets. For instance, if a company sells at a discount to a distributor in a Central American country because the local consumers cannot afford European or US price levels, there is a risk that the goods will be shipped back from this country to the United States and sold there through unofficial channels (Weigand, 1991). Fragmented national markets are geographically proximate, not only in Europe but also in West Africa, Latin America or South East Asia. Once different price levels are set in two neighbouring countries, consumers, and probably distributors, seek supplies from the cheaper sources, making the manufacturer compete with its own products. If the price differential is large enough to offset transaction costs, unauthorized intermediaries may compete with sole agents or exclusive dealers on national markets where a specific marketing strategy has been defined (see case A11.2). They can be seen as 'free-riders' who take advantage of the costly brand advertising and marketing costs borne by the company and its regular dealers, to cut prices and margins, and build volume without participating in the overall contribution of the channels to the brand's investments (Tan et al., 1997).

Many companies that manufacture home appliances and consumer durables struggle to control the ultimate destinations of their products. For instance, Belgian, Dutch and French agents in cities close to the German border sometimes buy from German wholesalers instead of their domestic distributor, who may sell at a higher price. When price policies implement country-specific prices, they should consider all the opportunities that may exist for consumer and/or distributor arbitrage. As Weigand (1991, p. 53) emphasized, consumer arbitrage is often effected through holiday travelling: 'An English tourist taking a holiday in Miami bought a place setting of bone china made in Britain. She didn't pay Britain's substantial value added tax. Further the dollar was cheaper that day'. Weigand notes that British manufacturers recognize that these personal imports affect their domestic sales. However, they have not found a way to stop them.

The same problem applies to products whose novelty is their major commercial argument. For example, a new music album is marketed in Britain before being put on sale in Italy. In such cases it is difficult to avoid a grey market flourishing, since a segment of well-informed Italian fans receive the news as soon as the album is on the market and will happily pay a premium to be among the first to have the album. The inflated profit margin is pocketed by the 'smart' people who organize the parallel market but who, in doing so, show that they understand the mechanics of urgent demand. Sales by the record company suffer as a result because the company may run out of stock in Britain and, a short time later, may be unable to sell its surplus Italian stock.

The objective of monitoring product price positioning across markets is a difficult issue. Indeed, in certain countries, agents may be forced to sell at prices lawfully dictated by producers. In other countries, however, legislation may consider such practices contrary to effective competition. Resale price maintenance laws prohibit the imposition of prices by the producer on an agent, even though this may be required by marketing strategy. Firms then manoeuvre around these laws through recommended retail price labelling, thus controlling agents' discretionary margin. The agent could, for example, try to sell the product at an offer price (e.g. to promote the agent's store) and come into conflict with the producer's pricing strategy.

Exclusive distribution agreements in home markets would appear to be a plausible solution to the problems of the grey market. But the implementation of such clauses of exclusivity is somewhat difficult. In the United States, there is some reluctance to limit competition by granting enforceable exclusivity rights to dealers. In the United States parallel importers, competing with authorized dealers in leading brands, were accorded an almost complete victory by the K-Mart ruling handed down by the US Supreme Court. Large companies with well-known brands, such as Cartier and Seiko, were struggling against parallel importers, but the Supreme Court judged that they cannot prevent unauthorized importation of products bearing their brand name, since their right to control the trade mark is exhausted by the sale.

European Union legislation also restricts exclusive distribution agreements. EU competition rules (Article 85 of the Treaty of Rome) prohibit any kind of market-sharing agreement by which a company could limit the sales of its distributors exclusively to their domestic market. In order to increase competition across EU countries, Article 85 and several jurisdictional decisions of the European Court of Justice have legitimized parallel imports. A company cannot prevent its 'exclusive' German distributor from selling to Italian customers, even if this company has also appointed an 'exclusive' distributor in Italy. It is therefore difficult to prevent distributors from seeking arbitrage opportunities. Hence grey markets have developed in Europe and other areas, seeking to overcome the many non-tariff barriers whenever price differentials offset the costs of parallel importing.

Possible solutions to the problems of grey markets, that is, solutions which may counter parallel imports, are as follows:

1.   Lower the price in a national market where it is too high and/or inflate it where it is too low, in order to offset not all, but enough, of the price differential, so that there is no longer any profit in parallel importing. This, however, may be at the expense of the global coherence of the marketing strategy in either one or both countries. In the view of Tan *et al.* (1997), authorized dealers, provided that they have a cost advantage, should be encouraged to engage in a price war with parallel importers in order to drive them out of the market. Similarly, authorized dealers could scale down their promotional expenses in order to regain advantage over the grey dealers.

2. Change the product so that the official product is favourably differentiated against the parallel imported product. If changes are only superficial, importers and consumers will not be fooled. If changes are more significant, economies of scale are lost. Other possibilities entail changing minor product attributes: extended warranties can be granted only to authorized dealers, so that parallel importers will offer products with little or no after-sales service and guarantee. A label 'not for export' or 'for domestic sale only' may be attached to the packaging (which also clearly identifies the national origin). This may prevent some dealers from re-exporting. The effectiveness of these labels is very limited, since in most countries it is not legal for a manufacturer to prohibit the export sales of its own products.

3. Tan *et al.* (1997) propose a number of guidelines that allow for the authorized dealers and the parallel importers to live in relative peace when the manufacturer considers both as sources of volume. They may target different consumer segments, determined on the basis of degree of risk aversion; or the unauthorized dealer may scale down its product, warranty and service offering.

4. Educate the dealer (Cavusgil and Sikora, 1988): weaker dealers may be prime targets for grey markets attacks and may, at first, react with an outburst of anger, because it may seem to them that the manufacturer is making excess profit at their expense. Explaining why such price differences exist is part of the manufacturer's role although the dealer may not consider such explanation to be credible.

5. Terminate the dealer agreement (or threaten to do so) when the dealer buys from unauthorized parallel sources. Weigand (1991) cites the case of Apple, which prints the following statement: 'Any Apple dealer or VAR (Value Added Retailer) found to be in violation of the mail-order or transhipping prohibitions will be stripped of its authorized status.'

6. A provisional solution for stopping the flow of unauthorized parallel imports is to buy back the grey market goods. This is positively perceived by authorized dealers, who feel actively protected by the brand owner. Generally, this solution is possible only when a permanent solution to parallel imports has been found and is quickly implemented after a short – and costly – period of buy-back.

Finally it is important to emphasize the risk that consumer perceptions of product positioning may be adversely affected by discrepancies in price for the same good across markets. For example, a Toyota Celica (1990 model coupé with a 16-valve engine) cost US$17,000 in October 1990 (that is, about 85,000 French francs or £8,500). The American market is a competitive one in which indirect taxes are about 10 per cent lower than those in the French market. The same car was sold (without options, like a compact-disc player, as in the United States) for 150,000 French francs (approximately £15,000) in France where Japanese cars were limited by agreement to 3 per cent of the market. It is in the interests of the Japanese car manufacturers to position their cars in the luxury bracket by setting higher prices. Taking into consideration the differences in indirect taxation in order to make a fair comparison, the same car was being sold at a 60 per cent premium in France compared to the United States.

For informed consumers (currently a rather rare species), buying in the home market is no longer attractive when they become aware that home-market prices are artificially inflated. Today, it is generally accepted that consumers are poorly informed as to international price differentials, and even when they are informed, they resign themselves to the idea that tariff and non-tariff barriers are set so that customers remain 'prisoners' of their home market prices. In the future both these assumptions may not continue to hold. Regional integration, in South America, Europe and South East Asia, is speeding up. Consumers are slowly becoming aware of the price levels for similar goods and services in neighbouring countries. They are also being offered increased opportunities for buying abroad, with no customs duties or clearance formalities.

11.5   MARKET SITUATIONS, COMPETITION AND PRICE AGREEMENTS

Ideal versus actual competition

One may wonder what the status of price is in the exchange process: is it an objective equilibrium point of a contract between the two parties or is it the instrument of a social relationship, a subjective equilibrium resulting from the social interaction between buyer and seller? In classical economic terms, the social exchange relationship disappears behind Adam Smith's 'invisible hand' of the market. However, it is debatable whether human nature tends more to alliance or to fighting. Both form part of human nature. The 'invisible hand' of the market puts the real behaviour of competitors in a 'black box', as if their innate tendency is to battle it out to bankruptcy. Is it quite normal for firms to engage in fierce competition? Is it not more in keeping with human nature to seek agreement, to divide territory between companies and to sign pacts, even though their duration may be limited?

On the world-wide market for household cleaning products four main firms compete strongly against each other: Procter & Gamble, Colgate-Palmolive, Unilever and Henkel; to this list the Japanese Kao should probably be added. They are competing head to head for market share on some segments, brands and national markets, whereas in other areas and for other brands armistices have been implicitly signed. Competition patterns have therefore to be surveyed case by case. In fact it is easy to appreciate that behind the normative position that we have largely adopted through its incessant repetition – it is essential to be competitive – a more complex reality exists. To varying degrees, competition and alliances between companies will always occur. Even more complex is the code which delineates to newcomers to the competitive scene (e.g. a national market) how they should behave towards those who are already established players on that scene. Large newcomers frequently face a combined attack from all the firms, domestic and foreign, already present in a national market: they, for instance, lower their prices, spread rumours about the newcomer's product or its service policies, and its real long-term commitment to local customers. This results in poor competition, which is somewhat detrimental to customers: such a (hidden) agreement exists on the French market for fire safety systems, where a norm stricter than the European standard (EN 54) bars outsiders from entering the market; as a result, prices for fire detectors in France are twice as high as in Britain. For all these reasons, the necessary customization of marketing strategies must be carried out according to the *actual* rather than ideal competition patterns.

Market situations and competition-avoidance patterns

Competition is not necessarily self-perpetuating. The dynamics of competition may lead to the concentration of supply amongst a limited number of companies and therefore to an actual decrease in the sum total of competing forces. The United States, the archetype of enacted liberalism, has been much more realistic in this regard than other countries since it introduced effective institutions at an early stage (for example, anti-trust legislation and the Sherman Act) to oversee the proper functioning of competition, to discourage dominant positions and the establishment of monopolies through mergers and acquisitions.

However as Cateora emphasizes, perhaps exaggerating (1983, p. 128): 'Except in the United States, 20th century orientation toward competition has been to avoid it whenever possible'. Inevitably one thinks of the large German cartels, Interessen Gemeinschaft Farben for example, which prior to the Second World War brought together the three major chemical companies, Bayer, BASF (Badische Anilin und Soda Fabrik) and Hoechst, that are now at the forefront of the world chemical industry. One also thinks of the Japanese *zaibatsus*, Mitsui, Mitsubishi and Sumitomo, industrial giants which, under the control of one extended family, encompass activities ranging from banking to car production, and from trading to shipbuilding. The Americans prohibited these *zaibatsus* after their victory over the Japanese in 1945. This has not stopped their continued existence on an informal basis, nor has it prevented competition from progressing extremely effectively within the Japanese market.

Abegglen and Stalk (1986) have demonstrated using the example of the motorcycle industry how competition between companies in Japan is often savage. Honda, which in the 1950s was far behind Tohatsu, completely overtook this firm and in 1964 Tohatsu went bankrupt. After entering the motor car sector during the 1960s, Honda suffered a relative loss of competitiveness in the face of competition from Yamaha, which achieved almost the same market share in 1981. At the beginning of the 1980s, Honda decided to attack Yamaha. Whereas Honda introduced 81 new models and ceased production of 32 (113 changes in product range in all), Yamaha 'only' introduced 34 new models and withdrew three (37 changes). This strategy, in combination with a fierce attack on prices and distribution, led to the collapse of Yamaha at the start of 1983. In addition to substantial losses, Yamaha announced redundancies and a restructuring programme as well as a reduction in stocks. Yamaha's chairman, Koike, was forced to acknowledge his failure publicly. This story, along with many similar ones, shows just how cut-throat the competition is in Japan, contrary to popular opinion. It is one of the principal sources of the strength of the Japanese when they enter foreign markets. This fierce domestic competition is also underestimated by foreign companies wanting to establish themselves in Japan (see for illustration case A9.1).

The simple truth is, however, that an industrialist's vocation is not to enjoy competition as an end in itself. Competition is imposed by public authorities through the opening up of frontiers, and ultimately by competitors themselves. If companies possess the legal and informal means to reduce competition, they will do so, as long as the type of agreement is stable and they do not allow the competing firm, with which the agreement is made, to take advantage of them.

TABLE 11.2   Basic forms of markets according to Von Stackelberg

Buyers	Sellers		
	One	Some	Many
One	Bilateral monopoly	Contradicted monopsony	Monopsony
Some	Contradicted monopoly	Bilateral oligopoly	Oligopsony
Many	Monopoly	Oligopoly	Pure competition

A German economist, Von Stackelberg (1940), had the idea of combining supply and demand situations to construct a typology of forms of markets. He distinguishes buyer and sellers according to whether they number one, several or many (see Table 11.2).

Every country has a few monopolies, some markets where pure and perfect competition reigns and a large number of oligopolies (large-scale consumption and durable consumer goods), oligopsonies and bilateral oligopolies (industrial input goods, such as steel, chemicals, rubber, and capital goods). What varies according to culture is the social approval or disapproval – the level of agreement and implicit consensus between local decision makers – as to whether a monopoly, through the restrictions on excessive competition, may be desirable for the community, or constitutes a danger to it. Intruders, coming from abroad, will then be seen either positively (from the point of view of the consumer) or negatively (from the point of view of the firm in competition with the foreign company, since ultimately the consumers are also often employees and thus potentially unemployed).

Indeed the Americans are often shocked by the amount of protection afforded to their flagship national companies by certain European governments. The Airbus-Boeing saga is typical of these conceptual differences that partly derive their roots from culture. The Europeans consider that the money lent by their governments, often viewed as sunk costs, was used wisely in view of the success of the Airbus aircraft, the number of jobs created, the positive effects on the trade balance and the preservation of the civil aeronautic industry in Europe which was previously under threat (a collective view, not purely liberal). However, for the Americans the affair was a costly mess that helped no one: the successful Boeing company was challenged by disloyal competition, the European taxpayer was further burdened and the standard rules governing international trade were distorted. In many respects, this is all true. Nevertheless, if Airbus did not exist, Boeing would be in a situation of monopoly. The lack of competition could also be seen as a problem.

11.6   MANAGING PRICES IN HIGHLY REGULATED ENVIRONMENTS

In many countries over the last twenty years, the annual rate of inflation has been a double digit one, and sometimes more than 100 per cent per year (which means several percentage points a month and, in some extremes cases, several percentage points a day). This sets definite constraints on pricing policies since prices cannot be increased every day or every week to adjust for inflation.

The case of high-inflation countries

Price stability, at the overall economic level, is a discipline based not only on macro-economic policies but probably also on definite cultural values. The necessary discipline is based on: (1) future time orientation, which provides the monetary authorities with real continuity in their fight against inflation; (2) control of the creation of money and credit; and (3) a belief in free market forces that may keep price increases under control because of active competition (such a belief is, in general, related to individualism and low power distance).

One of the main reasons for inflation being high, and remaining so, is that it profits some of the actors in the economic system: inflation transfers wealth fairly 'smoothly' from some social strata to others. When countries with high power distance (Table 3.3) are compared with those with high inflation, one may note a fairly high level of correspondence. With some notable exceptions (such as Japan), the higher the power distance in a country, the higher its inflation rate. The typical case for high inflation is a developing country, with a semi-authoritarian government and heavy financial regulation (price controls on most goods, foreign exchange control, strict import controls and high duties). High power distance at the society level is expressed in bureaucratic controls and restricted freedom for businesses unless they have the appropriate connections at the top.

High inflation rates generally result in the local currency being systematically weak against the main stable, and convertible, foreign currencies, because of a constant decrease of its nominal purchasing power. In this stereotypical portrait, which can nevertheless be found in at least one hundred countries, the local currency is non-convertible. Furthermore, the exchange rate is maintained at an artificial parity which has more to do with wishful thinking than with economic reality. This results in a parallel foreign exchange market, illegal but tolerated by the authorities most of the time. In comparison to the official exchange rate, parallel rates are favourable to foreign currency sellers and unfavourable to buyers. In Iran in 1993, after very high inflation in the previous years, the official exchange rate was about 1,500 more than the grey market exchange rate, before it was decided to align the official rate. In such situations, foreign exchange controls serve the purpose of enriching the most powerful (because they can buy foreign currencies at the favourable official rate), and restricting the capacity of local exporters to receive a real price (because they are obliged to sell their export receipts in hard currencies at the official rate which is most often grossly overvalued).

Inflation is supposed to be combated by price control, an expression of the power of regulatory authorities over companies. In a high power distance context, oppressive rules (see section 3.6) are the most frequent. Price increases, which are vital for companies to survive, can be delayed by the public authorities even though the last month's or the last week's inflation rate caused the entire industry to go into the red, costs having soared while sales figures stagnated because of controlled prices. For instance, the Brazilian automobile industry is subject to 'staircase' price increases by which Volkswagen, Fiat or Ford are suddenly allowed to increase their price by 50 per cent or more. The strong present orientation of the Brazilian public authorities' action favours high inflation, as is the case in many Latin American countries.

In these countries there is, literally, a high-inflation culture, and consumers and companies are used to living with this. Consumers delay their purchases after price increases occur, buy very large quantities just before increases occur (or because they may occur soon, as price increases are not officially announced). If possible, they stock up with items bought during favourable periods. As a result, sales are largely shaped by price increases or their announcement; the threat of an imminent price increase is used to motivate customers to buy 'now'. Customers must also have a present orientation: they must always be ready to buy at the best possible moment; in the extreme case, 'inflation bargains' are goods bought because they are currently cheap, rather than because they are actually needed. Such customer opportunism may be a problem for the consumers themselves, because they tend to be too price minded and to neglect other important criteria in their decision-making process. Furthermore, if they stock up on perishable items in excessive quantities, it may result in spoilt goods. On the other hand, companies do not depend on consumers for defining prices. The key for prices policy, which is mostly short term, is to negotiate price increases with public authorities. Pricing depends more on government authorization than on customers and competition.

The terms of discussion with price regulatory authorities is highly relational and manipulative, rather than strictly economic. In order to obtain price increases, and the highest possible ones, companies have to argue about losses incurred because of price limitation, and which now have to be compensated. Understandably, cost prices declared in negotiation with regulatory authorities will be systematically overestimated and losses in the previous period will be slightly exaggerated in order to get as favourable a new price as possible. A company will argue for a substantial price increase so to have a 'reserve' before the next increase. Naturally this whole process fosters inflation rather than slows it down. Another way of obtaining the necessary price allowances – to be mentioned, although it is illegal and unethical – is to propose baksheesh or some favours to the civil servants in charge of price control within the public administration.

Over- and under-invoicing

As explained above, many high-inflation countries have legislation aimed at controlling prices. The control may be effected either at retail, wholesale or production level, or at several levels simultaneously. Price increases may be curbed or limited, or even frozen. Trade profit margins may be monitored. The rationale for price control is usually a basic mistrust of free-market mechanisms, often augmented by a long-established tradition of state intervention in the economy.

The foreign exchange regulations also influence the practice of over- and under-invoicing. When countries experience balance-of-trade (and, more generally, balance-of-payments) problems, they often use administrative decrees which aim to stop outright the flow of foreign currency out of the country. Local exporters are controlled: they are forced to repatriate their earnings in foreign currencies as soon as possible and to exchange them for local currency at sometimes derisory exchange rates. Local importers are also under close scrutiny: the absolute necessity of their purchases abroad must be assessed before they are allowed to receive foreign currency to pay for their imports. Furthermore, they are often obliged to deposit a guarantee which may be more than the equivalent of their foreign purchase; this sum is deposited at the central bank in the months before payment, with little or even no interest. Where strict foreign exchange controls are enforced, there is no convertibility of the local currency into foreign 'hard' currencies.

A number of reasons clearly induce firms to practise under- or over-invoicing: they would not be willing to do this otherwise.

1.   When a country is exposed to a high level of political risk, as is the case with many developing countries, local business people seek to transfer funds to foreign banks as fears of political upheaval increase.

2.   Local business people may wish to expatriate money through under-invoicing, simply because they need cash to buy a prohibited (or scarce) product or equipment for their production facilities and particularly for the manufacture of products for export.

Verna (1989) describes various cases of over- and under-invoicing in international trade, relating to differences in currency convertibility. Total convertibility of a currency implies the possibility of its use in all international commercial and financial operations, whatever the object, place or sum concerned. Only a limited number of countries enjoy total convertibility of their currencies. The non-convertibility of local currencies (even more than quantitative restrictions which lead to smuggling) is responsible for over- and under-invoicing (Verna, 1989). Local business people ask their foreign customers to under-invoice, their foreign suppliers to over-invoice, and wait for the extra money to be paid into their bank account abroad. Currency black markets exist only in countries where the national currency is totally non-convertible. As a result, huge discrepancies may be found between the black market exchange rate and the official (central bank) exchange rate. Exporters, obliged to go through official channels, lose major benefits from their transactions. Either they have to sell foreign currency at the official rate, which is abnormally low, or they have to buy foreign currency for their purchases at the parallel rate which, conversely, is abnormally high. Local exporters are therefore tempted to under-invoice; the foreign customer will transfer to a foreign account the extra money in a fully convertible currency. To undertake such transactions the local exporter should have complete confidence in, or a forceful means of pressurizing, the foreign customer.

Over-invoicing works in a symmetrical way for imports. When local importers ask for an import licence from their national authorities, the face value should be as high as possible, since the allowance for buying foreign currency will be increased accordingly. They will ask their suppliers to over-invoice and to transfer the extra money into a convertible foreign account to maximize their overall profits. As Verna states (1989, p. 115):

An import licence will authorize the importer to order goods from a foreign supplier; a specified amount in foreign currency is paid by the local authorities in the name of the importer. In return, the importer should refund the authorities in local currency, at the official rate, and also pay customs duties on arrival of the goods. To obtain such an import licence may be a sort of 'windfall' because it allows the importer to buy foreign goods at a better price than is offered on the free market, mainly through the (favourable) exchange rate differential between the official and black markets . . . import licences can sometimes be transferable. They then become objects of exchange and even the subject of an auction . . . to the extent that some governments, which have become aware of this trade, sell import licences to the highest bidder.

QUESTIONS

1. To what extent does price bargaining involve friendship?

2. What is the relationship between bargaining and 'modern culture'?

3. Discuss the notion of 'economic rationality' from a cultural point of view.

4. How may price levels reflect Protestant as opposed to Catholic values?

5. What are the limitations on a consumer in displaying obvious price-mindedness when shopping? How do these limitations relate to culture?

6. In certain countries smuggling is fairly legitimate: customs officers are not very concerned with arresting smugglers, consumers buy smuggled products knowingly, and smugglers are known by everyone for what they do. Why and under which circumstances is this so? What are the consequences for marketing of smuggling being accepted as a legitimate activity?

7. Since the start of the Single European Market, UK citizens have been allowed to buy up to one hundred litres of alcoholic beverages (beer, wine and spirits) on the Continent and bring them back to Britain. Excise duties on alcohol are much higher in the United Kingdom than in France. UK consumers buy massive quantities of drinks in Calais, France, on the other side of the Channel, twenty miles (33 km) from Dover. French stores have opened special areas for these one-day British travellers who receive special fares from the ferry companies. What are the consequences for the UK brewing industry and for the distribution channels in the United Kingdom? What are possible responses for the UK brewing industry?

8. Is over- or under-invoicing legal? Why is it sometimes inevitable to do it?

APPENDIX 11: TEACHING MATERIALS

A11.1 Case: Saito Importing Company

Some years ago, Saito Importing Company, located in California in the United States, brought in a shipment of wood carving from Bali in Indonesia. At the time, the official exchange rate was 78 Indonesian rupias per US dollar. The 'black market' rate (as it was viewed by the Indonesian government), or 'free market' rate (as it was viewed by most of the rest of the world), was approximately 1,300 Indonesian rupias per US dollar.

The seller requested a letter of credit for one-half the value of the shipment, to be provided by a US bank and confirmed by an Indonesian bank. A request was made that the other half of the money be deposited in an account in a bank in New York.

Obviously, the 'half' that was received in New York had a value many times that of the 'half' received in Indonesia. The money in the bank account in New York was available for the seller to invest, to purchase goods for shipment to Indonesia or else-where, or to use if leaving Indonesia. Money which was held in Indonesia could, at that time, be used for such purposes only with the express approval of the Indonesian government. What the Indonesian exporter did was, of course, illegal under Indonesian law.

Saito Importing Company did not receive the goods until over a year later. Since Bali does not have a port which will accommodate ocean-going vessels, the letter of credit specified that transhipment was allowed. In the process of transhipment, the goods travelled around much of the world and were delayed while waiting for on-going vessels at points of transhipment.

When the wood carvings finally arrived in the US, Saito Importing Company declared the actual price paid for the goods, and indicated to customs why there was a discrepancy between purchase price and the value shown on the documents. The American company did not do anything illegal under US law.

(Source: Saito Duerr, 1989, p. 310.)

QUESTIONS

1. Should the US company have refused to agree to make the payments as requested by the Indonesian exporter? What would have been the expected effect on the price the Indonesian exporter demanded?

2. What effects would you expect the unrealistic official exchange rates to have had on Indonesian exports?

A11.2   Case: Riva International

Françoise Gain, the *directrice du marketing* at Riva in Brussels, Belgium, received aston-ishing results from the consumer panels and distributor panels for September and October 1995. It appeared that sales in Belgium and France of one of its main prod-ucts, the *crème base* Riva, were 20 per cent lower than the production level in the Belgian factory, which supplied both markets. No signs of excess inventories in the distribution in France or Belgium were noticed by the sales force during visits to the distributors.

Riva Belgium was the subsidiary of Riva Products Corporation, a large US-based multinational, whose main business lines were related to the cosmetics and beauty care industry. The Belgian subsidiary was in charge of both the French and the Belgian markets. In 1991 a scientific breakthrough by the corporate R&D laboratories had led to the development of a new skin care cream. Several patents had been filed and reg-istered to protect the property. In Europe, the industrial use of these patents had been licensed to Riva Belgium, which began producing and selling the new skin care cream in February 1992. Sales increased quickly and the new product was received favourably by Belgian and French consumers, who liked both its efficiency and good price–qual-ity ratio. Following instructions from international headquarters, the output of Riva Belgium was intended exclusively for supplying the Belgian and French markets as well as the markets of French-speaking Africa.

In January 1995 the English subsidiary of Riva, UK Riva Ltd, started producing the same *crème base* product. Hefty investments had been made in the English factory to ensure the best quality and a large production capacity. This product had been launched at the top end of the market for skin care cream. It was priced high and supported by heavy advertising and promotional expenses. After a promising start, deliveries had been falling off since August 1995. Actual deliveries to English distributors steadily diverged from target sales.

Françoise Gain knew about this situation as she had been engaged as an internal consultant in the launching of *crème base* Riva in the United Kingdom. However, what worried her most in November 1995 was the gap between sales to consumers in France and Belgium and ex-works shipments. She informed Jacques Graff, chief executive of Riva Belgium and a member of the international board.

At first he did not seem to be bothered by such a gap, and showed little interest in this 'problem': 'Françoise, you know: panel data, what does it mean really? Our product sells well and that is all that matters! Tell your panel company to reconsider their samples and their data collection procedures, and you will see that everything is in fact normal.'

Françoise Gain nevertheless took the decision to undertake an audit by an external consultant. His findings exactly confirmed those of the panels and brought evidence of no sizeable excess inventory at the distribution level. Furthermore it followed from the auditor's investigations that deviations had to be ascribed mostly to deliveries to two large wholesalers, who ranked among the five largest customers of Riva Belgium.

One month after his talks with Françoise Gain, Graff received a confidential note, issued by the chief executive of UK Riva Ltd. It stated that a member of his sales force had accidentally seen, at an English wholesaler, a carton containing *crème base* Riva with country-of-origin label 'Made in Belgium'. The wholesaler had been evasive if not reluctant to tell the sales representative where it came from. Jacques Graff asked Françoise Gain to come to his room, and handed her the note without comment.

'I am not surprised by this note', answered Françoise. 'On the contrary, it is evidence for my suspicions about parallel imports of our Belgian products to England. I have noticed that our sales which vanished from Belgium and France were precisely equal to the drop in the deliveries of UK Riva Ltd. It is now quite clear that some of our wholesalers export to English distributors and that, before doing this, they did not warn our sales and marketing group. I examined the cost structure of UK Riva production and found that our product made in Belgium could be sold by Belgian wholesalers to English distributors at a profit. Belgian distributors may price it at 15 per cent below the English list price, even though there are transport costs.'

'How is that possible?' asked Graff, amazed.

'The English *crème base* Riva was launched with heavy production and promotion costs,' explained Françoise Gain. 'It is positioned at the high end of the market. Its price is higher than any of the competing products. I told them, before launching it, that this retail price level was too high. But I faced disapproval. The finance department at UK Riva Ltd wanted a quick return on investment, taking into account the large cash outflows at the start. The marketing people, backed by the advertising agency, claimed the opportunity to seize a segment which was at the very top end of the market and which had been, up to then, neglected by competitors. Consequently my opinion was put aside.'

Jacques Graff started to walk back and forth. 'As a chief executive of the Belgian subsidiary, I am delighted. Our plant works at full capacity. But, as a member of the international board, I cannot let the English subsidiary plunge. What can we do?'

'One thing is certain', answered Françoise Gain. 'We cannot prevent our customers, namely independent wholesalers, from exporting to England, if they wish to do so. As for the English distributors, one cannot blame them for seizing a better-priced offer and simultaneously taking advantage of the promotional effort of UK Riva! I know it is more easily said than done, but you should have defined, a long time ago, an international pricing strategy at the international board level.'

'It is never too late to do the right thing! Françoise, please prepare a report on your suggestions to cope with this problem of parallel imports of the *crème base* Riva', said Graff in conclusion.

QUESTIONS

1. Why are there problems of parallel imports? Where do they come from?

2. What can be done to stop wholesalers exporting to England?

3. Is it necessary to change the marketing strategy of *crème base* Riva, and especially its price? Where and how?

4. How should one organize to co-ordinate international marketing strategy across national markets? Prepare the suggestions Françoise Gain is supposed to present to Graff and to the international board.

(Source: Adapted from a case written by Alain Ollivier, Ecole Supérieure de Commerce de Paris. Reproduced with the kind permission of the author.)

A11.3 Critical incident: Taman SA

At Taman SA, a Spanish company, sales systematically exceed production. Is this a fortunate situation that arises from the know-how and energetic efficiency of the marketing and sales department? Or is it an unfortunate situation that arises from the lack of production capacity, or the inability of the production department to plan demand peaks effectively? Nobody knows the exact answer.

To tell the truth, one should excuse both the production department and the sales department. In fact the market for high-technology products, in which Taman has built a strong European share, is growing rapidly, at about 50 per cent p.a. Not only is Taman experiencing difficulties in trying to supply its clients, but its competitors also face the same problems.

Costs, be they direct or total, are somewhat uncertain and fuzzy. In spite of a rather elaborate cost accounting system, accountants may endlessly argue about the real cost price of a given order. Diverse and changing factors tend to blur the calculation of costs, such as the allocation of R&D expenses, the cost of components, shared expenses between different orders, the price–volume relation, etc.

The director of marketing and sales and the director of production and operations are constantly in conflict. Conflicts focus on such cases as that of Magnusson AB.

Magnusson AB is a new customer from whom Taman has never, up to now, received an order. Following technical tests of Taman products by Magnusson people at their factory, and after a successful certification procedure, Magnusson is ready to place a fairly large order.

The marketing and sales director argues that getting a new client is something you have to pay for. The director of production and operations considers that the largely positive margin that this order brings is smaller than that of other orders. Besides, he fears that it could disturb the production schedule for the coming weeks and consequently that it could result in numerous delivery delays.

QUESTION

Write in thirty lines how you would describe this problem. What ways and means would you suggest to these two directors for solving their conflict and/or serving their customer base better?

REFERENCES

Abegglen, James and George Stalk Jr (1986), 'The Japanese corporation as competitor', *California Management Review*, vol. 28, no. 3 (Spring), pp. 9–7.

Allen, David Elliston (1971), 'Anthropological insights into customer behavior', *European Journal of Marketing*, vol. 5, no. 3, pp. 45–57.

Becker, Gary S. (1965), 'A theory of the allocation of time', *Economic Journal*, vol. 75 (September), pp. 493–517.

Cateora, Philip R. (1983), *International Marketing*, 5th edn, Richard D. Irwin: Homewood, IL.

Cavusgil, S. Tamer (1990), 'Unraveling the mystique of export pricing', in Hans B. Thorelli and S. Tamer Cavusgil (eds.), *International Marketing Strategy*, 3rd edn, Pergamon: Oxford, pp. 503–21.

Cavusgil, S. Tamer and Ed Sikora (1988), 'How multinationals can counter grey market imports', *Columbia Journal of World Business*, vol. 23, no. 4 (Winter), pp. 75–85.

Curry, David J. and Peter C. Riesz (1988), 'Price and price-quality relationships: A longitudinal analysis', *Journal of Marketing*, vol. 52 (January), pp. 36–51.

Dawar, Niraj and Philip M. Parker (1994), 'Marketing universals: Consumers' use of brand name, price, physical appearance, and retailer reputation as signals of product quality', *Journal of Marketing*, vol. 58, no. 2, pp. 81–95.

Fauld, David J., Orlen Grunewald and Denise Johnson (1994), 'A cross-national investigation of the relationship between the price and quality of consumer products: 1970–1990', *Journal of Global Marketing*, vol. 8, no. 1, pp. 7–25.

Jacoby, Jacob R. and Jerry C. Olson (1977), 'Consumer response to price: An attitudinal, information processing perspective', in Y. Wind and P. Greenberg (eds.), *Moving Ahead with Attitude Research*, American Marketing Association: Chicago, pp. 73–86.

Johansson, Johny K. and Gary Erickson (1985), 'Price-quality relationships and trade barriers', *International Marketing review*, vol. 2, no. 3, pp. 52–63.

Johansson, Johny K. and Ikujiro Nonaka (1990), 'Japanese export marketing: Structures, strategies, counterstrategies', in Hans B. Thorelli and S. Tamer Cavusgil (eds.), *International Marketing Strategy*, 3rd edn, Pergamon: Oxford, pp. 585–600.

Keegan, Warren J. (1984), *Multinational Marketing Management*, Prentice-Hall: Englewood Cliffs, NJ.

Khuri, Fuad I. (1968), 'The etiquette of bargaining in the Middle-East', *American Anthropologist*, vol. 70, pp. 693–706.

Oxenfeldt, A. R. (1950), 'Consumer knowledge: Its measurement and extent', *Review of Economics and Statistics*, vol. 32, no. 4, November, pp. 300–16.

Palia, Aspy P. and Charles F. Keown (1991), 'Combating parallel importing: Views of US exporters to the Asia-Pacific region', *International Marketing Review*, vol. 8, no. 1, pp. 47–56.

Prus, Robert C. (1989a), *Pursuing Customers: An ethnography of marketing activities*, Sage Publications: Newbury Park, CA.

Prus, Robert C. (1989b), *Making Sales: Influence as interpersonal accomplishment*, Sage Publications: Newbury Park, CA.

Riesz, P. (1978), 'Price versus quality in the marketplace', *Journal of Retailing*, vol. 54, no. 4, pp. 15–28.

Roeber, Carter A. (1994), 'Moneylending, Trust, and the culture of commerce in Kabwe, Zambia', *Research in Economic Anthropology*, vol. 15, Greenwich, CT: JAI Press, pp. 39–61.

Saito Duerr, Mitsuko (1989) in Gerald Albaum, Jesper Strandskov, Edwin Duerr and Lawrence Dowd, *International Marketing and Export Management*, Addison-Wesley, Reading, MA.

Sjolander, Richard (1992), 'Cross-cultural effects of price on perceived quality', *European Journal of Marketing*, vol. 26, no. 7, pp. 34–44.

Sproles, George B. (1977), 'New evidence on price and quality', *Journal of Consumer Affairs*, vol. 11, Summer, pp. 63–77.

Steenkamp, Jan-Benedikt E. M. (1988), 'The relationship between price and quality in the marketplace', *De Economist*, vol. 136, no. 4, pp. 491–507.

Tan, Soo J., Guan H. Lim and Khai S. Lee (1997), 'Strategic responses to parallel importing', *Journal of Global Marketing*, vol. 10, no. 4, pp. 45–66.

Tellis, Gerard J. and Gary J. Gaeth (1990), 'Best value, price-seeking, and price aversion: The impact of information and learning on consumer choices', *Journal of Marketing*, vol. 54, April, pp. 34–45.

Veeck, Ann and Alvin C. Burns (1995), 'The formation of beliefs in a price-quality relationship: A study of urban Chinese consumers', *Asian Journal of Marketing*, vol. 4, no. 1, pp. 47–61.

Verna, Gérard (1989), 'Fausses facturations et commerce international', *Harvard-l'Expansion*, no. 52 (Spring), pp. 110–20.

Von Stackelberg, H. (1940), *Die Grundlagen der Nationalökonomie*, Springer Verlag: Berlin.

Weber, Max (1958), *The Protestant Ethic and the Spirit of Capitalism*, Charles Scribner's Sons: New York.

Weigand, Robert E. (1991), 'Parallel import channels: Options for preserving territorial integrity', *Columbia Journal of World Business*, vol. 26, no. 1, pp. 53–60.

Yamada, Y. and N. Ackerman (1984), 'Price-quality correlations in the Japanese market', *Journal of Consumer Affairs*, vol. 18, no. 2, pp. 51–65.

Yucelt, Ugur and Nadeem M. Firoz (1993), 'Buyers' perception of the price-quality relationship: The Turkish case', *Proceedings of the 6th World Marketing Congress*, Istambul: Academy of Marketing Science, 564–8.

Zeithaml, Valarie A. (1988), 'Consumer perceptions of price, quality and value: A means-end model and synthesis of evidence', *Journal of Marketing*, vol. 52, July, pp. 2–22.

12 International distribution and sales promotion

This chapter considers, from a cross-cultural perspective, those elements of the marketing mix which are key in 'pushing' the product towards the customer. This does not mean, however, that no elements of channel and sales promotion management are of universal applicability across countries and cultures. The elements that help to 'push' the product to the customer are as follows: (1) the distribution channels; (2) sales promotion; and (3) the sales force (examined in Chapter 15).

Once again an eclectic approach has been preferred as exhaustiveness is not possible. I have chosen to present the Japanese distribution system (section 12.1) which has often been claimed to be complex and difficult to deal with. The Japanese *Keiretsu* distribution is, in some ways, very different from the western 'modern' style of distribution channels (i.e. depersonalized, simplified, efficient). Section 12.1 describes how the distribution system is rooted in the Japanese landscape (physically) and explains how it also depends on the Japanese national character. Although the distribution channels provoke negative reactions from the non-Japanese (*Gai-jin*), their deep embededness in Japanese business customs renders these criticisms largely invalid. These channels have been under attack from non-Japanese companies, for they supposedly favour Japanese goods and producers and they are reputed to act as a barrier to the entry of imported goods. Some of these disparaging comments have been frequently voiced at the GATT international negotiations; however, these comments reveal ignorance of the deep roots of *Keiretsu* in the Japanese culture. Since channels involve direct relationship with final customers, servicing and informing them, they deeply reflect cultural idiosyncrasies. The next two sections present the criteria for selecting foreign distribution channels (section 12.2) and examine the role of distribution as a 'cultural filter' (section 12.3). Section 12.4 relates to the considerable expansion of direct marketing world-wide; it explains how catalogues and direct marketing tools must be adapted for cross-border use and discusses how the World-Wide Web can be used for direct marketing, the Internet serving as an electronic platform for the international distribution of goods and services.

The last topic in this chapter, sales promotion (section 12.5), has some universal objectives: to let potential consumers try the product, to facilitate repurchasing, to increase the frequency of purchases, to reach a new segment of consumers, to reinforce brand loyalty, and so on. Sales promotion has developed a number of techniques, which have been well documented. Although this whole range of techniques is known in most countries, there is wide variation in their degree of local legitimacy and legal acceptance.

12.1   THE CULTURAL DIMENSION OF DISTRIBUTION CHANNELS: THE CASE OF JAPANESE *KEIRETSUS*

Distribution and Japan

Japan is an insular, heavily populated country, where only a small proportion of the land is inhabitable. A population of approximately 120 million people is effectively concentrated into an area of roughly 60,000 square kilometres, in other words a little under 20 per cent of the total area of Germany. As a result, for every 100 square kilometres of usable space, there are 18.95 retail businesses in Japan in contrast to 1.68 in France and 0.28 in the United States (1985). Distribution is highly fragmented: numerous retail firms with many levels of wholesale and semi-wholesale operations form a complex, confused and seemingly illogical network. There are at present more retail outlets in Japan, 1.62 million, than in the United States (1.5 million), and the average number of employees per retail outlet is 12 in the United States versus only 4 in Japan (Johansson, 1997)

The wholesalers and semi-wholesalers play a central role in the system. Yoshino (1971) gives a historical reason for this: in the past, the manufacturing sector was made up of small businesses which lacked sufficient marketing and management capabilities. The gap was filled by distributors who provided outlets, funding, raw materials and working capital. Similarly, at the other end of the chain, the wholesalers and semi-wholesalers added their expertise to a retail business that was very fragmented. Kuribayashi (1991) and Montgomery (1991) noted a change in the growth trend of retail stores: whereas it grew at 1–2 per cent p.a. until 1982, it is now declining at about the same annual rate (1 per cent). However, this process was largely slowed down by the 1974 large-scale retail store law, which was revised and in fact strengthened in 1979: the law limits the size of stores and requires the approval of smaller-scale retail stores, before a new large store (500 square metres or more) may open.

The retail trade has a close relationship with the customer. Because of the traffic problems (in town centres the speed limit is usually 20 kilometres per hour) and the lack of car parks owing to a shortage of space, many consumers go shopping on foot or by bicycle (Dupuis and de Maricourt, 1989). As a result, the relationship between the consumer and the retailer is a close one and they get to know each other well.

The high level of purchasing power in Japan contrasts with the quantitative limitations on consumption due to the lack of space. The area available actually restricts many forms of consumption: it is not possible to drive such long distances as in

Europe or the United States simply because roads and motorways would become completely jammed. Similarly, the purchase of pieces of furniture or household goods is limited by the availability of inhabitable space. However, as a means of reinforcing this restriction in a positive way, the Japanese are extremely keen on detail, aesthetics, quality and service (Turcq and Usunier, 1985). They therefore demand extensive services from their retailers even if they have to pay for them. Accordingly, they have the benefit of a wide range of services which, although straightforward, do make life easier for the Japanese consumer:

1. Daily opening times of up to 12 or 13 hours.
2. Very restricted periods of closure during the year, for both weekly and annual holidays.
3. Availability of free home delivery.
4. Easy acceptance of returned goods, even though the goods may not be defective.
5. Credit accounts with monthly payments for regular customers.

The compensation for the retailer is in higher gross profit margins which are about 30 per cent higher than the European average (Dupuis and de Maricourt, 1989, p. 129).

Description of the system

This strong relationship – service and loyalty, willingness to pay for the retailers, commitment to their customers – is passed along in the entire distribution structure right through the wholesalers and semi-wholesalers to the producers. Shimaguchi (1978) describes the principal characteristics of the relationships within the Japanese system of distribution by distinguishing both the practice of and the philosophy behind the system of vertical control in the distribution system that the Japanese call *Keiretsuka ryutsu*, or *Keiretsus*. This may be approximately translated into English as 'distribution channel arrangements' or 'integrated marketing networks' (Czinkota and Woronoff, 1991, p. 57).

The practical aspects revolve around a system of discounts, which is widespread and extremely complicated. These rebates operate on three levels: to encourage sales promotion (new consumers, support for products that are selling badly, clearing expensive stocks, etc.); as rewards (for the favourable placing of a product in the shop window or on the shop counter, in an attempt to increase sales); and finally as a means of control (limitation of turnover of competing products, reductions in the rate of return of sold goods, payments in cash or within a short period of time, respect for 'recommended' prices, etc.). These rebates are calculated either on a percentage basis or on a flat rate based on different kinds of sales calculation. Rebates are often confidential to encourage retailers to believe that they are receiving more than the others. However, to avoid frustration and jealousy, many producers have encouraged more explicit systems of rebate.

The system of *tegata* is the second aspect of these sales practices. *Tegatas* are deferred payment systems, based on promissory notes which allow the offer of extended credit periods to the operator at the next stage of the channel. The relationship between two successive layers in this vertical distribution network can be described as (financially) 'protected/obliged'. Trade credit is largely and liberally extended throughout the whole distribution system, rather like in Italy and France, but unlike the United States and Germany where payment times are much shorter. Payment periods range from 60 to 120 days and sometimes to 180 days. Glazer (1968, p. 20) remarks that 'everybody uses them [promissory notes] and some are referred to as "pregnancy" notes, in that they may not become due for nine months and more'. The practice of deferred payments has a snowball effect, whereby everybody in the network, financially strong or not, is threatened by notes which become uncollectable. Accounts receivable are made heavier by the *tegata* practices. Financial reliance becomes not only an individual, but also a collective issue: if one member fails, this may lead to a chain reaction of bankruptcies.

Japanese distribution's commitment *vis-à-vis* service to consumers

The right to return unsold products is extremely liberal because consumer complaints are seen as opportunities for learning rather than as a problem. Learning begins with the consumers at the end of the chain because retailers cannot afford to hold in stock products that have been returned by customers. The dedication *vis-à-vis* consumer complaints is real:

> In Japan, when a customer complains, the sales clerk realizes that the customer has a problem, and then tries to understand exactly what it is. She first empathizes with the customer and adopts the customer's viewpoint to gain a clear understanding of what the customer's problem is. This means listening more than talking, and avoiding judgemental or critical remarks. (Johansson and Nonaka, 1996, p. 33.)

Since distributors receive products to sell rather than order them, they must be given the capacity to provide full feed-back from the consumer to the manufacturer. If the producer does not receive an explicit order from the distributor, the producer will send a *mihakarai-okuri*, which is a delivery based on the producer's estimate of the level of stock held by the intermediary. The wholesalers accept these deliveries, although sometimes grudgingly. They then have to try to sell these extra consignments further on down the line within the network. This presupposes the fairly liberal right accorded to the intermediary and to consumers to return goods even when they are not defective.

A further aspect of the Japanese method of distribution is the high frequency of deliveries. Shimaguchi (1978) explains this high frequency (retailers and wholesalers are in contact daily) in terms of limited financial resources, powerful competition and a tradition of wide personal contact between those who trade with each other. As a result the wholesalers are obliged to sell to retailers in small quantities and at short and regular intervals. Although wholesalers have a tendency to regard the system as inefficient, they accept it because, on a global level, it achieves an economic compromise between increased delivery costs and decreased inventory costs. It is worth noticing the similarities with the *kanban* system of just-in-time deliveries in the field of industrial procurement and subcontracting. One might expect these quasi-affective relationships between channel members to translate into non-aggressive price negotiations and ultimately into non-competitive pricing. Nothing of the kind occurs: the whole distribution system is very much concerned with price levels. Distributors enforce competition, without the need to shift frequently from one supplier to another in order to compel them to keep product prices low. Thus Weigand (1970, p. 24) notes:

> As a consequence of the Japanese commitment toward their employees, Japanese sellers must view prices as a highly flexible marketing instrument. The notion of marginal pricing and the importance of selling at prices that contribute to costs is well understood both by businessmen and by academicians . . . Prices may be cut at any level in the marketing channel by firms that must have sufficient immediate income to meet their unavoidable costs, but the move ultimately will affect the retailers' cost of goods.

Furthermore, the setting of an initial price in Japan is a key decision. Raising the price afterwards may be as difficult as reducing it. The Japanese place a high symbolic meaning on prices; a price reduction may spoil the image of the product, especially when it is intended as a gift (Montgomery, 1991). In fact, Japanese traders in the distribution system fight over price a great deal, in spite of their loyalty to each other; this, in turn, stimulates demand.

'Traders . . . try to resolve their disputes flexibly not necessarily based on formal contacts but on their mutual trust and confidence which has been built up by human relationships and a long, stable continuity of transaction' (Kuribayashi, 1991, p. 55). The personal relationship and human association between the members of the system clearly introduce an emotive element. It is further supported by the practice of gifts. Twice a year, in the middle of the year at *ochugen* and at the end of the year at *oseibo*, the companies send out an enormous number of presents (Shimaguchi, 1978) whose cost, importance and nature conform to a complex code. This practice is further reinforced by business lunches and trips with clients, which are intended to win their friendship rather than to discuss directly any business. This would be considered the height of bad manners.

In addition to the practices cited above, producers often give support to the distribution channels in the area of sales promotion, for example by sending out extra demonstrators and salespeople to supermarkets, or 'kits' for product presentation within the department. There are incentive schemes for retailers whereby they are offered bonuses such as a *kabuki* show, a weekend in Hong Kong or even a week in Hawaii. Although the majority of these practices do exist in other countries to varying degrees (see Box 12.1), sources agree that in Japan they exist in the strongest and most systematic form (Weigand, 1970; Shimaguchi, 1978; Kuribayashi, 1991).

Traditional *Gai-jin* criticisms of the Japanese system of distribution

Numerous converging criticisms of the Japanese distribution networks are made by foreign firms. There are, first, complaints about the distribution system being in collusion with Japanese public authorities trying to protect local business. Cateora, for instance, explains the case of the Coca-Cola company when it introduced Fresca in Japan: 'The Japan Soft Drink Bottlers Association staged an anti Coca-Cola campaign in which they charged unfair marketing practices. Then, when the Coca-Cola company applied to

BOX 12.1

'Master's' retailers at Dunlop France (a subsidiary of Sumitomo Rubber): *Keiretsu* distribution in France

The sports division of Dunlop France (a subsidiary of the Japanese Sumitomo Rubber) manufactures and markets tennis balls. It has developed a system of privileged relationships with its dealers, which is very much like the *keiretsu* system.

The object is to select a limited number of retail shops that procure their articles from Dunlop France. In exchange for certain commitments, retailers receive advantages from Dunlop France. Dunlop aims to improve its brand image and to increase consumer brand awareness. Which retailers may apply for the 'Master's' label? They must be independent retail stores; this excludes large specialized sportshops and hypermarkets. They should have a good reputation with potential buyers and be recognized as experts in tennis equipment; they must also offer product lines for golf and squash. Moreover, they must enjoy total freedom of procurement.

'Master's' retailers enjoy beneficial trading conditions, as in *Keiretsu* distribution. Dunlop France is committed to informing them of new products before other retail stores, and supplying them with the new products first. Finally, Dunlop France publishes a complete list of the 'Master's' points of sale in the specialized tennis press (*Tennis de France* and *Tennis Magazine*). These benefits naturally imply some obligations for retail stores. Retail stores commit themselves to maintaining a defined level of inventory and products on display, both tennis rackets and tennis balls as well as lines for golf and squash. They also commit themselves to sell at least 70 per cent of their tennis balls annually under the Dunlop brand name.

Moreover the retailer must report to Dunlop France any remarks made by consumers that may lead to improvements in the quality of new products. Ultimately, the retail store manager provides a sponsor (usually a well-known tennis professional) with Dunlop France rackets and balls. Presently about 150 stores bear the 'Master's' label. Dunlop France carefully ensures that the selected stores fulfil their obligations. The outcome, as far as brand awareness and brand image are concerned, proves quite satisfactory, especially for tennis rackets.

(Source: Adapted from Eric Zeller, 1989, pp. 33–4. Reproduced with permission.)

introduce Fresca, the association put so much pressure on various Japanese ministries that the company withdrew the application' (Cateora, 1983, p. 622).

A second argument against *Keiretsu* distribution is that it creates such a chain of affective relationships operating vertically between producers, wholesalers and retailers that foreign producers find the systems impenetrable. One of the most heavily criticized aspects is the *itten itchoai* system ('single outlet, single account'), which requires retailers to order only from specified wholesalers and prohibits these same wholesalers from selling to other retailers, thus restricting competition to the whole-sale stage. In the same way, numerous territorial restrictions (exclusive distribution arrangements) are reinforced by the setting up of dealerships for specified areas, which co-operate amongst themselves and increase the producers' ability to impose their marketing strategies (Ishida, 1983). As a consequence, Japanese distribution systems are resented as one of the main obstacles encountered by foreign firms seeking to pen-etrate the Japanese market and even a cause of failure.

Third, Japanese channels are supposed to be inefficient: long, costly, complex and imposing an ultimate surcharge on the consumer. The main reason for their contin-ued existence, despite their inefficiency, must be the Japanese wish to exclude foreign competition, to protect 'Japan Inc.'. For this reason, the Japanese system of distribu-tion has become a major target of criticism from abroad.

Is the Japanese system of distribution impenetrable?

Czinkota and Woronoff (1991) emphasize that the *Keiretsus*, which also exist in the production system, aim to 'keep it all in the family': subcontracting networks are insti-tutionalized, whereas elsewhere they would be fluid and informal. Shimaguchi (1978) has described the main factors, deeply ingrained in the Japanese mentality, which underlie the *Keiretsu* distribution system:

A well-known Japanese psychoanalyst, Doi, wrote a famous book in 1973, entitled *Amae-no-kozo*, that is 'the anatomy of dependence'. Apparently *amae* is a unique fea-ture of Japanese society, which is diffused throughout society, including the distribu-tion channels. *Amae* is 'the indulgent, passive love which surrounds and supports the individual in a group, whether family, neighbourhood, or the world at large. Close dependency and high expectancy of others in a group seems to be the way of life in Japan' (Shimaguchi, 1978, p. 58). Nakane (1973) has also emphasized the role of *amae* in the building and the maintenance of group bonds in Japanese society. It means that relationships between channel members are not depersonalized ones, even when members belong to different companies. Frequent visits of suppliers (producers and/or wholesalers) to retailers are required for maintaining close human relationships in the channels and fostering the quality of the services rendered to the ultimate consumers.

A vertical structure is virtually inevitable in view of the Japanese mentality. The notion of social status is central to Japanese culture. In the field of interpersonal rela-tionships there are three distinct levels: the *sempai* are people of advanced years, highly respected, addressed by their name and the suffix *san*; younger, less experienced people (the *kohai*) are addressed by their name with the suffix *kun*; colleagues on the same level in the hierarchy (same age, experience and seniority) are the *doryo* and should be addressed without a suffix The determination of social status is extremely important and is one of the major reasons behind the widespread practice of exchang-ing business cards. Vertical relationships exist between organizations in much the same way as between individuals.

The Japanese are fairly long term oriented and their sense of time (*Makimono* time, see section 2.2) emphasizes continuity, stability and perseverance. According to

Inagaki (quoted in Turpin, 1990) persistence is instilled into Japanese people by their mothers from early childhood. A survey based on a representative sample of 3,600 Japanese (over 16 years old) has shown that, among the ten preferred words of the Japanese, *doryoku* (effort) ranks first, *nintai* (persistence) second and *kanjo* (tenacity) ranks fifth. As a consequence of its long-term orientation, Japanese business is much more turnover oriented than profit oriented. Japanese companies tend, as far as possible, to accept business as soon as the sales price covers direct costs and begins to cover fixed costs. This fact is illustrated by Hanawa (quoted by Shimaguchi, 1978): '*Kami yori usui Kosen* (margins thinner than paper) is a common saying in Japanese business circles. In certain cases, with a complete disregard for producers' price lists, Japanese distributors end up bargaining machines after harsh negotiations at a price lower than list. Why such low margins'? There is a Japanese business philosophy which believes that 'A deal done is better than none'.

The Japanese themselves (Yoshino, 1971; Shimaguchi, 1978; Ishida, 1983, Kuribayashi, 1991) admit that the *Keiretsu* system is infused with a sense of conservatism, and that it does not lead to innovation. They probably appreciate in the distribution system (a very relational and human sector, everywhere in the world) the warm, sensitive and emotional tradition which permeates marketing and business in Japan.

The question of whether *keiretsu* distribution is intentionally a barrier to the entry of foreign goods on the Japanese market is a difficult one. It seems to be an accusation against the Japanese for what is essentially their way of being. As stated above they are themselves quite critical of their distribution system. According to Ishida (1983, p. 322):

the formation of distribution keiretsu in oligopolistic markets for highly differentiated products has the following consequences: (1) elimination or reduction of interbrand and intra brand price competition, (2) strengthening of barriers against new entrants to the market, (3) restriction of dealer independence with a consequent loss of business enthusiasm, innovation, and rationalisation, and (4) preservation and strengthening of oligopolies.

It may be argued that the above aims to accord tokens of goodwill to the American negotiators (in the Americans' relations with their Japanese counterparts, and in the GATT arena in general), greatly irritated by the Japanese distribution channels which Americans clearly do not understand. This does not prevent the Japanese from recognizing the way in which they may be seen by the *Gai-jin*. But they are not really prepared to change that part of the system which is authentically Japanese, and which constitutes the major barrier resented by non-Japanese business people.

Overcoming the barrier of Japanese distribution

Do real-life examples indicate that foreign companies have achieved original and efficient market entry? Many instances tend to show that the barriers imposed by Japanese distribution channels may be overcome. Ohmae (1985) quotes the case of the US pharmaceutical company Shaklee, which has directly transferred its door-to-door sales system from the United States to Japan. Shaklee had noticed that there was no legal rule requiring vitamins and nutritive pills to be sold only through medical doctors or pharmacists. It was only a custom: no regulation had formally imposed it. The Japanese pharmaceutical companies observed the phenomenal growth of

Shaklee's sales but were unable to react. They were afraid of damaging relations with their traditional intermediaries, especially wholesalers and retail pharmacists. They were still obliged to rely on them for the sales of their drugs. Another US-based pharmaceutical company, Bristol-Myers, also implemented such a door-to-door sales programme, with their Japanese joint-venture partner (Cateora, 1983). The product was sold in a box which contained toothpaste, analgesics and other home remedies, and was offered to households on the basis of consignment sale: every six months a salesperson visited the household, replenished the collection and collected the payment for the products that had been used. Pahud de Mortanges *et al.* (1997) explain how many large pharmaceutical companies from western countries have been able successfully to enter the Japanese market. They have adapted to local selling practices, with one salesperson promoting pharmaceuticals per 2.5 practising physicians – whereas the ratio is one salesperson to every 10 physicians in the United States.

Such cases as Rosenthal (see Box 12.2) or ComputerLand (case A12.1) clearly prove that Japanese distribution channels are penetrable by foreign companies. Montgomery (1991) also provides evidence of US companies, such as Williams Sonoma, successfully circumventing the *Keiretsu* distribution system, via catalogue sales and limited retail stores of their own. Moreover, the Japanese distribution system does change, especially under the harsh competitive forces of the Japanese market. As Ohmae (1985) stated, it is not a 'stone statue', nor are there written rules which prohibit its change.

How to deal with the Japanese distribution system

What are the stages that must be followed to permit successful entry into Japanese channels while respecting the uniqueness of Japanese culture? A five-stage approach for the successful introduction of a foreign product into Japanese distribution channels can be recommended (Shimaguchi and Rosenberg, 1979, Montgomery, 1991):

1. Find a Japanese partner; this is the key to securing adaptability to the unique cultural environment. The *sogoshosha* (trading companies) are potential partners, provided that they do not represent a competing Japanese producer or export the products of a Japanese competitor, and are not related to a larger group (*zaibatsu*) which has competing lines of products. An important choice is to decide whether to ally with a company in the same industry or in a non-related industry. Whereas one may tend naturally to the former in order to ensure a smooth start (in that the two partners share the same business culture), it may prove much more dangerous in the long run. The Japanese local partner may become a competitor on world markets through new products which were originally designed by the joint venture and then transferred to the Japanese partner's main operations (Czinkota and Woronoff, 1991).

2. Find an original positioning on the market, either by offering a significantly higher level of quality or a significant price advantage, or by emphasizing the exoticism of the product as being foreign and imported.

3. Identify alternative opportunities for distribution channels. Philips, for instance, has succeeded in splitting its sales of electric shavers and small household appliances between two different types of channel: large department stores and chains on the one hand, small retailers on the other.

BOX 12.2

Rosenthal in Japan

Rosenthal, a German company, exports porcelain items, fine glassware and trinkets, which sell quite well on the Japanese market, more as gifts than for the buyer's use. The range of products offered in Japan is somewhat different to that in other countries: emphasis is put more on tea-drinking items, which may be offered as presents, than on dishes. Rosenthal constantly surveys the Japanese market, in order to adapt its product range to Japanese tastes and to find those items which could best be sold in Japan. Over the last twenty years, Rosenthal has established close relations with its Japanese distributors. They are frequently invited to visit Rosenthal's production facilities in Germany. Rosenthal assists them a great deal in the display of its products on the shelves and maintains a full-time team of window dressers in Japan. The main dealers, that is large department stores, are visited at least once a week. Moreover Rosenthal has initiated a special training session for Japanese retailers: each year a group of Japanese retailers is invited to a ten-day session in Germany, with all expenses paid by Rosenthal, in order to learn how to advise customers. Retailers greatly appreciate this support, and they willingly push Rosenthal's products, especially since margins are hefty.

(Source: Dupuis and de Maricourt, 1989, p. 152. Reproduced with kind permission.)

4. Be patient, aim for the long term and be prepared to wait for a long pay-back period (probably five to ten years).

5. Be aware that it is necessary to adopt the mentality of Japanese distribution channels. Build a network of personal relationships, develop loyalty, spend time and resources building relationships of trust.

12.2   CRITERIA FOR CHOOSING FOREIGN DISTRIBUTION CHANNELS

The method for selecting channels abroad is based on a checklist of issues that have to be dealt with in the choice of foreign distribution channels (Cateora, 1993, Czinkota and Ronkainen, 1990). The '9-Cs' criteria which seem most significant are as follows:

1. *Consumers and their characteristics.* Some geographical segments in a foreign market may be, for instance, more import oriented. Channels serving these segments should therefore be preferred. The French beer Kronenbourg, for example, entered the United States and was initially available only in the centre of New York, and then went on to reach the whole metropolis including the suburbs. The reason for this is that people within this area consume large quantities of imported as well as US beer. It was not until five years later that Kronenbourg became available throughout the whole of the United States.

2. *Culture.* This point has already been considered in relation to Japanese distribution networks. Distribution is the element of the marketing mix that is most deeply rooted in culture, because it is closely related to everyday life and human relationships (even in large-scale, self-service, apparently depersonalized stores). The next section describes in more detail the impact of culture on selected aspects of distribution.

3. *Character.* It is important that the image projected by the channel, its sales methods, shop locations and clientele as well as appearance, should correspond to the image and character that the product is intended to convey. An important reason for the success of Louis Vuitton-Malletier is the large-scale investment in a global network of exclusive retail outlets, located in high-profile areas in major cities throughout the world. Local consumers may also remain faithful to their traditional distribution outlets for specific segments of consumption, precisely because of their traditional character. In Spain for instance, Nueno and Bennett (1997) explain that despite the continuous development of hypermarkets, consumers make a clear distinction between the products sold in the different distribution channels and prefer to purchase perishable goods such as fish, fresh fruit and vegetables, meat and bread, in traditional stores.

4. Necessary *capital* relates to the issue of what financial resources are necessary to start and maintain the channel (fixed capital, working capital, possible initial losses which will need to be financed).

5. *Cost.* This criterion is strongly linked to the previous one, but relates more to trade margins than to overhead costs. It depends largely on the respective positions of strength of producers and distributors. In the United Kingdom, for instance, food distribution is in the hands of a very limited number of large stores chains such as Tesco, Sainsbury and Asda. These giants exert pressure on major manufacturers to make them bear part of the cost, in particular those relating to storage; they also request smaller, more frequent deliveries with mixed items. A similar situation exists in France where the powerful hypermarkets impose numerous constraints on the producers which increase their overheads: payments of fixed commissions in return for the right to carry the reference number, layout of the counter displays by the producer's own staff, direct help in sales promotion, etc.

6. *Competition* arises in channels either through competing products being placed side by side on shelves, or through competitors refusing other producers access to the distribution channels. Czinkota and Ronkainen (1990) cite the case of the American manufacturers of caustic soda, which is used in the manufacture of glass, steel and chemical products, who have proved incapable of successful entry into the Japanese market despite their price advantage. The Japanese union of manufacturers of caustic soda formed a cartel which apparently set the level of imports, specified which trading company was to work with which American supplier and bought up the cheap American imports in order to sell them through the intermediary of its members. The success of the operation was twofold since they received the profit in place of the American exporter and still managed to keep control of their market. The American exporters were equally unsuccessful in their attempts to deal directly through small distributors, since the industrial users

of the product were concerned about the risk of cutting themselves out from their main source of supply (the Japanese) if they placed orders directly with the American exporters.

7. *Coverage* is another important element. It is important to cover markets that are widely scattered. Furthermore, markets that are very concentrated tend also to concentrate maximum competition, since demand attracts supply. The coverage in terms of product range, sizes and options must also be considered, especially when channel members look for complementary products, spare parts and so on. The product coverage according to channel type varies across countries: a French *droguerie* doesn't sell the same products as a US *drugstore* or a German *Drogerie*, although there is overlap between the product ranges.

8. *Continuity*. It is vital that the channel in which investment is to be made does not turn out to be unusable for some reason (e.g. bankruptcy or financial difficulties, recapture of market share by more aggressive competition, the introduction of legal prohibitions on the sale of products through the channel, etc.). Continuity may be hampered by slick competitors. Cateora (1983) cites the example of an American firm which lost roughly half its local sales in South America. Two of its European competitors had unofficially agreed to force the American company out of the market. One of the two, which was selling a wide range of products, forced the distributors to stop representing the even wider range marketed by the American. The other competitor purchased shares in the company that distributed the American company's products.

9. *Control*. The ideal situation is of course where the company creates its own distribution network. This ensures maximum control. It appears that integrating the company's own distribution abroad should be considered, particularly when the product differentiation is large (i.e., where there are few substitutes) or where the network assets are transaction specific, such as a product which requires lengthy training for the consumer as well as the seller (Anderson and Coughlan, 1987). The alternative to control by equity is control set up by carefully drafted contract (the written base), or preferably through long-established trusting relationships with the local distributor (personal verbal base). For example, the Caterpillar company sells world-wide without sales subsidiary companies, by using a system of dealers. Some Caterpillar dealers have been in business for more than half a century.

12.3   THE ROLE OF DISTRIBUTION AS A 'CULTURAL FILTER'

Culture at the interface between shoppers and the stores

Distribution forms subtle relationships with consumers by means of direct contact. People get into the habit of buying certain products which are backed by fixed services, at clearly defined times, in particular shops. Table 12.1 presents guidelines for enquiring how distribution is affected by the prevailing cultural patterns in a particular country/culture context. The table refers to specific sections in other chapters where some of the underlying rationales have already been exposed. Naturally culture explains only part of the variance in distribution systems; another part is related to shoppers and their sociodemographic characteristics or to economic conditions.

Shopping behaviour differs in many ways according to culture. The first point to take into consideration is whether the shopping experience is partly experienced as a waste of time in the whole consumption process, as may be the case in countries where time is strongly economic. The differences in opening hours in northern and southern Europe clearly illustrate the influence of culture on the distribution system: in northern Europe, Sunday is sacred and a prevailing feminine orientation strives towards protecting store employees' quality of life (which would be spoilt by long opening hours).

Certain products may be banned from particular outlets for legal dispositions based on religious or social beliefs. In France, for instance, basic drugs, and more generally non-ethical drugs such as aspirin, can be sold only through pharmacies; in the United States, as in many countries, drugstores sell basic medicines. These practices correspond to differing views on whether people can have recourse to self-medication. The French legislators do not trust patients and require them to proceed in all cases through doctors and pharmacists, whereas the US system is confident of people's common sense and ability to distinguish what is a flu and what is a serious illness.

TABLE 12.1   Influence of culture on some aspects of distribution
**   *vis-à-vis* shoppers**

Selected aspects of distribution	Traits which *may* differ according to country/culture
(1) Shopping behaviour	Is time spent shopping experienced as wasted? (economic time; section 2.2)
	Is return of goods standard behaviour? (complaining behaviour; section 4.3)
	Who is the shopper? (sex roles, age, etc.)
	Degree of loyalty to the shop and the shopkeeper (section 4.2)
(2) Opening hours	Religion-based arguments in favour of restricted store opening hours
	Femininity-based arguments (store personnel should not be exploited)
(3) Product range	Products may be banned because of religious or legal prescriptions
(4) Willingness to service consumers	Human nature is good (friendliness towards shoppers) versus bad (indifference)/negative view of service to others (section 9.3)
(5) Waiting lines	Compliance with rules (see Tables 3.3 and 3.6 and section 9.3)
(6) Thefts by consumers or personnel	Ethical behaviour – ingroup orientation (see sections 2.3, 3.6 and 15.6)
(7) Self-service vs. personnel in contact	See section 9.3

Another example concerns the distribution of beer in Turkey, a Muslim country; up to June 1984, beer was considered a non-alcoholic beverage and thus sold in coffee-houses; beer consumption increased sixfold between 1969 and 1983. Under pressure from religious authorities, the government reclassified beer as an alcoholic beverage (which it is), banned its advertising on radio and television and prohibited its sales in outlets lacking alcohol licences. The prohibition of sales through the channel of coffee-houses resulted in a dramatic drop in beer sales in Turkey (Miller and Demirel, 1988).

Wide differences also exist in the waiting and service conditions at the cashier's desk: in the United States and Japan it is standard practice in supermarkets to help customers pack their purchases; an employee is often specifically in charge of packing; in most of Europe, where mass distribution is oriented towards low price rather than service, customers have to pack their things in a hurry while paying their bill (Turcq and Usunier, 1985).

Theft, either by customers or store employees, is an important phenomenon in distribution that has to be deciphered, country by country, in light of cultural differences. Naturally economic constraints (purchasing power per capita) play a certain role but they do not explain all: in France and Italy, theft is more developed than in Greece which has a much lower per capita income. In some countries, theft is not a problem because it is clearly understood as evil by everybody. The kind of consensus which brings about this favourable result is hard to explain, and probably even harder to replicate. Where the rate of theft to sales amounts to several per cent, it cannot be explained simply by economic conditions, namely poverty. Theft is regarded by some as a sport and is implicitly understood as a legitimate way of social redistribution. Another explanation is strong ingroup orientation whereby ethical behaviour is limited to the ingroup: in countries where retailers are immigrants belonging to a particular foreign group, thieving from a store that belongs to a foreigner may not be felt to be evil but rather as a way to recover one's own goods from this 'outlander'.

The influence of culture on the relationship between channel members

Depending on the country concerned, the relationships between domestic producers and distributors may be stronger, more loyal and collaborative, or weaker, more unstable and conflictual. Strongly established links between members of domestic channels generally make entry more difficult for foreign firms. France, which largely invented the concept of the hypermarket, benefits from a distribution set-up that is effective, powerful and strongly independent of producers. It is so strong that products bearing the store name compete head to head with the producers' brands, creating an atmosphere of conflict between producers and distributors where loyalty is difficult to maintain. The system is inherently susceptible to penetration by imports: foreign suppliers are perceived as more flexible and a good alternative to domestic producers. At the other extreme Japan is the place where links between producers and distributors are traditionally very strong and positive. Central to this are the *Keiretsus* of distribution, true vertical relationships, mixing business and emotion in typically Japanese fashion, described in section 12.1. These networks are based on a powerful sense of loyalty, with many services being rendered by one party for the other, and therefore more difficult for foreign companies to penetrate.

Kale and McIntyre (1991) posit a series of hypotheses on channel relationship based on Hofstede's (1980) four cultural dimensions. They first consider the initiation process where firms try to draft the distribution agreement. According to them companies coming from high uncertainty avoidance (UA) societies will be biased in favour of finding partners who have a solid reputation and can offer written performance guarantees; conversely, in the case of weak UA, partners will be sought more informally and more flexibility will be shown in negotiations. Firms in highly individualist and masculine cultures (typically the United States) will tend to choose partners on objective criteria, negotiate the terms of the agreement from an adversarial standpoint and engage in new relationships as well as divorce themselves from the old ones on the basis of economic criteria. Conversely, partners coming from collectivist and relatively feminine societies (for instance South Korea, Taiwan, Thailand) will be more relationship centred and will expect more harmony in the partnership, and dissolution will be less aggressive and less frequent.

During the implementation process, Kale and McIntyre hypothesize that high power distance (PD) will lead firms to use coercion in their influence attempts, whereas low PD firms will avoid coercion, will prefer face-to-face communication to memos and will engage in consultative rather than unilateral decision making. High individualism and masculinity will result in more frequent and manifest conflicts between channel members and lower co-operation. In contrast to these orientations, they cite a senior executive of Coca-Cola in Japan explaining that: 'Once the partnership was in place, it wasn't just the Coca-Cola company selling in Japan; it became a family, a spirit of togetherness, of common purpose.'

O'Grady and Lane (1992), by interviewing chief executive officers of almost 300 companies on both sides, show that Canadian retailers when they enter the US market have to face different values. Americans are significantly more competition oriented (more achievement oriented, more risk taking) and more oriented towards a Protestant work ethic than the Canadians. The Canadian retailers are shown to be less individualistic and masculine and higher in power distance and risk avoidance than the American distributors. These findings are largely consistent with the hypotheses of Kale and McIntyre in distinguishing competitive/confrontational distribution scenes from collaborative ones: 'The executives frequently commented that Americans were found to be much more competitive than Canadians. Frequently the executives voiced comments typically used to describe battles such as 'It was all out war' or 'Their arsenal was impressive' (1992, p. 8).

Shoham et al. (1997) have studied conflicts in international channels of distribution, that is, when channels members belong to different cultures and are separated by cultural distance. They show very clearly that the degree of channel conflict increases with cultural distance, whereas a high quality of distribution systems, in the form of visiting foreign markets frequently and providing channel support, tends to decrease channel conflicts. In the case of Greek exporters (collectivist/high UA and PD) and their British importers (individualistic/low UA and PD), Katsikeas and Piercy (1991) show that the relationships are fairly stable with a low degree of conflict and few communication problems, except on pricing issues. This is reinforced by the fact that, among the British importers, there are a good number of Greeks or Cypriots, which shows the strong value of having one's own countrymen as 'beachheads' in the target market.

12.4   DIRECT MARKETING WORLD-WIDE

One among millions of direct marketing purchasers in the world, I buy the family Christmas cake (a Deluxe medium, 2 3/4 pounds) from Collin Street Bakery in Corsicana, Texas, which is baked following the traditional recipe of Gus Weidman, a Bavarian who went to the United States at the end of the nineteenth century. Bought by credit card, the cake reaches my home in France within one month. Catalogue sales have been expanding world-wide at a very fast rate over the last ten to fifteen years. In 1993, *Catalog Age* reported that 37 per cent of US mail-order companies had international operations while another 20 per cent were considering the possibility of an overseas programme (Robles and Akhter, 1997). Lands' End, one of the leading US direct marketers world-wide, sends its products to more than 170 countries, while large European mail-order companies such as Otto Versand, Quelle, Bertelsmann and La Redoute have developed important cross-border operations, especially in Europe (Akhter, 1996). The development of international credit cards and the consequent facilitation of international payment have greatly decreased the transaction costs for both consumers and cataloguers. Restrictive legislation opening hours for stores may be an incentive for consumers to buy direct: Germany and Austria, two countries where store opening hours have been historically strictly limited in comparison to other developed countries, rank first and fourth world-wide as regards catalogue sales per capita (Mühlbacher *et al.*, 1997); the German catalogue industry is the strongest in the world relative to country size.

Among the problems involved in selling direct cross-border are, first, logistics issues: direct mail can be sent from the domestic country, from within the target country, or from a third country, with the objective of minimizing mailing costs while keeping speed and security of delivery at a fair level. Although it may seem the easiest solution to mail from within the target country because the local language and culture will be better understood, there may be constraints in the local postal service which make it more advantageous to mail from a third country; this can prove cheaper in terms of mailing costs (Desmet and Xardel, 1996). The second major issue about cross-border direct marketing deals with regulation, mainly postal regulations, customs and privacy issues, all of which are largely country specific (Rawwas *et al.*, 1996). They become, however, more and more standardized at the regional level, however, as in the EU, where a European Union Postal Service has been implemented in 1998 after six years of preparation. Customs may be a problem since goods sent to reach the foreign customer for a specific date (e.g. Christmas) can be delayed by customs; this will, however, not be the case when goods are shipped to industrialized nations.

The third issue is the availability of mailing lists, and their degree of reliability in terms of names and addresses, especially when they are not regularly updated. Rosenfield (1994) makes an international comparison of direct marketing in the USA and in other countries, and states that US marketing is different rather than better. Mailing costs in the USA are comparatively low, but mailing lists are sometimes of marginal quality, causing a low net response rate. Among the European countries, France appears as the highest-tech country in the world for direct mail but with expensive lists; Germany also has very high standards and world-class technology but

German lists are subject to stringent privacy rules (*Datenschutz*); Italy, on the other hand, with its inefficient postal service, is a relatively difficult context for direct marketing. In Latin America, Argentina and Chile are favourable countries with fairly good infrastructure, but Brazil lags behind because of post and phone problems.

Direct marketing has to be adapted for language and cultural reasons. The text, for catalogues, letters and so on, is generally prepared with the help of locals or even directly in the target country to ensure appropriateness of language. Some catalogues advertise directly world-wide in English. Examples are *the World's Best*, from Baltimore or *Shepplers*, which sells Western wear; they target an affluent English-speaking audience and use international mailing lists or selective national mailing lists. The Lands' End catalogue contains a four-page leaflet called 'Lands' End Glossary' which explains the basics in Arabic, German, Japanese and Spanish. Language adaptation must also target the addressee's name: 'Jean', a boy's first name in French, is a girl's first name in English, so that sometimes I receive international direct mail addressed to 'Mrs' or 'Ms'. The source culture is often indicated by the origin of the mail, the letter or the stamp, and it may be desirable to emphasize this culture if it is positively valued in the target country (which will be the case when there is a strong association of the source country with the products sold and a positive evaluation of it as a country of origin). Conversely, it may be better to fully localize operations when the name must be local: Germany's Bertelsmann sells books and records direct in France, under the name 'France Loisirs', because the original company name is not positively associated with cultural products in France. The Bertelsmann's book club operates in various European countries (Germany, France, the UK) and adapts its operations to suit each country, within the same basic formula (a two-year subscription with a minimum purchase of one book every three months): the catalogues are adapted for each market; in France it sells through 500 salespeople, a method that is totally ineffective in the UK; there are no shops in the UK but France and Germany maintain a network of 200 and 300 shops respectively (Desmet and Xardel, 1996).

Ethics are a problem in international direct mail; concerns with privacy, and the possible fraudulent uses of mailing lists are major concerns in a number of countries: Germany and New Zealand have very strict privacy regulations but some other countries are more lenient. Even in neighbouring countries, such as the United States and Canada, ethical views on direct marketing differ: Canadians tend to have more power distance than Americans and to resent letters in too direct a style; therefore, letters have to be written differently for Canadian audiences (Graves, 1997).

In 1999, only a very few countries are not connected to Internet. Direct marketing is increasingly using the Internet as a global medium. Lands' End, like many other direct mail companies, has a Web site from which everything in the catalogue can be ordered: it checks the inventory in real time, totals the order and provides for payment and shipment. CatalogSite, for instance, offers catalogues on line to both end customers and catalogue distributors, and 3M's Web site gives information on a growing number of its 60,000 products, provides access to further information on its products and world-wide operations, and offers items for sale. The growth of the Internet is exponential, probably doubling every six months, and even cautious China launched the China Web, in 1996; in 1995, 22 countries went on line (Quelch and Klein, 1996). Some companies have flourished on the Internet, such as the book distributor

Amazon.com, the leading bookseller on the Internet, which devotes a Web page to each book offered. The Web allows companies to display a considerable amount of information on their products: the AMP connect Web catalogue enables users to navigate among 70,000 different spare parts. Toyota's Web site offers text screens with detailed product specifications and dealer locations; potential consumers can also test a variety of colours and view their future car from a variety of vantage points as well as look at interiors (Hodges, 1997).

Although a fascinating instrument for international marketing, the Internet has a number of limitations, in terms of extensive use. The first key issue is that of the network infrastructure which was initially built for US national defence purposes and was then developed by academic users. The commercial development of the Web is a formidable challenge because the numbers of servers have to be regularly increased and jams on the Web are nowadays a reality. The second issue concerns the safety of payments by credit card on the Internet, specifically, the need to ensure that the card number is not used fraudulently by opportunistic Internet navigators. Although many potential customers see this as a problem, the use of encryption and the presence of specialized intermediaries between supplier and customers makes fraud more and more unlikely. Payment will be less of a problem in the future since it is now possible to load one's bank card with cash value using one's regular bank's Web site, and use electronic cash anonymously for on-line purchases (Hodges, 1997).

Quelch and Klein (1996) foresee that the main uses of the Internet for international marketing will be: sending company information to internal customers (employees and intermediaries), sending product information to and conducting transactions with customers, and providing marketing and sales support and information to internal users. Only a limited number of products can be sold on the Internet, because virtual shopping lacks the full scale experience of real shopping, especially the human encounter and the opportunity to see and buy the product directly. This alone explains the failure of some virtual shopping galleries which ceased operating within a few months. The word 'virtual', often advertised as if it were an 'open sesame', is far from inoffensive:

> The technology of virtual simulation cannot but reinforce this risk of de-realization by giving a pseudo-concrete and pseudo-palpable character to imaginary entities . . . On one hand, thus, they constitute tools to command complexity, propitiating a better intelligibility, on the other they have a certain propensity to encourage latent forms of illusion and even schizophrenia. The more we recur to simulation as a scriptural means and as a way of inventing the world, the greater the risk to confound the world with the representations we make of it. (Queau, 1993, pp. 98–9, cited by Ribeiro, 1997, p. 499.)

The characteristics of Internet users are very specific: they are generally higher educated and English-speaking, necessarily computer literate, and belong to the younger generations. As a consequence electronic commerce tends to market successfully those products which make sense for such an audience, many of the products being either computer related (from software to ink cartridges), or education (e.g. books) and leisure related. A more general limitation to the growth of the Internet is its almost exclusive use of English: unless people can read English, the majority of Web sites are irrelevant to them. While the quality of the Web as a global medium cannot be questioned if English is assumed to be its natural language, it is much less so when one considers the French, German or Spanish speaking sites, which are generally ignored. As Letts (1997, p. 16) emphasized: 'The irony of course is that until the World Wide Web localizes, it won't be a global medium. In localization, it will allow global companies to offer market relevant programs, and that . . . is the secret to successful globalization.'

12.5   SALES PROMOTION: OTHER CUSTOMS, OTHER MANNERS

Sales promotion techniques are fairly universal, but in their use and the conditions of their implementation they vary cross nationally and depend on cultural variables (see Box 12.3). Sales promotion targets some basic marketing objectives that are cross-culturally valid. It aims to engage the consumer in any of the following: (1) a first trial; (2) a first purchase; (3) an immediate purchase; (4) re-purchase; (5) an increase in frequency of purchases; and (6) entering a point of sale. Promotional techniques combine the sales proposal with the following:

1. Discounts or rebates of various kinds: coupons, 'in-pack' money-off, reimbursement offers, etc., mostly directed at immediate purchase.
2. Competitions: games, contests, lotteries, sweepstakes, etc.
3. Collection devices of various kinds (stamps and continuity plans), oriented towards increasing the frequency of purchases and building consumer loyalty.

BOX 12.3
Global transferability of sales promotions: Lego examples

A case in point is Lego A/S, the Danish toy marketer which undertook American-style consumer promotion in Japan a few years ago. Earlier, the company had measurably improved its penetration of U.S. households by employing 'bonus' packs and gift promotions. Encouraged by that success, it decided to transfer these tactics unaltered to other markets, including Japan, where penetration had stalled. But these lures left Japanese consumers unmoved. Subsequent investigation showed that consumers considered the promotions to be wasteful, expensive, and not very appealing. Similar reactions were recorded in other countries. Lego's marketers thus got their first lesson on the limitations of the global transferability of sales promotions.

In 1997, Lego is involved in a global promotion with Shell Oil since promotional Lego toys have been designed exclusively to be distributed at Shell's 44,000 service stations world-wide. The material for this global promotion will be the same world-wide but the tactics used, including giveaways, cash-back coupons and discount coupons, will be decided locally.

(Source: Kashani, 1989, pp. 92–3 and Koranteng, 1997. Reproduced with permission.)

4. Free samples or some kind of cross-product offer, for the purpose of consumer trial especially.

5. Gifts: 'in-pack' gifts, purchase with purchase, reusable packaging, product bonus, etc.

Cross-national differences in the use of sales promotion techniques

The first question to be addressed is: who is the target? It is not solely the end consumer. Sales promotion may also address store personnel by encouraging them to stock a product or to display it in a favourable position, or to promote a product directly. In some countries, the success of some batteries derives from the fact that store personnel put one brand in a more favourable display position than others; they do so because of the gifts they receive from the batteries' manufacturers, ranging from a camera to vacations abroad. In less developed countries, where retailers in rural areas lack resources, they may be more appropriate targets for sales promotion than the final consumers who have little choice but to buy what is actually in the only store available. Similarly, where people have servants who shop for food and household supplies, it may be better to target them, the actual buyers, rather than the members of the family who employs them (Foxman *et al.*, 1988).

A second question is whether a technique is considered ethical: sales promotion regulations differ cross nationally according to various assumptions about what is moral or immoral and what is fair or unfair in the relationship between a merchandiser/sales promoter and a customer/shopper. Most developed countries strictly regulate sales promotion in order to prevent abuses (Boddewyn and Leardi, 1989). There is also some fear, as with advertising, that sales promotion costs could result in overpricing of products. Czinkota and Ronkainen (1990) cite the example of AC Nielsen, which tried to introduce money-off coupons in Chile that had to be sent to the manufacturer for reimbursement. The supermarket union opposed the promotion on the grounds that it would raise costs unnecessarily and recommended its members not to accept the coupons.

The areas in which ethical issues are mostly raised are competitions, gifts and cross-product offers. The United Kingdom and the United States are the most favourable countries for sales promotions (Boddewyn and Leardi, 1989). Anglo-Saxon countries are generally more liberal than other countries, especially for competitions: most kinds of lotteries, free draws and sweepstakes are legally permitted. In most Anglo-Saxon countries, private betting organizations (bookmakers) are permitted whereas in most other countries, betting (horse races, lotteries) is state controlled, since it is seen as immoral for private individuals to profit from organizing lotteries and betting games. Italy authorizes lotteries and sweepstakes where prizes are not in cash but in kind. Prizes in competitions are often limited to small amounts: the Netherlands limits prizes to 250 guilders, which severely restricts the attractiveness of sales promotion competitions. France allows competitions, but they are carefully controlled so that no purchase is needed to enter the competition. This leads in many countries to precisely drafted regulations where terms such as 'purchase obligation' and 'chance' are strictly defined (see Box 12.4, which describes the regulation of sales promotion competitions

BOX 12.4

Sales promotion through competitions in Switzerland (Geneva)

Competitions for sales promotion are governed by the law on lotteries. The basic principle is fairly simple: *chance cannot be linked with an obligation to purchase.* On this basis there are three situations where a competition is considered lawful:

1. There is no purchase obligation and the right answers are not to be found by chance.
2. There is a purchase obligation and the right answers are not to be found by chance.
3. There is no purchase obligation and the right answers are to be found by chance.

Consequently, it is necessary to define the two expressions 'purchase obligation' and 'chance'.

Definition of 'purchase obligation'
1. A label, a cap, or any part of a packaging has to be sent by post.
2. The entry form for the competition is printed on the reverse of a label.
3. The entry form is inside the packaging.
4. There is a participation fee for the competition.
5. The competition is announced in a place where people are attending a paying performance.
6. Where the competition is organized by a newspaper and is publicly advertised and the newspaper or magazine has to be bought in order to cut out the entry form.
7. A piece of information is required which is on the label or packaging, and cannot be found by simply looking at the product on the shelves.
8. If, to obtain such information, people are compelled to enter a sales room where they cannot 'escape' the salesperson, the judge may consider that there is a 'moral constraint' on the purchase.

Definition of 'chance'
1. Random draw.
2. Random draw in the event of tied entries.
3. A question which cannot be answered by skill, science, calculus or knowledge, for instance: time taken by the winner of a race; flight time of a plane; number of cigarettes or matches which have to be put end to end in order to cover the distance between two cities; to be the tenth visitor to an exhibition, the twentieth buyer of a product, and so on.

(Source: Adapted from Gambiez *et al.*, 1988, pp. 12–13.)

in the canton of Geneva, Switzerland, where Swiss precision leaves little room for ambiguity).

Many national regulations prohibit gifts or limit their value. In France, the value of a promotional gift cannot be higher than 4 per cent of the retail price and must not exceed FFr. 10 ($2). The idea behind this prohibition is that consumers should buy products, not gifts. If the value of the gift is too high in comparison to the total price of the item, this could result in the consumers being fooled by the merchandiser. Collectors' items, as gifts, are subject to the same kind of regulatory ceiling: the value of the collector's item associated with the purchase is often legally limited. Sales promotions encouraging a first trial, such as cross-product offers and purchase with purchase offers, are often controlled by national legislation because, when consumers pay for two products at the same time, they cannot clearly assess the one for which they actually pay. A description of the sales promotion rules of the main countries (which are regularly updated) may be found in Boddewyn (1992).

Some sales promotion techniques are fairly resistant cross culturally, since they appear less questionable: free samples as a way to induce people to try the product; money off the next purchase as a way to induce consumers to repeat their purchase; point-of-purchase materials, product tastings or demonstrations as a way to increase consumer knowledge of the product, etc. However, some countries object to sales promotion techniques in general because of the risk of consumers being misled. Whereas some countries believe in the personal responsibility and ability of consumers to seek and evaluate information (the United Kingdom, the United States), others have less confidence in the capacities of individual consumers to make free and responsible choices (Latin European and northern European countries). In Scandinavian countries, sales promotions face the greatest obstacles, since every promotion has to be approved by an official body.

Sociocultural factors influencing the implementation of sales promotion techniques

Table 12.2 presents a series of sociocultural factors, some of them already mentioned above, which influence the implementation of sales promotion techniques. The level of literacy is obviously an important variable to be considered since promotion is often associated with text; if the target market is largely illiterate, people will not respond to a coupon campaign for instance. Level of literacy becomes crucial when the purpose of the campaign is consumer education. Visual and oral promotion should be given preference over written materials wherever the literacy rate is low. Promotional campaigns in some African countries travel from village to village showing a promotional movie film while the operator hands free samples of the product to the audience. Conversely, an increasing level of education and political awareness may be favourable for promotion that has a higher ambition: Thailand's state-owned oil company Bang Chak Petroleum, which offered two oranges or a copy of the Thai constitution as promotional gifts, was more successful with the constitution booklet (Wentz, 1997).

Retailer sophistication is required when the promotional techniques need some follow-up, such as redeeming coupons or dealing with stamps or collectors' devices, that is, the retailer needs to be an intermediary between the manufacturer and the

TABLE 12.2   Cross-cultural adequacy problems for selected sales promotion techniques

Technique	Culture-related features which may affect implementation
Coupons	Level of literacy, consumer and retailer sophistication/low social status implied
Contests and sweepstakes	Legal requirements/Prizes must suit target market tastes
Price-offers	Absence of price labelling and display/bargaining/trade misuse
Stamps and collections	Future orientation needed/high inflation/level of channel sophistication
Free samples	Interpretation of gratuity/trade misuse/theft of sampled products
Gifts (in, on or near packs)	Legal requirements/theft by channel employees or customers

final consumer in a fairly organized way (stocking coupons, reckoning, ordering premiums, etc.). If prizes are given, they must suit the target market's tastes: this is especially important in competitions where the prizes are advertised. Cars, trips, various household equipment or goods, or cash are possible prizes: whenever legally possible, cash is the most universally acceptable prize, since it allows further free spending.

Unethical trade behaviour *vis-à-vis* the manufacturer is possible in a number of cases: retailers can decide to sell what were supposed to be free samples or they can pocket price-off offers by increasing prices. Retailers' employees can put aside samples, gifts or premiums for themselves or others. Strict control of the retailers involved in a promotion is required wherever such opportunistic attitudes are possible.

Promotional techniques can be associated with images of social status. Foxman *et al.* (1988) give the example of Hong Kong where the response to coupons is very positive, whereas the use of stamps is popular in Thailand, both of these locally popular techniques being associated with middle-class status. In many countries coupons or price-off offers can be associated with low-class status, because the implied price consciousness mediates an image of low purchasing power. On the other hand, promotional techniques based on a price reduction cannot be implemented in countries where basic prices are not displayed and bargaining is the rule: the rebate has a meaning only inasmuch as a clear market price is known by the consumer. Once again, in such cases, it is better to target channel members rather than the end user, for instance by offering retailers a rebate for quantity sold after a certain period of time, as they will be obliged to make sales in advance to customers in order to build volume.

Some promotional techniques require extended involvement, such as collectors' devices, stamps or self-liquidating premiums, refunds after a series of purchases, etc. Cultures with a present time orientation respond poorly to these techniques which require future orientation because of delayed gratification (Foxman *et al.*, 1988). Similarly, high inflation is very detrimental to any sales promotion whose rewards are not virtually immediate: the face value of coupons, price-off offers and other rebates may have little meaning after the passage of the few weeks necessary for printing, distribution and claiming of the rebates.

The final caveat is that it is necessary to check that the purpose of the promotional technique is locally understood (this is a problem of conceptual equivalence). For instance, in many societies being given a free sample is difficult to interpret. The basic rationale, that a producer wants consumers to try a product in order to have them buy it, is not self-evident. A free sample is understood either as a sign of poor quality ('they give it because they cannot sell it') or as a sign of the naivety of the manufacturer ('let's take as much as possible'). P & G, which is now expanding rapidly in eastern Europe, experienced major problems with free samples in Poland in 1993, where some people ignored them whereas others broke mailboxes to steal as many samples as they could. In any case, it must be kept in mind that price reductions are by far the most popular sales promotion techniques (Boddewyn and Leardi, 1989).

QUESTIONS

1. A distribution formula is successful in the United States; you are asked to extend it through a franchise system to several countries around the world. How would you devise a policy for those franchisees who want adaptation to the standard recipe for their home market, in the following areas: size of the store, personnel recruitment, servicing, stocking, brands represented, display, store name, etc.?

2. What are the ways in which retailing know-how is transferred internationally?

3. Discuss the distinguishing features of the Japanese distribution system.

4. Why do exporting firms tend to have somewhat different distribution channels abroad compared to their domestic market, apart from the peculiarities of the local distribution systems?

5. Until recently, the typical store in Germany was open each day, from Monday to Friday, from 9 a.m. to 6.30 p.m. On Saturdays, German shops close at 2 p.m., and they all close on Sundays. Once a month there is a special shopping Thursday, and stores open till 8.30 p.m. Conversely, opening hours in the United States are much longer and some supermarkets have 24-hour opening, seven days a week. Stores employees in Germany are highly unionized and unions have traditionally opposed any increase in opening hours. To what extent do time-related cultural differences explain the huge difference in store opening hours between Germany and the United States?

6. Using a local catalogue (from your own country), explain how (in terms of language, size, photographs, prices, product information, delivery and payment conditions, etc.) it should be adapted to be sent to a culturally remote market with a similar level of economic development (choose the target market).

7. Discuss how store size can be related to culture.

8. Explain how cultural values can have a negative impact on self-service and auto-mated service in general (that is, without personnel in contact with the shopper/consumer).

9. Based on available statistics, review key differences in the retailing systems in the countries of the European Union.

APPENDIX 12: TEACHING MATERIALS

A12.1   Case: ComputerLand in Japan

ComputerLand recognized that they would need a Japanese partner in order to enter the Japanese market. Because of government regulations and attitude, it probably would not have been possible to obtain permission to establish a wholly owned subsidiary. Additionally, the complexities of the Japanese market would have made development of franchises there very difficult. (Both McDonald's and Kentucky Fried Chicken entered the market with Japanese partners.)

ComputerLand wanted a partner who had experience in both procurement and distribution of computer products. Though they talked with a number of companies, Kanematsu-Gosho Ltd emerged as the top candidate. Kanematsu-Gosho was a major trading company, had experience in the desired areas, and already had business dealings with IBM. ComputerLand entered into negotiations with the Japanese company in order to try to develop a joint venture. The discussions, which lasted for nine month, were detailed and difficult. The Chairman of ComputerLand was concerned that if his vice-president went to Japan to negotiate, he would be at a disadvantage trying to operate in the different culture. He therefore insisted that the negotiations be done in the United States by telephone from Japan.

This made it difficult for the Japanese to negotiate. The Japanese decision-making process requires much more consultation and agreement with the company than would normally be necessary in European and American firms. There were long delays and a lot that had to be done through telex correspondence. Among other things, the Japanese government had to be persuaded to allow the American partner to have a 50 per cent ownership rather than the customary (at the time) minority position. The agreement was finally concluded with ComputerLand contributing knowledge, trade mark, and technology and Kanematsu-Gosho contributing cash to start the joint venture, ComputerLand Japan Ltd. The Vice-President of ComputerLand then went to Japan to head the operation as Vice-President and Resident Director. A number of policy and operational problems had to be solved.

In the United States, franchisees were required to pay cash before merchandise would be shipped to them. An attempt was made to follow this policy in Japan. Retailers in Japan, however, are used to receiving credit from wholesalers – often for 0 to 90 days or even longer. A cash-in-advance policy proved to be impossible in Japan, so the company eventually went to a 10-day-open-credit policy.

In the United States, franchises were given only to individuals, not to corporations or other businesses. This was done so that the stores would be personally managed by the owners. ComputerLand Japan was not able to find a sufficient number of individuals who had or could obtain the necessary cash. Eventually the policy was changed to allow a company to own a minority interest. As in Europe, store locations and format were also a problem. Within the United States, ComputerLand insisted on a minimum size for a store of 2,000 square feet (185 m^2), a location with a large amount of traffic going by, and a parking lot in the rear. This was simply not possible in most locations in Japan.

It was also difficult to attract top-quality people as employees to work for a foreign company in Japan. Finally, there were simple problems of coordination between proprietor-owned ComputerLand and large, publicly owned Kanematsu-Gosho. In spite of these difficulties, ComputerLand Japan was very successful, growing to 50 franchises with annual sales of US$50 million. It was assisted greatly by the fact that, for the first two years of operation, ComputerLand had the exclusive distribution right in Japan for the IBM PC.

Over the years, Kanematsu-Gosho found it increasingly difficult to continue to accept some of ComputerLand's policy. Additionally, they felt that the American partner was simply exercising too much control. When ComputerLand offered to buy them out, Kanematsu-Gosho agreed. The operation then became a wholly owned subsidiary of the United States corporation. Eventually, this subsidiary was sold to one of the franchisees who continues to operate it under a license agreement with ComputerLand.

(Source: Written by John T. Sakai, Director, AZCA Inc., former Vice-President of ComputerLand.)

QUESTIONS

1. Was it wise for ComputerLand to insist on holding the negotiations in the United States? What were the advantages and disadvantages to each of the parties? Why did Kanematsu-Gosho agree to the location?

2. Analyze the differences between the Japanese and American distribution systems as they appear in this case. Which elements of the 'ComputerLand model' are transferable to Japan?

3. When exporting to another country or setting up a joint venture there, how can you decide which of the local customs and business practices you should accept, and which of your home country practices you should introduce?

A12.2   Case: Aunt Sarah's Fried Chicken

Early in March 1993, Jean Michel, president of Aunt Sarah's Fried Chicken–Europe, was faced with the problem of maintaining quality control among franchisees in Germany. He had received reports that several of the franchisees in Germany were serving potato pancakes instead of French fries. Also, there were reports of inconsistency in the size of the servings of chicken. Aunt Sarah's had built its reputation on its ability to offer a completely standardized product of high quality in every retail outlet.

Aunt Sarah's Fried Chicken was started by Sarah Browning in a little shop in Dallas, Texas, in 1958. The great popularity of her home-style fried chicken led to expansion to other locations in Dallas and in neighbouring cities. Because of limitations of capital expansion to other American markets was accomplished through franchises. By 1977, Aunt Sarah's had 760 franchise outlets in the United States. From the time she opened her second location in Dallas, Ms Browning had found that her most difficult continuing problem was in maintaining consistent standards of quality in all retail outlets. When she launched into franchising, she recognized that this problem of quality control would become even more serious, since the many individual franchisees lacked the same experience and commitment to a standardized product as did members of the Aunt Sarah's organization. Franchisee visitation and quality control were placed under the direction of a separate division headed by Ms Browning's daughter, Cynthia. In 1993, the American market was divided into nine regions, each with its own Sales, Site Selection and Construction, and Operations and Quality Control divisions.

In 1978, an entrepreneur in Paris, France, sought and received the first franchise outside the United States. As requests began to be received for other foreign franchises, it became necessary in 1981 to establish Aunt Sarah's Export Company, a wholly owned subsidiary. Aunt Sarah's chicken fitted into European eating preferences as well as being a popular foreign novelty item. It soon became evident that the European market was potentially large and should be actively cultivated. In 1983, the European division was set up with Jean Michel, a Belgian advertising executive, as the new director, with the headquarters office in Brussels. Michel was successful in establishing new franchise outlets at the rate of about ten per year. By 1987 there were sixty-one outlets in Europe, more than Michel could personally supervise. Since the Aunt Sarah reputation was just as dependent on high-quality food preparation and absolute consistency in Europe as in the United States, it was necessary to improve the system for maintaining careful supervision over the franchise outlets. Consequently, in 1988, Mr Michel divided the European division into four regions – England, Benelux, Germany and Italy – each headed by a regional manager.

From the start, the regional division managers had difficulty enforcing company operating procedures among the international franchisees. Mr Schmidt was having particular difficulty with the fifteen franchises in Germany. The franchisees had little confidence in Mr Schmidt and resented his attempts to control their activities. Most of the franchisees had been with the firm longer than he had. Each had gone through a company training programme, either in Dallas or in Brussels, and had subsequently operated his business without the help or advice of a German regional manager. During the period of minimal supervision, many had modified their product to fit what they felt were the unique needs of the local market. For example, three franchisees had decided that potato pancakes would be more popular than French fries in their parts of Germany. Two others had modified the carefully developed mixture of spices used in the chicken batter. Although these modifications had been accepted in the local markets where they were made (the franchisees involved had excellent sales performance), these aberrant outlets failed to present the standardized product and atmosphere expected by Aunt Sarah customers throughout the world. Mr Schmidt was a 1985 graduate of the INSEAD graduate programme in business in Fontainebleau, France. Before joining Aunt Sarah's in 1992, he worked for a large department store in Bonn. He was bright, well trained and 36 years of age. The typical franchisee in Germany was in his forties and had worked in the restaurant or food business for a minimum of 10 years. These entrepreneurs were reluctant to accept suggestions about how to run their business from Mr Schmidt.

QUESTIONS

1. Evaluate Aunt Sarah's policy of standardizing operations and recipes according to the American pattern in different cultures such as Germany and France.

2. How can Jean Michel help Mr Schmidt in his relations with the German franchisees?

(Source: Adapted from Cundiff and Hilger, 1988, pp. 295–7.)

REFERENCES

Akhter, Syed H. (1996), 'International direct marketing: Export value chain, transaction cost, and the triad', *Journal of Direct Marketing*, vol. 10, no. 2, pp. 13–23.

Anderson, Erin T. and Anne T. Coughlan (1987) 'International market entry and expansion via independent or integrated channels of distribution', *Journal of Marketing*, vol. 51, January, pp. 71–82.

Boddewyn, Jean-Jacques (1992), *Premiums, Gifts and Competitions*, International Advertising Association: New York.

Boddewyn, J. J. and M. Leardi (1989), 'Sales promotion: practices, regulation and self-regulation around the world, *International Journal of Advertising*, vol. 8, no. 4, pp. 363–74.

Cateora, Philip R. (1983), *International Marketing*, 5th edn, Richard D. Irwin: Homewood, IL.

Cateora, Philip R. (1993), *International Marketing*, 8th edn, Richard D. Irwin: Homewood, IL.

Cundiff, Edward W. and Marye Tharp Hilger (1988), *Marketing in the International Environment*, 2nd edn, Prentice Hall: Englewood Cliffs, NJ.

Czinkota, Michael R. and Illka A. Ronkainen (1990), *International Marketing*, 2nd edn, Dryden Press: Hinsdale, IL.

Czinkota, Michael R. and Jon Woronoff (1991), *Unlocking Japan's Markets*, Probus Publishing: Chicago, IL.

Desmet, Pierre and Dominique Xardel (1996), 'Challenges and pitfalls for direct mail across borders: The European example', *Journal of Direct Marketing*, vol. 10, no. 3, pp. 48–60.

Doi, T. (1973), *The Anatomy of Dependence*, Kodansha: Tokyo.

Dupuis, Marc and Renaud de Maricourt (1989), '*France/Etats-Unis/Japon, trois mondes, trois distributions*', Cahier ESCP no. 89–81, Ecole Supérieure de Commerce de Paris.

Foxman, Ellen R., Patriya S. Tansuhaj and John K. Wong (1988), 'Evaluating cross-national sales promotion approach strategy: an audit approach,' *International Marketing Review*, vol. 5 (Winter) pp. 7–15.

Gambiez, Chantal, Hélène Lelièvre and Véronique Surget (1988), La Promotion des Ventes en Suisse, Research paper for the International Marketing Seminar, Ecole Supérieure des Affaires, University of Grenoble.

Glazer, Herbert (1968), *The International Business in Japan: The Japanese image*, Sophia University: Tokyo.

Graves, Roger (1997), 'Dear Friend' (?): Culture and genre in American and Canadian direct marketing letters', *Journal of Business Communication*, vol. 34, no. 3, pp. 235–52.

Hodges, Mark (1997), 'Is Web business good business?' *Technology Review*, vol. 100, no. 6, August/September, pp. 23–32.

Hofstede, Geert (1980), *Culture's Consequences: International differences in work related values*, Sage: Beverly Hills, CA.

Ishida, Hideto (1983), 'Anticompetitive practices in the distribution of goods and services in Japan: The problem of distribution Keiretsu', *Journal of Japanese Studies*, vol. 9, no. 2, pp. 319–34.

Johansson, Johny K. (1997), *Global Marketing*, Chicago, IL: Irwin.

Johansson, Johny K. and Ikujiro Nonaka (1996), *Relentless: The Japanese Way of Marketing*, New York: HarperCollins.

Kale, Sudhir H. and Roger P. McIntyre (1991), 'Distribution channel relationships in diverse cultures', *International Marketing Review*, vol. 8, no. 3, pp. 31–45.

Kashani, Kamran (1989), 'Beware the pitfalls of global marketing', *Harvard Business Review*, September–October, pp. 91–8.

Katsikeas, Constantine S. and Nigel F. Piercy (1991), 'The relationship between exporters from a developing country and importers based in a developed country: Conflict considerations', *European Journal of Marketing*, vol. 25, no. 1, pp. 6–25.

Koranteng, Juliana (1997), 'Shell lets local decisions steer global promotion', *Advertising Age International*, October, p. 13.

Kuribayashi, S. (1991), 'Present situation and future prospects of Japan's distribution system', *Japan and the World Economy*, vol. 3, no. 1, pp. 39–60.

Letts, Alex (1997), 'If the Web is so worldwide why is it mainly in English?', *Advertising Age International*, May, p. 16.

Miller, Fred and A. Hamdi Demirel (1988), 'Efes pilsen in the Turkish beer market: marketing consumer goods in developing countries', *International Marketing Review*, vol. 5 (Spring), pp 7–19.

Montgomery, David B. (1991), 'Understanding the Japanese as customers, competitors and collaborators', *Japan and the World Economy*, vol. 3, no. 1, pp. 61–91.

Mühlbacher, Hans, Martina Botschen and Werner Beutelmeyer (1997), 'The changing consumer in Austria', *International Journal of Research in Marketing*, vol. 14, pp. 309–19.

Nakane, Chie (1973), *Japanese Society*, University of California Press, Berkeley.

Nueno, José Luis and Harvey Bennett (1997), 'The changing Spanish consumer', *International Journal of Research in Marketing*, vol. 14, pp. 19–33.

O'Grady, Shawna and Henry W. Lane (1992), 'Culture: an unnoticed barrier to Canadian retail performance in the United States', Academy of International Business Annual Conference, Brussels, 22 November.

Ohmae, Kenichi (1985), *La Triade, Emergence d'une stratégie mondiale de l'entreprise*, Flammarion: Paris.

Pahud de Mortanges, Charles, Jan-Willem Rietbroek and Cort MacLean Johns (1997), 'Marketing pharmaceuticals in Japan: Background and the experience of US firms', *European Journal of Marketing*, vol. 31, no. 8, pp. 561–82.

Queau, Philippe (1993), 'O tempo do virtual', in André Parente (ed.), *Imagem-Maquina*, Rio de Janeiro: Editora 34, pp. 91–9.

Quelch, John A. and Lisa R. Klein (1996), 'The Internet and international marketing', *Sloan Management Review*, vol. 37, no. 3, Spring, pp. 60–77.

Rawwas, Mohammed Y., David Strutton and Lester W. Johnson (1996), 'An exploratory investigation of the ethical values of American and Australian consumers: Direct marketing implications', *Journal of Direct Marketing*, vol. 10, no. 4, pp. 52–63.

Ribeiro, Gustavo Lins (1997), 'Transnational virtual community? Exploring implications for culture, power and language', *Organization*, vol. 4, no. 4, pp. 486–505.

Robles, Fernando and Syed H. Akhter (1997), 'International catalog mix adaptation: An empirical study', *Journal of Global Marketing*, vol. 11, no. 2, pp. 65–91.

Rosenfield, James R. (1994), 'Direct Marketing worldwide: One man's perspective', *Journal of Direct Marketing*, vol. 8, no. 1, pp. 79–82.

Shimaguchi, Mitsuaki (1978), *Marketing Channels in Japan*, Ann Arbor: Michigan.

Shimaguchi, Mitsuaki, and Larry J. Rosenberg (1979), 'Demystifying Japanese distribution', *Columbia Journal of World Business*, Spring, pp. 38–41.

Shoham, Aviv, Gregory M. Rose and Fredric Kropp (1997), 'Conflicts in international channels of distribution', *Journal of Global Marketing*, vol. 11, no. 2, pp. 5–27.

Turcq, Dominique and Jean-Claude Usunier (1985), 'Les Services au Japon: l'efficacité . . . par la non-productivité', *Revue Française de Gestion*, May–June, pp. 12–15.

Turpin, Dominique (1990), *World Competitiveness Report*, IMD/World Economic Forum: Lausanne.

Weigand, Robert E. (1970), 'Aspects of retail pricing in Japan', *MSU Business Topics*, vol. 18 (Winter), pp. 23–30.

Wentz, Laurel (1997), 'Global Village', *Advertising Age International*, October, p. 1–3.

Yoshino, Michael Y. (1971), *Marketing in Japan: A Management guide*, Praeger: New-York.

Zeller, Eric (1989), Masters thesis, Ecole Supérieure de Commerce de Paris, pp. 33–4.

Intercultural marketing communications

Introduction to Part 4

INTERCULTURAL MARKETING COMMUNICATIONS

Language plays a central role in marketing communications when they take place in an international and multilingual context, since communication styles as well as world-views are deeply influenced by the structure of languages. Part 4 reviews four major types of marketing communication tools in turn: advertising, personal selling, public relations, marketing and business negotiations. These tools are used to communicate not only with customers but also with all stakeholders in the market, including middlemen, business partners, public authorities, and even competitors.

Communication is never language-free. That is why, before we examine these communication tools, we look in Chapter 13 at intercultural communication, both verbal and non-verbal. This chapter explains how language shapes our world-views, inasmuch as the words we use and the way we assemble them in speech correspond to particular assumptions and experiences about the world in which we live. This naturally results in ethnocentrism, that is, a spontaneous tendency to refer to our own beliefs and values when interpreting situations and trying to make sense out of experience. Stereotyping is part of the game of reducing unfamiliarity to familiarity by oversimplifying foreign traits. It comes therefore as no surprise that misunderstandings in intercultural communication are quite frequent. The last section in this chapter explains how to avoid cultural misunderstandings and improve communication effectiveness in international business, especially when using interpreters.

The main tool for communicating marketing messages to customer audiences is advertising. For reasons of image consistency, many companies want now to promote their products globally through standardized advertising campaigns which use the same advertising strategy and execution world-wide. Thus, the question to be answered before transferring campaigns cross-nationally is: which elements should be localized and which ones can be similar world-wide? Chapter 14 first examines the general influence of culture on attitudes towards the social utility of advertising, especially when advertising adopts a comparative stance. International companies have to make decisions in two main areas, advertising strategy (information content, advertising appeals, etc.) and advertising execution (characters and roles represented, visual and textual elements, etc.). Based on a review of cross-cultural studies of advertisements, the chapter explains the extent to which both strategy and execution can be standardized or should be localized. The focus is then on the development of global media resources and the globalization of advertising agencies.

Much marketing information is also communicated directly to market stakeholders, that is, presented and explained directly by the sales force or indirectly through intermediaries or business partners in foreign markets. Chapter 15 starts by explaining what 'commerce' means from an intercultural perspective, that is, the ways and means to communicate effectively with the market in both directions, rather than in a one-sided exchange as is largely the case with advertising. The chapter therefore develops a number of issues that are central to personal selling in an international perspective: how to network in business markets, buyer–seller interactions, how cultural differences affect the management of the sales force, public relations across cultures, and, last but not least, the issue of bribery and business ethics in an international context.

The last two chapters in this book are dedicated to a topic that is generally ignored by international marketing textbooks, that of negotiating sales and business agreements. Good communication with business partners must be a key concern when marketing across borders, languages and cultures. Chapter 16 explains how trust is a sensitive asset in relational marketing and reviews the influence of culture on international marketing negotiations, using the framework developed in Part 1 of the book. It explains how divergence in the underlying concepts of negotiation, the preferred outcomes, the attitudes towards time, etc., may result in misunderstandings during the negotiation process. Chapter 17 presents some elements of the national style of business negotiation for different cultural groupings and proposes guidelines concerning international marketing negotiations.

13 Language, culture and communication

Glen Fisher, a distinguished scholar in the field of intercultural relations, has described a conversation with a Latin-American friend about the words used in English and Spanish for business relations. His friend first remarks that in English the word 'business' is positive. It connotes the fact of being 'busy' and emphasizes doings things. Expressions such as 'getting down to business' highlight people who have a responsible concern for their work. Fisher further explains that:

In Spanish the word is 'negocio' . . . The key is the 'ocio' part of the word, which connotes leisure, serenity, time to enjoy and contemplate as the preferred human condition and circumstance. But when harsh reality forces one from one's 'ocio', when it is negated, then one has to attend to 'negocio'. The subjective meaning is obviously much less positive than in English. (Fisher, 1988, pp. 148–9.)

In this chapter, several such examples show how a linguistic/cultural group, through words or language structure, expresses a definite world-view, '*eine Weltanschauung*' as the Germans express it. The anthropologist and linguist Benjamin Lee Whorf went even further, arguing that language shapes our world-views, our behaviour toward others, and our manner of acting. Language is obviously a major – though not the only – component of culture. However, it is for many reasons underemphasized in international business literature. First, language seems to be translatable: there are dictionaries and, if need be, professional translators. Unfortunately this ignores the fact that a part of the message which is culturally unique is lost in the translation process (as the Italian proverb says '*traduttore traditore*', translator betrayer). Second, management literature is in general centred on decision making and strategy formulation rather than the implementation of decisions. Language is important mostly in the implementation phase because implementation is largely based on communicating with others, buyers, employees, colleagues, superiors. The logic of the planning stage can overlook the significance of language and communication, because these items are related to implementation. The third argument is that language differences have been systematically underestimated in international business literature because of an understandable bias in American culture: since English really is the *lingua franca* of international business there is no major reason for native speakers of English to learn foreign languages. There is much more motivation for people from Germany, Japan, France and Italy to take the question of language seriously.

In this chapter we will review the main aspects of language and communication that have both a direct and an indirect impact on international business operations:

1.   Verbal communication styles and their relationship to contextual factors.

2.   Non-verbal communication, especially through gestures and eye and body language.

3.   The way language shapes and reflects particular world-views.[1]

4.   Ways of dealing with language differences in international business.

Awareness is even more necessary than knowledge in relation to the impact of language and communication differences on international business. Given the variety of national and regional languages, one cannot expect to be able to speak and write them all. Even multilingual business people will frequently be faced with language contexts in which they have little or no proficiency. What is needed then is an awareness that large chunks of reality will always be partly hidden from us because we are not native speakers.

13.1   VERBAL COMMUNICATION: THE ROLE OF CONTEXT

'Verbal' implies words and sentences and, in most of what follows, spoken discourse, not written communication. Written communication is a special case and it is treated in more detail in other sections of this book devoted to international negotiation and contracts. Verbal may be opposed to non-verbal communication, which is often said to occupy a dominant place in actual communication flows. However, language is legitimately seen as having a prominent place in communication, perhaps because it is largely explicit and therefore more easily amenable to consciousness. Thus linguistic differences are perceived as one of the main causes (though not the only one) of intercultural communication misunderstandings. Where differences in the coding/decoding process are ignored by the communicators, they may persist throughout the whole interaction process; instead of disappearing they may become more marked, even when people seem to be better acquainted with each other.

A first distinction in language-based communication is whether the messages sent by the speaker are explicit, that is, to be taken literally and not necessarily to be set 'in context'. Setting messages 'in context' would imply that what is literally said has to be in some way reinterpreted using various cues taken from the context, particularly the cultural context of the speaker.

The context of language-based communication

The use of the word 'context' and the emphasis that is put on the role of context in communication derive from Edward T. Hall, an American anthropologist. During the

1940s Hall studied the culture and social integration of Hopi and Navajo Indians. He first advised diplomats in the 1960s, and then later on business people in their dealings with other cultures. This naturally led him to an interest in intercultural communication, a field where he has been a major contributor during the last forty years. Hall is the kind of individual who is fascinated by foreign cultures, sometimes showing a certain prejudice in their favour and against his own native culture.[2]

The communication mode that first springs to mind is the verbal mode. Phrases and words in a single language have (more or less) a precise meaning; in any case, we live with the necessary assumption that words and their combinations have a particular meaning, and that the listener gets a clear message from the speaker. This assumption allows us to avoid the time-consuming task of constantly verifying that the message received is the same message that was sent. However, the communication mechanism incorporates many elements:

1. Even in an exchange that is primarily verbal, part of the message is non-verbal: gestures, gesticulations, attitudes, etc. The issue then is to know to what extent non-verbal/implicit messages (which will be discussed in the next section) *mix* with verbal/explicit messages.

2. Communication integrates feedback mechanisms to verify or improve the clarity of messages. In many cultures, the accuracy of the communication process needs to be checked by various means, including repetition, paraphrases, interruption, etc.

3. In most cases, communication is dependent on its context, that is, who says it and where and when it is said. Contextual factors may distort what actually seems to be said literally.

Although Edward Hall does not define context precisely, the following components can reasonably be presumed: location, people involved (age, sex, dress, social standing, etc.), the context of the conversation itself (at the workplace, in a showroom, during a round of labour negotiations, during a sales visit). He contrasts high context (HC) and low context (LC) in the following way: 'a high-context (HC) communication or message is one in which most of the information is either in the physical context or internalized in the person, while very little is in the coded, explicit, transmitted part of the message. A low-context (LC) communication is just the opposite; i.e. the mass of the information is vested in the explicit code' (Hall, 1976).

Context will often influence communication without the participants being aware of it. For example, cultural prejudices may intervene, with such unspoken questions as: does this young speaker deserve trust? The relationship assumed by a particular culture between age and credibility may be positive, negative or neutral, and therefore have an impact on the flow of communication. Another important issue is whether it is necessary to know one's conversation partner relatively well to be able to talk seriously to him or her about business. This relates to the intensity of the personalization, or conversely the depersonalization of the communication process.

Context brings together the sum of interpretation mechanisms that originate within a culture and allow the message to be explained. In his collection *The Snows of Kilimanjaro*, Ernest Hemingway (1976, p. 33) tells a story, entitled 'A day's wait', in which a young boy is told that he has a fever of 102 – in degrees Fahrenheit – though he does not know that the temperature is measured on this scale. Since he previously was in France, he thinks of the temperature as being on the Celsius temperature scale, and asks: 'About how long will it be before I die?' His mother does not know what is the matter with him and explains that people do not die of a fever of 102. The young boy goes on arguing: 'I know they do. At school in France, the boys told me you can't live with 44 degrees. I've got 102.' Finally his mother understands that he has been waiting all day to die and she explains that, like kilometres and miles, what is 37 degrees on one thermometer is 98 on another.

Low-context cultures and explicit communication

As explained above, in certain cultures, communication is based on low context and explicit messages. These messages are almost 'digital' and could be translated into simple computer units (bytes). The Swiss, for instance, have a reputation for talking quite literally, with explicit messages and low context. This implies a great deal of precision in the verbal aspect of communication, implying precision with respect to time commitments and so on. Thus, in Switzerland a speed limit is interpreted as literally just that. The speed limit on motorways is 120 kilometres an hour, and when a driver is caught speeding by the police, a speedometer error of 6 per cent is allowed and then the fine is given in proportion to the speed violation. When a patient arrives late for a doctor's appointment in certain Swiss cantons, he or she has to pay a cash penalty and reschedule the appointment if the doctor is unavailable.[3]

These two examples should be taken for what they are: not as illustrations of an unhealthy preoccupation with punctuality, exactness and respect for rules, but as evidence of a tight social order, a highly organized social system that is costly to run but is also greatly beneficial for all. In the case of the health service, a Swiss doctor who has made a preliminary assessment over the phone with a patient will schedule their time together very precisely. If each party makes an effort to keep the appointment, the result is a genuine saving. The patient will also avoid a long period in the waiting room, exposed to the germs of the other patients.

Appointments are one example of explicit messages that in low-context cultures must be taken literally. Another would be an arrangement such as: 'I can offer you a price of $140 per package of twelve, to be delivered in cases of 144 within five weeks' (an example of a seller's explicit message to a potential buyer). The North American cultures (United States and Canada) feature, together with the Germanic cultures (Germany, Switzerland and Austria) and the Scandinavians, among the cultures with explicit communication and low context.[4]

Contextuality of communication is partly related to whether the language itself expresses ideas and facts more or less explicitly. Japanese, for instance, is in general less precise than English or French. For example, personal pronouns are often not explicitly expressed in Japanese, and the number of tenses is much smaller (especially in comparison to French). In Japanese, both spoken words (that is, sounds) and written words (based on *kanji*, that is pictograms) often have multiple meanings, so that the listener needs some kind of contextual clarification. Sometimes, Japanese people write the *kanji* (ideographs) briefly on their hand to make clear what they are saying.

Naturally it would be a mistake to say that certain languages are vague and others precise. The real world is more complex. This has to be strongly nuanced when one looks more carefully at the structure of the language. For instance, German has many verbs that have quite different meanings according to context. It is easy to discover such examples just by consulting a German–English dictionary. For instance, the verb *absetzen* means, according to context, to deposit or deduct a sum, to take off a hat, to dismiss an official, to depose a king, to drop a passenger, to sell goods, to stop or pause, or to take off (a play).[5] The same holds true for the Finnish language, even though the Finns may have a reputation, like many northern Europeans, for their explicitness in communication. Finnish has a very special language structure which renders the use of context useful in communication, that of the Finno-Ugrian languages, which is really only shared with Estonia and Hungary. The Finnish language uses 16 cases which virtually replace all the prepositions used in other languages. Even proper nouns can be declined using these cases.

All languages share a common objective, that is, they have a common problem to solve, which is conveying meaning in an appropriate way from people to people. But they achieve it differently, relying to varying degrees on precise words, structured grammar or, in contrast, on contextual indications of how ambiguous meanings should be made precise. English is a precise and fairly context-free language. This holds especially true for 'international English'. The *lingua franca* of international business is context free, that is, both impoverished and made precise.

High-context cultures favour a more diffuse communication style

A notion that helps in the understanding of the differences in context-related communication styles is the distinction between specific and diffuse. In low-context cultures, people tend to focus on specific issues and address their counterpart in a specific role (as a buyer for instance), not really impersonally but with a specific view of what the person before them has to do. In high-context cultures, people generally address broader issues and move easily between different conceptions of their counterpart (as a private person, as a buyer, as a potential friend). Diffuse in style should not be equated with 'confused' in communication, but it is clear that to speakers from low-context cultures, communication with people from high-context cultures may at times appear complicated.

Among the high-context cultures, according to Hall, we find the Latin American, the middle East and the Japanese.[6] In Japan, context plays a significant role. One example is the rules of politeness; the manner of speaking perceptibly shifts in register between more than 20 subtly different forms according to the age, sex and social position of the conversation partner, as well as the relative positions of the speakers in the social hierarchy (pupil/teacher, buyer/seller, employee/employer). The word 'no' practically does not exist in the Japanese vocabulary – a 'yes' in certain circumstances can actually mean 'no'. Keiko Ueda (1974) distinguishes 16 ways to avoid saying 'no' in Japanese. The range of possible solutions varies from a vague 'no', to a vague and ambiguous 'yes', a mere silence, a counterquestion, a tangential response, exiting (leaving), making an excuse such as sickness or a previous obligation, criticizing or refusing the question itself, saying 'No, but . . .' or 'Yes, but . . .', delaying answers ('We will write you a letter') and making apologies.

No person belonging to cultures of this sort which use implicit messages and high context can communicate without a fairly good understanding of their conversation partner. Impersonal dealings (such as the style of an American businessman who comes for a day to discuss a contract, rapidly gets to the heart of the matter, and uses the limited time available for discussion, insisting on concentrating on crucial matters) will make a person from those cultures ill at ease and will impede their conversation.

A misunderstanding between the two communicators may arise over their differences of opinion as to what is truly important. The person from a high-context/diffuse communication culture will prefer to spend some time chatting about life in general with the very purpose of getting to know their negotiating partner. The person from a low-context/specific communication culture, on the other hand, will prefer to get straight down to business with the aim of avoiding wasting time on chatting, and proceeding directly to a rational discussion of the project.

Occasionally, some cultures, which fall in the middle range, may shift from an explicit/specific to an implicit/diffuse communication style and vice versa. The United Kingdom and France are examples of such a tendency. The British practice of 'understatement' values complicity between people at the expense of clarity. French has often been considered as a good language for diplomacy because it can be alternately vague and precise, according to the kinds of words and style chosen. Sometimes French can be written with very precise words, with simple sentences (subject–verb complement), but it can also, if need be, be styled in a very vague manner, starting with long dependent clauses describing circumstances and possibilities.

The cultural context of communication styles

So far, the discussion has been mostly about low- and high-context communication and their relationship to precision in languages, as well as to the specificity or the diffuseness of the communication focus. However, verbal communication styles include a series of other elements: tone of voice, frequency and nature of conversational overlap, speed of speech, degree of apparent involvement in what one says, emphasis on talking versus emphasis on listening, digressive and indirect speech styles, etc. These are marked by cultural norms which implicitly define what is 'good' communication ('good' meaning appropriate between members of the cultural community in so far as they share the same code). There are at least three areas where communication style is strongly culture bound:

1. The style may reflect a self-concept. In cultures where the self-concept is strong, one may expect a communication style based on talking and self-assertion; where, on the contrary, suppression of the self is valued, a modest, listening communication style is likely in a participant, all other things being equal (especially purely individual personality characteristics).

2. Communication styles reflect a view of what is appropriate interaction. The Latin style of interruption, for instance, is a lot about showing interest. Latins often find

themselves speaking when others have not finished their sentence, and those who have some familiarity with the Anglo-Saxon and the Nordic communication styles may feel sorry about what could seem an overlap or even an interruption, although it is really well intentioned and positive. In Latin cultures, interruption and overlap show empathy with the other speaker and shared interest in the topic. Furthermore, Latins are (or they believe they are) able to speak and listen at the same time.

3. Communication styles also reflect the appropriate emphasis put, according to cultural norms, on talking and listening respectively. Japanese top executives often behave like a 'sphinx': they are almost pure listeners. Their role is to hear people. With some exceptions, Japanese bosses often display a mediocre talent for making public speeches and appear to be poor spokesmen. In contrast with Latin cultures, for instance, where interactions may appear to be held between 'two speakers', the Japanese have often a tendency to display a 'two listeners' communication culture. Silence is in fact valued as a full element of communication. It conveys messages, which, although implicit, may be interpreted through contextual factors. In a novel entitled *Shiosai*, the Japanese writer Yukio Mishima features a young fisherman, Shinji, who takes his salary back to his mother, a widow with another, younger son. Shinji's salary is the family's only resource. Mishima recounts: 'Shinji liked to give his pay envelope to his mother without uttering a word. As a mother, she understood and always behaved as if she did not remember it was pay day. She knew that her son liked to see her looking surprised' (Mishima, 1969, p. 57).

Many messages are included in silent communication, and, in general, Europeans and Americans tend to fear them much more than Asians do. The issue of shared meaning attributed to communication behaviour inside the cultural group is important, whether the values are positive or negative. Silence may be experienced positively, as a moment for listening (especially to what is 'not said'), or negatively as a sign of possible loss of interaction, as a time-waster, or even as a sign of possible animosity on the part of the conversation partner. Similarly, conversational overlap may be seen as diluting the clarity of exchange, mere impoliteness, a lack of interest in what one says, or as fatuous on the part of the overlapper. Conversely, it may be interpreted as a sign of empathy, a quick feedback saving time, or even a necessary sign for pursuing the exchange.

As we hope to have shown, the rules of achieving 'good' communication are largely cultural. The feeling that the flow of messages is going smoothly between two conversation partners is based on their ability to avoid a 'bad' conversation, where messages would be altered or interrupted. The value judgement on the means that are 'good' or 'bad,' appropriate or inappropriate, is largely based on unconscious cultural standards. In a domestic setting, people agree implicitly on the appropriate rules of communication. In an intercultural situation, people have to allow themselves the informal opportunity to discuss and establish the rules of their communication (what is called meta-communication). It is quite clearly a difficult task. Box 13.1 illustrates the substantial difficulties involved in clarifying the rules of communication about what friendship means and involves.

BOX 13.1

The language of friendship

The American finds his friends next door and among those with whom he works. It has been noted that we take people up quickly and drop them just as quickly. Occasionally a friendship formed during school days will persist, but this is rare. For us (Americans) there are few well-defined rules governing the obligations of friendship. It is difficult to say at which point our friendship gives way to business opportunism or pressure from above. In this we differ from many other people in the world. As a general rule, in foreign countries friendships are not formed as quickly as in the United States, but go much deeper, last longer and involve real obligations. For example, it is important to stress that in the Middle East and Latin America your 'friends' will not let you down. The fact that they personally are feeling the pinch is never an excuse for failing their friends. They are supposed to look out for your interests. Friends and family around the world represent a sort of social insurance that would be difficult to find in the United States. We do not use friends to help us out of disaster as much as we do as a means of getting ahead – or, at least, of getting the job done. The United States systems work by means of a series of closely tabulated favors and obligations carefully doled out where they will do the most good. And the least that we expect in exchange for a favor is gratitude.

The opposite is the case in India, where the friend's role is to 'sense' a person's need and to do something about it. The idea of reciprocity as we know it is unheard of. An American in India will have difficulty if he attempts to follow American friendship patterns. He gains nothing by extending himself in behalf of others, least of all gratitude, because the Indian assumes that what he does he does for the good of his own psyche. He will find it impossible to make friends quickly and is unlikely to allow sufficient time for friendships to ripen. He will also note that as he gets to know people better, they may become more critical of him, a fact that he finds hard to take. What he does not know is that one sign of friendship in India is speaking one's mind.

(Source: Hall, 1960. Reproduced with permission.)

13.2 NON-VERBAL COMMUNICATION

Since much of what is exchanged in communication is only implicitly meant and agreed on, not talked about, non-verbal communication is largely used as an additional interpretative framework which allows people to overcome the shortcomings of verbal communication. The rules, rites and usage of non-verbal communication are also culture bound. When business people from different cultures communicate, they also exchange elements of non-verbal communication. This constitutes a large part of what Edward Hall calls 'context', which is used in the decoding of implicit messages. The elements of context can be separated into four levels:

1. The analogical components of verbal messages,[7] such as a way of saying 'yes' that makes it mean no, profuse thank-yous that contain a meaning other than their 'digital' content precisely because of their excess, etc.

2. Non-verbal communication such as gestures, gesticulations, eye contacts, etc.

3. Messages that are often emitted unknowingly by the speakers according to their personal characteristics of age, size, weight, sex, dress and so on. All of these characteristics are culturally encoded in the culture of the speaker, and decoded by the listener using his or her own cultural programme.

4. Elements of interpretation dictated by the circumstances of the conversation, including type of place, atmosphere of the meeting, how the space is organized in the office,[8] time, etc.

Although all four of these elements interact, this section focuses on the second aspect, non-verbal communication, while recognizing that status, circumstances and the other aspects of context combine with it in bringing about culture-bound interpretations.

Communication through gestures

Body language is an infinite source of differences and misunderstandings. Condon and Youssef (1975) give the following account. A professor who was of English origin and taught at the University of Cairo was sitting on his chair with his feet in front of him, the soles of his shoes facing toward his Egyptian students. A Muslim considers this to be one of the worst possible insults. A student demonstration followed, and it was taken up by the newspapers, which denounced British arrogance and demanded that the professor be sent back to his home country.

Ways of greeting people differ greatly between cultures. While the French have the custom of shaking hands the first time they meet a person each day, the Anglo-Saxon cultures use this custom much less extensively. They are surprised at the excessive (for them) use that the French make of the handshake. In Japan a bow is the appropriate manner of greeting. In certain large Japanese department stores there are hostesses whose sole job is to bow to each customer who comes into the store. Anyone who has observed bowing rituals in Japanese railway stations or airports cannot help but be struck by the complexity of these bowing ceremonies, where the number, depth and synchronization are accurately codified. As Ferraro emphasizes: 'In fact it is possible to tell the relative social status of the two communicators by the depth of their bows (the deeper the bow, the lower the status) . . . The person of lower status is supposed to initiate the bow, and the person of higher status determines when the bow is completed' (Ferraro, 1990, p. 73).

A challenge in intercultural communication is to understand what hand gestures mean in a particular culture. As Box 13.2 shows, a simple piece of advice would be to avoid gesturing with the hand for fear of being misunderstood. Yet there are circumstance and places where it may be adequate.

BOX 13.2

Avoid gesturing with the hand, and yet . . .

In general, avoid gesturing with the hand. Many people take offence at being beckoned this way, or pointed at, even if only conversationally. In parts of Asia, gestures and even slight movements can make people nervous. If you jab your finger in the air or on a table to make a point, you might find that your movements have been so distracting that you have not made your point at all. Unintentionally, Americans come across as aggressive and pushy. Yet, in other parts of the world, particularly in Latin America or Italy, gesturing is important for self-expression, and the person who does not move a lot while talking comes across as bland or uninteresting. As always, watch what local people do. Or ask. While in England we once asked, 'How do you point out someone without pointing?' Our companion dropped a shoulder, raised his eyebrows and jerked his head to the side, as though tossing it in the direction he meant to point. Clear as day, he pointed without pointing.

(Source: Copeland and Griggs, 1986, p. 111.)

The meaning of head gestures is also a point of great cultural difference. Moving the head back and forth means yes in most western European countries, but it means no in Greece and Bulgaria, and moving the head from left to right is a sign of negation for some and affirmation for others. In many western countries it is considered a gesture of affection to pat a child on the head, but in Malaysia and many Islamic countries the head is considered to be the source of spiritual and intellectual activity and is therefore sacred (Harris and Moran, 1987).

Another area of non-verbal communication where the importance of cultural variations cannot be denied is that of physical contact. Ferraro (1990) offers a complete description of forms of non-verbal communication involving physical contact: various groups kiss (the cheek, lips, hand, foot), take a person by the arm, clasp the shoulders, pinch the cheek, shake hands, tickle, stroke, give a little pat, etc. These gestures, running over into the realm of familiarity and sexual conduct, are subject to extremely varied codes of use. The kiss regarded as normal between Russian men or Arab men who hold hands in the streets may appear shocking to Anglo-Saxons. Ferraro (1990, pp. 85–6) recounts his own experience while conducting anthropological field research in Kenya:

After several months of living and working with Kikuyu, I was walking through a village in Kiambu district with a local headman who had become a key informant and a close personal acquaintance. As we walked side by side my friend took my hand in his. Within less than 30 seconds my palm was perspiring all over his. Despite the fact that I knew cognitively that it was a perfectly legitimate Kikuyu gesture of friendship, my own cultural values (that is, that 'real men' don't hold hands) were so ingrained that it was impossible for me not to communicate to my friend that I was very uncomfortable.

The significance of communication codes is complex, and it would be wrong to see as opposites people who are reserved in their physical contact (including Anglo-Saxons) and those who are more liberal. Nowhere does there exist true freedom from customs. The way in which American and European men and women show their feelings for each other by kissing in public may seem, to be the shocking demonstration of something that should be kept private, when seen by other peoples. Dancing, which is a part of social gatherings, may seem indecent to some and perfectly innocent to others.

Facial expressions and communication with the eyes

Laughing and smiling, frowning and knitting one's brow express communication. A smile can be a sign of satisfaction, of agreement, of embarrassment . . . or even not a sign at all. Certain cultures consider the spontaneous expression of attitudes and emotions by a facial expression to be normal. The reverse is true in other cultures, particularly in Asia where it is considered desirable not to show emotion; this has given rise to the impression of Asians as unreadable and stoic. According to Morshbach (1982):

Self control, thought of as highly desirable in Japan, demands that a man of virtue will not show a negative emotion in his face when shocked or upset by sudden bad news; and, if successful, is lauded as *taizen jijaku to shite* (perfectly calm and collected) or *mayu hitotsu ugokasazu ni* (without even moving an eyebrow) . . . The idea of an expression-less face in situations of great anxiety was strongly emphasized in the *bushido* (way of the warrior) which was the guide-line for samurai and the ideal for many others.

Visual contacts (looking someone straight in the eye, or, conversely, looking away, or lowering the eyes, or turning them away when they meet someone else's eyes, when they will also do the same) are all given different meanings in different cultures. This is proof that the same conduct (innocent as it may be) can be arbitrarily given totally opposite meanings. As Harris and Moran (1987) have remarked, Arabs often look each other straight in the eye because they believe that the eyes are the windows of the soul and that it is important to know the heart and soul of those one is working with. By contrast, Japanese children are taught in school not to look their teacher in the eye, but to look at the level of the neck. When they become adults, it is considered a gesture of respect to lower their eyes in front of their superiors. The French have a tendency to look people straight in the eye; like the Americans and other Europeans, they tend to associate a lack of honesty with someone who looks away, and see it as potentially signalling an unfriendly, defiant, impersonal or inattentive attitude.

Dealing with unknown communication styles, especially non-verbal ones, is not an easy task. Exhaustive knowledge of the wide range of cultural interpretations of physical behaviour, gestures and contact is impossible. Although it is clear that one can avoid major behavioural mistakes, it seems more difficult to develop adequate behaviour oneself unless one stays long enough in a particular country to have time to learn. Besides, part of the locally 'adequate' behaviour was learned in childhood, through rearing and education practices, and it translates into a physical demeanour which is profoundly ingrained. Once again, knowledge appears not to be enough. Awareness begins with the capacity to *unlearn*, that is, to discover progressively the cultural relativity of one's own verbal and non-verbal communication behaviour. The *unlearning process* is a key point, a condition, for the learning process to take place.

In everyday adjustment courtesy is a resource not to be ignored when discussing hard managerial topics. Politeness and courtesy are based on linguistic indirection used to show social consideration (Morand, 1996), by not being direct. Thus politeness is always a high-context kind of communication in every culture and has a certain core of universal rules such as not spitting at a person or slapping another's face. However, the degree of contextuality varies according to language and culture. The word courtesy is derived from the word 'court', meaning the residence of a king or emperor. It emphasizes the kind of noble behaviour that enhances self-respect through the respect of others. Most languages have such a word. German, for instance, has the word *höflich* (polite), based on the German word for court, *Hof*. Much is forgiven foreigners provided that they are not arrogant, and show consideration for their opposite numbers, even if ignorant of their customs. Modest, though firm, behaviour facilitates the acceptance of cultural mistakes by the other party.

13.3   LANGUAGE SHAPING OUR WORLD-VIEWS

Language tends to shape our world-views. It contains pre-shaped images of the real world which partly condition our experiences. In this section, we give examples that show that language shapes and reflects different assumptions in terms of time, emotions and feelings, attitude to action, social hierarchy, and how this is expressed in the colloquial phrases used in marketing communications. That language influences culture (shapes it), and thereby behaviour, is a major causal assumption which can be challenged (in many cases language simply reflects culture). That is why we set the limits of this assumption in the second part of this section.

Language influencing culture

The first proponent of the idea that language has a decisive influence on culture was the linguist Edward Sapir. Language creates categories in our minds, which in their turn directly influence the things we judge to be similar and those that *deserve* to be differentiated. It is our *Weltanschauung* that will be determined: our way of observing, of describing, of interacting and finally the way in which we construct our reality. Sapir (1929, p. 214) writes:

The fact of the matter is that the real world is to a large extent unconsciously built up on the language habits of the group. No two languages are ever sufficiently similar as to be considered as representing the same social reality. The worlds in which different societies live are distinct worlds, not merely the same world with different labels attached.

The linguist and anthropologist Benjamin Lee Whorf developed and extended Sapir's hypothesis. The Whorf–Sapir hypothesis contends that the structure of language has a significant influence on perception and categorization. But although the empirical testing of this hypothesis seems to have been fairly thorough,[9] it is not considered valid by many linguists. For example, the gender given to words is not necessarily indicative of a particular cultural meaning (for example the gender of the Earth, the sun and the moon, of vices and virtues, etc.); for most it often seems to reflect an arbitrary choice. It may be however that this attribution of gender had a certain meaning

BOX 13.3

Time patterns revealed by language

Representations of time are conveyed through the medium of language, as a means of communication and therefore collective action. Whorf comments about the Hopi language in the following terms:

After long and careful study and analysis, the Hopi language is seen to contain no words, grammatical forms, constructions or expressions, that refer directly to what we call 'time', or to past, present, and future, or to motion as kinematic rather than dynamic (i.e. as a continuous translation in space and time rather than as an exhibition of a dynamic effort in a certain process), or that even refer to space in such a way as to exclude that element of extension or existence that we call 'time', and so by implication leave a residue that could be referred to as 'time'. Hence, the Hopi language contains no reference to 'time', either implicit or explicit (Carroll, 1956, pp. 57–8).

The vocabulary of time also reveals much about the linkage between language and cultural representations. For those who have doubts about the existence of differences in cultural representations of time that are revealed, conveyed and reproduced by language, the example of the English/US word 'deadline' is very illustrative. A quick translation into French would give 'échéance [temporelle]' or 'délai de rigueur' (Langenscheidt, 1989) but would not render the intensity of this word. Taken literally, it seems to suggest something like 'beyond this (temporal) line, you will (there is a danger of) die (dying)'. It therefore gives a genuine notion of urgency to what was originally a very abstract notion (a point which has been agreed upon on a line of time). The word deadline is used in French by many businesspeople as such (*un deadline*), even though it is not in the official dictionary, because it conveys a typically Anglo-American sense of urgency that French people do not find in their own language.

Language also reflects (and pre-shapes) how people envision the future. In some African languages (Kamba and Kikuyu), there are three future tenses which express (1) action in two to six months; (2) action that will take place immediately; and (3) action 'in the foreseeable future, after this or that event.' Commenting on the uses of these African tenses, M'biti demonstrates how coherence and sophistication in the accurate use of the near future, are important to people.

You have these tenses before you: just try to imagine the tense into which you would translate passages of the New Testament concerning the Parousia of Our Lord Jesus Christ, or how you would teach eschatology. . . . If you use tense no. 1, you are speaking about something that will take place in the next two to six months, or in any case within two years at most. If you use no. 2, you are referring to something that will take place in the immediate future, and if it does not take place you are exposed as a liar in people's eyes. Should you use no. 3 you are telling people that the event concerned will definitely take place, but

BOX 13.3 *CONTINUED*

when something else has happened first. In all these tenses, the event must be very near to the present moment: if, however, it lies in the far distant future – beyond the two-year limit – you are neither understood nor taken seriously (1968, pp. 8–20).

Levine, conducting research on Brazilian versus US time, highlights the way concepts of punctuality are reflected in the language. He takes the example of the translation from English to Portuguese of a questionnaire containing the verb 'to wait':

Several of our questions were concerned with how long the respondent would *wait* for someone to arrive versus when they *hoped* the person would arrive versus when they actually *expected* the person would come. Unfortunately for us, it turns out that the terms *to wait*, *to hope* and *to expect* are all typically translated as the single verb *esperar* in Portuguese. In many ways our translation difficulties taught us more about Brazilian–Anglo differences in time conception than did the subjects' answers to the questions (Levine, 1988, pp. 48–9.)

There is a sort of continuum across languages in the accuracy of description of the waiting phenomenon (a fundamental issue in time experience!). French language, which lies somewhere between English and Portuguese in terms of temporal accuracy, uses two words: *attendre* (to wait) and *espérer* (to hope). To expect has no direct equivalent in French and must be translated by a lengthy circumlocution ('*compter sur l'arrivée de . . .*').

at the genesis of the language, but that the meaning has since been lost. Box 13.3 illustrates how languages reflect different patterns of time.

Languages in relation to actions, thoughts and emotions

Another example may be given of the language–culture link by the way – linguistic as well as cultural – in which an Anglo-American deals with action, especially in business. There is a rich vocabulary to be used, which is often difficult to translate into many other languages, if real equivalence of meaning is sought. The words might include, for instance: *problem solving, issue, matter of fact, down to earth, (empirical) evidence, completed, feed-back, to perform, achievement, individual, data, to check, to plan, deadline, cognitive, emotional, successful* and so on. Even such an elementary word as *fact* contains a rather demanding content: in English it must be an *established* piece of reality; its French equivalent, *fait*, is less demanding in terms of unanimously agreed-on reality (*les faits peuvent être discutés*, corresponding to a spirit of the facts being 'challenged' rather than just discussed); in German, a fact may be translated by *Tatsache, Wirklichkeit, Wahrheit* or *Tat* – it can mean equally a piece of *reality*, a piece of *truth* or a piece of *action*.

The following short passage caricatures the English way of acting:

This man is achievement and deadline oriented. He first reviews the issues at stake. Then he tries hard to gather data, to verify, measure. As much as possible he will bring hard facts, empirical evidence, not simple opinions. If and when his thoughts and his emotions are conflicting, he will choose to behave as a matter-of-fact and down-to-earth guy. Being individually rewarded, he is therefore eager to perform the task and complete the job. He (almost) always meets his schedule.

When trying to translate this small text into other languages,[10] the difficulties extend far beyond the pure lexical and grammatical ones. They are *cultural translation* difficulties. These problems correspond to what is often called the spirit of a language (in French, *Le génie de la langue*): far from being merely a linking of a chain of words, a language contains a series of stands taken on the nature of our relationship to reality.

Let us compare, for instance, the respective qualities of the three most important western European languages. By 'qualities of languages' we mean that one of these languages may be better at expressing ideas, facts or moods, etc. than the others. A comparison between English, French and German[11] suggests that German is stronger than English in the expression of abstractions.[12] In German, word endings such as *-heit*, *-keit*, *-ung*, *-schaft*, *-tum* and *-nis* allow the 'abstractification' of concrete notions. English is not only less able to express pure concepts, it is also less prone to. English is more action and more outward oriented, and takes the view that data-oriented and objective approaches to issues allow a separation between feelings (inner) and actions (directed toward the outside). French expresses inner states more accurately, with an emphasis on emotions rather than pure thoughts, describing the self and others. This corresponds to a view that any action is related to affectivity. Stereotypically, we could say that English is a language of action, French a language of emotions and German a language of thoughts.

Language as a reflection of status, hierarchy and a vision of appropriate social relationships

The way we address other people is another example of how language shapes or reflects a social hierarchy. There is only one word used in English for 'you', even when accompanying a first name, and this is most often considered as reflecting a society which has strong assumptions about equality between people. It is said to reflect informality. By contrast, the French often use the formal *vous* for people they do not know very well instead of the informal *tu* which they reserve for family and friends. Thus the French are reputed to be more formal. The Germans use *du* (second person singular) in informal and personal settings and *Sie* (third person plural) in formal address. The Germans, like the Spaniards, have three forms of address: while the second person plural (*ihr*) has been lost in practice in German, it remains in Spanish. In fact, a closer look at these forms shows that the English 'you' was not originally a second person singular, which was 'thou' in old English (as in Shakespeare's plays), but the more polite second person plural. That means that the only address kept in English is based on an assumption of full respect and formality and not on the everyday and less formal form of 'thou'. In fact, the assumed informality of English address, advocated by many native English speakers, is difficult to grasp for a Latin. The addressing of people by their first name and the use of 'you' appears to the Latin as a different kind of formalism rather than true informality. Language reflects quite complex assumptions about equality between people. It is true that the French use of *vous* reflects the strong emphasis on hierarchical and status differences in French society. But it can be very diversely nuanced, with the addition, for instance, of *Monsieur* (formal *vous*) or simply the first name (informal *vous*). It is naturally not simply because they have long used the polite form that the French have a fairly hierarchical society. But the language context contributes to a constant reframing of culture-bound assumptions about hierarchy in a society.

Language used in writing advertising messages

A function of language is to convey messages. A common problem for advertisers world-wide is how to use language in order to describe consumer benefits, suggest product qualities and convince potential buyers. It must be done using words that represent local world-views. That is why international advertising is very 'Whorfian', even if advertisers and their agencies are not conscious of it (see Box 13.4). The language input in marketing communications is much more significant than it may seem at first. It is directly useful in designing copy strategy and indirectly useful, when one is trying to understand consumer moods or viewers' emotions. For example, life insurance advertising implies the evocation of death, which may be taboo in certain cultures, or subject to the use of a particular vocabulary and subdued style. Advertising – especially when it comes to targets and strategies – is never as standardized as it appears to be at first sight. In Box 13.4 we illustrate the diverging cultural interpretations of a sign which *prima facie* seems universal (but is not so).

BOX 13.4
Global marketing communications?

The slogan 'Put a Tiger in your Tank', although often taken as the most perfect example of a standardized advertising campaign, is not as standardized as it might seem. It has been argued that it is standardized, because at first reading it looks as if it were fully equivalent across countries. However, studying the advertisements more closely, one sees that in some countries the power is located in the tank (northern Europeans: '*Pack den Tiger in den Tank*' in Germany, '*Stop'n Tiger in uw Tank*' in Holland). In other countries, the powerful tiger is located in the engine (in French, '*Mettez un Tigre dans votre moteur*'; in Italian, '*Metti un Tigre Nel Motore*'). The interpretation, as to where the power source is located, differs. Note, however, that an engine cannot work without fuel and vice versa. Nobody is really right, it is simply the interpretations that differ, the Anglo interpretation (tank) being more passive and the Latin interpretation (engine) more active. In Thailand and some neighbouring countries the tiger is experienced quite differently from how it is viewed in Europe, America or Japan. Until recently the tiger was a danger for the local population, especially in the countryside; therefore its image is that of jungle danger rather than of power. The image expressed by the word 'tiger' is not the same in a country where the tiger is experienced as a physical threat and sometimes as a source of terror for the local population as it is in countries where tigers have only been seen in books, films and zoos.

Languages and new international cultures

People have a great deal of leeway in using language. This is more clearly expressed in French than in English since two words correspond to 'language': la *langue* (in English, literally, 'tongue' – the same word serving in French to express both the physical organ and what it helps to create) and *le langage*. *La langue* is the language itself and *le langage* is largely how people use *la langue*, and possibly other means, in order to communicate.

The most obvious influence of culture on language is that of a vocabulary with its own particular capacities and limits. Specific examples of this are the new technological vocabularies from computer science, nuclear technology, audiovisual communication, aerospace technology, etc., which are largely borrowed and exchanged between linguistic and national cultures, the benefit being the creation of a nearly universal technical culture. There are also vocabularies which have been enriched because of physical occurrences that demand precise description, as in the huge number of terms for different types of snow that exist in the language of Eskimos and all peoples who live near the Arctic Circle. Another example is the rich culinary vocabulary in France, where a preoccupation with good food is an element of society that strongly influences daily life.

I do not intend to enter into a debate on the causality of language and culture, which is scientifically very complex and which also risks turning into a 'chicken and egg' argument. However, common-sense reasoning reveals limitations to the Whorfian hypothesis in relation to those who speak many languages, or those who were raised in various linguistic and cultural environments, or the Swiss who share a strong national culture in spite of language differences.[13] In a static scenario, that is, one where an individual or a certain group has been educated in a totally homogeneous cultural environment, language can have an influence on world-view and on one's actions when confronted with reality. But the theory is much less valid in a dynamic scenario, that is, one where language changes from generation to generation or where people travel abroad. Then they will encounter opportunities to borrow language and culture. Interaction between language and culture is reciprocal, in particular in the light of cultural borrowing.

13.4   ETHNOCENTRISM, STEREOTYPES AND MISUNDERSTANDINGS IN INTERCULTURAL COMMUNICATION

One may add that the cultural mechanism (living according to one's culture in one's daily life) is almost an unconscious action. The cost of adopting the cultural traits of the environment in which one lives is minimal. But there are generally high costs associated with the identification and adoption of the traits of another culture. This is shown clearly by the difficulties encountered by immigrants in integrating, even those who have immigrated voluntarily.

Ethnocentrism

Owing to the high cost of changing one's culture, most people live without even envisaging such a possibility. This causes what James Lee (1966) calls the SRC (Self-Reference

Criterion): we all have an automatic and unconscious tendency to refer to our own thought framework, which is mainly tied to our national culture (which in general we did not choose), to interpret situations, evaluate people, communicate, negotiate or decide which attitude to take. This framework is generally modelled by ethnocentrism. The concept of ethnocentrism was first introduced by G. A. Sumner (1906) more than eighty years ago, to distinguish between *ingroups* (those groups with which an individual identifies) and *outgroups* (those regarded as antithetical to the *ingroup*).

Ethnocentrism has been extended by psychologists at the level of the individual, where it relates to the natural tendency of people to refer themselves spontaneously to the symbols, values and ways of thinking of their own ethnic or national group (their ingroup). Ethnocentrism may lead to disinterest and even contempt for the culture of other groups (Levine and Campbell, 1972). Lee (1966) suggests the following steps in order to try to eliminate the decisional bias related to the SRC when dealing with international operations:

1. Define the problem or the objectives, as would be done according to the customs, behavioural standards and ways of thinking of the decision-maker's country.

2. Similarly, define the problem or the objectives, as would be done according to the customs, behavioural standards and ways of thinking of the foreign country (where the decision will be implemented).

3. Isolate the influence of the self-reference criterion on the problem, and identify the extent to which it complicates the decision-making problem.

4. Redefine the problem (and often the objectives), without the bias related to the SRC and then find the solutions and make decisions which fit with the cultural context of the foreign market.

In this way one can imagine the following situation. People are standing in line at an amusement park, such as Disneyland, where there are some very popular attractions. In the original context in the United States, discipline with respect to queues is strong. They are usually well organized and there are even tangible indicators for this (yellow line on the ground indicating to people where to stop to queue, visible corridors for queuing in line, etc.). In the foreign context of France, where there is a developed sense of 'free-for-all' and less of a habit of organized queues, combined with a reluctance towards anything that seems too socially structured, the problem will not present itself in the same terms.

Although it constitutes the first practical framework that allows us to attribute all operational value to cultural representation, the SRC also comprises a degree of naivety and inadequacy. It presupposes that it is possible easily to penetrate the mysteries of a culture without being a native. Cultural expertise is a complex reality. Sometimes neither marketing experts from the original country (in total ignorance) nor foreigners (through lack of consciousness of their own culture) are capable of diagnosis in the second and third phases. The effect of the effort of bias removal and the results achieved by the use of the SRC are not immediate.

Stereotypes

As pointed out by Gauthey and Xardel (1990, p. 20), if the French perceive Americans as being tough in business and arrogant, and see the British as insincere, it is for the most part due to stereotypes, which give a distorted view. American arrogance is, in fact, related to a different hierarchy of values: professional relations are centred on the task in hand, the object of discussion, to the exclusion of personal relations with the other party.

Stereotypes, although sometimes representing a simplification which is intellectually useful, none the less have the function of reducing and conserving our differences, which can make them dangerous. Gauthey (1989, p. 63) notes the personal aspect: 'It seems a thousand times easier to stay attached to our own values and to transfer onto the foreigner the responsibility to change his point of view than to decenter ourselves, that is to leave our system of reference and put ourselves in the place of the other.' Characteristic of stereotypes are a cognitive function (wherein they work as a simplified intellectual representation of other people) and also an emotional function (self-defence against a difference that provokes anxiety). Michel Droit, in his book *Chez les Mangeurs d'hommes* (With the Man Eaters), exposes the stereotype of the sorcerer in primitive societies. He describes the people of Papua New Guinea as seen by civilized observers who are necessarily their ideological enemies (1952, p. 124, author's translation):

Armed with tamed snakes which they use to execute their victims, with poisons enchanted prayers and medicinal herbs known only to them, sorcerers, through well-organized propaganda and strong co-operative solidarity, let entire populations live in fear and sometimes in terror of their '*nepou*', that is their evil powers.

The point is not to suggest that Michel Droit's description of the sorcerer is false His reading partially reveals reality but also ignores how the sorcerer is integrated into the Papuan community. Stereotypes are often used to capture the salient traits of a 'foreign' national character. Box 13.5 shows how French people are viewed (at least stereotypically) by people of other nations.

Self-shock

It is necessary to acknowledge that the problem of cultural representation is more complex than simply 'getting to know the other'. As shown by Zaharna (1989) in a review article on the culture shock experienced by people of different cultures, the problematic representation of the 'other' may evolve into a confrontation (equally problematic) with oneself. Zaharna calls this process 'self-shock'. Experiencing how others actually are may be somewhat destabilizing: identity confusion is a typical feature of culture shock (Oberg, 1960). Self-shock is probably one of the principal causes of stereotyping. Stereotypes often protect 'the self', much more than they really provide information on 'the other'.

When people from different cultures meet, as when expatriate managers meet local executives or international sellers meet local buyers, the encounter is an intercultural one where the absence of previous knowledge of the other's culture makes for uncertainty. At first, one might think that the basic problem is 'getting to know the other'. But in the intercultural encounter, there is in fact a 'progressive unfolding of the self' which can be attributed to 'a set of intensive and evocative situations in which the individual perceives and experiences other people in a distinctly new manner and, as a consequence, experiences new facets and dimensions of existence' (P. S. Adler, 1975, p. 18). In intercultural encounters, the necessary introduction of the 'other' risks disturbing one's personal identity, which is placed in question by the 'mirror effect'.

Within our own cultural context, we have unconsciously built our 'self-image'. We necessarily construct an image of ourselves from the observations that we make, based on the responses of others to our conduct. This is emphasized by Erikson (1950, p. 13): 'Identity is the confidence gathered from the fact that our own ability to maintain

---

BOX 13.5

Some stereotypes of the French (undeserved?)

How various nationalities perceive the French:

- The Germans: Pretentious and offhand. Fashionable, womanizing, frivolous, fickle, well-mannered, resourceful.
- The British: Nationalistic, chauvinistic, intransigent, centralist, dependent on the state, polite but not open-minded, humourless, short-tempered.
- The Dutch: Cultured, fond of good living, fidgety, talkative, not very serious, feelings of superiority.
- The Spanish: Pretentious, early sleepers, cold and distant, hypocritical, impolite, patronizing, hard working.
- The Swedish: In-built superiority complex, scornful, boastful, talkative, immoral, dirty, neo-colonialists, disorganized, cultured gastronomy, suffocating hierarchy.
- The Finns: Xenophobic, superficial, scornful, chauvinistic, courteous, romantic, enjoying life, patriotic, chaotic.
- The Americans: Chauvinistic, well-mannered. Combination of good food and good conversation, Paris. Curious about foreign people, pretentious, talkative, pleasant, intelligent.
- The Russians: Talkative, self-satisfied, lazy. Luxury, inequality, culture. Pleasant, intelligent, resourceful.
- The North Africans: Fairly racist, a little stingy, reasonably honest. Good education and good food. Selfish.
- The Asians: Exhibitionist, indiscreet. Reticent in making friends. Bureaucracy and red tape.
- The Black Africans: Racist, honest, lacking respect for elders and betters. At odds with themselves and nature. Not spontaneously hospitable.

(Source: Gruère and Morel, 1991, p. 51. Reproduced with permission.)

interior resemblance and continuity equals the resemblance and continuity of the image and the sense that others have of us.' But the process of the creation and maintenance of personal identity has two characteristics that make it problematic in the intercultural encounter: (1) it happens for the most part outside our consciousness, and (2) it requires a good capacity for interpersonal communication.

According to Zaharna 'self-shock', unlike culture shock which is seen as a reaction to difference between oneself and the other, is a concept that extends to differences with and inside the self. The root of 'self-shock' lies in the intimate workings of the relationship between the ego (that is, personal identity), our behaviour and the 'other' (as the 'other' actually is, and as perceived by us, and also as forcing us to reflect upon ourselves). Self-shock emerges as a deep imbalance between our need to confirm our identity and our ability to do so. In one way, this situation places the individual in a position of 'double-bind' (Bateson, 1971). The self-shock situation increases our need for the reinforcement of our personal identity, while at the same time resulting in a loss of ability to satisfy this need. Thus, one can understand more easily that certain stereotypes or abrupt judgements about foreigners result almost directly from our attempts to defend ourselves by avoiding the painful double constraint of self-shock.

Gauthey (1989, p. 64) cites the case of the general manager of a software company, a subsidiary of a French advertising and communications group, who says: 'I can't stand the English, and when I go to London, I never leave the airport.' This attitude is clearly defensive: in refusing to leave the airport, he stays on neutral international ground, with no risk of being confronted by the image of himself that he will be shown by the English.

International empathy: A naive concept

In the concept of international empathy we can catch a glimpse of the immense naivety of those who well-meaningly argue in favour of cultural empathy (being open-minded, sincerely interested in the other, ready to listen, etc.). This communication tactic, although well meant, may only last for a brief period – the time during which the personal identity of the 'empathizer' has not yet come into play. There are a series of concrete issues at stake, which are important for people involved in intercultural communication in business:

1. Which personality types and/or personal backgrounds are best suited to inter-cultural communication?

2. Related questions are: Are we able to communicate better with particular countries and cultures? How can we increase our abilities in this respect?

3. A question rarely dealt with is: If an adjustment must be made during the inter-cultural encounter, who should be the one to adapt? Quite apart from personal capacities, empathy or the position of strength, can the intercultural learning situation be led other than bilaterally? In other words, why learn if the other does not learn too? Why not learn simultaneously, rather than in two parallel learning situations that may never meet?

13.5   HOW TO IMPROVE COMMUNICATION EFFECTIVENESS IN INTERNATIONAL BUSINESS

A 'reasonable' version of the use of the Whorfian hypothesis

The first consequence of the Whorf–Sapir hypothesis, in so far as one chooses to adhere to it, is that business people from different cultures not only communicate in different ways, but also perceive, categorize and construct their realities differently. This therefore supposes a 'state of alert' in communication, a readiness to accept that words, even those that are translated with no apparent difficulty, offer only an illusion of sharing in the same vision of reality. It is necessary to retain as many foreign words as possible in their original form, in the following ways:

1. By forcing oneself to recognize their unique nature and therefore keeping culturally unique concepts in the native language form to signal their uniqueness.

2. By questioning the interpreters, or even one's foreign business partners, about the precise meaning of words or expressions in the context of a particular culture.[14]

3. By clearly identifying areas of shared meaning.

For instance, in the examination of contract clauses, it is necessary to try to extricate the true meaning of each clause, starting from the perspective that they are never exactly equivalent. This is true even in the case where a dictionary seems to indicate (falsely) that an English term such as 'act of God' is a strict equivalent of a French term (here *'force majeure'*).[15]

Linguistic ethnocentrism versus linguistic polycentrism

An unfortunate consequence of the Whorf–Sapir hypothesis is that linguistic ethnocentrism is largely inevitable. One might wonder whether it would be a more realistic approach to have only natives of a language and culture write about cultural topics for their fellow citizens. If we think of anthropology, a discipline with a high record of reporting on other cultures, it seems that the answer would be 'yes'. Famous anthropologists generally belonged to the cultures of their publishers and readers, not to the cultures they observed. The same holds true for area specialists. For instance, the two specialists on French culture who are best known are Theodore Zeldin of Harvard University and John Ardagh, a British journalist. Similarly, the most prominent specialist in Germany on French contemporary civilization is a German, Ulrich Wickert. It is often useful to be an outsider in relation to what is observed and, culturally and in language terms, an insider in reporting what has been observed. This evokes the issue of *cultural mediation*, which is discussed briefly in section 2.3. However paradoxical and provocative it may seem, it is sometimes more important to be understood than to understand, inasmuch as the *understanding* depends on the mindset of the observer as well as on the object to be understood. What is said by mere cultural insiders is often difficult to understand unless it has been in some way recalibrated in the linguistic background of the reader, which means more than simply translated.

For international business people to be linguistically non-ethnocentric does not mean that they have to have a full command of several foreign languages. It is more important, and in fact much easier than learning to read and speak fluently, to catch what is unique in the structure of the foreign language and some of its words. A look at a book of basic grammar and careful attention to specific words are a good start. Very often authors of books on Japanese business customs or management style keep Japanese words as they are originally pronounced when they want to signal a culturally specific meaning.[16] Sometimes words are forged that partly bridge the cultural divide. Boye de Mente cites for instance the Japanese word *nominication* which is made up of the first part of the Japanese word *nomimasu* (to drink) and the last half of 'communication': 'This Japlish word refers to business conversations and socializing that takes place in bars, cabarets, and other drinking establishments, and it is one of the institutionalized ways of "wisdom gathering" in Japan' (de Mente, 1990, p. 261).

Culturally unique life concepts have a major impact on decision-making processes inside companies and especially on the issue of labour–management relationships. They are signalled by words such as *management by objectives* for the Americans, *ringi* for the Japanese, *mitbestimmung* for the Germans and *concertation* for the French. The same holds for the managing institutions of a company: a German *Aufsichtsrat*, often translated into English as 'supervisory board', should be considered a specific institution, typical of German business culture, with particular consequences in the real life of real businesses (Schneider-Lenné, 1993). Although linguistic ethnocentrism is largely inevitable, we must strive for linguistic polycentrism, by trying to keep original words, understanding meaningful elements in the grammar (such as gender, tenses and sentence construction), and trying to behave as 'explorers' of the meanings and world-views expressed by different languages.

Taking the true measure of language and communication abilities in international business

In considering English as the *lingua franca* of international business, we have to differentiate two groups: native and non-native English speakers. Their positions are clearly different. For non-native English-speaking business people, learning English and often one or two other languages is a must. For instance, the Swedes, Finns, Danes and Norwegians often speak three or four foreign languages: English, another Nordic language and French, German or Spanish. The situation is very different for native English speakers. Simon observes: 'The United States continues to be the only nation where you can graduate from college without having had one year of a foreign language.' (Simon, 1980, p. 2). Although regrettable, this may be explained and understood. The United States is a vast country which is linguistically homogeneous in that nearly everyone shares the common language of English. There is no real need to learn foreign languages, whereas in Europe most large cities are located less than 200 miles (330 km) from a foreign-speaking area and a foreign language is an asset. Although the USA is now the fourth-largest Spanish-speaking country in the world and more than half the population of Miami is of Spanish-speaking origin, this does not necessarily require Americans to learn Spanish. Rather, Hispanics have to learn English. Moreover, there may be differences in the amount of effort required to learn certain foreign languages. If an American or a European wants to really learn Japanese, the characters have to be learnt, which implies a much larger effort than for the Japanese to learn the Roman alphabet: the *gai-jin* (non-Japanese) has to learn two syllabaries of about 100 characters each (*hiragana* and *katakana*, phonetic symbols) and about 1,850 *kanjis* (ideographic symbols), whereas the Roman alphabet to be learnt by the Japanese has only 26 phonetic characters, not a large addition given the skill needed to master Japanese writing. Lastly, Americans can fairly easily find English speakers during their travels, and they can count on their foreign business partners having – at least superficially – a good command of English. Furthermore Americans are tolerant and lenient towards the mistakes of their non-native counterparts: 'international English' sometimes has little to do with real English grammar and words.

Thus these are good reasons why native English speakers are somewhat lazy about foreign languages. Understandably, therefore, the impact of language differences has been systematically underestimated in international business literature because of an 'English-only' bias in Anglo-American culture. Most international business textbooks do not include a single reference in a foreign language. Even a text devoted to the cultural dimension of international business such as Ferraro (1990) does not have (among about 200 references) a single *truly* foreign reference, that is, from a foreign author in a foreign language, although some works by foreign authors are listed when they have been published in English.[17] This may imply a substantial bias, since these authors would not be read in their own linguistic contexts and any foreign authors who have not been translated into English are not even considered. However, there are naturally good and practical reasons for maintaining language homogeneity in sources, namely that the reader would not be able either to find or to read these references, so this should not be considered only as a reflection of linguistic ethnocentrism.

What is unfortunate, however, is that native English speakers are at a disadvantage, although the opposite may appear to be true. The main disadvantage for them is that they cannot grasp the features of the foreign language in terms of world-view and communication style. Furthermore, many native English speakers cannot imagine what it is like to express oneself in a language with little proficiency unless they themselves have tried to learn and speak a foreign language. Thus native English speakers have to develop an awareness of their paradoxical competitive disadvantage in terms of language. However, the message to be conveyed cannot be simply and plainly to learn foreign languages. It is a different thing to understand and speak a foreign language as such and to understand the consequences of languages being different. Absolute proficiency in many languages is not needed. International business people do not have to be multilingual; they do, however, need to have an awareness of what language differences imply.

On the other hand, non-native English speakers must not deceive those with whom they deal. Although many foreign business people seem to have a good command of English, they still have the kind of world-view that has been shaped by their native language and culture. Thus proficient non-native English speakers may be somewhat misleading partners for their opposite numbers: they look quite the same, but they are quite different. This may be especially true for northern Europeans. They may seem quite similar, especially to Americans, since their English pronunciation has largely been shaped by television viewing. Nevertheless, they may have in reality a different mindset and also a much greater proficiency for oral than for written communication. If so, this may cause problems when the written details of business contracts are discussed.

Some guidelines for effective communication in international business

The following are some guidelines for effective communication in international business:

1. Start by assessing as accurately as possible the possible intercultural obstacles that exist, such as language and problems of communication in general. Business people often underestimate or even completely overlook this point, since they often share a technical culture with their conversation partner. They are also deceived by an almost international atmosphere that can be quite misleading. Glen Fisher points out:

    > Obviously, the modern intensity of international interaction, especially in business and in technological, communication and educational fields, has produced something of an internationalized 'culture' which reduces the clash of cultural backgrounds and stereotyped images. Happily for us this *modus vivendi* is largely based on Western practices and even on the English language, so many otherwise 'foreign' counterparts are accommodating to the American style of negotiation.' (Fisher, 1980, p. 8.)

    Unfortunately, in the real world, the person who does not feel the need to adapt, especially as far as language is concerned, may be indulging in indolence. The result will be the mistaken impression that one's partner is just like oneself. That is to say that often similarities are illusions, especially when foreigners seemingly share the same 'international culture'. Those who adapt are aware of differences, whereas those who must be adapted to remain unaware.

2. Be aware that what is explicitly said is not necessarily what is implicitly meant. Check, verify. Spend time on checking communication accuracy, especially when the stakes are high (orders, delivery dates, contractual involvement in general).

3. Learning the non-verbal communication style of other cultures may prove very difficult. Deep cultural learning in this area is very hard after childhood. It is better to aim for a state of alertness so that one does not decode non-verbal messages erroneously, rather than try to gain full command of different types of non-verbal communication.

4. In many cases interpreters may serve a crucial purpose, that of transposers of meaning. They do not work 'like a dictionary', translating literally. They may translate better from one language to another than in the reverse direction, and this will depend not only on which language is their native one, but also on a personal leaning that they may have towards one party. It is also necessary to make sure that they are truly loyal to the party who has hired them. It may be advisable to hire several interpreters when the business at stake justifies it.

5. It must be clearly appreciated that there is always a part of the language which cannot be translated. Culture-specific meaning is conveyed by language as it reflects the culture. Always keep in mind the Italian adage, cited above, *traduttore/ traditore* (translator/traitor).

6. Develop a 'bomb squad' ability to defuse a conflict based on negative stereotypes. (Subjective) misunderstandings in intercultural communication often snowball and mix with purely interest-based (objective) conflicts, resulting in confrontations that may not be productive. There are sometimes necessary conflicts and even good ones, where confrontation should not be avoided. But in many other cases, cultural misunderstandings may have a purely negative influence on the dealings that follow, possibly even leading to the breaking off of negotiations.

7. Keep in mind that all this depends on advance preparation, and unfortunately cannot be improvised. An effort to help the other intelligently and agreeably to understand one's own culture is a prerequisite, and may often involve 'wine and dine' situations. When formal business negotiations or even preliminary business talks start and one side lacks even the barest knowledge of the partner's culture, relations will often turn sour. It will soon be too late to approach basic issues affected by common understandings and cultural differences. Then the only way to negotiate is to discuss on the substantive ground of 'business is business'. In this light, training in intercultural business seems more like a preliminary investment to improve the effectiveness of business deals than a way of resolving urgent problems. In medical terms, cultural understanding in business appears as the prevention rather than the cure.

QUESTIONS

1. Comment on the following sentences:

   it is the subjective meaning of words and expressions that needs to be captured. Time spent exploring why a given utterance does not translate well may be more productive for the one who is actually trying to communicate than concentration on technical excellence. (Fisher, 1988, p. 172.)

2. Give examples of low-context versus high-context communication.

3. Transform the following sentence into low-context and high-context sentences: 'Your price is too high compared with that of the competitors' (buyer).

4. Discuss the following statements from the perspective of stereotyping:

   Many Germans, for instance, do not like to converse much during their meals. Germans will ordinarily begin their meals by taking a sip of beer or soda and then picking up and holding knifes and forks throughout the meal, putting them down only when they are finished eating. For many Germans eating is a serious business that is not to be disturbed by trivial comments and animated conversation. Gannon, 1994, p. 5.)

   Germans also frequent the symphony on a regular basis; the former West Germany with its population of 62 millions boasts approximately 80 symphony orchestras . . . This societal and cultural love of music has produced some of the finest composers of classical symphonic music. In fact, many experts agree that the classical symphony reached its highest level of attainment and maturity in the works of Haydn and Mozart. (Gannon, 1994, p. 68.)

5. Why can the obvious showing of emotions be considered dangerous? Why do cultures vary in the degree of emotional restraint?

6. Consider the gender aspect of words in the following languages. In English almost everything is neutral except persons and some animals, and exceptionally an object such as a ship. French has feminine and masculine but no neutral. In German, persons, objects and concepts can be feminine, masculine or neutral. For instance 'sun', 'earth' and 'moon' are all neutral words in English; in French they are respectively masculine (*le soleil*) and feminine (*la terre, la lune*); in German the same words are feminine (*die Sonne, die Erde*) and masculine (*der Mond*). Elaborate on the possible cultural meanings of attributing gender to words. To what extent can we speak of more or less 'sexualized' languages (I mean here 'sexualized' and not simply 'gendered'). Outline the limitations of such an interpretive approach.

7. In Japanese there are no articles either definite or indefinite. *Hon*, for instance, means 'the book', 'a book', 'the books' or 'books'. What does this imply for the Japanese when they want to express their thoughts?

8. Consider gift-giving practices as an element of communication. What are the main dimensions of gift giving (consider the donor, the receiver, the size and nature of the gift, the circumstances and its meaning for either side)? How would cultural interpretations differ? Take into account the values involved. (You can base your discussion on elements found in articles about gift giving.)

9. Can you describe at least one circumstance when you had an ethnocentric attitude? If you find it hard, can you explain why?

APPENDIX 13: TEACHING MATERIALS

A13.1 Exercise: Multicultural class

Look at the person seated next to you in class, or anyone with whom you have frequent interaction. Then select somebody originating from a foreign culture. List three examples of non-verbal communication that she or he uses, describe them accurately and decode their meaning. Now ask this person to look at you and do the same. Then work together and compare both interpretations and try to understand why meaning was shared or, possibly, not shared.

(This exercise can be implemented only with a good degree of cultural diversity within the student group.)

A13.2 Exercise: I 'love' cake

Start from the English verb 'to like' and find its equivalents in French, German and Spanish. Do not hesitate to translate them back into English in order to detect differences in meaning. Include in your search some basic etymological grounds (e.g. *gusto* in Spanish is based on the word for 'taste'). What differences in terms of world-views are suggested by the different conceptual dimensions of 'liking' (preference, affective, pleasure, love, enjoyment, eating/ingesting, etc.) and their attributions to people, things or situations? Suggest possible consequences for international marketing and advertising strategies.

A13.3 Exercise: Following directions

Objective
To clarify for participants the formats of their communication and the difficulties and inaccuracies encountered when implementing those formats.

Participants
Any number of dyads, each individual in a given dyad representing a different culture. Facilitator.

Materials
1. One or more index cards for each participant (see Figure 13.1).
2. Answer sheets and pencils for each participant.

Setting
Dyads should be seated around a table. If there are several dyads, each should be seated at a different table.

Time
Variable, depending on participant characteristics, number of cards per participant and processing phase; anywhere from ten minutes to an hour or more.

Procedure

1. Participants are divided into culturally mixed dyads and seated around tables.
2. At each table, one participant sits on one side of the table and is designated as source. The other is seated on the other side and is designated as 'respondent'.

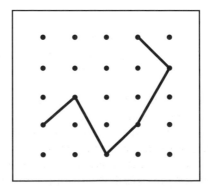

FIGURE 13.1 Index card.

3. Each participant is given an answer sheet and one or more index cards. The index card, as shown in Figure 13.1, contain eight matrices of 25 dots each. The cards contain one matrix of 25 dots, on which six of the dots are connected by five lines. Each card design is unique.

4. Each source must verbally communicate the design on one of his cards to the respondent seated across from him who must reproduce it on one of the blank matrices on his answer sheet within a recommended time limit of ten to fifteen seconds.

5. Participants alternate being sources and respondents and may change their partners with each new round of activity.

6. Facilitator leads discussion, tying in participants' experience with the exercise objective, emphasizing the role cultural difference may play in confounding communication.

7. Suggestions on variations of this exercise are:
    (a) Ask participants to draw their own designs and then communicate them to each other.
    (b) Draw and communicate more complex designs (nine dots and eight lines) in the same amount of time.
    (c) Communicate designs drawn on irregular matrices.
    (d) If several dyads take part in the exercise, make each correct communication worth one point. Besides the element of inter-dyad competition, the success of each dyad member becomes contingent upon the success of the other. Some interesting effective data may be generated for discussion.

(Source: Royal Freuhling, of the University of Hawaii, 1975, in Weeks *et al.*, 1987, pp. 10–13. Reproduced with the kind permission of the publisher.)

A13.4   Case: Supreme Canning

The Supreme Canning Company (the true name of the company is disguised) is an independent United States packer of tomato products (whole peeled tomatoes, chopped tomatoes, katsup, paste, pizza and other sauces, and tomatoes and zucchini). The company is located in the State of California. Although it produces some cans with its own brand label, much of its output is canned for others and their brand names and labels put on the cans. It produces shelf-size cans for eventual sale at retail, gallon-size cans for use by restaurants and industrial users, and 55 gallon drums for use by others for repacking or further processing. Its annual processing capacity is in excess of 100,000 tons of tomatoes (processed during an operating season of approximately three months in length).

During the decade before 1987, the California canning industry had suffered from heavy competition from abroad and inadequate local demand. A somewhat increasing domestic demand for specialty tomato products, especially pizza and other sauces, was not adequate to absorb increasing imports. The high value of the US dollar, through 1985, had made it difficult for United States companies to sell abroad. Excess capacity and the resulting depressed prices had led to bankruptcy for a number of Californian canners. With the decline of the value of the dollar during 1986 and 1987, and the efforts of Japan to reduce its trade barriers and increase imports, it appeared that Supreme Canning Company might be able to get into the Japanese market. An inquiry received from a foodpacker and distributor in Japan indicated interest from that side. The Japanese firm produced and distributed a large number of products, was well known in Japan, and was much larger than the US company.

Since Supreme Canning Company did not have well-known brand names of its own, the company was interested in acting as a large-scale supplier of products made to customer specifications for use by the customer or distribution under the customer's label. Thus, the inquiry from Japan was most welcome.

The Japanese company invited senior executives of the American firm to visit their production facilities and offices in Japan. Both the president and chairman of the board of Supreme Canning Company had a four-day visit with the executives of the company in Japan. The president of the US company, who had some knowledge of Japanese business practice from studies at Stanford University and from his widespread reading, attempted to act as a guide to Japanese business practice. The chairman of the board had little knowledge of Japan, and viewed himself as a decisive man of action. Although there were a few minor misunderstandings, the visit was concluded successfully and the Americans invited the Japanese to visit their plant in California for four days.

The Japanese indicated their interest in the signing of a mutual letter of cooperation. The American chairman of the board was not interested in this, but rather wanted some specific agreements and contracts. As the time for the Japanese visit to the United States drew near, the Japanese indicated that their president would not be able to come. Some senior executives would be able to meet, but they would only be able to spend two days instead of four. The vice-chairman of the board of the California company wrote asking why the Japanese were not going to send their president, and inquiring why they could not spend four days instead of two, 'as we did in Japan'. The letter was frank and direct. The tone was that of a person talking to an equal, but not with any great deal of politeness. The Japanese company decided to cancel the visit, and no further negotiations or serious contacts were made.

Some months later, a local businessman of Japanese extraction asked the president of Supreme Canning Company if some representatives of another (and even larger) Japanese food products producer and distributor could visit the plant. Four Japanese showed up along with the local businessman, who acted as interpreter and go-between. The three middle-aged Japanese produced their *meishi* (business cards) and introduced themselves. Each spoke some English. The older man did not present a card and was not introduced. When the president of the American company asked who he was, the go-between said, 'He's just one of the company's directors'. The visit concluded without discussion of any business possibilities, but this was to be expected in an initial visit from Japanese businessmen.

Supreme's president later found out the family name of the unknown visitor and immediately recognized it as being that of the president of the Japanese company. He assumed that the president of the Japanese company had come but had hidden the fact. He felt that he had been taken advantage of. He telephoned the go-between and told him that he never wanted anyone from that company in his plant again. From a description of the unknown visitor, a consultant to the company realized that the visitor was not the president of the Japanese company. Rather, it was the semi-retired father of the president. The father retained a position on the board of directors and maintained an active interest in company activities, but was not active in day-to-day affairs. Unlike his son who was fluent in English, he spoke only Japanese.

(Source: Saito Duerr, 1989, pp. 85–7.)

QUESTIONS

1. Was the chairman of the American company wrong for not having found out in advance about Japanese business practices? Why did he not do so? (Answer the same questions in relation to the Japanese companies and US business practices.)

2. What are the principal cultural mistakes made (a) by the Americans from the Japanese perspective, and (b) by the Japanese from the American perspective?

3. What should the president of the American company do now?

A13.5   Case: Doing business in China: a failure in getting paid

In recent years, the People's Republic of China (PRC) has become much more open to trade with the West, and has also made substantial internal economic reforms. Companies in Japan, the Western European countries, the United States and elsewhere have viewed the Chinese market as having enormous potential. With a population of a billion and a growing economy, it has appeared to many to be worthwhile to make a major effort to gain a foothold in the market. Both direct exports and joint ventures have been used.

In spite of the economic reforms, however, the PRC remains a tightly controlled, centrally directed economy. Most commercial enterprises and almost all production facilities are state owned and state run. Only a small number of designated organizations are allowed to engage in international trade, and all of these are state owned.

All contracts for trade must receive several government approvals. Larger contracts receive more approvals than smaller ones. It is not always apparent to the outsider, or perhaps even to some of the Chinese, what specific approvals will be required in particular cases. While letters of credit may be issued to companies exporting to China, these do not provide the same level of assurance that a letter of credit issued by, say, a London bank would. The Chinese bank will simply not release foreign exchange, regardless of the existence of a letter of credit, without the approval of appropriate government agencies. Foreign companies selling to the government may not receive a letter of credit, but may feel that they can rely on the good faith of the government.

A major United States exporter recently called upon the US Embassy in Beijing requesting assistance in solving a problem. About one year earlier they had sold approximately US$8.0 million worth of equipment to the China National Technology Import Company for use by the Chinese Ministry of Petroleum Industries (MOPI). To date, no payment had been received, and the company did not seem to be getting anywhere in its attempts to collect. The commercial attaché at the embassy called the

Technology Import and Export Department of the Ministry of Foreign Economic Relations and Trade (MOFERT), the Chinese department which would appear to be in charge of the transaction. MOFERT agreed to a meeting at 10.00 a.m. the next day. After the commercial attaché had briefed MOFERT representatives on the problem, they indicated that they were not in charge of the transaction; it came under the jurisdiction of the Import and Export Department, not the Technology Import and Export Department. Nevertheless they agreed to see what they could do to help. The commercial attaché expressed hope that the problem could be resolved as expeditiously as possible since the payment was already a year overdue.

At 2.00 p.m. the same afternoon, MOFERT officials called and informed the commercial attaché that the problem had been resolved and that payment would be forthcoming. They explained that MOPI had delayed submitting the request for initial contract approval and had sent that along with the request for payment. This had caused a delay. The rules had been changed so that, in addition to the approvals required when a contract is to be signed, an additional set of approvals is required from the same organizations when the goods are delivered. In the case of this contract, two separate sets of approvals were required from each of the following:

1. MOPI;

2. MOFERT;

3. the State Planning Commission;

4. the State Administration for Foreign Exchange Control.

(Source: George Lee of San Francisco State University, and formerly commercial attaché, US embassy, Beijing, PRC. Reproduced with the kind permisssion of the author.)

QUESTIONS

1. Why does the People's Republic of China have a State Administration for Foreign Exchange Control, and so many approvals required for a purchase of goods from overseas?

2. Is the additional difficulty involved in trying to sell to the People's Republic of China, compared with trying to sell to France or Taiwan, worth the trouble? Why or why not?

3. If you wanted to export to the People's Republic of China, would you go to your own government or embassy in China for assistance? Why or why not?

4. If the United States company had a similar problem in France, is it likely they would have contacted their embassy for assistance? Why or why not?

A13.6 Critical incident: Scandinavian Tools Company

A major Swedish company that specialized in metal tools and factory equipment had created a French subsidiary a few years ago, based in Lyons, France. This plant was at first supplied with inputs (specialty steels, high-speed steels for blades and saws, etc.) from Sweden. It mostly produced and sold for the French markets and for exports to southern European markets, namely Italy, Spain and Portugal. The drive and energy for creating this new venture came from a young Swedish executive, Bo Svensson. Svensson had spent part of his time as a student, and then as a young engineer, in France. Thereafter he had been in a position to convince the top management of this large Swedish multinational company to launch a new subsidiary in France.

Svensson was very enthusiastic about France. He liked the country very much and had learnt the language, which he spoke fluently with a slight northern European accent. In the rush of starting the new company everything went smoothly. Svensson, who was chief executive officer of the French venture, knew how to secure customers and make them loyal; he also knew how to deal with the headquarters in Sweden. The market was growing quickly and competition was not particularly fierce. At the beginning, products were made in Sweden and then exported to France, where Svensson and the subsidiary dealt with marketing and distribution.

After a few years demand began to swell, so the parent company in Sweden decided to build a production plant in France. Machines and factory equipment for the new plant came from Sweden, and the factory was quickly operating at normal capacity. Svensson then hired a vice-president for administration, André Ribaud, an ambitious young executive, also in his thirties, with a law background. The two men got on well together, although their backgrounds and personal profiles were quite different. They shared the work and responsibilities: Svensson was in charge of relations with headquarters, marketing and the monitoring of financial performance; as plant manager, Ribaud was in charge of production operations, human resource management, cost accounting, monitoring cost prices and delivery delays.

After a few years it appeared that Svensson felt more and more relaxed in his job. Quite independent in his profitable subsidiary of (at that time) 200 employees located in a place remote from Sweden, he was able to have a very flexible timetable. He was also very free with personal expenses, which he was entitled to have reimbursed by the subsidiary: he simply had to sign his own expenses receipts. Svensson did not hesitate to use this facility: he did not make a clear distinction between his own money and the company's money. Svensson gradually got into the habit of abusing company-paid personal expenses. Ribaud was shocked. Svensson even went so far as to have the expenses of his mistress paid by the subsidiary.

Meanwhile Ribaud was still working as efficiently as during the initial years. Growth had been impressive. Starting with a few employees in a two-room office in Lyons, the subsidiary had grown to a dynamic medium-sized company with more than 500 people on the payroll; Scandinavian Tools France had bought two plants from competitors. Following these changes, Ribaud's responsibilities quickly increased. He had involved himself completely and passionately with the company. He knew each member of staff personally and was respected by them.

Over time the relationship between the two men had considerably worsened. Svensson saw that Ribaud was winning more and more influence and power inside the company, and was well known by the customers. He felt jealous of him and tried his best to make Ribaud's life in the company difficult. Ribaud, on the other hand, increasingly resented the excessive expenses and the catty remarks of his boss, for whom he no longer felt any esteem. Svensson was a complex, energetic and whimsical character. His charisma and stamina had enabled him to seduce the French clients as well as the management staff at the headquarters in Sweden. The excellent financial performance of the French subsidiary had enabled him to retain the confidence of his superiors, who were also Swedish compatriots. They had trust in his management talents and therefore they allowed him a large degree of freedom. He had also established friendships with some of the senior directors at headquarters, especially with the director in charge of public relations. Svensson was well known at headquarters level, and he understood company 'politics' quite well.

After fifteen years of almost steady growth, the market was reaching the stage of maturity. With the removal of borders within the EU, there were many acquisitions by large European and American competitors. The French subsidiary had lost some of its profitability. The middle managers were complaining to Ribaud about Svensson's lack of interest in the subsidiary and his mismanagement. Everybody believed that emergency decisions had to be taken before the situation got even worse. But Svensson turned a deaf ear to their complaints and remained unwilling to enter into discussion with either Ribaud or the other executives. The French were also amazed, and somewhat shocked, to see that there was no reaction from headquarters. It looked as if headquarters had little interest in the destiny of the French subsidiary. People at headquarters still seemed to have confidence in Svensson, who knew how to make them feel secure.

Ribaud did not feel comfortable in this situation. He felt that the financial balance of the subsidiary was threatened and that one factory would probably have to close in the near future. It also seemed to him that the interests of Swedish shareholders were not being adequately taken into account. Relations between Svensson and Ribaud were so damaged that Svensson was convinced that Ribaud was plotting against him. Svensson therefore systematically took a contradictory stance to Ribaud, at the risk of making inappropriate decisions which could possibly lead the subsidiary almost to the brink of bankruptcy.

Each time Ribaud brought up these problems during meetings with people from headquarters, Svensson abruptly interrupted him, shifting from English to Swedish in order to keep him out of the conversation. Under heavy pressure from some of the executives of the subsidiary who were about to resign and leave the company, Rihaud felt obliged to react. He had tried, during visits by members of the Swedish headquarters, to give them, indirectly, an idea of the situation. But he got the impression that he was not being heard. They had their own image of the chief executive officer which was clearly different.

In desperation, Ribaud decided to send an official note to the top management in Stockholm, in which he told them that he would be obliged to resign if nothing was done to put an end to the present disorder. He tried to write it as objectively as possible in a matter-of-fact style, citing evidence and hard facts. This was not an easy task since objectivity may prove difficult in such circumstances and, moreover, he was denouncing his boss, which is never very pleasant. He called one of the members of the top management in Stockholm whom he knew a little better than the others, explained about the letter and sent him a copy.

QUESTION

What answer could Ribaud expect?

NOTES

1. Depending on your own linguistic background, in reading this chapter you may be wondering how the linguistic mix (original French text, English translation) has influenced the kind of arguments put forward and the way in which they have been expounded. The Whorfian hypothesis, briefly explained in section 13.3, is presented in detail in the writings of Benjamin Whorf, collected after his death by John B. Carroll (1956).

2. A good example is the following assertion in Hall (1966, p. 50): 'In the Northern European tradition most Americans have cut themselves off from a powerful communication channel: olfaction. Our cities lack both olfactory and visual variety . . . During World War II in France I observed that the aroma of French bread freshly removed from the oven at 4:00 A.M. could bring a speeding jeep to a screaming halt . . . In the typical French town, one may savor the smell of coffee, spices, vegetables, freshly plucked fowl, clean laundry, and the characteristic odor of outdoor cafés.' Although there is some truth in Hall's words, I am not so sure that France is so odourful and the Americans so cut off from olfactive communication.

3. The example made known to me took place in Geneva, where the penalty was 15 Swiss Francs (about $12).

4. I am not arguing that these national cultures have a great deal in common. The concept of low context/explicit messages relates only to communication; in other aspects they may differ widely.

5. Langenscheidt, *German–English Dictionary* (New York: Pocket Books, 1970).

6. Hall posits the American as being more HC (or less LC) than the Swiss, the Germans and the Scandinavians (1976, p. 91), and the French and the English as more HC than the Americans but less than the Japanese. A possible tentative ranking on a scale starting with LC and moving across to HC would be: Swiss-Germans, Germans, Scandinavians, Americans, English, French, other southern Europeans, Latin Americans, Middle Easterners, Japanese.

7. Analogical components of verbal messages are those which work by imitation of existing models or regular patterns, but which cannot be reduced to binary, digital information. First, a 'yes' is '1' as opposed to 'no' which is '0' (digital component); second, the meaning derived from how this 'yes' is said is the analogical component of the message.

8. In this chapter, we have not paid special attention to the 'language of space'. This includes the codes concerning social distance: how far should one stay from another person in order to respect their area of private space and does such an area even exist? A complete approach to these relations of space was proposed by Hall (1966) in *The Hidden Dimension*, where he developed the concept of 'proxemics' – the grouping of observations and theories dealing with the use of space by human beings, especially as far as private space and social space are concerned. Hall further developed an interesting cross-cultural comparison of proxemics between the Germans, the English, the French, the Japanese and the Arabs.

9. The verifications of the Whorf–Sapir hypothesis seem to have been fairly conclusive, in particular those related to the comparative experiments based on Navajo children on the one hand and Anglo-Americans on the other. They shared all the principal socio-cultural characteristics (education, family income, religion, etc.) except language (see the experiments reported by Ferraro, 1990, pp. 54–5).

10. I wrote this short English text myself, therefore it is not a 'valid text' but a caricature or exercise in reflection. Native anglophones will notice the 'Gallic' style with respect to idioms.

11. This is related to English, French and German intellectual styles, which are described in more detail in Chapter 3, using the typology of Galtung (1981).

12. What is said here is fairly tentative; there are no definitive proofs, and so there are at best illustrations, and many people may disagree with what I say here. Think of it as proposed rather than imposed.

13. However, in Japan I had a student who was the son of the Turkish ambassador to the United Nations. Having been raised in France, Belgium, Italy and Brazil, he was studying for a Master's Degree in International Management at the American Graduate School of International Management in Phoenix, Arizona. Already a fluent speaker of Turkish, French, English, Italian and Portuguese, he was learning Japanese. But he was quite unable to move with ease from any one of these languages to another. When in the middle of a conversation I asked him for the English translation of a French word (I taught in English), he could never do this without a considerable delay. In fact *he thought separately in each one of these languages*, which is fairly consistent with the Whorfian hypothesis.

14. Sussman and Johnson (1996), based on a qualitative analysis of critical incidents provided by professional interpreters (in German, French, Japanese and Spanish), highlight three major roles for interpreters: editor, cultural coach and monitor/checker. In their view, international executives should be informed consumers of interpretation services. Executives conducting business through the services of an interpreter should hire an interpreter with proven or accredited skills and try to avoid using multiple interpreters since the use of many interpreters results in confused and protracted business transactions. It is also necessary to determine whether the interpreter should be a passive or an active participant taking on more than the strict interpreting role.

15. To investigate the equivalence/non-equivalence of terms, take two dictionaries and look in each of them at the translations in both directions. The Langenscheidt compact dictionary translates *act of God* as *force majeure*, but it translates *force majeure* as *overpowering circumstances*; Harrap's Concise Dictionary does not include the expression *act of God* in the English section and translates *force majeure* as 'circumstances outside one's control'. The next step is to consult a lawyer to arrive at the meanings of all these expressions, and find their respective legal consequences. *Force majeure* is used, as such, in English and US contracts.

16. It is naturally impossible to keep Japanese words in their original, spoken and written, form; they need to be transliterated into the Roman alphabet. The system often used is the *Hyojunshiki* (standard system), which is an adaptation of the Hepburn system.

17. The total unawareness of language differences in intercultural encounters is a general feature of the English-speaking cross-cultural literature. In an article about cross-cultural groups at work, Smith and Berg (1997, pp. 9–10) give many cues about how to improve intercultural effectiveness, but totally ignore language. People have to 'learn how to learn together', to discover 'other members' unique cultural contributions', to 'explore group polarities'. That native language is our main asset, learnt spontaneously, and is a main cultural differentiator across different linguistic areas is ethnocentrically ignored because everyone in the global world is supposed to speak fluent English. Language diversity as an opportunity for improving intercultural encounters is denied. Period.

REFERENCES

Adler, Peter S. (1975), 'The transitional experience: An alternative view of culture shock', *Journal of Humanistic Psychology*, vol. 15, pp. 13–23.

Bateson, Gregory (1971), introduction to *The Natural History of an Interview*, University of Chicago Library Microfilm Collection of Manuscripts in Cultural Anthropology, Series 15, Nos 95–98.

Carroll, John B. (1956), *Language, Thought and Reality: Selected writings of Benjamin Lee Whorf*, MIT: Cambridge, MA.

Condon, John C. and Fahti Youssef (1975), *Introduction to Intercultural Communication*, Bobbs Merrill: Indianapolis.

Copeland, Lennie and Lewis Griggs (1986) *Going International*, Plume Books/New American Library: New York.

De Mente, Boye (1990), *How to Do Business with the Japanese*, NTC Books: Chicago, IL.

Droit, Michel (1952), *Chez les Mangeurs d'hommes*, La Table Ronde: Paris.

Erikson, Erik (1950), *Childhood and Society*, Norton: New York.

Ferraro, Gary P. (1990), *The Cultural Dimension of International Business*, Prentice Hall: Englewood Cliffs, NJ.

Fisher, Glen (1980), *International Negotiation: A cross-cultural perspective*, Intercultural Press: Yarmouth, ME.

Fisher, Glen (1988), *Mindsets*, Intercultural Press: Yarmouth, ME.

Galtung, Johan (1981), 'Structure, culture and intellectual style: An essay comparing Saxonic, Teutonic, Gallic and Nipponic Approaches', *Social Science Information*, vol. 20, no. 6, pp. 817–56.

Gannon, Martin J. (1994), *Understanding Global Cultures: Metaphorical Journeys through 17 Countries*, Sage Publications: Thousand Oaks, CA.

Gauthey, Franck (1989), 'Gérer les différences dans l'entreprise internationale', *Intercultures*, no. 6, April, pp. 59–66.

Gauthey, Franck and Dominique Xardel (1990), *Le Management Intercuturel*, PUF, Collection 'Que Sais-Je?': Paris.

Gruère, Jean-Pierre and Pierre Morel (1991), *Cadres Français et Communications Interculturelles*, Eyrolles: Paris.

Hall, Edward T. (1960), 'The silent language in overseas business', *Harvard Business Review*, May–June, pp. 87–96.

Hall, Edward T. (1966), *The Hidden Dimension*, Doubleday: New York.

Hall, Edward T. (1976), *Beyond Culture*, Doubleday: New York.

Harris, Philip R. and Robert T. Moran (1987), *Managing Cultural Differences*, 2nd edn, Gulf Publishing Company: Houston, TX.

Hemingway, Ernest (1976), *The Snows of Kilimanjaro and Other Stories*, Charles Scribner's and Sons: New York.

Langenscheidt (1989), *Compact Dictionary French–English/English–French*, by Kenneth Urwin.

Lee, James A. (1966), 'Cultural analysis in overseas operations', *Harvard Business Review*, March–April, pp. 106–11.

Levine, Robert A. and Donald T. Campbell (1972), *Ethnocentrism: Theories of conflicts, ethnic attitudes, and group behavior*, John Wiley: New York.

Levine, Robert V. (1988), 'The pace of life across cultures', in Joseph E. McGrath (ed.), *The Social Psychology of Time*, Sage Publications: Newbury Park, CA, pp. 39–60.

M'biti, John (1968), 'African concept of time', *Africa Theological Journal*, vol. 1, pp. 8–20.

Mishima, Yukio (1954), *Shiosai* (French translation), Gallimard: Paris (original Japanese edition, 1954).

Morand, David A. (1996), 'Politeness as a universal variable in cross-cultural managerial communication', *International Journal of Organizational Analysis*, vol. 4, no. 1, pp. 52–74.

Morschbach, Helmut (1982), 'Aspects of non-verbal communication in Japan', in Larry Samovar and R. E. Porter (eds.), *Intercultural Communication: A reader*, 3rd edn, Wadsworth: Belmont, CA.

Oberg, Kalvero (1960), 'Culture shock: Adjustment to new cultural environments', *Practical Anthropology*, vol. 7, pp. 177–82.

Saito Duerr, Mitsuko (1989) in Gerald Albaum. Jesper Strandskov, Edwin Duerr and Laurence Dowd (1989). *International Marketing and Export Management*, Addison-Wesley: Reading, MA.

Sapir, Edward (1929), 'The status of linguistics as a science', *Language*, vol. 5, pp. 207–14.

Schneider-Lenné, E. (1993), 'The governance of good business', *Business Strategy Review*, vol. 4, no. 1 (Spring), pp. 75–85.

Simon, Paul (1980), *The Tongue Tied American*, Continuum Press: New York.

Smith, Kenwin and David Berg (1997), 'Cross-cultural groups at work', *European Management Journal*, vol. 15, no. 1, pp. 8–15.

Sumner, G. A. (1906), *Folk Ways*, Ginn Custom Publishing: New York.

Sussman, Lyle and Denise Johnson (1996), 'Dynamics of the interpreter's role: Implications for international executives', *Journal of Language for International Business*, vol. 7, no. 2, pp. 1–14.

Ueda Keiko (1974), 'Sixteen ways to avoid saying "no" in Japan', in J. C Condon and M. Saito (eds), *Intercultural Encounters in Japan*, Simul Press: Tokyo, pp. 185–92.

Weeks, William H., Paul B. Pedersen and Richard W. Brislin (1987), *A Manual of Structured Experiences for Cross-cultural Learning*, Intercultural Press: Yarmouth, ME.

Zaharna, R. S. (1989), 'Self shock: The double-binding challenge of identity', *International Journal of Intercultural Relations*, vol. 13, no. 4, pp. 501–26.

14 Intercultural marketing communications 1: Advertising

In the mid-1970s, when Polaroid introduced its cameras in Europe, it used the same advertising strategy, including TV commercials and print advertisements, as in the United States; these campaigns never achieved much impact in either raising awareness of instant photography or pulling customers into the stores. Later on, Polaroid developed very successful European campaigns on the basis of the strategy of one of its smallest subsidiaries, that in Switzerland, a multicultural and central country in Europe. The strategy of Polaroid Switzerland, promoting the functional uses of instant photography as a way to communicate with family and friends, proved to be transferable in European countries (Kashani, 1989). Advertising, being based on language and communication, is the most culture-bound element of the marketing mix.

This chapter could be subtitled 'national cultures, technological advances and the globalization of marketing communications'. Indeed it attempts to show, as Chapters 5 to 8 did, that globalization is not the very simple process that it is often believed to be. The first sections of this chapter describe cultural differences as they pertain to various aspects of advertising: what are the general attitudes *vis-à-vis* advertising (14.1)? How are advertising strategy (14.2) and creative standards (14.3) affected by local culture? How is media selection affected by differences in media availability and style (14.4)? Section 14.5 examines the globalization of advertising.

Since advertising is largely based on language and images, it is influenced by culture. Cross-national differences continue to exist, for the simple reason that we have not yet ceased to have different languages. Moreover language, be it through words or images, is the strongest link between advertisers and their potential audiences in marketing communications. The management process for marketing communication *per se* does not depend on the particular country where the advertising campaign is launched. It is composed of six steps (Figure 14.1). Logically, these steps should be taken in order, although feedback at any step is possible and often necessary, especially after testing the campaign. The six basic steps are as follows:

1. Isolate the communication problem to be solved: increase brand awareness, change the brand image, increase sales, differentiate from rival brands, take market share from the competition, etc.

2. Identify the relevant target population: which consumer segments? What are their sociodemographic characteristics, consumption habits, psychographic characteristics (consumer lifestyles and values), etc.?

3. Define the marketing communication objective in terms of influencing the target population, at either the attitudinal or the behavioural level. Communication objectives may be, for instance, to convince consumers that they like the product (to improve product acceptance), to let people try a product again (to increase sales by building consumer loyalty), to let people act, or to educate the consumer, etc.

4. Select the advertising themes and a creative strategy: how will the brand name be emphasized? Which copy strategy should be used?

5. Design a media plan: which media to use, how to optimize the best media to reach the target audience, etc.

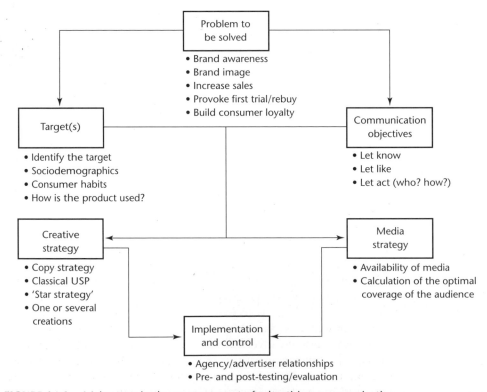

FIGURE 14.1   Main steps in the management of advertising communication.

6. Implement and monitor the advertising campaign: pre- and post-tests of advertisement effectiveness; research on different aspects (message recall, brand recall, aided brand recognition, actual influence on sales); etc.

The international dimension naturally has an influence on the implementation of each of these steps, but not an equal influence on each step. Let us take an example: to advertise life insurance in Tunisia, it should be taken into account that the life insurance market is a new one, where consumers have little knowledge of this kind of financial service. For this reason, the message shows a man and a woman watering a tree which grows by leap and bounds. Finally, a large pine tree protects them with its branches, while they sit happily in its shade. Certainly culture will influence the objective: the education of the consumer would be a basic objective in a country where life insurance is almost unknown. But the changes caused by cultural differences are most obvious with respect to the creative strategy (step 4). One should acknowledge and respect the values of Tunisian consumers who belong to an Arab-Muslim culture which is nevertheless strongly linked to two European cultures (Italy and France). The complex mix of Muslim and western culture has to be considered, since values that involve important matters (life and death, protecting one's family, betting on the future) are at stake.

The media plan will also be strongly influenced by local idiosyncrasies: media availability, viewing habits and media regulations still differ a great deal across countries. Conversely, the other steps in Figure 14.1 are not strongly affected by local factors: defining a communication problem or a communication objective, or testing the effectiveness of a campaign, calls for a similar approach in each country. Although the first three sections of this chapter favour customization of advertising, section 14.4 may appear to be in contrast to this. Technological advances that are now in progress world-wide, such as satellite television and the global reach of the media, have an undeniable impact on local attitudes and purchasing behaviour. The emergence of world wide advertising media partly breaks down cultural resistance. In fact, they open different lines of communication between cultures that previously were geographically and culturally separated, such as western and eastern Europe, or southern Europe and North Africa. Furthermore they open the way to new marketing communications in areas of the world which are culturally fragmented, for ethnic, linguistic or political reasons: Europe, South East Asia, Central and Latin America. In this new style of international marketing communication, strictly national segments and audiences must be differentiated from cross-border regional segments and audiences. The choice of the appropriate media as well as the choice of the language in which to advertise are therefore key success factors. The final section of this chapter deals with the issue of advertising globalization.

14.1   INFLUENCE OF CULTURE ON ATTITUDES TOWARDS ADVERTISING

General attitudes towards the role and functions of advertising

Advertising, which is a large part of marketing communications, is a field that is constantly changing. On the one hand it is closely dependent on the cultural and linguistic attitudes of the local target population. On the other hand, in so far as social representations are not fixed, advertising is a privileged method of cultural borrowing; advertising mirrors changing social behaviour. The relative freedom of advertising creation and the need to capture the audience imply that advertising is sometimes challenging and often innovative. It is therefore the ground for societal debates. This is illustrated below by several advertising-related issues, e.g. 'publiphobia' (social criticism and rejection of advertising) and attitudes towards comparative advertising.

General attitudes towards publicity and 'publiphobia'

'One view that has always existed is that advertising is nothing more than wasted money. This negative view of advertising is vaguely rooted in the ideas of the Saint-Simonist doctrine, in which anything that does not involve the production of material goods is considered to be socially unproductive. (Saint Simon was a nineteenth-century social philosopher who advocated the view that distribution and services in general were economically unproductive activities.) Retail sales and the service industry, including advertising, are considered to be parasitic activities. This view is often reinforced by the (misleading) argument that consumers pay for advertising costs which are included in the price of the product they buy.

This social representation was a part of the Marxist doctrine, and its influence on real socialism often produced disastrous consequences, such as shortages of basic staple items. This was largely caused by the absence of any effective distribution system through which products would have been made available to consumers. The shortage was further reinforced by the absence of a marketing communication system to inform people which goods and services were available to them, when, where and at what price (traditional and useful functions!).

In many European countries, especially in northern Europe and in France, there are still some traces of 'publiphobia'. The advertising profession in France was even forced to launch a huge poster and billboard campaign about fifteen years ago, against those known as 'publiphobes'. In certain countries such as Kuwait, advertisements for pharmaceutical products are strictly controlled or even forbidden. It is often considered immoral to spend too much on advertisements and sales promotions for ethical drugs, on the assumption that it unduly increases the final price of a drug and thereby reduces the chances of the poorest people to buy essential medical supplies and regain their health. As a consequence, many countries put a ceiling on pharmaceutical advertising, or subject it to a special tax.

At the international level, more attention is now being given to the idea that advertising, though undeniably useful to society, can also have negative results such as the encouragement of conspicuous consumption and the creation of needs that cannot be satisfied, or that advertising may be deceptive. Therefore the economic and social committee of the UN (United Nations) has proposed a resolution that would protect consumers in developing nations. Wills and Ryans (1982) have looked at how consumerists, students, academics and managers differ in their attitudes towards advertising, across 14 countries. They show that, across all the countries, the views held by consumerists and managers are quite different. Managers often find advertising to be quite factual (75 per cent), providing important information about products or services (71 per cent) and both entertaining and informative (78 per cent), whereas consumerists rate it at a lower level on these dimensions (61, 48 and 50 per cent respectively). On the other hand, the attitudes of consumerists and managers do not differ significantly on various aspects of advertising: whether the advertisements are humorous, aesthetically pleasing or informative about prices. In all these aspects consumerists have a slightly less positive opinion. More than 50 per cent of the consumerists, on average (across the 14 countries), tend to have a negative opinion about the information content of advertising.

Andrews *et al.* (1991) show that there are substantial differences among young people from various countries (the United States, Denmark, Greece, India, and New Zealand) in the perception of advertising in general. US students were shown to have more affective responses towards advertising, using statements such as 'stupid', 'entertaining', 'annoying'; they were also the least critical of advertising among the five nations surveyed. The potentially negative effects of advertising, in economic as well as social terms, represented only 22 per cent of US students' statements, compared with 60 per cent for the Greeks and 51 per cent for the Indians. New Zealand students, who come from a country where advertising regulation is quite strict, were those with the most negative views of advertisements; they emphasized their view that advertisements were 'meaningless repetition' or that they 'interrupt good programmes'. It seems that people from developing countries are more concerned with the impact of advertising on product costs, leading to more social criticism of advertising than in developed countries (Darley and Johnson, 1994).

Attitudes towards comparative advertising

Attitudes towards comparative advertising basically depend on the responses that are given in a particular society to the following questions:

1. What is the social function of comparative advertising?
2. What are the prevailing arguments concerning the legitimacy of comparative advertising?
3. How should competition between brands be facilitated?
4. Does comparative advertising result in fooling the consumer by using disputable information to praise one's own brand and put down others?

Socially dominant responses to these questions directly influence comparative advertising regulations in a given country. In some countries, comparative advertising is held in low esteem. This is the case in France, where it has traditionally been considered a denigration of competing brands. It is therefore forbidden under Article 1382 of the Civil Code. In order for the advertisement to be considered comparative, there need only be a comparison of two competing products, even if the terms are not inaccurate, tendentious, or antagonistic. For instance, about twenty years ago Lip, the top French watchmaker, was forced to pay heavy penalties to Timex, the top company in the American watch industry. The main feature of Timex's Kelton brand was its distribution through tobacconists, whereas Lip was confined to the more traditional channel of watch and jewellery stores. Lip was under attack from Kelton which, through the tobacconists, caused Lip huge sales losses. With the purpose of counter-attacking in order to regain market share Lip began an advertising campaign that showed a broken watch in an ashtray surrounded by a thick cloud of smoke, with a slogan that read: 'The watches sold in tobacconists are like cigarettes: they go up in smoke.'

Belgium, Italy and Germany are some other European countries that forbid comparative advertising. It is sometimes argued that some countries forbid comparative advertising as an indirect way of protecting their national products from unfavourable comparisons with imported goods. According to Boddewyn (1984) the French authorities, who were about to legalize comparative advertising, took a step backwards, fearing that Japanese car manufacturers would use comparative advertising to communicate aggressively the advantages of their cars, thereby increasing their share of the French market where competition with other European producers is already active.

However, in the United States comparative advertising is legally permitted. The basic arguments in favour of comparative advertising seem to make sense: it facilitates consumer information, choice and competition between brands. Hence automobile advertising frequently gives performance statistics of competing models, such as fuel consumption, speed and comfort. Opponents of comparative advertising take the argument further and cast doubt on the possibility of using truly objective measures, which would be handled by completely independent testing organizations. As a consequence, comparative advertising would often end up giving either no information at all or partly misleading information to the consumer. Opponents of comparative advertising also implicitly support the idea that it is necessary to enforce moral business relationships between competitors. The role of marketing communications, by means of advertising, is to praise the virtues of their own product, not to put down (however indirectly) the virtues of competing products.

James and Hensel (1991, p. 55) emphasize the possibility that malicious comparative advertising can turn into negative advertising. They take the example of a Kentucky Fried Chicken advertisement which made explicit reference to McDonald's.

The first ad, sponsored by Kentucky Fried Chicken, opens with a red-haired Ronald McDonald surrogate (sans clown outfit) being interrogated by a Senate 'subcommittee' rivalling the likes of that faced by Oliver North. Allegations are raised as to the defendant's lack of expertise and questionable ability to provide quality chicken (McNuggets) to the public. When pressed as to how he expects to be able to sell chicken given this lack of expertise, 'Ronald' responds, 'Toys, lots of toys!', while the man who appears to be his legal counsel buries his head in his hands.

Allowed in the United States, but forbidden in many countries, comparative advertising is in a process of change at the European level. It is already permitted in some European countries, and a European Union directive has allowed comparison under definite constraints. Legislation requires that advertising be based on features of the competing products or services that are material, relevant, verifiable and fairly chosen. Comparisons should be objective and should not discredit competitors or their brands.

14.2   CULTURE AND ADVERTISING STRATEGY

The function of an advertisement is to communicate a message to an audience based on two major elements: strategy and execution. While there is some overlap between these categories, advertising strategy comprises 'what is said' and execution concerns more 'how it is said'. Advertising strategy relates to the types of appeals used, the themes developed and the overall communication style, whether (1) direct or indirect, (2) explicit or implicit or (3) rational or emotional. Advertising style in communicating with the audiences of viewers, readers or listeners can be roughly divided into three basic categories: (1) persuasive, (2) informative and (3) oneiric, that is dream-oriented.

Advertising appeals

A limited number of different advertising appeals can be identified based on common themes and concepts. Although all of them are used world-wide, cultural sensitivity is portrayed through the varying usage of these same appeals (Agrawal, 1995). A comparison of US and Japanese advertising strategies shows, for instance, that the same ten basic appeals are used. The Japanese preference for implicit, indirect communication is reflected by a relative lack of hard-sell appeals. Instead, there are four times as many soft-sell appeals in Japanese as in US advertisements. In accordance with Japanese values, there also are more advertisements which stress tradition and veneration of the elderly (Javalgi *et al.*, 1995). The product-merit appeal, on the other hand, is dominant in US advertisements (Mueller, 1987). As stated by Lin (1993, pp. 44–5), Japanese cultural values stress status symbols in advertising whereas Americans place emphasis on individual determinism:

Japanese advertisements reveal an indulgence with sensitive crafting of product image and appearance slated within a subtle frame of reference. This contrasts sharply with the American fixation on presenting facts and attributes to showcase product superiority . . . [In Japan] 'boasting' of product quality and 'bribing' consumers into submission are not in line with the custom of respectful treatment of consumers and respectable projection of company image. These same rationales explain why comparative and testimonial messages are not a desirable form of advertising in Japan.

Several other characteristics have been noted which distinguish Japanese from US creative strategy: little relationship between advertisement content and the advertised product, only brief dialogue in TV commercials with minimal explanatory content, priority placed on company trust rather than product quality, etc. (Kishii, 1988; Di Benedetto *et al.*, 1992). Different advertising strategies in Japan and the USA are also observed with regard to corporate advertisements (McLeod and Kunita, 1994).

A comparison of the USA, the UK, France, Korea and India reveals that Korea uses a significantly higher percentage of descriptive advertising appeals whereas France can be characterized by symbolic advertising and the USA and the Asian countries by a larger use of associative appeals than the European countries (Cutler *et al.*, 1992). Similar differences between Asian, US, and European creative strategies are confirmed by a study by Zandpour *et al.* (1992) who found a dominant use of argument and imitation in US commercials, higher levels of information and obligation strategies in Taiwan and, again, most symbolic association strategies in French advertisements. Swedish ads also depend more on symbolic associations than the US ads (Martenson, 1987).

A significant degree of similarity in advertising strategies only appears in culturally close countries like the USA, the UK and Canada. Overall, advertising agencies in all three places use the same strategies in the same number of cases. Problem solution is most popular, followed by USP (unique selling proposition), emotion, brand image and brand identity (West, 1993; Appelbaum and Halliburton, 1993).

Relying on the dream-oriented part of the advertising audience is typical of the 'Séguéla' doctrine. The dream-like dimension that surrounds the product is favoured at any price. Italian and French advertisements often appear as very dream oriented: viewers and readers are supposedly willing to escape from the real world. The oneiric style of advertisement enhances the fantasy of the consumer and emphasizes the imagination of satisfaction and enjoyment. It does so in a rather holistic way (the product and its benefits tend to be implied rather than actually shown). The oneiric style does not really concentrate on actual buying and consumption experiences. Germans, unlike the French or the Italians, are known to have a taste for highly informative advertising. A young German advertising specialist, Konstantin Jacoby (quoted in *Communication et Business*, 1988, p. 18) criticizes French advertising, and especially the most well-known publicist Jacques Séguéla (co-founder of the RSCG agency, reputed for oneiric, dream-oriented copy strategies):

Certainly it [French advertising] is better than German advertising, but the French should take care not to sink in art for art's sake or in *séguélomania*. The message of the Citroen advertising campaign is horrible. What is the link between the Great Wall of China and Citroen? Are Citroen cars manufactured there now?

The information content of advertising: Cross-national differences

The information content of advertising is a key issue since it shows whether the strategy follows the informative option, rather than the persuasion or dream-orientation avenues. The information content will naturally be lower when the two last avenues are followed. Ever since the first systematic evaluation of information content by Resnik and Stern (1977), the informativeness of advertising has received considerable attention all over the world. Many researchers compared their country's advertising situation to that of the United States. The most important findings of these studies are that information content varies by country – but also by broadcast time, product type and medium. Stern and Resnik (1991), based on a review of existing evidence, found that the information content (the number of information cues contained in advertisements) varies cross nationally.

Overall, it appears that US television advertising is less informative than most other television advertising world-wide. US television advertising contains less information than Australian (Dowling, 1980), French-Canadian (Johnstone *et al.*, 1987), Spanish (Bigne *et al.*, 1993), Ecuadorian (Renforth and Raveed, 1983), Irish (Ward and McQuirk, 1987), French and German (Schroeder, 1991) and Japanese television advertising (Lin and Salwen, 1995). Only British TV advertisements seem to contain less information than US advertisements (Weinberger and Spotts, 1989a). However, Keown *et al.* (1992), comparing the information content of advertising across four countries (the United States, Japan, South Korea and the People's Republic of China) found the highest level of information cues in the United States, followed by Japan and the People's Republic of China, whereas South Korean advertising scores lowest in informative content. In all countries, television and radio advertising were generally less informative than print advertising. Cross culturally, print media are more informative than radio and television: comparing the information content of media in the USA, Japan, China and South Korea, it was found that magazine and newspaper advertisements have a larger number of information cues than television and radio advertisements (Keown *et al.*, 1992). Similarly, in comparing the information content of American and Swedish advertising, by using a systematic analysis of the content of television commercials, Rita Martenson (1987) shows that Swedish advertisements have less information elements than American advertisements. She attributes this fact to the atmosphere of intense competition for the attention of television viewers that exists in the United States. The consumers change channels to avoid commercials, use commercial breaks to look at the programmes on other channels, etc. 'This means that [in the US] any commercial that does not have a very clear and simple message will strongly reduce its chances of getting the slightest amount of attention' (Martenson, 1987, p. 141).

In a meta-analysis of 59 studies about information content, an interesting result from a cross-cultural perspective is that advertising in developed countries is more informative than in developing countries (Abernethy and Franke, 1996). A closer look at some of the studies quoted above offers additional valuable insights. Information content varies strongly from one country to another. Although product types and other environmental factors such as the competitive environment have an influence on information content, culture is the most important factor in explaining how much and what kind of information can be found in an advertisement. Both the types of information cues and the quantity of information are culture bound. Whereas some targets prefer more rational, tangible cues – as in the USA – others expect emotional and more 'subjective' information. This is why many Japanese advertisements present 'company-sponsored research', an element that is much less important in western countries. Even in neighbouring countries with a similar economic environment, such as France and Germany, information content varies fundamentally (Schroeder, 1991). Because information reduces uncertainty, cultures known to avoid uncertainty such as the German culture (Hofstede, 1991) will always have a tendency to ask for more information than cultures which have a lower uncertainty avoidance score. Furthermore, communication in Germany is based on explicit messages. It thus naturally scores high on the Resnik and Stern procedure which counts explicit information cues.

When comparing advertising practices in Turkey, Canada and Sweden, Kaynak and Ghauri (1986, p. 127) explain that in developed countries advertising copy in general contains more writing and technical information, because most consumers have a high level of literacy and education: 'Unlike Canada and Sweden, most of the advertising copy used by the Turkish agencies is persuasive in nature rather than informative.' The Turkish word for advertising is *Reklam*: this corresponds to a more traditional vision of advertising, where persuasion and slogans are the key issues.

Assuming that consumers are rational information seekers (which is not true in most cultural contexts), advertising content should be related to information sought by consumers in order to improve the relevance of their choices. If for any reason consumers are not 'good' (motivated and educated) information seekers, they will be less sensitive to the information content of an advertisement. This is the case if they do not directly use advertising information in their brand evaluations in order to reduce perceived risks when purchasing. Hoover *et al.* (1978) compared Mexican consumers with their American neighbours: they found that Mexicans generally displayed a much lower level of perceived risk related to their purchases. Hoover *et al.* argue that the lower level of perceived risk is related to a somewhat fatalistic tradition which exists in Mexican society. Conversely, in the United States a more 'master-of-destiny' orientation implies a greater perceived risk of being disappointed by any purchase. Thus Mexican consumers and, more generally, consumers belonging to fatalistic-oriented societies react more easily to persuasive message (the brand name repeated numerous times) and also oneiric messages (a dream which allows one to escape from a daily life which is not always bright).

Finally, it should be noted that the types of information cues vary by country. While Japanese advertisements, for example, have very few price, warranty and guarantee cues compared to US advertisements, they carry a much higher number of packaging cues (Lin, 1993; Lin and Salwen, 1995; Javalgi *et al.*, 1995). Korean advertisements include the price 38 per cent of the time, whereas in other countries the average is between 8 per cent (India) and 16 per cent (France) (Cutler *et al.*, 1992). While 'The British don't even want to mention money' (Reinhard and Phillips, 1985, p. 46), French commercials present more quality information and new ideas, and in Taiwan information about product availability and special offers are significantly higher than average (Zandpour *et al.*, 1992).

As a general rule, advertising strategy must fit with the local orientation concerning information content and style of advertising. Advertising strategies which follow purely informative, oneiric or persuasive routes will have to be considered cautiously as applicants for cross-border transfer.

14.3   CULTURE AND ADVERTISING EXECUTION

Once the advertising strategy is defined, execution remains a quite significant cross-cultural 'filter', since meaning transfer is fine-tuned through executional details, most of which are strongly culture bound. This section reviews the empirical literature in the following domains of advertising execution: (1) language; (2) use of humour; (3) characters and roles represented; (4) religion and social taboos as obstacles to the use of provocative, sexy or non-conformist creations; (5) visual elements of advertising: colours, background themes used in execution, etc.[1]

Language

Advertisements usually have several text elements (catch phrase, product description, slogan) and use colloquial language, very subtle yet precise in meaning. The character and structure of these elements heavily influence the advertisement's effectiveness, while language differences are the strongest barrier to effective communication. Duncan and Ramaprasad (1995) show for instance that, in a sample of companies advertising international brands which tend to favour standardized strategy (68 per cent) and standardized execution (54 per cent) the percentage of cases (across all countries) where they standardize language is only 11 per cent.

In a French context, for example, in order to be effective, 50 per cent of all words in an advertisement should be nouns and verbs, the percentage of words exceeding three syllables should not be higher than 10 per cent, most of the long words should be familiar words, and sentences should have an average length of about 10–13 words (Tixier, 1992). Furthermore advertising language is often based on quite slangy words, particular to local people, and difficult to find in dictionaries. The viewer or the listener understands messages all the more readily when colloquial speech expresses the delicate messages of daily life – sentiments, sensations, family relations, friendships, love affairs – that are reflected in advertising. Translating colloquial speech is difficult since it uses idiomatic expressions, which change from one language to another.

Marcel Bleustein Blanchet (quoted in *Reader's Digest*, 1987, pp. 42–3), a publicist for more than sixty years, notes a change in the role of slogans, which have become both simpler and more sophisticated, and less frequently used. He explains that 'when the public was less demanding and less blasé, slogans were the best means of launching a brand. Especially when radio began to advertise . . . pre-war slogans were a sort of *comptines* [little nursery rhymes]. They were assonantal forms that the ear picked up instinctively.'

Effective textual elements, including the use of foreign vocabulary in an advertisement, are defined differently from one culture to another. A very large percentage of Asian advertisements contains English – and in some rare cases French – words (Mueller, 1992; Sherry and Camargo, 1987). Since the most important function of this foreign vocabulary ultimately is to achieve positive country-of-origin effects, its use depends on product type and product origin. Within a sample of ads from Hong Kong, Japan, South Korea and Taiwan, the likelihood of encountering foreign words is highest for advertisements in Hong Kong and Taiwan featuring western-made personal care products (Neelankavil *et al.*, 1995). However, it would be fundamentally wrong to conclude from the heavy use of foreign words in Asian countries that there is a trend towards a globalization of advertising language. The Japanese culture in particular has demonstrated that English loanwords are used for their symbolic weight but are embedded in Japanese traditions. 'The loanwords are Japanized, becoming a distinctive communication neither entirely alien nor entirely traditional' (Sherry and Camargo, 1987, p. 185).

As argued in the previous chapter, the slogan 'Put a tiger in your tank', for instance, is not as standardized as it might seem. At first reading, it looks as if it were fully equivalent across countries, but the interpretation differs as to where the power source is located – engine or tank. Examples of translation and conceptual equivalence problems abound, especially for advertising campaigns in which message standardization has been attempted (for examples see Ricks *et al.*, 1979). A full rewrite is usually needed to transpose slogans from one language to another. This implies a thorough search for words which have the same intended meaning as in the source language, provided that these can be found (see section 7.2).

For advertisements that must be easily internationalized, one should avoid at all costs any problems related to language, for instance by using a merely visual TV commercial on which a voice-over in the local language can be added for each country. Another problem concerns the comprehension of foreign words, since a minority of persons world-wide can understand English. Even the translation of a message into each target country's language does not guarantee uniform comprehension. The meaning attributed to certain words depends on cross-culturally differing association norms. If the English word 'quiet' is translated into German ('ruhig') and French ('tranquille'), German consumers mostly think of a forest (41 per cent), sleep (35 per cent), church (20 per cent), but also of a cemetery (13 per cent) and a bed (8 per cent). The pictorial associations of their French counterparts are fundamentally different and less homogeneous (countryside: 13 per cent; forest: 11 per cent; house: 9 per cent; library: 5 per cent, etc.). The congruency coefficient between both groups for the word 'quiet' is only 0.17 (Kroeber-Riel, 1992).

The visual element of the message can be emphasized to the detriment of the textual component. As a consequence, television commercials aimed at a European audience often use a script where the characters speak neither to the audience nor to each other. Then a voice-over message on a sound track can be added to the image track. This avoids the drawbacks associated with dubbing. Most people lip-read unconsciously, at least in part. When watching a dubbed commercial, many people feel uneasy about the lag between lip movements and sounds. Written communication should also be avoided in messages targeted at a multilingual audience. For instance, a commercial for a detergent where a housewife is handed a packet of '*Waschpulver*' will be identified by British, Italian or French viewers as foreign or German. A few years ago, IBM used the character of Charlie Chaplin and the mode of a silent film in a multinational campaign, the goal of which was to foster corporate image. This allowed the advertisement to be used in any country of the world. The same can be applied to magazine advertisements where the text can be reduced or even virtually deleted. It may sometimes be kept in its original language in advertisements for ethnic products. The text must then be short and must strongly support an ethnic image (French for perfume, English for a large international newspaper, Italian for luxury leather shoes, etc.). The text must be universally understood, although not necessarily in full detail; the message should at least make sense with respect to the halo of meanings around the product proposal.

In cases where translations lead to the desired associations, space considerations have to be taken into account when conceiving an advertisement. Differing language structures mean that, the textual part of advertisements grows by about 25 per cent when English is translated into Roman languages, and by 30 per cent when translated into Germanic languages (Grüber, 1987). This can alter the overall layout of the advertisement, and possibly decrease the relative impact of visual elements.

Humour

The basic concept of humour is universal since it can be found in every culture and in any country's advertising; however, preferences for types of humour vary cross culturally (McCullough and Taylor, 1993). Globally, most humour has an incongruity-resolution structure: people develop expectations based on category norms that are capable of being violated, sometimes in a humorous way (Suls, 1983); a naked businessman or a clothed ape speaking to the audience are examples of incongruity-based humour. Some cross-cultural support exists for a positive affect-based effect of humour in advertising. For groups of Finnish and US students a linkage between perceived funniness of an advertisement, liking the advertisement, and liking the product can be established (Unger, 1995). However, a closer look at the use of humour also reveals notable cultural differences.

First, the percentage of advertisements intending to be humorous varies across countries. There is for example a significantly higher percentage of humorous advertisements in television commercials in the UK than in the United States whereas French commercials use humour about as frequently as US spots but clearly more often than German spots (Weinberger and Spotts, 1989b; Appelbaum and Halliburton, 1993). Second, although the incongruity principle can be found in the advertising of different countries, the relative importance of such humour varies. Alden *et al.* (1993) related Hofstede's values to the use of humour in advertising, by comparing two individualist cultures (the United States and Germany) with two collectivist and high-power-distance cultures (Thailand and South Korea). More incongruent contrasts are found in German (92 per cent) and Thai (82 per cent) than in American (69 per cent) and Korean advertisements (57 per cent). Additionally, in countries with high collectivism scores, significantly more characters are depicted in humorous advertisements than in more individualistic countries. Similarly, in countries high on the power distance dimension (i.e. Korea, Thailand) characters portrayed in humorous advertisements are much more likely to have an unequal status than in low-power-distance countries such as the USA and Germany (Alden *et al.*, 1993).

The kind of humour preferred by each target culture differs: while English people are known for their black humour, Germans seem to prefer humour based on gloating (Huth and Unger, 1988). The latter would not be much appreciated in Japan where slapstick or demeaning humour is seldom seen in advertising. Instead the Japanese make humorous dramatizations of situations involving family members, colleagues, neighbours, etc. to create a bond of mutual feelings between the advertiser and the viewer (Hanna *et al.*, 1994). Additionally, black and earthy humour is also present in Japanese commercials. Subjects such as diseases, wars or funerals which are taboo themes in the USA are treated with humour in some Japanese advertisements (Di Benedetto *et al.*, 1992). It thus appears that humour can be an element of standardization in cross-cultural advertising, especially when it is based on the incongruity principle which has a fairly global appeal. Nevertheless, the creative presentation of humour in advertisements needs considerable adaptation to be effective (Alden *et al.*, 1993).

Characters and roles represented in advertisements

When depicting characters, advertising must be extremely careful. Whether it is the age, dress or situation of a character that is represented, nothing should be left to chance in advertising messages. In general, target audiences prefer characters with which they can identify. Since the physique of a person – and even more so a hero-like person depicted in an advertisement – is a clear manifestation of a particular culture, the choice of characters needs particular attention in cross-cultural advertising.

Advertising is often accused of perpetuating traditional social roles, sometimes even acting as a vehicle for outdated ideas. However, the real situation is much more ambiguous: in most countries advertising acts as an agent of both social change and social maintenance. Advertising creation sometimes acts as an agent of change because social challenge is a method of capturing the attention of the audience, and because social innovators are also opinion leaders for new products and new ways of life. Advertising also reinforces traditional and sometimes old-fashioned social patterns: it is the mirror of society as a whole.

One important issue related to characters in advertising is the portrayal of gender role. Several cross-cultural investigations have examined role portrayal in magazine and

TV advertising. They all found that advertising reflects traditional stereotypes of male and female roles to varying degrees. Overall, women for example are mostly shown in non-working roles, often in the home, and in decorative roles. When women appear in working roles, they are more likely than men to be depicted in clerical, blue-collar or secretarial roles. Sex stereotyping is relatively consistent in nature world-wide although it may vary in degree; for instance, in both Hong Kong and Singapore, males are more likely to be portrayed as product authorities and females as product users (Siu, 1996). Yeung and Lau (1993), looking at magazine advertising, show that Hong Kong and Taiwan treat gender role similarly, putting half of the men in working roles; in contrast, Japanese advertisements put 93.6 per cent of women in non-working roles.

In a comparative study (Australia, Mexico, the United States) of the advertising industry's attitude towards sex roles, Mary Gilly (1988) analyzed, for each country, 12 hours of programmes: 275 American, 204 Mexican and 138 Australian commercials were viewed. In neither the United States nor Mexico (as opposed to Australia) were women pictured in professional or executive positions. In these two countries men, more often than women, were shown in roles of authority or expertise with respect to the product, whereas women were more often shown in the role of the consumer. Finally, the only country where there is a difference in the situations in which men and women appear is the United States, where a woman is more likely to be shown at home. One would have expected a more traditional image in Mexico and a more modern image in the United States, with Australia somewhere in between. These results show that our basic intuitions as to which country gives the most 'modern' image of women are not necessarily backed up by facts. Similarly, Huang (1995) shows that in a more masculine society (the United States) there is more sex role stereotyping, women are less frequently portrayed in working situations and there is less frequent use of female voice-over than in a feminine society (Taiwan).

Important differences are also found in neighbouring Asian countries. A Malaysian television channel, oriented towards a mostly Muslim target audience, typically depicts men in exciting and independent top executive roles. 'The woman was frequently a young housewife who stayed at home to mind the house and the children' (Wee et al., 1995, p. 62). On Singapore television, on the other hand, men are over-represented in middle management roles, while the woman stereotype was more modern: a young, attractive woman, concerned with beauty, and depicted in white-collar and service occupations. Interestingly, the portrayal of women on a second Malaysian channel, targeted both to Malaysian and to Singaporean audiences, is a compromise between the stereotypes held by both audiences.

In Swedish magazine advertisements, women are more likely to be depicted in working roles, far more likely to be portrayed in recreational roles, and far less likely to be depicted in decorative roles than in US magazine advertisements (C. Wiles and Tjernlund, 1991); a further study showed that women were never depicted in housework and childcare activities in Swedish advertisements whereas they were shown twice as often as males in such situations in American advertisements (C. Wiles et al., 1995). Some countries display a stronger tendency to depict women in traditional roles related to the family and the home: Rose et al. (1993), for instance, show that German and Japanese people emphasize more traditional roles for women than do people in Denmark, France, New Zealand and the United States. However, across all six countries, the traditional view of female roles decreases from older to younger generations, which shows consistent cross-national convergence.

Although the studies show that sex role stereotypes are found in all cultures, local differences exist. It seems that Australia and Sweden have a more balanced and non-traditional representation of men and women in their advertising than for example the USA and Singapore. Malaysia, and to a lesser extent Mexico, where religious values and tradition are more important, display the biggest sex-role differences in advertising. Whereas on Malaysian (Muslim) television the portrayal of the sexes lags behind changes in society (i.e. the number of housewives is grossly exaggerated – Wee *et al.*, 1995), marketers in countries like Sweden have a more proactive approach in defining sex roles, thus creating new trends. Even across countries with quite similar levels of development, stronger traditional values in the society, such as in Japan compared with the United States, cause women's roles to be portrayed more traditionally (Javalgi *et al.*, 1995).

In the European countries and in the USA, men and women predominantly appear in non-working roles. There is room for some standardization if both genders are depicted in recreational (men more than women) or decorative roles (women more than men). This would be acceptable, for example, in the USA, Sweden and The Netherlands (J. Wiles *et al.*, 1995). Besides, in any country's advertising, women should ideally be young. However, the preference for types of beauty presented in advertising differs across societies (Bjerke, 1995). Although standardized across Europe as concerns core themes, the Wash & Go shampoo advertising campaign by Procter & Gamble was adapted locally using different beauty presenters according to country.

A certain degree of standardization can be found regarding the use of western models in Asian countries. Such models can be found in more than one-third of magazine advertisements in Hong Kong, Taiwan, Japan and South Korea, and they are particularly frequent in advertisements for products from the West, notably personal care products (Neelankavil *et al.*, 1995). At the same time however, many advertisements reviewed in those countries had a completely local character.

With regard to the portrayal of the elderly in advertising, cross-cultural differences are also observed. A country's degree of orientation towards traditional values has an impact on the portrayal of the elderly in advertising messages. For instance, Japanese magazine advertisements show more respect towards the elderly than their American counterparts (Mueller, 1987; Javalgi *et al.*, 1995). However, common stereotypes are not always confirmed. For example, the elderly are not presented more frequently in a family setting in Latin America than in the USA and there is neither a greater proportion of portrayals of elderly males nor a more frequent use of the elderly as celebrity endorsers in Latin American advertisements (Bates and Renforth, 1987).

Traditional roles that are not present in the source culture may unintentionally appear when they are used in the target culture. A 'spurious' meaning may appear in the target culture which was not intended by the advertiser in the source culture. Douglas and Dubois (1980) give the example of a brandy advertisement which was targeted at the South African Bantu market. It showed a couple seated at a table with a bottle superimposed over them. Many Bantus thought that the woman was carrying the bottle on her head, as many traditional African women do. This created an unintended and confusing contrast between the traditional, local aspect of the characters and situation and the modern, imported aspect of the product. It therefore prevented clear and effective marketing communication.

As a consequence, one should study a representative sample of local advertising messages, whether commercials or magazine advertisements. This will give a good idea of the sex roles, age roles, typical everyday situations and social relations in a particular country. It can be achieved in a systematic way by a content analysis of newspaper, magazine and television advertisements, at least several dozen of each type. An advertisement should always be created in co-operation with a native of the target culture, who would act as a test audience; in the case of internationally standardized advertisements, messages in the various linguistic/cultural contexts should be reviewed by natives of each target culture.

In order to avoid creating spurious associations, the advertising script may go so far as not to present any characters at all, the target audience being not clearly defined or too large – making the choice of characters a difficult one. For instance, in a Renault advertisement, a car without a driver was shown moving in the middle of a scale-model city. This avoided the choice of a specific character, whose age, sex or appearance would influence the product's positioning undesirably. A car without a driver may, however, be negatively interpreted in countries where such a situation is associated with a safety issue (runaway car) or a distortion of reality (how can a car drive without a driver?). This may inhibit a positive response to the message.

The influence of mores and religion

It is crucial to choose the appropriate symbolic elements by which cultural meanings about products and services may be communicated to the audience. Mores and religion act as filters of advertising messages, transforming factual information into culturally interpreted meaning (e.g. a naked woman washing her hair in her bathroom) into elements of culture-based meaning (it incites people to sexual debauchery). If one focuses on information rather than meaning, it is difficult to become aware of the influence of mores and religion on advertising messages. This point is illustrated by the example of advertising in Saudi Arabia (Box 14.1).

BOX 14.1

The influence of religion on advertising in Saudi Arabia

The Saudi legal system is unique in the sense that it identifies law with the personal command of the 'one and only god, the Almighty'. The Islamic laws known as *Sharia* are the master framework to which all legislation, existing and proposed, is referred and with which it must be compatible. The *Sharia* is a comprehensive code governing the duties, morals and behaviour of all Muslims, individually and collectively in all areas of life, including commerce. *Sharia* is derived from two basic sources, the Quran or Holy Book, and the *Hadith*, based on the life,

BOX 14.1 *CONTINUED*

sayings, and practices of the Prophet Muhammed . . . At the very minimum, an understanding of fundamental *Sharia* laws as contained in Quranic injunctions is necessary in order to gain insights into advertising regulation and content. . . .

Three sets of Quranic messages have special significance for advertising regulation. First there are strict taboos (*haraam*), such as alcohol, gambling, cheating, idol worship, usury, adultery and 'immodest' exposure . . . For example alcoholic products are banned. There are no local advertisements, and foreign print media are only allowed into the country after all advertisements of alcoholic beverages have been censored. Promotions involving games of chance are illegal . . .

Other dangers for advertisers include messages which may be considered as deceptive by religious standards. According to Islam, fraud may occur if the seller fails to deliver everything promised, and advertisers may need to use factual appeal, based on real rather than perceived product benefits. Statuary should not appear in advertising, since it may be perceived as a symbol of idol worship. Since religious norms require women to be covered, international print advertisements may have to be modified by superimposing long dresses on models or by shading their legs with black. Advertisers of cosmetics in Saudi Arabia refrain from picturing sensuous females; instead, in typical advertisements a pleasant-looking woman appears in a robe and headdress, with only her face showing . . .

A second set of Quranic injunctions governs the duties a Muslim must perform, such as praying five times daily, fasting during the month of Ramadhan, giving *zakaat* (charity) to the poor, and respecting and caring for parents and the disadvantaged. Advertisers have to ensure that they do not hinder the performance of these obligations. For example, during the five prayer times, which last from 10 to 20 minutes, products cannot be promoted on radio or TV, retail shops close, and no commercial or official transactions are permitted. Advertisements should not depict, even humorously, children being disrespectful to parents and elders, whereas the image of a product could be enhanced by advertisements that stress parental advice or approval . . .

A third set of Quranic injunctions remind the faithful of God's bounties and enjoins them to thank Him for such blessings as good health, peace of mind, food, water and children. It is legal and sometimes recommended practice for advertisers to introduce their messages with Quranic words: 'In the Name of Allah, the Most Gracious, the Most Merciful'; 'By the Grace of God'; 'God is Great (Allah-o-Akbar)'; Al-Rabiah and Nasser, a manufacturer of water pumps, uses a Quranic verse: 'We made from water every living thing.' Such verses may also be used to legitimise operations or to assure that services are in accord with Islamic principles.

(Source: Luqmani *et al.*, 1988, pp. 61–4. Reproduced with permission.)

Al-Mossawi and Michell (1992) have measured the influence of observance of Islamic rules on attitudes towards contentious and non-contentious commercials in Gulf countries. Their findings show that strict Muslims show more interest in, and especially a higher recall of, non-contentious ads whereas there is no difference in the responses of lenient Muslims, regardless of whether the advertisement contains elements considered to be against the principles of Islam or not. The influence of religion on advertising, exemplified by the Muslim religion, although strong, is uniform neither across countries nor across individual viewers within a particular country (see Al-Makaty *et al.* (1996) in the case of Saudi Arabia). Furthermore, sensitive issues such as family planning can be treated successfully if creation adequately goes beyond traditional beliefs and taboos (Wafai and El Tigi, 1994).

Many of us have some superstitions, even though we may deny it. Rarely will advertisements show people walking under ladders, unless, for the sake of humour, something happens to them. This is proof of the force of superstition. The social habits of daily life also play a role, particularly those that are related to what is (locally) considered polite, courteous or hospitable. In this way, a well-known brand of tea alienated the Saudi public when it showed a Saudi host using his left hand to serve tea to one of his guests. Moreover, the guest was wearing shoes, which is considered in Saudi Arabia to be the height of rudeness.

Attitudes towards nudity can differ from one country to another. French advertising is considered to have more nudity than that in nearly any other country. It is well accepted in French society, since the meaning conveyed by nudity there is very much related to beauty, excellence and nature. At opposite end of the spectrum one can cite the example of the advertisements for the Guy Laroche perfume Drakkar Noir in France and Saudi Arabia (Czinkota and Ronkainen, 1990, p. 616). The original French advertisement showed a man's bare forearm, held at the wrist by a woman's hand, with the man's hand holding a bottle of cologne. The Saudi advertisement showed the man's forearm covered by a suit jacket, with only the cuff of the shirt showing, while the woman lightly touched his hand with one of her fingers. Respect for the existing social conventions in the target society will long remain a prerequisite for the localization of advertising messages. Furthermore, the role of advertising has never been (at least officially) to change a society's mores, but rather to sell a product.

Generally the relationship between men and women, depicted by advertising, is a ticklish problem. For instance, Miller and Demirel (1988) depict advertising for beer on the Turkish market which portrays men and women drinking the beer in social activities at home. Emphasizing a family setting as the consumption situation is a response to the problem that showing men and women together in coffee houses and beer pubs, predominantly male institutions, would violate Turkish customs of courtship and social interaction.

Visual elements

Advertising copy is complex and inevitably tends to reflect the cultural background of those who have created it. For instance, Huang (1993) showed that colour is used differently in US and Taiwanese industrial advertising: yellow, the favourite colour of the Chinese, meant to be the colour of royalty, is found more often in Taiwanese advertisements, whereas brown was preferred in many American advertisements. Background themes, the setting and roles depicted are also important aspects of the copy. By systematically comparing Brazilian and US advertisements for cars over a ten-year period, Tansey *et al.* (1990) showed that Brazilian advertisements use significantly more urban themes and depict more leisure situations than US advertisements. Product use conditions which are most often depicted by the advertising visual should also be considered; for instance, individualistic as compared with collectivist settings for product use have been shown to be significant elements of contrast between Chinese and American advertising (Zhang and Gelb, 1996; Zhang and Neelankavil, 1997).

Many visual elements commonly found in print advertisements (size of the visual, use of photographs, use of black and white advertisements, presentation of children) vary across countries. Cutler *et al.* (1992) have investigated the visual component of print advertising across five countries (the United States, the United Kingdom, France, Korea and India) through a detailed content analysis of about 250 advertisements per country. Indian advertisements use significantly more black and white and show more children than those in any other country; Korean advertisements show price two or three times as frequently as those in other countries, and significantly represent more elderly persons, whose wisdom is valued in Far Eastern cultures; French advertisements are by far the most oriented towards aesthetics: five times more than US, Korean or Indian advertisements, but only twice as much as British advertisements. US advertisements appear by far the most comparative, ten times more frequently than those in France for instance. Furthermore, US advertisements depict children in more idealistic settings – clean and smiling – than French advertisements, where they are more likely to appear quite realistic (Hall and Hall, 1989).

Standardization of magazine advertisements in the countries mentioned will not be easy for durable or non-durable products since there are more differences than similarities for product types. Each country is unique on one or several visual characteristics. But overall, no systematic differences between industrialized and developing countries appear. Interestingly, within the western countries analyzed, the use of visual elements in the UK more closely resembles practice in the United States than in France. This means that there may be standardization barriers within the European Community (Cutler and Javalgi, 1992; Cutler *et al.*, 1992).

When comparing language to pictorial elements in advertising, many pretend that pictures are understood everywhere. This is certainly true but does not help the international advertiser much since the issue is not *whether* pictures are understood but rather *how* they are understood. As with language elements, pictures also present culture-specific association norms (Hung and Rice, 1995). While rain evokes freshness for certain persons, it is associated with coldness by others. This, again, can certainly not be characterized as a positive factor for global advertising (Kroeber-Riel, 1992). In fact, people from different cultural origins have different attitudinal reactions when exposed to foreign television commercials (Martenson, 1987). Besides, people from different cultures do not evaluate information in the same way. Hornik (1980) has emphasized that, while concepts like product attributes are probably universal, and while the product function is similar across nations, the exact form of attribute perception in each society might differ considerably. After being exposed to photographs of and a verbal briefing on a new car, British, German, French and Swedish respondents had different perceptions of the product. The car's styling scored well in Germany and Sweden, but poorly in Britain and France. With regard to safety, the new car scored well only in Britain. At the same time it was perceived as particularly unreliable in Sweden (Colvin *et al.*, 1980). Walle (1997, p. 702) explains how the Marlboro man, a global promotional icon, is understood differently world-wide and re-invested with local meanings; it is, for instance, considered as a symbol of wealth and prosperity by Africans and was a symbol of freedom to East Germans in the time of communism:

To this East German woman, the Marlboro man was a seductive icon, but to her it did not represent the heritage of the American frontier. Juxtaposing the image of a man who lives without fences to the realities of her own life and the shadow of the Berlin wall, she viewed the Marlboro man as an alternative to the oppressive dictatorship in which she lived. We both saw the same ad; I interpreted it as an American while she processed it in ways which fit into her life. The product and promotion were homogeneous; the meaning and response were not.

Advertising in societies experiencing quick change

China has witnessed a dramatic change in the place of advertising in the overall business and social scene.[2] In societies where people have been told for a long time that advertising is simply capitalist propaganda and as such evil and deceptive, advertisers today still face some degree of distrust and cannot just use the same approach as elsewhere. Recently, the role of history has clearly come through in China where many consumers feel that good products sell themselves and that only bad products need advertising. In such a context, foreign companies have to target long-run acceptance, stressing product availability and building brand reputation (Liang and Jacobs, 1994). They cannot just imitate what is done elsewhere. The case of China also illustrates that product meaning changes over time. Luxury goods evolved from hated symbols of decadent capitalism to consumption incentives for those who work hard (Tse *et al.*, 1989; Swanson, 1996). This goes along with a shift in the dominant values in Chinese advertising. Between 1982 and 1992, utilitarian values decreased and more symbolic values – with both eastern and western origins – increased (Cheng, 1994). Cultural values depicted by Chinese advertisements tend to reflect both Chinese culture and western imports and have much to do with product categories and country of origin. The value of 'tradition', for instance, is more used for food and drink whereas 'modernity' is a value found in a large number of Chinese advertisements for promoting products which fit into the new affluent society (Cheng and Schweitzer, 1996). Over time, product availability as the main emphasis in Chinese advertisements has decreased. Simultaneously, emphasis on brand superiority and comparative advertising has become more frequent (Zhou and Belk, 1993).

Cross-national transferability of advertising copy

Transfer of promotional materials is a practice which is frequent in multinationals (Hill and James, 1991): they are adapted as necessary. When attempts are made to transfer advertising copy cross culturally, the first issue is the grouping of countries within which cross-national transfers are easier. For instance, Zandpour and Harich (1996) have grouped countries according to whether they value more rational (think) or more emotional (feel) advertising appeals. The second issue deals with the precautions to be taken when transferring copy. Even between countries that look culturally very similar, such as the United States and the United Kingdom there are very significant differences in the style of advertising copy. The first obvious differences is that broadcast television is more commercialized in the United States than in the United Kingdom. Katz and Lee (1992) looked at differences in US and UK prime-time television advertising: they found that the categories of product advertised differ significantly: personal care, travel and cars are more frequently advertised in the United States, whereas services are more frequently advertised in the UK. Even within Europe there is no evidence that the content of advertising copy is converging; it seems on the contrary that the cultural content, specific to each country, is even increasing over long periods of time (Snyder *et al.*, 1991).

An interesting approach is to try to cluster countries according to cultural values (Hofstede's ones being the most appropriate) in order to determine whether it is possible to transfer part or the whole of an advertising creation or even a full campaign. Kale (1991) gives the example of the promotion of tourism in India for the US tourist market. When trying to adapt, both the target (US) and the source (India) cultures have to be considered: they differ mostly on power distance (40 versus 77) and individualism (91 versus 48). Kale insists that the (Indian) message must be targeted to the (US) individual: the message must reflect friendliness and informality, and it must value autonomy, variety and pleasure, all positive values for highly individualistic cultures, such as that of the United States. He further suggests that, since democracies are perceived as small-power-distance institutions, the message should emphasize that India has a democratic government, which would help bridge the gap of power distance between the source and the target country. Albers-Miller and Gelb (1996) have shown that advertising appeals used in business advertising largely match with cultural values as represented by Hofstede's four cultural dimensions. For instance status appeals in advertisements are significantly more used in a high-power-distance society such as Korea than in a low-power-distance society such as the United States (Cutler *et al.*, 1995). Masculinity in Mexico (*Machismo*) seems to be an influential force in the advertisements for traditional male-oriented products such as automobiles (Gregory and Munch, 1997, 115).

Since Hofstede's dimensions seem to be meaningful, it is interesting to try to cluster countries according to them. Sriram and Gopalakrishna (1991) have combined them with economic and demographic indicators, on the one hand, and media availability indicators (televisions per 1,000 people, radios per 1,000 people, advertising spending per capita, etc.). They cluster countries, for advertising strategy, into six groups: Japan is isolated in one group, and most other groups are fairly heterogeneous geographically, except northern Europe and a sort of central Asian area extending from Iran to the Philippines. The two Hofstede dimensions that discriminate significantly between these groups are once again power distance and individualism. They should however be used with caution, since individualism/collectivism has been shown to be only a minor predictor of whether advertisements portray single persons versus groups (Cutler *et al.*, 1997): they have a broad rather than a precise influence on advertising and should be used for defining strategy rather than executional details.

If a transfer has been decided upon, the following elements have always to be carefully checked to ensure the cultural adequacy of the final copy: (1) comparative advertising or not; (2) degree and type of informative content, style; (3) adequacy of basic copy themes in relation to local mores and customs; (4) execution: background themes, colour, use of words (puns, suggestive words), use of humour, use of symbols, type of characters and roles (age, sex, status), situations and types of relationship depicted; and (5) implementation constraints, such as lack of a medium available locally.

14.4 MEDIA WORLD-WIDE: TECHNOLOGICAL ADVANCES AND CULTURAL CONVERGENCE

World-wide differences in advertising expenditure

One cannot help but be struck by the difference in advertising expenses across countries, even though these countries may have comparable levels of economic development. This can be partially attributed to media availability (radio, television, newspapers, magazines, film, billboards). Where some media are non-existent or their availability is limited, expenses are automatically restricted by the lack of space for advertising. In the mid-1990s, the world average per capita advertising expenditure was about US$60. In 1997, the United States has the leading edge with US$362 advertisement spending per capita, followed by Japan with US$347, Germany and the United Kingdom with US$266 per capita, and France with US$175. The same five countries rank in the same order on total advertisement spending, being followed by Brazil, South Korea, China, Italy and Mexico. Per capita advertising expenditure is much lower in developing nations: in 1997, only US$32 in Mexico, US$41 in Brazil and a small US$3 for China despite its rank of eigth for total advertisement spending (*Advertising Age International*, 1997a). In the poorest African countries, the figures for annual per capita advertising expenditure barely exceed US$1.

Cross-cultural differences in media availability and use

The availability of advertising media is influenced by the level of a country's economic development and also by its view of the appropriate mix between business/commercial activities, on the one hand, and cultural/recreational activities on the other hand. Tuncalp (1992, 1994) gives the example of Saudi Arabia, where traditional values do not permit the showing of films to public gatherings; as a result, the cinema medium does not exist in Saudi Arabia. Ethical debates about whether certain products can be advertised have an influence on regulations, for instance about media space available for cigarette and alcohol advertising (see Box 14.2).

Advertising is largely based on news and entertainment media. The communication support systems such as television and audiovisual equipment, printing presses, photographic equipment, etc. are costly and need to be balanced by sales, advertising or other sources of revenue. Financial support in countries where banks have limited lending capacity is often based on political influence (which may prove unstable). In many countries the Press is even more dependent on politics than on advertisers.

BOX 14.2

Advertising regulations globalize steadily but slowly

Marlboro Man is headed for a showdown at the Brussels corral. The European Commission is trying to round up a posse to run the Stetson-wearing hero of the cigarette industry's leading brand and the rest of its most potent symbols off the Community's advertising hoardings. It would also curb the use of brand names to market non-tobacco products such as lighters and fashion accessories. If the Commission has its way, the directive on 'advertising of tobacco products in the press and by means of bills and posters' will be approved . . .

From that date cigarette manufacturers would be expected to comply with standard Single Market rulings on the size and content of health warnings on cigarette packets, the presentation of tobacco products themselves and a ban on indirect advertising . . .

As in many a Hollywood Western, the lawmakers are up against some powerful vested interests. The market is divided between multinationals and state-owned companies. The multinationals led by the UK's BAT industries, Switzerland's Rothman's International, and US giants Philip Morris and RJ Reynolds, account for almost half the 560 billion cigarettes sold annually in the EU. Advertising is a vital weapon in their fight for market share. State-owned, or recently privatized tobacco companies, though, have little interest in siding with the multinationals. Cigarette advertising in four countries is banned (Italy, Portugal), soon to be abolished (France), or severely restricted (Spain). Within the Commission the UK, Germany, Greece, Denmark and The Netherlands are opposed to the draft proposal, on the grounds that it encourages restrictive practices. But as the Commission tries to unite its forces it is coming under pressure from other interested parties. The sharpest shouting comes from advertising groups. 'For the first time, Community legislation is purporting to restrict indiscriminately the fundamental principle of freedom of speech', declares European Advertising Tripartite (EAT), a Brussels-based group representing media, advertisers and agencies.

In November 1997, EU officials are still discussing an EU-wide ban of tobacco advertising and the directive cannot be adopted before the end of 1998 due to parliamentary debate. If it is decided, member states have up to 30 months to implement the ban locally.

(Source: Adapted from: 'Tobacco warning', *International Management*, February 1991, p. 56, and
Advertising Age International, 1997c, p. 2)

Apart from purely economic factors, the availability of the media is also influenced by two social representations concerned with the relationship between the media and its audience. The first deals with what is considered a reasonable ratio between advertising and entertainment time (news and programmes) by the local audience and what they consider the appropriate sequencing between advertising and entertainment, for instance in terms of television movies being sliced up by advertising. The second social representation is whether advertising is considered an entertainment in itself. If entertaining the target audience is a necessary condition for capturing their interest, creative effort may have to be devoted to entertainment rather than mere advertising messages. This may reduce the effectiveness of the advertisement because the viewers' attention is attracted by the creative side of the message and diverted from the product that is being presented. Responses to the issue of how entertainment and advertising interrelate probably differ in the United States and Europe.

Many countries have instituted rules which place limits on television advertising. Sweden has no advertising on its national channels. Germany limited advertising to 20 minutes per day over three to five time periods. There are now several private television stations such as Sat 1, Pro 7 or Vox, with no limitation on advertising time, while the limitations on public channels (ARD and ZDF) have been loosened. France controls all its channels, public and private, with regulations (*cahier des charges*) that limit television commercials to about an hour per day. New Zealand has two state-controlled television stations which forbid advertising on Sunday, and a third station, totally commercial (Andrews *et al.*, 1991).

Conversely, where little or even no advertising regulation exists, there can sometimes be such an invasion by advertising that viewing television programmes becomes little more than watching advertisements, a reproach frequently addressed by Europeans to American, Brazilian or Canadian television channels. The general contrast here seems to be between the Americas (the United States, Mexico, Brazil and Canada), with liberal advertising regulations, and most other countries, where audio-visual media availability is more limited by regulation. Saudi Arabia, for example, bans commercial advertising on radio (Tuncalp, 1992).

In many countries, radio stations have flourished with extensive advertising space, that is, up to 20 minutes of commercials per hour; programmes are constantly interrupted by advertising. This hectic schedule may be resented by listeners who constantly change stations, obliging advertisers to buy media space for the same time blocks across several radio stations. The question of finding the acceptable proportion of advertising to total time is an important one. Studies have shown that in the United States an increasing number of consumers consider that television advertising is sometimes stupid and tends to be less intelligent than previously. US television viewers are therefore dissatisfied (Martenson, 1987). The situation is fairly paradoxical: as the number of media channels increase, it becomes more difficult to reach and monitor a target audience since viewers' saturation with advertisements leads them to reduced ability to listen to advertising and to zapping reactions. It is surprising that the issue of whether the viewer/listener is entertained by advertising is rarely addressed, given its practical importance. Zapping has been widely studied, but most studies have only sought to demonstrate how an advertiser can avoid its unfortunate results. It is taken for granted that the audience has no saturation threshold, or at the very least an extremely high one. This assumption suggests the absolute legitimacy of mass advertising communication within a society that willingly portrays itself as being free-market oriented. In contrast, many European countries started from the opposite assumption, and advertising therefore took a long time to assert itself on television.

The emergence of global media

The previous sections have placed much emphasis upon differences in advertising across countries. These differences do not offset certain similarities and convergence. Diverse media combine into a 'media landscape' which is primarily shaped by the freedom of choice of the audience. Some media have achieved almost world-wide recognition and a truly global audience. Among the international advertising media that have achieved the most impressive world-wide reach is the monthly *Reader's Digest*. It is the world's most widely read magazine, with a circulation of 28.7 million in 15 languages and 169 countries. It was founded in 1920 by DeWitt Wallace and his wife Lila Acheson. The first issue came out in February 1922 (see Box 14.3).

BOX 14.3

The internationalization of the *Reader's Digest*

'Since the formula of the Digest is so effective in the United States, why not attempt to repeat it elsewhere?' thought DeWitt Wallace. But exporting the formula of a magazine requires that the obstacle of language be overcome. The simplest solution was to begin in England, which could serve as a gateway into Europe. Accordingly, the first foreign edition of the *Reader's Digest* appeared in Great Britain in 1937. The second foreign edition, however, did not appear in Europe. In 1940, in the midst of the Second World War, the first issue of *Selecciones del Reader's Digest*, the Spanish-American edition, came out in Cuba. Why Cuba? The long-term objective was to attack the South American market, even if sales had to be made at a loss (as indeed occurred for many years). But for the time being, DeWitt Wallace's objective was more of a missionary one, for he sought to combat the Nazi advance. In 1942, a Portuguese edition in Brazil followed. This edition reached a print run of 300,000 copies. In 1943, there was a return to Europe with the publication of a Swedish edition. The war was not yet over, but DeWitt Wallace was already contemplating market entry into Europe. He offered cut-price subscriptions of the *Digest* to families of young Americans who had been called up. Along with chewing gum and nylon stockings, the *Reader's Digest* was to arouse the interest of young Europeans. After the war, in 1947, *Sélection du Reader's Digest* finally appeared in France under the management of General Thompson. There was an initial print run of 275,397 copies, which almost doubled for the second issue. The global expansion of the *Reader's Digest* did not stop . . . Germany, Italy, Switzerland and Belgium, as well as India, South Africa, Australia and New Zealand, were all in turn to have their edition of the magazine. Today, thirty-nine editions of the *Reader's Digest* are published, including one for schoolchildren, another in large type for those with sight problems and an edition in Braille. It can justifiably claim the distinction inscribed on every cover of being the most widely read magazine in the world.

(Source: Adapted from Reader's Digest, 1987, pp. 10–11, and *Reader's Digest* news release 'Products and services', June 1988.)

There are now some 'global' newspapers such as the *International Herald Tribune*, the *Wall Street Journal* and the *National Geographic* magazine. Their circulation covers almost the entire world. *Time* magazine publishes 133 different editions, which enables advertisers to reach precise target audiences in a large number of locations throughout the world. Many French magazines such as *L'Express*, *Le Point* and *Elle* and German magazines such as *Der Spiegel* and *Burda Moden* also publish international editions. The advertising clientele of these world-wide publications nevertheless remains fairly limited. It consists of 'global' advertisers who are themselves mostly targeting a global clientele, namely a segment of well-off consumers who travel internationally. Industries that use media with global reach are basically airlines, banks and financial services, consumer electronics and telecommunications, cars, tobacco and alcohol, perfumes and luxury products. Such is the case in Asia where Pan-Asian advertising media reach an upper-scale audience composed of affluent business people and travellers (Ha, 1997). However, advertisers should be cautious when using similar media globally since media perception, in terms of being enjoyable, informative, annoying and offensive, has been shown to vary cross culturally (Somasundaran and Light, 1994).

The global media landscape has two facets: while local media survive because language differences remain a pervasive reality, a globalized supply of media is emerging which greatly serves the globalization of advertising. The best example of such breakthroughs in international telecommunications is the growth of the World Wide Web as an advertising medium. The Web is most attractive for reaching people under 35, called 'generation X', who have over US$200 billion purchasing power world-wide and comprise nearly 75 per cent of Web users. Industries such as telecommunications, computers, electronic entertainment equipment, publishing and financial services are the most intense users of the Web as a global medium (Kassaye, 1997).

The influence of television satellites

Television satellites now offer media with regional or global coverage. The United States is a pioneer in this field – no fewer than 30 satellites were in service in the United States in 1990 (Mariet, 1990) serving an impressive number of television channels. Examples in this section mostly focus on Europe and Asia which tend to remain fragmented audiences, because of language diversity. Previously, television channels were purely national, mostly state owned, and with some development of private hertzian (transmission of hertzian waves by ground stations) and cable channels during recent years. Europe is now following the United States. Programmes such as MTV, CNN, TNT Cartoon and BBC World-wide now reach millions of homes on all continents through satellite television.[3]

Many satellites covering most of Europe are now available for transmission, such as Astra (Luxemburg) and TDF and TVSAT (French-German). Daily newspapers are also becoming globalized as a result of information transmitted by satellites and computerized typesetting; the core parts of the global newspaper are common to all local editions and are sent as digital information to local printing workshops, which add local news and advertising. Whereas satellite television has developed considerably in Europe, its penetration rate is still low in Asia, despite some inroads made by the Hong Kong-based Star TV satellite (Ha, 1997).

There are different possibilities for the use of television satellites. They can transmit images that will be used to make up programmes (primarily news and sports) which are then re-broadcast in a traditional form, e.g. hertzian ground television. The broadcasting of satellite images to viewers can be achieved via a cable network. An infrastructure of ground receiving stations is then needed, before the images are sent to viewers through the cable. Ground stations can receive signals of minimal strength, amplify them and redirect them through cable to private homes. Cable channels can be scrambled and paid for with the purchase of a decoder, by subscription or hourly fees. The third solution is a broadcast which is directly received by the viewer with a parabolic antenna (dish). In this case the satellite must broadcast much stronger signals so that they can be picked up on the ground.

The problem of the satellite and cable network infrastructure is just as complex as the creation of new programmes to fill the screens of the new television channels. For the television industry the problem is acute: television channels cannot show just news from international news agencies and cheap talk shows, with the overall purpose of reducing the hourly cost of programmes. Television channels must set up some really entertaining programmes in order to attract viewers who then have a reason to watch the commercials. Europeans as well as Asians have difficulties creating and selling television series and soap operas internationally, in comparison to the United States (Sarathy, 1991). It is estimated, for instance, that the changes in the European televisual industry necessitate over 50,000 hours of new programmes per year. In 1987 the rights to one hour of the *Dallas* series cost US$32,000, compared to US$400,000 for the production of one episode of the series *Chateauvallon* by a European consortium led by the French state-owned station Antenne 2. In 1989, the re-broadcast rights to an American television film cost US$70,000, compared with almost a million dollars for the production of a comparable European film (Sarathy, 1991). This situation has not changed over the last ten years: the American TV industry still has a leading edge on prices.

Media giants have emerged which are likely to take control of large parts of the global media industry, such as Ted Turner, Berlusconi, Leo Kirsch, Springer, Bertelsmann, Hachette, the Luxemburg television company (RTL), Australian press magnate Rupert Murdoch and the Canadian ITC group. The bulk of these groups are multimedia interests and are equally engaged in the development of the press media covering regional areas. Many countries have invested in cable systems, which are competing with direct television (DBS). Some countries are already equipped with dense cable networks, such as Ireland, Belgium and Germany, where more than half of all households are linked in. Other countries such as France are lagging behind and attempting to catch up. In general, there has been little European consensus on standards for telecommunication technologies such as high-definition television (HDTV), fibre optic networks, electronic transmission standards, etc. Technological, industrial, media, cultural and legal interests overlap in a realm of complex influences, where national state influence is still strong, as is the tradition in the European media and television industries.

Certain European regulations aim to protect the cultural identity of European audiovisual networks. The French, in particular, were somewhat disturbed by the invasion of American programmes, to the detriment of European culture and creation.

(Once again, self-contradiction is possible: some people may be both faithful viewers of American television series and opponents of imported television programmes as a whole.) This implies an increasing influence of the English language, which the French and other Europeans fear could further damage the influence and reach of their own languages. In May 1989, the EU adopted a directive that required at least half of the programmes on European television to be produced in Europe. Nevertheless the text of this directive was fairly vague and allowed loose interpretation by the member countries. Similarly, some Asian countries tend to protect their cultural identity often by prohibiting or discouraging the installation of satellite dishes, thus limiting the potential coverage of pan-Asian media.

Enlargement and overlapping of media

The influence on marketing communications of media globalization and potential media overlap is quite significant. There is a large increase in the available media space on television; the new channels are almost all private, and must finance their operations either by advertising or by subscription (cable and/or scrambler/decoder). Satellites such as Astra cover a significant number of countries in western Europe. This produces great overlap zones where viewers are able to receive a large number of channels with a simple dish and decoder. This phenomenon can be observed world-wide, especially in Europe and Asia. However, it is questionable whether media overlapping has been a problem in Europe for advertisers, especially since 1993, when the physical borders between the then 12 member states of the EU were progressively abolished. Some people tend to underrate the importance of media overlapping:

Much is made of overlapping media particularly in classroom situations. Yet the impact of imported overlapping media has only a marginal beneficial effect on audiences. Evidence from Ireland, Austria and Switzerland indicates that where advertising comes in from adjacent countries it is largely ignored unless the product is also advertised locally, thus undermining the increased coverage potential. There is a need to harmonize creative presentation where overlaps occur to prevent confusion in the minds of potential customers. (Dudley, 1989, pp. 287 and 290.)

One has to address the issue of whether media overlapping in Europe may lead to a compulsory standardization of brands and of the creative themes and presentation of ads. Sarathy (1991) illustrates this issue by citing Unilever's difficulties in creating Euro-advertising for its household cleanser which is called Vif in Switzerland, Viss in Germany, Jif in the United Kingdom and Greece and Cif in France. Mourier and Burgaud (1989) suggest that companies that adapt marketing plans to each European market risk being misunderstood by consumers. Indeed in switching channels, consumers would be disturbed if the same product were advertised under different brand names and had diversified packagings, and if different product uses and benefits were emphasized. However, not all viewers watch foreign channels, and not all products are marketed throughout Europe. Only 25,000 French households have chosen to orient their satellite dish towards Astra satellites, which transmit overwhelmingly German-speaking programmes which 99 per cent of French people just do not understand.

Technological and social changes open the door for more specific and segmented marketing

There are increasing numbers of standard brand names across Europe, especially within industries that are potential candidates for regional marketing globalization in Europe – such as banks and financial services for private clients, airlines, mass market consumer goods, as well as many consumer durables such as cars, household appliances, stereo and video systems and photographic equipment. Until now, domestic markets were considered to be the most likely units to be segmented; however, complex segments emerge where country is not necessarily the segmentable unit *par excellence* (see section 8.4 on intercultural marketing strategies based on cultural affinity zones and classes).

Pan-European market segments account for a homogeneous population across countries – for example, age groups. This is the case in relation to products for young people. Television stations such as MTV and Sky are well prepared for this. The rock radio image, supported by the emergence of European rock, is carefully cultivated by MTV. As pointed out by Tom Freston, the president of MTV: 'Music crosses borders very easily, and the lingua franca of rock'n'roll is English. Rock is an Anglo-American form.' Freston further indicates what he considers to be the mission of MTV: 'We want to be the global rock and roll village, where we can talk to youth world-wide' (cited by Sarathy, 1991).

Ethnicity plays an increasing role in Europe, and pan-European market segments may be fairly effective when cultural and linguistic minorities are targeted. At the national level, these minorities do not reach critical numbers which could justify the creation of specific media, since they are scattered all over the countries of Europe. But minorities may be more significantly served at the European level. Mariet (1990) cites the case of the development of Hispanic television in the United States. There are two principal networks: Univision-SIN, started in 1961, now reaches 5.1 million households, that is, 85 per cent of Spanish-speaking Americans; the other large Hispanic network, Telemundo, covers 77 per cent of these households and is present in 35 states. In 1989, US$305 million was invested in advertising on the Spanish-speaking media. Such initiatives are also likely to flourish in Europe, in that they can fulfil the need for television communication of Arabic-speaking North African immigrants, Turks, Armenians or Jews. Erbil (1995) describes the case of ethnic community viewers in Germany: the largest foreign group is the Turks, with 1.9 million people and seven channels (one on cable); the Italians number 560,000 and have three channels available; the Greeks 350,000 with two channels; the Poles 260,000 with five channels; the Spaniards 135,000 with six channels (four on cable); the Japanese community has 27,000 members and can have access to a Japanese-speaking channel (JSTV) both on cable and by satellite.

Cross-border segments may also be based on classes of cultural affinity (section 8.4). In these groupings, consumers share similar buying habits or a common language; segments may be further divided on the basis of traditional criteria such as sociodemographics (age, sex, income, etc.). For example, a relevant segment may consist of beer drinkers in the zone of cultural affinity of Mediterranean Europe, identified by several common sociodemographic characteristics and/or by criteria linked to their consumption habits and psychographics. MTV, TNT Cartoon and Eurosport are typical media for reaching classes of cultural affinity.

Some market segments and advertising audiences will remain mostly domestic ones. As a consequence, they will be only slightly influenced by market globalization in Europe. Ethnic food products such as the German *Knödel* would fall into this category. Regional and local marketing have developed alongside global marketing and are able to target very precise and quite small populations through local radio stations which have emerged over the past ten years. The marketing strategy of small segments of the service industry could be supported by emerging local media, for instance for local cultural products such as sports events, shows, private tutoring, etc. When marketing at the local level, cross-border geographical segments can be designed such as a county in northern France grouped with a neighbouring county in French-speaking Belgium (Walloon).

14.5   THE GLOBALIZATION OF ADVERTISING

Agencies internationalize

Advertising agencies are nowadays largely internationalized. The largest agencies, such as Young & Rubicam, McCann-Erickson, FCB, Ogilvy & Mather, BBDO, J. Walter Thompson, B. Lintas, Grey, Saatchi and Saatchi, etc., have built up a network of subsidiaries covering most countries over the last twenty or thirty years. The largest advertising agency in the world, Dentsu Inc., is Japanese while the largest Japanese agencies are now present in a growing number of countries, mostly in Asia. The Japanese advertising market is a large one: it remains very attractive to Japanese agencies, which then target South East Asia and Australia in the first stages of their international expansion.

It is not always easy to launch 'triadic' agencies successfully. HDM, an attempt at merging European (Havas), Japanese (Dentsu) and American assets (Marsteller, a large subsidiary of Young & Rubicam), aimed to become a specialist in global marketing communication due to its triadic position. At the beginning of 1991, the European part of HDM (Eurocom-Havas) withdrew from the alliance with Dentsu and Young & Rubicam/Marsteller, to form a joint venture with the British group WCRS.

Large national agencies are compelled to follow the route towards the internationalization of marketing communications, media and audiences. As well as having to be able to organize cross-border campaigns for advertisers, they also try to remain knowledgeable experts on local idiosyncrasies in the implementation of marketing communication strategies. National agencies, because of limited financial resources, may acquire minority stakes in agencies in neighbouring foreign countries or may build international networks of national agencies through alliances or joint ventures. The French Publicis group, for instance, has become associated with the American group FCB. Large independent agency networks such as Advertising and Marketing International Network from Cleveland, Ohio, or Affiliated Advertising Agencies International from Aurora, Colorado, had respectively US$1.8 and US$3.4 billion advertising volume world-wide in 1994 (*Advertising Age*, 1995).

Relationships between advertisers and agencies

Following the internationalization of advertisers, agencies have increased their foreign operations. In large multinational corporations with diversified product lines, this can lead to a complex advertiser/agency organization. The various organizational levels (national, regional and world-wide) within both the multinational agency and the multinational advertiser must be in constant contact with each other, increasing the usual communication problems within large international organizations. Different approaches may be chosen for the organization of international marketing communication with respect to the agency/advertiser relationship (see Case A14.1). One possibility is to use just one large international advertising agency, which allows for centralization of communication; this can be implemented for each product division separately, or for large brands or for the purpose of managing the corporate image world-wide. An opposite solution is to hire local agencies that are well acquainted with local constraints as they affect media and consumers. Intermediate solutions between these two extremes attempt to find an effective trade-off between world-wide co-ordination and the local tailoring of advertising campaigns. Ford has decided to regionalize its brand advertising in Europe with central co-ordination and five sub-regional teams which adapt advertising strategy to clusters of local European markets (*Advertising Age International*, 1997b).

Advertising standardization: feasibility and desirability

After a review of arguments for and against advertising standardization world-wide, Onkvisit and Shaw (1987, p. 51) conclude that a more meaningful question is whether standardized advertising should be used or not, even if it is feasible. Harvey (1993) considers the following arguments in favour of standardized advertising: (1) provides consistent image across markets; (2) avoids confusing mobile consumers; (3) may decrease the cost of preparing campaign themes, copy and materials; and (4) enables firmer control over the planning and execution of campaigns across markets. He gives a complete checklist of factors to be considered in order to assess whether the standardized approach is appropriate. These include product factors, competition, organization variables, media infrastructure, regulations and market/societal variables; some aspects of the advertising process may be standardized while others are not. The danger of this approach is that it does not distinguish desirability of standardization (which has to be assessed first) from its feasibility; he states initially that 'given the strong economic and administrative rationale it is assumed that, if possible, advertisers would prefer to standardize advertising' (Harvey, 1993, p. 58).

Evidence from companies concerning advertising standardization shows a mixed picture. For instance, Ryans and Ratz (1987) analyzed 34 usable responses from international advertising/marketing managers who were delegates at an international advertising conference. They self-reported on their company's practices, in the framework of a questionnaire survey. Ryans and Ratz's findings indicate relatively high levels of advertising standardization for campaign themes, creative execution and media execution. Only parent company managers were interviewed and their quantitative reports (based on levels of agreement or disagreement on a rating scale) may be rather distanced from actual local decisions. An interpretive key to their findings is offered by Ryans and Ratz themselves (1987, p. 157) who observe that 'the majority of respondents thought that usage situations for their products were very similar world-wide . . . [an] explanation is that international advertising managers have adopted the position of the globalists and assume it holds true for their products'. However, it seems that advertising standardization, as reported by major international agencies, has increased over the last thirty years especially under pressure from clients (Rosenthal, 1994).

In order to determine the level of standardization, Mueller (1991) analyzed print and television campaigns for American consumer goods and services advertised in the United States and either in Germany or Japan (for which market distance with the United States is larger than for Germany). Between the United States and Germany, the highest level of advertising standardization was exhibited by Mars Candy bars, followed by Marlboro cigarettes; the lowest levels were associated with Camel cigarettes and credit cards. In the case of Japan the level of adaptation was on average much larger, signalling the more important role of market distance compared with product type. Across Chinese-speaking countries, standardization is feasible only for some strategic decisions (target segments, positioning, core themes) but cannot be used for tactical decisions such as executional style and media planning (Tai, 1997).

The global campaign concept

One cannot underestimate the complexity of managing an international campaign (Clark, 1987), especially in the realm of agency/advertiser relations, which are often difficult to manage even when both agency and advertiser are excellent companies. For instance, Procter & Gamble has always been reputed to be a demanding advertiser for its agencies, but also very loyal to them. P & G, like many large companies, has had very stable relationships (sometimes for forty years or more) with a group of agencies; some of them have world-wide responsibility for a product line and/or a major brand (*Advertising Age*, 1987). But the creative work is sometimes a source of conflict between major advertisers and their agencies when their views diverge as to the strategy to be followed. Most advertisers then try to adopt a democratic style, by discussing opinions, facts, data and drafts of potential advertising campaigns. The final say always comes when campaigns are actually put into practice and their impact on various objectives may be monitored (brand awareness, brand image, sales increase, etc.). Van Raaij (1997) adopts the view that the globalization of marketing communications is less pervasive than it seems at first sight; therefore the necessary degree of adaptation should increase over a continuum of four levels: *mission* (long term, identity and vision of the communicator), *proposition* (campaign themes), creative *concepts* (how themes are translated in the language and cultures of the target groups) and *execution*. While mission can rather easily be globalized, execution will need much local tailoring.

The objective of a global advertising campaign has to be clearly defined: it does not seek to save on creative costs. It aims to promote a global brand name and image. Accordingly, the creative director for McCann-Erickson world-wide, Marcio Moreira, emphasizes that an advertiser should not pursue a global advertising strategy as a way of saving money, trying to achieve in only one campaign what may in fact require 12.

The correct implementation of a global campaign requires a great deal of effort and creative time, and ultimately its cost may prove higher than the sum total of individual campaigns (Marcio Moreira, quoted by Hill and Winski, 1987). Dean M. Peebles (1988), who was for many years the manager of international communications for Goodyear, the world's leading tyre manufacturer, recommends the following steps for the design and implementation of a global advertising campaign:

1. Choose a large advertising agency with subsidiaries all over the world; select in this agency an international account manager, who reports to the advertiser's headquarters.

2. Establish multinational planning meetings between the client and the agency, as well as a multinational creative team.

3. Brand managers and headquarters level should conduct and supervise consumer research and the pre-tests of the draft communication.

4. The resulting draft global campaign should be sufficiently finalized in order to facilitate discussion, but flexible enough to be transposed (rather than translated) into the various cultures and lifestyles of the target audiences.

Figure 14.2 presents a flowchart of headquarters–subsidiary relations for the planning and co-ordination of world-wide advertising at Goodyear. This flowchart indicate the tasks to be performed and the (tight) time schedule imposed (Peebles and Ryans, 1984, p. 83).

Practical implementation of global advertising campaigns is not an easy task. The organization must be completely interactive and use both bottom-up and top-down communication flows. Communication between headquarters and subsidiaries should not be a 'sham' dialogue in which decisions already taken at the very top level would have to be accepted by local executives as if they were their own. This issue is all the more complex because interaction problems between various levels within the multinational advertiser (international headquarters, regional headquarters, country subsidiaries) may snowball, leading to difficulties of communication and co-ordination with the international agency.

Global communication is primarily intended to establish the corporate image of a company or to foster recognition of one of its major brands across a large number of countries (e.g. McDonald's, Goodyear, Michelin, Nestlé). For instance, the Subtitles campaign of IBM was introduced globally in 1995 with the aim of promoting the universality of the brand imagery of IBM. The message was that IBM delivers simple and powerful solutions anywhere, at any time and for anyone; the use of subtitles and voice-overs allowed for both a global message and a localized communication (McCullough, 1996). The next step is to advertise the products themselves, and at this point the creative input of local subsidiaries and regional headquarters, as well as their influence on the advertising strategy, is much more significant. But local campaigns, even if they advertise local products and local brand names, must be carefully co-ordinated so that they make a positive contribution to the global message. The core values which are conveyed by the company's corporate image (e.g. high technology, robustness, innovativeness, style, social responsibility) should also be recognizable in its brand and product advertising at the local level. Finally, communication with

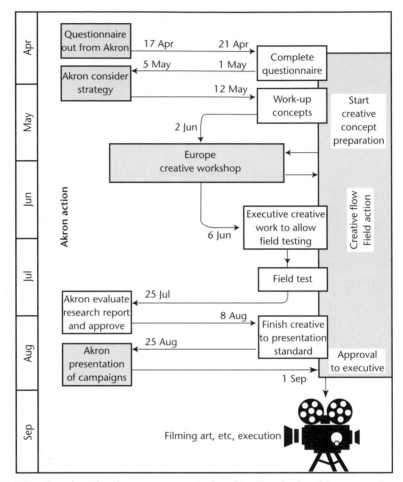

FIGURE 14.2 Flowchart for the management of multinational advertising campaigns at Goodyear.

(Source: Peebles and Ryans, 1984, p. 83. Reproduced with the kind permission of the original publisher, the *Journal of Marketing*.)

market segments which remain specific to certain countries should be fully delegated to the local level. Not every piece of communication can be globalized.

QUESTIONS

1. The English word 'hair' corresponds to two (totally different) French words: *cheveux* (of head) or *poil* (on body). Interpret the difference in concepts of what 'hair' is. What might be the consequences in terms of marketing for personal care products?

2. Describe the respective cultural adequacy of persuasive, informative and oneiric messages.

3. Why does the acceptance of comparative advertising vary cross culturally?

4. What are the target audiences of satellite television in Europe?

5. Give examples of mores which vary cross culturally and outline their possible consequences in terms of advertising adaptation.

6. What are the real benefits of a global advertising campaign?

7. Wella, a German giant in personal hair care, has recently decided to globalize a brand of its subsidiary Mühlens in Cologne (Germany) – 4711, which is the original *Eau de Cologne* perfumed water. The 4711 brand, although well known in the German-speaking area, has an old image and *Eau de Cologne* seems to be associated in the minds of consumers in many countries with cheap perfume rather than tradition or luxury. How would you tackle this issue?

APPENDIX 14: TEACHING MATERIALS

A14.1   Case: Levi Strauss Company: World-wide advertising strategy or localized campaigns?

The Levi Strauss Company, manufacturer of the famous LEVI'S jeans and other wearing apparel, markets its products in 70 countries. The company owns and operates plants in 25 countries and has licensees, distributors and joint ventures in others. The company is now in the process of evaluating its advertising policy to determine whether to apply a worldwide strategy to all advertising or settle on localized campaigns for each country in which it sells its products.

You have been asked to evaluate their present programs and to make recommendations that will assist management in deciding whether it is better (1) to create advertising campaigns locally or regionally but with a good deal of input and influence from headquarters as they presently do, (2) to allow campaigns to be created independently by local advertising companies or (3) to centralize at national headquarters all advertising and develop a consistent worldwide advertising campaign. You are asked to do the following:

1. Prepare a report listing the pros and cons of each of the three approaches listed.

2. Make a recommendation as to the direction the company should take.

3. Support your recommendation and outline major objectives for whichever approach you recommend.

The following information should be of assistance in completing this assignment.

Company objectives

In a recent Annual Report, the following statement of objectives of Levi Strauss International was made:

In addition to posting record sales, Levi Strauss International continued to advance toward two long-term objectives. The first is to develop a solid and continuing base of regular jeans business in markets throughout the world, thus proving a foundation for product diversification into women's-fit jeans, youthwear, menswear, and related tops. The second objective is to attain the greatest possible self-sufficiency in each of the major geographic areas where Levi Strauss International markets: Europe, Canada, Latin America, and Asia/Pacific. This requires the development of raw material resources and manufacturing in areas where the products are marketed thus reducing exposure to long supply lines and shipping products across national borders.

Unlike some competitors, Levi Strauss International does not, in its normal markets, seek 'targets of opportunity,' that is, large one-time shipments to customers it may never serve again. Rather, the goal is to develop sustainable and growing shipment levels to long-term customers.

Organization

Western European group. The company's European operations began in 1959 with a small export business, and, in 1965, an office was opened in Brussels. The company now has 15 European manufacturing plants and marketing organizations in 12 countries. This group includes all Western Europe served by the Continental and Northern European divisions.

The Continental European Division is headquartered in Brussels and is responsible for operations in Germany, France, Switzerland, the Benelux countries, Spain and Italy.

The Northern European Division is headquartered in London and is responsible for all marketing and production in the United Kingdom and the Scandinavian nations.

Other international group. The divisions in this group report directly to the president of Levi Strauss International. They are Canada, Latin America, and Asia/Pacific. *The Canadian Division* consists of two separate operating units: Levi Strauss of Canada and GWG. Levi Strauss and Company is sole owner of GWG which manufactures and markets casual and work garments under the GWG brand.

The Latin American Division traces its origins to 1966 when operations began in Mexico. In the early 1970s, the business was expanded to Argentina, Brazil, and Puerto Rico. In addition to these countries, the division now serves Chile, Venezuela, Uruguay, Paraguay, Peru, Colombia, and Central America. Plans call for the division to explore new markets in Central America and the Andean Region.

The Asia-Pacific Division had its beginning in the 1940s when jeans reached this market through US military exchanges. In 1965, a sales facility was established in Hong Kong. Markets now served include Australia and Japan, the two largest, as well as Hong Kong, the Philippines, Singapore/Malaysia, and New Zealand. Business in Indonesia and Thailand is handled through licensees. The markets served by this division present opportunity for growth in jeanswear. However, diversification potential in Asia/Pacific is centered in Japan and Australia.

Other operating units. One other unit, EXIMCO, not aligned with either Levi Strauss USA or Levi Strauss International, reports directly to the president. EXIMCO has two major responsibilities; market development and joint ventures in Eastern Europe, the USSR, and the People's Republic of China, and directing offshore contract production for the company's divisions.

Comments

The director of advertising and communications for Levi Strauss International shares with you the following thoughts about advertising:

The success of Levi Strauss International's advertising is derived principally from their judging it consistently against three criteria: (1) Is the proposition meaningful to the consumer? (2) Is the message believable? and (3) Is it exclusive to the brand? A set of core values underlies their advertising wherever it is produced and regardless of strategy: honesty/integrity, consistency/reliability, relevance, social responsibility, credibility, excellence, and style. The question remains whether a centralized advertising campaign can be based on this core of values.

Levi Strauss' marketing plans must include 70 countries and recognize the cultural and political differences affecting advertising appeals. Uniform advertising (i.e., standardized) could ignore local customs and unique product uses, while locally prepared advertising risks uneven creative work, is likely to waste time and money on preparation, and might blur the corporate image. Consistency in product image is a priority.

International advertising now appears in 25 countries. Levi currently uses seven different agencies outside the United States, although one agency handles 80 percent of the business worldwide. In Latin America, they use four different agencies, and still a different agency in Hong Kong. Levi is not satisfied with some of the creative work in parts of Latin America. The company wants consistency in Latin American strategy rather than appearing to be a different company in different countries. They are not satisfied with production costs and casting of commercials, and the fact that local agencies are often resistant to outside suggestions to change. They feel there is a kneejerk reaction in Latin America that results in the attitude that everything must be developed locally. The risks of too closely controlling a campaign result in uninteresting ads compared with decentralizing all marketing which produces uneven creative quality.

Competition

At the same time that Levi is looking at more centralized control of its advertising, another jeans maker is going in the opposite direction. Blue Bell International's Wrangler jeans company has just ended a six-month review of its international advertising and decided against coordinating its advertising more closely in Europe. The concept of one idea which will work effectively in all markets is attractive to Wrangler. Yet the disadvantages are just as clear; the individual needs of each market cannot be met, resistance from local managers could be an obstacle, and the management of a centralized advertising campaign would require an organizational structure different from their present one. To add to the confusion, a leading European jean manufacturer, the Spanish textile company Y Confecciones Europeas, makers of 'Louis' jeans, recently centralized its marketing through one single advertising agency. Louis, fourth largest jeans maker after Levi, Lee Cooper, and Wrangler, is intent on developing a worldwide international image for its Louis brand.

Review of current ads

A review of a selection of Levi advertisements from around the world provided the following notes:

European television commercials for Levi's were super-sexy in appeal, projecting, in the minds of some at headquarters, an objectionable personality for the brand. These commercials were the result of allowing complete autonomy to a sales region. Levi's commercials prepared in Latin America projected a far different image than those in Europe. Latin American ads addressed a family oriented, Catholic market. However, the quality of the creative work was far below the standards set by the company.

Ads for the United Kingdom, emphasizing that Levi's are an American brand, star an all-American hero, the cowboy, in fantasy wild West settings. In Northern Europe, both Scandinavia and the U.K., they are buying a slice of America when they buy Levi's. In Japan, where an attitude similar to that in the U.K. prevails, a problem confronted Levi's. Local jeans companies had already established themselves as very American. To overcome this, Levi's positioned themselves against these brands as legendary American jeans with commercials themed 'Heroes Wear Levi's,' featuring clips of cult figures like James Dean. These commercials were very effective and carried Levi's from a 35 percent to a 95 percent awareness level in Japan.

In Brazil, unlike the United Kingdom, consumers are more strongly influenced by fashion trends emanating from the European Continent rather than from America. Thus, the Brazilian-made commercial filmed in Paris featured young people, cool amidst a wild traffic scene – very French. This commercial was intended to project the impression that Levi's are the favored brand among young, trend-setting Europeans.

Australian commercials showed that creating brand awareness is important in that market. The lines 'fit looks tight, doesn't feel tight, can feel comfortable all night' and 'a legend doesn't come apart at the seams' highlighted Levi's quality image and 'since 1850 Levi jeans have handled everything from bucking bronco . . .' amplified Levi's unique positioning. This campaign resulted in a 99 percent brand awareness among Australians.

(Source: Cateora, 1983, pp. 525–9. Reproduced with permission.)

QUESTIONS

1. Based on the various copy strategies described in the case, analyze the possible themes that can be used to support Levi's image.

2. How should one operationalize the set of core values: across the various countries/cultures where Levi advertises its products, how can precise criteria be set which enable one to judge whether a commercial respects the core values?

3. Prepare a comparative table showing the pros and the cons of each of the three approaches listed at the beginning of the case.

4. Make a recommendation as to the choice which should be made by Levi's (one of the three approaches or a combination of them). Please support your choice with arguments.

A14.2   Case: Excel and the Italian advertising campaign

Excel is a multinational company, based in northern Europe, which produces television sets, video recorders and other consumer electronics. In the 1980s it went through a phase of external growth by the take-over of the German and French subsidiaries of a large US-based company which had decided to divest itself of this industry. Within two years this Nordic company tripled in size. It changed from having a mainly Scandinavian base to having a complete European spread, with an 11 per cent share of the European market. The group, built in successive layers, inherited numerous local brands, namely those of the companies taken over. These brands are basically localized marketing assets, with only national coverage and brand recognition. Excel plans to have only one pan-European brand in the long run, with one local brand for each individual country.

The European headquarters were installed in Switzerland, near Lausanne. This location was chosen so that headquarters would be situated in central Europe but not in a country where Excel already had a plant, as this might imply some sort of 'national preference'. Over a period of two years an important reshaping of the industrial base was undertaken, with massive lay-offs in some plants and industrial investment aimed at increasing productivity.

Excel wanted to minimize advertising expenses while simultaneously giving its brand a strong, similar image across Europe. In fact it inherited some very diverse brand names, which were those of the companies most recently acquired in their home markets. Excel was therefore willing to design a pan-European advertising campaign. The national subsidiaries were invited either to join this campaign or to design their own campaign. In the latter case, they would have to finance it with their own money. The campaign was scheduled for autumn 1990.

Because of the World Cup which was taking place in Italy in June 1990, the Italian subsidiary decided that it could not wait until the autumn, as this type of sports event usually generates increased demand for television sets and video recorders. They managed to go ahead by themselves: they made an advertisement which proved to be a real hit and generated a significant sales increase. A television commercial was created and a poster also. The same advertising theme was used for sales promotion. The advertisement showed a superb television set with a video recorder as an integral part, encircled by a red ribbon which largely hid the screen. The slogan was '*Venite a veder lo; dal vero*' (come and see it; for real).

This campaign was a success soon after it started, and was presented to the general managers of the subsidiaries, who met for a residential seminar in Switzerland with the people at European headquarters in Geneva. Reactions were very positive. They proposed the idea of using the same campaign, themes and creation in other European markets. At the beginning of March, Mr Makinen, in charge of marketing communications at the European headquarters, decided to send a memo to the marketing/advertising managers of each subsidiary. A poster and a video presenting the Italian campaign were also enclosed. This memo made a concrete suggestion to the subsidiaries that they should adopt the themes and creation of this campaign. It asked them for their opinions. Makinen invited them to study the feasibility of using such a campaign in their home market and to send their comments back quickly, so that a pan-European campaign could possibly be launched in August. The Italian advertising manager, Signor Ragoli, was available if the European headquarters or national subsidiaries wanted any additional information.

Responses from the subsidiaries (that is, the answers plus the course of action finally adopted) were as follows. It took quite a long time for answers to come back, which could be explained by the overload of work experienced by people in the subsidiaries during this period of reorganization. Some countries never answered the proposal. Otherwise reactions were quite positive, except for that of France. The Spanish answer came quickly. The advertising and public relations manager, Senor Gonzales, sent a copy of the letter to his Italian colleague at European headquarters. He wrote that Spain had decided to use the campaign created in Italy, in order to unify Excel marketing communication. The Spanish wanted to use five different television channels for a total of 22 slots. They supported this with a press campaign and sales promotion in distribution channels. They needed the original version of the Italian television commercial, with music on one track and speech on another (one image track plus two sound tracks). In Spain the final version of the Excel campaign was launched in May 1990. The image track remained unchanged, but the music had been modified and there were several other minor changes. What seemed, at first sight, to be a straight copy of the Italian concept, finally turned out to be a largely modified version. Nevertheless Spain was the only country where the marketing team made the decision to use the experience of their Italian colleagues.

Sweden and Norway also responded quickly to the memo in similar terms. In neither of these two countries was advertising allowed on national television channels; furthermore, they traded under the Scandinavian brand name Scantel, rather than Excel. The Swedish response explained that the subsidiary did not advertise on television, since TVl and TV2 did not offer any space; but with the growth of satellite television the Italian proposal might be interesting for the future. The Swedes thought that the Italian campaign was well designed and implemented. The model presented (Excel 7181) was usable with their brand name since they had the same make. The Norwegians' answer had also been very positive. They promised to keep in mind the concepts of the Italian campaign and further indicated that they would recommend its implementation for 1991.

In France the advertising and public relations manager, Monsieur Dubois, initially contacted by telephone, expressed a positive but rather cautious opinion. He said that he had first to discuss the themes and creation with his advertising agency. He called back to make it clear that even if he had any advertising funds left (in fact they were already entirely spent), he considered that the Italian campaign was not appropriate for Ariane (the brand name of the recently acquired French subsidiary). According to him, it did not fit in with the French criteria of what actually makes good advertising. In his opinion Ariane had a fairly traditional image in France, and French consumers would need more serious arguments to change their views. Consequently 'good' advertising for the Ariane brand had to emphasize, first of all, the high-technology image. Ultimately, he thought that the Italian campaign was not sophisticated enough, and that French people prefer more in-depth, sophisticated and detailed campaigns.

QUESTION

How can the failure of the European headquarters to have the Italian campaign adopted by the other European subsidiaries be explained? What is the right way to go about this in the future? What has to be changed?

A14.3   Exercise: Borovets – a Bulgarian ski resort

Compare the two short texts below (each dated the beginning of 1990). Both depict the Bulgarian ski resort Borovets. The first one is an extract from the magazine *Actuel* (no. 122), from an article entitled 'Guide des bons plans à l'Est' (A guide to travelling in Eastern countries), p. 69. The other is an extract from the trade brochure of the Bulgarian state tourist corporation, *Balkanturist*, entitled 'Bulgaria welcomes you', p. 10. This short exercise is not meant to serve any other purpose than a pedagogical exercise; it does not aim to describe any real situation and should not prejudice readers concerning holidays in Bulgaria.

Text 1: A charter flight to Bulgaria

The phenomenon already exists, it never stops swelling. Bulgaria is a hospitable place for exhausted proletarians in quest of cheap snow and sun. For the time being, most of the troop comes from Britain: 75 per cent of the tourists are English, 20 per cent are German, the remaining 5 per cent are Dutch, Swedish or French.

The Bulgarian government rubs its hands. The blaze of freedom which blasts through the East has already brought hordes of capitalist tourists. Bulgaria is in urgent need of foreign currencies. The country hopes to have its holiday resorts working at full capacity. Borovets is the most famous resort: in fact, it is a concrete boil encrusted on the mountains. The eight hotels, of luxurious appearance, offer limited comfort: water shortages, telephones out of order, ghost reception desks, bad-tempered staff and rooms where the cleanliness is somewhat dubious. Infrastructure, equipment and service do not meet minimum requirements.

Bulgarian tourism turns out dissatisfied customers. Like Franco's Spain of the 1970s, it is the same reinforced concrete everywhere. Varna and Burgas on the Black Sea coast look like Benidorm. The sea coast is built up with concrete rabbit hutches which swarm with Bulgarian city-dwellers, Greek spendthrifts or drunk Britons. Apocalypse! The rare night-clubs are inaccessible. Meals in the 300-place restaurants have all the style and allure of gymnasium banquets.

Text 2: Borovets

In Bulgarian, Borovets literally means 'beautiful place'. Borovets during the winter has pure, ozone-rich air; it has 150 days of snow cover which provides exceptional ski slopes, from 1,300 to 2,500 meters high.

Each year Borovets is host to numerous international ski championships. Ingemar Stenmark, the Mahre brothers, Girardelli and many other famous skiers have spoken highly of this resort which welcomes everyone.

It is a very fashionable ski resort, with its numerous comfortable and cosy hotels, its enticing restaurants and various entertainment facilities for day and night. Borovets is located 50 miles from Sofia, and it has been enjoyed by children and adults since the end of the nineteenth century, when it was only a small holiday centre.

It is no exaggeration to say that Borovets can compete with the Swiss or the French ski resorts. Now why wait any longer to visit us? We wish only to welcome you.

QUESTIONS

1. Why is there such a difference between these two pictures? Do these two articles refer to the same reality?

2. How can one get an idea of the level of service in this resort?

3. How should the state company for Bulgarian tourism (which manages the resort) communicate? What prevents them from doing so?

A14.4   Exercise: Slogans and colloquial speech

Marketing communications (advertising copy, slogans, promotional offers, text on coupons, etc.) are language based. The quality of reception of the marketing messages by the target audience is very sensitive to the accuracy of the wording. Marketing communication is based on everyday – colloquial – speech, often very idiomatic.

The basic purpose of this exercise is fairly simple: it may be implemented with a group of people who have different linguistic backgrounds, but yet have a capacity to communicate with each other since some of them speak several languages. It does not imply that total fluency is necessary. Participants should simply take care to translate *into* the language(s) which they speak fluently (not *from*).

The exercise consists of the following:

1. Collecting slogans (and, more generally, short marketing communication texts) from magazines, billboards, posters, television commercials, sponsor announcements or short texts such as those found in greeting cards; translating them into other languages, with the objective of finding the equivalent meaning and local wording. The translation techniques explained in section 7.2 (back-translation, parallel translation and a combination of the two) should be used.

2. Collecting 'identical' slogans (again, generally any short marketing communication text) that push the same international brand in different countries, then analyzing and comparing how similar propositions and concepts are conveyed in the different languages. Bookshops that sell foreign newspapers and magazines will be useful places to find the basic data.

NOTES

1. I do not comment here on music and lyrics because these are widely used cross nationally and necessarily borrow somewhat from the local style of music but also quite often use global music, ranging from classic to pop, disco, reggae, etc. Murray and Murray (1996) show for instance a small difference in frequency of music in commercials between the United States (84.5 per cent) versus the Dominican Republic (94.3 per cent). International advertisers in the Dominican Republic tend to use more fast tempo/non-Latin music whereas domestic advertisers made greater use of lyrics with Latin music, especially the local *merengue*.

2. See for instance the striking contrast between Ho and Sin (1986) or Stewart and Campbell (1986) and Swanson (1996, 1997).

3. For statistics on the global reach of television channels, and media in general, see *Advertising Age International* which regularly publishes data on satellite television, major advertising spenders world-wide and major advertising agencies.

REFERENCES

Abernethy, Avery M. and George R. Franke (1996), 'The information content of advertising: A meta-analysis', *Journal of Advertising*, vol. 25, no. 2, pp. 1–17.

Advertising Age (1987), 'The house that built ivory', 20 August, pp. 26–27.

Advertising Age (1995), 'Independent agency networks', 15 May, p. i15.

Advertising Age International (1997a), 'Top global ad markets', pp. i7–i10;

Advertising Age International (1997b), 'Brand management goes regional at Ford', October, p. i2.

Advertising Age International (1997c), 'EU Officials to vote on compromise of tobacco ad ban', November, p. 2.

Agrawal, Madhu (1995), 'Review of 40-year debate in international advertising: Practitioner and academician perspectives to the standardization/adaptation issue, *International Marketing Review*, 12(1), pp. 26–48.

Albers-Miller, Nancy D. and Betsy D. Gelb (1996), 'Business advertising as a mirror of cultural dimensions: A study of eleven countries', *Journal of Advertising*, vol. XXV, no. 4, Winter, pp. 57–70.

Alden, Dana L., Wayne D. Hoyer and Chol Lee (1993), 'Identifying global and culture-specific dimensions of humor in advertising: a multinational analysis', *Journal of Marketing*, vol. 57, April, pp. 64–75.

Al-Makaty, Safran S., G. Norman Van Tubergen, S. Scott Whitlow and Douglas A. Boyd (1996), 'Attitudes towards advertising in Islam', *Journal of Advertising Research*, vol. 36, no. 3, pp. 16–26.

Al-Mossawi, Mohammed and Paul Michell (1992), 'The impact of cultural factors on the response of viewers to TV commercials in the Gulf countries: An empirical study', *Proceedings of the first Conference on the Cultural Dimension of International Marketing*, Odense, pp. 443–69.

Andrews, J. Craig, Steven Lysonski and Srinivas Durvasula (1991), 'Understanding cross-cultural student perceptions of advertising in general: implications for advertising educators and practitioners', *Journal of Advertising*, vol. 20, no. 2, pp. 15–28.

Appelbaum, Ullrich and Chris Halliburton (1993), 'How to develop international advertising campaigns that work: The example of the European food and beverage sector', *International Journal of Advertising*, vol. 12, pp. 223–41.

Bates, Constance, and William Renforth (1987), 'The elderly in magazine advertising: An inter-country comparison between the U.S. and Latin America', in Charles F. Keown and Arch G. Woodside (eds.), *Proceedings of the Second Symposium on Cross-Cultural Consumer and Business Studies*, Honolulu, Hawaii, 14–18 December, pp. 30–3.

Bigne, Enrique, Marcelo Royo, and Antonio C. Cuenca (1993), 'Information content analysis of TV advertising – The Spanish case', *Proceedings of the 6th World Marketing Congress*, Istambul, pp. 324–29.

Bjerke, Rune (1995), 'An experimental study in standardisation of Euro advertising: A beauty type as advertising presenter', unpublished PhD thesis, University of Otago, New Zealand, October.

Boddewyn, Jean J. (1984), 'The regulation of advertising around the world in the 1980s and beyond', in Gerald M. Hampton and Aart P. Van Gent (eds.), *Marketing Aspects of International Business*, Kluwer-Nijhoff Publishing: Boston, MA, pp. 73–83.

Cateora, Philip R. (1983), *International Marketing*, 5th edn, Richard D. Irwin: Homewood, IL.

Cheng, Hong, (1994), 'Reflections of cultural values: A content analysis of Chinese magazine advertisements from 1982 and 1992', *International Journal of Advertising*, vol. 13, pp. 167–83.

Cheng, Hong and John C. Schweitzer (1996), 'Cultural values reflected in Chinese and US television commercials', *Journal of Advertising research*, vol. 36, no. 3, pp. 27–44.

Clark, Harold F. Jr (1987), 'Consumer and corporate values: Yet another view on global marketing', *International Journal of Advertising*, vol. 6, pp. 29–42.

Colvin, Michael, Roger Heeler and Jim Thorpe (1980), 'Developing international advertising strategy', *Journal of Marketing*, vol. 44, Fall, pp. 73–9.

Communication et Business (1988), *Numéro 'Spécial Europe'*, no. 70, 14 March.

Cutler, Bob D., Rajshekhar G. Javalgi and M. Krishna Erramilli (1992), 'The visual component of print advertising: a five-country cross-cultural analysis', *European Journal of Marketing*, vol. 26, no. 4, pp. 7–20.

Cutler, Bob D., Rajshekhar G. Javalgi and Dongdae Lee (1995), 'The visual component of print advertising: a five-country cross-cultural analysis', *Journal of International Consumer Marketing*, vol. 8, no. 2, pp. 45–58.

Cutler, Bob D., S. Altan Erdem and Rajshekhar G. Javalgi (1997), 'Advertiser's relative reliance on collectivism-individualism appeals: A cross-cultural study', *Journal of International Consumer Marketing*, vol. 8, no. 2, pp. 43–55.

Czinkota, Michael R. and Illka A. Ronkainen (1990), *International Marketing*, 2nd edn, Dryden Press: Hinsdale, IL.

Darley, Willam K. and Denise M. Johnson (1994), 'An exploratory investigation of beliefs towards advertising in general: A comparative analysis of four developing countries', *Journal of International Consumer Marketing*, vol. 7, no. 1, pp. 5–21.

Di Benedetto, C. Anthony, Mariko Tamate and Rajan Chandran (1992), 'Developing creative advertising strategy for the Japanese marketplace,' *Journal of Advertising Research*, vol. 32, January–February, pp. 39–48.

Douglas, Susan and Bernard Dubois (1980), 'Looking at the cultural environment for international marketing opportunities', in P. Kotler and K. Cox (eds.), *Marketing Management and Strategy: A reader*, Prentice Hall: Englewood Cliffs, NJ, pp. 388–96.

Dowling, G.R. (1980), 'Information content in U.S. and Australian television advertising', *Journal of Marketing*, vol. 44, no. 3, pp. 34–7.

Dudley, James W. (1989), 1992: *Strategies for the Single Market*, Kogan Page: London.

Duncan, Tom and Jyotika Ramaprasad (1995), 'Standardized multinational advertising: The influencing factors', *Journal of Advertising*, vol. 24, no. 3, Fall, pp. 55–68.

Erbil, Kurt (1995), 'Ein Stückchen Heimat', *TV Spielfim*, vol. 10, pp. 30–1

Gilly, Mary (1988) 'Sex roles in advertising: A comparison of television advertisements in Australia, Mexico, and the United States', *Journal of Marketing*, vol. 52, April, pp. 75–85.

Gregory, Gary D. and James M. Munch (1997), 'Cultural values in international advertising: An examination of familial norms and roles in Mexico', *Psychology and Marketing*, vol. 14, no. 2, pp. 99–119.

Grüber, Ursula (1987), 'La communication internationale a sa langue: l'adaptation', *Revue Française du Marketing*, no. 114, 1987/4, pp. 89–96.

Ha, Louise (1997), 'Limitations and strengths of Pan-Asian advertising media: A review for international advertisers', *International Journal of Advertising*, vol. 16, no. 2, pp. 148–63.

Hall, Edward T. and Mildred Reed Hall (1989), *Understanding Cultural Differences*, Yarmouth, Maine: Intercultural Press.

Hanna, Nessim, Geoffrey L. Gordon and Rick E. Ridnour (1994), 'The use of humor in Japanese advertising', *Journal of International Consumer Marketing*, vol. 7, no. 1, pp. 85–106.

Harvey, Michael G. (1993), 'Point of view: A model to determine standardization of the advertising process in international markets', *Journal of Advertising Research*, vol. 33, no. 4, pp. 57–65.

Hill, John S. and William L. James (1991), 'Product and promotion transfers in consumer goods multinationals', *International Marketing Review*, vol. 8, no 4, pp. 6–17.

Hill, J. S. and J. M. Winski (1987), 'Goodbye, global ads', *Advertising Age*, 16 November.

Ho, Suk-ching and Yat-ming Sin (1986), 'Advertising in China: Looking back at looking forward', *International Journal of Advertising*, vol. 5, pp. 307–16.

Hofstede, Geert (1991), *Culture and Organizations: Software of the mind*, McGraw-Hill: Maidenhead, Berkshire.

Hoover, Robert J., Robert T. Green and Joel Saegert, (1978), 'A cross-national study of perceived risk', *Journal of Marketing*, July, pp. 102–8.

Hornik, Jacob (1980), 'Comparative evaluation of international and national advertising strategies', *Columbia Journal of World Business*, vol. 15, no. 1, pp. 36–45.

Huang, Jen-Hung (1993), 'Color in US and Taiwanese industrial advertising', *Industrial Marketing Management*, vol. 22, pp. 195–8.

Huang, Jen-Hung (1995), 'National character and sex roles in advertising', *Journal of International Consumer Marketing*, vol. 7, no. 4, pp. 81–96.

Hung, Kineta, and Marshall D. Rice (1995), 'A comparative examination of the perception of ad meanings in Hong Kong and Canada', in Scott M. Smith (ed.), *Proceedings of the 5th Symposium on Cross-Cultural Consumer and Business Studies*, Provo, UT: Brigham Young University, pp. 262–6.

Huth, Sabine and Fritz Unger (1988), 'Eine vergleichende Untersuchung zur humorvollen Werbung: BRD vs. USA', *Planung und Analyse*, vol. 5, pp. 197–200.

James, Karen E. and Paul J. Hensel (1991), 'Negative advertising: the malicious strain of comparative advertising', *Journal of Advertising*, vol. 20, no. 2, pp. 53–67.

Javalgi, Rajshekhar, Bob D. Cutler and Naresh K. Malhotra (1995), 'Print advertising at the component level: A cross-cultural comparison of the United States and Japan', *Journal of Business Research*, vol. 34, pp. 117–24.

Johnstone, Harvey, Erdener Kaynak and Richard M. Sparkman, Jr. (1987), 'A cross-cultural/cross-national study of the information content of television advertisements', *International Journal of Advertising*, vol. 6, pp. 223–36.

Kale, Sudhir H. (1991), 'Culture-specific marketing communications: an analytical approach', *International Marketing Review*, vol. 8, no. 2, pp. 19–30.

Kashani, Kamran (1989), 'Beware the pitfalls of global marketing', *Harvard Business Review*, September–October, pp. 91–8.

Kassaye, W. Wossen (1997), 'Global advertising and the World Wide Web', *Business Horizons*, vol. 40, no. 3, pp. 33–42.

Katz, Helen and Wei-Na Lee (1992), 'Oceans apart: an initial exploration of social communication differences in US and UK prime-time television advertising', *International Journal of Advertising*, vol. 11, pp. 69–82.

Kaynak, Erdener and Pervez N. Ghauri (1986), 'A comparative analysis of advertising practices in unlike environments: A study of agency–client relationships', *International Journal of Advertising*, vol. 5, pp. 121–46.

Kaynak, Erdener and Ugur Yucelt (1987), 'A cross-national/cross-cultural study of radio listening preferences: American and Canadian consumers contrasted, *International Journal of Advertising*, vol. 6, pp. 331–38.

Keown, Charles F., Lawrence W. Jacobs, Richard W. Schmidt and Kyung-Il Ghymn (1992), 'Information content in advertising in the United States, Japan, South Korea, and the People's Republic of China', *International Journal of Advertising*, vol. 11, pp. 257–67.

Kishii, T. (1988), 'Message vs. mood: A look at some of the differences between Japanese and Western television commercials', in: *Dentsu Japan Marketing/Advertising Yearbook*, Dentsu: Tokyo.

Kroeber-Riel, Werner (1992), 'Globalisierung der Euro-Werbung. Ein konzeptioneller Ansatz der Konsumentenforschung', *Marketing ZFP*, vol. 14, no. 4, pp. 261–7.

Liang, Kong and Laurence Jacobs (1994), 'China's advertising agencies: Problems and relations', *International Journal of Advertising*, vol. 13, pp. 205–15.

Lin, Carolyn A. (1993), 'Cultural differences in message strategies: A comparison between American and Japanese TV commercials', *Journal of Advertising Research*, vol. 33, no. 4, pp. 40–8.

Lin, Carolyn A., and Michael B. Salwen (1995), 'Product information strategies of American and Japanese television advertisements', *International Journal of Advertising*, vol. 14, pp. 55–64.

Luqmani, Mushtaq, Ugur Yavas and Zahir Quraeshi (1988), 'Advertising in Saudi Arabia: Content and regulation', *International Marketing Review*, vol. 6, no. 1, pp. 59–71.

McCullough, Wayne R. (1996), 'Global advertising which acts locally: the IBM subtitles campaign', *Journal of Advertising Research*, vol. 36, no. 3, pp. 11–5.

McCullough, Lynette S. and Ronald E. Taylor (1993), 'Humor in American, British and German ads', *Industrial Marketing Management*, vol. 22, pp. 17–28.

McLeod, Douglas M. and Motoko Kunita (1994), 'A comparative analysis of the use of corporate advertising in the United States and Japan', *International Journal of Advertising*, vol. 13, pp. 137–52.

Mariet, François (1990), *La Télévision Américaine*, Editions Economica: Paris.

Martenson, Rita (1987), 'Advertising strategies and information content in American and Swedish advertising: A comparative content analysis in cross-cultural copy research', *International Journal of Advertising*, vol. 6, pp. 133–44.

Miller, Fred and A. Hamdi Demirel (1988), 'Efes pilsen in the Turkish beer market: marketing consumer goods in developing countries', *International Marketing Review*, vol. 5, Spring, pp. 7–19.

Mourier, Pascal and Didier Burgaud (1989), *Euromarketing*, Editions d'Organisation: Paris.

Mueller, Barbara (1987), 'Reflections of culture: An analysis of Japanese and American advertising appeals', *Journal of Advertising Research*, vol. 27, no. 3, pp. 51–9.

Mueller, Barbara (1991), 'Multinational advertising: factors influencing the standardised vs. specialised approach', *International Marketing Review*, vol. 8, no. 1, pp. 7–18.

Mueller, Barbara (1992), 'Standardization vs. specialization: An examination of westernization in Japanese advertising', *Journal of Advertising Research*, vol. 32, January–February, pp. 15–23.

Murray, Noel M. and Sandra B. Murray (1996), 'Music and lyrics in commercials: A cross-cultural comparison between commercials run in the Dominican Republic and the United States', *Journal of Advertising*, vol. XXV, no. 2, Summer, pp. 51–63.

Neelankavil, James P., Venkatapparao Mummalaneni and David N. Sessions (1995), 'Use of foreign language and models in print advertisements in east Asian countries: A logit modelling approach', *European Journal of Marketing*, vol. 26, no. 4, pp. 24–38.

Onkvisit, Sak and John J. Shaw (1987), 'Standardized international advertising: a review and critical evaluation of the theoretical and empirical evidence', *Columbia Journal of World Business*, Fall, pp. 43–55.

Peebles, Dean M. (1988), 'Don't write-off global advertising: A commentary', *International Marketing Review*, vol. 6, no. 1, pp. 73–8.

Peebles, Dean M. and John K. Ryans (1984), *Management of International Advertising*, Allyn and Bacon: Boston, MA.

Reader's Digest (1987), 40th anniversary special edition, *Sélection du Reader's Digest*, Paris.

Reinhard, K. and W. E. Phillips (1985), 'Global marketing: experts look at both sides', *Advertising Age*, vol. 56, no. 15, p. 46.

Renforth, W. and S. Raveed (1983), 'Consumer information cues in television advertising: A cross country analysis', *Journal of the Academy of Marketing Science*, vol. 11, no. 3, pp. 216–25.

Resnik, Alan J., and Bruce L. Stern (1977), 'An analysis of information content in television advertising', *Journal of Marketing*, vol. 44, no. 1, pp. 50–3.

Ricks, David A., Jeffrey S. Arpan and Marilyn Y. Fu (1979), 'Pitfalls in overseas advertising', *Journal of Advertising Research*, reprinted in S. Watson Dunn and E. S. Lorimer (eds.), *International Advertising and Marketing*, Grid: Columbus, OH, pp. 87–93.

Rose, Gregory M., Lynn R. Kahle, and Fredric G. Kropp (1993), 'A woman's place is in the home: A cross-cultural analysis of attitudes towards women', in Gerald Albaum et al. (eds.), *Proceedings of the 4th Symposium on Cross-Cultural Consumer and Business Studies*, University of Hawaii, pp. 213–7.

Rosenthal, Walter (1994), 'Standardized international advertising: A view from the agency side', *Journal of International Consumer Marketing*, vol. 7, no. 1, pp. 39–62.

Ryans, John K., and David G. Ratz (1987), 'Advertising standardization: A re-examination', *International Journal of Advertising*, vol. 6, pp. 145–58.

Sarathy, Ravi (1991), 'European integration and global strategy in the media and entertainment industry', in Alan M. Rugman and Alain Verbeke (eds.), *Global Competition and the European Community*, vol. 2, JAI Press: Greenwich, CT, pp. 125–48.

Schroeder, Michael (1991), 'France-Allemagne: la publicité. L'existence de deux logiques de communication', *Recherche et Applications en Marketing*, vol. 6, no. 3, pp. 97–109.

Sherry, John F. Jr. and Eduardo G. Camargo (1987), ' "May your life be marvelous": English language labelling and the semiotics of Japanese promotion', *Journal of Consumer Research*, vol. 14, September, pp. 174–88.

Siu, Wai-Sum (1996), 'Gender portrayal in Hong Kong and Singapore television advertisements', *Journal of Asian Business*, vol. 12, no. 3, pp. 47–61.

Snyder, Leslie B., Bartjan Willenborg and James Watt (1991), 'Advertising and cross-cultural convergence in Europe, 1953–1989', *European Journal of Communication*, vol. 6, pp. 441–68.

Somasundaram, T. N. and C. David Light (1994), 'Rethinking a global media strategy: A four country comparison of young adults' perceptions of media-specific advertising', *Journal of International Consumer Marketing*, vol. 7, no. 1, pp. 23–38.

Sriram, Ven, and Pradeep Gopalakrishna (1991), 'Can advertising be standardized among similar countries? A cluster-based analysis', *International Journal of Advertising*, vol. 10, pp. 137–40.

Stern, Bruce W. and Alan J. Resnik (1991), 'Information content in advertising: A replication and extension', *Journal of Advertising Research*, vol. 31, no. 3, pp. 36–46.

Stewart, Sally, and Nigel Campbell (1986), 'Advertising in mainland China: A preliminary study', *International Journal of Advertising*, vol. 5, pp. 317–23.

Suls, J. (1983), 'Cognitive processes in humour appreciation', in: *Handbook of Humour Research*, J. Goldstein (ed.), New York: Springer, pp. 39–57.

Swanson, Lauren A. (1997), 'China myths and advertising agencies', *International Journal of Advertising*, vol. 16, no. 4 pp. 277–83.

Swanson, Lauren A. (1996), 'People's advertising in China: A longitudinal content analysis of the *People's Daily* since 1949', *International Journal of Advertising*, vol. 15, pp. 222–38.

Tai, Susan H. C. (1997), 'Advertising in Asia: Localize or regionalize', *International Journal of Advertising*, vol. 16, no. 1, pp. 48–61.

Tansey, Richard, Michael R. Hyman and George M. Zinkhan (1990), 'Cultural themes in Brazilian and U.S. auto ads: a cross-cultural comparison', *Journal of Advertising*, vol. 19, no. 2, pp. 30–9.

Tixier, Maud (1992), 'Comparison of the linguistic message in advertisements according to the criteria of effective writing', *International Journal of Advertising*, vol. 11, pp. 139–55.

Tse, David K., Russell W. Belk and Nan Zhou (1989), 'Becoming a consumer society: A longitudinal and cross-cultural content analysis of print ads from Hong Kong, the People's Republic of China, and Taiwan', *Journal of Consumer Research*, vol. 15, March, pp. 457–71.

Tuncalp, Secil (1992), 'The audio-visual media in Saudi Arabia: Problems and prospects', *International Journal of Advertising*, vol. 11, pp. 119–30.

Tuncalp, Secil (1994), 'Outdoor media planning in Saudi Arabia', *Marketing and Research Today*, vol. 22, no. 2, May, pp. 146–54.

Unger, Lynette S. (1995), 'A cross-cultural study on the affect-based model of humor in advertising', *Journal of Advertising Research*, vol. 35, no. 1, January–February, pp. 66–71.

Van Raaij, W. Fred (1997), 'Globalisation of marketing communications', *Journal of Economic Psychology*, vol. 18, pp. 259–70.

Wafai, Mohamed and Jehan El-Tigi (1994), 'Selling beyond belief – How to use advertising to promote non-traditional concepts', *Marketing and Research Today*, vol. 22, no. 2, May, pp. 128–38.

Walle, A. H. (1997), 'Global behaviour, unique responses: Consumption within cultural frameworks', *Management Decision*, vol. 35, no. 10, pp. 700–8.

Ward, James W. and Jim McQuirk (1987), 'Information content in television advertising: Ireland, United States and Australia', in: C. F. Keown and A. G. Woodside (eds.), *Proceedings of the Second Symposium on Cross-Cultural Consumer and Business Studies*, Honolulu, Hawaii, December 14–18, pp. 37–40.

Wee, Chow Hou, Mei-Lan Choong, and Siok-Kuan Tambyah (1995), 'Sex role portrayal in television advertising. A comparative study of Singapore and Malaysia', *International Marketing Review*, vol. 12, no. 1, pp. 49–64.

Weinberger, Marc G. and Harlan E. Spotts (1989a), 'A situational view of information content in TV advertising in the U.S. and U.K.', *Journal of Marketing*, vol. 53, no. 1, pp. 89–94.

Weinberger, Marc G. and Harlan E. Spotts (1989b), 'Humour in U.S. versus U.K. TV commercials: A comparison', *Journal of Advertising*, vol. 18, no. 2, pp. 39–44.

West, Douglas C. (1993), 'Cross-national creative personalities, processes, and agency philosophies', *Journal of Advertising Research*, vol. 33, no. 5, September–October, pp. 53–62.

Wiles, Charles R. and Anders Tjernlund (1991), 'A comparison of role portrayal of men and women in magazine advertising in the USA and Sweden', *International Journal of Advertising*, vol. 10, no. 3, pp. 259–67.

Wiles, Charles R., Judith A. Wiles and Anders Tjernlund (1996), 'The Ideology of advertising: the United States and Sweden', *Journal of Advertising Research*, vol. 36, no. 3, pp. 57–66.

Wiles, Judith A., Charles R. Wiles, and Anders Tjernlund (1995), 'A comparison of gender role portrayals in magazine advertising: The Netherlands, Sweden and the USA', *European Journal of Marketing*, vol. 29, no. 11, 35–49.

Wills, James R. and John K. Ryans Jr (1982), 'Attitudes toward advertising: A multinational study', *Journal of International Business Studies*, Winter, pp. 121–41.

Yeung, Kevin and K. F. Lau (1993), 'Gender role stereotyping in print advertisements: A comparison of Hong Kong, Taiwan and Japan', in Gerald Albaum *et al.* (eds.), *Proceedings of the 4th Symposium on Cross-Cultural Consumer and Business Studies*, University of Hawaii, pp. 225–31.

Zandpour, Fred, Cypress Chang, and Joelle Catalano (1992), 'Stories, symbols and straight talk: A comparative analysis of French, Taiwanese and U.S. TV commercials', *Journal of Advertising Research,* vol. 32, January–February, pp. 25–37.

Zandpour, Fred, and Katrin Harich (1996), 'Think and feel country clusters: A new approach to international advertising standardization', *International Journal of Advertising*, vol. 15, no. 4, pp. 325–44.

Zhang, Yong and Betsy D. Gelb (1996), 'Matching advertising appeals to culture: The influence of products' use conditions', *Journal of Advertising*, vol. XXV, no. 4, Winter, pp. 29–40.

Zhang, Yong and James P. Neelankavil (1997), 'The influence of culture on advertising effectiveness in China and the USA: A cross-cultural study', *European Journal of Marketing*, vol. 31, no. 2, pp. 134–49.

Zhou, Nan and Russell W. Belk (1993), 'China's advertising and the export marketing learning curve', *Journal of Advertising Research*, vol. 33, no. 6, November–December, pp. 50–66.

15 Intercultural marketing communications 2: Personal selling, networking and public relations

'Mouth smiles, money smiles better' is a Ghanaian saying. Money is always at the very centre of personal selling, as price is discussed as well as 'side price'. Person-to-person relationships are also at stake in this part of marketing communications which is based on personal selling and public relations, which mix rational and non-rational arguments, hard business facts and human relationships. There are four ways of achieving marketing communications: advertising (examined in the previous chapter), sales promotion (section 12.5), personal selling and public relations. Understandably enough, cultural differences (time and space assumptions, interaction models and attitudes towards action, as described in Chapters 2 and 3) have a major impact on how relationships start and develop. It is argued in section 15.1 that people who want to take into account cultural differences have to be *relationship* centred rather than purely *deal* centred (commerce rather than simply marketing). Section 15.2 develops this argument by comparing the western view of business networks to the Chinese *guanxi*. We then discuss how culture impacts an buyer–seller interactions (section 15.3), which, involving personal contact, are more culture bound. Personal selling issues are afterwards examined in an organizational perspective focusing on how a sales force can be managed in a cross-cultural perspective (15.4). Section 15.5 deals with public relations, which, even if they do not directly contribute to sales, may be of prime concern for defending corporate image before various publics. In the last two sections we examine ethical issues related to selling, first by presenting facts about bribery (15.6) and second by suggesting some ways of appreciating the cultural relativity of ethical attitudes (15.7).

15.1   INTERCULTURAL COMMERCE

Commerce as implementation of marketing programmes

Commerce is about personal selling and establishing continuity in the relationship with individual customers, organizational buyers and intermediaries. Commerce is defined by the *Collins Dictionary* as follows: '1. the activity embracing all forms of the purchase and sale of goods and services; 2. social relationships; 3. *Arch.* sexual intercourse.' Commerce favours the social interaction between vendor (producer and/or distributor) and consumer. The quality of this social interaction, including marketing strategies which respect cultural integrity, guarantees the effective implementation of global strategies. Commerce is simply non-technocratic marketing.

The '4P's model (McCarthy, 1964) of the marketing mix (product, price, place and promotion) has been extensively used; as a paradigm it continues to assist greatly in the design of marketing strategies, serving to question their coherence and soundness. But, little by little, it has led to rather ritualized marketing practices where functions and their content are seen as fairly independent. Market research specialists are not product managers, nor are they advertising managers or sales promoters; as we have argued in section 7.6 an atomistic view of reality leads to decisions made by experts, each one having precisely defined tasks. An issue that does not fall clearly within their explicit responsibility will not even be considered. For instance, when questions arise as to consumer complaints management, it is not always clear who should be in charge of it. The correct answer should be that *everybody* is in charge of consumer complaints and great care should be taken to avoid having *nobody* in charge of consumer complaints.

Technocratically oriented market research treats the customer too impersonally, like abstract units in a sample. Messages from consumers are filtered by close-ended questions, which pre-shape what people actually say. A large part of what they *would be willing to say* is in fact often ignored. The '4P's paradigm of marketing theory has led to practices which are sometimes totally ignorant of the company environment (Zeithaml and Zeithaml, 1984). Various segments of the public (consumers, actual buyers, competitors, etc.) are often ignored simply because there is no established communication channel to hear their voice.

Continuity in commercial relationships: Learning from consumers

Firms, and their employees, often have a tendency to try to maintain the *status quo*, thereby avoiding difficult choices: this process of 'knowledge disavowal' consists in not being prepared to ask questions and avoiding exploratory and developmental research (Barabba and Zaltman, 1991; Fournier *et al.*, 1998). A new style of marketing, more consumer and relationship oriented, less strategy oriented, recommends that the voice of the market should be heard. There are indeed many reasons why the relationship and the lines of communication between a producer and the ultimate consumer may be broken. The preoccupation with *marketing continuity* is a directly operative one and Day (1994) explains that a company needs to activate sensors at the point of customer contact:

In most organizations front-line contact people – who handle the complaints, hear requests for new services, cope with lead users, or lose sales due to competitor initiative – are seldom motivated to inform management on a systematic basis. They may fear [to] have their job load increase, suspect the information won't be used, or not know where it should be sent . . . Channels for the upward flow of information need to be established and incentives need to be offered for useful insights.

Distribution often acts as a filter; consumers complain but there is no specific communication channel to the manufacturer and complaints are not taken seriously or are simply ignored (see Box 15.1). When the distributor is independent, located in a foreign country, and paid by commission on sales rather than rewarded for key consumer or competitor information, it is likely that the upward flow will be nil unless specific action is taken. A product may, for instance be refused by distribution, for substantive reasons which remain ignored, such as store employees experiencing difficulties in opening cardboard boxes which are stapled in such a way that they are injured when trying to open them. Similarly, a class of potential consumers may be neglected by marketing communications, since only actual buyers are targeted and research has failed to examine alternative segments.

BOX 15.1
'Tubeless tyres', you said . . .

A consumer bought a leading European make of tyre for his car. He asked his garage to fit the tyres. In fact they fitted tubeless tyres since they were supposed to be cheaper (as they did not need air chambers). These tyres, however, kept deflating. When complaining for the first time, the consumer was told by the garage to be slightly more careful in inflating the tyres. They had to be reinflated roughly twice a week. The customer contacted his garage again but was merely told that it 'didn't usually happen'. The customer asked if the tyre manufacturer would take back the defective tyres but the garage told him that that was impossible and that in any case the tyres did at least stay inflated for a couple of days.

Finally, after going backwards and forwards several times, the customer had air chambers put into the tyres. The problem immediately ceased. When he spoke to his garage, they informed him that the wheel rims had warped slightly owing to the 30,000 miles (48,000 km) that the car had done. Other cars (the garage mentioned a German make) had rims made out of a thicker steel which was more resistant and therefore did not warp. Such a car could have tubeless tyres fitted successfully, whatever its age. The customer asked the garage to pass on this information to the tyre manufacturer so that it could inform tyre centres which cars were not suitable for tubeless tyres after a certain mileage had been covered. The garage said that this was impossible. The information was not passed on. Tubeless tyres continue to deflate in a fairly large number of cases. Customers either fit air chambers or buy a different car . . . or they change their make of tyre.

The example of Japanese *Keiretsu*, presented in section 12.1, demonstrates the value of building communication channels which help in the design and implementation of marketing strategies. Where opportunities for the return of products are liberal, distributors may warn producers about products which are defective or with which consumers are simply not happy. When, conversely, producers or retailers reject consumer complaints and therefore the return of products, they will often shift responsibility for the failure on to the consumers. They will, for instance, tell them that they have not read the instructions, or have misused the product, or fixed it incorrectly.

A negotiation and human resource emphasis

A commerce orientation means that not only personnel but also clients should be seen by a company as its human resources. The frontiers of the organization should be less clear-cut. Most companies are very dichotomous in that they develop impermeable boundaries between their 'inside' and their 'outside'. Insiders are generally people listed on the payroll. It is often claimed in slogans emanating from within the company that consumers are 'kings' (to be found everywhere: *le client est roi, der Kunde ist König*, etc.), but in reality they are treated as pure *outsiders* and there is little personal knowledge of who the consumers actually are. A consumer who wants to meet a manager (just to explain something about the product or the service, with a positive view towards its improvement) will generally not even be received. Very often distribution channels will be used as 'shock-absorbing mattresses'. As distribution channels are in direct contact with customers, if something goes wrong, it is *their* job to deal with it. Splendid isolation of manufacturers is too often the rule of non-commerce-oriented organizations, whenever they claim to be marketing oriented. To avoid this bias, consumers must be viewed as one of the key human resources of the company. They are not kings, but suitable people with whom to negotiate reasonable changes to the buyer–seller relationship. Personal selling is the main tool of commerce: it allows direct relationships and communications with distributors and final customers and must convey messages in both directions, from the manufacturer to the market and vice versa.

Making contacts

Commerce puts equal emphasis on the marketing offer (product, price, delivery dates, etc.) and on the quality of the social relationship between buyer and seller, manufacturer and consumer. That is why making appropriate contacts and developing relationships is an essential part of commerce, this being true for personal selling and public relations as well as marketing negotiations. The issue is at what level of the organization and with which people must contacts be made to maximize the chances of a successful outcome. When making contacts, in a cross-cultural perspective, people should be aware of the following: (1) status is not shown in the same way in all cultures; (2) influential persons are not the same and individual influence is not exerted in the same way; and (3) the decision-making process differs. Box 15.2 illustrates the first two points with an African example.

BOX 15.2
The little man in rags and tatters

The story takes place in the corridor to the office of the minister of industry of the Popular Republic of Guinea at the beginning of the 1980s. Whether you had an appointment or you came to solicit a meeting, you had to be let in by the door-keeper. Besides, the door was locked and he had the key. This little man looked tired and wore worn out clothes; his appearance led foreign visitors to treat him as negligible and to pay little attention to him. When visitors had been waiting for a long time while seeing others being given quick access to the minister, they often spoke out unrestrainedly, voicing their impatience to the old man, who seemed to have only limited language proficiency. In fact, the door-keeper spoke perfect French and was the uncle of the minister, which gave him power over his nephew according to the African tradition. It was notorious that the minister placed great confidence in his uncle's recommendations. Thus some foreign contractors never understood why they did not make deals although they had been developing winning arguments with the minister himself.

(Source: Gérard Verna, Laval University, Quebec.)

Credibility is an initial condition for building trust in relational marketing. According to Slatter (1987), the salesperson's job in competitive bidding situations (which are quite common in international sales of equipment, turnkey plants and in the case of public procurement) consists of five main tasks:

1. Establishing the salesperson's personal credibility.
2. Undertaking market research.
3. Influencing design and specifications.
4. Establishing the firm's credibility.
5. Establishing a communication system.

There are clearly two levels where credibility has to be established: personal and organizational. The credibility of a particular person is linked to cultural codes. People emit messages about their own credibility which are linked to physical, status and/or behavioural attributes (see sections 3.1 and 15.3). The vendor will try to become personally acquainted with key decision makers in potential target companies. There may be some problems in clearly identifying the key decision makers, and establishing one's credibility with them. They may resent dealing with 'mere salespeople', especially in countries where sales status is low and power distance is high, because it conflicts with their self-image and their organizational position. Hierarchical relationships *across* organizations are a very sensitive issue; all the more so because they supposedly exist only subjectively. Complex codes of interpersonal relationships

PERSONAL SELLING, NETWORKING AND PUBLIC RELATIONS **507**

govern the establishment of credibility: it is therefore often necessary to use sales assistants or market researchers as 'door-openers', who will quickly be succeeded by higher-ranking sales executives or sales managers (Box 15.3).

Any 'detail' may be of importance in establishing credibility in the absence of more profound informational cues which come only when the relationship is more established. Business cards are important because they provide clear information on business persons: their family and first names, how to reach them, their status within the company etc. A foreign-language card will also reflect sensitivity to the host culture (Freivalds, 1991) and when one is working mostly with a particular culture (e.g. a US business person exporting to Japan), it is advisable to have a card printed in English on the one side with the Japanese transliteration on the other side. Credibility is often based on first impressions: accent has been shown to influence the credibility and effectiveness of an international business person. Tsalikis *et al.* (1992) have compared the effect of accent type on credibility of business people in a Latin American context: in Guatemala, for instance, Guatemalan Spanish evokes more favourable judgements than the same sales pitch in foreign-accented Spanish.

BOX 15.3

The Japanese 'message-boy'

During research into the key factors surrounding the success of Japanese engineering companies in world markets, I had the opportunity to interview several Japanese engineering specialists. One of them had worked for C. Itoh, a large Japanese trading company, on the sale and project follow-up of an oil refinery in Algeria. He explained by the use of a diagram (Figure 15.1) the Japanese 'method' for selling turnkey factories.

He stressed the central role of the *sogoshosha* (GTC: general trading company) as an *organizer*, a function that includes the responsibilities of information source, business intermediary and co-ordinator. An *organizer* is roughly equivalent to a 'sales prospection expert before, during and after the sale of a large and highly complex item'. One of C. Itoh's small offices in Algiers, which specialized in import–export, principally of textile products, learned of the existence of a new tender for an oil refinery which was shortly to be published. The Algiers office sent a fairly detailed fax to Tokyo – step (1) in Figure 15.1 – where the engineering company(ies) and the manufacturing companies (MFG) who would be in a position to tender for the project were sought out – step (2).

Even at this early stage, a project team will begin to assemble from among the different companies involved (3). The trading company contacts the official bodies: first, the foreign insurance division of the Ministry of International Trade and Industry (GOV) to determine whether the project has a chance of being covered for political and commercial risk (4). The Japanese Exim-Bank, the public export-

BOX 15.3 *CONTINUED*

finance body (BKG), will also be contacted for a preliminary study into financing options. These bodies will not make any firm commitment, but they will give a preliminary response: if the project risks not being covered by official guarantees, or receiving only limited cover, the project team instituted by the trading company may decide to abandon the tender. While all this is going on, and even before the bid documents are available, a preliminary team will be sent to the site to examine the possibilities of water and energy supply, transport facilities, etc. Already the Japanese are gaining time (5). Once the bid documents are available to companies (6), the trading company's local representative will go to collect them personally from the future owner and dispatch the documents to Tokyo after having summarized the main points in a long and detailed fax or E-mail. The representative will not hesitate to stay up most of the night to draft this text. By this stage, the Japanese have already gained 15 days on their international competitors (7).

Once the detailed fax or E-mail has been received, a larger team will go to examine the technical and economic conditions on site. The results of this survey, and the consultation with various engineering partners, heavy equipment manufacturers (MFG) and carriers (TRP), will enable the formulation of a detailed bid, which very often has to be submitted within a fairly short time span (thirty days) after the publication of the tender. The bid will not be sent, but handed over by a young executive, who will be 25 to 30 years old: a 'message-boy' (8). His task is an important one: thanks to him, there is no risk of the documents being blocked by customs; he also has the job of 'sizing up' the people being dealt with and of discerning the people who will really make the final decision. Once more the Japanese have gained time; they are never late in submitting a tender, whereas a number of their foreign competitors submit theirs after the deadline. Although late delivery of a bid is usually accepted (bidding times are fairly short), it does not necessarily reflect favourably on the capacity to meet delivery dates.

Now the negotiation phase begins (9). This will easily last several months and in extreme cases will stretch, with long interruptions, over several years. Much shuttling back and forth between the various levels (10) will allow the finalizing of an offer. If successful, the offer will lead to the signature of the contract for a large-scale project (11), in which the trading company and the engineering company will generally be joint contractors. As a result, the trading company will adopt the role of co-ordinator between the various companies carrying out the project (12).

According to my Japanese informant, Nobuhiko Suto, now a professor at Tokai University, who had been personally involved in the deal, the 'message-boy' is typical of the Japanese way of doing business. He is even requested to scrutinize the face of the people to whom he submits the offer to determine their reaction

BOX 15.3 *CONTINUED*

to the Japanese bid. In the West, it is difficult to conceive of such care being taken to assess subjective reactions objectively.

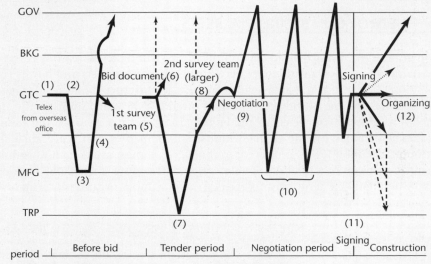

FIGURE 15.1   The role of Japanese general trading companies as 'organizers' in the negotiation and implementation of international turnkey operations: a Japanese view.

The decision-making process in the buyer's organization is a key issue for making adequate contact. Power distance (PD) plays an important role in the style of organizational decision making: the higher it is, the more centralized it is. In a French context, for instance, with high PD, individualism and uncertainty avoidance, decision making and budgetary power are located at the top of the organization. Most people cannot make a decision by themselves, including buying a pencil, without referring to the top. Thus, for personal selling, one has to target contacts at the top while keeping friendly contacts with people at intermediate levels because they could resent their lack of power being openly manifested by the seller's attitude and could therefore obstruct. In countries where power distance is small, decision making is more decentralized, and there are financial thresholds for decisions at each level of the hierarchy, especially when there is also an individualistic orientation in the culture. In such a context the level of contact is roughly proportionate to the financial amount of the sales contract.

The Japanese style of reaching decisions by committee can disorientate people of other nationalities who are used to decisions being made by a boss, a great deal of power being thereby concentrated in one person's hands. There are many examples of firms which, after protracted negotiations with Japanese firms, heard nothing more for several months. They assumed that they had lost the deal, but to their surprise they ultimately received an agreement: the process of *ringi* had been at work in the Japanese company – a procedure of written consultation which requires the input of various interested parties, meetings and careful consideration of objections and suggestions. Box 15.3 shows how the Japanese manage the process of preliminary contacts in a situation where both the seller's and the buyer's organization are complex.

15.2   NETWORKS IN BUSINESS MARKETS

For many reasons, firms tend to develop networks; among these reasons is the long-term nature of business relationships between industrial suppliers and buyers (Dwyer *et al.*, 1987). An airline and an aircraft company, for instance, build regular relationships over the lifetime of the aircraft, which often last 25 years; similarly the aircraft company is closely connected to the engine manufacturer because the design of the aircraft includes specific engines. Industrial companies also build alliances for developing common R & D projects or to manage common assets such as commonly developed software or a joint distribution system. Therefore, since companies do not work in isolation, the term network refers to two or more organizations involved in long-term relationships.

Generically, a network may be viewed as consisting of 'nodes' or *positions* (occupied by firms, households, strategic business units inside a diversified concern, trade associations and other types of organization) and *links* manifested by interaction between the positions . . . Networks may be tight or loose, depending on the quantity (number), quality (intensity), and type (closeness to the core activity of the partners involved) of interactions between the positions or members. (Thorelli, 1986, p. 38.)

The network approach to business has been developed by the IMP group with the view that relationships between companies, built out of the history of the companies' dealings with each other, matter as much as mere elements of the deal itself, that is the hard data on product specifications, price and terms of contract (see Ford, 1990; Johansson and Mattsson, 1988). In business networks, personal contacts matter because they serve to reduce the uncertainty linked to complex deals by face-to-face exchange of information on technical, organizational and commercial matters. 'Mutual trust, respect and personal friendship between participants allows confidential information to be exchanged' (Ford, 1990, p. 81). Personal contacts also enable interacting partners in the network to assess each other's competence, to negotiate implementation issues and beyond-the-letter-of-the contract issues in the case of highly complex products and turnkey plants. If there is a critical problem, they offer a framework for the quick exchange of information and rapid decisions about corrective measures. Personal contacts also play a social role. However market rationality and the 'doing' orientation maintain the lead in the western view of networking. People are there to 'close the deal', not to enjoy the pleasures of social life:

companies are not likely to encourage interaction which is only socially based. There is an expectation that other elements of interaction (such as information exchange, product sales or purchases and adaptations) would also result. There is evidence from the research that buyers are more inclined to maintain 'good but distant' relationships than salesmen. Yet some suppliers see the dangers of too close an involvement of their salesmen with customers, in that they may lose their objectivity and take actions in the interests of the social relationships, rather than in the wider interests of their company. (Ford, 1990, p. 83.)

Broadly considered business networks are a fairly universal reality. The very notion of *guanxi* can to a large extent be considered the Chinese, and more broadly the East Asian form of business connection, consisting in maintaining relationships with the appropriate organizations and individuals within these organizations. The Chinese *guanxi* corresponds to *Kankei* in Japan and *Kwankye* in Korea, that is, after-hours socialization which become important forums for meeting and convincing key decision makers in a socially more comfortable atmosphere (Tung, 1996). *Guanxi* mixes social behaviour and business practices in a complex set of disinterested and interested personal interactions. It is not necessarily directed at short-term results and consists in an investment in relationships which may or may not be called upon in the future. The practice of *guanxi* translates into large sales forces for maintaining contacts and large accounts receivables (in a way similar to the liberal credit policy in Japan, see section 12.1). Firms engaged in a connected set of companies, called *guanxihu*, do their best to avoid embarrassing a business partner experiencing temporary financial problems. *Guanxi* has been shown to be strongly favourable to the performance of international joint ventures in China (Luo, 1995) as well as for foreign-invested enterprises in China and Chinese domestic firms (Luo, 1997, Luo and Chen, 1997).

The Chinese concept of *guanxi* shares some common traits with the Western concept of networking, especially the continuity of business relationships and a framework for understanding the relationships between firms engaged in co-operative rather than competitive behaviour. There are, however, some significant differences which Luo and Chen (1997, pp. 3–4) explain as follows.

guanxi primarily relates to personal, not to corporate, relations, and exchanges that take place amongst members of the *guanxi* network are not solely commercial, but also social, involving the exchange of *renqing* (social or humanized obligation) and the giving of *mianzi* (face in the society), or social status. This feature often leads *guanxi* to be named 'social capital'. In contrast, networking in Western marketing and management literature is the term primarily associated with commercially based corporate-to-corporate relations. Because of this difference, many Western business people are often in danger of overemphasizing the gift-giving and wining-and-dining components of *guanxi* relationships, thereby coming dangerously close to crass bribery or to [being] perceived as 'meat and wine friends' which is a Chinese metaphor for mistrust.

15.3   BUYER–SELLER INTERACTIONS

Seller's status and the status of trade

In many countries sales work has a low status. Selling is implicitly associated with persuasion techniques and taking money from people rather than usefully bringing products and services to them. Trade has some negative connotations in Latin countries for instance, where it was traditionally associated with exploitation, especially when buying for resale, leading to the view that distribution, and services in general, were economically unproductive activities. Those who adopt this view consider engineering and production noble activities, in contrast to marketing and sales which are devalued. Such poor status often makes people think that personal selling requires no formal training, but rather innate communication talents, a certain lack of scruple and a good deal of opportunism.

The value placed on money is also central to the status of trade since sellers sell goods and services *against* money. In fact most cultures have a problem with money, which is often implicitly viewed as depriving activities of a higher sense of purpose, making people *bassement intéressés* (meanly self-interested). A range of possible solutions are shown by the different values placed on price bargaining, presented in section 11.2: either explicit reference to price is avoided whenever possible, explicit discussions about price come quite late (which may at times be embarrassing), or a supposedly 'favourable' price is ritually associated with friendship or common belonging.

The seller's status is in fact often related to membership of a particular group such as the Chinese, who have been prominent merchants in many South East Asian nations, or the Lebanese in West Africa. The reader will recognize here some of the basic assumptions presented in Table 2.2, especially the being/doing divide. The status of a minority as 'commercial group', reflecting strong being orientation, is ambiguous: members of this minority may have taken this role because it was somewhat rejected by the majority, but their success and influence as tradespeople may be resented. On the other hand, in many countries, it is an absolute necessity for the seller to be personally acquainted with the buyer, and common membership in the same ingroup may be required. The buyer might find some personal characteristics of the seller difficult to accept, such as a European export saleswoman selling to a Saudi buyer.

Power distance also has an influence on the seller's status: in high-power-distance countries, the seller is often responsible for conveying the producer's conditions to the customer, with very limited leeway for negotiation – especially about price and delivery conditions. Jolibert and Tixier (1988, p. 11), both French, coming from a high-power-distance society, give a good example of the distinction between sales (understood as a low power/low status situation) and marketing negotiation (considered a high power/high status role):

> During sale the business conditions are fixed by the vendor. The purchaser is not in a position to debate them . . . The job of the vendor therefore consists of convincing the purchaser of the worth of his offers, of the appropriateness of the product offered to meet the needs of the purchaser . . . Negotiation begins when there is a *possible discussion* about the terms of business between the purchaser and the vendor.

In this definition the salesperson's role is only to convince; he/she is given no role in representing the customer's needs and making them known to his or her company! More paradoxically, in this definition, the purchaser is also in a subordinate situation to the supplying company.

Selling styles: Arguments and presence

Let us begin with a question framed in radical terms: what must a salesperson do when asked to sell poor-quality products, or less radically, when the seller perceives the weaknesses of a product through clients' comments? Should the salesperson inform the company, in particular the production department, or merely consider the terms of the business offering as fixed and stick to the role of persuasion? In fact, when preparing arguments, a salesperson has two main concerns: one is for the customers and their needs; the other is for achieving the sale, for 'closing the deal'. Adcock *et al.* (1993, p. 306) combine these as shown in Figure 15.2.

If one regards the seller's role as strictly separate from that of the business negotiator, sales staff being supposed to obediently sell products as they are and not to debate the marketing mix, then the role of salespeople is principally that of persuasion, the art of persuasion being subject to highly significant cultural variations. The following questions outline possible ways of differentiating the sales persuasion technique:

1. How far can one take persuasion without becoming insistent, annoying, irritating?

2. Is one persuasive merely by listening, where clients appreciate salespeople to whom they can talk, or by talking?

3. What arguments will be the best and the quickest for persuading the prospective purchaser?

Cateora (1983) proposes some stereotypes of selling styles:

1. In Asian countries, where people mind arrogance and the showing of extreme self-confidence, vendors should make modest, rational, down-to-earth points; they should avoid winning arguments against the buyer, who could suffer a 'loss of face', and react quite negatively.

2. In Italy, on the contrary, the lack of self-confidence would be perceived as a clear sign of lack of personal credibility and reliability; thus one needs to argue strongly in order to be considered a serious partner.

3. In Switzerland, you have to speak precisely and your words will be taken quite literally.

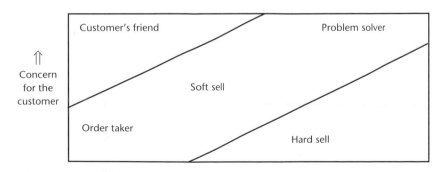

FIGURE 15.2   Selling orientations.

4. In the United Kingdom, it is advisable to use the *soft sell* approach (do not be pushy with your prospective buyer). The very favourable position of the 'soft sell' approach in Figure 15.2 (which is drawn from British authors) gives some support to this.

5. In Germany, you should use the *hard sell* approach (make visits, offer trials, be very visible).

6. When selling to a Mexican buyer, one should emphasize price.

7. In Venezuela, a vendor will have to emphasize the quality of goods.

If a true variety of selling styles related to national culture exists, it is not to be denied that the style of selling depends also on the personality of the salesperson and the type of industry, from the market trader to the executive, selling billion-dollar contracts, from the friend to the distant acquaintance. However, culture dictates assumptions about their role adopted by the majority of sellers. For instance if the view is that a good salesperson should be able to close the deal, then the job is that of short-term persuasion at any price. Conversely, if the seller is viewed as the representative of the client within the company, salespeople should have a long-term outlook, listen to the client and even be willing to lose an order once in a while. Selling styles also depend on which type of concrete results (winning new customers, reaching a sales target) and/or more subjective achievements (getting on well with clients, maintaining a friendly atmosphere in the sales team) are considered as evidence of the seller's efficiency or inefficiency.

Equality in the buyer–seller relationship

Some of the basic conditions of the buyer–seller interaction are partially dictated by culture, especially the relative position of strength of buyer and seller. Numerous empirical studies have been undertaken to determine which role, buyer or seller, holds the *ab initio* position of strength in intracultural marketing negotiations. Graham (1981) suggests that one of the reasons for the American trade deficit with Japan was the difference, in the representation of the buyer–seller relationship, regarding the position of strength. The Japanese believe that strength lies with the purchaser whom the salesperson must do the utmost to satisfy, whereas the Americans envisage a more egalitarian position, as Graham (1981, p. 9) points out in his examination of which party adapts to the other in the relationship of intercultural business negotiation:

Anthropologists tell us that power relations usually determine who adopts and adapts behavior in a cross-cultural setting. Japanese executives in an American setting are likely to be the ones to modify their behavior . . . However, if an American seller takes his normative set of bargaining behavior to Japan, then negotiations are apt to end up abruptly. The American seller expects to be treated as an equal and acts accordingly. The Japanese buyer is likely to view this rather brash behavior in a lower status seller as inappropriate and lacking in respect. The Japanese buyer is made to feel uncomfortable, and he politely shuts the door to trade, without explanation. The American seller never makes the first sale, never gets an opportunity to learn the Japanese system.

Table 15.1 gives a summary of the influence of culture on buyer–seller interactions.

TABLE 15.1   A summary of the influence of culture on buyer–seller relationships

Cultural value	Influence on seller and buyer
Inferior status for trade	Poor status for sales/selling is reserved to a minority group
Being/doing	More personal relationship orientated/more impersonal deal orientated
Money	Price bargaining as friendship ritual
Ingroup orientation	Only people from a certain ingroup are considered as adequate for sales roles/transactions have to be made preferably between ingroup members
Family orientation	Buyer–seller relationships are viewed as an element of a larger family network
Short-term orientation	Achieving the sale is the paramount goal
Long-term orientation	Keeping the client is the paramount goal
Low/high power distance	Equality/inequality between buyer and seller
Listening versus talking	Soft sell versus hard sell

15.4   SALES FORCE MANAGEMENT IN A CROSS-CULTURAL PERSPECTIVE

Several authors in the field of international marketing have stressed the influence of cultural differences on sales force compensation systems (Still, 1981; Hill *et al.*, 1991, Cateora, 1993). Cross cultural differentiation is an important variable for improving the effectiveness of the sales function: Lackman *et al.* (1997), based on data from four cultural groupings (western Europeans, Americans, Japanese and Latin Americans) have shown that substantial differentiation in line with Hofstede's parameters is required in the industrial sales function to generate effective marketing results.

The idea that the promotion of sales personnel is done on merit and that decisions are made on an objective basis is very strong in the United States. This is linked with a 'master of destiny' philosophy which underlies much of US management thinking (Cateora, 1993). People are in control of their own destiny and therefore responsible for the effective use of their own resources. In many cultures which have a more fatalistic approach to life, controlling individual performance does not seem to make sense. Uncontrollable higher-order forces largely shape our acts and future. Ali and Schwiercz (1985), for instance, report that Saudi Arabian performance and evaluation control systems work informally, without systematic controls, established criteria or definite procedures.

The question of the influence of culture on sales force management is not considered exhaustively here. Many of its facets are infused with human resource management and therefore subject to significant cross-cultural variance. For instance, many enquiries considered in the United States as discriminatory when recruiting sales people according to a US 'affirmative action compliance program' (e.g. Chonko *et al.*, 1992, p. 410) would never be considered as discriminatory in most countries.

The birthplace of applicants, their marital status, age, citizenship or language competencies are standard, non-discriminatory enquiries in most cultures where there is still
some *being* orientation. The 'affirmative action, equal opportunity' programme is
derived from extremely strong *doing* and *outgroup* orientations, whereby it is seen as
almost evil to describe persons as they *are*.

This section does not consider the question of whether to employ local or international sales representatives, the expatriation of sales and marketing personnel or
companies that sell to international customers with highly qualified and often multilingual 'selling globe trotters' who deal with equipment, advanced technology or
turnkey projects. This section relates to companies that sell durable or non-durable
consumer goods, equipment for small businesses or intermediate industrial goods. In
each country where they are established, such companies have a local consumer base
and local sales representatives, and therefore the influence of culture on sales force
compensation systems is much stronger. Problems arise when multinational companies try to unify the remuneration systems of local sales staff and when they attempt
to apply a standardized incentive system linked to the parent company's culture to
local sales representatives.

Incentives for sales representatives

Hofstede's (1991) parameters can be used (section 3.2) as well as Hall's theory of communication (1976) to clarify the incentives issue, which is an organizational one. The
organization must encourage its sales representatives and/or the sales team to attain
specific objectives (turnover target, profit target, promotion of certain products, gaining market share at the expense of competitors, etc.). There are therefore several steps
which are influenced by cultural differences:

1. Setting objectives.
2. Evaluation, i.e. setting up a system to calculate target-to-actual-sales deviation
   followed by feedback to the salespeople.
3. Compensating the sales force achievements: designing the incentive system and
   attempting to standardize it across countries.
4. Implementing the sales force compensation system.

Two incentive systems for monitoring the sales force (models 1 and 2 in Table 15.2)
are described below. They are Weberian 'ideal types', not necessarily to be found in
their pure form in the real world. The first model is appropriate for a firm belonging
to an individualistic society where communication is fairly explicit (low context, see
section 13.1), power distance is small and uncertainty avoidance is weak (e.g.
the United States). Model 2 is appropriate for a company originating from a society
where communication is implicit (high context), power distance is high and uncertainty avoidance is strong (e.g. Japan). One can hypothesize that the masculinity/
femininity cultural dimension also influences the practical implementation of these
two models of sales force compensation: assertive (masculine) and nurturing (feminine) feedback to low-performing salespeople and corrective actions are carried out
differently.

TABLE 15.2   Contrast models

Cultural traits	Model 1	Model 2
Power distance	Low	High
Individualism	High	Low
Uncertainty avoidance	Low	High
Context of communication	Low	High

Attitudes towards the setting of objectives and their use in performance measurement

The first step is the setting of sales objectives. Here, differences in the preciseness and contextuality of communication style across societies (Hall, 1976) affect the setting of objectives. Objectives that are precisely set, quantified and openly negotiated correspond to societies where people communicate fairly explicitly with a weak context. On the other hand, the stronger the tendency to communicate with a high context, the poorer will seem a system based solely on numbers. 'Number crunching' is not a trait of high-context societies: figures are not assumed to depict correctly the complexities of the real world. In high-context societies, numbers are considered as efficient, but oversimplified. Despite that, some kind of quantified objectives are needed, but they are not considered as accurate and do not serve the same purpose. Depending on which model (1 or 2) is appropriate, objectives may have different roles.

The first role is that of *formal and realistic evaluation* (model 1), where the sellers must deserve their salary. In societies where relations have been relatively depersonalized people can be evaluated by figures: the bottom line is related to what an average seller is expected to attain. Target levels of sales are negotiated with the salesperson. Only results are relevant. The deviation of actual sales from target is measured precisely. Corrective actions, sanctions and rewards result from the monitoring (carried out by the boss) of the salesperson's performance.

The second major role is that of *internal incentive* (model 2), if the seller cannot easily be dismissed (societies with lifetime employment and strong uncertainty avoidance, emphasizing a high level of job security). Staff turnover is low and closer personal ties exist within a stable work force. The risk is that sellers may seek security and lack personal initiative and drive. The objective is not openly and truly negotiated, as in model 1, since high-power distance clashes with the idea that task objectives should ideally be set by oneself. It is assumed that the boss knows what the sales staff should achieve, not the salespeople themselves. The objective then is not necessarily as realistic as in model 1. The boss may manipulate the situation by setting 'instrumental' objectives: excessively high target levels are set which serve as an ultimate level of attainment. Although everybody knows (implicitly) that a lower performance level will be achieved, this will still be a better performance than if such an ambitious objective had not been set.

Accuracy of goal setting

After objectives have been set, deviation from the target must be measured. The accuracy of systems of performance evaluation and incentive calculation is always higher in a situation of explicit communication, corresponding to model 1. This orientation rewards individual merits, even more so when the company emphasizes individual rather than team achievements. In other words, the individual is seen as the very source of the performance (see the individualism assumptions detailed in section 3.1). In the case of high context/implicit communication (model 2), the evaluation phase is not necessarily precisely and formally implemented since the objective may be significantly higher than that which can realistically be attained. In failing to attain the set objectives, sellers will, none the less, have made their very best efforts. If model 1 were applied at this step only, they would be considered as underperforming. However, owing to the implicit system of evaluation, they are not considered so. There is unspoken awareness in the organization that sales objectives are not wholly realistic. No formal and quantified evaluation is implemented. Furthermore, what constitutes a good sales performance is implicitly clear within the company, making it relatively useless to assess performance very precisely.

Individualism/collectivism, uncertainty avoidance and performance measurement

The individualist or collectivist orientation in a society is a meaningful axis of cultural differentiation (Hofstede, 1991). In the United States, where individualism is very strong, the cultural emphasis is put on individual achievements (Kotabe *et al.*, 1992). It implies precise and individualized sales targets, fostering competition within the sales force. Competition between the salespeople, within the sales team, is considered legitimate, even though it may undermine the coherence of collective action when this is needed (e.g. in exchange of information on customers and accounts, training other salespeople in sales practices, transfer of experience from senior salespeople to junior ones, etc.).

More traditional societies tend not to engage in individual goal setting and variable commission rewarding. Still (1981) argues that, in Thailand, family background largely determines social position, much more than money which confers only limited status. Therefore, fixed salaries, which demonstrate social status, stability and group belonging are more respectable and desirable than a larger income that includes a substantial but variable commission component, which emphasizes individualism and instability. Hill *et al.* (1991, p. 23) point out:

Tradition is also an important determinant of Japanese compensation plans. Because their social system is based on hereditary and seniority criteria, salary raises, even for sales forces, are based on longevity with the company. Similarly commission systems are tied to the combined efforts of the entire sales force, fostering the Japanese team ethic and downplaying the economic aspirations of individuals.

Precise measurement of salespeople's performance may even be considered almost evil in some countries. In South East Asia, the ethics of non-confrontation clearly clash with an objective review of performance. It could cause the subordinate to 'lose face' and would infringe a societal norm (Redding, 1982). Motivation theories, which in fact underlie sales force compensation systems, are culturally bound, because they were developed in the United States by Americans and for Americans (Adler, 1991). They put a strong emphasis on individualism and rationalism as bases for human behaviour. According to Hofstede's empirical description of work-related values, collectivist societies such as Japan tend to favour global stimulation of the sales force as a team. Intrinsic rewards are favoured. Conversely, more individualistic societies such as the United States will favour individual performance variables (individual sales, profits per area, etc.) and extrinsic rewards. As a consequence the marketing information systems needed to run these stimulation methods are rather different. The same retrieved information may serve different functional purposes according to the country. In Germany, very detailed market information will be sought in an attempt to reduce uncertainty in decision making, since Germans fear uncertainty and try to avoid it (Hofstede, 1991). In the United States, where a high value is put on assertiveness and personal achievement (masculine society, with low uncertainty avoidance) the same detailed information will be used for the precise control of salespeople.

Femininity/masculinity and ways of remedying underperformance

When sellers are clearly underperforming, there are different methods to deal with the problem, particularly from the point of view of the immediate superiors. In a masculine society, the absence of results will be emphasized in a fairly crude manner. In a company where the individual is supposed to be efficient and to perform well, unsatisfactory achievements will probably lead first to a clear warning that performance must be improved. Then, if the salesperson fails to come up with arguments relating to factors outside his or her control and if underperformance continues, the employee will be dismissed. This hard-line method does not, on balance, lead to better sales performance than the methods employed by companies based in feminine countries.

In countries that are more femininity oriented (Sweden, northern European countries, France), values are placed more strongly on quality of life. There is a protective and maternal attitude on the part of the organization towards its members. This does not mean, however, that these societies strive less for efficiency than masculine societies. Sellers who underperform will simply be entitled to more understanding. Checks are initially made to see if there are any explanations, apart from their abilities as salespeople, which may excuse their weak performance, such as poor definition of a sales area with too small a potential, or particularly strong competition within the sector, etc. When the reasons for their underperformance have been assessed with them (formally or informally), they receive assistance from colleagues and from the organization (especially in the form of additional training). It is only after the organization has done everything within its power to help the salesperson to increase his or her performance that a final decision is taken.

Compensation systems based on cultural values and industry characteristics

Table 15.3 describes some basic sales force compensation systems according not only to the cultural values involved but also to the type of goods sold. Fixed salaries, for instance, will be preferred where uncertainty avoidance is high. Employees who enjoy

TABLE 15.3   Basic sales force compensation systems, sectors and the cultural values involved

Objectives/type of goods	Compensation plans	Values involved
Long-term sales efforts; equipment, turnkey sales	Fixed salary and promotions	Lifetime employment; co-operation within the sales team; collective performance
Reach precise sales quotas; consumer goods	Pure (or quasi-pure) commission	Own business: no loyalty to the company; individualistic and competitive
Achieve more precise goals (sales of certain products, new territories or segments)	Fixed salary, plus monetary and non-monetary incentives	Mixed values: contract and long-term orientation; loyalty but not unlimited commitment

job security have a preference for a fixed salary, possibly with a limited part of it related to variable commissions. Salespeople accept pure commission payments, with no fixed salary at all, only in model 1. Cultural dimensions combine with the type of industry, which also has a strong influence on the compensation system: sellers are not rewarded in the same way for the sale of nuclear plants, batteries and photocopiers. Large individual sales, requiring lengthy sales efforts and sales force teamwork, tend to be in line with straight salary compensation, as do the cultural values of model 2. Smaller individual sales, requiring individually identifiable sales efforts, tend to correspond with commission payments and the cultural values of model 1.

The rewards can be intrinsic or extrinsic. Intrinsic rewards are related to the satisfaction of inner needs. They are rewards which individuals give to themselves (Anderson and Chambers, 1985). They involve no pecuniary element and have no influence on material life. People may be intrinsically motivated by a job well done, the esteem of their colleagues or even the securing of a contract *per se.*

On the other hand, extrinsic rewards are material and are generally made in cash or in kind. They involve different forms of bonuses and commissions. Extrinsic rewards can be linear (in direct proportion to sales exceeding the objective), progressive or degressive, or can be triggered once a single objective has been attained; the criteria and formulae for calculating variable extrinsic rewards are very varied (Hill *et al.*, 1991; Chonko *et al.*, 1992). Purely extrinsic rewards, such as variable commissions on sales, are motivators which work 'from the outside'. Some rewards are on the fringe of intrinsic and extrinsic rewards: for example, medals or titles (best salesperson for the period). Rewards can be centred on the individual, on the group (e.g. a leisure trip for the whole sales team) or on a mix of both (e.g. awards for the best sales teams). As is frequently the case in Japan, group rewards may take the form of a joint holiday for the sales team which is both an individual and a group reward simultaneously, contributing to the consolidation of the intra-group relationship. Various forms can be considered for rewarding individuals: short breaks or long holidays, presents to the sellers or their relatives, payment by the company of certain personal expenditures, etc.

Models 1 and 2 depict extreme characteristics, but real-world compensation systems combine intrinsic and extrinsic, individual and collective rewards. Rewards such as promotion and salary increases combine recognition (intrinsic) and money (extrinsic). A large range of possibilities for compensation exists which can be used to design a sales-force compensation system adapted to the local culture. Two caveats must be added: (1) model 2 is not the paradise of salespeople in contrast to the extreme pressure to achieve in model 1 – nothing may be derived from these models in terms of different salespeople's satisfaction across cultures, and/or perception of being treated fairly; and (2) standardization of sales-force compensation is possible at the regional level where cultural variance is limited.

Kotabe *et al.* (1992) show that the perception of equity in pay, promotion and other employment-related criteria is higher for US salespeople than for either their Japanese or Korean counterparts. US salespeople perceive that they are treated more fairly by their organizations than the Japanese, especially in terms of the pace at which their sales managers require them to perform their tasks and assignments. Japanese employees, traditionally regarded as highly motivated and productive, are also under strong pressure to perform, as a way to maintain their place in the group. As for Koreans, Kotabe *et al.* (1992, p. 45) note that

many Korean employees appear to have little control over their destinies in their organizations because of the seemingly autocratic management style and the use of non-contingent reward-based systems. Management decisions, as they relate to employees, apparently are often predicated on criteria unrelated to an individual's performance. This kind of situation may lead employees to experience inequity.

Programmes aiming at the improvement of sales-force productivity can be standardized at the regional level, as shown by the example of Digital Equipment Corporation, for the 2,500-strong sales force of its 17 European subsidiaries (Kashani, 1989, p. 94); they must be prepared carefully, with respect for people and their cultures:

sales managers were at first predictably unenthusiastic about using the system. It was considered an infringement on their authority. What gradually sold them on it was the continuity of attention the program got in the two years after its highly visible launch, through watchful monitoring of progress toward full implementation, coordinating sessions among local sales managers, and periodic messages of reinforcement from top management . . . The coordinating sessions for subsidiary sales managers were particularly helpful, highlighting the payoffs from use of the system and furnishing a forum for dealing with common problems.

15.5   PUBLIC RELATIONS ACROSS CULTURES

Public relations (PR) consists of a set of co-ordinated communication programmes between an organization and its publics, designed to improve, maintain or protect a company product or image. The 'publics' concerned by PR can be internal, such as employees, or external to the firm, such as the general public, customers, suppliers, distributors or the media. Other targets for PR actions are government, for the purpose of lobbying about new or existing legislation, or stockholders and the financial community. The function of PR in a cross-national, and therefore most often a cross-cultural context, is made difficult especially in terms of *mutual* understanding. The functions of PR are twofold: (1) in normal situations, to create and enhance a favourable corporate image with the various publics concerned, with the view that a foreign firm is particularly susceptible to nationalistic criticism; (2) in crisis situations such as boycotts, accidents, strikes, product recalls and so on, to maintain goodwill by responding to criticism, explaining remedial action that is taken to overcome the problem, and anticipating and countering messages that may damage the corporate image.

Cross-cultural differences can been noted in the way companies react to disasters such as plane crashes, major pollution, etc. They reflect the prevailing sense of responsibility *vis-à-vis* the community but also the companies' sense of secrecy and the view of what is culturally appropriate for dealing with these events: adopting a very low profile and waiting for the tempest to calm down or adopting a high profile, pleading either guilty or not guilty. Swiss pharmaceutical companies, when confronted with major pollution incidents in the Rhine river, which were allegedly their fault, adopted an extremely low profile, engaging in very little communication, reflecting the Swiss penchant for secrecy and dislike of public display. When JAL suffered its worst-ever plane crash in 1985, with 520 dead, the JAL response was very elaborate, going far beyond what westerners would expect in such situations, including the dismissal of its president and public apologies to the Japanese people (Pinsdorf, 1991).

PR enters the scene as a very different form of communication: it is not advertising, or salesmanship. PR people, whether full-time officers or outside PR consultants, have nothing to sell. They use publicity as a means of conveying messages to the publics (whether by securing editorial space or the use of any kind of films, videotapes or slides), as well as the organization of events, meetings, conferences, sponsorship. The Channel Tunnel for instance, burdened with financial problems and construction delays, had to undertake PR with the two basic stockholder communities, French and British, and with the international banks financing the project. There may be many cross-cultural differences, including the very notion of PR which is rooted in modern corporate culture, and may be unknown in some cultural contexts.

Cultural variance may occur in the following aspects of the PR process: (1) the recommendations for making contact are basically the same as in section 15.2, except that a PR officer is selling nothing, which may make the contact both easier (there being no money involved) and less efficient (PR may be considered purposeless); (2) managing relationships; (3) disclosing information, especially in the case of private, secret or sensitive information; (4) developing arguments, some of which cannot be understood locally; and (5) dealing with nationalistic feelings.

Managing relationships: Thinking locally

People from western countries, where outgroups are strong, do not naturally think in terms of who is a member of which group: working with the key ethnic groups is, however, a key element for good PR in many foreign contexts. The model of a free press must also be partly abandoned: in many countries its freedom is curtailed by the government, often in much more subtle ways than mere censorship. The influence of local competition should not be underestimated: the lack of antitrust laws in many countries reflects the legitimacy of making market-sharing or price agreements with competitors and the lack of concern with the benefits for consumers of 'fair trade'; consequently, PR officers may be involved in talks with competing firms which would be considered unethical in the United States because they infringe US antitrust legislation. Such discussions are all the more important when the local competitors are technologically inferior to the foreign firm but can use their legitimacy as a national firm as a weapon against a foreign intruder.

When making agreements, PR officers should avoid: (1) disclosing unnecessarily information which local parties regard as secret, the sense of confidentiality being culturally relative; (2) using arguments which are not understood because their basic logic clashes with the host country culture; and (3) conveying messages about local people and culture that are perceived as negative.

Foreign firms have to face nationalism: being foreign makes things slightly worse for a company when it is under attack. When Audi cars faced the problem of sudden acceleration with its 5000 series in the United States, the German company, a subsidiary of the Volkswagen group, did not adopt a low profile, convinced as it was of the high quality of its engineering. It took a very negative stance against the CBS television programme *60 minutes*, which showed the problems of sudden acceleration and interviewed drivers. Audi criticized the tests made for this programme and, further, denied the allegations, attributing sudden acceleration to the negligence of the drivers. Finally Audi took action too late and recalled 25,000 cars in January 1987. The market response was dramatic and sales in the United States dropped from 74,000 in 1985 to 23,000 in 1988 (Czinkota and Ronkainen, 1990).

Ambiguous arguments are as much to be avoided as taking too strong a position. If the local employees of a multinational company receive better pay than the average worker in the country, this can be seen as beneficial to these people individually but detrimental to the collectivity as a whole, because, for instance, it lures farmers to the industrial sector, or it causes merchants to raise their prices because of the purchasing power of a small affluent group.

Emphasizing local citizenship is always necessary: it must be done with unambiguous arguments such as those used by IBM which emphasized in the mid-1980s in the European countries its importance as a local employer, citing the number of employees in each country and the local R & D efforts. Such a view of local citizenship embodied in a global attitude was expressed by Percy Barnevik, the Swedish-born president and chief executive officer of ABB (the merger of Asea (Sweden) and Brown Boveri (Switzerland)), when he was asked by William Taylor (1991, p. 91), the associate editor of the *Harvard Business Review*, what it means to be a global company:

ABB is a company with no geographic center, no national axe to grind. We are a federation of national companies with a global coordination center. Are we a Swiss company? Our headquarters is in Zurich, but only 100 professionals work at headquarters and we will not increase that number. Are we a Swedish company? I'm the CEO and I was born and educated in Sweden. But our headquarters is not in Sweden, and only two members of our board of directors are Swedes. Perhaps we are an American company. We report our financial results in U.S. dollars, and English is ABB's official language. We conduct all high-level meetings in English. My point is that ABB is none of those things – and all of those things. We are not homeless. We are a company with many homes.

The case of product liability

Product liability is an area where PR is needed. Nestlé, the Swiss food company, one of the largest in the world, faced a boycott because its infant feeding formula had allegedly caused many deaths of babies in the Third World. In 1974, a report by a British journalist and a pamphlet entitled 'Nestlé kills babies' started an accusation process that developed during the mid-1970s. Nestlé withdrew its infant formula advertising and decided to participate in consumer education programmes. The key reasons for the problems experienced by Nestlé's Third World consumers were cultural: the belief in the magic properties of western products and the pressure to give what is the best, the most modern, as a sign of love for babies. A more down-to-earth reason was the poor use of the product, mixed with contaminated water. Nestlé should have anticipated the key reasons for misuses of its, otherwise excellent, product: (1) illiteracy – people just cannot read the instructions for use; (2) even when literate, people rarely rely on written materials, which have an abstract image; and (3) the inability to cope with ambiguous messages (the product is good but can be bad). This is a problem for pharmaceutical companies, in that most drugs have side effects. However, in many countries it is dangerous to mention them too explicitly since people will not believe in a drug whose manufacturer clearly acknowledges the potentially adverse consequences (most of which can be avoided by proper use!).

15.6   BRIBERY: FACTS

Bribery is associated with selling, obtaining favours, making things work: it is a practice which can be found in almost all cultures. The Germans call it *Schmiergeld* ('grease money'), the French *pot-de-vin* (literally, jug of wine), in the Middle East it is a *baksheesh*, in Italy a *Bastarella* (little envelope) and in Mexico a *mordida* (a bite). These practices know few borders and even the Japanese construction industry has been heavily plagued with bribery scandals in recent years. Naturally every country officially prohibits bribery, but laws are locally enforced. Principles are often universal, whereas their enforcement may be a matter of place (see Tables 3.6 and 3.7 on the types of rules).

Types of bribery

Information and data on illegal payments are very sparse and often fragmentary. Such issues are sensitive and companies remain very secretive. Factual data have, however, been collected, both through the investigations carried out by financial journalists (Péan, 1988) and academic researchers (Walter, 1989), and, more systematically in the United States, as a consequence of prosecutions under the Foreign Corrupt Practices Act 1977 (Gillespie, 1987).

The practice is too widespread to be ignored. It takes various forms:

1. *Small and large gifts*. A common practice is to offer influential foreign officials a stay, fully paid, at a four-star hotel with a limousine for the duration of their stay; these stopovers may cost the host several thousands of dollars a day when one

takes into account all the additional expenses involved, such as receptions, restaurants and recreation.

2. *Percentages* paid, based on the contract value. Here the illegal payments result in much larger sums being paid, in proportion to the size of the contract (whether this is for the sale of a squadron of fighter planes, or a turnkey plant, etc.). Indeed, in the United States, in the public disclosure of the illegal payments involving American multinationals in the 1970s, sums of up to US$70 million were mentioned. The companies involved included Lockheed, United Brands, Gulf Oil. Many other firms were implicated, principally in the mining, aeronautical and engineering sectors. The notorious Lockheed scandal destabilized Japan's Prime Minister Tanaka, Prince Bernhardt in The Netherlands, the Christian Democrat parties in Germany and Italy, and even President Lopez of Honduras. Venezuela, Mexico and Paraguay are known in South America for the practice of making baksheesh payments. A significant percentage in these countries of large deals with foreign companies are laundered through nominee companies which act as figureheads, keeping the money safe before its collection by high-ranking officials (Usunier and Verna, 1994).

3. *Tips*. When civil servants are poorly paid, but hold authority and responsibility (e.g. a police officer, a customs officer or a tax inspector) it may be 'implicitly understood' that in exchange for carrying out poorly rewarded public duties, such officials may supplement their income. Thus to pass through customs or to obtain a tax form (for a mandatory declaration) may require some 'greasing' payment, which may be seen as a form of implicit salary, in so far as the authorities are perfectly well aware of the existence of such practices. In China in 1993, more than 60,000 cases of corruption of civil servants were revealed, with more than half a million people being under investigation and more than 10,000 already tried before a court (Galtung, 1994).

Methods

There is wide variation between countries, and between industrial sectors, as to whether illegal payments are made and the sums involved. Payments are much more substantial, for example, in the construction industry or in Nigeria than in electronics or in Australia. An important caveat must be made: not everyone is corrupt. There is nothing worse than attempting to bribe someone who strongly disapproves of such immoral behaviour. This last point is clearly illustrated by Agpar (1977) who quotes the case of the managing director of a large American multinational who offered 500 Saudi Riyals in cash to a Saudi police officer (about US$140) so as to ensure that a decision on a fairly minor offence against labour law would be favourable. In a fury, the officer reported the attempted bribe to his superiors. After spending 20 days in prison, the businessman was fined 25,000 Riyals and was fortunate to escape a more serious penalty.

This case clearly demonstrates the danger and also the ineffectiveness of the direct method (passing cash from one hand to another). Accordingly, more indirect methods exist instead:

1. Slush funds are set up to effect small payments by cheque, nominally as payment for services rendered. In the 1980s, for instance, Braniff Airlines sold 3,500 plane tickets in South America for a total of US$900,000 without making any record of the transactions in their accounts. This money was used to set up a slush fund that in turn fed a secret bank account. This money was mentioned neither in the parent company accounts, nor in those of the subsidiary. This secret account was used to pay additional commissions to organizers and travel agents in clear breach of the Federal Aviation Act.

2. The transfer of 'brown paper packets' (an English expression) is often made by an intermediate consultancy company. These companies often have their head office in Luxemburg or Liechtenstein, or in some other tax haven. The consultancy company is often involved right from the tender stage in the case of a factory or turnkey project. Consider the scenario where one of the key decision makers for the final selection of the foreign contractor controls a local construction consultancy company. During a reception, this person will whisper to the head of the negotiating team of a large engineering or construction company he is dealing with that it would be advantageous if his consultancy company were to be requested to carry out preliminary technical studies. These studies will in fact be largely fictitious. The fees paid for these studies will correspond to the commission. If these studies are further sub-contracted to a nominee company in Luxemburg, the baksheesh money will be transferred to a 'safe place'.

3. Nominee and local consultancy companies, to which 'phoney' consulting contracts are given, may be used in different ways. For example an approach may be made to an adviser to the transport minister for country X who is well placed to influence the decision on an underground railway project in town Y. It will be suggested that he be made a part-time employee of the Luxemburg-based nominee company. Without having to move at all he will receive a salary each month which, for reasons of discretion and convenience, will be paid into an account in Switzerland. When he goes skiing with his family, the adviser/consultant will take the money out of his bank account in Geneva, then discreetly spend it in an exclusive ski resort. Money spent abroad is less compromising than money brought back home.

4. Two other accounting solutions are frequently employed: the over-invoicing of certain transactions, expenditure or receipts, and the recording of fictitious transactions. For example, the American Hospital Supply company was obliged to pay a 10 per cent commission to obtain the contract for the construction of a hospital in Saudi Arabia. AHS artificially inflated the price of the contract, then recorded a commission for consultancy fees, even though no service of this type had been rendered. This allowed the 10 per cent commission to become tax-deductible expenditure, and made the payment apparently legitimate, whereas in fact it remained illegal (Daniels *et al.*, 1982).

15.7   BRIBERY: ETHICAL ASPECTS

Bribery is considered by most business people as a key ethical issue in international marketing. According to Mayo *et al.* (1991), more than one-third of a sample of US executives ranked bribery as the most serious of ten possible ethical problems that may arise in international marketing operations.

The first ethical position is that of cultural relativism: whether it is right or wrong, good or bad, depends on one's culture. This is based on the view that rules are applicable locally in the ingroup territory and thus when in Rome, one should do as the Romans do. In relativistic terms, words such as 'right' or 'wrong', 'good' or bad', only have a meaning within a specific cultural context. The first part of this section tries to give a view of cultural relativism in the case of Africa where corrupt money is largely, but not completely, redistributed in society. However, one cannot ignore the negative consequences of such widespread corrupt practices. Galtung (1994) and others show the heavy burden placed by corruption on economic development: for instance, the property of President Mobutu Sese Seko of Zaire is said to be equivalent to the whole of the external debt of the country. A second position was therefore cultural universalism, which is based on the view that there are core ethical principles which are universally applicable, whenever and to whomever, independently of territory and group membership. The USA's Foreign Corrupt Practices Act of 1977, revised in 1988, is an example of such a universalist approach to ethics *and* rules. The third possible view is a pragmatic and respectful view of how ethical behaviour can be developed in a cross-cultural context.

Cultural relativism: The bribe as bonanza

There is often a tendency to oversimplify the issue of international corruption to one of a face-to-face meeting between two people, a donor and a recipient. In reality the donor of the baksheesh often faces a group of recipients. The benefit of an illegal payment has a group aspect. It rarely benefits one single person. As a result bribery is intermingled with a dense network of social relationships. Bonds of fraternity and complicity develop between people of the same ethnic background or tribe. These people are necessary intermediaries for ensuring that the influences, the information search and the handing over of the baksheesh may all be effectively implemented. The bonds built on everyday co-operation call for redistribution of small parts of the bribe. The secretary who guesses the existence of the baksheesh, the customs officer who intercepts a 'brown paper parcel', etc. However, each should take their share in proportion to their level of influence and power in the society and should take care not to exaggerate (Box 15.4).

Bonds may also be forged by the possibility of retaliation; those who have not requested a baksheesh, but who have a strong suspicion as to its existence, may either inform the authorities or exert a sort of implicit blackmail by demanding their 'cut'. They may even take no action by simply closing their eyes to what is happening. They are guided by their rationality: they can take the risk of participating in illegal remuneration and benefit personally; exert blackmail and thereby risk offending those in power, leading to ultimate punishment; or lastly inform against the person who has accepted the bribe and suffer any adverse consequences that may result.

Primitive hunterer/gatherer societies, as described by ethnologists, can be used as an archetype for the redistribution of a bribe considered as plunder. While the men hunt (symbolically: those who hold power and go 'hunting' for large sums), the

BOX 15.4

'Article 15'

On the banks of the large Zaire river just as in the province of Shaba, no one in Zaire is surprised to see a civil servant demanding a 'matabiche' in return for a passport or some other official document. On the contrary, people would be worried if such a request was not made. No Zairian would take offence at having to pay for an official hearing, or to have a letter sent to a department head. Seals and headed note paper are bought and are even sometimes forged. In Zaire, civil servants are 'resourceful people' and know how to supplement their income. The police set up roadblocks when they need money: drivers never have the requisite paper and are therefore obliged to put their hands in their pockets.

At the main post office in 'Kin' (Kinshasa, the capital), letters and parcels may – like anywhere else in the world – be posted in a box, but it is less than certain that they will ever arrive at their destination. The 'citizen' (in Zaire, the 'Supreme Guide' has brought into fashion this revolutionary title) greatly increases the chances of this occurring if he greases the palm of the postman. Likewise, a citizen may make a telephone call to the other end of the planet for the price of a tip. All this comes under 'Article 15' a shameful way of designating the small scale corruption practised by civil servants. This corruption is institutionalised and widespread; it also goes under the name of 'matabiche': bribe, backhander, a 'little something', brown paper packet.

The practice is so ingrained that President Mobutu did not shy away from encouraging it in a speech on the 20th May 1976: 'If you are going to steal, steal a small amount and do it intelligently, in a nice way. If you are going to steal so much that you become rich in a single night, you will be arrested.'

(Source: Excerpt from Péan, 1988, pp. 139–140.)

women, children and the elderly devote their efforts instead to gathering wild fruits and vegetables (symbolically: those who collaborate at a menial level, but who are still aware of what is happening). Ultimately the bribe/plunder is divided up according to fairly precise rules. Redistributing plunder and crops among the members of one's tribe is basic moral behaviour in many countries (see Box 15.5). However, the tendency to think that developing countries have 'lower' ethical standards should be resisted, even though the extent of bribery in some developing nations and evidence from research would suggest it. For instance, Burns and Brady (1996), show lower ethical perceptions among Malaysian students than American students; Al-Khatib *et al.* (1996) show that Egyptians are more lenient towards 'questionable actions' than Americans. There is, however, a systemic effect: sellers' markets, high inflation, low wages and economic hardship explain questionable practices while they obviously do not excuse them. Very often, the bribery issue is not one of ethical standards, but a mere matter of

BOX 15.5

A Good minister in Senegal

For the man in the street, a good minister is a demagogue, someone who is adept at by-passing the law and its rulings to keep the voters from his region, his parents and his friends happy. If you try to behave like a minister acting objectively by treating your cousins, your allies, members of the branch of your party in the same way as all other citizens, even political opponents, the people will be totally confused. You will not be understood. You are not respecting the rules of the game. You will be the object of public contempt. You are not a minister for the purpose of serving the nation or carrying out the policies of a government which is in power for the good of all its citizens. You are first and foremost a minister for your own good, so that you may take advantage of your position, and enable your parents and allies, your friends and the members of your party to benefit too. No one will reproach you, everyone will understand. Those who are out of office are the only ones who will criticise this behaviour although if they were in office themselves they could not be sure of resisting the demands of their own tribe, family, or parents-in-law. There is nothing wrong in taking advantage of one's position to help out one's relatives; the ideal would be to consider all citizens as your own relatives.

(Source: Ndao, 1985, pp. 34–5.)

survival. Arnould (1995, p. 130) gives the example of West African traders who refuse to pay the bribes asked for by customs agents or policemen: 'A truck and its contents were burned at the border between Benin and Togo under mysterious circumstances when the driver working for one onion trader in Lomé refused to pay.'

Anti-corrupt action and cultural universalism: The FCPA

The United States has been brave enough to look into the problems of business ethics posed by illegal payments. In the mid-1970s the Attorney General's inquiry into the Watergate affair revealed that suspect payments had been made to foreign politicians by large American companies. In 1977 the FCPA (Foreign Corrupt Practices Act) made it illegal for companies to influence foreign officials by personal payments or transfers of money to political groups. This law obliges firms to institute internal accounting controls. The FCPA's definition of what constitutes bribery is very wide. It does, however, exclude small payments known as 'backhanders' and tips paid to minor civil servants to speed up customs clearance or any administrative formalities.

After the introduction of this legislation, over forty articles appeared in the management literature in the United States criticising the FCPA on the grounds that it was detrimental for American companies abroad (Gillespie, 1987). Kaikati and Label (1980) claimed that the FCPA placed American companies at a competitive disadvantage as compared with European or Japanese competitors. In France, Switzerland or Germany, although illegal payments paid to nationals were illegal and not tax deductible, those paid to foreign officials were. Jacoby *et al.* (1979) pointed out that in response to the FCPA the majority of American multinationals substantially reduced or eliminated these practices. Either they abandoned certain export businesses, or they turned their former agents into separate companies, independent of themselves, who could buy and sell in their own right, or sometimes they even abandoned their long-standing competency as a prime contractor and acted as a simple sub-contractor for French, German, Japanese or Korean companies. A further frequent criticism of the FCPA is that it has destabilized political regimes that are friendly to the United States. It is alleged that the leaders of these countries were sometimes forced into making compromising revelations.

Gillespie (1987), studying matters involving corruption in the Middle East for the previous ten years, carried out an analysis of about 60 cases of corruption where foreign companies were involved. She concluded that the arguments made against the FCPA were not strictly borne out by the facts. Some regimes remained stable despite major scandals (e.g. Turkey, Egypt, Saudi Arabia), others fell (in the case of the Shah of Iran) for more deep-rooted reasons. Furthermore, her study of the changes in the export market share of the United States (in comparison with its major international competitors) showed that US foreign trade with the Middle East had not been adversely affected by the FCPA.

Comparison of ethical attitudes across industrial nations

Ethical attitudes within the major developed countries towards illegal payments are not uniform (Lee, 1981). Until recently, in France, Germany and Switzerland bribery was simply seen as a cost of doing business abroad and could be claimed as a corporate tax deduction. The French call it FCE, *frais commerciaux exceptionnels* ('exceptional sales expenses'), and it was not only deductible from corporate income but also eligible for export credit insurance in cases where the foreign client takes the bribe but does not pay for the contract (Usunier and Verna, 1994). US managers tend to adopt stronger ethical standpoints than their European and Japanese counterparts. Becker and Fritzsche (1987) suggested a scenario which posed a business ethics problem linked to an illegal payment. Three sample groups of businessmen were interviewed, one from the United States (124 respondents), one from West Germany (70 respondents) and one from France (72 respondents). The scenario was as follows:

The Rollfast Bicycle company has been barred from entering the market in a large Asian country by collusive efforts of the local bicycle manufacturers. Rollfast could expect to net 5 million dollars per year from sales if it could penetrate the market. Last week a business man from the country contacted the management of Rollfast and stated that he could smooth the way for the company to sell in his country for a price of US$500,000. If you were responsible, what are the chances that you would pay the price? (Becker and Fritzsche, 1987, p. 89.)

While the replies from the French and German managers differed little, those of the Americans indicated that they were, by and large, less prepared to pay the secret payment. Whereas 47 per cent of the American respondents gave as an explanation that this was unethical, illegal and contrary to the corporate code of conduct, 38 per cent of Germans and 55 per cent of the French thought either that 'the competition would force us to accept', or that 'it's simply the price you have to pay for doing business'.

France and West Germany have legislation prohibiting the bribing of public civil servants, but these regulations do not apply extraterritorially. French and German businessmen cannot be prosecuted for bribes effected outside their national territory. Conversely, the FCPA as well as numerous other American regulations (anti-trust, fiscal, and so on) do have extraterritorial application. Despite the fact that the FCPA increases the probability of disclosure, the corruption scandals in the Middle East by no means involved only the United States. Gillespie (1987) notes that the corruption affairs in the Middle East involving European or Asian multinationals were revealed either locally or by newspapers in the countries making the payments. In not one of the scandals that she studied (for the period 1970–85, there were 42 involving American companies, 29 involving European or Asian companies) were Americans imprisoned, whereas Europeans or Asians were put in prison in seven instances.

A pragmatic and respectful view of ethical behaviour in a cross-cultural context

As noted by Berenbeim (1997, p. 26) host country conditions have to be taken into account:

You cannot say to a country manager, 'Don't do this, don't do that, now here are your goals for country X where all of your competitors do this and that. I don't want to hear any excuses if these objectives are not met.' Under those circumstances, either rules will be have to be broken or ambitious goals will not be achieved. The way to avoid this kind of impossible situation is to build a consensus among practitioners for enforceable rules . . . The example of the FCPA is a case in point. Although it would be more satisfying to punish the person who demands the bribe than the company that pays it, obtaining legal prohibitions in the major industrial countries and targeting the companies that bribe rather than the local citizens who demand payment is likely to have greater impact.

The first consideration is pragmatic: business people who make illegal payments take (real) personal risks for (potential) organizational benefits, either through company loyalty or personal interest (sales commission or promotion). Doing this, they (1) involve their company in the risk of being implicated in a scandal; and (2) themselves risk being implicated, indicted, imprisoned and ultimately sentenced to a long term of imprisonment. In the case of turnkey sales, the favourite domain for big bribes, it is important to clarify the mandate for negotiation that is given to the project negotiators by the engineering company or consortium of contractors. One may put it in straightforward terms: 'If you must grease palms do it right.' Unless the negotiators actually raise the bribery issue directly and openly, the exact extent of their powers and responsibility will be insufficiently clarified. The executives who sell factories or turnkey equipment often 'go into battle' with little prior warning or protection.

The payment of a baksheesh always involves the individual responsibility of the donor, even if his or her company, or the consortium that he or she represents, also risks being drawn into the scandal. As Graham (1983) states: 'From a legal standpoint, the recommendation is clear – avoid questionable deals. The loss of the few "questionable" contracts is not worth the risk of indictment, prosecution, conviction . . . Moreover, if you are indicted, will your company support you or opt to plead guilty and accept the fine?' A pragmatic view for an individual requires reference to a personal norm, not a corporate one. Useful guidelines for those confronted with this issue are provided by the definition of a 'moral personality' proposed by John Rawls in his *A Theory of Justice* (1971). A moral personality is characterized by two capacities, namely the capacity to conceive good and the capacity to develop a sense of justice. The first is realized through a rational project for one's life. The second implies a continuing desire to act in a way that one believes is just. Thus for Rawls, a moral personality has chosen his or her own goals; and he or she prefers those conditions which enable him or her to fully express his or her nature as a rational, free and equal being. The unity of the person is then manifested by the coherence of his or her project. This unity is based on a higher order aspiration to follow the principles of rational choice in a manner that suits his or her sense of justice. It means that if you are asked to do something which violates your sense of right and wrong, it is better not to do it, even if it means not behaving as a Roman in Rome.

A final remark: Rawls's definition of a 'moral personality' remains a rather western one, in that it emphasizes rationality, individualism and the sense of equality with others. In many other cultural contexts, where moral personalities actually exist, these traits would not be emphasized in such a definition.

There is unfortunately no common international legal framework which can circumvent bribery. Moreover, legal texts based on the regimes of particular rations, since they simply prohibit or permit certain acts, do not explain how to behave in the real world. The only universal sources for guiding one's behaviour are for instance the guidelines which stem from United Nations codes and from some analyses which provide the basis for the identification of ethical issues, based on case studies. Ethical conflicts must therefore largely be documented on a moral rather than purely legal basis, keeping in mind that moral judgements are partly universal, partly culturally relative.

QUESTIONS

1. Indicate elements of variation in selling styles (including basic views of what is a buyer–seller interaction, the kind of arguments developed and the communication style).

2. Personal selling often plays a more important role in foreign than in domestic markets. Why?

3. Discuss the limitations to the standardization of a sales-force stimulation system.

4. Discuss how a strong emphasis on group belonging in a particular culture may influence the recruitment of salespeople.

5. Discuss the cultural relativity of the following statements about salespersons (excerpt from Hill *et al.*, 1993, pp. 68–9):

   – Our salespersons are very achievement-oriented.
   – Salespersons need patience to be successful.

– Our salespersons consider the source of income, whether salary or commission, to be more important than the size of income.

– Our sellers should have definite call schedules and planned routes.

– Our salespersons are very time-oriented.

– Our salespersons need a lot of supervision.

– Selling is a prestigious job in the country.

– Salespersons are regarded as future managers.

– A salesperson's social class can limit his/her contacts and effectiveness.

– Family connections often help salespersons in their work.

– A salesperson's religious beliefs can limit his/her contacts and effectiveness.

6.   What is the borderline between a 'gift' and a 'bribe'? Outline possible criteria for defining such a border which allow for some cross-national flexibility.

7.   How can bribery be related to space-related cultural assumptions?

8.   WTD, a large US multinational chemical company, has been recently attacked in several large Latin American countries where it has plants. The company has been attacked by the local press for alleged pollution and poor safety conditions for employees. It has been argued that WTD has much lower standards in these areas than in the USA and that the company shows its Yankee and imperialist orientation in such choices. The company executive officers think these criticisms are largely wrong: inadequate local legislation and poor respect of safety rules by local employees have caused problems rather than a deliberate neglect on WTD's part. Advise the firm on a public relations programme.

9.   Discuss the cultural relativity of the framework for a manager facing an ethical dilemma, who should ask the following questions:

- What are the **facts**; what are **my alternatives**?
- What parties will be affected?
- What do I owe to each of these parties?
- What would produce the greatest **benefits** for **all** parties?
- What **rights** does each party have, and how can these rights best be **respected**?
- Are all parties treated **fairly** and **justly**?
- On balance, what is the most **ethical** alternative?
- How do I best **implement** this alternative?

The words in **bold** are those which offer the best route for questioning the cultural relativity of this framework.

APPENDIX 15: TEACHING MATERIALS

A15.1   Case: When international buyers and sellers disagree

No matter what line of business you're in, you can't escape sex. That may have been one conclusion drawn by an American exporter of meat products after a dispute with a German customer over a shipment of pork livers. Here's how the disagreement came about:

The American exporter was contracted to ship '30,000 lbs. of freshly frozen U.S. pork livers, customary merchandisable quality, first rate brands.' As the shipment that was prepared met the exacting standards of the American market, the exporter expected the transaction to be completed without any problem. But when the livers arrived in Germany, the purchaser raised an objection: 'We ordered pork livers of customary merchantable quality – what you sent us consisted of 40 percent sow livers.

'Who cares about the sex of the pig the liver came from?' the exporter asked.

'We do,' the German replied. 'Here in Germany we don't pass off spongy sow livers as the firmer livers of male pigs. This shipment wasn't merchantable at the price we expected to charge. The only way we were able to dispose of the meat without a total loss was to reduce the price. You owe us a price allowance of US$1,000.'

The American refused to reduce the price. The determined resistance may have been partly in reaction to the implied insult to the taste of the American consumer: 'If pork livers, whatever the sex of the animal, are palatable to Americans, they ought to be good enough for anyone,' the American thought.

It looked as if the buyer and seller could never agree on eating habits.

(Source: Reproduced with the kind permission of the Dun and Bradstreet Corporation.)

QUESTIONS

1. What does 'customary merchandisable quality' mean? Where? In which language and cultural context?

2. Discuss how ethnocentrism and SRC (self-reference criterion) are at work in this case.

3. In this dispute, which country's law would apply, that of the United States or of Germany?

4. If the case were tried in US courts, who do you think would win? And if tried in German courts? Why?

5. Is formal litigation justified in such a case? How can one solve this problem? How can one avoid this type of conflict in the future?

A15.2   Critical incident: Setco of Spain

Planning sales targets for the sales force is a universal practice. Nobody questions it. So it was when Mr Gonzales, a Spaniard, was recruited by Setco of Spain, the Spanish subsidiary of a large US multinational company. Soon after his job began, he was assigned a product line, of which he had some experience, in a new sales territory. The sales manager of Setco of Spain did not know precisely the market potential of this new area. Until then, potential customers in this area had never been regularly visited. Moreover few indicators were available in order to estimate the market potential of this new area in a quantified and precise manner.

When he first met the sales manager for Spain, Gonzales was amazed by his friendly tone; dialogue within the sales team and horizontal communication were the rule. Instead of being set an objective, he was invited to give his opinion on the matter. In fact, he could set his quarterly sales target himself, after visiting the area and making some preliminary contacts with prospects. Because of the newness of this area, the sales manager made no comment. Gonzales was confronted with a new freedom: in his previous positions as sales representative, he had never fixed his own sales targets by himself. He had always been given targets by his boss. His reaction was therefore to reduce significantly the objective relative to the sales he was reasonably expecting, in order to retain some leeway.

After four months, actual sales per area were released. Gonzales was used to this kind of report, since it provided basic data for computing possible bonuses. However, he was surprised to see that his actual sales figures was compared to target sales, and the difference between actual and target sales was explictly presented. It looked flattering. The individual achievements of the other members of the sales team were mentioned in this memo as well. They did not match that of Gonzales.

At the meeting of the sales force, quarterly sales were examined, as well as the targets for the next quarter and the marketing programme. Gonzales was surprised to see how embarrassing his 'performance' appeared to the other sales representatives. Never had any sales representative at Setco of Spain so largely overshot the mark. He was teased by his colleagues, who made some bittersweet remarks and jokes. He felt bad about it, especially because he had been trying hard. He had used all his skills as a salesman, which were considerable and had been proved in his previous positions.

During the discussions, he acknowledged that his area's market potential had been largely underestimated. His sales target was therefore revised and increased by a large amount. This was done in full agreement with all the members (including him) of the sales team, who democratically discussed targets and achievements together during the quarterly sales meetings.

In the companies for which he had worked before, sales objectives were settled in a somewhat hierarchic way. The objectives were, fortunately, too high to be achieved. Being out of reach, the objectives worked as a sort of line of sight, an ideal level. It worked as a way of forcing lazy people to do more and of motivating the achievers to surpass themselves. Logically enough, actual sales were not carefully monitored, nor were individual achievements calculated by comparisons of target sales and actual sales.

At the end of the third quarter, Gonzales began to think that he had been set too high an objective. He had been working extremely hard for almost six months, pushed by enthusiasm for his new job. Moreover an unusually large order from a company in his sales area had swollen his first quarterly sales. This did not happen during the second and third quarters.

When the quarterly sales meeting took place, Gonzales once again appeared as the 'star' of the meeting: he had a record shortfall. No sales representative at Setco of Spain had ever experienced such a wide negative gap between target and actual sales. His colleagues made fun of him. They were slightly relieved to see him bite the dust. Some days later he received a personal memo from the marketing director, who made it clear that he had to adapt quickly or leave the company. 'You should know that in our company a salesman has to be able to settle his own objectives in a precise, realistic and dynamic way. Targets are the result of negotiations with the sales manager: they are based on market data. Individual sales targets are summed up, at every level in the corporation. They are the basis for the quarterly corporate sales figure forecast. The stocks of our company are registered on the New York Stock Exchange. Operators on the Stock Exchange are extremely sensitive to this kind of data. If every salesman in this company performed like you, our forecasts at the corporate level would be meaningless. Our headquarters simply cannot accept this.'

QUESTION

What should Gonzales do?

A15.3 Case: Union Carbide at Bhopal

In the 1970s, Union Carbide Corporation (UCC), one of America's largest chemical multinationals, had established production facilities in India. Its Indian subsidiary, Union Carbide India Limited (UCIL), under pressure from the Indian authorities, had built a new factory in 1978 to produce pesticides in Bhopal, the capital of Madhya Pradesh, a town situated 375 miles (600 km) south of New Delhi. It produced Sevin, a pesticide composed primarily of methyl isocyanate, extremely dangerous for humans and to be carefully kept in liquid form below 25 degrees Celsius. The project was plagued by problems of safety from the outset: in 1978, its year of construction, a huge fire broke out. Five major gas leaks in 1981 and 1983 left one dead and 47 injured. In 1982, a detailed inspection by American experts uncovered ten serious faults in the factory's safety systems. In fact, the factory's alarm system was ringing so often that people living in the vicinity of the factory treated it almost as background noise.

The Indian government imposed restrictions on foreign companies, limiting their direct participation by requiring that they negotiate local partnerships. UCC was able to continue operating in India only by agreeing to the formation of a new company, Union Carbide India Limited (UCIL), in which UCC was reduced to a majority shareholder with 50.09 per cent of the share capital. A further 22 per cent went to the government and the remainder was divided amongst 23,500 private Indian investors. Bhopal's social and political environment developed rapidly as a result of the factory. Attracted by the availability of work and the water and electricity which were supplied to the site at reduced rates, people poured in to the surrounding area. As a consequence, the population grew from 385,000 in 1971 to 671,000 in 1981. By 1984, it stood at nearly 800,000. From its original position of isolation, the factory was soon totally enveloped by the town's growth. Creaking under the strain of this huge influx of population, the town struggled to accommodate everyone. In the absence of a better alternative, the poorest of the new arrivals congregated in 'Khasi Camp', a shanty town situated between the centre of Bhopal and the factory.

Links between UCIL and the local Indian political establishment were mutually rewarding in many ways. The factory's legal adviser, for instance, was a former local head of Indira Gandhi's Congress Party. The former local police chief magically won the contract to guard the factory. One of the nephews of the former state education minister was the head of public relations at the factory.

There were also financial difficulties. In 1982, a slump in sales of its products resulted in the factory suffering a dramatic reduction in profitability. UCC, the parent company of UCIL, even considered shutting the plant down completely, but the Indian government refused to countenance such a possibility for fear of frightening away potential foreign investors. To balance the books, UCIL determined to reduce the factory's overheads. They chose to make many of their most qualified personnel redundant. These vacant posts were then either filled by less experienced personnel or simply scrapped. The consequent loss of morale and expertise amongst the workforce adversely affected work at the factory. News of these unfortunate mishaps was carefully suppressed thanks to the close working relationship between UCIL and the local authorities. The Indian authorities even extended UCIL's operating licence for a further seven years despite objections from the Press and opposition members in the state parliament.

The incident took place in the night of 2 December 1984. Water in substantial quantities was mixed by error with methylisocyanate, causing high pressure, the explosion of the vessel and massive leaks of lethal gas in the surroundings of the factory. The local population had no idea of what to do in the event of a serious incident at the factory: simply putting a wet cloth on the face would have protected a great many people. Even the local doctors were completely ignorant about the effects of the product being manufactured on their doorsteps. Warren Anderson, the chief executive officer of UCC, courageously decided to go to India.

Following the disaster, the state government of Madhya Pradesh carefully drew up an initial list of the human cost of this night of horror. The toll was a heavy one: they estimated that 3,828 people had been killed and 358,712 injured. Of these, 22,955 were left with a permanent disability. A single night of tragedy in Bhopal had claimed 362,540 victims. Ten years later, the government believed that about 6,600 people were killed in the incident. Bhopal pressure groups put the death toll at 16,000 and still rising by a few each week. They claimed that up to 600,000 people – more than half the city – suffered damage to their lungs, eyes and immune systems.

On 4 December 1984, Warren Anderson flew to Bhopal with a team of experts to try and discover the cause of the tragedy. His efforts were in vain. Anderson was arrested and imprisoned, then finally expelled. It was not until 20 December that the Indian authorities allowed a commission of inquiry to begin its work on site. They arrived to find that the factory had been closed since 6 December and was already being dismantled.

Public relations in such a context were extremely difficult to organize since most 'hard facts' arguments might have seemed insults to the Indian management, public authorities, doctors or even to the general Indian public. The solution was found in complex litigation: each party argued that the case should be heard in the jurisdiction of the other. Finally, UCC came out with the favourable decision that the final judgements be made in India where relevant jurisprudence was almost non-existent. On 14 February 1989, the Indian Supreme Court rendered its judgement: the American defendants were found liable and ordered to pay a total of US$470 million, US$50 million was to be paid in rupees by UCIL and US$415 million by UCC; the remaining US$5 million had been paid under the previous order of the American Federal Court as first aid to the victims. Many people found that the final award was rather low. For example, if this sum represented only those killed in the incident, it would be roughly equivalent to US$130,000 per victim. If it included those permanently disabled, the amount would represent only US$18,000 per person and if it was intended to compensate every injured person, it would represent an average of US$1,350 per person.

Its reputation heavily tarnished by the Bhopal affair, UCC realized in 1986 that a great deal of time and effort would be needed to regain lost confidence. During a speech delivered to the Davos Economic Forum on 5 February 1991, the new Chief Executive Officer of UCC, Robert Kennedy, affirmed 'Care for the planet has become a critical business issue – central to our jobs as senior managers'. UCC prioritized respect for the environment and safety concerns and established a health, safety and environment committee staffed by independent outsiders and an executive vice-president was given specific responsibility for environmental issues. The global performance of UCC in tackling pollution and improving safety and respect for the environment is regularly checked by independent experts. The company now has drawn up a strategic environmental plan with specific verifiable goals.

QUESTIONS

1. What are the problems involved in facing social responsibility in a culturally alien context?

2. Was Warren Anderson's trip to Bhopal a 'good' decision? Why? On the basis of which behavioural standards, home or host country's, should a company react?

3. How would you describe Union Carbide's corporate responsibility in the Bhophal case?

A15.4   Case: Houston Oil Supply

Fred Allman, director of marketing and sales for Houston Oil Supply, was faced with the difficult job of penetrating the Mexican oil market. The Mexican market consisted of a single firm, PEMEX, the government-owned oil production and marketing monopoly. Allman had had no previous experience with foreign buyers until last June, when he was approached by a representative of British Petroleum, who was interested in Houston's new service station pump for its Canadian stations. This started him thinking about the enormous potential for sales abroad, and he immediately focused his attention on the rich Mexican market south of the border. Houston Oil Supply had operated in the oil-producing regions of the south-western United States since 1946. The company was founded by Jake Grashof, an unsuccessful wildcat oil producer, to supply the needs of oil producers in the field. The company prospered over the years, and by 1980 was one of the leading oil well supply firms in the industry. At that time, Grashof, who had surrendered active management of the company to his two sons, was approached by the inventor of a revolutionary new electronic gasoline pump for service stations. Recognizing a potential winner in the market-place, Grashof obtained production and distribution rights to the pump and established a new division to produce and market it. It was at this time that Fred Allman was hired to sell the new product. By 1985, the new pump was being sold in all major markets in the United States, and sales for the division had climbed to US$11 million. Allman was attracted by the Mexican market because of the PEMEX monopoly. Although the Mexican market was large and growing rapidly, it was nowhere near as rich as the American or Canadian markets because of the lower percentage of ownership and usage of automobiles. However, it was still a large user of gasoline pumps, and its unique attraction lay in the fact that the entire market could be reached through a single buyer, PEMEX. Fred Allman had no idea how PEMEX officials made their buying decisions, but, from reading newspaper accounts of the US Justice Department action against Gary Bateman and Crawford Enterprises, he was aware that their methods of doing business were very different from those of American buyers. (See Exhibit 1 for a description of the *Bateman/Crawford Enterprises* case.) The parties involved apparently had obtained purchase orders from PEMEX through pay-offs to officials of the government-owned company. Although such action is not legal, he understood that Mexico's political and business infrastructures have permitted monetary 'subsidies' to influence and/or dictate transactional decision making. Known as the *mordida* or 'bite', public corruption had permeated all socioeconomic levels, becoming a 'way of life' among Mexicans. Since bribes are effected in various forms, no country is immune to their existence. In Mexico, however, pay-offs were conducted more openly – a catalyst for prompt, assured action.

Exhibit 1 US v. Gary Bateman/Crawford Enterprises

In October 1982 the US Justice Department brought an action against Crawford Enterprises and Gary Bateman, former marketing vice-president of Crawford Enterprises, for bribery and corruption of two PEMEX officials. PEMEX is a petroleum production and distribution monopoly owned and operated by the Mexican government. The indictments charged that the parties involved had obtained purchase orders from PEMEX through pay-offs to officials of the Mexican oil monopoly. Late in 1981, Gary Bateman, former marketing vice-president of Crawford Enterprises of Houston, Texas, pleaded guilty to making pay-offs totalling US$342,000 in bribes to Guillermo Cervera, administrative secretary to the chief of purchasing at PEMEX. When fired from Crawford Enterprises on 9 February 1979, Bateman had opened his own business – Applied Process Products Overseas, Inc. – with the idea of transacting business with PEMEX. Bateman had offered to pay Cervera 30 per cent of Applied's gross profit in exchange for assistance in obtaining business. Cervera presumably agreed and became 'administrator and handler' of the money, which would be divided with other PEMEX officials. Bateman's company obtained approximately US$5 million in purchase orders from PEMEX until March 1981, when Bateman signed a co-operation agreement with the US government bribery investigation in return for a reduction in the charges against him, to a minor offence only.

However, the US government stated that while marketing vice-president at Crawford Enterprises, Gary Bateman handled company dealings with PEMEX and usually carried large amounts of currency from Houston to Mexico City. This led to further investigation, and in October 1982, the US Justice Department alleged that a bribery scheme had been set up by Crawford Enterprises which paid US$10 million in bribes to two former PEMEX officials to secure orders for gas compression equipment totalling US$225 million between June 1977 and March 1979. The US government contended that Crawford Enterprises funnelled cash to a Mexican intermediary company, Grupo Industrial Delta, to be passed on to the PEMEX officials. Crawford

Enterprises, Inc. had been accused of representing the additional interests (in submitting bids to PEMEX) of Solar Turbines International, a subsidiary of Caterpillar Tractor Co., and Ruston Gas Turbines, Inc., a subsidiary of General Electric England Ltd. Crawford Enterprises has denied any wrongdoing in connection with the allegations.

Although corruption had been overemphasized as the cause of the current state of the economy of Mexico, the new administration of President de la Madrid, which took office in 1983, was striving for a 'moral renovation' that would include an attempt to reduce waste and political graft. To set an example, the Mexican government formally charged and subsequently dismissed three PEMEX officials for accepting over US$42,000 in bribes from the US firms in the Crawford Enterprises affair. Allman found himself in somewhat of a quandary. The US government had taken a consistent stand against the corruption and bribery of foreign buyers and particularly foreign government officials. And the Justice Department had followed an aggressive course of action against American offenders. Yet it seemed evident that despite current Mexican government opposition, the *mordida* was still a part of the Mexican culture and might be a necessary requirement for getting the attention of PEMEX buyers.

(Source: Adapted from a case prepared by Carol G. Spindola, in Cundiff and Hilger, 1988, pp. 123–5.)

Questions

1. Why are there differences in business practices between the United States and Mexico? What are these differences?

2. Is bribery the same thing as corruption? A bribe is defined as 'money or favour given or promised to a person in a position of trust to influence his judgment or conduct: something that serves to induce or influence'. Corruption is defined as 'the impairment of integrity, virtue or moral principle; morally degenerate and perverted'.

3. How are ethics established and whose ethics prevail in a foreign environment? Must foreigners comply with local customs, or can traditional business practices be challenged? Should marketers behave as 'change agents' in foreign markets?

4. If you were Fred Allman, competing for foreign contracts worth millions of dollars in sales, what would your ethical parameters be? Which actions would you take?

A15.5 Critical incident: The *Brenzy nouveau* has arrived!

Legritte Company was founded just after the Second World War by a skilful engineer, Monsieur Legritte. Aided by the reconstruction boom which was followed by the rapid economic growth of the 1960s, the Legritte Company developed more by improving the quality of its products than by investing money in marketing and sales. The intrinsic quality of the products, namely electrical connections for industrial use, has been the strong point of the business from the very beginning.

The company is located near Lyons (France) and employs about 200 people, with an annual turnover of 80 million francs. Two years ago Legritte was taken over by a US-based multinational company, Brenzy. Monsieur Legritte, drawing near to retirement age and with no qualified successor, sold his property to the Brenzy Corporation, which now owns the full 100 per cent. Brenzy has progressively introduced more up-to-date management methods in this traditional family business. Inventory management, cost accounting and delivery systems have all been changed to fit with Brenzy's procedures.

Sales promotion in France, and Europe generally, is based on nicely printed catalogues, technical instructions and directions for use. Unit prices reduce according to the size of orders. Products are promoted through small gifts given to the purchasers. Thus the launch of a new pre-insulated line of products, recently certified by EDF (Electricité de France, the public utility for electricity), came with a free gift (electrical pliers) for any order higher than 10,000 francs. This offer was open for six months. In order to receive the gift, the buyer simply had to fill in the gift voucher and enclose it with the order, provided the amount was sufficient.

Brenzy-Legritte was a newcomer to advertising. Being a fairly traditional medium-sized industrial company, they had not up to now invested a lot of money in advertisements. When they decided for the first time to advertise their products they did it by promoting their products along with what they called '*le Brenzy nouveau*', with a play on words between Brenzy and Beaujolais, a freshly harvested red wine and a fashionable drink.

An advertisement in a specialist journal showed a bottle of Beaujolais nouveau, with the following slogan above the image: 'The Brenzy nouveau has arrived!' Text in bold characters at the bottom stated: 'You are thirsty and craving a new line of effective products! Brenzy-Legritte is happy to join you in ordering Beaujolais nouveau!' It was indicated that a minimum order of 3,500 francs entitled buyers to receive three free bottles and a minimum order of 5,000 francs entitled them to receive six free bottles. The expiry date for this offer was stipulated. The new line of Brenzy-Legritte products was shown on the label of the bottle of Beaujolais.

EDF, which is a large customer of Brenzy-Legritte, was not very happy about this humorous advertisement. It seems that EDF experienced problems amongst its personnel when the boxes of Beaujolais arrived at its offices.

Brenzy-Legritte is now undergoing drastic changes in its organization. Computers have been linked to the European headquarters in Brussels. Strictly defined management procedures have been imposed by headquarters. Brenzy has issued a professional code of conduct, the implementation of which is compulsory for the French subsidiary as well as for all the other subsidiaries around the world. It is a complete code of business ethics, comprising precise and detailed prescriptions. Below are some extracts.

Suffice it to say that this code of conduct is perceived by most people at Brenzy-Legritte, especially the salespeople, as largely inappropriate to the French context and a mere interference in their business. They prefer to disregard it.

Excerpts from the code of conduct at Brenzy-Legritte

Correct use of company funds

1. Company funds will not be used in order to make payments, or concealed loans, with the purpose of dishonestly influencing a supplier, a client or a civil servant.

This prohibition applies not only to direct use of company money, but also to any kind of indirect payments, by the means of consultants/intermediaries, or by reimbursing to employees payments made by them.

2. No payment shall be made, for and in the name of the company or one of its subsidiaries, with the intent or knowledge that part of such a payment will serve other purposes than those described in the documents related to this payment.

Gifts, favours and entertainment

Small gifts of symbolic value, minor favours and modest receptions may be offered at the company's expense only when they meet all of the following conditions:

1. They must be compatible with the rules of the company and current business practices.

2. Their monetary worth must be limited; they must be presented in such a form as not to appear as a bribe or remuneration; they must not give rise to suspicions about the impartiality of the beneficiary.

3. They must be approved by the general manager of the subsidiary or by a vice-president at Brenzy Corporation; they must be compatible with the instructions previously approved by the direct superior, the managing director and a senior vice-president at Brenzy Corporation.

Gifts and entertainment for civil servants

As indicated above, gifts, other than symbolic ones or gifts of a very modest value, whatever their nature, or a sumptuous reception, whatever its motives, are not allowed.

Issues related to these procedures and their violations

1. Any employees who want to ask questions about this code and its implementation shall discuss it with the head of the department. If it entails legal or accounting matters, they shall refer to qualified personnel from the legal services and the accounting department, who shall be consulted.

2. The discovery of a case which is fraudulent, illegal, or which violates the rules of the company, shall immediately be reported to the legal counsellor. If such cases are identified, which implicate senior executives in the corporation, this case shall be reported to the executive vice-president, for examination by the chairman of the board, the chief executive officer, and the chairman of the audit committee.

3. No derogation to this procedure will be accepted in these matters. There will probably be some 'business opportunities' in the future, when it would be necessary to make questionable payments in order to succeed against a competitor, for one reason or another. The duty of the employee, in this case, is to reject such 'opportunities'.

4. Any infringement of the above-mentioned principles will result in disciplinary sanctions, including dismissal, a suing of the employee and a detailed report to competent regulatory authorities.

5. Moreover, disciplinary sanctions will be directed against any executive who initiates or approves such actions, or knows about them, or may have known about them, and did not quickly act to rectify them in accordance with this code. Adequate disciplinary sanctions will also be directed against any executives who neglect their hierarchical responsibilities, by not ensuring that their subordinates have been properly informed about the rules established in this code.

REFERENCES

Adcock, Dennis, Ray Bradfield, Al Halborg and Caroline Ross (1993), *Marketing, Principles and Practice*, Pitman: London.

Adler, Nancy J. (1991), *International Dimensions of Organizational Behavior*, 2nd edn, PWS-Kent: Boston.

Agpar, M. (1977), 'Succeeding in Saudi Arabia', *Harvard Business Review*, January/February, pp. 14–33.

Ali, Abbas and Paul M. Schwiercz (1985), 'The relationship between managerial decision styles and work satisfaction in Saudi Arabia', in Erdener Kaynak (ed.), *International Business in the Middle East*, De Gruyter: New York, pp. 138–49.

Al-Khatib, Jamal A., Scott J. Vitell and Mohammed Y. A. Rawwas (1996), 'Consumer ethics: A cross-cultural investigation', *European Journal of Marketing*, vol. 31, no. 7, pp. 750–67.

Anderson, Paul F. and Terry M. Chambers (1985), 'A reward/measurement model of organizational buying behavior', *Journal of Marketing*, vol. 49, Spring, pp. 7–23.

Arnould, Eric J. (1995), 'West African marketing channels', in John F. Sherry, Jr. (ed.), *Contemporary Marketing and Consumer Behavior*, Sage Publications: Thousand Oaks, CA, pp. 109–68.

Barabba, Vincent P. and Gerald Zaltman (1991), *Hearing the Voice of the Market*, Harvard Business School Press: Cambridge, MA.

Becker, Helmut and David H. Fritzsche (1987), 'A comparison of the ethical behavior of American, French and German managers', *Columbia Journal of World Business*, Winter, pp. 87–95.

Berenbein, Ronald E. (1997), 'Can multinational business agree on how to act ethically?', *Business and Society Review*, vol. 98, pp. 24–8.

Burns, David J. and John T. Brady (1996), 'Retail ethics as appraised by future business personnel in Malaysia and the United States', *Journal of Consumer Affairs*, vol. 30, no. 1, pp. 195–217.

Cateora, Philip R. (1993), *International Marketing*, 8th edn, Richard D. Irwin: Burr Ridge, IL.

Chonko, Lawrence B., Ben M. Enis and John F. Tanner (1992), *Managing Sales People*, Allyn and Bacon: Boston, MA.

Cundiff, Edward W. and Marye Tharp Hilger (1988), *Marketing in the International Environment*, 2nd edn, Prentice Hall: Englewood Cliffs, NJ.

Daniels, John D., Ernest W. Ogram and Lee H. Radebaugh (1982), *International Business: Environments and Operations*, 3rd edn, Addison-Wesley: Reading, MA.

Day, George S. (1994), 'Continuous learning about markets', *California Management Review*, vol. 36, no. 4, pp. 9–31.

Dwyer, Robert F., Paul H. Schurr and Sejo Oh (1987), 'Developing buyer–seller relationships', *Journal of Marketing*, vol. 51, April, pp. 11–27.

Ford, David (ed.) (1990), *Understanding Business Markets*, London: Academic Press.

Fournier, Susan, Susan Dobscha and David Glen Mick (1998), 'Preventing the premature death of relationship marketing', *Harvard Business Review*, vol. 76, no. 1, January–February, pp. 42–51.

Freivalds, John (1991), 'Foreign-language business cards', *Agri Marketing*, vol. 29, no. 3, pp. 48–9.

Galtung, Frederick (1994), *Korruption*, Göttingen: Lamuv Verlag.

Gillespie, Kate (1987), 'Middle East response to the US Foreign Corrupt Practices Act', *California Management Review*, vol. 24, no. 4 (Summer), pp. 9–30.

Graham, John L. (1981), 'A hidden cause of America's trade deficit with Japan', *Columbia Journal of World Business*, Fall, pp. 5–15.

Graham, John L. (1983), 'Foreign Corrupt Practices Act: A manager's guide', *Columbia Journal of World Business*, vol. 18, no. 3, pp. 89–94.

Hall, Edward T. (1976), *Beyond Culture*, Doubleday: New York.

Hill, John S., Richard R. Still and Ünal O. Boya (1991), 'Managing the multinational sales force', *International Marketing Review*, vol. 8, no. 1, pp. 19–31.

Hill, John S., Arthur W. Allaway, Colin Egan and Ünal O. Boya (1993), 'Perceptions of foreign field sales forces: An exploratory factor analysis of their characteristics, behaviors and sales', *Proceedings of the 6th World Marketing Congress*, Istambul, pp. 67–70.

Hofstede, Geert (1991), *Culture and Organizations: Software of the mind*, McGraw-Hill: Maidenhead, Berkshire.

Jacoby, N. H., P. Nehemkis and R. Eells (1979), 'Naivete: Foreign payoffs law', *California Management Review*, vol. XXII, no. 1 (Fall), pp. 84–7.

Johansson, Jan and Lars-Gunnar Mattsson (1988), 'Internationalization in industrial systems – a network approach', in N. Hood and J. E. Vahlne (eds.), *Strategies in Global Competition*, Croom Helm: New York.

Jolibert, Alain and Maud Tixier (1988), *La Négociation Commerciale*, Editions ESF: Paris.

Kaikati, J. G. and W. A. Label (1980), 'American bribery legislation: An obstacle to international marketing', *Journal of Marketing*, Vol. 44 (Fall), pp. 38–43.

Kashani, Kamran (1989), 'Beware the pitfalls of global marketing', *Harvard Business Review*, September–October, pp. 91–8.

Kotabe, Masaaki, Alan J. Dubinsky and Chae Un Lim (1992), 'Perceptions of organizational fairness: A cross-national perspective', *International Marketing Review*, vol. 9, no. 2, pp. 41–58.

Lackman, Conway L., David P. Hanson and John M. Lanasa (1997), 'Social relations in culture and marketing', *Journal of Marketing Theory & Practice*, vol. 5, no. 1, pp. 144–52.

Lee, K. H. (1981), 'Ethical beliefs in marketing management: A cross-cultural study', *European Journal of Marketing*, vol. 15, no. 1, pp. 58–67.

Luo, Yadong (1995), 'Business strategy, market structure, and performance of IJV', *Management International Review*, vol. 35, no. 3, pp. 249–64.

Luo, Yadong (1997), 'Guanxi and performance of foreign-invested enterprises in China', *Management International Review*, vol. 37, no. 1, pp. 51–70.

Luo, Yadong and Min Chen (1997), 'Does guanxi influence firm performance?', *Asia Pacific Journal of Management*, vol. 14, pp. 1–16.

McCarthy, E. Jerome (1964), *Basic Marketing: A managerial approach*, Prentice Hall: Englewood Cliffs, N.J.

Mayo, Michel A., Lawrence J. Marks and John K. Ryans Jr (1991), 'Perceptions of ethical problems in international marketing', *International Marketing Review*, vol. 8, no. 3, pp. 61–75.

Ndao, Cheikh Alioune (1985), *Excellences, vos épouses!*, Les Nouvelles Editions Africaines: Dakar.

Péan, Pierre (1988), *L'Argent Noir*, Librairie Arthème Fayard: Paris.

Pinsdorf, Marion K. (1991), 'Flying different skies: How different cultures respond to airline disasters', *Public Relations Review*, vol. 17, no. 1, pp. 37–56.

Rawls, John (1971), *A Theory of Justice*, Belknap Press of Harvard University: Cambridge, MA.

Redding, S. Gordon (1982), 'Cultural effects of the marketing process in Southeast Asia', *Journal of the Market Research Society*, vol. 24, no. 2, pp. 98–114.

Slatter, Stuart St P. (1987), 'The salesman's job in competitive bidding situations', *Industrial Marketing Management*, vol. 16, pp. 201–5.

Still, Richard R. (1981), 'Cross-cultural aspects of sales force management', *Journal of Personal Selling and Sales Force Management*, vol. 1, no. 2, pp. 6–9.

Taylor, William (1991) 'The logic of global business: an interview with ABB's Percy Barnevik', *Harvard Business Review*, March–April, pp. 90–105.

Thorelli, Hans B. (1986), 'Networks: Between markets and hierarchies', *Strategic Management Journal*, vol. 7, pp. 37–51.

Tsalikis, John, Marta Ortiz-Buonafina and Michael S. Latour (1992), 'The role of accent on the credibility and effectiveness of the international business person: The case of Guatemala, *International Marketing Review*, vol. 9, no. 4, pp. 57–72.

Tung, Rosalie (1996), 'Negotiating with East Asians', in P. N. Ghauri and J.-C. Usunier (eds.), *International Business Negotiations*, Oxford: Pergamon/Elsevier, pp. 369–81.

Usunier, Jean-Claude and Gérard Verna (1994), *La Grande Triche: Ethique, Corruption et Affaires Internationales*, Editions La Découverte: Paris.

Walter, Ingo (1989), *Secret Money*, 2nd edn, Unwin-Hyman: London.

Zeithaml, Carl P. and Valarie Zeithaml (1984), 'Environmental management: Revising the perspective,' *Journal of Marketing*, vol. 48, Spring, pp. 46–53.

16 Intercultural marketing negotiations 1: People, trust and tasks

In international marketing, negotiation skills are needed. Many agreements have to be negotiated, drafted, signed and finally implemented: sales contracts, licensing agreements, joint ventures and various kinds of partnerships, agency and distribution agreements, turnkey contracts, etc. Negotiation is based not only on legal and business matters, corresponding to the *doing* orientation, but also on the quality of human and social interactions, corresponding to the *being* orientation (section 2.3). Goldman (1994) emphasizes for instance the importance for the Japanese of *ningensei*, which literally translates as an all-encompassing and overriding concern for and prioritizing of 'humanity' or *human beingness* (see Box 16.2). According to Japanese specialists in international marketing negotiations:

The North American and U.K. negotiators failed to communicate ningensei at the first table meeting. Rushing into bottom lines and demanding quick decisions on the pending contract they also overlooked the crucial need for ningensei in developing good will . . . Hard business facts alone are not enough. . . Ningensei is critical in getting Japanese to comply or in persuading Japanese negotiating partners. (Nippon Inc. Consultation, quoted in Goldman, 1994, p. 31.)

There are various kinds of 'distances' between the potential partners: physical distance certainly, but also economic, educational and cultural distance, which tend to inflate the cost of negotiating internationally. Negotiations for large contracts may take years, but fortunately not continuously. Most international deals incur transaction costs which are disproportionate to the costs related to domestic deals: people in the domestic market usually share the same language and cultural background, which acts as a common knowledge base. For instance, it is much easier within the native cultural setting to guess who will be a good payer, a reliable partner or a trustworthy supplier.

Thus it would be a mistake to go flitting about like a butterfly on the international market: always looking for new partners, new customers and new ventures, without following up. This results in a great deal of 'one-off' business. Business people and companies perform poorly if they do not understand the golden rule of international marketing negotiations which is: have few partners and conduct few negotiations, but make the stakes meaningful. This will enable both parties to build a durable partnership. One should 'marry' well rather than often (section 16.1).This chapter seeks to develop two simple ideas. The first is that trust between buyer and seller is a key variable when structuring and developing any relational exchange. The second is that trust in an international sale or business venture is heavily dependent on culturally coded signs, and may ultimately be withdrawn precisely because these cultural codes have been ignored. These difficulties in interacting, negotiating sales, planning common ventures, working out agreements and achieving them together are deeply rooted in the cultural, human and social background of business people. They are not related to a superficial variance of business customs.

Simple 'empathy' is not enough for the avoidance of misunderstandings. In fact, people with different cultural backgrounds often do not share the same basic assumptions, as we have shown in Chapters 2 and 3. This may undermine the process of building and maintaining trust between culturally uneven partners (section 16.2). Subsequent sections deal with the various aspects of cultural differences which affect the trust-building process, particularly misunderstandings about personal and institutional credibility (section 16.3); differences in the underlying concept of negotiation: cultural predispositions to integrative negotiation, that is, the preference for maximizing the common cake before looking at one's own portion, or to a distributive orientation – maximizing one's own portion of the cake, rather than the cake itself (section 16.4); time-based misunderstandings during the negotiation process (16.5); the existence of a common rationality between the parties (section 16.6). Section 16.7 outlines the possibility of differences in outcome orientation and compares oral and written agreements as support for trust between the parties. The following chapter complements this one by examining some elements of national negotiation styles.

16.1   THE DYNAMICS OF TRUST IN RELATIONAL MARKETING

The motto of the Deutsche Bank, the largest German bank and a quite successful organization internationally, is '*Vertrauen ist der Anfang von allem*': trust is the beginning of everything. Trust is indeed a necessary condition for smooth and efficient business between partners, but is also a highly intangible, volatile asset, difficult to create, easy to destroy. Pursuing the Whorfian perspective introduced in Chapter 13, let us look first at how trust is expressed in various languages.

What is trust?

The English concept of *trust* is the reliance on and confidence in the truth, worth and reliability of a person or thing. Reliance is central in the Anglo-Saxon concept of trust, which is why the legal institution of trust has been highly developed in the common law tradition, whereas it was non-existent in the Roman-Germanic tradition until very recently. The German concept is based on two verbs: *trauen* and *vertrauen*, both of them meaning literally to 'trust'. But in fact the Germans use the first form, *trauen*, mostly in the negative sense, *'Ich traue Dir nicht'* ('I do not trust you'), and the second in the positive sense *'Ich vertraue Dir'* ('I trust you'). The prefix *Ver* indicates a transformation and this explains what lies behind the German concept of trust: (1) the initial position is distrust and (2) only after a favourable change has occurred can trust be established. The French notion of *confiance*, as in other Romance languages, is based on the Latin *confidentia*, a compound of *cum* (with, shared) and *fides* (faith, belief): the notion of sharing common beliefs is central to the Latin concept of trust. The Japanese word for trust is *shin-yô* meaning literally: sincere business; it is based on a compound of *shin*, a character for 'sincerity' and *yô* which means literally 'something to do, a business,' (Sakade, 1982).

Assuming that the very concept of trust is the same cross culturally and that languages only favour a facet of it, we have the following elements:

1. Trust is reliance on and confidence in people, words and things.

2. Trust is inseparable from distrust: since obvious showing of distrust is detrimental to the establishment of trust, every culture has to deal with the paradox of their inseparability.

3. Trust is about sharing common faith, beliefs, possibly education or group membership.

4. Trust is directed to the future and to common achievements, even though this does not deny the value of the lessons of the past.

Fukuyama (1994, p. 26) defines trust as 'the expectation that arises within a community of regular, honest, and cooperative behavior, based on commonly shared norms, on the part of other members of that community'.[1] Trust basically saves transaction costs in interpersonal and interorganizational relationships. The savings result from smooth communication: one does not need to write everything down, to invest in control systems; meetings are quicker: mutual understanding and consensus are reached more easily. But there are major obstacles to the establishment of trust in an *intercultural* perspective: (1) people do not always share the same communication style; (2) they may not share the same beliefs; (3) they do not necessarily agree on what are adequate control systems; and (4) their interpretation of a control system as signalling trust, distrust or a reasonable combination of both differs. Since the process of building and withdrawing trust is a very dynamic one – it can be killed in a few minutes – trust must be seen as an infant to be protected rather than an independent self.

A marriage between buyer and seller: The dimensions of relational marketing

Many successful international marketing partnerships share the following characteristics: (1) a long time span over which transactions occur, (2) a large size in terms of unit sales (i.e. compared to total turnover) and (3) a long-term relationship established between buyer and seller (Jackson, 1985). These characteristics all fit quite well with the concept of the 'domesticated market' (Arndt, 1979). In this type of market 'transactions are planned and administered, instead of being conducted on an ad hoc basis' (p. 70). Marketing is viewed from this perspective as an ongoing exchange relationship. Exchange is no longer studied as if it were a time-series of independent, discrete transactions. Buyer–seller relationships are seen to extend far beyond the short time horizon of discrete, small-scale transactions. Relational exchange marketing is almost inevitable in industrial markets, especially in the large world-wide market for international turnkey projects and systems, ranging from the turnkey brewery to the ready-made airport. These contracts are international by nature since the contractor (or contracting consortium of companies) and the owner belong to different nationalities. Turnkey operations may even be seen as a continuous sales process when the owner is planning expansion or a new project, subject to the performance achieved by the contractor in the present project. Trust is then an asset of prime importance in that it enables negotiation partners to overcome short-term conflicts of interest, personal confrontations or even communication misunderstandings (Dwyer *et al.*, 1987). This holds true for the negotiation phase itself, that is, before the signing of the contract(s), as well as for the negotiation process during the implementation phase. Different national/cultural backgrounds are then the source of communication problems and possible misunderstandings.

In relational marketing switching from one supplier to another incurs high transaction costs. This may be contrasted with discrete-transactions marketing, the case traditionally considered in marketing, which applies mainly to consumer goods and is characterized by (1) oligopolistic markets, where a few vendors face a multitude of buyers, and (2) standardized obligations, which are often embedded in a unilateral contract where price cannot be challenged by the buyer. Each transaction in relational marketing may be viewed as having its own history as well as encompassing its future, in as far as it may be anticipated by each partner (Macneil, 1980). Future collaboration (new orders, future common ventures, an extension or revamping of the actual plant, etc.), as well as the conditions, atmosphere and end results of the actual co-operation, are dependent on the assumptions each partner makes about the *trustworthiness* of the other party.

One may easily argue that relational marketing is applicable far beyond the domain of industrial and equipment goods. The negotiations of consumer goods companies with their foreign agents, licensees and distributors for making agreements belong to relational marketing. For instance, some of the relations between the Coca-Cola Company and its foreign dealers, or Procter & Gamble and its advertising agencies, have been established for several decades. Even with the individual consumer, discrete transaction marketing is not the only type of possible relationship: one may form a more personalized relationship with individual consumers by establishing contact with them on a more personal basis through distributors and their employees, in order to build long-term consumer loyalty, which is for instance largely the goal of the Japanese *Keiretsu* distribution system.

Development stages in the process of relational exchange

There are five main phases in the development of a relational exchange (Scanzoni, 1979): (1) awareness; (2) exploration; (3) expansion; (4) commitment; and (5) dissolution. The practical interest of Scanzoni's model is its validity across cultures. It breaks down the exchange relationship into phases, where trust always appears as the 'central asset'. The first phase – awareness – deals with the recognition of the other party as a feasible partner for exchange. Short distances, whether cultural, geographic or linguistic, facilitate this process. It is easier to trade with 'local buyers' than with 'distant merchants'. The intercultural situation renders this phase more difficult: many deals fail at this level; for instance, if they receive a letter written by a non-native speaker in poor English, most native English speakers will fear further communication difficulties and decide to abandon the project as early as possible, before real costs have been incurred. Case A13.4 (Supreme Canning) illustrates such a failure in the awareness phase.

In the second phase – exploration – the exchange relation begins. It remains a tenuous one. Partners are exploring the potential benefits and costs of an exchange. Several means are possible: trial purchase, installing a prototype plant, lending a machine or offering a technical visit to an existing plant. Five subprocesses are at work in exploration: attraction, communication and bargaining, power and justice, norm development and expectations development. Most of these subprocesses are subject to a certain cultural variance. For instance, bargaining attitudes, functions and rites vary according to cultures (section 11.2). Moreover the development of common norms is more easily attained if potential partners in the exchange belong to the same cultural background. During the expansion phase partners reap the benefits of their relationship and simultaneously become increasingly interdependent. The subprocesses of the preceding phase are still at work during the expansion. If each party has a strong positive perception of the other party's performance, the motivation to maintain and increase the exchange relationship is strong. This in turn reduces the probability that parties are looking for alternative partners, because of a lack of confidence in the future of the present exchange relationship ('unfaithfulness').

Such a process of exploration took place in the case of Euro-Disney [now called Disneyland Paris], between the Disney Corporation and its European partners. Initially the decision was made to transfer the basic successful Disneyland recipe to France – the same amusements, themes and policy guidelines, including the no-alcohol policy. However, while the project was under way, from 1986 to 1992, strong criticism from some French media called Euro-Disney *'un Tchernobyl culturel'* (a cultural Chernobyl), invoking the risk of cultural invasion, while other parts of the French population were in favour of Euro-Disney. Progressively the park has been Europeanized, emphasizing European characters such as Pinocchio (Italian), Cinderella (French) and Peter Pan (British), as well as European history.

Signing one or more contracts is not a necessary step for the commitment phase. The parties exchange implicit or explicit signs (either written or oral) of their willingness to continue their exchange relationship. One of these signs may be the allocation by both partners of large resources to the joint venture, starting a pilot plant or sharing personnel.

Dissolution is a possibility at any moment of the exchange relationship. It rests on an internal evaluation made by each partner of the costs of discontinuing the exchange. If these costs outweigh the benefits, the partners may negotiate a dissolution. These costs are difficult to estimate. The potential benefits of a new exchange relationship are also fairly uncertain and difficult to forecast. Breaking off is a complex process, often related to a crisis initiated by one of the partners. If the other party is willing to enter this separation ritual, dissolution becomes feasible. This 'divorce' is the counterpart of the relational marriage. Ohmae (1989, p. 148) gives a lively example of a dissolution of a joint venture between a US firm (N.O. in Box 16.1) and its Japanese partner (the soon-to-be former partner, F.P., in Box 16.1)

BOX 16.1

Intercultural discord

(Soon to be) New Owner: You guys never make decisions in time.

(Soon-to-be) Former Partner: Speedy decisions are not everything. Consensus is more important.

N.O.:   Well, just tell the dealers that our products are the best in the world. Tell them that they sell everywhere except here.

F.P.:   But the dealers complain that your products are just okay, not great. Even worse, they are not really tailored to the needs or aesthetic preferences of local customers.

N.O.:   Nonsense. What customers buy, everywhere in the world, is the physical performance of the product. No one matches us in performance.

F.P.:   Perhaps. Still the dealers report that your products are not neatly packaged and often have scratches on the surface.

N.O.:   But that has no effect on performance.

F.P.:   Tell that to the dealers. They say they cannot readily see – or sell – the performance difference you're talking about, so they have to fall back on aesthetics, where your products are weak. We will have to reduce the price.

N.O.:   Don't you dare. We succeeded in the United States and in Europe by keeping our prices at 5% above those of our competitors. If we're having trouble in Japan it's because of you. Your obvious lack of effort, knowledge, even confidence in our products – that's what keeps them from selling. Besides, your parent keeps on sending our joint venture group a bunch of bumbling old incompetents for managers. We rarely get the good people. Maybe the idea is to kill off our relationship entirely so they can start up a unit of their own making imitation products.

F.P.:   Well, if you feel that way, there is not much point in our continuing on together.

N.O.:   Glad you said that. We'll buy up the other 50% of the equity and go it on our own.

F.P.:   Good luck. By the way, how many Japanese-speaking managers do you have in your company – that is, after we pull out all the 'bumbling old incompetents' from our joint venture?

N.O.:   None. But don't worry. We'll just hire a bunch of headhunters and get started up in record time.

(Source: Ohmae, 1989, p. 148. Reproduced with permission.)

16.2   THE INFLUENCE OF CULTURE ON MARKETING NEGOTIATIONS

Culture and negotiation examined in the academic literature

The influence of culture on international business negotiations has often been studied using a comparative and cross-cultural setting (Graham, 1985; Graham, 1996) based on a dyadic simulated negotiation[2] (Kelley, 1966) where nationality is a proxy and summary variable for culture. Each nationality's negotiation style is described, on the basis of the contrast between different national groups observed in the simulated negotiation. Caution is necessary in directly transposing data on the behaviour or negotiation strategies of people from a particular country, collected during intracultural negotiations (with their compatriots). For instance, when Italians negotiate together, or with the French, they may not adopt exactly the same behaviour and strategies as they do when negotiating with Americans. Adler and Graham (1989) address the issue of whether these simple international comparisons are fallacies, when and if researchers are trying to describe cross-cultural interactions accurately. They demonstrate that negotiators tend to adapt their behaviour in intercultural negotiation and do not behave completely as predicted from observations in intracultural settings. They show, for instance, that French-speaking Canadians are more problem-solving oriented when negotiating with English-speaking Canadians than they normally are between themselves. Therefore their behaviour as observed in intracultural negotiations can only serve as a partial basis for the prediction of their style and strategies when negotiating with people belonging to different cultures. Hence the word 'intercultural' in this text directly relates to the study of interaction between people with different cultural backgrounds. The word 'cross-cultural' relates to a research design that is generally comparative.

General influence of culture on business negotiations

Culture mostly has an indirect influence on the outcome of negotiations (see for instance the models of McCall and Warrington, 1990 and Graham and Sano, 1990). It works through two basic groups of mediating variables: (1) the situational aspects of the negotiation (time and time pressure, power and exercise of power, number of participants, location, etc.) and (2) the characteristics of the negotiators (especially personality variables and cultural variables). These two groups of factors in turn influence the negotiation process, which ultimately determines the outcome. However, it is my contention that culture also has an influence on the outcome orientation: certain cultures are more deal/contract oriented whereas others favour relationship development. A review of the impact of culture on international business negotiations is given in Table 16.1. It indicates where in other chapters, especially Chapters 2 and 3, these topics are treated at more length.

An intercultural approach to building trust in international business negotiations

Trust is the mediating variable in the influence of culture on the process of international business negotiations. Relevant issues for building trust in international business negotiations are as follows:

TABLE 16.1   The impact of cultural differences on international marketing negotiations

Cultural difference	Impact on negotiations
(1) Behavioural predispositions of the parties	
Concept of the self and others	Impact on credibility in the awareness and exploration phases (Table 3.1 (b) and (c))
Interpersonal orientation	Individualism versus collectivism/Relationship versus deal orientation
Ingroup orientation	Similarity/'Limited good' concept/(Table 2.2 (a) and (b))
Power orientation	Power distance/Roles in negotiation teams/Negotiators' leeway
Willingness to take risks	Uncertainty avoidance /Degree of self-reliance of negotiators (Table 3.2 (d))
(2) Underlying concept of negotiation/Negotiation strategies	
Distributive strategy	Related to ingroup orientation/Power distance/Individualism/Strong past orientation
Integrative strategy	Related to problem-solving approach and future orientation
Role of the negotiator	Buyer's and seller's respective positions of strength (section 15.2)
Strategic time frame	Continuous versus discontinuous/Temporal orientations (Table 2.1 (c) and (d))
(3) Negotiation process	
Agenda setting/Scheduling the negotiation process	Linear-separable time/Economicity of time/Monochronism/ Negotiating globally versus negotiating clauses (Table 2.1 (a), (b) and (c))
Existence of a common rationality between the partners	Ideologism versus pragmatism/Intellectual styles/Wishful thinking/(Table 3.5 (b), (c) and (d))
Communication	Communication styles (Chapter 13)/Degree of formality and informality
Negotiation tactics	Type and frequency of tactics/Mix of business with affectivity
(4) Outcome orientation	
Partnership as outcome	Making a new ingroup – marriage
Deal/Contract as outcome	Rules between the parties (Table 3.5 (g))/Legal systems
Profit as outcome	Accounting profit orientation (economicity)
Winning over the other party	Distributive orientation
Time line of negotiation	Continuous versus discontinuous/There is no real time line to negotiation

1. How partners use their own cultural codes, as people and as representatives of organizations, to rate each other's credibility.

2. Their respective preference for the adoption of a 'problem-solving' orientation, embedded in an integrative and collaborative rather than a distributive/ competitive strategy.

3. How cultural patterns of time affect negotiation phases, scheduling, plans and deadlines.

4. The partners' approaches to formulating problems, identifying relevant issues and alternative solutions, and the extent to which this 'common rationality' is shared by both parties.

5. Differences in communication style and in the degree of formality/informality during the negotiation process.

6. The type of negotiation tactics used and the extent to which certain tactics can be misinterpreted and damage trust.

7. The basis for trust, whether is it oral ('my word is my bond') or written (only what has been laid down on paper and signed is viewed as binding).

8. The attitudes towards possible litigation; some cultures are litigation oriented as a result of the 'get-it-in-writing' mentality.

9. Differences in business ethics concerning illegal payments (see sections 15.6 and 15.7).

16.3   BEHAVIOURAL PREDISPOSITIONS OF THE PARTIES

Who is seen as a credible partner?

The issue of credibility has already been examined several times in this text. It is a key one in international marketing, and it depends on which personal attributes in a particular culture provide an individual with credibility for certain tasks and interactions (see section 3.1). Triandis (1983, p. 147) has emphasized three dimensions of the self-concept which may have a strong influence on the coding/decoding process of credibility: (1) self-esteem – the extent to which people think of themselves as very good or not too good; (2) perceived potency – the extent to which people view themselves as powerful, able to accomplish almost any task; and (3) perceived activity – the person sees the self as a doer, an active shaper of the world.

Since people generally live in homogeneous cultural settings (i.e. countries or regions within countries with one language, a dominant religion and shared values) they use the same cultural codes. When people do not share the same codes there may be problems in assessing their partner's credibility/trustworthiness. For example, the emitter (the decoder) may consider as a credible person somebody who shows a low self-concept profile (modest, patiently listening to partners, speaking little and cautiously, etc.); if, conversely, the receiver (the decoder) considers as a credible person somebody with a high self-concept profile (showing self-confidence, speaking arrogantly, not paying much attention to what the other is saying, etc.), there will be a credibility misunderstanding.

One of the main reasons for the seriousness of the Cuban missile crisis at the beginning of the 1960s was a misinterpretation by the Soviet leader Khrushchev of the credibility of the American president, John F. Kennedy. Kennedy and Khrushchev had held talks in Vienna, after the unsuccessful attack by US soldiers resulting in defeat at the Bay of Pigs. During their meeting, the young President Kennedy recognized that this attack had been a military and political mistake, which he regretted. Khrushchev saw this confession of error as a testimony of Kennedy's frank naivety and lack of character. He therefore inferred that it was possible to gain advantage by installing nuclear missiles in Cuba, which would have been targeted at the United States. This led the world to the brink of nuclear war between the superpowers. The events which followed showed that Khrushchev had been wrong in evaluating Kennedy's credibility. Ultimately, Kennedy showed great firmness and negotiating skill.

Khrushchev's mistake may be explained by differences in the cultural coding of credibility. Whereas in the United States, reaching a high position while still young is positively perceived, Soviet people associate age with the ability to carry responsibilities. Moreover, the admission of a mistake or a misjudgement is also positively perceived in the United States. US ethics value frankness and honesty. It is further believed that individuals may improve their behaviour and decisions by taking into account the lessons of experience. On the other hand, in the Soviet Union, to admit errors was rare. It generally implied the very weak position of people subjected to the enforced confessions of the Stalinist trials.

Signs of credibility

Personal credibility is decoded through the filter of numerous physical traits, but these are not often considered as they seem to be only appearances or because we tend to use these reference points unconsciously. The credibility signs clearly have a symbolic dimension: the associative links between personal characteristics and credibility are, in part, fixed arbitrarily by culture. Being tall may, for instance, be perceived as a sign of strength and character. Stoutness may be considered a positive sign for a partner in societies where starvation is still a recent memory. Where malnutrition is a reality for a section of the population, it is better to be fat, that is, well nourished and therefore rich and powerful-looking. Naturally these signs have a relative value: weight, height, age and sex cannot be considered as adequate criteria for selecting negotiators. Furthermore, negotiators may in fact be partly aware of or even share the cultural code of their partner. Each of these basic signs plays a role in the initial building of a credibility profile: age, sex, height, stoutness, face, tone and strength of the voice, accent and fluency in a particular language, self-esteem, perceived potency, perceived activity, etc. This profile only influences credibility in early contacts, that is, in the awareness and exploration phases.

Collective credibility: Relating personal trustworthiness to institutional credentials

Collective (company and ingroup) credibility is complementary to personal credibility. There are objective elements which permit assessment of the credibility of the firm, such as its balance sheet, annual reports, reference lists, technical specifications and all those elements that allow assessment of the financial and technical quality of a potential partner. Data and information increase the objectivity of the exchange relationship, but are not enough. For instance the Japanese, like many Europeans, do not emphasize financial performance measured by profits or dividends as a sign of company credibility as strongly as the Americans do. The Japanese and Europeans tend to place more emphasis on turnover, the company's connection with the government, its social reputation and its history.

As emphasized in the previous chapter, finding the appropriate level to establish contact may be an important issue. In societies where decision making is decentralized, it may sometimes be better to contact the people who have the required authority for making decisions, even though they may be at intermediate hierarchical levels (small power distance). In more centralized societies credibility is established on both sides by the top decision-makers meeting. Where committee decision making is the rule, the firm's credibility must be developed by contacts with many people, since it is often impossible to identify who is the ultimate individual decision maker. There may be no such person. US and European companies often believe that they have lost a deal negotiated with the Japanese because they do not receive a 'yes' for weeks or sometimes months. During this time, the *ringi* process has been at work in the Japanese company. Proposals are circulated among everyone involved in the deal, so that they can discuss it and ultimately affix their own seal of approval. Since (objective) credibility is based on power and decision making, a capacity to understand the influence process in the other party's decision making is therefore a key asset for effective negotiation.

In any national environment there are always some institutions which enable potential partners in joint ventures to assess each other as credible (business schools, engineering schools or law schools, professional associations and meetings, clubs, etc.). Laton McCartney (1989), for instance, describes 'The Grove', an annual three-day encampment, organized by the Bohemian Club of San Francisco, which has played a significant role in the growth of the Bechtel empire, the world leader in turnkey operations for many years:

But the real business of The Grove, where a favorite pastime was figuring out the corporate connections and interlocking directorates of incoming members, was just that: business. Not business by contract or by deal – both of which were barred on The Grove's grounds – but business by sheer association, by men spending time with, getting to know and like each other. 'Once you've spent three days with someone in an informal situation,' explained John D. Ehrlichman, who attended Grove encampments while a chief aide to Richard Nixon, 'you have a relationship – a relationship that opens doors and makes it easier to pick up the phone. (McCartney, 1989, p. 14.)

Interpersonal orientation

The reproach made to western business people by the Japanese, quoted in the introduction of this chapter, illustrates differences in interpersonal orientation. The concept of *Ningensei* (Box 16.2) presented at the beginning of this chapter has to do with the Confucian ethics which favour smooth interactions and the underplaying of conflict to the benefit of social harmony; it is typical of collectivist values of interpersonal relationships. For instance, the interpersonal sensitivity of Japanese people and their sincere interest in foreign cultures and people may make them friendly hosts at business lunches or dinners. As pointed out by Hawrysh and Zaichkowsky (1990, p. 42): 'Before entering serious negotiations, Japanese business-men will spend considerable time and money entertaining foreign negotiating teams, in order to get to know their negotiating partners and establish with them a rapport built on friendship and trust.' But it should never be forgotten that Japanese negotiators remain down to earth: they are strongly aware of what their basic interests are.

BOX 16.2

The Confucian logic in *Ningensei*

Ningensei exemplifies four interrelated principles of Confucian philosophy: *jen*, *shu*, *i* and *li*.

1. Based on active listening, *jen* is a form of humanism that translates into empathetic interaction and caring for the feelings of negotiating associates, and seeking out the other's views, sentiments and true intentions.

2. *Shu* emphasizes the importance of reciprocity in establishing human relationships and the cultivation of 'like-heartedness'; in Matsumoto's (1988) words it is 'belly communication', a means of coding messages within negotiating, social and corporate channels that is highly contingent upon affective, intuitive and non-verbal channels.

3. The dimension *i*, also termed *amae*, is concerned with the welfare of the collectivity, directing human relationships to the betterment of the common good. 'The *i* component of *ningensei* surfaces in Japanese negotiators' commitment to the organization, group agendas, and a reciprocity (*shu*) and humanism (*jen*) that is long-term, consistent and looks beyond personal motivation.'

4. *Li* refers to the codes, corresponding to precise and formal manners, that facilitate the outer manifestation and social expression of *jen*, *shu* and *i*. The Japanese *meishi* ritual of exchanging business cards is typical of *li* coded etiquette.

(Source. Adapted from Goldman, 1994, pp. 32–3)

Ingroup orientation

Concern for the other party's outcome is not necessarily to be found equally across cultures. Cultures place a stronger or weaker emphasis on group membership (the other party is/is not a member of the 'ingroup') as a prerequisite for being considered a trustworthy partner. In cultures where there is a clear-cut distinction between the 'ingroup' and the 'outgroup' (according to age, sex, race or kinship criteria), people tend to perceive the interests of both groups as diametrically opposed. This is related to what has been called the concept of 'limited good' (Foster, 1965).

According to the concept of 'limited good', if something positive happens in favour of the outgroup, the wealth and well-being of the ingroup will be threatened. Such reactions are largely the outcome of culture-based collective subjectivity: they stem from the conservative idea that goods and riches are by their very nature restricted. If one yields to the other party even the tiniest concession, this will directly reduce what is left for the members of the ingroup. The concept of 'limited good' induces negotiators to adopt very territorial and distributive strategies. It is a view which clearly favours the idea of the zero sum game, where 'I will lose whatever you may win' and vice versa. In Mediterranean and Middle Eastern societies where the ingroup is highly valued (clan, tribe, extended family), the concept of 'limited good' is often to be found. It slows the adoption of a problem-solving orientation, since co-operative opportunities are simply difficult to envisage.

Power orientation

One must distinguish between the formal power orientation on the one hand and the real power/decision-making orientation on the other. The first has to do with demonstrating status and how this may enhance credibility, especially in high-perceived-potency societies. It relates to the kinds of meetings, societies, clubs, alumni organizations and so on that assemble potentially powerful people. Belonging to such circles gives an opportunity for socializing and getting to know each other. The simple fact of being there and a member of a certain *club* is the main credibility message. The signs of formal power orientation differ across cultures; they may range from education and titles (English public schools, French *Grandes Ecoles*, *Herr Doktor*, Ivy League alumni in the United States, Todai graduates in Japan, etc.) to belonging to a particular social class or caste as in India.

Real power orientation is a somewhat different issue. As evidenced by Box 15.2 ('The little man in rags and tatters'), there may be wide differences between formal and actual influence on the decision-making process. When making contacts, in a cross-cultural perspective, people should be aware that in different cultures: (1) status is shown in different ways; (2) influential persons are different and individual influence is exerted in different ways; and (3) the decision-making process differs.

Hofstede (1989), in an article about the cultural predictors of negotiation styles, hypothesizes that larger power distance will lead to a more centralized control and decision-making structure because key negotiations have to be concluded by the top authority. And in fact Fisher (1980) notes in the case of Mexico, a typically high-power-distance country (score of 81 on Hofstede's scale; see Table 3.3), that one finds relatively centralized decision making, based on individuals who have extended responsibility at the top of organization. They become frustrated when confronted by the Americans who tend to have several negotiators in charge of specific issues:

In another mismatch of the systems, the Americans find it hard to determine how much Mexican decision making authority goes with which designated authority. There, as in many of the more traditional systems, authority tends to reside somewhat more in the person than in the position, and an organization chart does little to tell the outsider just what leverage – *palanca* – the incumbent has. (Fisher, 1980, p. 29.)

Willingness to take risks

Harnett and Cummings (1980), using a risk-aversion scale ranging from 16 to 48, have shown Americans to be risk takers (31.9) in comparison to the Thais who are highly risk averse (38.2), with the Japanese (34.1) and the Europeans (around 35.7) being in the middle.[3] A high level of uncertainty avoidance is noted by Hofstede as being associated with a more bureaucratic functioning and a lower tendency for individuals to take risks. This may be a problem for business negotiators when they have received a mandate from top management. For instance, the bureaucratic orientation in ex-communist countries has imposed strong government control on industry. As a consequence, Chinese negotiators, for instance, tend not to be capable of individual decision making. Before any agreement is reached, official government approval must be sought by Chinese negotiators (Eiteman, 1990). The same has been noted in the case of Russian negotiators by Beliaev *et al.* (1985, p. 110): 'Throughout the process a series of ministries are involved . . . Such a process also limits the degree of risk taking that is possible . . . the American who does see it from (the Soviet) perspective may well interpret it as being slow, lacking in initiative and unproductive.' Tse *et al.* (1994) confirm this tendency in the case of Chinese executives, who tend to consult their superior significantly more than Canadian executives, who belong to a low-uncertainty-avoidance society.

16.4 UNDERLYING CONCEPTS OF NEGOTIATION AND NEGOTIATION STRATEGIES

Integrative orientation versus distributive orientation

In business negotiations the purchaser (or team of purchasers) and the vendor (or group of vendors) are mutually interdependent while their individual interests clash. The ability to choose an effective negotiation strategy largely explains the individual performance of each party on the one hand, and the joint outcome on the other. In pitting themselves against each other, the parties may develop opposing points of view towards the negotiation strategy they intend to adopt: distributive or integrative.

In the distributive strategy (or orientation), the negotiation process is seen as leading to the division of a fixed 'cake' which the parties feel they cannot enlarge even if they were willing to do so. This orientation is also termed 'competitive negotiation' or 'zero sum game'. It leads to a perception of negotiation as a war of positions – territorial in essence. These are negotiations of the 'win–lose' type: 'anything that isn't yours is mine' and vice versa. The negotiators hold attitudes and objectives that are quasi-conflictual: interdependence is minimized whereas adverseness is emphasized.

At the opposite end of the spectrum is the integrative orientation (Walton and McKersie, 1965). The central assumption is that the size of the 'cake' (the joint outcome of the negotiations) can be increased if the parties adopt a co-operative attitude. Negotiators may not be concerned purely with their own objectives, but may also be interested in the other party's aspirations and results, seeing them as almost equally important. The integrative orientation has been termed 'co-operative' or 'collaborative'. It results in negotiation being seen as an attempt to maximize the joint outcome. The division of this outcome between the parties is to a certain extent secondary or is at least perceived as an important but later issue. Here negotiation is a 'positive sum game', where the joint outcome is greater than zero.

In practice, effective negotiation combines distributive and integrative orientations simultaneously, or at different stages in the negotiation process (Pruitt, 1981). The 'dual concern model', presented in Table 16.2 (Pruitt, 1983), explains negotiation

TABLE 16.2   Dual concern model

	Concern for one's own outcomes	
Concern for the other party's outcomes	Low	High
High	Yielding	Integrative strategy
Low	Inaction	Contending

strategies according to two basic variables: concern for one's own outcome and concern for the other party's outcome. This leads to four possible strategies. According to this model, the ability to envisage the other party's outcome is a prerequisite for the adoption of an integrative strategy.

Factors favouring an integrative strategy

The adoption of an integrative strategy is facilitated by the following:

1. A higher level of aspirations on both sides: the negotiators want to reach a better outcome or are under pressure from their principals who have defined increased outcome objectives while still allowing them explicit autonomy and room for manoeuvre (Pruitt and Lewis, 1975).

2. The ability to envisage the future; this permits the discovery or 'invention' of new solutions, which enables both partners to overcome the problem of the fixed size of the 'territorial cake'.

3. The existence of 'perceived common ground' (Pruitt, 1983); if sufficiently wide, this overlap between the interests of the two parties allows new solutions to be explored.

If one seeks to develop relational marketing, an integrative negotiating strategy is required. The nature of transactions imposes it. Business is fairly continuous and sometimes stretches over several years, and therefore implies a very strong buyer–seller interdependence. The performance level depends largely on the extent and quality of the collaboration between the partners. In studying the styles of negotiation of industrial purchasers, Perdue *et al.* (1986) have found, on the basis of a sample of 195 industrial purchasers, that the majority of them saw themselves as adopting an integrative strategy towards vendors.

A problem-solving approach

The integrative orientation is directly linked to a problem-solving approach in negotiation (Pruitt, 1983). The problem-solving approach (PSA) can be defined as an overall negotiating behaviour that is co-operative, integrative and oriented towards the exchange of information (Campbell *et al.*, 1988). Fair communication and the exchange of information between negotiators are important. 'Problem solvers' exchange representative information, that is, honest and objective data. There is no desire to manipulate the partner, as in instrumental communication (Angelmar and Stern, 1978). Empirical studies (involving experimental negotiation stimulation) have shown that this orientation positively influences the common results of negotiation (Pruitt, 1983). Rubin and Carter (1990), for instance, demonstrate the general superiority of co-operative negotiation by developing a model whereby a new, more co-operative contract provides both the buyer and the seller with cost reduction, compared with a previous adversarial contract. There are, however, some conditions: the first is the availability of cost-related data, the second is the release of the data to the other party during negotiation. The sharing of data is obviously conditioned by culture, language and communication-related issues.

The very concept of PSA is based on culturally relative assumptions: the first one is that the *doing* orientation is very strong in PSA – to solve a problem is to *do* something – and quite often PSA is posited as the *task*-related part of negotiation. Second, it assumes that both partners are *fair*, an English word untranslatable in many languages – *fair play* is used as such in French, for instance; 'fair' means something like 'open and honest in communication and interaction', a value which is not shared by many other cultures, as shown in the next chapter on national negotiation styles. Third, PSA assumes a view of *reciprocity*, based on *quick* response to the other party's openings, on a give-and-take basis, where concessions on each side are precisely *measured* and balanced.

As noted by Graham *et al.* (1994), PSA appears to make sense for American negotiators, but this framework may not work in all cases when applied to foreign negotiators. Graham *et al.* (1994) developed an empirical comparison across ten countries/cultures (the United States, Anglophone Canada, Francophone Canada, Mexico, the United Kingdom, France, Germany, the former USSR, Taiwan, China, Korea), starting from three rival hypotheses: (1) the PSA framework is universal; (2) there exist variations within the PSA framework when applied to foreign groups; and (3) the PSA framework does not work at all when applied to non-US negotiators. They show that on average the model works 'differently', and a claim for universality cannot be made. If we think in terms of *ningensei*, it is easy to imagine how, on the one hand, negotiation can be seen universally as problems to be solved, and on the other hand, the ways and means of problem solving may differ: PSA favours task orientation whereas *ningensei* favours a sense of being on the 'same wavelength', that is, a relationship orientation.

Cultural dispositions to being integrative

Even though one may accept the increased effectiveness of integrative strategies, in as far as they aim to maximize the joint outcome, the problem of how this joint outcome is divided between the two sides remains a key issue. Three questions then merit consideration:

1. Do the parties tend to perceive negotiations as being easier, and do they tend to adopt an integrative orientation more readily, when they both share the same culture?

2. Do negotiators who originate from particular cultures tend towards an integrative or a distributive orientation? Furthermore, do negotiators who originate from cultures which favour a problem-solving orientation risk seeing their personal

results heavily diminished by a distributive partner who cynically exploits their 'goodwill'?

3. Do cultural differences and intercultural negotiation reduce the likelihood of an integrative strategy?

Greater difficulties in being integrative in an intercultural negotiation situation than in an intracultural negotiation situation

There is general agreement that the results of negotiation are less favourable when the negotiation is intercultural as opposed to intracultural, all other things being equal (Sawyer and Guetzkow, 1965; Ghauri and Usunier, 1996). Van Zandt (1970) suggests that negotiations between Americans and Japanese are six times as long and three times as difficult as those purely between Americans. This increases the costs of the transaction for American firms in Japan, owing to the relative inefficiency of communication. The subjective satisfaction of the negotiators (measured by a questionnaire) in their result tends to be lower for intercultural negotiation than for intracultural negotiation (Weitz, 1979; Graham, 1985).

Problem solving depends on a collaborative attitude which is easier with a partner from the same culture: similarity leads to more trust and an enhanced level of interpersonal attraction (Evans, 1963; Graham, 1985). It facilitates awareness and exploration between parties and leads to more co-operative behaviour in negotiation. As a result, each side considers communication from the other as more representative, that is, objective information with little or no manipulative influences. *Perceived* as well as *actual* similarity can influence the parties: if similarity is perceived, but not based on strictly objective indications (such as shared nationality, language or educational background), a dissymmetrical view of similarity may arise between the buyer and the seller. For instance, many business people in the Middle East have a good command of either English or French. Middle Eastern business people are often perceived by their American or European counterparts as being similar to themselves, whereas Middle Eastern negotiators know that their western counterparts are different.

The role adopted in negotiation, whether buyer or seller, combines with perceived similarity: if sellers perceive a greater similarity, this can lead to a stronger problem-solving orientation on their part. Although appealing, similarity-based hypotheses have been poorly validated by the empirical study carried out by Campbell *et al.* (1988). No significant relationship was found among American and British buyer/seller pairs: similarity did not favour problem-solving orientation. In the case of the French and the Germans, the perceived similarity only led to a stronger problem-solving orientation on the part of the seller. However, in Campbell *et al.* (1988), the actual dissimilarity between negotiators was strongly reduced by the fact that all the simulated negotiations were intracultural.

As noted above, in intercultural encounters, misunderstandings may arise from perceptions of similarity which are not shared by both parties, such as a negotiation where the seller (e.g. American, for instance) perceives the buyer as similar (e.g. a westernized Arab buyer) while the reverse is not true: the Arab buyer is perfectly aware that the American seller knows very little about Arabic culture. The seller will adopt a problem-solving approach because of a fallacious perceived similarity, whereas the buyer may exploit the seller without feeling obliged to reciprocate and may ultimately maximize his personal outcome by adopting a covert distributive strategy. However, the *dynamics of similarity* (showing to the other side that one understands them and thus laying the foundation for an integrative attitude on both sides) can work in the other direction, and *adaptation* can bring a positive result. Harris and Moran (1987, p. 472) cite the case of a US banker from the midwest invited by an Arab sheikh to a meeting in London. The banker demonstrates unusual patience and deep awareness of the other party's power:

The banker arrives in London and waits to meet the sheikh. After two days he is told to fly to Riyadh in Saudi Arabia, which he does. He waits. After three days in Riyadh, he meets the sheikh and the beginning of what was to become a very beneficial business relationship between the two persons and their organizations began.

National orientations favouring the integrative strategy

The second question concerns the adoption of integrative strategies by some nationalities more than others. Studies tend to show that American business people show trust more willingly and more spontaneously than other cultural groups and have a stronger tendency towards a problem-solving and integrative orientation (Druckman *et al.*, 1976; Harnett and Cummings, 1980). The level of their profits as sellers depends on the buyer's responding positively by also adopting a problem-solving approach (Campbell *et al.*, 1988).

American negotiators have a stronger tendency to exchange representative communication, making clear and explicit messages a priority, and to exhibit less suspicion towards the other party, than most other cultures (Harnett and Cummings, 1980). This is in line with the American appreciation of frankness and directness and their low-context communication style (see section 13.1) which Graham and Herberger (1983) call the 'John Wayne Style' (Box 16.3). They often encounter certain difficulties in cultures where people take more time in the preliminaries: getting to know each other, that is, talking generally and only actually getting down to business later. As a result, Americans may not foster feelings of trust in negotiators from other cultural groups who feel it necessary to get to know the person they are dealing with (Hall, 1976).

Graham and Meissner (1986) have shown in a study comparing five countries that the most integrative strategies are adopted by the Brazilians, followed by the Japanese. On the other hand the Americans, the Germans and the Koreans choose intermediate strategies that are more distributive. This is consistent in the case of the Germans who are reputed for using the hard-sell approach, where the seller is fairly pushy and adopts an instrumental communication and a distributive strategy (Campbell *et al.*, 1988).

There is no empirical study that has shown, for example, that the Arabs from the Middle East have a tendency to be more distributive than the Americans. Americans tend to see the world as problems to be solved whereas Arabs see it more as a creation of God. The concept of integrative strategy, like the problem-solving approach discussed above, is strongly culturally influenced by the American tradition of experimental research in social psychology applied to commercial negotiation. It is based on a 'master of destiny' orientation which feeds attitudes of problem resolution. This presupposes a simultaneous concern for one's own outcome as well as for that of the negotiating partner (the 'dual concern model').

BOX 16.3

The 'John Wayne Style': Just call me John

Americans, more than any other national group, value informality and equality in human relations. The emphasis on first names is only the beginning. We go out of our way to make our clients feel comfortable by playing down status distinctions such as titles and by eliminating 'unnecessary' formalities such as lengthy introductions. All too often, however, we succeed only in making ourselves feel comfortable while our clients become uneasy or even annoyed. For example, in Japanese society interpersonal relationships are vertical; in almost all two-person relationships a difference in status exists. The basis for such distinction may be one or several factors: age, sex, university attended, position in an organization, and even one's particular firm or company . . . Each Japanese is very much aware of his or her own position relative to others with whom he or she deals . . . The roles of the higher status position and the lower status position are quite different, even to the extent that Japanese use different words to express the same idea depending on which person makes the statement. For example a buyer would say *otaku* (your company), while a seller would say *on sha* (your great company). Status relations dictate not only what is said but also how it is said.

(Source: Graham and Herberger, 1983, p. 162. Reproduced with permission.)

Ignorance of the other party's culture as an obstacle to the implementation of an integrative strategy in negotiation

One of the most important obstacles to effective international business negotiation is ignorance of all or at least the basic elements of the other party's culture. This barrier should be obvious, but is often forgotten by international negotiators. It refers not only to cognitive ignorance of the main features of the other party's culture, but also to the unconscious prejudice that differences are minor (that is, ignorance as absence of awareness). This favours the natural tendency to refer implicitly to one's own cultural norms, especially for the coding/decoding process of communication.

Lucian Pye (1986), in the case of business negotiations between American and Chinese people, and Rosalie Tung (1984a, 1984b) in relation to US–Japanese business negotiations, note the American negotiators' lack of prior knowledge of their partner's culture. Before they come to the negotiation table, Americans do not generally read books, nor do they train themselves for the foreign communication style, nor do they learn about the potential traps which could lead to misunderstandings. As Carlos Fuentes states (in a rather harsh aphorism): 'What the U.S. does best is understand itself. What it does worst is understand others' (Fuentes, 1986). French negotiators also tend to be underprepared in terms of cultural knowledge (see Chapter 17 on national negotiation styles), whereas the Japanese seemingly try to learn a lot more than the French or the Americans about the other party's culture before negotiation takes place.

The negotiation and implementation of many international ventures often imply ongoing negotiations that may last for several years. In this case, national cultures tend to disappear as the two teams partly merge their values and behaviour in a common 'venture culture'. In order to improve intercultural negotiation effectiveness, it is advisable to build this common culture between the partners/adversaries right from the start of the negotiation process. Adaptation should, however, be done cautiously: it does not mean wholesale adoption of strategies that work for natives, and the advice 'when in Rome do as the Romans do' has to be applied with due caution (Francis, 1991). It means rather establishing common rules and communication codes, and finding people on each side who will act as go-betweens. Parties should also try to agree on a common interpretation of basic issues, facts and solutions and on a joint decision-making process. This process is largely informal and built on implicit communication. Furthermore, it relies heavily on those individuals who have been involved in the joint venture over a long period of time and who get on well together. A core group of people is to be maintained on both sides over the necessary period of time in order to preserve the shared understanding.

16.5   TIME-BASED MISUNDERSTANDINGS IN INTERNATIONAL MARKETING NEGOTIATIONS

When reading this section, the reader should have in mind the time-related cultural differences presented in section 2.2.

A continuous versus a discontinuous view of time

Cultures which have a cyclical and integrative view of time will tend to have an underlying concept of negotiation whereby it is only one round in a recurrent relational process, with little sequencing, as compared with people holding a linear/separable view of time. This differentiation is also to be found in the outcome orientation where the time line of negotiation is less important for people with a cyclical/integrative view of time: for them the fact that a contract has been signed is no real reason not to pursue the negotiation process. The *strategic time frame* also depends on temporal orientations: the lack of future orientation, for instance, may be a serious impediment to the genuine involvement of a party.

Time for preliminaries

The importance of spending time for establishing personal relationships, especially in Asia and South America, has been noted by many authors (Hall, 1983, Pye, 1986; Graham and Sano, 1990, Hawrysh and Zaichkowski, 1990). There are a number of reasons for needing a personal relationship: (1) establishing the context of communication (Hall, 1976), acquaintance with the other persons being part of the necessary context; (2) a less strict separation between personal and professional spheres than in the West; and (3) the importance of personal status: this necessitates spending time in exploring (discreetly) who is who in order to avoid offending partners. This is all summed up in Burt's comments (1984, p. 7) that an American negotiator will be well advised to develop personal relations away from the negotiation room. 'The usual intense and rather dry approach to doing business must be supplemented with a social relationship. The Japanese are accustomed to the use of entertainment as a means of becoming better acquainted and of developing goodwill.'

The cultural time concept of Americans, strongly economic, partly explains why spending time in building personal relations is implicitly seen as bad. Time being seen as a resource not to be wasted, spending time on non-business matters, non-task related issues, is experienced as a violation of their cultural norms. What Adler *et al.* (1987) call 'non-task sounding', that is, establishing rapport and getting to know each other, the first phase in the process of business negotiations, not only needs a relaxed sense of economic time but also some past orientation. The Japanese, for instance, feel that an understanding of their past is necessary in order to understand them as negotiation partners today; thus it will make sense to spend time visiting Japanese shrines or learning the basics about *Zen* or *Ikebana*, the Japanese floral art.

Setting the agenda *and* scheduling the negotiation process

Most negotiation literature considers setting the agenda and scheduling the negotiation process as necessary tasks for the second step in Graham's four-stage model: the task-related exchange of information. An agenda is a schedule and list of items to be discussed during the negotiation process. In many cultures the very notion of 'agenda setting' is unheard of: cutting the process into pieces in advance and allocating time lots to each 'task' is at best theoretical. Hall's (1983) differentiation between monochronic and polychronic use of time (see section 2.2) is highly relevant for the scheduling of negotiation. An agenda-oriented negotiation team, basically monochronic, tends to try to negotiate clauses sequentially, whereas the other party, polychronic, may skip from one issue to another, coming back to points which had apparently been already settled, because they tend to negotiate globally. Graham and Herberger (1983) call it 'One thing at a time': Americans usually attack a complex negotiation task sequentially, that is they separate the issues and try to settle them one at a time.

Managing temporal clashes in intercultural business negotiations

Depending on the aim of a joint venture, partners from different cultures may be working together to develop a low-cost operation, or a new R & D project, or distribution and sales facilities. In such settings, issues to do with time will inevitably arise, both at an everyday level, simply in order to meet at the same time, and at a deeper level, that of assigning a common time frame to business operations.

Different time perspectives, be they organizational or cultural, result in temporal clashes. The conflicts that result from the inability to merge different ways of dealing with time may be located at an individual level, that of business people interacting with foreign partners and negotiating with them. Temporal clash at the level of individual interaction results from differing answers given to the following questions: How is somebody treated when he or she arrives half an hour late for a negotiation session? Do sessions have a finishing time in addition to their starting time? Is time also structured during the meeting by setting an agenda and a definite time limit for discussion on each point?

To illustrate the synchronization problem in negotiation, let us take the example of a French meeting versus a US one (a fairly polychronic versus a fairly monochronic culture; see section 2.2). In France some people arrive quarter of an hour late, and some half an hour late. Not only does the meeting not start on time, but those people who were on time have to wait for those who are late. Rarely do people who are late present apologies. Some, not all, simply explain why they are late. It is not unusual, when somebody arrives quite late, for most other people to halt their discussion and spend five or ten minutes explaining to the latecomer what has been said so far! Moreover, unlike US meetings, French meetings are almost never assigned a finishing time. This means that quite often, if there are several successive meetings, the reason why some people arrive late is that the previous meeting finished one or two hours after the (more or less vaguely and implicitly) agreed-upon finishing time.

Time-based tactical moves: Exerting time pressures in the bargaining process

Pressure can be exerted on economic-time minded negotiators by postponing the beginning of the negotiation, delaying meetings, concealing from them the time for concluding the negotiation, etc. Cohen (1980, p. 94) gives a classical example of how the Japanese manipulate their western partner's excessive time consciousness. When he arrives at Tokyo airport the Japanese ask him:

'Are you concerned about getting back to your plane on time?' (Up to that moment I had not been concerned.) 'We can schedule this limousine to transport you back to the airport.' I thought to myself, 'how considerate.' Reaching into my pocket, I handed them my return flight ticket, so the limousine would know when to get me. I didn't realize it then, but they knew my deadline, whereas I didn't know theirs.

The place where the negotiation takes place has an obvious influence on time-scarcity. Those who are 'at home' can monitor their regular business tasks while also participating in the negotiations. Those who have left their home country to negotiate at their partner's location can be for many reasons, both professional and personal, impatient to go home. The pressure of 'wasted time' can be used to take advantage of negotiators who have an economic pattern of time and are far from their home base.

The expression 'to waste time' has little meaning for many cultures, including the Bantus whose time patterns were described in reading A2.4. One may lose something tangible, like a ring or a pencil. But in order to waste and lose time, time should be a thing or – at least – it would be necessary to be able to separate time from the events with which it is inextricably bound up. Indeed the Bantus find it difficult to equate abstract time with a monetary unit of measurement. As outlined previously, within their culture Bantu people know nothing comparable to a linear Newtonian time, where events take place. There are events, and each one of these events carries its own desire and its own time. Time cannot be wasted or lost, because time has simply to be lived or experienced, whatever may be the way to experience it. No one can steal time, not even death.

The same quietness in the face of time may be seen in the Orient, in constrast to the Western anguish and guilt about time that might be wasted or lost. Several authors in the field of international business negotiations note that time pressure is strongly felt by American negotiators, whether they negotiate with the Chinese (Pye, 1982) or with the Japanese (Graham, 1981; Graham and Sano, 1990; Tung, 1984a, 1984b). American negotiators are eventually forced to yield because they view time as wasted or lost if not optimally allocated. When pushed to its extreme this logic may result in total inefficiency. People spend their whole time thinking of alternative uses for their time and assessing which alternative offers the best marginal return. As noted by Adler (1986, p. 162):

Americans' sense of urgency disadvantages them with respect to less hurried bargaining partners. Negotiators from other countries recognize Americans' time consciousness, achievement orientation, and impatience. They know that Americans will make concessions close to their deadline (time consciousness) in order to get a signed contract (achievement orientation).

Making plans together: Co-ordinating and planning the common venture

In many international negotiations planning a common venture, the various stages – the steps in the construction of a turnkey plant, or the implementation phases of a joint-venture or licence agreement – need explicit reference to dates, deadlines and the sequencing of interdependent tasks, in other words, planning. Planning is such a basic function of management that it is extremely difficult to admit that there are other models of time than those on which it implicitly stands. Naturally it would be naive to consider that business people have purely traditional time patterns. In fact, complex patterns of time-related behaviour may be used by people who share several cultural backgrounds, both the original in-depth background, and other more superficial backgrounds. Furthermore the native cultural background may be undervalued because it is supposed to be 'inefficient' or it is unknown to foreigners. Accordingly, people belonging to non-linear/economic time cultures often tend to imitate the cultural way of life that they tend to favour as the 'best' way. It might result in buying a superb watch as an item of jewellery or a diary because it is fashionable. But the functional behaviour which is in line with the watch or the diary will not be adopted. After these objects have been bought, they lose their cultural value as practical tools of the economic, monochronic, linear or separable time pattern. People involved in such cultural borrowing might prove unable to take any appointment seriously and probably experience difficulties in following any preset schedule.

The fallacy of imported economic time: Ideal and actual temporal behaviour

Ideal patterns of time and actual temporal behaviour may differ widely for negotiators who apparently use their partners' time culture rather than their own. Bista (1990), in the case of Nepal, highlights the conflict between time-based behaviour related to foreign education and the traditional influence of fatalistic beliefs on the lack of future orientation and sense of planning:

Planning involves the detailing of the connections between resources, objects and events, and the determination of an efficient course of action to attain desired results . . . Control is placed in the hands of the planner. But fatalism does not allow this kind of control, and is inherently antithetical to pragmatic thought . . . Over the past few decades, many Nepali students have travelled abroad to study in other countries, and have returned with advanced degrees in various professional capacities . . . Upon their return many are placed in positions of authority, as they represent the cream of Nepal's manpower resources. Though they may be initially inspired by a high degree of idealism, the new values that they bring back with them immediately confront fatalism and are typically defeated by it . . . After forty years of planning and an accumulation of foreign trained graduates, Nepal, then, still has little manpower to effectively bridge the disparities between the culture of the foreign aid donors and that of their own. (1990, pp. 137–8.)

In many countries, there is much cultural borrowing in relation to time management, that is, appointments, scheduling and meetings: the actual patterns of time management in industrialized countries such as the United States or northern Europe have been imported by other nations as ideal patterns (Usunier, 1990). In Latin-European countries, the PERT technique, which is designed for the scheduling of inter-related tasks, has been implemented mostly for its intellectual appeal. PERT, which is based on graph theory and looks for the 'critical path' in a set of tasks, has an appealing US 'management science' look. In France, where many managers and top executives have been trained as engineers, there has been great interest in this scientific management technique. However, actual project planning in France and Latin-European countries often works with high discrepancies relative to PERT dates: French people tend to be intellectually monochronic but actually behave in a polychronic manner (Hall, 1983).

Sometimes people even use two completely different time-management systems in parallel. This somewhat schizophrenic situation is most easily recognized when one looks at the construction of some turnkey projects in developing countries. At first, during the negotiation process and on signature of the contract, everybody genuinely agrees about using an economic-time/monochronic pattern. In fact the partners share the same beliefs as to what 'appropriate' time management should be and do not discuss the matter. This is, however, an ideal view on one side and actual behaviour on the other, and extreme confusion occurs when the project is being implemented.

16.6 CULTURAL MISUNDERSTANDINGS DURING THE NEGOTIATION PROCESS

Existence of a common rationality between the partners

As explained in section 3.4 people differ in their way of relating thinking to action: whereas ideologists tend to think broadly and relate to general principles, the pragmatist orientation values focusing on detailed issues that are to be solved one by one. Typical of pragmatists are the Americans, as noted by Weiss (1987, p. 31), in the case of the GM–Toyota negotiations for their joint venture in California: 'the Japanese tended to start talks with statements of general principle and usually did not respond to proposals before checking with their headquarters. The Americans preferred specific proposals and responses at the table.'

When negotiating a large contract (for a nuclear plant or a television satellite, for instance), ideologists see arguments that favour their 'global way of thinking': it is a unitary production, it is a complex multi-partner business, it often involves government financing and also has far-reaching social, economic and political consequences. Pragmatists, on the other hand, see many arguments that favour their way of thinking: the technicalities of the plant and its desired performance require an achievement and deadline orientation (pragmatist values).

Pragmatism is associated with a tendency to look at the details of facts, to measure, to validate empirically. Ideologists on the other hand have a liking for speech, words and ideas. They will be more oriented towards instrumental communication. Inasmuch as they aim to manipulate other people, ideologists may be as effective as pragmatists, since they may influence their counterparts through nicely worded general communications. In relational marketing, especially in the first two phases of the relational exchange, negotiation between ideologists and pragmatists may create misunderstandings (see Box 16.4) which will be difficult to overcome during subsequent phases.

Indeed, developing common norms will be fairly difficult, although necessary, if partners want to be able to predict the other party's behaviour. A frequent comment in such situations will be: 'One never knows what these people have in mind; their behaviour is largely unpredictable.' An American (pragmatist oriented) describes negotiations with the French (more ideologist oriented) in the following terms (Burt, 1984, p. 6): 'The French are extremely difficult to negotiate with. Often they will not accept facts, no matter how convincing they may be.'

BOX 16.4

Cartesian logic in negotiation

Rather imprecisely defined, the idea is that one reasons from a starting point based on what is known, and then pays careful attention to the logical way in which one point leads to the next, and finally reaches a conclusion regarding the issue at hand. The French also assign greater priority than Americans do to establishing the principles on which the reasoning process should be based. Once this reasoning process is under way, it becomes relatively difficult to introduce new evidence or facts, most especially during a negotiation. Hence the appearance of French inflexibility, and the need to introduce new information and considerations early in the game. All this reflects the tradition of French education and becomes the status mark of the educated person. In an earlier era observers made such sweeping generalizations as: 'The French always place a school of thought, a formula, convention, a priori arguments, abstraction, and artificiality above reality; they prefer clarity to truth, words to things, rhetoric to science . . .' [Quotation from Zeldin, 1977].

(Source: Fisher, 1980, p. 50. Reproduced with the kind permission of the publisher.)

Communication

Most of the content of Chapter 13 applies directly to the process of international marketing negotiations. For instance, the role of high context versus low context is to be noted. When messages are exchanged, the degree to which they should be interpreted has to be taken into account. For instance, silence is a form of communication for the Japanese, and Graham (1985) reports twice as many silences in Japanese interaction as in American. Westerners often have the impression that they 'do all the talking'. In fact, being open to different styles of communication is a key negotiation skill. This is especially true for non-verbal communication. For instance a lack of eye contact for the Americans is a signal that something is amiss and 'American executives reported that the lack of eye contact was not only disconcerting but reduced their bargaining performance [with Japanese]' (Hawrysh and Zaichkowsky, 1990, p. 34).

Negotiators must be ready to hear true as well as false information, discourse based on facts as well as on wishful thinking or pure obedience to superiors. Frankness and sincerity are relative values: they can be interpreted as mere naivety, a lack of realism or a lack of self-control in speaking our one's own mind. Furthermore, waiting for reciprocation when one has disclosed information useful for the other party makes little sense in an intercultural context. Frankness and directness are positive values for the Americans and to a lesser extent for the French, but they are not so for Mexicans in formal encounters, nor for the Japanese at any time (Fisher, 1980).

The issue of formality versus informality is a difficult one. Frequently a contrast is made between cultures that are supposed to value informality (e.g. American) and those that would be more formal (most cultures which have long historical roots and high power distance). 'Informality' may be simply another kind of formalism and the 'ice breaking' at the beginning of any typical US meeting between unknown people is generally an expected ritual. It is more important to understand the degree of formality required in particular circumstances. Away from formal negotiation sessions, people belonging to apparently quite formal cultures can become much more informal. Formalism in communication sometimes takes the form of diplomatic language, a highly coded type of speech, sometimes apparently quite remote from actual reality, known in French as *langue de bois* (literally 'wooden tongue' or 'wood language'). George Orwell, in *Animal Farm*, gives a good example of *langue de bois* concerning the pig Napoleon who had taken control of the farm and imposed its power on other animals.

Napoleon was now never spoken of simply as 'Napoleon'. He was always referred to in formal style as 'our Leader, Comrade Napoleon', and the pigs liked to invent for him such titles as Father of All Animals, Terror of Mankind, Protector of the Sheepfold, Ducklings' Friend, and the like. In his speeches Squealer would talk with the tears rolling down his cheeks of Napoleon's wisdom, the goodness of his heart, and the deep love he bore to all animals everywhere, even and especially the unhappy animals who still lived in ignorance and slavery on other farms. It had become usual to give Napoleon the credit for every successful achievement and every stroke of good fortune. You would often hear one hen remark to another, 'Under the guidance of our Leader, Comrade Napoleon, I have laid five eggs in six days'; or two cows, enjoying a drink at the pool would exclaim, 'Thanks to the leadership of Comrade Napoleon, how excellent this water tastes!' (1945, p. 62.)

Langue de bois, although a very non-American concept given the emphasis on direct, frank and honest speech in US culture, is practised in many organizations world-wide, either in relation to powerful people or groups, or concerning taboo issues; for instance, a previous failure with a foreign partner that would shed some useful light on actual negotiations.

Negotiation tactics

Graham (1993) has studied the negotiation tactics used in eight cultures, using video-taped negotiations where statements were classified into 12 categories using the framework of Angelmar and Stern (1978). His results show very similar negotiation tactics across cultures: most use a majority of tactics based on an exchange of information, either by self-disclosure or by means of asking questions (more than 50 per cent in all cases). The Chinese score the highest on posing questions, an outcome which is consistent with Pye's comments about them: 'Once negotiation begins the Chinese seem passive. They simply ask questions, probe for information, and conceal any eagerness they may feel' (1986, p. 78). On the other hand, the Spaniards are the best at making promises. The proportion of 'negative' tactics, including threats, warnings, punishments and negative normative appeals (statements in which the source indicates that the target's behaviour is in violation of social norms) is fairly low in all cases, never exceeding 10 per cent of the information exchange. Finally, cross-national differences are not great as concerns the type of tactics used or their frequency but rather at the level of how they are implemented.

   The use of theatricality, threats of withdrawal and tactics based on time, such as waiting until the last moment to obtain further concessions by making new demands, are based in national styles of negotiations, discussed in the next chapter. Tactics are also related to the ambiguous atmosphere of business negotiations where implied warm human relations are supposed to be mixed with business. This relates to the divide between affective and neutral cultures (Trompenaars, 1993) presented at the end of section 3.5. Negotiations are always interspersed with friendship and enmity, based on personal as well as cultural reasons.

16.7   DIFFERENCES IN OUTCOME ORIENTATION: ORAL VERSUS WRITTEN AGREEMENTS AS A BASIS FOR TRUST BETWEEN THE PARTIES

It would be naive to believe that profits, especially future accounting profits for each party, are the only possible outcome of the negotiation process. Others include: relationship building, personal satisfaction and alliances for future ventures. One reason that profits are not the sole possible outcome is that they are not fully foreseeable. However, since profits are often considered the sole motive, the negotiation partners are unaware of basic differences in outcome orientation. This can generate increased misunderstandings since many cultures are more relationship than deal oriented, as Weiss (1987) and Hawrysh and Zaichkowski (1990) point out in the case of the Japanese, and Pye (1986) and Eiteman (1990) in the case of the Chinese. People from these cultures prefer the outcome of the negotiation process to be a gentleman's agreement, a loosely worded statement expressing mutual co-operation and trust between

the parties, rather than a formal western-style contract which embodies expected profits in words, numbers and clauses.

Opportunism, misunderstandings and the perceived degree of agreement

It is generally considered that agreements are mostly in writing. They are achieved by
negotiation and by the signing of a written contract, which is often termed 'the law
of the parties'. This is unfortunately not always true. Keegan (1984) points out that in
some cultures 'my word is my bond' and trust is a personal matter, which he contrasts
with the 'get-it-in-writing' mentality where trust is more impersonal. The former
would be typical of the Middle East, whereas the latter would be found in the United
States where hundreds of thousands of lawyers help people negotiate written agreements and litigate within the framework of these written agreements.

This does not mean, however, that people rely *entirely* on either an oral base or a
written base. The main problem in making agreement work is to avoid opportunistic
behaviour on one side which would exploit the other side, or, even worse, opportunism on both sides. Keeping one's word can be achieved by the taking of oaths and
the existence of confidence between people who belong to a common group where
perjury is considered a crime. Within the boundaries of such an ingroup-oriented business community, the indelicate merchant is punished by being outlawed as a potential partner.[4] But this works well only within the ingroup and on a personal basis. That
is why, in an international setting where business people belong to different cultural
communities, such 'words' cannot be considered as reliable enough for committing
oneself. Written agreements, that is, formal contracts, offer a different avenue for
avoiding opportunistic behaviour; they are more precise and more impersonal, both
low-context and outgroup oriented. They offer predictability because details of each
party's obligations and rights have been discussed and put on paper. The impersonal
mediation of a third party, a national court or ICC arbitration guarantees that disputes
between the business partners will be examined on the basis of proven evidence and
contradictory arguments. Provided that a party's behaviour can be observed (i.e.
opportunistic behaviour cannot be hidden) and verified (proofs of breach of contract
can be brought), the court can oblige the infringing party to conform to a contract or
to pay compensation. Generally, litigation serves only as a threat: even in the USA
only a very small proportion of lawyers in large law firms are involved in litigation
(about 10 per cent).

Therefore, exploring, maintaining and checking the bases for trust is a complex
process. An agreement may be non-symmetrical, such as when party A perceives that
it agrees with B, but B does not agree with A; either B conceals the disagreement or
there is some sort of misunderstanding, usually language based. People may agree in
broad terms but hold different views of 'executional details' and may not perceive
their divergence, which may relate to different interpretations of clauses or of a tacit
part of the agreement. Although much may be written down, some aspects of the
agreement will remain unwritten and will seem, to one party but not the other, obviously in line with a written clause. If the parties do not find an opportunity to confront their interpretations, they will not be aware of such differences of opinion. A last
caveat is that the agreement may not be understood by both parties as implying the

same kind of commitment, the same stability over time of the exchange relationship; the parties may also be unaware that they do not share the same views of how precisely clauses should be interpreted in the future, whether broadly or to the letter.

Written documents as a basis for mutual trust between the parties

There is a fundamental dialectic in written agreements between distrust and confidence. At the beginning there is *distrust*. It is implicitly assumed that such distrust is natural. This has to be reduced in order to establish *confidence*. Trust is not achieved on a global and personal basis but only by breaking down potential distrust in concrete situations where it may hamper common action. Trust is built step by step, with a view towards the future and *real trust* is achieved only gradually. Trust is deprived of its personal aspects and, thanks to the written agreement, the parties may trust each other in business, although they do not trust each other as people. Trust is taken to its highest point when the parties sign a written agreement.

On the other hand, cultures that favour oral agreements tend not to hypothesize that trust is constructed by the negotiation process. They see trust more as a prerequisite to the negotiation of written agreements. Naturally they do not expect this prerequisite to be met in every case. Trust tends to be mostly personal and ingroup based. Establishing trust requires that people know each other. That is probably why many Far Eastern cultures (Chinese (Pye, 1982); Japanese (Graham and Sano, 1990; Tung, 1984; de Mente, 1987)) need to make informal contacts, discuss general topics and spend time together before they get to the point, even though all this may not appear task related.

Subsequently, the negotiation process will be lengthy because another dialectic is at work. Since people are supposed to trust each other, the negotiation process should not damage or destroy the basic asset of their exchange relationship – trust. They will avoid direct confrontation on a specific clause, and therefore globalize the negotiation process. Global friends may be local foes, provided trust is not lost as the basic asset of the negotiation process.

The ambiguity of the cultural status of written materials as a basis for building trust between the parties

That one should always 'get it in writing' is not self evident. The contrary idea may even emerge ('if they want it written down, it means that they don't trust me'). Regina Traoré Sérié (1986, quoted in Ollivier and de Maricourt, 1990, p. 145) explains, for instance, the respective roles of oral communication (spoken, transmitted through personal and concrete communication, passed from one generation to another by storytellers) and written materials (read, industrially printed, impersonally transmitted, with no concrete communication) in African culture.

Reading is an individual act, which does not easily incorporate itself into African culture. Written documents are presented as either irrelevant to everyday social practices, or as an anti-social practice. This is because someone who reads, is also isolating himself, which is resented by the other members of the community. But at the same time, people find books attractive, because they are the symbol of access to a certain kind of power. By reading, people appropriate foreign culture, they get to know 'the paper of the whites'. As a consequence, reading is coded as a positive activity in the collective ideal of Ivory Coast society, since it is a synonym for social success. This contradiction between 'alien' and 'fetish' written documents encapsulates the ambiguity of the status of books in African society.

Does writing produce irreversible commitments?

In cultures where relationships are very personalized, confidence cannot be separated from the person in whom it is placed. The basis for mutual trust is no longer the detailed written contractual documents, but a man's word which is his bond. It is not 'just any word', but a special kind of word, which is heavily imbued with cultural codes (Hall, 1976). These words as bonds cannot easily be transferred from one culture to another. Adler (1980) describes the case of an Egyptian executive who, after entertaining his Canadian guest, offered him a joint partnership in a business venture. The Canadian was very keen to enter this venture with the Egyptian businessman. He therefore suggested that they meet again the next morning with their respective lawyers to fill in the details. The Egyptians never arrived. The Canadian businessman wondered whether this was caused by the lack of punctuality of the Egyptians, or by the Egyptian expecting a counteroffer, or even the absence of lawyers available in Cairo:

None of these explanations was true, although the Canadian executive suggested all of them. At issue was the perceived meaning of inviting lawyers. The Canadian saw the lawyer's presence as facilitating the successful completion of the negotiation; the Egyptian interpreted it as signalling the Canadian's mistrust of his verbal commitment. Canadians often use the impersonal formality of a lawyer's services to finalize an agreement. Egyptians more frequently depend on a personal relationship developed between bargaining partners for the same purposes. (Adler, 1980, p. 178.)

If agreements are mostly person based, then their written base may be less important. Thus the demand by a Middle Eastern buyer for renegotiation of clauses, in a contract already negotiated and signed, should not be seen as astonishing. It should not necessarily lead to litigation. Behind the demand for renegotiation is the assumption that, if people really trust each other, they should go much further than simple and literal implementation of their written agreements. This leads to the following question: to what extent should the contract signature date be considered a time line which signals the end of the negotiation?

Written agreements as a time line for negotiations

As noted above, there are two different ways to look at the influence of the written agreement on the time line of the exchange relationship. Those favouring written-based building of trust tend to see a written agreement as the key point in the exchange relationship. It completes a phase during which potential relations have been carefully discussed and explored. It establishes a strict contractual code, which has then to be implemented quite literally. Written words, sentences, numbers and formulas have to be strictly observed. If a party feels free to depart from what has been written down, the Damocles sword of litigation will hang over the parties – and nobody likes litigation, supposedly.

Those favouring oral-based personal trust consider the signing of a written agreement an important step, but only one of many in a continuous negotiation process. The negotiation process was active before signature and will be active afterwards. A continuous negotiation process, where the contract is only one step, not the major step, is seen as the best basis for maintaining trust. As Edward Hall (1960, p. 94) stated:

Americans consider that negotiations have more or less ceased when the contract is signed. With the Greeks, on the other hand, the contract is seen as a sort of way station on the route to negotiation, that will cease only when the work is completed. The contract is nothing more than a charter for serious negotiations. In the Arab world, once a man's word is given in a particular kind of way, it is just as binding as, if not more so than, most of our written contracts. The written contract therefore violates the Moslem's sensitivities and reflects on his honour. Unfortunately, the situation is now so hopelessly confused that neither system can be counted on to prevail consistently.

Different attitudes towards litigation

It is easy to understand that the function of litigation will be different for both sides. Recourse to litigation will be fairly easy for those favouring written-based agreements as the ultimate means of resolving breaches of contract. The oral and personal tradition is less litigation prone because of its drawbacks: (1) it breaks the implicit assumption of trust, and (2) it breaches the required state of social harmony, especially in the Far Eastern countries, and may therefore be quite threatening for the community as a whole. As David (1987, p. 89, my translation) states:

. . . in Far Eastern countries, as well as in Black Africa and Madagascar . . . subject to the westernization process which has been attempted, one does not find, as in Hinduism or Islam, a body of legal rules whose influence may be weakened by the recognized influence of other factors; it is the very notion of legal rules which is challenged. Despite authorities having sometimes established legal codes, it is well known and seems obvious that the prescriptions of these codes are not designed to be implemented literally. They should only be considered as simple patterns. The judge will be able to moderate their strictness and, moreover, it is hoped that this will not be necessary. The 'good judge', whether Chinese, Japanese or Vietnamese, is not concerned with making a good decision. The 'good judge' is the one who succeeds in not making any award, because he has been skilful enough to lead the opponents to reconciliation. Any dispute, as it is a threat to social harmony, has to be solved by a settlement through conciliation. The individual only has 'duties' towards the society. Recognition of 'subjective rights' in his favour is out of the question. Law as it is conceived in the West is seen as good for barbarians, and the occupation of lawyer, in the limited extent that it exists, is regarded with contempt by the society.

These remarks by a specialist in comparative law give a good idea of the differences in the tradition of litigation between the Far East and the West. The western saying, 'the contract is the law of the parties', dominates the practices of international trade but this is in part window-dressing. In international marketing, a set of written contracts is always signed. This is not to say that people choose either oral or written agreements as a basis for trust. The real question is rather: how should the mix of written and oral bases for trust, as they are perceived by the parties, be interpreted? People do not deal with the real world in exactly the same way. Negotiating together requires changing one's views of reality. Not only differences in rationality and mental programmes, but also differences in time representations, may lead to a partner 'who thinks differently' being considered a partner 'who thinks wrongly'.

The greatest caution is recommended when interpreting the bases of trust, whether written documents or oral and personal bonds. Even in the Anglo-Saxon world, where it is preferred to 'get it in writing', a number of business deals, sometimes large ones – in the area of finance, for instance – are based on a simple telex or fax, or a phone agreement between two key decision makers. It would be a mistake to believe that personal relationships do not exist in places where written contracts are generally required. Moreover, in cultures where 'my word is my bond', it should never be forgotten that it is difficult to trust outgroup people, regardless of whether the agreement is based on words or a contract. Trust has therefore to be established and monitored on both bases, while keeping in mind a clear awareness of the limits of each base.

QUESTIONS

1. Discuss the principal foundations of trust and their cultural variability.

2. What is the role of time pressure in international marketing negotiations? How can you take advantage of time in the negotiation process?

3. Explain how frankness and directness in marketing negotiations can be diversely interpreted.

4. Why is seeing negotiation as a set of problems to be solved culturally relative?

5. How can the adoption of an integrative strategy be hindered by cultural factors?

6. To what extent is a written and detailed contract the basis of an agreement?

7. Discuss the value of introducing lawyers in intercultural negotiations.

8. Your company has signed a contract for a 10,000-student turnkey university in Saudi Arabia. A number of its facilities are designed for science and engineering schools and the remaining parts of the buildings will be designed for arts. The construction has not yet started. The Saudis send a fax telling you that an additional facility, a 500-student business school, is now planned and it must be integrated in the construction due to start in two months. What do you do?

APPENDIX 16: TEACHING MATERIALS

A16.1   Case: McFarlane Instruments

An American firm, the McFarlane Instruments Company, had delivered approximately US$400,000 worth of instruments to a People's Republic of China government agency. The agency refused to pay for the instruments, so the US company contacted the American Embassy in Beijing for assistance. The American commercial attaché arranged a meeting between the PRC industrial ministry representatives, company representatives, and himself.

In the meeting, the government officials stated that they would not pay because the instruments did not conform to the guarantee of accuracy of plus or minus 0.2 per cent. The US firm found this to be very strange since they had not encountered accuracy problems with their instruments sold in other countries. They finally inquired as to the temperatures at which the tests had been conducted. The Chinese officials indicated that tests had been conducted at 10°C and at 50°C.

The American firm replied that international practice and standards called for such tests to be conducted at 25°C. The instruments were normally used at approximately room temperature. Because of differential expansion and contraction coefficients of the materials in the instruments, use under much lower or higher ambient temperatures resulted in different levels of precision and need for recalibration.

The Chinese officials then produced a copy of the company's brochure which stated the plus or minus 0.2 per cent precision, but did not specify the test temperature. After approximately one hour of discussion, which consisted mainly of each side reiterating its position, the US firm attempted to break the deadlock. While avoiding any admission that the instruments failed to conform to international standards, they agreed to reduce the price by 30 per cent 'in order to maintain good relations'. Their only other choice was to attempt to reclaim the machines, and then attempt to re-export them through potentially difficult Chinese customs administration to the United States or elsewhere. The Chinese officials requested that a written proposal be submitted. This was done and the offer was made valid for a period of sixty days.

Three months later the Chinese government organization rejected the proposal, stating again that the instruments did not meet the promised precision. The US firm, after several more attempts at reconciliation, gave up and took back the machines. They now faced the difficult task of obtaining permission to re-export them, and the additional cost of doing that and paying for shipping costs.

Subsequent investigation indicated that the real problem had not had anything to do with the instruments themselves. Between the time the original contract had been signed and when the instruments were delivered, the PRC currency had been devalued. The contract was written in US dollars, and the Chinese organization had been allocated a given amount of the PRC currency, the *renminbi*, to pay for it (through the appropriate foreign exchange agency). With the new exchange rate, the Chinese government organization did not have enough money to pay for the instruments. The discount offered by the American company had not been sufficient to make up for the difference in exchange rates. The Chinese found it easier to reject the instruments than to admit what had happened.

(Source: Adapted from Albaum *et al.*, 1989, pp. 388–9.)

QUESTIONS

1. How can you determine the real problems which impeded the negotiations? What are they, in your opinion?

2. Would you expect it to be easy to get appointments with Chinese government officials? Why or why not?

3. Would you expect it to be easy to obtain information from Chinese officials? Why or why not?

4. What important lesson for negotiations does this case illustrate? How would you have approached this problem?

A16.2 Negotiation game: Kumbele Power Plant

A consortium, BDH, has been established between a US-based engineering company, a French company belonging to the same sector and a German firm producing heavy industrial equipment. This consortium is in the final phase of negotiations to win a contract for building a turnkey electric power plant. The owner is the National Electricity Authority, a state-owned corporation which holds a monopoly on the transport and distribution of electricity in an English-speaking country in Africa. National Electricity Authority has issued the tender.

The tender procedure was initiated 18 months ago. At first there were about twenty potentially qualified contractors which submitted bids. Most of them were engineering companies originating from the main industrial countries, and some came from newly industrialized countries such as South Korea, Brazil and Turkey. After a preselection phase, the number of potential contractors was reduced to a short list of five companies or consortia. The final selection process lasted for several months, as bids that were technologically not comparable had to be taken into account.

The consortium created by Brown Engineering Corp. (US), Duponval SA (French) and Horst BauTechnik AG (German) was chosen as the organization with which the final negotiations would take place. But a Japanese competitor has also made a very attractive offer and is in a position to supplant BDH, if BDH should prove to be too demanding for National Electricity Authority. In fact BDH has a strong reference list, supported by similar plants it has built which are working effectively. Moreover, in addition to its offer, BDH provides a low-rate, long-term financing scheme for the buyer, which has been created by putting together export credits issued by public organizations from the countries of the three members of BDH: US Eximbank for Brown, BFCE (Banque Française du Commerce Extérieur) for Duponval and KfW (Kreditanstalt für Wiederaufbau) for Horst BauTechnik.

The final price has not yet been settled, as there are still some important clauses to be discussed:

1. The supply of basic materials by the consortium, during the start-up of the power plant.

2. The possibility of signing a 'products in hand' contract. A 'products in hand' contract is a particular kind of turnkey operation, where part of the payment by the owner to the contractor is subject to the level of performance reached by the plant. After the start-up phase has been finished and individual pieces of equipment have been shown to work effectively, a phase begins where the contractor is assigned to operations. This means that a management contract has been signed. The variable fee may cover part or all of the turnkey operations as such and/or the management contract. In this case the consortium would agree to sign a

management contract to run the operation until it reaches 100 per cent of its target capacity (400 megawatts).

The proposal which served as a starting base for the final bargaining process was priced at US$105 million. Each of the partners-to-be has naturally retained its right to improve its position, either by obtaining a rebate (the buyer) or by increasing this base price level by astutely negotiating supplementary services (the consortium).

Since the inception of this tender, National Electricity Authority has made it known that the first power plant will be followed by the construction of two similar plants, all this being stated in the ten-year plan for the electrification of the country. It seems very likely that the contractor selected to build the first unit, if effective, will be well positioned for the next two orders which may possibly be placed by direct agreement between contractor and owner, that is, without a competitive bidding procedure.

At the negotiating table are three representatives of the buying organization and three representatives of the BDH consortium, each one an employee of one of the companies:

1. For the buyer:

    (a) Mr Ozuwu, who is in charge of project financing for industrial development at the Ministry of Finance. He might be a useful and even necessary go-between for many red-tape problems related to administrative and financial issues which could arise when the project is under way: payments, clearing customs for imported equipment, fiscal and social problems of expatriates, etc.

    (b) Mr Kempele, who is the director in charge of energy at the Ministry of Industry. He is concerned with the co-ordination of this project with the other industrialization projects being undertaken in the country. There have been many negative experiences of poor co-ordination in recent years: two years ago, some ships with a full load of cement were stranded in the main sea port of the country because there was not enough unloading equipment such as docks and cranes. This caused severe delay on several projects.

    (c) Mr Bura, the third representative, is 38, much younger than both Ozuwu, who is about 50, and Kempele, who is 60. He has been trained in the United Kingdom and the United States and holds a Master of Science degree in Electrical Engineering. At National Electricity Authority he is in charge of new plants and investment projects. He is reputed to be ambitious but also capable and hard-headed. In the long run he is seen as a possible chief exec-utive for National Electricity Authority. Bura has confidence in the country's development projects and in the capacities of local managers to run the new plants effectively.

2. For the consortium:

    (a) Mr Smith, a project manager aged 42, who has worked for many years at Brown, the US member of the consortium. Brown will take charge of the boiler part and the plant monitoring system. Brown is ranked among the leading US engineering companies. It has a high reputation for technical excellence as well as for cost control. Project managers at Brown are partly compensated with a bonus based on the profit generated by the project. A sophisticated cost accounting system monitors actual and forecast costs and margins regularly during the project. After the completion of projects lasting two to three years or more, final costs are calculated, with a minimal deviation from target costs.

(b) Mr Robin from Duponval SA, a French engineer who has worked for this company for the last ten years. Duponval has already formed several joint ventures with Brown, and Robin knows Smith because they have already worked together. Duponval SA is in charge of civil engineering and the total co-ordination of the work. This firm has established a good reputation worldwide for meeting delivery times.

(c) Mr Dietermeyer, a Doctor of Law, aged 55, has worked for the last twenty years for Horst BauTechnik. Although he has not been formally trained in engineering, he has built up a good knowledge of industrial engineering on the job. In addition to this he has attended many training sessions which have provided him with an in-depth knowledge of the technologies of a large variety of turnkey plants. He is considered in his company a skilful, experienced and effective business negotiator. His law background is very useful in discussing precise clauses, understanding what is at stake and the possible legal consequences of a specific clause. Horst is in charge of supplying and installing turbo-alternators and all the electrical parts in the plant.

BDH consortium has been chosen as the contractor with which National Electricity Authority is willing to negotiate the final agreement under the supervision of the Ministry of Finance and the Ministry of Industry. A sum of US$105 million is the starting point for the discussion; until now it has been considered a lump sum for a turnkey operation contract. But things have not yet been fully settled.

The African team wishes to negotiate either a rebate on this price level, arguing that there will be future projects which could be awarded to BDH, or complementary services or guarantees, which could be granted at no cost. These might possibly be the following:

1. The free supply of materials required for production during the start-up phase, which will last one month.

2. Free technical assistance for the industrial management of the power plant, to ensure correct service to consumers and proper management of the electricity distribution network.

3. A commitment from BDH to subcontract part of the job locally, especially the less sophisticated part of the civil engineering work.

BDH naturally would prefer to maintain its price, for which it had been selected from harsh competition. In fact there were some cheaper competitors, whose bids were up to $15 million less. But neither their reference lists nor their financing deals matched BDH's bid.

BDH has one concern – the delay penalty clause which National Electricity Authority wants to include. The fine is supposed to be 1 per cent of the total price for each construction month beyond the agreed completion time. The consortium foresees that there could be some delay. It fears that it might be difficult to assign clear responsibilities to either the contractor or the owner (or the state authorities of the country, or a large subcontractor, especially if it was a local business). Usually turnkey contracts include a customs franchise for all the equipment imported in order to build the plant. But it is not particularly unusual for customs officers to fail to apply these rules immediately, thereby delaying customs clearance of components and equipment, and consequently delaying the completion of the plant.

The parties have agreed to discuss the issue of transforming this pure turnkey operation, paid for by a lump sum, into a 'products in hand' contract. Under this scheme, part of the payment will be subject to a variable scale related to the level of capacity reached during the management contract period after the plant has been completed and started up. The possibility of a management contract has been discussed. It will probably be added to the turnkey contract (which includes the construction start-up phase, but no more). This management contract will encompass handling the industrial management procedures, the accounting system, setting salaries, customer service and providing training programmes for local executives. Progressively, local management is supposed to take over the management of the project. The basis on which the variable payment would be calculated has not been clearly settled up to now. This basis could be: the whole amount of the management contract, part of it, or the whole amount of the management contract plus part of the $105 million turnkey project.

The African proposal for this final negotiation includes the following elements:

1. The price of the management contract plus US$10 million (on top of the turnkey price) to become a variable and conditional payment, subject to the capacity level reached within a certain time span. This scheme would extend throughout the total 36 months of the management contract period.

2. For this variable part the proposed payment scheme is as follows:
    (a) 15 per cent after 6 months if the output reaches at least 50 per cent of the target capacity;
    (b) 15 per cent after 12 months if the output reaches at least 60 per cent of the target capacity;
    (c) 15 per cent after 18 months if the output reaches at least 70 per cent of the target capacity;
    (d) 15 per cent after 24 months if the output reaches at least 80 per cent of the target capacity;
    (e) 20 per cent after 30 months if the output reaches at least 90 per cent of the target capacity;
    (f) 20 per cent after 36 months if the output reaches 100 per cent of the target capacity.

3. The management contract may grant decision-making powers to the consortium in the following matters: recruiting personnel (workers, not the management), operating the plant and choosing supplies of appropriate quality and price. The selling price of the output as well as the operating costs are to remain the sole responsibility of National Electricity Authority.

The negotiation takes place at the headquarters of National Electricity Authority in Port Kumbele, where the power plant will be built. The talks simply aim at finalizing an agreement for beginning the construction as soon as possible. No detailed agenda has been prepared for the negotiations.

Discussion begins . . .

Recommendations for playing the Kumbele Power Plant negotiation game

The objective is to simulate business negotiations for international turnkey operations.[5] It may be played in four half-days, preferably in half-day sessions, with some time between them. Participants should first discuss between themselves as a team in order to prepare their negotiation strategies and tactics. The discussion should be centred on the business negotiation. Participants should not discuss technical matters related to the plant: this is because first, the necessary information is not included in the text and, second, it is not meant to be an engineers' discussion.

The intercultural aspect may be adapted to suit the participants. The characters in the game may easily be changed to women.

This game may be played as a competitive game, where two teams compete for the contract with National Electricity Authority. One team representing BDH and one team representing the Japanese engineering company (let's call it Chikoda) will face the Kumbele team.

Participants should conduct research to obtain some information about selling turnkey projects and management services internationally. See for instance Brooke (1985).

NOTES

1. Fukuyama's book, *Trust*, develops the idea that trust, or social capital as a propensity of people to co-operate beyond the borders of their limited ingroup (i.e. family, clan) is a key determinant of a nation's economic success. Fukuyama contrasts high-trust societies (prototypes: Germany, Japan) with low-trust societies (prototypes: China, France, Italy, Korea). In high-trust societies, economic actors can develop larger organizations, especially multinational firms, because people dare to trust 'strangers', that is professional managers and owners of other companies with which they merge their own business. In low-trust societies, the state is often obliged to intervene in order to create the large organizations needed for international competitiveness since local businesses find it difficult to create such organizations because they tend not to trust non-family associates. There is much more in Fukuyama's book than can be mentioned in these few lines. Suffice it to say that, after heavy criticism due to the alleged lack of empirical support, Fukuyama's theses have been strikingly confirmed on a sample of 40 nations by La Porta *et al.* (1997).
2. Kelley's game is a face-to-face simulated negotiation where a seller and a buyer negotiate a deal based on three products. Both buyer and seller have a profit sheet which they are instructed not to exchange. The rules can be learnt quickly and this price-bargaining exercise lasts generally about half an hour. It allows measurement of a number of negotiation variables both in terms of outcomes (each player's profit and their joint profit; each negotiator's satisfaction based on post-exercise questions) and process (duration, tactics used and verbal exchanges are videotaped and coded afterwards).

3. Although the national differences do not appear very large, the authors note that 'the difference between the Spanish (33.4) and the Greek managers (35.6) is large enough so that it could be expected to occur by chance less than one time in fifty if there were no real differences between these managers' (Harnett and Cummngs, 1980, p. 22). Differences are statistically significant between the Americans and the Thais but not between the Japanese and the Europeans.

4. Greif (1994) gives a very good account of how different societies solve the issue of trust and opportunism in business relationships, especially in the case of international trade. His analysis, both historical and based on game theory, relies on the comparison between two trading communities in the Mediterranean area during the late medieval area, the Maghribi traders and the Genoese merchants. Both faced the same kind of business environment and traded in similar goods; but they employed different solutions to the problem of agent's opportunism in the agency–principal relationship. While the Maghribis, a collectivist society, traded within their ingroup network and used the threat of collective economic punishment to reduce opportunistic behaviour, the individualistic Genoese 'ceased to use the ancient custom of entering contracts by a handshake and developed an extensive legal system for registration and enforcement of contracts' (p. 937).

5. There is a detailed teaching note available in the instructor's manual, which also contains personal and team role instructions, a standard contract form and an evaluation sheet for the negotiators.

REFERENCES

Adler, Nancy, J. (1980), 'Cultural synergy: the management of cross-cultural organizations', in W. Warner Burke and Leonard D. Goodstein (eds), *Trends and Issues in OD: Current theory and practice*, University Associates: San Diego, CA, pp.163–84.

Adler, Nancy J. (1986), *International Dimensions of Organizational Behavior*, PWS-Kent: Boston.

Adler, Nancy J. and John L. Graham (1989), 'Cross-cultural comparison: The international comparison fallacy?', *Journal of International Business Studies*, vol. 20, no. 3, pp. 515–37.

Adler, Nancy J., John L. Graham, and Theodore Schwarz Gehrke (1987), 'Business negotiations in Canada, Mexico and the United States', *Journal of Business Research*, vol. 15, pp. 411–29.

Albaum, Gerald, Jesper Strandskov, Edwin Duerr and Laurence Dowd (1989), *International Marketing and Export Management*, Addison-Wesley: Wokingham.

Angelmar, Reinhardt, and Louis W. Stern (1978), 'Development of a content analysis scheme for analysis of bargaining communication in marketing', *Journal of Marketing Research*, vol. 15, February, pp. 93–102.

Arndt, Johan (1979), 'Toward a concept of domesticated markets', *Journal of Marketing*, vol. 43 (Fall), pp. 69–75.

Beliaev, Edward, Thomas Mullen and Betty Jane Punnett (1985), 'Understanding the cultural environment: U.S.–U.S.S.R. trade negotiations', *California Management Review*, vol. 27, no. 2, pp. 100–12.

Bista, Dor Bahadur (1990), *Fatalism and Development*, Orient Longman: Calcutta.

Brooke, Michael Z. (1985), *Selling Management Service Contracts in International Business*, Holt, Rinehart and Winston: London.

Burt, David N. (1984), 'The nuances of negotiating overseas', *Journal of Purchasing and Materials Management*, Winter, pp. 2–8.

Campbell, Nigel C. G., John L. Graham, Alain Jolibert and Hans Günther Meissner (1988), 'Marketing negotiations in France, Germany, the United Kingdom and United States', *Journal of Marketing*, vol. 52, April, pp. 49–62.

Cohen, Herb (1980), *You Can Negotiate Anything*, Bantam: New York.

David, René (1987), *Le Droit du commerce international, réflexions d'un comparatiste sur le droit international privé*, Economica: Paris.

De Mente, Boye (1987), *How to do Business with the Japanese*, N.T.C. Publishing: Chicago, IL.

Druckman, D., A. A. Benton, F. Ali, and J. S. Bagur (1976), 'Culture differences in bargaining behavior', *Journal of Conflict Resolution*, vol. 20, pp. 413–49.

Dwyer, Robert F., Paul H. Schurr and Sejo Oh (1987), 'Developing buyer–seller relationships', *Journal of Marketing*, vol. 51, April, pp. 11–27.

Eiteman, David K. (1990), 'American executives' perceptions of negotiating joint ventures with the People's Republic of China: Lessons learned', *Columbia Journal of World Business*, Winter, pp. 59–67.

Evans, Franklin B. (1963), 'Selling as a dyadic relationship: A new approach', *American Behavioral Scientist*, vol. 6, May, pp. 76–9.

Fisher, Glen (1980), *International Negotiation: A cross-cultural perspective*, Intercultural Press: Yarmouth, ME.

Foster, G. M. (1965), 'Peasant society and the image of limited good', *American Anthropologist*, vol. 67, pp. 293–315.

Francis, June P. (1991), 'When in Rome? The effects of cultural adaptation on intercultural business negotiations', *Journal of International Business Studies*, vol. 22, no. 3, pp. 403–28.

Fuentes, Carlos (1986), cited in 'To see ourselves as others see us', *Time*, 16 June, p. 52.

Fukuyama, Francis (1994), *Trust: The Social Virtues and the Creation of Prosperity*, New York: Free Press.

Ghauri, Pervez N. and J.-C. Usunier (1996), *International Business Negotiations*, Pergamon/Elsevier: Oxford.

Goldman, Alan (1994), The centrality of 'Ningensei' to Japanese negotiating and interpersonal relationships: implications for U.S.–Japanese communication,' *International Journal of Intercultural Relations*, vol 18, no. 1, pp. 29–54.

Graham, John L. (1981), 'A hidden cause of America's trade deficit with Japan', *Columbia Journal of World Business*, Fall, pp. 5–15.

Graham, John L. (1985), 'Cross-cultural marketing negotiations: A laboratory experiment', *Marketing Science*, vol. 4, no. 2, pp. 130–46.

Graham, John L. (1993), 'Business negotiations: Generalizations about Latin America and East Asia are dangerous', *UC Irvine Research*, pp. 6–23.

Graham, John L. (1996), 'Vis-a-vis International Business Negotiations', in P. N. Ghauri and J.-C. Usunier Eds., *International Business Negotiations*, Oxford: Pergamon/Elsevier, pp. 69–90.

Graham, John L. and Roy A. Herberger Jr (1983), 'Negotiators abroad: Don't shoot from the hip', *Harvard Business Review*, vol. 61, no. 4, pp. 160–68.

Graham, John L. and Hans G. Meissner (1986), 'Content analysis of business negotiations in five countries', Working Paper, University of Southern California.

Graham, John L. and Yoshihiro Sano (1990), *Smart Bargaining: Doing Business with the Japanese*, 2nd edn, Ballinger: Cambridge, MA.

Graham, John L., Alma T. Mintu, and Waymond Rodgers (1994), 'Explorations of negotiation behaviors in ten foreign cultures using a model developed in the United States, *Management Science*, vol. 40, no. 1, January, pp. 72–95.

Greif, Avner (1994), 'Cultural beliefs and the organization of society: A historical and theoretical reflection on collectivist and individualist societies ', *Journal of Political Economy*, vol. 102, no. 5, pp. 912–50.

Hall, Edward T. (1960), 'The silent language in overseas business', *Harvard Business Review*, May–June, pp. 87–96.

Hall, Edward T. (1976), *Beyond Culture*, Anchor Press/Doubleday: Garden City, NY.

Hall, Edward T. (1983), *The Dance of Life*, Anchor Press/Doubleday: Garden City, NY.

Harnett, Donald L. and L. L. Cummings (1980), *Bargaining Behavior: An international study*, Dame Publications: Houston, TX.

Harris, Philip R. and Robert T. Moran (1987), *Managing Cultural Differences*, 2nd edn, Gulf Publishing Company: Houston, TX.

Hawrysh, Bryan Mark and Judith Lynn Zaichkowsky (1990), 'Cultural approaches to negotiations: Understanding the Japanese', *International Marketing Review*, vol. 7, no. 2, pp. 28–42.

Hofstede, Geert (1989), 'Cultural predictors of national negotiation styles', in Frances Mautner-Markhof (ed.), *Processes of International Negotiations*, Westview Press: Boulder, pp. 193–201.

Jackson, Barbara B. (1985), *Winning and Keeping Industrial Customers: The dynamics of customer relationships*, D. C. Heath and Company: Lexington, MA.

Keegan, Warren J. (1984), *Multinational Marketing Management*, 3rd edn., Prentice Hall: Englewood Cliffs, NJ.

Kelley, Harold H. (1966), 'A classroom study of the dilemmas in interpersonal negotiations', in K. Archibald (ed.), *Strategic Interaction and Conflict*, Institute of International Studies, University of California: Berkeley, CA.

La Porta, Rafael, Florencio Lopez-de-Silanes, Andrei Shleifer and Robert W. Vishny (1997), 'Trust in large organizations', *American Economic Review*, vol. 87, no. 2, May, pp. 333–8.

McCall, J. B. and M. B. Warrington (1990), *Marketing By Agreement: A cross-cultural approach to business negotiations*, 2nd edn, John Wiley: Chichester.

McCartney, Laton (1989), *Friends in High Places: The Bechtel story*, Ballantine Books: New York.

Macneil, Ian R. (1980), *The New Social Contract: An inquiry into modern contractual relations*, Yale University Press: New Haven, CT.

Matsumoto, M. (1988), *The unspoken way: Haragei – silence in Japanese business and society*, Kodansha International: New York.

Ohmae, Kenichi (1989), 'The global logic of strategic alliances', *Harvard Business Review*, March–April, pp. 143–55.

Ollivier Alain and Renaud de Maricourt (1990), *Pratique du marketing en Afrique*, Edicef/Aupelf: Paris.

Orwell, George (1945), *Animal Farm*, Penguin: London.

Perdue, B. C., R. L. Day and R. E. Michaels (1986), 'Negotiation styles of industrial buyers', *Industrial Marketing Management*, vol. 15, no. 3, pp. 171–6.

Pruitt, Dean G. (1981), *Bargaining Behavior*, Academic Press: New York.

Pruitt, Dean G. (1983), 'Strategic choice in negotiation', *American Behavioral Scientist*, vol. 27, no. 2, pp. 167–94.

Pruitt, Dean G. and Steven A. Lewis (1975), 'Development of integrative solutions in bilateral negotiations', *Journal of Personality and Social Psychology*, vol. 31, no. 4, pp. 621–33.

Pye, Lucian (1982), *Chinese Commercial Negotiating Style*, Oelgeschlager, Gunn and Hain: Cambridge, MA.

Pye, Lucian (1986), 'The China trade: making the deal', *Harvard Business Review*, vol. 46, no. 4, pp. 74–84.

Rubin, Paul A. and J. R. Carter (1990), 'Joint optimality in buyer–seller negotiations', *Journal of Purchasing and Materials Management*, Spring, pp. 20–6.

Sakade, Florence, editor (1982), *A Guide to Reading and Writing Japanese*, Tokyo: Charles E. Tuttle.

Sawyer, J. and H. Guetzkow (1965), 'Bargaining and negotiation in international relations', in H. Kelman, (ed.), *International Behavior*, Holt, Rinehart and Winston: New York.

Scanzoni, J. (1979), 'Social exchange and behavioral interdependence', in R. L. Burgess and T. L. Huston (eds.), *Social Exchange in Developing Relationships*, Academic Press: New York.

Traoré Sérié, Régina (1986), 'La Promotion du livre en Côte d'Ivoire', Paper presented to the conference on 'Marketing and Development', Abidjan (Ivory Coast), December.

Triandis, Harry G. (1983), 'Dimensions of cultural variation as parameters of organizational theories', *International Studies of Management and Organization*, vol. 12, no. 4, pp. 139–69.

Trompenaars, Fons (1993), *Riding the Waves of Culture*, Nicholas Brealey: London.

Tse, David K., June Francis and Jan Walls (1994), 'Cultural differences in conducting intra- and inter-cultural negotiations: A Sino-Canadian perspective', *Journal of International Business Studies*, vol. 25, no. 3, pp. 537–55.

Tung, Rosalie L. (1984a), 'How to negotiate with the Japanese', *California Management Review*, vol. 26, no. 4, pp. 62–77.

Tung, Rosalie L. (1984b), *Business Negotiations with the Japanese*. Lexington Books: Lexington, MA.

Usunier, Jean-Claude (1990), 'Négociation commerciale des projets: une approche interculturelle', *Revue Française du Marketing*, nos 127–128, pp. 167–84.

Van Zandt, H. R. (1970), 'How to negotiate with the Japanese', *Harvard Business Review*, November–December, pp. 45–56.

Walton, Richard E. and Robert B. McKersie (1965), *A Behavioral Theory of Labor Negotiations*. McGraw-Hill: New York.

Weiss, Stephen E. (1987), 'Creating the GM-Toyota joint venture: A case in complex negotiation', *Columbia Journal of World Business*, vol. 22, no. 2, Summer, pp. 23–37.

Weitz, B. (1979), 'A critical review of personal selling research: the need for contingency approaches', in G. Albaum and G. A. Churchill Jr (eds.), *Critical Issues in Sales Management: State of the art and future needs*, University of Oregon: Eugene.

Zeldin, Theodore (1977), *France 1848–1945*, vol. 11, Oxford University Press: Oxford.

17 Intercultural marketing negotiations 2: Some elements of national styles of business negotiation

Identifying a set of strategic archetypes used by foreign negotiators may enhance one's negotiating power. For instance, Asians, driven by low self-esteem and perceived potency, may open a negotiation by dwelling on their company's vulnerability, small size and other alleged weaknesses, to swell westerners' confidence and induce them to ask less and yield more. In marketing negotiation the image of the other negotiating party is based on a collection of stereotypes, often meaningful, a portrait of their national culture. This exercise in mutual reflection has to be reciprocal and particular for each bilateral relationship. It is unlikely, for example, that Germans or Italians would have an identical perception of the French negotiation style. Similarly the view held by the Japanese of westerners, remarking their lack of *ningensei*, cannot be considered as simply inverse and complementary to the view held by US negotiators of their Japanese counterparts. US negotiators do not complain of the excessive *ningensei* orientation of their Japanese partners! Therefore a matrix would be necessary to effectively describe the negotiating style of a particular country as perceived by other nationalities: for example, the Italian style being defined in terms of how it is perceived by the Americans, the French, etc. However the use of multiple perspectives would be too complex. Because of the necessity to reduce complexity, it must be recognized that archetypes of negotiation styles are most often an average of what is seen through western eyes.

This chapter complements the previous one. It describes some elements of national or regional styles of business negotiation. At the risk of adopting what could be termed a western stereotyping classification, this chapter describes the salient traits of the following 'nationalities' (listed in alphabetical order): African, American, British, Chinese, French, German, Japanese, Mexican, Middle Eastern and Russian. Section 17.1 describes Oriental, section 17.2 western negotiation style, section 17.3 deals with other areas of the world, and the last section proposes recommendations for effective intercultural marketing negotiations.

17.1   ORIENTALS

Chinese style

One of the main experts on business negotiation with the Chinese, Lucian W. Pye (1982, 1986) lists the following factors, which combine to demonstrate that the Chinese are tactical, skilful and fairly tough negotiators:

1. 'As hosts, the Chinese take advantage of their control over the pace of negotiations. First they set the agenda, then they suggest that the Americans start the discussions . . . their proposals become the starting point from which all compromise follows' (Pye, 1986, p. 177).

2. The Chinese deliberately adopt a fairly passive attitude, taking care not to show enthusiasm, concealing any feeling of impatience, playing their game impassively so as to force their opponents to be the first to show their hand.

3. They do not shy away from appearing very manipulative: with a view to disconcerting the other side and in the ultimate hope of obtaining further concessions, they will attribute an exaggerated importance to minor details, which in reality are of no consequence to them, or return to discussion of points where full agreement seemed to have previously been reached.

4. The bureaucratic orientation of the PRC is often noted: socialism has imposed strong government control on industry. As a consequence, Chinese negotiators tend not to be capable of individual decision making. Before any agreement is reached, official government approval must be sought by Chinese negotiators (Eiteman, 1990).

5. Chinese business people tend to overrate the advantage offered by their large population in terms of market opportunities. However, per capita purchasing power remains quite low. The Chinese promote their country as being 'the last big market on the planet' but underestimate the opportunities offered to their foreign partners by other countries (Eiteman, 1990).

6. Like the Japanese, the Chinese are less economic-time minded and less short-term oriented than westerners. 'The Chinese use time shrewdly. If they sense that business people are in a hurry to leave China, they may slow down negotiations and turn the deadline to their advantage' (Pye, 1986, p. 78).

7. The Chinese networking system, *guanxi* (see section 15.2; Luo, 1995; Luo and Chen, 1997), needs to be taken into account, as the development and maintenance of appropriate connections is key to business and may help in negotiating beyond the negotiation table itself. As emphasized by Tung (1996), most of these relationships are based on a combination of blood (immediate and extended families), educational ties and geography, that is, common membership in the same clan or village. Ingroup orientation is strong and people from outgroupist cultures must regard the Chinese networking activities without prejudice.

8. Pye also notes the role played by differences of attitude relating to the concept of 'friendship'. Thus it seems that whereas the Americans view friendship in terms of

a feeling which rests on a natural mutual exchange, in other words on a principle of reciprocity, the Chinese view friendship in terms of loyalty. The idea is that of a long-lasting obligation:

> What the Chinese neglect in terms of reciprocity they more than match in loyalty. They not only keep their commitments, but they also assume that any positive relationship can be permanent. A good example of this is the number of Chinese who have tried to establish pre-1949 ties with U.S. companies and individuals – as though nothing had happened in the intervening days. (Pye, 1986, p. 79.)

Japanese style

Numerous books are devoted to consideration of the Japanese style of negotiation and more generally to the Japanese mentality and style of management. Several major traits can be distinguished:

1. The Japanese are well prepared, particularly from the point of view of familiarity with the culture of the people with whom they are dealing (Tung, 1984a). They are a highly ethnocentric people who are, paradoxically, at the same time very conscious of this ethnocentrism. They are also well prepared in terms of definition of their basic interests and are willing to struggle quite determinedly to defend them.

2. The purchaser's role is predominant. Vendors must be fully aware of this fact and adapt their behaviour accordingly (Graham, 1981).

3. Although at heart they are very sensitive and emotional, they seek to conceal their true emotions as far as possible (Burt, 1984; see also sections 3.5 and 13.2). Like all Asians they must not be made to 'lose face': in practice (at the very least) their foreign counterparts should avoid a style of communication that would be resented by the Japanese as being too direct.

4. Within a group of Japanese negotiators it is difficult to determine who really performs what function and who holds what power; it is always unwise to rely solely on 'who says what' as a clear indication of 'who holds power'.

5. Japanese negotiators display quite a high level of tolerance of ambiguity. Whereas ambiguity may be perceived by Americans as a sign of weakness and a lack of masculinity and assertiveness, the Japanese do not see ambivalent behaviour as contradictory to masculinity (Hawrysh and Zaichkowsky, 1990).

6. Japanese people are very long-term oriented. In large companies lifetime employment is the rule. These companies are often backed by large banks which, as shareholders, do not strive for a quick return. They are more concerned with the soundness of the long-term business strategy of the company to which they lend. This partly explains why Japanese negotiators do not feel as strongly pressured by time lines as do their western counterparts.

7. Like most Asians, the Japanese tend to prefer an agreement based on trust to a written contract. Even though this agreement may be loosely worded, in their view it is a better expression of the mutual trust that has developed between the parties (Oh, 1986).

8. The empathy of Japanese people may be very high: the interpersonal sensitivity of Japanese people and their sincere interest in foreign cultures and people may make them friendly hosts at business lunches or dinners. As noted earlier Japanese businessmen spend time and money entertaining their negotiating partners to establish with them a rapport built on trust. However, Japanese negotiators remain strongly aware of what their basic interests are. They are reputed to be tough negotiators.

Middle Eastern style (Arab-Islamic world)

If a 'Middle Eastern style' truly exists, the following caveat should be borne in mind. The countries considered here are almost exclusively Arab-Islamic countries, except for Iran which is Shiite Islam but not Arab, and Turkey which is Ottoman and Islamic but not Arab and has dominated the Arab world for centuries. Yet it would be a mistake to ignore the enormous diversity of the Middle East. Christian minorities (Lebanese Maronites, Egyptian Copts, Iraqi Nestorians, Armenians, members of the Orthodox churches, etc.) are present almost everywhere and influential in some countries. These religions are in fact fully integrated in the Middle East. It is therefore essential to be fully aware of the fact that a world that is somewhat hastily classified as Arab-Islamic is also composed of Arabs who are not Muslims and Muslims who are not Arabs.

Some of the characteristics of 'Middle Eastern style' are as follows:

1. The importance of 'concrete territorialities': knowledge of the subgroup to which the negotiator belongs is essential; the relationships between the parties must be explored with great care, to find out who is who and what relationship each negotiator has with the different groups.

2. The role of intermediaries ('sponsors' in Saudi Arabia) is very important. As a result of European colonization over the last two centuries, the majority of 'Middle Eastern' business people speak French or English and understand European civilization; whereas the reverse is rarely true. Intermediaries must be employed for a simple reason: we (the Europeans and Americans) systematically underestimate the cultural divide.

3. It must always be borne in mind that members of Middle Eastern civilizations were largely the founders of those in Europe. They have left many traces behind, and as far as art and culture are concerned, their influences were dominant for many centuries during the Middle Ages. The pride of the person with whom you are dealing must be – genuinely – respected.

4. One must expect a great deal of emotion, theatricality and demonstrativeness, interspersed with true pragmatism. The mixture is often bewildering. Friendship is sought, relationships are personalized, and the idea of a cold 'business-like' relationship is difficult to envisage. Once a true friend has been made (which is far from straightforward), the sense of loyalty can be very strong.

5. As has already been emphasized, Islamic values permeate daily life. For example, if the negotiations lead to consideration of a loan and interest rate, although this problem is not insurmountable, a great deal of caution is essential. The question

of *riba*, which is usually translated as 'interest', never fails to pose problems for Koranic law and the different legislative assemblies entrusted with its interpretation. These assemblies have been more or less strict in their interpretation of *riba*, which is mentioned several times in the Koran, as being forbidden. Thus specific financial operations, excluding the imposition of a method of repayment for loans which is fixed in advance, have been settled in accordance with Islamic law and on the basis of ancient practices. Rather than loans, they are joint operations where the banker brings the financing and clients their facilities and business talents. *Mudhâraba* corresponds to a project financing with no recourse for the banker; *musharaka* is similar except that the client brings part of the financing; *murabaha* is a sort of leasing agreement.

17.2 WESTERN STYLES

American style

The American style is oriented towards several major aspects which are linked to the US national character, namely individualism, with the emphasis on ability, competence, professionalism, decision making and explicit communication. As a consequence American negotiators usually possess the following qualities: seriousness, pragmatism and accuracy in writing clauses. American negotiators have fairly well-defined autonomy and room for manoeuvre, but clear limits are also set, and they have to report to their principals. In the negotiation process, Americans often consider that decisions have to be made on the spot by the individual who has the most expertise or responsibility in a given area (Beliaev *et al.*, 1985).

The following characteristics have been often noted:

1. Professionalism is a quality that is very widely recognized in Americans. In business negotiation, it means careful selection of the negotiators and methodical preparation of files.

2. In their failure to take sufficient account of the culture of other parties (Tung, 1984b), the Americans, like the French, are an 'ethnocentric-missionary' people. They are quite convinced (as are the French) that their system is the 'one best way', and that the other peoples of the world would do well to adopt their system of values and behaviour.

3. A great deal of attention is (pragmatically) paid to precise issues to be debated, to facts and evidence, to an attitude oriented towards matter-of-fact discussions and to a tight negotiation time schedule. This renders them susceptible to becoming irritated by negotiating parties who are more interested in general principles or even logical reasoning (the French, for example; Burt, 1984). This may also lead to their interpreting the attitudes of their negotiating counterparts who have a non-linear style as delaying tactics. They will resent global negotiation as a way of reconsidering what has already been decided and as a failure to respect a pre-set agenda.

4. A strong positive emphasis is placed on frankness and sincerity; Americans show willingness to make the first move by disclosing their position in the hope (some-

times unfulfilled) that their adversary will do likewise. They are also prepared to adopt the 'John Wayne Style' (Graham and Herberger, 1983; see Box 16.3), by pushing frankness to the bounds of arrogance. This can shock people from cultures where self-assertion must be contained within strict limits.

5. A genuine naivety, ingenuousness and a 'retarded adolescent' style (noted by Margaret Mead) can sometimes lead Americans to choose positions that are very tough because they are – genuinely – disappointed. This occurs mainly when, having demonstrated their – genuine – sincerity, they then feel that they have been badly treated, since their open-mindedness has been taken advantage of. However, sincerity and frankness are by no means universal cultural values, contrary to what a good number of Americans may believe.

6. Equality between purchaser and vendor, and 'let the best man win'. This can surprise people who deal with Americans, since Americans value personal assertiveness and can therefore appear tough: there is little sympathy for anyone who loses. In the US business mentality, no consolation prizes are won by 'losers'.

7. The Americans are supposed to be informal in everyday life. In fact, compared to other peoples, they are formal in different areas. When it comes to negotiating agreements, they are quite formal and anxious about the preciseness and explicitness of written contracts which are therefore drawn up with care. These contracts, the law between the parties, are also the basis for attitudes which are readily oriented towards recourse to litigation and legal battles with the assistance of lawyers.

8. As noted earlier, Americans tend to be short-term oriented. At the end of the Vietnam War, the Vietnamese were at a time advantage in the US–Vietnamese peace talks in Paris, because they had rented a villa with a two and a half years' lease, whereas the Americans rented hotel rooms on a week-to-week basis. The US time pressure in business may be easily explained by the system of quarterly reporting to shareholders and the Stock Exchange. US companies depend heavily on the financial markets; labour mobility is high. Accordingly people must get quick results, and show a faster return than their foreign counterparts. This 'short-termism' tends to disadvantage them in negotiations.

British style

Like the French, the British have been strongly affected by their tradition of diplomatic negotiation and their country's position as head of a far-flung empire. The British style is characterized by the following:

1. A 'soft-sell' approach which is essential for negotiating. British coolness is not an empty phrase. An air of confidence, restraint and calm is essential for any negotiators in the position of seller. They must never be seen to be pushy in negotiation.

2. The British have the reputation of being less motivated by money than the Americans; with the relative decline of Great Britain, they have become more inclined to make the most of their free time; companies are often full of adminis-

trative personnel. This situation has a tendency to slow down the decision-making process significantly (Burt, 1984).

3. The study carried out by Campbell *et al.* (1988), using the vehicle of a simulated negotiation, demonstrates that the factor that has the strongest influence on negotiation in the United Kingdom is the role of negotiator (purchaser or vendor). In the negotiation simulation, British purchasers obtained slightly superior results to vendors of the same nationality. This is consistent with the British reputation of having a 'soft-sell' type of approach, where the vendor must take care not to annoy the purchaser by being too pushy, turning up too often, making too many proposals or by adopting an attitude that is too action oriented.

4. Although seemingly closest to the Americans, the British are not necessarily those who resemble them the most in the field of business practice. They are usually more contextual in communication, and indirect, hence a willingness to try to interpret the British position in business negotiation is essential.

5. Language-related issues (the style in which they write clauses, for instance) are treated very differently by the British and the Americans. Whereas US people easily accept a somewhat simplified 'international English' that will be used for drafting agreement, the British, like the French, take pride in correct language, and are sensitive to style for style's sake.

French style

1. The French are said to be somewhat difficult to negotiate with. As noted earlier, the French tend to be ideologists and find it difficult to 'accept facts, no matter how convincing they may be. Although they may consider themselves to be experts at negotiating, at times they tend to be amateurish and inadequately prepared' (Burt, 1984, p. 6).

2. The fact that the French are conflict prone, do not mind confrontation and sometimes even enjoy it, is confirmed by Weiss and Stripp (1985) who describe the French negotiating style as competitive and inherently confrontational. They also tend to use emotional and theatrical ways of behaving in negotiation.

3. In France (as in the United Kingdom) social class remains an important feature of society. Consciousness of social status is very strong in France, as is power distance (see Chapter 3). French negotiators are sensitive to the organizational status of their foreign counterparts, and require equivalence.

4. France is still one of the most centralized nations in the world, with a very long tradition of Paris-based decision making (inaugurated by Hughes Capet, in 987). High-ranking civil servants (*énarques* and *polytechniciens*) have a substantial say in business deals which involve large companies and their subsidiaries.

5. At times, some French negotiators may be resented as arrogant and disdainful: in a very high-power-distance society, which is at the same time individualistic, power display may be exacerbated, to the detriment of politeness and courtesy.

6. Burt (1984, pp. 6–7) complements his view of the French negotiation style as follows:

The French seem to enjoy negotiating for its own sake. When they are in the mood some-times for several days – very little progress is made. Sooner or later though, they tire of the game and want to reach closure. A careful count of the numbers of cigarettes consumed per hour serves as an indication of the restlessness and the willingness to make concessions in order to reach closure. Leisure time and the desire for the 'good life' are key motivators. An awareness of these motivators can be useful in reaching agreement, as is indicated in the following dialogue:

American: 'We need to reach agreement, since I've booked us at (the Frenchman's favourite restaurant). But we can't go until we reach agreement on these remaining issues.'

Frenchman: 'I agree. Let's go!'

German style

1. One of the striking aspects of the German national mentality is its relatively high level of uncertainty avoidance (score of 65 on Hofstede's index of uncertainty avoidance; see Table 3.3). A key term is *sicher* (sure, safe). The Germans do not like *unsicherheit*, a sense of insecurity which makes them feel uneasy in business, as well as in their whole life. In front of partners who generate such uncertainty, Germans will quickly develop *Mißtrauen* (mistrust). They need to be *versichert*, that is, assured, and this cannot be done through superficial and wordy arguments, but only with hard facts, sound arguments, tests and so on.

2. The German love of formality is one of the first elements that stands out clearly. For example, the title of *Doktor*, even *Professor Doktor*, is a recognized sign of abil-ity and will be employed. Formality and the presence of constraining rules (which are generally respected) in the decision-making process on the German side are characteristics of the German system, which seeks to avoid uncertainty (as defined by Hofstede, 1980). These rules are often the end result of a reasonably solid con-sensus. The respect for accepted rules is more internalized by the Germans than forced upon them.

3. Decisions in a German company are taken at a fairly slow pace. The machine is 'well oiled', but it is also rather cumbersome. A fairly substantial number of signatures will be required for any final agreement.

4. Great pride is taken in the technical quality of products manufactured in Germany; thus a reaction of disbelief is instinctively provoked when a German is faced with something that originates from abroad and which fails to conform, for example, to the DIN standards. As a result, readiness to participate in detailed discussions with technical experts is essential.

5. German earnestness is no myth. The Germans are people who keep their word, and who will respect the agreement made, whether it takes a written or an oral form. They loathe anything that approaches flippancy, in particular negotiation for negotiation's sake, or indeed the failure to keep appointments. Germans, when they negotiate with the Italians or the French, often resent their Latin counter-parts' unreliability in keeping to their commitments.

6. They prefer explicit communication, and display a temporal style that is clearly monochronic. In negotiations, Germans wait for the schedule and agenda to be respected.

7. The role of emotions and friendship (in negotiations) is fairly limited: in the process of negotiations, Germans keep their distance. They feel that a personal relationship could interfere with the result of their work (Schmidt, 1979).

8. There is ambiguity about the perception of Germans by other people: Germans are both admired and disliked. As stated by Barzini (1983, p 94), this 'has its roots not only in their less amiable traits – arrogance, tactlessness and obtuseness – but also in their great virtues, their excellence in almost all fields'. Germans should be considered as individuals more than any nationality in the world. This is the best way to avoid negative biases when negotiating with Germans, who, after all, are not personally responsible for every event of German history.

17.3   NEGOTIATION STYLES IN OTHER AREAS OF THE WORLD

Black African style

1. Black Africans' love of talking always amazes those used to useful speech. Africans simply do not have the same relationship to the universe as Europeans and Americans do. Differences relate to basic concepts such as time and space (see sections 2.2, 2.3 and A2.4). Poetry has a powerful meaning for Africans. The African is a very verbal person: language (Africans are almost all polyglots) is an instrument for the enjoyment of the pleasure of speaking. As a result, negotiations can sometimes seem to be rather ill directed, not purely because Africans enjoy debating, but also because they enjoy speaking.

2. There is an absence of a strictly economic individual motivation:

    Money does not have the same value as in Europe. Westerners are accustomed to an age-old tradition of exchange based on money which has acquired a strong symbolic value as reward for work, as a means of saving, as a measure of personal success and as the fair price of things . . . [in Africa] attitudes towards money follow different rules. Money is only a means of obtaining enough for survival and projection of self-image, whereas its other attributes fade into the background . . . this money is taken without remorse, and in good humour [the 'baksheesh' that is – see Chapter 15], and usually benefits, not just the person who receives it but also the whole family. The African system of distribution functions in such a way that money goes to the one who needs it: the employee whose salary does not allow him to live decently, the high-ranking civil servant who supports a large family in the village for example. (Gruère and Morel, 1991, pp. 122-3)

3. The reality of tribes and the group is never to be ignored: during the process of business negotiations, the influence of the family and ethnic background will inevitably make its presence felt, whether through the participants or the beneficiaries of the negotiations.

4. The concept of time is simply not the same. This has a direct influence on the progress of business negotiations. As noted by Weiss and Stripp (1985, p. 39) in the case of Nigeria, 'Time is simply considered flexible. Lateness to meetings (even of several hours) is common. In the same vein, the foreigner who hurries through a negotiation – even after a very late start – will often be suspected of cheating.'

5. As Gruère and Morel (1991) emphasize, Black Africa is a mosaic, involving various characteristics of diversity: ethnic, religious (Christianity, Islam, animism) and linguistic. There too, as in the Middle East, a map of the 'human landscape' must be prepared in advance. In the West, we rarely consider people first as members of their tribe. People tend to be considered purely as individuals. The advantage of such a view has been a growth in tolerance and a reduction in violence between groups whose identity conflicts. The disadvantage has been the increase in individual isolation, since individuals are significantly less supported in their personal life by the ingroup.

Mexican style

1. As in many South American societies, family and political ties are extremely important in Mexico for determining individual influence. Strong ingroup orientation is expressed in bonds of loyalty and solidarity among the top people in both business and government. The dominant political party, PRI, is also a structure allowing patronage and networking in Mexican society, where relationships are a key issue. *Ubicacion*, that is, where one is plugged into the system, is important for determining a negotiator's status (Weiss and Stripp, 1985).

2. As noted earlier Mexico is a high-power-distance country, ranking second or third highest world-wide, depending on the countries considered; as a consequence, decision making is fairly centralized and 'Mexicans logically prefer to deal abroad at the higher levels of government and business and on a personal and private basis' (Fisher, 1980, p. 28).

3. Personal leverage – *palanca* – is important, and influential Mexican negotiators tend to be well positioned in their society, exhibiting their status and stamina.

4. Like most Latins, body language is important: it conveys emotions, especially when a negotiation is trying to persuade the other party. To their American neighbours in particular, Mexicans appear at times overly dramatic, emotional and sentimental. Conversely, Mexican negotiators may resent some of their foreign partners as reserved, unexpressive and cold.

5. Truthful communication is not to be expected always from Mexicans and frankness should not be taken for granted. Paz (1962) explains that: 'The Mexican tells lies because he delights in fantasy, or because he is desperate, or because he wants to rise above the sordid facts of his life' (quoted by Weiss and Stripp, 1985, p. 33). The use of instrumental strategies by Mexican negotiators is confirmed by Adler *et al.* (1987). This allows them to increase their profits, by manipulating their negotiation partner.

6. According to Graham (1993), in a comparative study across 17 countries, Mexicans appeared as competitive negotiators (this being evidenced by a fairly low level of joint profits) and the Mexican buyers were those who obtained the lion's share of the profits (almost 57 per cent of the joint outcome), the highest position for buyers out of the 17 countries.

7. The Mexicans have a relaxed concept of time, expressing a polychronic pattern whereby schedules are not given precedence over relations with people. The

mañana philosophy of time is based on a strong present orientation, which is detrimental to the accuracy of long-term planning and to real commitment *vis-à-vis* dates and deadlines. As the example of 'ocio' and 'negocio', at the beginning of Chapter 13, has shown, extreme activity, workalcoholism and high time consciousness are not strong values in Spanish-speaking Mexico.

8. Mexicans have a problematic identity problem with their big neighbour, the United States, and there is high sensitivity 'to their perceived dependent relationship with the United States and their long memory of patronizing and demeaning actions taken by the U.S. as a government, by American companies and by Americans as individuals (Fisher, 1980, p. 40).

9. Although corruption has been combated by public authorities in recent years, bribery remains frequent in Mexico.

Russian style

1. Given the more than seventy years of communist regime, the Soviet system has left some deep impressions on Russian society. As emphasized in section 6.5, this results in a lack of understanding of basic economic concepts such as the free-market price, company valuation or balance sheet. The lack of knowledge of the free-market mechanisms is progressively being redressed by management education.

2. The low level of individual initiative and the strong aversion for risk taking are explained by Beliaev *et al.* (1985, p. 105) in the following terms:

> Each negotiator will be well trained in the party discipline; obedient, with a well-developed sense of hierarchy; hard-working and trained for stress, but with narrow horizons; loyal to the state and fearful of mistakes because of the risk of falling to the level of the average Soviet citizen; cautious, tough, and inflexible because of the strictness of their instructions; and willing to subordinate personal life to the demand of the position.

3. As a result the Soviet style, still a part of the Russian style even after the fall of the communist regime, has been described as fairly tough and unilateral. Negotiators tended to make extreme initial demands, to view adversaries' concessions as weakness, to make only minimal concessions and to ignore deadlines (Cohen, 1980). On the other hand, the Soviet-style Russians were good payers and did respect contracts which were drafted in a very detailed way.

4. Graham *et al.* (1992) note the consensus of descriptions of Soviet negotiators as 'competitive' and 'uncompromising'. They show in a laboratory experiment that Russian negotiators tend to prefer a distributive strategy, and this with minimal negative effects on their (Russian) partner's satisfaction, which tends to suggest that such competitive behaviour is considered locally as standard practice.

5. The ethical system of Russians widely differs from that of Americans according to Lefebvre (1983):

> Something that an American considers normative positive behavior (for example, negotiating and reaching a compromise with an enemy, and even any deal with another individual), a Soviet man perceives as showing Philistine cowardice, weakness, as something unworthy

(the word 'deal' itself has a strong negative connotation in contemporary Russian). (Quoted in Graham *et al.*, 1992, p. 396.)

6. Communist centralized planning, based on detailed five-year plans, did not infuse Soviet Citizens with a sense of economic time (Beliaev *et al.*, 1985). Given the complexity of co-ordination between government bodies, the Soviet citizen gave up trying to meet exact schedules. In Russia today, this logically results in a highly present and short-term-oriented society.

7. Russia is now undergoing fundamental transition. The bureaucratic controls have progressively been relaxed, giving birth to a new society with deep contrasts. New entrepreneurs are almost western in style, full of initiative but lacking professionalism and reliability, and may appear very different from the Soviet style described above. However, what has been gained in terms of flexibility is largely compensated by the prevailing lack of reliability, opportunistic behaviour and the confusion between business and wild capitalism. Incidents involving payment defaults and failure to enforce negotiated contracts are now frequent. Many new Russian entrepreneurs do not feel bound by normal business norms and contracts because either they ignore them or they view them as foreign and therefore inapplicable in their context.

17.4   SOME BASIC RULES FOR INTERNATIONAL MARKETING NEGOTIATIONS

In short, the international business negotiator should follow some basic rules:

1. Be well prepared; define in advance your basic interests, objectives and bottom line, and allow room for manoeuvre. Before participating in a negotiation, learn the basics about the behavioural norms in your partner's culture, especially those concerning appointments, punctuality and planning.

2. Allow time for adequate preliminaries: getting to know the other party is most often crucial. More time is needed than in domestic business negotiations, since cultural as well as personal knowledge has to be acquired. Allow yourself plenty of time, and even more. Patience is an asset in negotiation and it is destroyed by time pressure.

3. Be flexible with the negotiation agenda if the other party does not stick to it.

4. If necessary, be prepared to withdraw from a negotiation if the stakes are too low, or send lower-level, less expensive executives. If possible, negotiate at home where you have a competitive advantage over your foreign partner, in terms of time control.

5. Be ready for different communication styles and be cautious in interpreting silence, emotionality, threats and any kind of manipulative communication.

6. Never tell the other side when you are leaving because this gives them control over your time.

7. Respect the sensitivities of your partner in the area of (a) personal status; and (b) national pride.

8. Do not be deceived by the other party seeming to share your time pattern: try to set realistic dates and deadlines and plan modestly and realistically. Tight deadlines may result into major delays that ruin the credibility of the whole planning process.

9. Try to balance relationship orientation and deal orientation: wait for the negotiation process to extend beyond the signature of the deal.

QUESTIONS

1. What sort of cultural misunderstandings could arise from a negotiation between Japanese buyers and French sellers?

2. Discuss the influence of group orientation (as presented in Chapter 2 and illustrated in this chapter for some national groups) on behaviour during the negotiation process.

3. Negotiations between Russians and Chinese: are they easy? Why?

4. Imagine a negotiation between a (stereotypical) Mexican businessman and a (stereotypical) US businesswoman: which cultural misunderstandings may appear between them in the negotiation process?

5. Discuss similarities and differences between US and British business negotiation styles.

6. American business people meet potential Japanese partners in California to discuss a joint venture project. The joint venture would sell US-made products on the Japanese market. One of the Americans starts the first meeting by saying to his Japanese counterpart: 'Since we are going to work together in the future, we had better get to know each other now. My name is John. What is your name?' Is this form of address adequate? If so, why? If not, why not?

APPENDIX 17: TEACHING MATERIALS

A17.1   Case: Tremonti SpA

Tremonti SpA was a small company located in the suburbs of Milan. Like many small and medium enterprises in the northern part of Italy, it specialized in special machines and mechanical engineering. Tremonti SpA had developed a sophisticated knowledge in the production of machines for assembling electronic components.

The company had been founded by an engineer, Mr Stefanini, who owned the business and gave it its technological drive. Until now he had always made the choice to invest more money in R & D than in production operations. The company therefore cared more about prototypes than about mass production (if that means anything in an industry where world-wide markets rarely exceed tens or hundreds of machines).

A large part of the production was in fact subcontracted. This made factory investments lighter and gave production flexibility in the face of unsteady demand. But subcontracting about 60–80 per cent of the parts and a large amount of the assembly work was not satisfactory in that it made it difficult to follow and monitor production schedules accurately.

The export manager, Mr Lesca, had considerably increased export sales during the last five years. Export sales at Tremonti SpA were 80 per cent of the total corporate sales figure. Clients were mostly located in the United States and in Europe, with a very small proportion in Japan. Lesca's team was composed of two export salesmen, who had a technical background and provided maintenance for machines located abroad, and two English-speaking secretaries who were in charge of export logistics and paperwork.

I

Lesca was worried by a problem with an American customer. The American had already bought one machine from Tremonti SpA and was very satisfied with it. It worked at full capacity, it had been delivered on time and it was reliable. Then he ordered a second machine, which was now in the production process.

Unfortunately, according to the manufacturing department, the production of this machine seemed to be delayed by four to six weeks from the agreed delivery date. Yet the American customer was willing to order a third machine, since the first one had been working satisfactorily for the last six months. He did not know about a possible delay to the second machine.

Lesca wondered what he should do:

1. Should he tell the American customer about the delivery delay of the second machine during his next visit to negotiate the sale of the third machine? The agreed delivery date for the second machine is six weeks after the next visit of Lesca to his American customer.

2. If yes, how should he announce it?

II

Finally, after the visit had taken place, Lesca was satisfied with the tactics he had adopted. He felt a need to extract some more widely applicable principles out of this communication experience. When flying back from the United States, he wondered how he should have acted with people from the following national/cultural backgrounds: German, Japanese and Saudi Arabian.

III

Demand had been growing quickly. Since Tremonti SpA's machines were up to date and reliable, they were especially sought out. But delivery delays were increasing. A conversation with a German customer, Herr Weisslinger, gave him another opportunity to become aware of the high level of sensitivity of clients to their suppliers meeting delivery dates.

'You Italians,' began Weisslinger, 'you do not really know what a delivery date is. There are huge differences between the delivery date agreed upon when signing the contract and the actual delivery date. And you wait until the last minute to tell us that you won't be able to meet your delivery date. Sometimes you do not even report it and we have to send you a fax to try to find out when the machine will be delivered. Yet it should already have been delivered, and we are not even informed.'

'No, you carry it too far,' answered Lesca. 'I do not believe that we deliberately miss delivery dates. You have to understand: a delivery date is indicative. When ordering, a date is fixed that best suits the client. We indicate the delivery date that we think we are able to meet. Numerous hazards may then occur. Our suppliers and subcontractors do not adhere strictly to their delivery dates, and this causes a large part of our own delays.'

'If I understand you correctly, we have to accept things as they are,' said Weisslinger.

'I am afraid so,' replied Lesca. 'I am the personal advocate of our clients within the company. But, you know, my authority is limited, and the Italian national character values deadlines and time precision far less than Anglo-Saxons do. Moreover it is an organizational problem: everybody has to feel committed if we want to achieve a greater respect for delivery dates.'

'Yes indeed,' said Weisslinger, 'I think your machines are of good quality and your maintenance and after-sales service are OK. But your competitors provide equal qualities and they meet their deadlines. We have to make rational choices. You do not meet your delivery dates.'

Mr Lesca is now wondering how he should allocate his efforts. Should he go on playing the role of a 'trade ambassador', trying diplomatically to make the foreign clients accept delays? Should he, on the other hand, spend more time in the company and undertake action to improve the organizational functioning for delivery dates? How should he tackle the issue with Stefanini? What ways and means would be sufficient to improve the commitment to delivery dates?

IV

Some time after this conversation with Weisslinger, Lesca went to Japan on a business trip, and had the opportunity to present Tremonti SpA's technical achievements. On his return from Japan, he went to Stefanini's office to discuss the potential of the Japanese market. 'We did place some orders there, but they are small compared with the total Japanese market, and particularly small when compared with the sales we achieved in the United States. I have had preliminary talks with a large electronics company called Nokan. We examined the possibility of a marketing joint venture, which would be responsible for selling and servicing our machines on the Japanese market. It looks fine; but I know that Japanese people are not easy to deal with. They are extremely polite, courteous and gentle, but what are their real intentions? Frankly, I do not trust them. Besides, they have a reputation for ransacking technologies, and it is a fundamental that we protect our knowledge base.' Stefanini wanted to prepare for the negotiation of this marketing joint venture. He asked Lesca the following questions:

1. 'How can we get information about Japanese culture?'

2. 'Which aspects are relevant to our problem?'

REFERENCES

Adler, Nancy J., John L. Graham and Theodore Schwarz-Gehrke (1987), 'Business negotiations in Canada, Mexico and the United States', *Journal of Business Research*, vol. 15, pp. 411–29.
Barzini, Luigi (1983), *The Europeans*, Penguin Books: London.

Beliaev, Edward, Thomas Mullen and Betty Jane Punnett (1985), 'Understanding the cultural environment: U.S.–U.S.S.R. trade negotiations', *California Management Review*, vol. 27, no. 2, pp. 100–12.

Burt, David N. (1984), 'The nuances of negotiating overseas', *Journal of Purchasing and Materials Management*, Winter, pp. 2–8.

Campbell, Nigel C. G., John L. Graham, Alain Jolibert and Hans Günther Meissner (1988), 'Marketing negotiations in France, Germany, the United Kingdom and United States', *Journal of Marketing*, vol. 52, April, pp. 49–62.

Cohen, Herb (1980), *You Can Negotiate Anything*, Bantam: New York.

Eiteman, David K. (1990), 'American executives' perceptions of negotiating joint ventures with the People's Republic of China: Lessons learned', *Columbia Journal of World Business*, Winter, pp. 59–67.

Fisher, Glen (1980), *International Negotiation: A cross-cultural perspective*, Intercultural Press: Yarmouth, ME.

Graham, John L. (1981), 'A hidden cause of America's trade deficit with Japan', *Columbia Journal of World Business*, Fall, pp. 5–15.

Graham, John L. (1993), 'Business negotiations: Generalisations about Latin America and East Asia are dangerous', *UCI Irvine/Research*, pp. 6–23.

Graham, John L. and Roy A. Herberger Jr (1983), 'Negotiators abroad: Don't shoot from the hip', *Harvard Business Review*, vol. 61, no. 4, pp. 160–8.

Graham, John L., Leonid I. Ivenko and Mahesh N. Rajan (1992), 'An empirical comparison of Soviet and American business negotiations', *Journal of International Business Studies*, vol. 23, no. 3, pp. 387–418.

Gruère, Jean-Pierre and Pierre Morel (1991), *Cadres Français et Communications Interculturelles*, Eyrolles: Paris.

Hawrysh, Bryan Mark and Judith Lynn Zaichkowsky (1990), 'Cultural approaches to negotiations: Understanding the Japanese', *International Marketing Review*, vol. 7, no. 2, pp. 28–42.

Hofstede, Geert (1980) 'Motivation, leadership and organization: Do American theories apply abroad?' *Organizational Dynamics*, Summer, pp. 42–63.

Lefebvre, Victorina D. (1983), 'Ethical features of the normative hero in Soviet children's literature of the 1960s–70s', *Studies of Cognitive Sciences*, vol. 20, School of Social Sciences: Irvine, CA.

Luo, Yadong (1995), 'Business strategy, market structure, and performance of IJV', *Management International Review*, vol. 35, no. 3, pp. 249–64.

Luo, Yadong and Min Chen (1997), 'Does guanxi influence firm performance?', *Asia Pacific Journal of Management*, vol. 14, pp. 1–16.

Oh, T. K. (1986), 'Selling to the Japanese', *Nation's Business*, October, pp. 37–8.

Paz, Octavio (1962), *The Labyrinth of Solitude*, Grove: New York.

Pye, Lucian W. (1982), *Chinese Commercial Negotiating Style*, Oelgeschlager, Gunn & Hain: Cambridge, MA.

Pye, Lucian W. (1986), 'The China trade: Making the deal work' *Harvard Business Review*, vol. 46, no. 4, pp. 75–84.

Schmidt, Klaus D. (1979), *Doing Business in France, Germany and the United Kingdom*, pamphlets published by the Business Intelligence Program, SRI International: Menlo Park, CA.

Tung, Rosalie L. (1984a), 'How to negotiate with the Japanese', *California Management Review*, vol. XXVI, no. 4, pp. 62–77.

Tung, Rosalie L. (1984b), *Business Negotiations with the Japanese.* Lexington Books: Lexington, MA.

Tung, Rosalie (1996), 'Negotiating with East Asians', in P. N. Ghauri and J.-C. Usunier (eds.), *International Business Negotiations*, Pergamon/Elsevier: Oxford, pp. 369–81.

Weiss, Stephen E. and William Stripp (1985), 'Negotiating with foreign businesspersons: An introduction for Americans with propositions for six cultures', Working Paper no. 85–6, Graduate School of Business, New York University: New York.

Postscript

Globalization as 'modernism' brought to backward nations

As Ernest Dichter emphasized in an article entitled 'The World Customer', which is considered a seminal article in the field of international marketing, particularly as it was the first to picture the phenomenon of the globalization of world markets:[1]

Only one Frenchman out of three brushes his teeth. Automobiles have become a must for the self-esteem of even the lowliest postal clerk in Naples or the Bantu street cleaner in Durban . . . Four out of five Germans change their shirts but once a week. (1962, p. 113.)

The explanation is to be found some papers later: 'The fact that 64% of the Frenchmen don't brush their teeth is in part caused by the lack of running water in many communities' (p. 116). The Germans rank first for the 'self-illusions' a nation can have about itself. Dichter proposes the following illustration: 'Germans still refer to themselves as a nation of poets and thinkers; yet the largest selling newspaper, the *Bildzeitung*, has a circulation of 2 million based largely on sensationalism and tabloid treatment of news' (p. 117). According to Dichter (at the beginning of the 1960s) Dutch housewives would serve instant coffee, making the verbal excuse that instant coffee is used only in an emergency. 'What happens, however, is that the number of emergencies has increased amazingly' (p. 117).

One might think that globalization emerged from the advances in modernity and cleanliness accomplished by these backward people when they overcame their resistance to change. One may also wonder whether there is any real connection between Goethe, Schiller, Kant and Heidegger on the one hand and the *Bildzeitung* on the other, other than the fact that they are all German. It is necessary to highlight the first paradox in this approach: many arguments in favour of the globalization of markets are totally ethnocentric; as such, they are in contradiction with the spirit of globalization, which is based on the rejection of ethnocentrism.

Some true reasons for the globalization of markets

Globalization is, first of all, based on technological advances, which in turn explain globalization on the supply side: economies of scale and experience effects, drastic changes over the past forty years in transportation and also new telecommunications technologies. The globalization of consumers and demand will certainly occur in the future, but it will happen much later than its early defenders imagined. Moreover the process of world-wide globalization of demand may be quite different from what they visualized: a steady extension of the 'American way of life' throughout the world which would contribute to the global happiness of humankind.

But cultural coherence should not be forgotten and marketers still have to be aware of it. Consumers buy meanings, not just products. Meaning is intersubjectively shared in the cultural community. The process of globalization of demand will be long term because of the local nature of culture and its contribution to collective identity. Moreover, this evolution can be achieved only by individuals who *learn*. Learning is a large part of culture. Globalization implies that consumers throughout the world have to borrow foreign ways of life, experience new behaviours and construct shared meanings with people from other cultures. At present, a great many things are shared among the cultures of the world, but just as many remain culture specific. *Amnesty* International, the practice of *judo*, playing or listening to *jazz*, the *Olympics* and many other cultural artefacts, even though they were born in particular cultures, are probably bearers of future universal values. Obviously each national culture has a specific contribution to make to the movement towards globalization. If there is any true (and sincere) way of being *global* it is not by denying differences, but by being aware of and responsive to them.

We face a second paradox, the two sides of which must be constantly kept in mind: on the one hand, lifestyles are apparently tending to become global; on the other, the claims for recovering cultural identity are stronger than ever. Numerous peoples who have been denied a sovereign state are demanding their independence as nations, emphasizing the uniqueness of their culture. The concept of a nation-state, although a fairly recent one historically,[2] remains very strong for many individuals. Although it is not the only way of protecting cultural identity, it is still the most elaborate and the most efficient one.

The law of comparative advantage, described in Chapter 5, has almost completely eliminated the concept of culture from international trade theory. One may remark, as Galtung (1990) does, that: 'In short, this "law" [of comparative advantage] is a piece of cultural violence buried in the very core of economics.'[3] Ignoring cultural differences, the law of comparative advantage imposes a paradigm of international trade, which is excessively utilitarian: it assumes the *complete pre-eminence of utility over identity*. Yet real people do not live only with what is useful to them, they also live out of the maintenance and self-actualization of their identity, of which their cultural identity is a significant part. Thus it is necessary to integrate the dimension of culture in marketing strategies and in their implementation, when they focus on international markets.

Designing tailored marketing strategies and implementing them with respect for the local context

As this book (it is hoped) shows: marketing strategies tailored to national/cultural markets are not in contradiction with the choice of a global business strategy. On the contrary, cultural tailoring is a basic element of a global business strategy. The reality of cultural exchanges world-wide is now so complex and so inextricable that any over-simplification is dangerous. Let us take a concrete example: using instant coffee does not imply that one has, once and for all, adopted ready-made standardized consumer goods. Coffee beans and ground coffee have made a tremendous come-back against instant coffee, regaining lost market share in most coffee-drinking countries. No evolution is fixed; consumers change from 'tradition' to 'modernism', but also back to (almost) traditional ways of consuming. Among the segments targeted in an intercultural marketing strategy there will be both transnational market segments and national market segments, to which specific offers will be made. National culture will continue to influence strongly many aspects of the implementation of marketing strategies: choice of distribution channels and trade partners, setting of prices, sales and marketing negotiations, etc.

This is fortunate because, if cultural differences were to disappear, I suspect that life would be boring.

NOTES

1. I am sorry for the unkind use of certain sentences that appear in this article. It is a superb example of sincere ethnocentrism, as well as of relative lack of long-term vision. The article does, however, contain many insightful remarks.
2. The concept of a nation-state emerged clearly at the end of the seventeenth century and developed further during the nineteenth century. Germany and Italy, for instance, were not united as nation-states before the end of the nineteenth century, under the auspices of Bismarck in Germany and Cavour in Italy. Decolonization was the heyday of the concept of the nation-state: many countries were formed which corresponded not to a nation, not to a shared culture among the various groups of citizens, not even to a geographical unit.
3. Johan Galtung thoroughly defines what the process of cultural violence encompasses. In particular, one section of his article (4.5) argues that Ricardo's doctrine (developed further by Heckscher and Ohlin, and others) justifies the world division of labour: 'The principle of comparative advantage sentences countries to stay where the production-factor profile has landed them, for geographical and historical reasons' (p. 300). However, marketers are not economists: their pragmatism may induce them to choose *culturally non-violent* marketing strategies, if they prove successful.

REFERENCES

Dichter, E. (1962), 'The World Customer', *Harvard Business Review*, vol. 40, no. 4, pp. 113–22.

Galtung, J. (1990), 'Cultural violence', *Journal of Peace Research*, vol. 27, no. 3, pp. 291–305.

Author Index

Aaker, David A., 340, 349
Abe, Shuzo, 132
Abegglen, James C., 371, 338, 347, 380
Abernethy, Avery M., 461, 494
Ackerman, N., 361, 381
Adcock, Dennis, 513, 543
Adler, Keith, 352
Adler, Nancy J., 63, 88, 95, 519, 543, 552,
    566, 568, 575, 584, 597, 602
Adler, Peter S., 434, 450
Advertising Age, 474–5, 482–4, 494–5
Agpar, M., 525, 543
Agrawal, Madhu, 459, 495
Ahmed, Sadrudin A., 323, 347
Ahuvia, Aaron, 57, 60, 96, 108, 110, 132, 135,
    150, 177
Akhter, Syed H., 397, 409–10
Albaum, Gerald, 244, 578, 584
Albers-Miller, Nancy D., 473, 495
Alden, Dana L., 132–3, 465, 495
Ali, Abbas, 515, 543
Ali, F., 585
Al-Khatib, Jamal A., 528, 543
Al-Makaty, Safran S., 470, 495
Al-Mossawi, Mohammed, 470, 495
Allaway, Arthur W., 544
Allen, David Elliston, 356, 380
Alpay, Guvenc, 320, 352
Amine, Lyn S., 185, 207, 225, 243, 285, 314
Ancel, Marie-Odile, 199–200
Anderson, B., 349

Anderson, Erin T., 393, 409
Anderson, Paul F., 520, 543,
Anderson, William T., 325–6, 347
Andrews, J. Craig, 457, 476, 495
Angelmar, Reinhard, 221–2, 245, 561, 572,
    584
Appelbaum, Ullrich, 460, 465, 495
Applbaum, Kalman, 132, 149, 152, 173
Arndt, Johan, 548, 584
Arnould, Eric, 132, 135, 529, 543
Arpan, Jeffrey S., 499
Arunthanes, Wiboon, 132–3
Askegaard, Søren, 133
Attali, Jacques, 27, 54
Avlonitis, G., 175

Baalbaki, Imad B., 282, 314
Badhuri, Monika, 243
Bagozzi, Richard P., 120, 132–3
Bagur, J. S., 585
Ballah, R.N., 106, 133
Ballon, Robert J., 32
Bamossy G. J., 175, 328, 347
Bannister, J. P., 173
Barabba, Vincent P., 503, 543
Bartlett, Christopher, 141, 173, 266, 279
Barzini, Luigi, 596, 602
Bates, Constance, 467, 495
Bateson, Gregory, 435, 450
Baudrillard, Jean, 121–2, 133
Baumgartner, Gary, 173

Beatty, Sharon E., 132–3
Becker, Gary S., 359, 380
Becker, Helmut, 530, 543
Beliaev, Edward, 559, 584, 592, 598–9, 603
Belk, Russell W., 57, 95, 104, 131–4, 145, 157,
        173, 175, 472, 500–1
Bell, Daniel, 119, 133
Bell, David, 136, 172–3
Bennett, Harvey, 392, 410
Benton, A. A., 585
Beracs, Joszef, 175–6
Berenbein, Ronald E., 531, 543
Berg, David, 450, 452
Berger, Brigitte, 181, 207
Berne, Eric, 71, 94–5
Berning, Carol K., 54
Berry, John W., 22, 55
Beutelmeyer, Werner, 410
Bhandari, Labdhi, 174
Bhuian, Shahid N., 327, 347
Bigne, Enrique, 460, 495
Bilkey, Warren J., 320, 347
Bista, Dor Bahadur, 61, 95, 568, 584
Bitterli, Urs, 21
Bjerke, Rune, 467, 495
Blackwell Roger D., 134
Bleek, W., 51
Bleustein-Blanchet, Marcel, 463
Bliemel, F., 175
Boas, Franz, 17
Boddewyn, Jean Jacques, 267, 280–1, 351,
        401, 403, 405, 409, 458, 495
Bodur, Muzzafer, 281
Bohnet, Michael, 217, 243
Bon, Jérôme, 158, 173, 207, 321, 347
Bond, M. Harris, 202, 207
Boston Consulting Group, 252
Botschen, Martina, 410
Bouchet, Dominique, 118–19, 133, 147,
        173–4
Boya, Unal O., 544
Boyd, Douglas A., 495
Bradfield, Ray, 543
Brady, John T., 528, 543
Brannen, Mary Yoko, 161, 165, 174
Brislin, Richard W., 22, 50–1, 54, 93, 95–6,
        452
Brooke, Michael Z., 583–4
Burgaud, Didier, 480, 498
Burns, Alvin C., 361, 381, 528, 543
Burt, David N., 566, 570, 584, 590, 592, 594,
        603
Buske, Erwin, 263, 280
Buzzati, Dino, 122
Buzzell, Robert D., 262, 279

Cabat, Odilon, 334, 347
Cadix, Alain, 207
Calantone, R., 119, 133, 273, 279
Callison, John R., 175
Calvert, Stephen, 133
Camargo, Eduardo, 43, 55, 463, 499
Campbell, David, 133
Campbell, Donald T., 218–19, 243, 432, 451
Campbell, J.B., 243
Campbell, Nigel C. G., 494, 499, 560, 562–3,
        584, 594, 603
Camphuis, Pierre-Arnold, 287, 314
Carey, George, 270, 279
Carroll, Collette, 349
Carroll, John B., 6, 21, 449–50
Carter, J. R., 561, 586
Catalano, Joelle, 500
Cateora, Philip R., 371, 380, 387, 390–1, 393,
        409, 490, 495, 513, 515, 543
Cattin, Philippe, 334, 347
Cavusgil, S. Tamer, 114, 133, 159, 175, 185,
        207, 212, 225, 234, 243, 358, 369,
        380
Cecchini, Paolo, 193, 207, 261
Chambers, Terry M., 520, 543
Chan, Allan K.K., 332, 349
Chan, T.S., 148, 174
Chandran, R., 245, 496
Chang, Cypress, 500
Chang Dae Ryun, 325, 347
Chao, Paul, 348
Chapman, Malcolm, 132–3
Chen, Dongling, 141, 172, 174
Chen, Min, 511, 544, 589, 603
Cheng, Hong, 472, 495
Chéron, Emmanuel, 177
Cherrie, Craig, 54, 95
Chiaramonte, Joan, 279
Chien, M., 106, 133
Child, John, 5, 22
Chiou, Jyh-Shen, 110, 133
Chonko, Lawrence B., 515, 520, 543
Choong, Mei-Lan, 500
Chun, K. T., 230, 243
Chung, Kae H., 324, 327, 350
Clark, Harold F. Jr, 156, 174, 339, 347, 484,
        495
Clements, Kenneth W., 141, 172, 174
Cohen, Herb, 567, 585
Cohen, Judy, 297–8, 314
Colombat, Catherine, 333, 347
Colvin, Michael, 472, 495
Condon, John C., 423, 451
Contensou, François, 338, 348
Copeland, Lennie, 301, 314, 424, 451

Costa, Janeen Arnold, 175
Coughlan, Anne T., 393, 409
Council of the European Communities, 195,
    207
Craig, C. Samuel, 212–13, 222, 224–8, 243–4
Crawford, John C., 326, 348, 350
Cuenca, Antonio C., 495
Cummings, L. L., 558, 563, 584, 586
Cundiff, Edward W., 131, 133, 324, 328, 344,
    346, 348, 352, 409, 540, 543
Cunningham, William H., 325–6, 347
Curry, David J., 361, 380
Cushner, Kenneth, 54, 95
Cutler, Bob D., 459, 462, 471, 473, 496–7
Czinkota, Michael R., 140, 169, 172, 174, 277,
    279, 332, 348, 384, 388, 390–2, 401,
    409, 470, 496, 523

D'Andrade, Roy G., 120, 133
d'Astous, Alain, 347
Daniels, John D., 165, 174, 526, 543
Darbelet, Michel, 188, 207
Darley, William K., 457, 496
Darling, John B., 158, 174, 327, 348
Das, Ajay, 212, 243
Dasen, Pierre R., 22, 55
David, René, 576, 585
Davis, H. L., 220, 243
Dawar, Niraj, 131, 133, 144, 149, 174, 361,
    380
Day, Ellen, 175
Day, George S., 253, 279, 503, 543
Day, R. L., 586
Dayan, Armand, 186, 207
De Maricourt, Renaud, 207, 383–4, 391, 409,
    574, 586
De Mente, Boye, 437, 451, 574, 585
De Mooij, Marieke K., 270–1, 280
De Ruyter, Ko, 292, 315
Deher, Odile, 264–5, 279
Demidov, V. E., 199, 209
Demirel, A. Hamdi, 395, 410, 470, 498
DeMoss, Michelle, 132, 134
Derr, C. B., 87–8, 95
Desmet, Pierre, 397–8, 409
Deutscher, I., 218, 243
Dholakia, Ruby Roy, 157, 174
Di Benedetto, C. Anthony, 459, 465, 496
Diamantopoulos, A., 283, 315
Diaz Del Castillo, Bernal, 21
Dichter, Ernest, 123, 605, 607
Dietl, Jerzy, 198, 207
Djursaa, Malene, 161–2, 174
Dobscha, Susan, 544
Doi, T., 388, 409

Domanski, Tomasz, 198, 207
Doran, Kathleen Brewer, 150, 174, 181, 207
Dornoff, Ronald J., 325–7, 348
Douglas, Susan P., 151, 174, 212–13, 222,
    224–30, 242–6, 281, 349, 467, 496
Dowd, Lawrence, 584
Dowling, G.R., 460, 496
Droit, Michel, 433, 451
Druckman, D., 563, 585
Du Preez , J.P., 315
Dubé, Laurette, 350
Dubini, Paola, 197, 208
Dubinsky, Alan J., 544
Dubois, Bernard, 102–3, 133, 467, 496
Dudley, James W., 480, 496
Duerr, Edwin, 584
Duncan, Tom, 462, 496
Dupuis, Marc, 383–4, 391, 409
Dupuy, Francois, 338, 348
Durkheim, Emile, 18
Durvasula, Srinivas, 495
Dwyer, Robert F., 510, 543, 549, 585

Easterby-Smith, Mark, 242, 244
Eastman, Jacqueline K., 132, 133
EC Committee of the American Chamber of
    Commerce in Belgium, 191, 207
Eden, David, 279
Eells, R., 544
Egan, Colin, 544
Eiteman, David K., 559, 572, 585, 589, 603
El Adraoui, Mustafa, 347
El Haddad, Awad B., 185, 207
El-Tigi, Jehan, 470, 500
Eliade, Mircea, 10, 22
Engel, James F., 111, 134
Enis, Ben M., 543
Erbil, Kurt, 481, 496
Erdem, S. Altan, 496
Erickson, G. Scott, 347–8
Erickson, Gary M., 321, 329, 348, 361, 380
Erikson, Erik, 21–2, 434, 451
Eroglu, Sevgin A., 323–4, 326, 348, 350
Erramilli, M. Krishna, 496
Eshghi, Abdolezra, 141–2, 174
Esposito, Odile, 194, 207
Essad Bey, Mohammed, 76, 95
Etchegoyen, Alain, 340, 348
Ettenson, Richard, 159–60, 174, 323, 325, 348
Etzel, Michael J., 320, 348
Evans, Franklin B., 562, 585

Farr, Robert M., 18, 22
Fauld, David J., 360–1, 380
Fay, T., 245

Fei, X. T., 106, 134
Feldman, Lawrence P., 53–4
Ferraro, Gary P., 31, 49, 54, 92, 95, 423–4,
    438, 449, 451
Firat, Fuat, 147, 160, 175
Firoz, Nadeem M., 361, 381
Fisher, Glen, 415, 439–40, 451, 558, 570–1,
    585, 597–8, 603
Ford, David, 510–11, 543
Foster, G. M., 557, 585
Fournier, Susan, 503, 544
Fournis, Yves, 193, 207
Fox, Richard J., 175
Foxman, Ellen R., 401, 404, 409
Francis, June P., 565, 585, 587
Franke, George R., 461, 494
Frazer Winsted, Kathleen, 292, 315
Fredenberger, Bill, 133
Freivalds, John, 507, 544
Frese-Weghöft, Gisela, 60, 95
Freud, Sigmund, 95
Freuhling, Royal, 443
Friederes, Geroen, 176
Frijda, N., 215, 242, 244
Fritzsche, D.H., 530, 543
Fu, Marilyn Y., 499
Fuentes, Carlos, 564, 585
Fukuyama, Francis, 548, 583, 585

Gaedeke, Ralph, 173, 175, 324, 348
Gaeth, Gary J., 174, 348, 361, 381
Galtung, Frederick, 525, 527, 544
Galtung, Johan, 79–80, 94–5, 449, 451, 606–7
Gambiez, Chantal, 402, 409
Gannon, Martin J., 440, 451
Gans, Herbert, 118, 134
Garland, B. L., 348
Garcia Marques, Gabriel, 58
Garner-Earl, Bettina, 349
Garreau, J., 273, 280
Gauthey, Franck, 433, 435, 451
Geertz, Clifford, 94–5, 152, 175, 213, 244
Gelb, Betsy D., 471, 473, 495, 501
Gentry, J. W., 273, 280
Gephart, Werner, 153, 175
Ger, Güliz, 132, 134, 157, 175
Ghauri, Pervez N., 198, 207, 461, 497, 562, 585
Ghoshal, Sumantra, 263, 280
Ghymn, Kyung-Il, 315, 497
Gillespie, Kate, 524, 529–31, 544
Gilly, Mary, 466, 496
Gilmore, James H., 264–5, 280
Giordan, Alain Eric, 287, 315, 336, 348
Glazer, Herbert, 385, 409
Glenn, E., 77, 95

Glowacka, Aleksandra E., 325, 351
Godiwalla, Yezdi M., 234, 243
Goldman, Alan, 546, 557,
Goodenough, Ward H., 5, 12, 22
Goodyear, Mary, 225, 228–9, 244
Gopalakrishna, Pradeep, 325, 348, 473, 499
Gordon, Geoffrey L., 496
Gorman, Thomas M., 151, 175
Gorn, Gerald J., xii, xv
Graby, Françoise, 158, 173, 175, 325–6, 348
Graham, John L., 234, 244, 514, 531, 544,
    552, 561–7, 571–4, 584–5, 590, 593,
    597–9, 602–3
Graham, Robert J., 31–2, 54
Graves, Roger, 398, 409
Green, Paul E., 241–2, 244
Green, Robert T., 132–3, 212–3, 225, 244, 497
Gregory, Gary D., 473, 496
Greif, Avner, 584–5
Griggs, Lewis, 301, 314, 424, 451
Grønhaug, Kjell, 234, 244
Grüber, Ursula, 464, 496
Grubbs Hoy, Mariea, 208
Gruère, Jean-Pierre, 434, 451, 596–7, 603
Grunert, Klaus G., 244
Grunert, Suzanne C., 215, 244
Grunewald, Orlen, 380
Guetzkow, H., 562, 587
Gurevitch, A. J., 27, 54

Ha, Louise, 478, 496
Halborg, Al, 543
Haley, Eric, 208
Hall, Edward T., 25, 29, 32, 34, 40, 54, 295,
    315, 417, 419, 422, 449, 451, 471,
    496, 517, 544, 563, 565–6, 569,
    575–6, 586
Hall, Mildred Reed, 471, 496
Halliburton, Chris, 460, 465, 495
Hamanishi, Craig M., 175
Hamel, Gary, 263, 280
Hampton, Gerald M., 175, 263, 280, 322, 348
Hanna, Nessim, 465, 496
Han, C. Min, 159, 175, 323, 328–9, 349
Hansen, D. M., 267, 280
Hanson, David P., 544
Hanson, John H., 131, 134
Hao, J., 243
Harich, Katrin, 473, 500
Harnett, Donald L., 558, 563, 584, 586
Harris, Philip R., 31, 54, 424–5, 451, 563, 586
Harris, Richard Jackson, 317, 349
Harvey, Michael G., 483, 496
Häubl, Gerald, 176
Hawking, Stephen W., 10, 22

Hawrysh, Bryan Mark, 556, 565, 571–2, 586, 590, 603
Hayashi, Shuji, 32–3, 54
Hayek, F.A., 179, 207
Heckscher, Eli, 607
Heede, Søren, 141–2, 176
Heeler, Roger, 495
Hemingway, Ernest, 417, 451
Hensel, Paul J., 458, 497
Herberger, Roy A. Jr, 563–4, 585, 593, 603
Hernandez, S. L., 245
Heslop, Louise A., 173, 175–6
Hilger, Marye Tharp, 131, 133, 344, 346, 348, 409, 540, 543
Hill, John S., 263, 267–8, 280, 472, 485, 496, 515, 518, 520, 532, 544
Hirschmann, Elisabeth C., 102, 134, 232, 244
Ho, Suk-Ching, 181, 203, 207, 494, 497
Hodges, Mark, 399, 409
Hoff, Edward J., 263, 281
Hofstede, Geert, 25, 54, 63–71, 95–6, 141, 201–2, 207, 225, 396, 409, 461, 473, 497, 516–19, 544, 558, 586, 595, 603
Holden, Nigel, 198, 207–8
Hollensen, Svend, 259, 280
Holzmüller, Hartmut H., 268, 280
Homer, Pamela, 133
Hooley, Graham J., 324, 349
Hoover, Robert J., 461, 497
Hornik, Jacob, 53–4, 471, 497
Hout, Thomas, 263, 280
Howard, J., 111, 134
Howes, David, 161, 175
Hoyer, Wayne D., 132, 495
Hsieh, Y. W., 106, 134
Hsu, F. L. K., 106, 134
Huang, Jen-Hung, 466, 470, 497
Huang, Yue Yuan, 332, 349
Hughes, M. A., 273, 280
Hung, Kineta, 471, 497
Huszagh, Sandra M., 144, 175
Huth, Sabine, 465, 497
Hyman, Michael R., 499

Inkeles, Alex, 14, 21–2
Ishida, Hideto, 388–9, 409
Ishihara, Shintaro, 46, 54
Ivenko, Leonid I., 603

Jackson, Barbara B., 548, 586
Jackson Jr. Donald W., 245
Jacobs, Laurence, 301, 315, 472, 497–8
Jacoby, Jacob R., 29, 53–4
Jacoby, N. H., 530, 544

Jaffé, Eugene D., 324, 327–8, 348–51
Jahoda, G., 215, 242, 244
Jain, Subhash C., 145, 175
Jamal, Ahmad, 132–3
James, Karen E., 458, 497
James, William L., 268, 280, 472, 496
Javalgi, Rajshekhar G., 459, 462, 467, 496–7
Joachimsthaler, Erich, 208, 340, 349
Jodelet, Denise, 18, 22
Johanson, J., 259, 281, 510, 543
Johansson, Johny K., 160, 175, 183, 186, 208, 230–1, 242, 244, 322–4, 326, 329, 348–9, 361, 366, 380, 383, 385, 409
Johar, J., 133, 279
John, J., 280
Johnson, Denise, 380, 450, 452, 457, 496
Johnson, Lester W., 410
Johnstone, Harvey, 460, 497
Jolibert, Alain, 173–4, 320, 324, 328, 347, 349, 351, 512, 544, 584, 603
Jordt, Ingrid, 132, 149, 152, 173
Jung, Carl Gustav, 74, 96

Kadima, K., 51, 54
Kagame, Alexis, 51, 54
Kahle, Lynn R., 133, 273, 280, 499
Kaikati, J. G., 529, 544
Kale, Sudhir H., 396, 410, 473, 497
Kamamoto, Mitsuko, 293–5, 295, 315
Kamins, Michael A., 327, 349
Kapferer, Jean-Noel, 338, 349
Karns, David, 350
Karsaklian, Eliane, 116, 134
Kashani, Kamran, 266–7, 280, 400, 410, 453, 497, 521, 544
Kassaye, W. Wossen, 478, 497
Katsikeas, Constantine S., 396, 410
Katz, Helen, 473, 497
Kaufman, Carol Felker, 32, 54
Kaynak, Erdener, 114, 133, 159, 175, 461, 497
Keegan, Warren J., 233, 244, 270–1, 280, 364, 380, 573, 586
Kelley, Harold H., 552, 583, 586
Keown, Charles F., 315, 367, 381, 460–1, 497
Khanna, Sri Ram, 327, 349
Khera, Inder, 327, 349–50
Khrutskogo, V. E., 199, 208
Khuri, Fuad I., 356, 381
Kieser, A., 5, 22
Kim, C. Y., 349–50
Kim, Dong Han, 177
Kim, G., 350
Kishii, T., 459, 497
Kitayama, Shinobu, 108, 132, 134
Klein, Lisa R., 398–9, 410

Kluckhohn, Clyde, 4, 22
Kluckhohn, Florence R., 4, 19, 22–5, 87, 96, 113
Koh, Anthony C., 234, 244
Kopytoff, Igor, 139, 152, 175
Koranteng, Juliana, 400, 410
Kosaka, Hiroshi, 96, 134, 208
Kotabe, Masaaki, 518, 521, 544
Kotler, Philip, 102, 134, 185, 187, 208, 340, 350
Kracmar, J. Z., 228, 244
Kraft, Frederick B., 158, 174, 324, 327, 348, 350
Kragh, Simon Ulrik, 161–2, 174
Krieger, Nathalie, 349
Krishnakumar, Parameswar, 320, 350
Kristensen, Kai, 244
Kroeber, Alfred L., 4, 22
Kroeber-Riel, Werner, 464, 471, 498
Kropp, Fredric, 411, 499
Kunita, Motoko, 459, 498
Kuribayashi, S., 383, 386, 389, 410
Kushner, J. M., 131, 134, 228, 244

La Porta, Rafael, 583, 586
Label, W. A., 529, 544
Lackman, Conway L., 515, 544
Lagerlöf, Selma, 23, 53
Lamb, Charles W. Jr, 320, 326, 348, 352
Lambin, Jean-Jacques, 338, 350
Lampert, Shlomo I., 350
Lanasa, John M., 544
Lane, Henry W., 396, 410
Lane, Paul M., 32, 54
Langeard, Eric, 212, 244
Lascu, Dana-Nicoleta, 199, 208
Latour, Michael S., 545
Lau, K.F., 466, 500
Lauginié, Jean-Marcel, 188, 207
Laurent, André, 63, 87–9, 95–6, 161, 165, 177
Laurent, Clint R., 105, 131, 134,
Lazarde, Michelle M., 326, 350
Lazer, William, 76, 96, 112, 121, 134, 186, 208
Le Clézio, J. M. G., 21–2
Leardi, M., 401, 405, 409
Leclerc, France, 316–17, 350
Lee, Byoung-Woo, 349
Lee, Chol, 495
Lee, Dongdae, 496
Lee, George, 446, 578
Lee, James Λ, 431–2, 451
Lee, Kan Hom, 530, 544
Lee, Khai S., 381
Lee, Wei-Na, 473, 497

Leeflang, Peter S. H., 140, 173, 175, 191, 208
Lefebvre, Victorina D., 598, 603
Lehmann, Donald R., 294, 315
Lelièvre, Hélène, 409
Lemak, David J., 133
Lemmink, Jos, 315
Lessem, Ronnie, 191, 208
Lesser, J. A., 273, 280
Letts, Alex, 400, 410
Leung, K., 212, 244
Levine, Robert A., 432, 451
Levine, Robert V., 428, 451
Levinson, Daniel J., 14, 21–2,
Levitt, Theodore, 101, 134, 139–40, 146–7, 175
Levy-Bruhl, Lucien, 17
Lewis, Steven A., 560, 586
Li, Tiger, 267, 280
Lian, Brad, xv
Liang, Kong, 472, 498
Light, C. David, 478, 499
Lillis, Charles M., 173, 176
Lim, Chae Un, 544
Lim, Guan H., 381
Lim, Jee-Su, 351
Lin, Carolyn A., 459–60, 462, 498
Linton, Ralph, 4, 15, 22, 84, 96
List, Friedrich, 139
Littler, Dale, 346, 350
Littré, Emile, 4
Litvin, Deborah R., xv
Liu, Raymond, 132, 135
Lohnes, Colleen, 174, 347
Longworth, John W., 299, 315
Lopez-de-Silanes, Florencio, 586
Louis, Ernst A., 351
Lowe, Andy, 244
Ludlow, Peter W., 260, 280
Lumpkin, J. R, 321, 323, 350
Lumwanu, F., 51, 54
Luo, Yadong, 511, 544, 589, 603
Luqmani, Mushtaq, 469, 498
Lysonski, Steven, 495

Maalouf, Amine, 42–3, 54
Machleit, K. A., 323–4, 348
Macrae, Chris, 340, 350
McCall, J. B., 552, 586
McCarthy, E. Jerome, 503, 544
McCartney, Laton, 556, 586
McClelland, David, 67
McCornell, J. D., 297, 315
McCracken, Grant, 120, 134, 149, 152, 176
McCullough, Lynette S., 464, 498
McCullough, Wayne R., 485, 498

McDonald, William, J., 132, 134
McIntyre, Roger P., 396, 410
McKersie, Robert B., 559, 587
McLeod, Douglas M., 459, 498
McQuirk, Jim, 460, 500
MacLean Johns, Cort, 315
Macneil, Ian R., 549, 586
Madden, Thomas J., 351
Maheswaran, Durairaj, 321, 350
Malhotra, Naresh K., 282, 314, 497
Malinowski, Bronislaw, 5, 8–9, 22,
Malliaris, P., 175
Manrai, Ajay K., 208
Manrai, Lalita A., 208
Manzer, L. Lee, 280
Marcel, Claude, 351
Marchetti, Renato, 218–19, 244
Mariet, François, 478, 481, 498
Marks, Lawrence J., 544
Markus, Hazel Rose, 108, 132, 134
Martenson, Rita, 168, 176, 459, 461, 471, 476,
    498
Martin, Ingrid M., 326, 350
Maruyama, Magoroh, 228, 234, 245
Maslow, Abraham H., 103–4, 134
Mather, Anne, 277–9, 281
Matsumoto, M., 557, 586
Mattsson, Jan, 315, 510, 543
Mauviel, Maurice, 46–7, 53–5
Mayer, C. S., 218, 245
Mayo, Michel A., 526, 544
M'biti, John, 427, 451
Mead, Margaret, 12, 15, 22, 59, 90–2, 96, 593
Meissner, Hans Günther, 563, 584–5, 603
Mendenhall, Mark, 104, 134
Merton, Robert, 30, 55
Michaels, R. E., 586
Michell, Paul, 470, 495
Michon, Christian, 207
Mick, David Glen, 132, 134, 544
Milhomme, Albert J., 165, 176
Miller, Fred, 395, 410, 470, 498
Miniard, Paul W., 134
Mishima, Yukio, 421, 451
Mintu, Alma T., 585
Mitchell, V. W., 111, 134
Montesquieu, Charles de, 15–16, 22, 45, 55
Montgomery, David B., 253, 279, 383, 386,
    390, 410
Moran, Robert T., 31, 54, 424–5, 451, 563,
    586
Morand, David A., 425, 451
Morel, Pierre, 434, 451, 596–7, 603
Morello, G., 173, 176, 321, 350
Morganosky, Michelle A., 326, 350

Morris, Jon D., 222, 245
Morris, Michael, 133, 279
Morsbach, Helmut, 425, 451
Moscovici, Serge, 18, 22
Mourier, Pascal, 480, 498
Mueller, Barbara, 459, 463, 467, 484, 498
Mühlbacher, Hans, 397, 410
Mullen, Thomas, 584, 603
Mummalaneni, Venkatapparao, 498
Munch, James M., 473, 496
Murata, Shoji, 96, 134, 208
Murray, Noel M., 494, 498
Murray, Sandra B., 494, 498
Mussey, Dagmar, 206, 208
Myrdal, Gunnar, 201, 208
Mytton, Graham, 213, 226–7, 245

Nagashima, Akira, 173, 176, 327, 349–50
Nakane, Chie, 388, 410
Naor, Jacob, 197, 208
Napoleon-Biguma, Constantin, 52, 55
Narayana, Chem L., 173, 176
Naumann, Earl, 242, 245
Ndao, Cheikh Alioune, 529, 544
Nebenzahl, Israel D., 160, 175, 323–4, 327–8,
    348–51
Neelankavil, James P., 463, 467, 471, 498, 501
Nehemkis, P., 544
Nes, Erik, 320, 347
Neubauer, Fred, 191, 208
Nishina, Sadafumi, 318, 350
Nonaka, Ikujiro, 186, 208, 230–1, 242, 244,
    349, 366, 380
Nueno, Jose Luis, 208, 392, 410

Oberg, Kalvero, 433, 452
Ofir, Chezy, 294, 315
O'Grady, Shawna, 396, 410
Ogram, Ernest W., 543
Oh, Sejo, 543, 585
Oh, T. K., 590, 603
Ohlin, Bertil, 607
Ohmae, Kenichi, 256, 281, 389–90, 410,
    550–1, 586
Oliver, Lauren, 352
Ollivier, Alain, 158, 173, 207, 321, 347, 379,
    574, 586
Olsen, Barbara, 132, 134
Oneal, John R., xv
Onkvisit, Sak, 332, 350, 483, 498
Ortiz-Buonafina, Marta, 545
Orwell, George, 571, 586
Ottosen, Rune, 94, 96
Oxenfeldt, A.R., 360, 381
Ozsomer, Aysegul, 268, 281

Pahud de Mortanges, Charles, 289, 315, 390, 410
Palia, Aspy P., 367, 381
Pan, Yigang, 337, 350–1
Papadopoulos, Nicolas G., 159, 175–6, 328, 347
Parameswaran, Ravi, 220, 245, 328, 351
Parker, Philip M., 133, 144, 149, 174, 206, 208, 361, 380
Paz, Octavio, 597, 603
Péan, Pierre, 524, 528, 545
Pearson, Emil, 51, 55
Pedersen, Paul B., 22, 96, 452
Peebles, Dean M., 340, 351, 485–6, 498
Perdue, B. C., 560, 586
Perlmutter, Howard, 281
Perrin, Michel, 324–5, 351
Peterson, Blyth, Cato Associates Inc., 151, 176
Peterson, Robert A., 320, 328, 351
Petit, Karl, 53, 55
Phillips, W.E., 462, 498
Philpot, J. W., 242, 245
Picard, Jacques, 267, 281
Pichene, B., 134
Piercy, Nigel F., 396, 410
Pike, K., 212, 245
Pimblett, Carole, 265, 281
Pine, B. Joseph II, 264–5, 280
Pinsdorf, Marion K., 522, 545
Plummer, Joseph, 211, 245
Pohl, Manfred, 201, 208
Poortinga, Ype H., 22, 55, 212, 242, 245
Porter, Michael E., 252, 262, 280–1
Prahalad, C. K., 263, 280
Pras, Bernard, 221–2, 245
Price, Lydia J., 133
Pruyn, Ad, 209
Pruitt, Dean G., 559–61, 586
Prus, Robert C., 353, 357, 381
Punnett, Betty Jane, 134, 584, 603
Pye, Lucian W., 564–5, 568, 572, 574, 586, 589–90, 603

Queau, Philippe, 399, 410
Quelch, John A., 200, 208, 263, 281, 398–9, 410
Quraeshi, Zahir, 498

Radebaugh, Lee H., 165, 174, 543
Rajan, Mahesh N., 603
Ramaprasad, Jyotika, 462, 496
Ramuz, Charles Ferdinand, 21
Rao, C.P., 321, 351
Ratz, David G., 483–4, 499
Raveed, S., 460, 499

Rawls, John, 532, 545
Rawwas, Mohammed Y.A., 397, 410, 543
Redding, S. G., 105, 131, 134, 518, 545
Reierson, Curtis, 173, 176, 320, 329, 351
Reilly, Michael D., 119, 135
Reinhard, K., 462, 498
Reischauer, Edwin O., 41, 53, 55
Renforth, William, 460, 467, 495, 499
Resnik, Alan J., 460, 499
Ribeiro, Gustavo Lins, 399, 410
Ricardo, David, 137–8, 176, 607
Rice, Marshall D., 471, 497
Richins, M., 108, 113–14, 135
Ricks, David A., 134, 263, 281, 463, 499
Ridnour, Rick E., 496
Riesz, Peter C., 360–1, 381
Rietbroek, Jan-Willem, 315
Rim, Ik-Tae, 325, 347
Ritzer, George, 145–6, 156, 158, 163, 176
Ro, Kong-Kyun, 349
Robinson, Chris, 110, 131, 135
Robles, Fernando, 397, 410
Rodgers, Waymond, 585
Rodrik, Dani, 157, 176
Roeber, Carter A., 357, 381
Rogers, E. M., 289, 315
Ronkainen, Illka A., 140, 172, 174, 169, 172, 174, 277, 279, 332, 348, 391–2, 401, 409, 470, 496, 523
Rose, Gregory M., 411, 466, 499
Rosen, Barry-Nathan, 330, 351
Rosenberg, Larry J., 390, 410
Rosenfield, James R., 397, 410
Rosenthal, Walter, 484, 499
Ross, Caroline, 543
Roth, Kendall, 265, 281
Roth, M. S., 282, 315
Rotter, J. B., 71, 96
Royo, Marcelo, 495
Rubin, J. Z., 561, 586
Rudden, Eileen, 280
Ryans, John K., 483–6, 498–9, 544

Sadarangani, Pradip, 132
Saegaert, Joel, 131, 273, 281, 497
Saghafi, Massoud M., 325, 351
Sahagun, Bernardino de, 21
Saito Duerr, Mitsuko, 377, 381, 445, 452
Sakade, Florence, 548, 587
Sakai, John T., 407
Salles, Robert, 351
Salwen, Michael B., 460, 462
Samiee, Saeed, 173, 176, 265, 281–2, 315, 320–1, 351
Samli, A. Coskun, 315

Sano, Yoshihiro, 552, 565, 568, 574, 585
Sapir, Edward, 212, 245, 426, 449, 452
Saporito, Bill, 261, 266, 281
Sarathy, Ravi, 479, 481, 499
Saunders, J. A., 173
Sawyer, J., 562, 587
Scanzoni, J., 549, 587
Schaefer, Anja, 321, 351
Schein, Edgar H., 87, 96
Schlegelmilch, Bodo B., 315
Schlieper, Katrin, 346, 350
Schmidt, Klaus D., 596, 603
Schmidt, Richard W., 497
Schmitt, Bernd H., 337, 350–1
Schneider-Lenné, E., 437, 452
Schooler, Robert D., 320, 325, 351
Schroeder, Michael, 460–1, 499
Schurr, Paul H., 543, 585
Schwarz Gehrke, Theodore, 584, 602
Schweiger, Günther, 173, 176
Schweitzer, John C., 472, 495
Schwiercz, Paul M., 515, 543
Sechrest, L., 216, 245
Segall, Marshall H., 17, 21–2, 45, 53, 55
Sentell, G. D., 242, 245
Sessions, David N., 498
Sehti, S. Prakash, 147, 176
Shalofsky, Ivor, 339, 351
Sharif, Mohammed, 174
Sharma, S., 159, 176
Shaw, John J., 332, 350, 483, 498
Sherry, John F., 43, 55, 157, 176, 463, 499
Sheth, Jagdish N., 111, 134, 141–2, 147, 174, 176, 262, 281
Shimaguchi, Mitsuaki, 384–6, 389, 410
Shimp, Terence A., 159, 176, 326, 351
Shipley, David, 349
Shleifer, Andrei, 586
Shoemaker, Robert, 230, 244
Shoham, Aviv, 282, 315, 396, 411
Sikora, Ed, 369, 380
Silk, A. J., 243
Simon, Paul, 437, 452
Sin, Yat-ming, 494, 497
Sinatra, Alexandro, 197, 208
Singh, Jagdip, 114, 124, 135
Sissmann, Pierre, 272, 281
Siu, Wai-Sum, 466, 499
Sjolander, Richard, 361, 381
Slatter, Stuart St P., 506, 545
Smith, Adam, 56, 96
Smith, David E., 141–2, 176
Smith, Kenwin, 450, 452
Snyder, Leslie B., 473, 499
Soehl, Robin, 281

Solomon, Michael R., 104, 118, 124, 135, 297, 315, 343, 351
Somasundaram, T.N., 478, 499
Sondergaard, Michael, 64, 96
Sood, James H., 143, 177, 222, 245
Sorokin, Piritim, 30, 55
de Souza, Marianne, 243
Spar, Deborah L., 143, 177
Sparkman, Richard M., 497
Spindola, Carol G., 540
Spotts, Harlan E., 460, 465, 500
Sprick, Sara J., 349
Sproles, George B., 360, 381
Sriram, Ven, 473, 499
Stalk, George Jr, 338, 347, 371, 380
Stanton, J. L., 215, 226–8, 245
Stayman, Douglas M., 132
Steele, Murray, 161, 177
Steenkamp, Jan-Benedikt E.M., 361, 381
Stern, Bruce L., 460, 499
Stern, Louis W., 561, 572, 584
Stewart, Sally, 494, 499
Still, Richard R., 263, 267–8, 280, 515, 518, 544–5
Stobaugh, Robert B., 264, 281
Stoetzel, J., 193, 208
Stöllnberger, Barbara, 268, 280
Strandskov, Jesper, 584
Straus, Karen, 119, 135
Stripp, William, 596–7, 604
Strodtbeck, Frederick L., 4, 19, 22–5, 87, 96, 113
Strutton, David, 410
Suk, Jong, 351
Suls, J., 464, 499
Sumitomo Corporation, 261, 281
Sumner, G. A., 432, 452
Sunoo, D. H., 320, 351
Surget, Véronique, 409
Sussman, Lyle, 450, 452
Suto, Nobuhiko, 508
Swanson, Lauren A., 472, 494, 499
Sweeney, Tim, 243
Swinder, Janda, 321, 351
Szybillo, George J., 54

Tai, Susan H. C., 270, 281, 484, 499
Takashi, S., 230, 246
Tam, Jackie L. M., 270, 281,
Tamate, Mariko, 496
Tambyah, Siok-Kuan, 500
Tan, Soo J., 367–9, 381
Tankersley, Clint B., 348
Tanner, John F., 543
Tanouchi, Koichi, 121, 135

Tansey, Richard, 471, 499
Tansuhaj, Patriya S., 133, 280, 409
Taylor, Humphrey, 226, 245
Taylor, Ronald E., 183–4, 208, 464, 498
Taylor, William, 523, 545
Telesio, Piero, 264, 281
Tellis, Gerard J., 361, 381
Terpstra, Vern, 323, 349
Thoenig, Jean-Claude, 338, 348
Thorelli, Hans B., 510, 545, 323, 325, 329,
    349, 351
Thorpe, Jim, 495
Thorpe, Richard, 244
Tiano, André, 287, 315
Tietz, B., 198, 208
Tixier, Maud, 463, 500, 512, 544
Tjernlund, Anders, 500
Tongberg, R. C., 325, 351
Traoré Sérié, Régina, 574, 587
Triandis, Harry C., 25, 35, 55, 61, 77, 96, 554,
    587
Trompenaars, Fons, 25, 55, 82, 96, 296, 315,
    572, 587
Tsalikis, John, 507, 545
Tse, David K., 472, 500, 559, 587
Tull, Donald S., 244
Tuncalp, Secil, 226–7, 245, 282, 315, 474, 476,
    500
Tung, Rosalie L., 203, 208, 511, 545, 564, 568,
    574, 587, 589, 603–4
Turcq, Dominique, 384, 395, 411
Turpin, Dominique, 312, 389, 411
Tylor, Edward, 5, 22

Ueda, Keiko, 419, 452
Unger, Fritz, 465, 497
Unger, Lynette S., 464, 500
Urban, Christine D., 151, 174
Usunier, Jean-Claude, 29, 31, 55, 81, 96, 150,
    172, 177, 179, 198, 207–8, 218–19,
    232, 244–5, 260–1, 272, 281, 324,
    326, 352, 384, 395, 411, 525, 530,
    545, 562, 569, 585

Vahlne, J. E., 259, 280
Valentine, Gill, 136, 172–3
Valette-Florence, Pierre, 31, 55
Valla, Jean-Paul, 351
Van Herk, Hester, 212, 229, 245
Van Maanen, John, 161, 165, 177
Van Mesdag, Martin, 263, 281
Van Raaij, W. F., 102, 111, 135, 140, 173, 175,
    185, 191, 208, 215, 245, 484, 500
Van Tubergen, G. Norman, 495
Van Zandt, H. R., 562, 587

Vandenbergh, Bruce, 335, 352
Varvoglis, Fanis, 351
Veblen, Thorstein, 104
Veeck, Ann, 361, 381
Vega, Tomas, 351
Ven, Sriram, 473, 499
Verhage, B., 113–14, 135
Verhallen; Theo M., 212, 229, 245
Verna, Gérard, 375, 381, 506, 525, 530, 545
Vernon, Raymond P., 259, 281
Vishny, Robert W., 586
Vitell, Scott J., 543
Von Stackelberg, H., 372, 381
Vuursten, Karel, 242, 246

Waarts, Eric, 209
Wafai, Mohamed, 470, 500
Wagner, J., 174, 348
Walker, Bruce J., 320, 348
Walle, A.H., 472, 500
Wallendorf, Mélanie, 119, 132, 135
Walls, Jan, 587
Walsh, Len, 44, 55
Walter, Ingo, 524, 545
Walton, Richard E., 559, 587
Wang, Chih-Kang, 320, 326, 352
Ward, James W., 460, 500
Warrington, M. B., 552, 586
Watkins, Harry S., 132, 135
Watt, James, 499
Wayne-Saegaert, M.,
Weber, Max, 363, 381
Webster, Cynthia, 228, 246
Wee, Chow Hou, 466–7, 500
Weeks, William H., 19–22, 53, 55, 90, 96, 443,
    452
Weigand, Robert E., 367, 369, 381
Weinberger, Marc G., 460, 465, 500
Weiss, Brad, 241, 246
Weiss, Stephen E., 569, 572, 587, 596–7, 604
Weitz, B., 562, 587
Wentz, Laurel, 403, 411
Werner, O., 218–19, 243
Wesley, John, 363
West, Douglas C., 460, 500
Wetzels, Martin, 315
White, Gregory P., 213, 215, 244, 348
White, Phillip D., 324, 328, 352
Whitelock, J. M., 194, 209, 265, 281
Whitlow, S. Scott, 495
Whorf, Benjamin Lee, 5, 21, 415, 426–7,
    449–50
Wierenga, Berend, 193, 195, 209
Wildt, A. R., 320, 351
Wiles, Charles R., 466, 500

Wiles, Judith A., 467, 500
Wilk, Richard, 105, 135
Wilke, Margaritha, 336–7, 352
Willenborg, Bartjan, 499
Williams, Stephen C., 299, 315
Wills, James R., 285, 315, 456, 500
Wilsher, Peter, 330, 352
Wind, Yoram, 242, 246, 255–6, 263, 281
Winski, J. M., 485, 496
Wolfe, Alan, 195, 209
Wolfe, William G., 245
Wong, John K., 409
Wong, Nancy, 57, 60, 96, 108, 110, 132, 135, 150, 177
Woods, Walter A., 144, 177
Woronoff, Jon, 384, 388, 390, 409
Worthley, Reginald, 315

Xardel, Dominique, 397–8, 409, 433, 451

Yamada, Y., 361, 381
Yamin, Mo, 134
Yan, Chen, 41, 55
Yang, Chung-Fang, 105–6, 111–12, 131, 135
Yang, M.C., 106, 135
Yaprak, Attila, 220, 245, 328, 351–2

Yau, Oliver H. M., 105, 112, 131, 135
Yavas, Ugur, 320, 352, 498
Yeung, Kevin, 466, 500
Yong, Mahealani, 54, 95
Yoshimori, Masaru, 332, 338, 340, 352
Yoshino, Michael Y., 383, 389, 411
Youssef, Fahti, 423, 451
Yucelt, Ugur, 361, 381, 497

Zaharna, R. S., 433, 435, 452
Zaichkowsky, Judith L., 143, 177, 556, 565, 571–2, 586, 590, 603
Zaidi, S. M., 245
Zaltman, Gerald, 222, 246, 503, 543
Zandpour, Fred, 459, 462, 473, 500
Zax, M., 230, 246
Zayavlov, P. S., 199, 209
Zeithaml, Carl P., 503, 545
Zeithaml, Valarie A., 343, 352, 359, 361, 381, 503, 545
Zeldin, Theodore, 436, 570, 587
Zeller, Eric, 387, 411
Zhang, Yong, 471, 501
Zhao, Xiaoyan, 279
Zhou, Nan, 472, 500–1
Zinkhan, George M., 499

Subject index

Act of God, 436, 450
Advertiser–agency relationships, 164, 483,
    485–6
Advertising agencies, 183, 203, 482–4
Advertising appeals, 459–60, 473
Advertising expenses *per capita*, 473–4, 494
Advertising legislation, 112, 456–8, 469, 475–6
Advertising standardization, 430, 462–3,
    471–3, 483–5
Affective cultures, 73, 82, 572
Afghanistan, 227
Africa,
    advertising, 180–1, 297, 403, 472
    consumer behaviour, 152, 204, 292
    culture, 59, 68–9, 301, 574–5
    negotiation style, 506, 512, 596–7
Age, 59, 109, 223, 296, 325–6, 417, 467, 474
Algeria, 322
Amae, 388, 557
American way of life, 147–8, 196, 606
Anglo-Saxon, 81, 88, 194, 401, 420, 424, 428,
    438, 547
Anti-trust legislation, 191
Arabs, 41–2, 49, 68, 92–3, 161–2, 301, 424–5,
    455, 481, 562–3, 591
Arbitrage, 367, 573
Argentina, 68, 143, 317
Armenians, 46, 481, 591
ASEAN, 190
Asia, 61, 63, 195, 108, 200–3, 301, 327, 421,
    424–5, 459, 463, 466

Assimilation, 118–19, 269
Atomistic view, 231–3, 242
Attitude towards action, 24, 72–86
Australia, 68, 143, 269, 299, 317–18, 321, 326,
    361, 460, 466–7, 525
Austria, 68, 143, 205, 272, 397, 480
Azerbaidjan, 46

Back-translation, 218–19
Baksheesh, 524
Bali, 92
Bantu (People), 31, 34, 51–2, 222, 467, 567,
    605
Barbados, 143
Bargaining, 355–7, 512
Beer, 141–2, 154–5, 161, 194, 395, 470
Being orientation, 35, 57, 74, 82, 147, 296,
    512, 515–16
Belgium, 46, 68, 88, 144, 161, 272, 321,
    377–8, 458, 479
Body gestures, 423–4
Bolivia, 226
Brand loyalty, 110, 354
Brand names, 330–2
Brand, 144, 316–19, 330–41, 483
    functions of the, 337–9
    global, 339–41
    linguistic aspects of, 331–7
Brazil, 68, 71, 85, 273, 373, 428, 563
    advertising, 471, 474–5
    consumer behaviour, 116–17, 180, 286, 301

Brazil *Continued*
　　Made in Brazil, 318, 322, 324–5, 328
Bribery, 524–30, 598
Bulgaria, 182, 197, 319, 424, 492–3
Business ethics, 182, 526–32, 540–3
Buy National campaigns, 158–60
Buyer–seller relationships, 511–15, 548–9

Calibration equivalence, 213, 222–3
Cameroon, 287
Canada, 68, 322, 396
　　advertising, 398, 459, 461, 479, 488
　　consumer behaviour, 143–4, 361
　　negotiation style, 559, 561, 575
Cartesian logic, 570
Cassis de Dijon ruling, 193, 289
Castes, 60–1
Catalogue sales, 105, 183, 397
Catholic, 105, 362–3
Chile, 68, 71, 143
China, 217, 273
　　advertising, 460–1, 470–2
　　brands, 332, 336–7
　　consumer behaviour, 105–6, 143, 149–50, 270
　　culture, 41, 60, 88, 112, 201–3, 273, 299, 333, 583
　　Made in China, 323, 325–6
　　negotiation style, 445–6, 511–12, 525, 559, 561, 572, 574, 576–8, 589–90
Climate (adaptation to), 16, 152, 194, 287–8, 291
Code law, 77
Cognitive styles, 87, 102, 111–12
Collectivism, 26, 62–3, 86–7, 104–6, 108–10, 132, 190, 201, 396, 465, 471, 473, 518, 553, 555, 584
Colloquial speech, 462, 494
Colombia, 68, 143
Colonization, 41–2
Colours (cultural meaning of), 221–2, 470–1
Commerce, 503–5
Common Law, 77, 143
Common sense, 78
Communication and context, 416–20, 594
Communication styles, 420–1, 553, 564, 571–2, 590, 599
Comparative advantage (law of), 138–9, 606–7
Comparative advertising, 457–8, 472, 474
Competencies (cultural relativity of), 15–17
Competition, 392
　　avoidance, 370–1
　　globalization of, 251–63
Competitions (sales promotion), 400–4

Conceptual equivalence, 212–15, 463
Confucian values, 202, 556–7
Conspicuous consumption, 104, 150, 201
Constructs, 215
Consumer,
　　cultural resistance of the, 156–7
　　culture, 145–8, 157
　　dissatisfaction, 103, 113–14, 124, 503–4
　　ethnocentrism, 159
　　involvement, 102, 111
　　loyalty, 102, 110–11, 132
Consumerism, 102, 112, 124–5, 180, 360, 456
Contextual equivalence, 213, 227–8
Copts, 591
Copy strategy, 454, 458–72
Corn Laws, 138
Corporate culture, 87–8, 523–4
Corporate image, 483
Costa Rica, 68
Costs, 251–4, 284–5, 296, 365–6, 392, 397
Cost–volume relationships, 253
Country of origin images, 157–60, 220, 318–30
Courtesy bias, 228
Credibility,
　　collective, 555–6
　　personal, 417, 506, 553–5
Creolization, 161
Cross-border cultures, 11–13
Cross-cultural equivalence, 211–30, 242, 450
Cuba, 327, 554–5
Cultural affinity classes, 270–2
　　zones, 270–1
Cultural assumptions, 24–6, 41, 57–8, 71–2, 87–8
Cultural borrowing, 41–4, 184–8, 455
Cultural consumption, 118–19
Cultural hostility, 45–7, 54
Cultural identification, 57, 270
Cultural identity, 9, 118–20, 139, 606
Cultural relativism, 427–9, 565
Cultural resistance, 156–7
Cultural violence, 606–7
Culture and consumer behaviour, 101–60
　　definitions of, 4–5
　　elements of, 5–9
　　and nationality, 11–15
Culture-bound products, 149–55
Culture shock, 433–4
Custom duties, 189
Customs union, 189–90
Czech Republic, 198, 321

Data collection, 213, 227–35, 242
Decentring, 219

Decision-making process, 76, 505, 510, 556, 565, 594, 597
Delivery dates, 80–1, 600–2
Denmark, 68, 88, 116, 140, 215, 259, 261, 272, 321, 457, 466
Developing countries, 114, 157–8, 172, 180, 228–9, 267, 401, 456, 461, 471
Direct marketing, 397–9
Discounts, 400
Distribution,
    channels, 195, 383–96, 504
    choice of foreign distribution channels, 391–3
    exclusive distribution agreements, 368
    Japanese, 383–91
Distributive orientation, 553, 559–61
Doing orientation, 35, 57, 74, 82, 147, 296, 512, 515–16, 561
DPPO (*Direction participative par objectifs*), 69
Dual concern model, 559–60
Dumping, 365–6

Eastern Europe, 190, 197–200
Eating habits, 6, 105, 107–8, 141–3, 146–55, 161–2, 172
Economicity of time, 27–9, 147, 190, 293, 359–60, 553, 567–8, 589
Economies of scale, 253, 284–5
Economies of scope, 253
Ecuador, 68, 460
Educational practices, 15–17, 56, 116–17
Egypt, 69, 181, 185, 423, 530, 575
El Salvador, 68, 327
Emic, 212, 242
Empathy (international), 435
Eskimos, 431
Ethiopia, 11, 69
Ethnic consumption, 103, 118–20
Ethnicity, 118–20, 181, 228, 464, 481–2, 596–7
Ethnocentrism, 39, 103, 255–7, 286–7, 299, 364, 431–2, 436
Etic, 212, 242
Etymology, 333, 346
Euro-brands, 265–6, 346
Europe, 148, 372, 467, 475, 483, 558
    culture, 195–6
    internal market, 191–7, 261, 289
European audience, 464
European consumer, 111, 115, 193–6
European trademark, 341
European Union, 140, 188–97, 267, 290, 397, 458, 475, 480
Exchange rates, 373–5
Expatriates, 150, 286

Experience effects, 253, 284–5
Experiential equivalence, 213, 216–17
Extended family, 109, 213
Extraterritoriality, 86
Extrinsic rewards, 520–1

Face giving, 511
Familism, 106, 515
Fatalism, 73–5, 515
FCPA (Foreign Corrupt Practices Act), 86, 524, 527, 529–31
Femininity, 64, 66–9, 72, 212, 124, 141, 190, 394, 396, 466, 516, 519
Finland, 68, 143, 158, 272, 327, 464
Food and Drug Administration (FDA), 163, 285
Force majeure, 436, 450
Foreign exchange controls, 84, 373–6
France,
    advertising, 183–4, 186–7, 455–66, 470–2, 474–5, 479–80
    business ethics, 524, 530–1, 540–1
    consumer behaviour, 105, 115–17, 143–4, 151–5, 158–9, 173, 266, 271–2, 291, 295, 301, 395, 605
    culture, 32, 35, 38, 49–50, 68–70, 79, 82, 84, 88, 93, 273, 420, 423, 425, 583
    Made in France, 158, 173, 306, 317, 320–1, 323–4, 326–7
    marketing management, 185–6, 192, 210, 257–9, 338, 387, 398, 446–8, 519
    negotiation style, 548, 550, 561–2, 567, 569–71, 588, 592, 594–5
    sales promotion, 401, 403
Franchise, 406–8
Free-trade area, 189–90
Friendship, 57, 59, 356, 422, 572, 589–91, 595
Functional equivalence, 213, 215–16
Future orientation, 25, 28, 31–2, 52, 147, 373, 404, 565

Gai-jin, 34, 121, 382, 386
GATT (General Agreement on Tariffs and Trade), 39, 178, 188–9, 262
Geocentrism, 255–6, 364
Germany, 217
    advertising, 183, 204, 458, 460–1, 463, 465, 472, 474–5, 470–80, 484
    business ethics, 524–5, 530–1
    competition, 371
    consumer behaviour, 105, 116, 144, 151–5, 194, 204–6, 266, 271–2, 301, 605
    culture, 69–70, 79, 84, 88, 94, 583
    Made in Germany, 158, 220, 317–25, 327
    management style, 192, 437

Germany *Continued*
    marketing management, 391, 397–8,
        407–8, 523
    negotiation style, 547–8, 561, 563, 588,
        595–6
    selling style, 514, 519
    technical standards, 285, 288
Ghana, 69, 301, 502
Gifts (promotional), 401, 403–4
Global advertising campaigns, 484–6
Global marketing, 139–56
Global media, 400, 477–9
Global strategy, 262
Globalization of markets, 101, 136–7, 139–48,
        156–7, 252, 257–9, 289, 605
Grammatical equivalence, 213, 216
Greece, 68, 229, 272, 395–6, 424, 457, 480–1,
        576, 584
Grey markets, 367–9
Group membership, 33–9, 512, 518
Guanxi, 511, 589
Guatemala, 68, 507

Hard sell approach, 513–15
Hierarchy of needs, 67, 103–4
Hierarchy, 9, 64–7, 69, 429
High context, 417, 419–20, 516–18
Hinduism, 11, 61, 116, 576
Hiragana, 121, 305, 337, 438
Hispanics, 18, 31, 120, 127–31, 273, 481
Home country rule, 193
Honduras, 525
Hong Kong, 68, 105, 202, 270, 322, 463, 467,
        478
Hopi Indians, 427
Human rights, 63
Humour, 464–5
Hungary, 190, 197–9

Icon, 297, 333–4
Ideologism, 73, 77–8, 553, 569–70
Idiomatic equivalence, 213, 216
Implicit messages, 419–20
Implicit salary, 525
Import licence, 375–6
Incentives, 516–17, 520–1
India, 12, 173, 563–8
    advertising, 457, 459, 462, 471, 473
    culture, 61, 68, 74, 94, 227, 422
    Made in India, 320, 337
Indians (American), 21, 25
Individualism, 26, 62–3, 86–7, 104–6, 108–10,
        132, 147, 190, 201, 396, 465, 471,
        473, 517–21, 553, 584
Indonesia, 68, 88, 191, 201, 228, 376–7

Industrial products (images of), 324–5
Inflation, 191, 222–3, 354, 372–4, 404
Informative advertising, 459–62, 474
Ingroup, 34–9, 118, 120, 132, 432, 515, 553,
        557–8, 573, 584, 589, 596–7
Insh'Allah, 49, 92
Instructor's manual, xiv, 584
Instrumental communication, 561
Integrative orientation, 553, 559–64
Intercultural communication, 436–40
Intercultural marketing, 251, 258–73
Intercultural approach, xii, 552
International diffusion of innovations, 289
International trade, 137–9
Internet, 203, 398–400, 478
Interpreters, 439, 450
Interviews, 214, 221, 228, 234–6, 328
Intracultural setting, 552
Intrinsic rewards, 520–1
Involvement (consumer), 111
IQ tests, 17, 45
Iran, 11, 158, 321, 373, 473
Iraq, 11, 69, 94
Ireland, 68, 230, 272, 312, 460, 479–80
Islam, 75–6, 214, 424, 460–70, 576, 591–2
Islamic law, 592
Israel, 68
Italy,
    advertising, 455, 458, 474
    consumer behaviour, 118, 121–3, 152, 154,
        161, 215, 229–30, 266, 271–2, 286,
        291, 395
    culture, 46–7, 68, 82, 84, 88, 273, 301, 583
    Made in Italy, 220, 317, 319, 322, 324, 327
    marketing management, 367–8, 401, 524–5
    selling style, 513, 600–2
Ivory Coast, 301

Jamaica, 68
Japan bashing, 46
Japan,
    advertising, 183, 459–63, 465, 467, 473–4,
        481–2, 484
    brands, 337–8
    competition, 259, 338
    consumer behaviour, 41, 110, 121, 132,
        141, 143, 149, 153, 173, 292–4, 299
    culture, 32–4, 38, 40–2, 49–50, 53, 59, 68,
        76, 80, 82, 87–8, 93, 112, 203, 301,
        388–9, 423, 583
    distribution, 303–12, 383–91, 406–7
    language and communication, 41–2, 217,
        333, 419–21, 425, 437, 444–5, 507
    Made in Japan, 158, 173, 220, 320, 322–5,
        327

Japan *Continued*
  management style, 522
    market research, 228, 230–1, 242
    marketing management, 186, 252–4, 282,
        289, 347, 360–1, 366, 516, 519–21
    negotiation style, 507–9, 511, 514, 546,
        548, 550–1, 556, 562, 564, 566–7,
        569, 571–2, 574, 576, 588
    sales promotion, 400
    technical standards, 303–12
John Wayne Style, 564, 593
Joint ventures, 198, 390, 482

Kamei, 338
Kanji, 121, 305, 337, 438
Katakana, 305, 337, 438
Keiretsu, 382, 384–90
Kenya, 69, 424
Kikuyu, 424, 427
Knödel, 482
Koran, 76, 214, 469–70
Kultur, 4
Kuwait, 69

Language, 6–7, 116, 120–1, 148, 195–6, 212,
        216–22, 243, 297, 331–7, 397–8,
        415–31, 453, 462–4, 507, 548–9, 593
Latin America, 32, 63, 71, 215, 223, 227–8,
        325, 373, 415, 422, 467, 507, 565,
Latin Europe, 190–1, 194, 272–3, 403
Latins, 296, 420–1
Law of one price, 353
Learning, 253, 259, 285, 296, 606
Lebanon, 69, 512
Legal systems, 77, 180, 191–2, 553, 576–77
Lexical equivalence, 213, 216
Libya, 69
Life insurance, 214–15
Lifestyles, 145, 270, 606
Literacy, 109, 290, 403–4
Litigation, 576–7
Local marketing knowledge, 178–84, 188,
        199–200
Locus of control, 71
Logo, 334
Long-term orientation, 31, 151, 515, 520,
        548, 589–90, 593, 597
Lotharingian Europe, 272
Lotteries, 112, 400–2
Low context, 132, 179, 417–19, 461, 516–18
Loyalty, 37, 364
Luxemburg, 272, 478–9, 526

MBO (management by objectives), 69
McDonaldization, 146
'Made in' label, 317–20

Madrid Agreement, 341
Mailing lists, 397–8
Makimono time, 32–3
Malaysia, 19, 68, 181, 201–2, 228, 270, 424,
        466–7
Maronites, 591
Masculinity, 64, 66–9, 72, 124, 190, 396, 466,
        473, 516, 519
Mass customization, 264–5
Mastery over nature, 25, 73–4, 124, 515
Material culture, 40, 63, 116
Materialism, 132
Mauritania, 228
Media availability, 474
Media planning, 454
Meiji era, 42
Mercatique, 187–8
Meta-communication, 421
Metalanguage, 120
Metaphysical world, 74
Metempsychosis, 30, 75
Methodism, 363
Metric equivalence, 213, 221–3
Mexico, 10, 20–1, 68, 143, 301, 323, 325,
        345–6, 461–2, 466–7, 474–5, 514,
        524–5, 538–40, 558, 561, 597–8
Middle East,
    business ethics, 530–1
    culture, 422, 558
    negotiation style, 562–3, 573, 575, 591–2
Misunderstandings (cultural), 431, 547, 551
MNCs (multinational companies), 87–9, 265,
        268
Modal personality, 14
Modern culture, 26, 30, 141, 147–8, 472
Monochronism, 27–32, 553, 566–8, 595
Monopoly, 372
Monopsony, 372
Morocco, 225
Motivation, 67, 104, 109, 116, 123–4
Movie films, 145, 150–1, 164, 173
Mozambique, 227
Multidomestic, 252, 262
Multilingual persons, 431, 450
Muslims, 11, 214, 423, 455, 466–7, 470, 591

NAFTA (North American Free Trade
        Agreement), 189–90
National character, 14, 21
Nationality (and culture), 11–14, 35, 87–8
Nation-state, 13, 607
Negotiation, 505, 546–83
Negotiation styles, 588–99
Negotiation tactics, 553, 572
Nepal, 40, 569

Nestorians, 591
Netherlands, 321, 401, 467
    consumer behaviour, 113–14, 144, 266,
        272, 292, 605
    culture, 68, 82, 88, 201
Networking, 505–11, 589
Neutral cultures, 73, 82, 296, 572
New Zealand, 68, 326, 457, 466, 475
Nigeria, 47, 69, 213, 525
Ningensei, 546, 556–7, 588
Non-tariff barriers, 189, 260
Non-verbal communication, 422–6, 439
Northern Europe, 88, 141–2, 158, 190–1,
        362–3, 394, 403, 438, 456, 519, 569
Norway, 68

Objectives of communication, 454
Oligopoly, 372, 549
Oneiric style of advertising, 459–60
Oral agreement, 572–6
Oral behaviour, 95
Organization of international advertising,
        485–6
Organizational structure, 266–7
Outgroup, 34–9, 189, 432, 516, 589
Over- and under-invoicing, 374–5
Overlapping of media, 480

Packaging, 300, 302
Pakistan, 68, 322
Palanca, 597
Panama, 68
Pan-European market segments, 271–2, 481
Paraguay, 525
Parallel imports, 367–9
Paris Union, 341
Past orientation, 25, 28, 31–2, 52, 190, 553
Perceived potency, 58, 61, 554
Perceived risk, 111, 215, 273, 321–2
Perception, 17, 213, 220–1, 297–8
Peripheral consumption contexts, 161–2
Personalization, 35–7, 295, 356–7, 417, 549,
        565–6
Peru, 68
Philippines, 68, 270, 301, 322–4, 473
Phonology, 333, 347
Planning, 568–9
Poetry, 76
Poland, 197–9, 325, 361, 405, 481
Polycentrism, 255–6, 364, 436
Polychronism, 27–32, 563, 566–8, 597
Portugal, 68, 272, 317
Postmodernism, 147, 160, 173
Potential reality, 79–81
Potlatch, 104, 131

Power distance, 64–72, 181, 190–1, 293, 373,
        396, 465, 473, 512, 515–17, 553,
        558, 594
Pragmatism, 73, 77–8, 553, 569–70, 591
Present orientation, 28, 31
Price, 144, 353–75
    declaring prices, 358–9
    manipulating prices, 364
Price–quality relationships, 359–63
Problem solving, 553, 560–3
Procedural traditional time, 32
Product adaptation, 194–5, 282–6
Product liability, 288, 524
Product life cycle (international), 259
Product standardization policy, 283–4
Production flexibility, 263–5
Protestants, 362–3
Proxemics, 40, 449
Psychographic variables, 145, 220, 273
Public relations, 521–3
Publiphobia, 456

Quality, 308, 312, 359–62
Québecois, 144, 273, 460, 552, 561
Questionnaire, 219, 221, 235–41, 328, 428

Racism, 45–6
Rationality, 362–3, 553, 569
Record industry, 259, 272, 367–8
Regiocentrism, 255–6
Regional differences, 273
Relational exchange, 354, 549–50
Relational marketing, 548–9
Reliability (of a research instrument), 215,
        220, 235, 242
Religion, 12, 30–1, 59–60, 74–5, 148, 273,
        468–70
Representative communication, 561
Resale Price Maintenance, 368
Respondents, 213, 224–30, 234–5
Response style, 213, 228–30
Riba, 591
Ringi, 510, 556
Rituals, 557
Romania, 46, 182, 190, 197, 199
Rules, 74, 83–6, 292–4, 553, 595
Russia, 198–200, 217, 554–5, 559, 561, 598–9

Saint-Simonism, 456
Sales force compensation systems, 515–21
Sales objectives, 516
Sales promotion, 112, 400–5
Salespeople, 511–21
Sample, representativeness of, 224–6, 468
    size, 226, 242

Sampling equivalence, 213
Sampling unit, 213, 224
Satellite television, 478–9
Saudi Arabia, 94, 287
    advertising, 468–70, 474, 476
    business ethics, 525, 530
    culture, 49–50, 69, 92–3, 214
    marketing management, 161–2, 327, 515,
        591
Scale (psychometry), 124–5, 221
Scale effects, 253
Scandinavia, 227, 271–2, 317
Secrecy bias, 227
Segmentation of markets, 268, 272–4, 481–2
Self-concept, 56–61, 108–10, 132, 420, 553–4
Seller's status, 512
Selling styles, 512–14
Semantic differential, 221
Semantics, 333–6, 347
Senegal, 529
Service attributes, 283–4, 290–6
Sex cultures, 12, 59–60
Sex roles, 60, 108–9, 465–7
Sexual bias, 228
Sharia, 468
Shipping charges, 254
Sierra Leone, 69
Similarity hypothesis, 553, 562–3
Singapore, 68, 105, 201–2, 270, 301, 466–7
Slogans, 462–3
Social class, 12, 57–8, 60–1, 109
Social representations, 17–19, 353, 360, 455
Sociodemographic variables, 270, 274, 325–6
Soft sell approach, 513–15, 593–4
Sogo-shosha (general trading company), 304,
        507–8
Sourcing, 255
South Africa, 68, 467
South Korea, 144, 201
    advertising, 459–63, 465, 467, 471, 474
    culture, 68, 201, 203, 230, 301, 583
    Made in South Korea, 320, 323–4, 327
    marketing management, 343–4, 396, 511,
        521, 561, 563
Soviet Union, 158, 559
Space-related assumptions, 33–41, 51–2
Space (cultural language of), 40, 449
Spain, 44, 69, 140, 152–4, 272–3, 288, 291,
        317, 324, 379, 392, 460, 534–6, 572,
        584
SRC (Self Reference Criterion), 431–2
Sri Lanka, 12, 181
Standardization, 139, 145–6, 142–8, 296, 302
Standards, international, 140, 193, 288–90
    technical, 285–6, 288, 595

Stereotypes, 433–5, 466–7
Swahili, 116
Sweden,
    advertising, 459, 461, 466–7, 472
    culture, 13, 53, 88, 272–3
    Made in Sweden, 317, 325
    marketing management, 143, 158, 210,
        292, 361, 446–8, 519
Switzerland, 11, 205, 273, 522, 524, 530
    advertising, 453, 480
    culture, 21, 60, 69, 84, 88
    Made in Switzerland, 318–19
    sales promotion, 402–3
    selling style, 513
Symbolic aspects of
    colours, 297, 299–302
    money, 596
Symbols, 7, 10, 297–8, 301, 472
    definition of, 283, 297

Taiwan, 69, 270, 325, 327–8, 396, 459, 462–3,
        466–7, 470, 561
Tamil, 12, 181
Tanzania, 69, 241
Temporal equivalence, 213, 223
Tender, 506–7
Territoriality, 8, 37, 39, 591
Thailand, 69, 74, 94, 201, 270, 396, 403–4,
        518, 558, 584
Theory of climates, 15–16
Third World, 84, 104, 288, 524
Third World consumer, 157
Time (cultural patterns of), 27–31, 53, 427–8
Time orientations, 24–5, 27–33, 51–2, 190,
        292–3, 553, 565–9, 596–7, 599–600
Tokugawa era, 41, 53
Trade mark, 304, 334, 340–1, 347
Transaction costs, 364
Translation, 196, 213, 216–22, 243, 428–9,
        463–4
Transliteration, 332, 507
Transportability, 254–5
Treaty of Rome, 189, 191
Triad, 256
Tribe, 8, 596–7
Trust, 547–51, 583, 590
Tunisia, 455
Turkey, 268, 361, 395, 530
    advertising, 461, 470, 481
    consumer behaviour, 157, 220
    culture, 41–2, 69, 301
    Made in Turkey, 322
Turnkey operations, 507–8, 510, 549, 568,
        579–83
TV programmes, 476, 479

Uncertainty avoidance, 64, 67–70, 72, 190,
        396, 461, 516–17, 553, 558–9, 595
United Arab Emirates, 69
United Kingdom,
    advertising, 459–60, 462, 465, 471–4, 480
    consumer behaviour, 115, 144, 161–2, 173,
        215, 266, 271
    culture, 63, 68, 79, 82, 88, 230, 273, 301,
        420
    Made in the UK, 158, 173, 320, 323, 327
    marketing management, 143, 192, 269,
        282, 360–1, 367–8, 392, 398
    negotiation style, 561, 593–4
    sales promotion, 401, 403
    selling style, 514
United States, 11
    advertising, 183, 457–62, 470–1, 473–5,
        478, 481, 484
    business ethics, 523, 527–32
    consumer behaviour, 40, 110, 113–15,
        118–19, 143–4, 148, 151, 153,
        159–60, 162, 173, 215, 220, 291–2,
        295, 301
    culture, 35, 38, 40, 57, 59, 69, 71, 79, 82,
        87–8, 93, 273, 422, 425, 437–8
    Made in the USA, 148, 158, 173, 185, 318,
        320, 322, 325, 327, 329
    market research, 223, 230–1, 233–4, 242–3
    marketing management, 143, 151, 184–6,
        234, 262–8, 287, 289, 302, 338,
        360–1, 372, 389–91, 397 9, 515–16,
        519, 521
    negotiation style, 396, 514, 551, 554–6,
        558, 561–4, 566–7, 569–71, 573,
        576, 588, 592–3, 597
    parallel imports, 267–9

    sales promotion, 401, 403
    technical standards, 285–6
Universalism, 529–30
Uruguay, 69
Utilitarianism, 139, 147–8, 189, 472, 606

Validity, 215, 242, 328
Values, 5, 432, 459, 472, 520
Veblen effect, 104
Venezuela, 69, 514, 525
Vietnam, 89, 576
Visual illusions, 17

Waiting, 292–4, 428
Wasps, 102, 118
Walloon, 46, 482
Weltanschauung, 415, 426
Whorfian hypothesis, 6–7, 426–7, 436, 449
Wishful thinking, 73, 80–1, 95, 553
Word-of-mouth communication, 111, 113,
        145
World Intellectual Property Organization
        (WIPO), 341
World market share, 257–8
World production (growth of), 260
World Trade Organization (WTO), see GATT
Written agreement, 572–5

Yea-saying, 229–30
Yemen, 60
Yugoslavia, 69, 143

Zaibatsus, 371
Zaire, 527–8
Zambia, 69
Zapping, 476